INSIDE

WINDOWS NT©
WORKSTATION 4

CERTIFICATION ADMINISTRATOR'S RESOURCE EDITION

KATHY IVENS

BRUCE HALLBERG

New Riders Publishing, Indianapolis, Indiana

Inside Windows NT Workstation 4, Certification Administrator's Resource Edition

By Kathy Ivens and Bruce Hallberg

Published by:
New Riders Publishing
201 West 103rd Street
Indianapolis, IN 46290 USA

Printed in the United States of America 1 2 3 4 5 6 7 8 9 0

Library of Congress Cataloging-in-Publication Data

CIP data available upon request

ISBN: 1-56205-790-1

Warning and Disclaimer

This book is designed to provide information about the Windows NT Workstation 4 computer program. Every effort has been made to make this book as complete and as accurate as possible, but no warranty or fitness is implied.

The information is provided on an "as is" basis. The author(s) and New Riders Publishing shall have neither liability nor responsibility to any person or entity with respect to any loss or damages arising from the information contained in this book or from the use of the disks or programs that may accompany it.

Associate Publisher	*David Dwyer*
Publishing Manager	*Julie Fairweather*
Marketing Manager	*Mary Foote*
Managing Editor	*Sarah Kearns*
Director of Development	*Kezia Endsley*

Product Development Specialist
Sean Angus

Acquisitions Editor
Sean Angus

Senior Editor
Suzanne Snyder

Development Editor
Stacia Mellinger

Project Editor
Daryl Kessler

Copy Editors
Amy Bezek, Jennifer Clark, Krista Hansing, Matt Litten, Karen Walsh, Michelle Warren

Technical Editor
Lyle Bryant

Software Product Developer
Steve Flatt

Software Acquisitions and Development
Dustin Sullivan

Assistant Marketing Manager
Gretchen Schlesinger

Acquisitions Coordinator
Amy Lewis

Editorial Assistant
Karen Opal

Manufacturing Coordinator
Brook Farling

Cover Designer
Dan Armstrong

Cover Production
Nathan Clement, Louisa Klucznik

Book Designer
Glenn Larsen, Sandra Schroeder

Director of Production
Larry Klein

Production Team Supervisors
Laurie Casey, Joe Millay

Graphics Image Specialist
Kevin Cliburn

Production Analysts
Erich J. Richter, Dan Harris

Production Team
Lori Cliburn, Kim Cofer, Linda Knose, Malinda Kuhn, Elizabeth SanMiguel, Scott Tullis

Indexer
Kevin Fulcher

About the Authors

Kathy Ivens has been a computer consultant since 1984, and has authored and co-authored numerous books on computer subjects. She is a frequent contributor to national magazines, writing articles and reviewing software. She has three brilliant daughters, three terrific sons-in-law, and the most beautiful granddaughter ever born.

Bruce Hallberg is the Director of Information Systems for a biotechnology company located in Redwood City, California. He has been heavily involved with PCs since 1980 and has specialized in accounting and business control systems for the past seven years. He has consulted with a large number of local and national companies in a variety of areas and has expertise in networking, programming, and system implementations. He works with a wide variety of PC computer platforms, including DOS, Windows, OS/2, Unix, and the Macintosh.

Trademark Acknowledgments

All terms mentioned in this book that are known to be trademarks or service marks have been appropriately capitalized. New Riders Publishing cannot attest to the accuracy of this information. Use of a term in this book should not be regarded as affecting the validity of any trademark or service mark.

Dedications

This book is dedicated to Allen Lewites, Bill Telepan, and Mike Bernardi, with love and respect and in the interests of equal time.

Kathy Ivens

This book is dedicated to my dear friend, Tova Sweet.

Bruce Hallberg

Acknowledgments

The people at New Riders are the best in the business. We never stop feeling deep appreciation to be working with them. Don Fowley is a publisher of incredibly wonderful qualities. Stacia Mellinger is one of the most capable professionals in the publishing industry and we always drool at the chance to work with her (okay, we actually beg people to rearrange her schedule to accommodate us). Sean Angus is an editor of rare and marvelous substance, combining a quick sense of humor with a commitment to quality in addition to a couple of other terrific characteristics, and therefore qualifies as an author's dream editor. Daryl Kessler, a delightful, charming, and highly skilled professional, managed somehow to keep herself and us sane as she juggled more details than anyone should be expected to handle. (And she never gets upset when she has to listen to us whine and complain.) Lyle Bryant is one of the most competent technical editors we've had the pleasure to work with, and his expertise is so solid that we learned to look through our manuscripts eagerly to find his notes and suggestions for added material. Amy Bezek (who has been one of our favorite editors for a long time), along with Matt Litten, Jenny Clark and Krista Hansing (new to us for this book, in case you're wondering why we singled out Amy) took on the onerous job of checking copy for authors who usually type too fast, forget half the punctuation (except dashes—we love dashes, but they remove most of them), and never think of running a spell checker.

Contents at a Glance

Part V: Networking with NT 4

Part VI: Communicating with NT 4

Part VII: Administering NT Workstation 4

Part VIII: Understanding Server Features

Part IX: Appendices

Table of Contents

Part VII: Administering NT Workstation 4   787

26   Understanding Shared Resources   789

27   Protecting Your Workstation   815

Objectives List for Implementing and Supporting
Microsoft Windows NT Workstation 4.0

A. Planning

Objectives	Page References
A.1 Create unattended installation files.	Chapter 2 page 86, Doing a Network Roll-Out
A.2 Plan strategies for sharing and securing resources.	Chapter 27 page 824, Planning a Backup Strategy Chapter 32 page 974, Using the Workstation's Server Properties
A.3 Choose the appropriate file system to use in a given situation. File systems and situations include: NTFS FAT HPFS Security Dual-boot systems	Chapter 1 page 54, Choosing a File System Chapter 30 page 908, Converting NTFS Chapter 33 page 1002, Understanding NT Server and NTFS

B. Installation and Configuration

Objectives	Page References
B.1 Install Windows NT Workstation on an Intel® platform in a given situation.	Chapter 2 page 62, Mandatory Installation Factors Chapter 2 page 62, CD-ROM/Network Share Access Chapter 2 page 63, Floppy Support

continues

continues

Objectives	Page References

continues

C. Managing Resources

continues

continued	
Objectives	**Page References**
	Chapter 26 page 790, Sharing Drives
	Chapter 26 page 793, Sharing Folders
	Chapter 26 page 794, Setting Drive, Directory, and File Permissions on NTFS Drives
	Chapter 27 page 839, Setting Permissions for Backup
C.4 Set permissions on NTFS partitions, folders, and files.	Chapter 26 page 794, Setting Drive, Directory, and File Permissions on NTFS Drives
	Chapter 26 page 797, Changing Ownership
C.5 Install and configure printers in a given environment.	Chapter 8 page 305, Use the Resources
	Chapter 12 page 423, Exploring Parallel Ports
	Chapter 17 page 544, Installing Printers
	Chapter 17 page 545, Installing a Local Printer
	Chapter 17 page 548, Sharing Local Printers
	Chapter 17 page 555, Schedule a Shared Printer's Use
	Chapter 17 page 556, Install a Network Printer from Network Neighborhood
	Chapter 17 page 558, Install a Network Printer with the Wizard
	Chapter 17 page 565, Understanding Banners

D. Connectivity

Objectives	**Page References**
D.1 Add and configure the network components of Windows NT Workstation.	Chapter 20 page 636, Installing Network Protocols
	Chapter 20 page 667, Reviewing Bindings and Changing the Network Access Order

Objectives	Page References
D.2 Use various methods to access network resources.	Chapter 8 page 302, Navigate the Network
	Chapter 8 page 305, Use the Resources
	Chapter 8 page 306, Find Computers from the Start Menu
	Chapter 8 page 307, Map Drives Using Network Neighborhood
	Chapter 17 page 564, Print from DOS
	Chapter 20 page 675, Understanding Administrative Shares
	Chapter 21 page 684, Accessing Other Network Computers
D.3 Implement Windows NT Workstation as a client in a NetWare environment.	Chapter 20 page 643, Client Services for NetWare
D.4 Use various configurations to install Windows NT Workstation as a TCP/IP client.	Chapter 20 page 652, DHCP and WINS
	Chapter 22 page 713, TCP/IP for Internet Connections
D.5 Configure and install Dial-Up Networking in a given situation.	Chapter 22 page 698, Installing and Configuring DUN Services
	Chapter 22 page 701, Using Phonebook
	Chapter 22 page 701, Creating Phonebook Entries
	Chapter 22 page 705, Advanced Phonebook Entries
	Chapter 22 page 706, Editing Phonebook Entries
	Chapter 22 page 706, Basic Tab
	Chapter 22 page 708, Server Tab

continues

E. Running Applications

F. Monitoring and Optimization

continued

Introduction

Windows NT Workstation 4 is the newest, most robust operating system from Microsoft Corporation. It has been adopted by corporations all over the world as the standard for client computers on networks.

We wrote this book to help administrators understand and work with the computers running Windows NT Workstation on their network systems.

An additional purpose of this book is to provide all the necessary information for computer professionals who need to prepare for the *Implementing and Supporting Microsoft Windows NT Workstation 4.0* certification exam #70-73.

Who Should Read This Book?

This book is for network administrators and users who are responsible for installing and administering network systems that include Windows NT 4 workstations. It covers basic, intermediate, and advanced concepts for the operating system. Users who are comfortable with earlier versions of Windows NT will find the changes in the operating system so broad and significant that even reading about basic functions and features will reveal new information. Windows 95 users will find the interface familiar, but the scope and power of Windows NT is far beyond what they are used to.

This book is also for computer professionals who need to pass the *Implementing and Supporting Microsoft Windows NT Workstation 4.0* certification exam as they move toward Microsoft Certified Systems Engineer (MCSE) certification or Microsoft Certified Product Specialist (MCPS) certification.

◆ MCSE is the Microsoft Certified Professional category for those computer professionals who work with Microsoft networks.

◆ MCPS is the Microsoft Certified Professional category for those computer professionals who want to be certified specifically for a particular Microsoft product.

This book is a comprehensive volume for the knowledge base required for the NT Workstation exam, which is a core exam for both certification programs.

If you are interested in the certification exam, we offer the following assistance:

◆ Throughout the book we'll cover the information needed to pass the Windows NT Workstation exam as part of our discussion of any topic that is related to the exam.

◆ An icon appears before every topic that includes information you'll need for the exam.

◆ Hands-on, step-by-step instructions on performing tasks will help you gain practical knowledge about the skills required for the exam.

◆ Questions and answers at the end of each chapter provide an opportunity to test your understanding of the material in the chapter.

Objective
B.22

◆ A matrix of test topics and where they are covered within this book is located before the introduction of the book. An icon such as this one in the margin pinpoints the corresponding information on the page indicated in the matrix. Together, the matrix and icons make it easy for you to find exactly what you need as you make sure you've covered all the knowledge bases you need.

We don't expect you to read this book as if it were a novel (or we'd have developed a running plot). You can flip from chapter to chapter, section to section, as your needs demand. Between the test topic matrix and the index, we're confident you'll easily find exactly what you're looking for.

About the Windows NT Workstation Certification Exam

The *Implementing and Supporting Microsoft Windows NT Workstation 4.0* certification exam measures concepts and skills that are rather comprehensive. An overview of the concepts and skills you'll need to master is presented in this section. Complete information about the Microsoft Certification program is found in Appendix B, "Overview of the Certification Process."

Planning

You should be prepared to answer questions about the following topics:

- Creating files for unattended installation

- Planning strategies for resource sharing, including security for shared resources

- Choosing the appropriate file system (NTFS, FAT, HPFS) to use in situations that are described as part of the test (security considerations, dual-boot systems)

Installation and Configuration

You will need to answer questions that test whether you have sufficient knowledge to perform the following tasks in a given situation (the test will describe the situation):

- Install NT Workstation on an Intel platform

- Set up dual-boot systems

- Remove Windows NT Workstation

- Install, configure, and remove hardware components, including Network adapter drivers, SCSI device drivers, Tape device drivers, UPS, Multimedia devices, Display drivers, Keyboard drivers, and Mouse drivers

- Use the Control Panel applications to configure a Workstation computer

- Upgrade to Windows NT Workstation 4.0

- Configure server-based installation in order to provide wide-scale deployment of the operating system

Managing Resources

You must be prepared to answer questions that test your ability to do the following tasks:

- Create and manage local user and group accounts

- Set up and modify user profiles

- Set up shared folders as well as their permissions

- Set permissions on NTFS partitions (including folder and file permissions)

- Install and configure printers (specific situations will be established on the test)

Connectivity

Exam questions will include a test of your ability to do the following tasks:

- Install and configure the network components of Windows NT Workstation

- Use a variety of methods to access network resources

- Implement Workstation as a NetWare client.

- Install Workstation as a TCP/IP client using a variety of configurations

- Install and configure Dial-Up Networking

- Configure Microsoft Peer Web Services

Running Applications

The exam questions relating to applications are geared toward testing your ability to launch applications. (The exam may require knowledge of RISC-based computers.)

- Launch applications in a variety of environments

- Launch applications with a variety of priorities

Monitoring and Optimization

You will be asked to display your knowledge on a variety of operating system tools that are included with the operating system. In addition, you are expected to understand the results these tools display when you use them. Exam questions will test your skills in the following areas:

◆ Monitoring performance with the use of the system tools

◆ Identifying and fixing specific performance problems

◆ Optimizing performance in a variety of operating system areas

Troubleshooting

The questions on the exam will test your ability to solve problems that are established on the exam, including these:

◆ Choosing the right action to take if a computer fails to boot properly

◆ Choosing the appropriate action when there is a failure in printing

◆ Selecting the appropriate action when there is a failure in the installation process

◆ Choosing the right action in the event of application failure

◆ Selecting the right action to resolve the problem of a user's inability to access a resource

◆ Using the appropriate tool to modify the Registry in a specific situation

◆ Using advanced techniques to solve any of a variety of problems that may be presented on the exam

All the knowledge you need to learn how to perform all the actions and make all the decisions necessary during the exam is in this book.

Special Elements in this Book

Inside Windows NT Workstation 4, Certification Administrator's Resource Edition is packed with numerous and notable special elements and textual features aimed at enhancing the presentation of the material herein. It is our goal that this enhanced presentation will clarify coverage (Chapter Snapshots), add meaning in terms of the "type" of information presented (Notes, Tips, Cautions, and Sidebars), provide frame of reference (full-frame figures), and wrap-up information with valuable, author-generated insight (End Notes).

Chapter Snapshots

Each chapter begins with what is called a Chapter Snapshot. A Chapter Snapshot has two basic parts:

- Introductory text

- A list of topics

The introductory text escorts you into the concepts covered in the specific chapter. If the chapter focuses on a new concept or term, the text begins with a thorough definition. It goes on to spell out the significance of the topic as it stands against the larger force of Windows NT Workstation 4, therefore justifying its coverage. Finally, the introductory text found in the Chapter Snapshot nails down exactly how the chapter's subject will be explained. It does so by introducing the second half of the Chapter Snapshot—the list of topics.

The list of topics is really nothing more than the main headings within the chapter pulled out and placed in one spot for your convenience. This list offers a quick breakdown of exactly what you can expect from the chapter's discussion.

The Chapter Snapshot clarifies coverage for you and creates expectations eventually fulfilled by the actual text within the chapter.

Notes, Tips, Cautions, Sidebars

Inside Windows NT Workstation 4, Certification Administrator's Resource Edition features several special "asides" set apart from the normal text. These asides add extra meaning by illustrating graphically the kind of information being presented. This book offers four distinct asides:

- Notes

- Tips

- Cautions

- Sidebars

Note A Note includes "extra"—and useful—information that complements the discussion at hand rather than being a direct part of it. A Note might describe special situations that can arise when you use Windows NT Workstation 4 under certain circumstances, and tells you what steps to take when such situations do arise. Notes also might tell you how to avoid problems with your software or hardware.

Tip A Tip provides you with quick instructions for getting the most from your Windows NT 4 system as you follow the steps outlined in general discussion. A Tip might show you how to conserve memory in some setups, how to speed up a procedure, or how to perform one of many time-saving and system-enhancing techniques.

Caution A Caution tells you when a procedure might be dangerous—that is, when you run the risk of losing data, locking your system, or even damaging your hardware. Cautions generally tell you how to avoid such losses, or describe the steps you can take to remedy them.

Sidebars Offer Additional Information

A Sidebar, conceptually, is much like a Note—the exception being its length. A Sidebar is by nature much longer than a Note but offers the same extra, complementary information. Sidebars offer in-depth insight into the topic under discussion.

Full-Frame Figures

Most computer books offer readers illustrations to drive home the idea featured in the text. Some books, however, tend to limit the reader visually. When the text talks about a specific dialog box, for example, the accompanying figure shows that specific dialog box and nothing further. For most discussions, this type of illustration is satisfactory. Not quite so here. Because *Inside Windows NT Workstation 4, Certification Administrator's Resource Edition* tackles a completely new operating system version, catering not only to those users experienced in NT 3.51 (moving to NT 4) but also to those migrating from a completely different OS, the figures in this book extend the reader's frame of reference to the entire screen. The specific OS item being discussed is highlighted within each illustration with darker ink, but the rest of the screen that would be observed by a user is also included (lighter ink used). Basically, you see the entire screen in each figure, with the specific image of note highlighted visually.

End Notes

Each chapter wraps up with a special paragraph or two offering a final piece of insight into the chapter's topic area.

End Note: End Notes are aimed at giving you, the reader, just a little bit more—sometimes an inside scoop, sometimes a suggestion for implementing features effectively. This short bonus section contains information that perhaps did not fit neatly into the chapter's determined discussion structure but is valuable nonetheless. Enjoy.

New Riders Publishing

The staff of New Riders is committed to bringing you the very best in computer reference material. Each New Riders book is the result of months of work by authors and staff who research and refine the information contained within its covers.

As part of this commitment to you New Riders invites your input. Please let us know if you enjoy this book, if you have trouble with the information and examples presented, or if you have a suggestion for the next edition.

Please note, though: New Riders staff cannot serve as a technical resource for Windows NT Workstation 4 or for questions about software- or hardware-related problems. Please refer to the documentation that accompanies NT 4 or to the applications' Help systems.

If you have a question or comment about any New Riders book, there are several ways to contact us. We will respond to as many readers as we can. Your name, address, or phone number will never become part of a mailing list or be used for any purpose other than to help us continue to bring you the best books possible. You can write us at the following address:

New Riders Publishing
Attn: Publisher
201 W. 103rd Street
Indianapolis, IN 46290

If you prefer, you can fax New Riders Publishing at (317) 581-4670.

NRP is an imprint of Macmillan Computer Publishing. To obtain a catalog or information, or to purchase any Macmillan Computer Publishing book, call (800) 428-5331.

Thank you for selecting *Inside Windows NT Workstation 4, Certification Administrator's Resource Edition*!

PART I

Introducing Windows NT Workstation 4

Chapter Snapshot

In this chapter, you learn about Windows NT Workstation's architecture, including the following:

Windows NT
Workstation 4

CHAPTER 1

Understanding Windows NT Workstation 4

Microsoft now offers two fundamentally different families of operating systems: Windows 95 and Windows NT. Each system is built on entirely different code bases—they appear similar, but the underlying operating systems are completely different. Windows 95 is hosted only on Intel 80386 and greater processors, and is intended for the broadest marketplace, running on the lowest common denominator of Intel-based platforms. Windows NT, on the other hand, runs on a wide variety of processor families, and in different versions to meet very diverse needs.

There are two versions of Windows NT: Workstation and Server. Both use the same kernel and other low-level operating system code, but each contains different add-on features that enable their different missions. Server is designed to run as a server, letting many users share the server's resources. Workstation, on the other hand, is intended to run on users' desktops and serve as their primary desktop operating system.

Inside Windows NT Workstation 4, Certification Administrator's Resource Edition explores the version of Windows NT intended to be run on users' desktops, whether business desktop computers, home computers, or even portable notebook computers.

The key to mastering any operating system—beyond just being a proficient user—is to understand the design, architecture, and broad features of the system. Using the knowledge you gain in this chapter as a base, you'll be well prepared to move to later chapters in this book, thereby gaining a full understanding of Windows NT Workstation 4.

> **Note** You will see references to Windows NT Workstation and Windows NT Server in this chapter, as well as some that just refer to Windows NT. When Windows NT is used, you can safely assume that both products are being referred to. Because both products are built on identical bases, much is shared between the two product levels.

Understanding the Microsoft Operating System Family

If you are planning on getting an MCSE certification from Microsoft, you should be able to identify the key differences between Windows NT Workstation and Windows 95. Both are client operating systems, both offer certain strengths and weaknesses relative to the other, and as an expert on Windows NT Workstation 4 you should be able to understand and elaborate these differences. In the following sections you'll learn about the key differences between these two client operating systems. You will also learn about Windows NT Server 4, another important operating system in the Microsoft Operating System family.

Understanding Windows 95

Windows 95, the successor to Windows 3.1 and Windows for Workgroups, is designed to be the mainstream desktop operating system for Intel-based computers. It is generally more versatile than Windows NT Workstation in its ability to run more types of software programs, but this versatility comes at the cost of being much less robust than Windows NT Workstation.

The key features of Windows 95 are as follows:

◆ Supports *preemptive multitasking* for 32-bit Windows programs (those based on the Win32 programming model) and DOS-based programs.

◆ Does not support multiple processors, and does not support processors other than those in the Intel 80386, 80486, and Pentium families.

◆ Supports *cooperative multitasking* for 16-bit Windows programs (typically, those programs designed for Windows 3.x).

Note To learn more about preemptive and cooperative multitasking, read the section "Understanding Multitasking" later in this chapter.

◆ Includes Internet Explorer, an Internet Web browser.

◆ Includes Microsoft Messaging, a versatile e-mail client application.

◆ Is more compatible than Windows NT Workstation 4 with older Windows- and DOS-based applications. It can support programs that must take control of the computer's hardware.

◆ Will run well on the widest variety of PCs, even those that are several years old.

◆ Maintains hardware profiles for different configurations.

◆ Supports Plug and Play, a technology that automatically recognizes and reconfigures hardware devices in the computer. Plug and Play also supports removable hardware, such as devices used with portable computers.

◆ Can share its files and attached printers with other computers across a network.

Windows 95 also requires less extensive hardware than Windows NT Workstation. You can run Windows 95 on the following minimum hardware platform:

◆ Intel-based PC with an 80386 or higher processor running at 20 MHz or faster

◆ 4 MB of Random Access Memory (RAM)—though 8 MB is the recommended minimum

◆ 40 MB of free disk space

Note The preceding requirements are those provided by Microsoft and are important to know if you intend to take the test for MCSE certification. In reality, however, most users will benefit from 12 MB to 16 MB of RAM, and at least 100 MB of free disk space.

Understanding Windows NT Workstation 4

Windows NT Workstation 4 is the premium client operating system offered by Microsoft. It is designed around the Windows NT operating system, and key system components are shared between Windows NT Workstation 4 and Windows NT Server 4. Broadly speaking, Windows NT is designed to be the most reliable operating system available for desktop computers. This reliability comes at the price of having some limits, however, not shared by Windows 95.

The key features of Windows NT Workstation 4 are as follows:

◆ Supports preemptive multitasking for all applications.

◆ Supports multiple processors, and supports not only the Intel-based processors supported by Windows 95, but also the DEC Alpha AXP family, and the IBM/ Motorola PowerPC family.

◆ Includes Internet Explorer, an Internet Web browser.

◆ Includes Microsoft Messaging, a versatile client e-mail application.

◆ Includes Peer Web Services, which lets you develop a personal Web server on your Windows NT Workstation 4 computer.

◆ Has extensive security over the computer's resources, including files, folders, printers, and other hardware. You can control access by user and group either on the local computer, or through a domain controller (usually a Windows NT Server computer that manages security in a network).

◆ Supports the FAT file system, as well as the much more advanced NTFS file system. Limited support is also included for drives formatted using HPFS (OS/2's High Performance File System).

◆ Increased stability relative to Windows 95 (and to most other operating systems from any source). Each application runs in its own memory address area and is protected from the effects of other applications running. Similarly, the computer hardware and operating system is protected from the effects of application programs.

In order to run Windows NT Workstation 4, you need the following minimum hardware:

◆ Intel-based PC with an 80486 or higher processor running at 33 MHz or faster

◆ 12 MB of Random-Access-Memory (RAM)—though 16 MB is the recommended minimum

◆ 120 MB of free disk space

Note The above requirements are those provided by Microsoft and are important to know if you intend to take the MCSE certification test. In reality, however, most users will benefit from 24 MB to 32 MB of RAM, and at least 200 MB of free disk space.

Choosing Between Windows NT Workstation 4 and Windows 95

As the old saying goes, there is a time and place for everything. There is also a time and place for both Windows 95 and Windows NT Workstation 4. Each is suited to different classes of users and desktop computers, and both are appropriate in different circumstances.

Generally, Windows 95 is the easiest way to get the benefit of a 32-bit operating system onto a desktop computer, and Windows NT Workstation 4 is designed to be the most powerful 32-bit operating system for desktop computers.

In your company—or if you intend to become MCSE-certified—you may be called on to offer advice on which operating system someone should choose. Notice that there are similarities between Windows 95 and Windows NT Workstation 4. Specifically, they share their user interface, include some of the same applications such as Windows Messaging and Internet Explorer, and have some similar features such as hardware profiles, system policies, and user profiles.

There are also some key differences:

◆ Windows 95 requires less advanced hardware than Windows NT Workstation.

◆ Windows 95 will be compatible with a wider variety of application progams.

◆ Windows 95 is better suited to portable computers, including any computer that can use Advanced Power Management (APM).

◆ Windows NT Workstation 4 can offer higher performance in many cases.

◆ Windows NT Workstation 4 is more reliable than Windows 95.

◆ Windows NT Workstation 4 has much better security than Windows 95.

To choose one of these operating systems over another, you should start by examining the hardware compatibility requirements. Generally, Windows 95 will support just about any PC hardware currently available. For Windows NT Workstation, you should consult the Hardware Compatibility Guide (HCL) that is available on Microsoft's Web site (http://www.microsoft.com).

You should then check the compatibility with the applications that need to be run. Most application vendors will state whether their applications are compatible and are supported on Windows NT Workstation, perhaps by using the Windows NT logo on their packaging.

If the preceding two requirements are met by Windows NT Workstation 4, then it is generally a superior choice to Windows 95.

Understanding Windows NT Server

The "big brother" of the Windows NT family is Windows NT Server 4, an operating system designed to support many users in a networked environment. Windows NT Server 4 can be used to offer file and print services to a network client base, or to provide other network services such as acting as an application or messaging server, and to operate in these capacities in a large network.

The key features to understand about Windows NT Server are the following:

◆ Performance is tuned for a server role.

◆ Windows NT Server 4 supports up to four processors in its retail version, and even more (up to 32) in special OEM versions available from multiprocessor computer vendors. (Windows NT Workstation 4 only supports up to 2 processors in its retail version.)

◆ Supports up to 256 inbound Remote Access Service sessions, those that can support remote users dialed into the server.

◆ Includes built-in support for RAID technology, which increases fault-tolerance.

◆ Includes Internet Information Server, a service that lets you deploy HTTP (HyperText Transfer Protocol), FTP (File Transfer Protocol), and Gopher services over the Internet.

◆ Supports Macintosh client computers over a network.

◆ Includes some network services not found in Windows NT Workstation 4, such as routing for multiple protocols, DNS, DHCP, and WINS.

◆ Includes Windows NT Directory Services (NTDS) for managing an enterprise-wide directory database.

In order to run Windows NT Server 4, the minimum requirements are as follows:

◆ Intel-based computer with an 80486 or better processor running at 33 MHz or faster

◆ 16 MB of RAM

◆ 130 MB of free disk space

| Note | The above requirements are those provided by Microsoft and are important to know if you intend to take the MCSE certification test. In reality, however, most sites that are using Windows NT Server in a server capacity will benefit from at least 64 MB of RAM (128 or 256 MB is often not too much for larger networks), and will probably require many gigabytes of total disk storage. |

Exploring What's New (versus NT 3.51)

Windows NT Workstation 4 is a major upgrade from version 3.51, the previous version of Windows NT Workstation. In the new version, you can see how Windows NT Workstation is evolving into a more powerful system that provides an even wider variety of uses than previous versions.

> **Note** In the following sections, the new features of Windows NT Workstation 4 are overviewed. Elsewhere in the book, you learn how to master these features.

New Desktop Design

Key among the new features is the addition of the desktop first introduced with Windows 95. (Previous versions of Windows NT Workstation used the same user interface as Windows 3.1x.) The new user interface makes Windows NT Workstation easier to use, and makes it more accessible to a wider variety of users.

From a business standpoint, the new interface reduces support and training costs for organizations that wish to deploy both Windows 95 and Windows NT Workstation throughout their user bases. Because both share an identical user interface, users in the company don't even really need to know which one they are running, and training costs are reduced; train users on Windows 95, and you've also trained them on Windows NT Workstation 4. Moreover, the new interface provides a much more graceful way to migrate users from Windows 95 to Windows NT Workstation when the need arises. From the user's perspective, when moving from (or between) Windows 95 and Windows NT Workstation 4, the operating system appears to be unchanged. However, the user will appreciate the stronger multitasking and greater reliability that Windows NT Workstation offers.

> **Note** Windows NT Workstation 4 is a more "industrial strength" operating system. Two key benefits of its design include more powerful multitasking (the ability to run multiple programs at once) and greater reliability (the ability to gracefully handle program errors without affecting other running programs).

Figure 1.1 shows the Windows NT Workstation 4 desktop. Notice that the design is identical to the default Windows 95 desktop.

Use My Computer to browse
locally connected drives, the
Control Panel, printers, and
Dial-Up Networking

Network Neighborhood
lets you browse and use
network resources

Exchange Inbox
provides a universal
e-mail client

Figure 1.1

*The Windows NT
Workstation
desktop is
identical to that of
Windows 95.*

Recycle Bin deletes files (and
holds them in case of mistakes)

My Briefcase lets you painlessly
synchronize files between your
desktop and portable computers

Use the Start button on the
Taskbar to access programs
and other features of the system

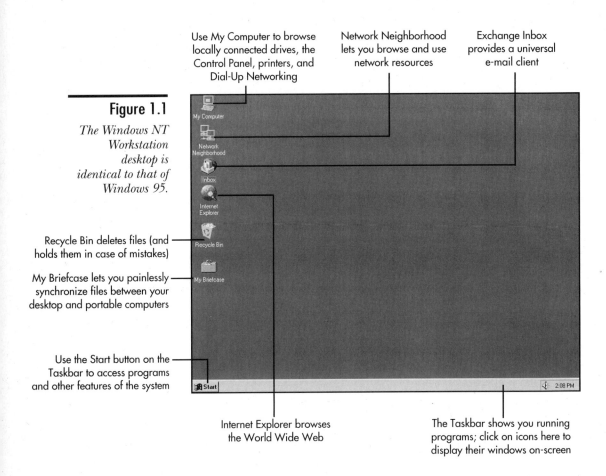

Internet Explorer browses
the World Wide Web

The Taskbar shows you running
programs; click on icons here to
display their windows on-screen

Note   Avoid minimizing the impact of the new desktop; it's an important feature of
Windows NT Workstation 4. Although the desktop does not reflect new
fundamental underlying technology, it does offer a number of usability features that
weren't available in previous versions of Windows NT Workstation, as well as
important benefits for all users of Windows NT Workstation.

Windows Explorer

Computer users once delighted in calling File Manager "File Mangler." Windows
Explorer (see fig. 1.2) replaces File Manager. Though you can duplicate all the
functions found in Explorer by using the icons found in My Computer and Network
Neighborhood, Windows Explorer lets more advanced users work more efficiently
with files and folders than they can using My Computer and Network Neighborhood.

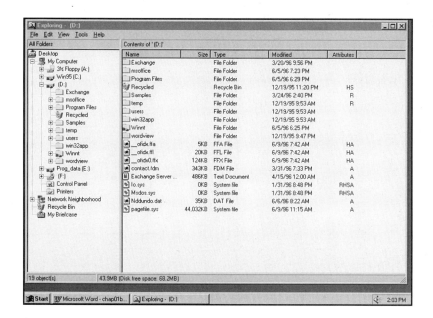

Figure 1.2

Windows Explorer replaces File Manager in Windows NT Workstation 4.

Start Menu and Taskbar

Working with your computer is made easier with the Start menu, which enables you to access virtually every part of your system through a series of hierarchical menus that are fast and convenient to navigate. Figure 1.3 shows the Start menu open.

The Start menu is located on the Taskbar, the solid gray bar shown at the bottom of the screen. All open windows and objects appear on the Taskbar; click on them to bring them into the foreground. By default, the Taskbar is visible on the desktop at all times, even when you're working with an application. You can make the Taskbar invisible when windows are open if you like, or you can relocate it to other places on your screen.

Note   Multitasking operating systems run programs in the foreground and the background. A program is said to be in the *foreground* when the program is running, is on your screen, and is usable by you. A program is said to be in the *background* when the program is running, but may not be visible. It's still doing work, but you just can't immediately access its commands or data without bringing it into the foreground by clicking on it. When a program is in the foreground and can accept input from a user (through the keyboard or mouse), it is said to "have the focus" on the desktop.

Figure 1.3

The Start menu lets you access programs and objects on your computer.

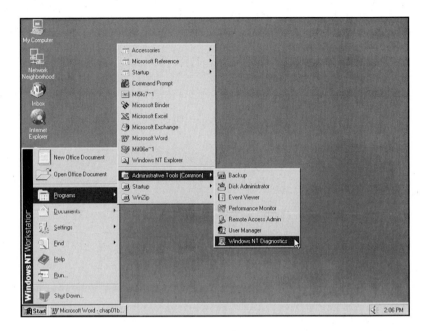

The Taskbar also has a small status window in the lower-right corner of the desktop. Often, this area displays the current time and any small control programs that are running. Figure 1.3 shows the system volume control with the small speaker icon. Double-clicking on these small icons (or right-clicking) lets you access their features.

Long File Names on FAT Volumes

Windows NT Workstation 4 has the capability to store long file names on disks formatted using the File Allocation Table (FAT) file system. Using a similar mechanism as Windows 95, your documents can use long file names with spaces, multiple periods, and other special characters on FAT-formatted disks.

 While the mechanism that Windows NT Workstation 4 uses to store long file names on FAT disks is similar to Windows 95's, it is not the same. Using Windows 95 disk utility programs, such as Norton Utilities or those packaged with Windows 95, can damage the long file names so that Windows NT Workstation 4 can no longer see them. It's important that you use disk utilities designed for Windows NT Workstation 4 instead of those designed for Windows 95.

Properties Settings

Windows NT Workstation 4 is much more object-oriented in its user interface than previous versions. Virtually all objects visible on the desktop, and often even objects inside other objects (such as the volume control in the Taskbar), can have their individual properties changed. To do this, right-click on the object and choose Properties from the resulting pop-up menu. Figure 1.4, for example, shows the pop-up menu for My Computer and the resulting dialog box that appears after choosing Properties from the menu.

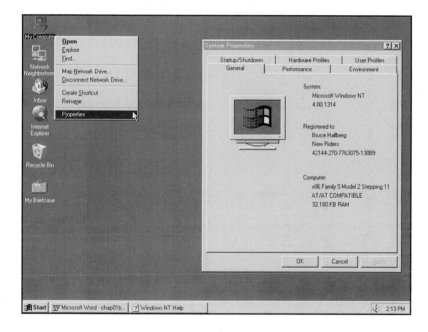

Figure 1.4

Almost all objects have Properties dialog boxes that contain object-specific settings.

Different types of objects display different properties dialog boxes. You are always shown only the dialog box and tabs that are appropriate for any given object. A file's Properties dialog box, for example, is completely different from a device's Properties dialog box.

New User Interface Elements

The basic Windows user interface has been improved, both in Windows 95 and in Windows NT Workstation 4. Every window now has a close button in its upper-right corner, usually found to the right of the minimize and maximize buttons (refer to fig. 1.2); it's the button that has the "X" in the center.

Shortcut menus, discussed in the previous section, are another new benefit in the user interface. To access shortcut menus, right-click on an object. The resulting menu displays only commands that are appropriate for that object. A device's object shortcut menu, for example, does not have a Rename command, while a folder's or file's shortcut menu does.

Note Throughout this book you'll see references to both the right and left mouse buttons. Windows NT Workstation enables you to swap the functions of the two mouse buttons, to allow for left-handed people. If you have switched your mouse buttons, you'll need to remember that right means left and vice-versa when mouse buttons are mentioned.

Shortcut icons offer another new feature. Any object in the system can be made into a shortcut icon, which is simply a reference to the original object. Figure 1.5, for example, shows shortcuts added to the desktop for the locally connected drives on the computer. You also see a number of shortcuts in the Microsoft Office applications window.

Figure 1.5

Shortcuts enable you to access objects from wherever you want.

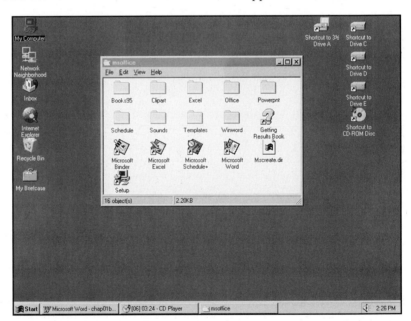

By default, shortcuts are created with the name "Shortcut to" followed by the name of the object. You can also recognize shortcuts by the small arrow box in the lower-left corner of the icon.

Note Windows NT Workstation 4's new user interface contains a myriad of new features. In the preceding sections, you learned about the key additions. For more details on the finer points, see the chapters in Part II, "Exploring the Windows NT 4 Desktop." These chapters explain how to work with the Windows NT Workstation 4's desktop, menus, and windows.

Portable Computer Capabilities

Previous versions of Windows NT Workstation could not be installed onto portable computers because its resource requirements exceeded the capabilities of the portable computers of that time. Previous versions of Windows NT also did not support PC Card (PCMCIA) devices, docking stations, and the like. Windows NT Workstation 4 adds these capabilities, making the operating system usable on portable computers in addition to desktop machines.

Internet Capabilities

Windows NT Workstation 4 now includes two important Internet programs: Internet Explorer and Peer Web Services. Internet Explorer, also available for Windows 95, lets you browse pages on the World Wide Web, or those on your own network that are formatted using HTML (HyperText Markup Language). Peer Web Services lets you create HTML pages on your own network (or even on your own computer) and lets other network users access them through your network.

Knowing Windows NT Workstation Design

Windows NT is the most ambitious operating system ever developed. The goals for its design were very aggressive and were meant to meet a wide variety of needs. Windows NT Workstation 4 can be run on portable computers, modest desktop computers, and even on multiprocessor workstation computers that rival most minicomputers. This section takes a look at some of the highlights of Windows NT's design, such as how it multitasks, how it provides compatibility with programs written for other operating systems, how it remains secure (unable to have its security broken), and so on.

Compatibility

The early versions of OS/2 from Microsoft and IBM taught both companies several important, though painful, lessons. One of the chief lessons surrounded compatibility with existing software. Organizations spend much more money on application software than on operating systems, or even the computer hardware on which they run. In many cases where much custom software is written, these costs exceed even the costs of training and supporting all of the users and systems. Early versions of OS/2 had very poor compatibility with existing DOS applications. In fact, the situation was so difficult that many took to calling the OS/2 1.x "DOS compatibility box" the "penalty box."

One of the design goals for Windows NT is that it be as compatible as possible with existing applications. Considering, however, that Windows NT is also supposed to be a highly secure operating system—in which applications do not have any direct access to the system's hardware or other running programs—makes such compatibility difficult. Still, Windows NT does a far better job of meeting the needs of existing applications than OS/2 1.x was able to.

Windows NT Workstation includes subsystems that let you run DOS, OS/2 1.x, Windows 3.x, Windows 32-bit, and POSIX applications. Also included is the ability to use the FAT and NTFS file systems. The FAT file system supports MS-DOS, Windows 3.x, Windows NT, and OS/2 applications.

Portability

The Intel x86 platform is perfectly adequate for almost any desktop computing need, but falls far short of having the type of horsepower that larger business and government applications need. When you need, for instance, to administer a payroll system for tens of thousands of employees, perform complex modeling of weather patterns, calculate engineering tolerances to a fine degree, or use a computer to design and edit a motion picture, you need much more powerful hardware than that offered by any PC.

Also, consider a business in which people need to use both engineering-level workstations as well as PCs. It would be much less expensive and difficult if the people who needed the high-level workstation performance could use the same operating system and applications as others who use simpler PCs.

For these reasons, and many others, Windows NT is designed to be portable to different hardware architectures. Both Complex Instruction Set Computing (CISC) processors (such as the Intel x86 family), as well as Reduced Instruction Set Computing (RISC) processors are supported by Windows NT. Presently, Windows NT runs on the Intel x86 family, MIPS R4000-based computers, Digital Alpha AXP-based computers, and IBM/Motorola PowerPC-based systems.

Scalability

Windows NT is designed to be scalable in order to take advantage of systems with multiple processors. Scalability means that you can run the same operating system and same programs on more powerful hardware when you need to. You can run Windows NT on systems having from 1 to 32 processors. This capability enables you to install the right amount of processing power for your needs, while also enabling you to increase the power of your hardware as your needs grow—without having to invest in new software.

Note The retail version of Windows NT Workstation 4 supports up to two processors, while the retail version of Windows NT Server 4 supports up to four processors. To support more than four processors, special versions of Windows NT are available from the manufacturer of the multiprocessor computer.

Security

Windows NT is designed to be one of the most secure network operating systems on the market today. Windows NT Server is organized using a hierarchy of Organization, Domain, and Site; security for users is maintained within each Domain and is replicated to each server in the Domain. User accounts are then assigned certain specific rights to resources such as printers, directories, and such, either individually or as part of a group assignment. Default security can be maintained for different groups to which each user may be assigned, and many groups are automatically defined in the system (administrator, domain user, backup administrator, and so on). These groups can be assigned specific resources, and then a user inherits the rights of the assigned group. You can also create security policies in the network and use those policies with groups and users.

In evaluating the security of a given operating system for client/server deployment, it's helpful to have an objective way of clearly evaluating the merits of the products being considered. One such method relies on the U.S. Government's security guidelines, set forth by the National Security Agency. Though business implementations generally are not required to fit within these guidelines, the guidelines do offer a useful yardstick for comparison.

Windows NT Server and Workstation client/server operation provide you with full C2-level security in the operating system. In fact, in August 1995 the NSA rated Windows NT (version 3.5 with Service Pack 3 installed) at the C2 security level. Windows NT is the first widely available graphical operating system to achieve this rating. Keep in mind, though, that this rating does not mean that your particular installation will be certified at the C2 level because certification is always done on a site-by-site basis and takes into account more than the rating of the operating system itself. But, provided your site has met other requirements in areas such as physical access and hardware security, Windows NT can be part of a C2-certified site.

Note Windows NT Workstation and Server do not comply with the C2 security rating when actually connected to a network. This, however, happens to be more of a shortcoming in the current networking standards (including the design of popular protocols like TCP/IP and IPX/SPX) than in Windows NT itself.

What Is C2-level Security?

In order to understand what C2 security means, you first need to understand the context of the National Security Agency security ratings. The NSA sets out requirements for different levels of security for government installations. These levels are assigned a letter from A to D, and the requirements for each are spelled out in a book called the Trusted Computer System Evaluation Criteria, otherwise known as the "Orange Book" (it has an orange cover). These requirements change over time, and are open to interpretation. In fact, each vendor negotiates with the NSA about the details of how its particular products may meet different security levels.

C-level security is based on the concept of Discretionary Access Control (DAC). This means that users are individually authenticated, but are then trusted to know to whom they can and cannot give access. For example, you can be given access to a set of files, but you are then trusted to know whether it's okay to grant others access to those files, and nothing stops you from doing so. B-level security, on the other hand, implements Mandatory Access Control (MAC), such that the operating system has to validate every access granted to ensure that the person being given access has a high enough security rating to access the resource. In a MAC environment, for example, you are not allowed to give others access to your files unless the operating system can validate that the other person has sufficient security clearance for those files. In a commercial enterprise, MAC security is typically overkill (remember a rule of thumb: the stronger the security system is that must be followed, the more effort that is needed to maintain it). And, indeed, no widely available commercial NOS provides B-level security.

Under Windows NT, every object (for example, a file, window, or other system object) has an owner and can be audited. The operating system can audit all actions relating to those objects, such that the administrator can track accesses, or even failed attempts at access. This ability to audit access gives you accountability for the security in the system, and a method for finding out what happened if something goes wrong and information gets into the wrong hands.

User accounts in Windows NT are doubly encrypted in a database that's part of the system. The first encryption is performed on the password itself and uses a one-way function that's computed using an RSA encryption algorithm. Passwords can be up to 128 characters long, use the Unicode character set (a standard that allows for many different languages), and are case-sensitive. The second encryption is performed with the user's relative ID, which is assigned by the system when his account is created. This second encryption increases the difficulty of decrypting a user's password.

Networking

Windows NT was designed from the ground up to operate as a networked platform. Because the requirements for a server are very different from a workstation, however, Microsoft makes two different versions of Windows NT: Server and Workstation. Although both are built on identical foundations, the Server product includes more functionality dedicated to serving large numbers of client computers. Windows NT Workstation, on the other hand, is designed to be a client operating system, which also has the capability to act as a server in a peer-to-peer networking scheme.

Windows NT supports many different networking protocols:

- ◆ **TCP/IP.** The standard for the Internet and Unix machines.
- ◆ **IPX/SPX.** The standard for Novell NetWare networks.
- ◆ **NetBEUI.** A Microsoft protocol used primarily in peer-to-peer networks.

Windows NT also supports a variety of network client/server technologies, such as remote procedure calls (RPCs), NetBIOS, and Windows Sockets.

Understanding Windows NT Workstation System Components

Windows NT Workstation is a modular operating system, in which key components of the system are separate from other components. Contrast this with a monolithic operating system in which most of the operating system resides in a single, large kernel. Figure 1.6 illustrates an overview of the Windows NT architecture.

> **Note** An operating system's kernel is the collection of software functions that reside at the lowest level of the operating system. The kernel is the very core of any operating system.

This section explores the different components of the Windows NT Workstation architecture and how those components work together.

Hardware Abstraction Layer

Because Windows NT is designed to be portable to different computer platforms—all of which use different devices and even different types of devices—some mechanism is needed to insulate the main part of the operating system from the hardware on which it is running. Otherwise, the operating system becomes dependent on the hardware in such a way that it becomes impossible (or nearly so) to port it to other platforms.

Figure 1.6

Windows NT uses many components, all working together seamlessly.

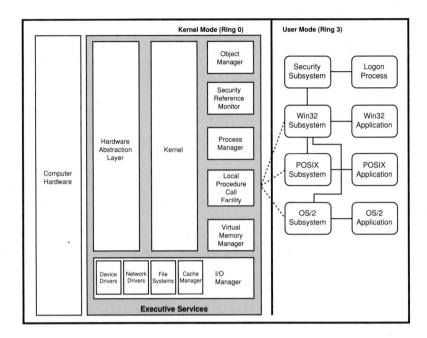

To solve this problem, Windows NT's bottommost layer is designed to shield upper-level parts of the operating system from the hardware. This layer is called the Hardware Abstraction Layer, or HAL. The HAL virtualizes the interfaces between the operating system and the hardware. You might say that it hides the hardware from the rest of the operating system. The kernel, for instance, makes its hardware requests through the HAL. The HAL layer is then responsible for performing the actual hardware interface necessary to achieve the desired result. In this way, most of the programming instructions for the operating system do not need to be customized to work with the different hardware available on different computer platforms.

Because of the HAL, Windows NT can be easily ported to other computer architectures. During the porting, the HAL needs to be modified extensively, but other parts of the operating system (OS) can remain fundamentally unchanged. This is how Windows NT is made to be as portable as possible.

The HAL's main jobs are to service hardware requests from both the kernel and device drivers. The HAL also takes care of the details of symmetric multiprocessing (SMP).

Kernel

The next layer is called the kernel. The kernel is primarily responsible for task scheduling (coordinating when each task in the system runs and how much of the processor it consumes) and for synchronizing work among the processors in the system. It does so by dispatching threads (parts of a task) to the different processors in the system in such a way that the processors operate as efficiently as possible; the kernel tries to run program threads on each processor in a balanced way so that you realize the greatest possible performance from the system.

Higher layers in the system use the kernel to synchronize various activities, and also rely on some kernel functions called kernel objects. These objects are accessible through various Application Programming Interfaces (APIs) and can be used by programmers.

Note Objects—in the context of software—can be a tricky concept to understand. Basically, every part of the system—where a "part" can be a location in memory, a file, a folder, a system component, a hardware device driver, and so on—is treated as an individual object that is distinct from other objects in the system. Each object can contain both programming code that runs, and data that is specific to the object.

Objects benefit programmers and users because they allow programming styles that, at a fundamental level, force programmers to design their programs so that they are more modular than otherwise, are more reliable, and are easier to program. Entire books are available that discuss the details of object-oriented programming if you're interested in learning more about how software objects work, and how to program and use them.

There are two types of objects managed by the kernel: dispatcher objects and control objects. Dispatcher objects are used to control and coordinate access to system resources, and control objects are used to perform control actions on the system. Tables 1.1 and 1.2 list the available dispatcher and control objects, respectively.

TABLE 1.1
Dispatcher Objects

Type of Object	Description
Event	Event objects record the occurrence of events, and are used by other threads to coordinate actions.
Mutant	Mutant objects control access to resources where the access needs to be mutually exclusive. Mutant objects can be used in both kernel and user modes of the system.

continues

TABLE 1.1, CONTINUED
Dispatcher Objects

Type of Object	Description
Mutex	Mutex objects also provide for mutually exclusive access to resources, but are used only in kernel mode.
Semaphore	Semaphores are used to coordinate access to resources, even in a shared fashion (as opposed to mutually exclusive). Semaphore objects exist in signaled and unsignaled states.
Thread	Threads in Windows NT are objects that are dispatched by the kernel. Thread objects exist only within defined process objects.
Timer	Timer objects are used to measure time between events and also are used as timeout mechanisms for procedures that are not able to accomplish their tasks.

TABLE 1.2
Control Objects

Type of Object	Description
Asynchronous Procedure Call	APC objects are used to halt the execution of a given thread object.
Interrupt	Interrupt objects tie processor interrupts to the service routines associated with the interrupts.
Process	Process objects contain the virtual memory address space and other information associated with a process, such as a list of thread objects in the process and their current status.
Profile	A profile object is a special object that is used to profile, or measure, how long program functions take to execute.

NT Executive

The Windows NT Executive is made up of a number of components working together that provide services to the environment subsystems. Broadly grouped, these Executive Service Components include the following:

- ◆ **Device Drivers.** Lets the operating system interface with specific hardware devices.

- ◆ **Hardware Abstraction Layer (also called the HAL).** Interfaces the computer hardware with the operating system.

- ◆ **Managers.** Manages Input and Output, processes, objects, security, and window management.

- ◆ **Microkernel.** Handles the lowest-level of the operating system services, including scheduling activities on the operating system and hardware interrupts.

Specific components of the NT Executive include the Object Manager, Process Manager, Virtual Memory Manager, Local Procedure Call Facility, I/O Manager, Cache Manager, and the Security Reference Monitor (refer to fig. 1.6). Collectively, these components support a layer of software called System Services, which in turn provides an interface between user-mode subsystems (such as the DOS or Win32 subsystem) and the NT Executive.

Object Manager

The Object Manager manages system objects. Objects in this context are run-time instances (objects that are created when the object is invoked) that are used by the operating system. The Object Manager creates object handles (pointers that programs use to reference the objects) for the system objects, as required by applications that need access to the system objects.

The Object Manager also controls the Windows NT namespace and manages system objects on an ongoing basis. The namespace lets processes access objects that have names. Examples of named objects are file objects, port objects, thread objects, and so on.

Process Manager

Two types of objects, process objects and thread objects, are controlled by the Process Manager. The Process Manager creates and deletes processes, and provides application services for managing process and thread objects.

> **Note** A process is comprised of a memory address space, a collection of objects associated with the process, and the thread objects of the process. There is always at least one thread associated with every process.

Virtual Memory Manager

Windows NT's memory model accommodates up to 4 GB (4096 MB) of virtual memory for each process. The memory is called virtual because it can be composed of both physical RAM and temporary storage residing on the hard disk. The Virtual Memory Manager manages this memory so that applications running are not aware of whether their memory address spaces exist in RAM or in the virtual memory file on the disk; the entire process of managing the virtual memory is transparent to the applications.

In Windows NT's memory model, each process has 4 GB of allocated virtual memory space—2 GB for program storage and 2 GB for system storage. This memory is broken down into 4 KB pieces, called *pages*. There are therefore over 1 million virtual 4 KB pages for each process. Each individual page can be located either in RAM or in the virtual memory area on the hard disk. Accordingly, Windows NT is said to use a *paging virtual memory architecture*. Paging contrasts with swapping, which Windows 3.1 used and which works with larger pieces of memory (64 KB in the case of Windows 3.1). Windows NT's virtual memory is stored in a file called PAGEFILE.SYS, which can be located on any of the system's disks. In fact, Windows NT can have multiple paging files, each located on a different disk, and the system can coordinate the paged memory located in all of the different virtual memory files.

The Virtual Memory Manager controls the pages of memory so that all pages needed by a process are, if necessary, moved from the paging file into RAM so that the process can run as efficiently as possible. Unused pages may be kept in the paging file, and frequently used pages are kept in RAM. This process is called *demand paging*.

> **Note** The Windows NT kernel is not pagable, and always resides in physical RAM.

The paging work done by the Virtual Memory Manager can grow quite complex because it keeps track of where each page of each process's memory is located and manages the pages accordingly. The processes themselves are ignorant of this information; the Virtual Memory Manager "shows" them their allocated memory and takes care of the details of managing that memory.

The approximate steps that the Virtual Memory Manager takes look like this:

1. An application stores data to memory.

2. The Virtual Memory Manager (VMM) handles the request. It calculates how many pages are needed for the request and then creates a map connecting

unused RAM to the memory address space the application uses. It ensures that the RAM pages used do not conflict with any other uses.

3. If RAM is being completely used, the VMM then examines how recently the pages of RAM have been accessed and moves the necessary number of pages to the paging file and then assigns those pages to the application that made the most recent storage request.

When an application subsequently requests memory that has been moved to the paging file, the VMM transparently reverses the process, moving the page of memory back into RAM and updating the memory map for the affected applications.

Local Procedure Call Facility

Each running application is supported by an appropriate environment subsystem. There are subsystems for Win16, Win32, POSIX, OS/2, and DOS applications. Applications communicate with the appropriate subsystem in a client/server fashion, where they make requests of the subsystem and receive responses that satisfy those requests. Windows NT includes a component called the Local Procedure Call Facility that acts as a communication conduit between applications and their subsystems.

Note   The Local Procedure Call Facility functions similarly to the Remote Procedure Call Facility that network applications can use.

Applications in Windows NT are isolated from the subsystems that they rely on. If this weren't the case, an errant application could crash the subsystem in question, possibly affecting other running applications that are also relying on the subsystem.

Applications do not directly make calls to their subsystems. Rather, the application contains stub functions that mirror the functions in the subsystem. When the application makes a particular operating system API call, it actually only executes one of these stub functions. The stub function then packages the request and sends it to the subsystem in question using the Local Procedure Call Facility. The subsystem then unpacks the request, fulfills it, and packages a message to the application with the results of the API call (again, using the Local Procedure Call Facility). As far as the application can tell, it executed the function directly. In reality, the program and the subsystem were kept at arm's length.

Note   If you're not familiar with programming, a *call* is simply a request from a program to the operating system that asks to get something done. An application, for example, makes calls to create and destroy windows, display text, or use one of the devices connected to the computer.

There is only one disadvantage to this approach: it adds overhead to the system, which impacts performance. However, it also drastically improves the reliability of the system. Remember that the fastest application in the world does no good if it regularly gets halted by other applications in the system. In the long run, the reliability of this approach outweighs the performance impact.

I/O Manager

Windows NT uses a layered device driver model. At the bottom layer are the device drivers, which communicate directly with the computer hardware. Above device drivers are network drivers, which send and accept network information. Next up the line are file system drivers, such as those that support FAT or NTFS disks. One more level up is the Cache Manager, discussed in the next section. And at the top level is the I/O Manager, which is responsible for managing all input and output for Windows NT.

This architecture creates a standard mechanism for handling all I/O in the system. From an application's perspective, all devices fundamentally operate the same way because it is the lower levels of drivers that actually take into account how to communicate with different types of devices, such as network cards or hard disks. The I/O Manager helps pass information back and forth between the lower-level drivers and the application subsystems, and simplifies the application programmer's job.

Applications can use two methods to access information through the I/O Manager. The simplest method is called synchronous I/O, where the application's processing is directly tied to getting information back from the driver. An application, for example, might request data from a disk. The I/O Manager accepts the request and halts further processing by the application (the application is said to be I/O blocked). Once the request is fulfilled by the disk device driver, the application is started again and the information it requested is sent.

For many applications, synchronous I/O is perfectly suitable. Because most devices in the system are much slower than the processor, an application might have to wait a long time (relatively speaking) until it can continue doing work. In some cases, an application might be able to accomplish a significant amount of other work while its I/O request is being fulfilled. In cases such as these, asynchronous I/O solves the problem. When an application is programmed to use asynchronous I/O, the I/O Manager accepts the requests and puts them into the queue of waiting requests. It does not block the application from further processing. When the request is fulfilled by the device, the I/O Manager signals the application that its data is ready and sends the data back to the application.

| **Note** | The I/O Manager fulfills I/O requests in the most efficient order possible, which is not necessarily in the order in which they were received. For instance, a series of requests to the disk might be sent to the disk controller before requests bound for a network board are processed. The I/O Manager is designed to get the most work accomplished in the least amount of time, and sometimes you get more work accomplished in less time if you structure it differently.

Here's a real world example: when you make a list of things you need from the supermarket, you don't walk through aisles only grabbing things in the order in which they're listed on your shopping list; instead, you walk through each aisle and get the items on the list in that aisle so you only have to make one pass through each aisle. If you only grab things in the order in which they're listed, you would be in the store for a long time! The I/O Manager follows similar rules to optimize performance.

Cache Manager

Between the I/O Manager and the lower-level device drivers is a component called the Cache Manager, which manages all of the device caching in the system.

A cache is an area of system memory (RAM) that keeps frequently accessed data readily available. When data previously requested from a disk is in the cache, and an application requests that data from the disk again, rather than the request being sent to the actual hard disk, the cache provides the data. Because system memory is many times faster than hard disks, applications using cached data run much faster than they would if they had to rely on the disk to satisfy all of their data requests. Caching can also apply to data requested from a network or from other devices working the same way.

The Cache Manager has a variety of features that improve its effectiveness:

◆ **Dynamic sizing.** Grows and shrinks the size of the cache in response to system demands and available memory.

◆ **Lazy writing.** Lets the cache record make changes to data, and then writes those changes to the device when the system is less busy. This feature enables the application to continue processing instead of waiting for the new data to be completely written to the device.

◆ **Lazy commit.** Similar to lazy writing, but used when transactions (such as those for a database application) are written by an application.

Note For information on controlling the behavior of Windows NT's caching, see Chapter 30, "Managing Disks."

Windows NT Environmental Subsystems

Windows NT contains a number of different environmental subsystems that provide compatibility for various types of applications. Using these subsystems, Windows NT Workstation 4 can run applications originally written for DOS, OS/2 1.x, Windows 3.x (also known as Win16), POSIX, and Win32.

Each subsystem resides in its own user-mode process. Each of the environmental subsystem processes is protected from the other subsystems so that, for example, a crash in the Win16 subsystem doesn't bring down other subsystems.

Note The Win32 subsystem handles screen, keyboard, and mouse I/O for all subsystems. If the Win32 subsystem crashes, the other subsystems also crash.

The Win32 subsystem is always loaded and running when the system is up. The other subsystems are only loaded when an application of that type is started. For this reason, you can realize some operating efficiencies (slightly lower RAM requirements and faster overall system speed) by using applications that make use of as few subsystems as possible.

DOS Subsystem

DOS programs behave poorly on the whole; they were written for an operating system that allowed them to completely take over the computer's hardware. In order for Windows NT to be a secure environment, this sort of behavior cannot be permitted. Many DOS communications programs, for example, are designed to take complete control of the computer's serial ports while communicating. Under Windows NT, this setup would compromise the rest of the system's ability to use the serial ports. Similar problems exist for other devices in the computer, such as the hard and floppy disk drives and even installed RAM. Plus, if a DOS program had access to direct control of any of the hardware in the system, it could mistakenly crash the rest of the system. If Windows NT's design is to be as crash-proof as possible, it doesn't make sense to allow this sort of behavior from DOS programs. Yet most DOS programs won't operate unless they can take control of the hardware. So what's the solution?

In order to protect an operating system such as Windows NT from DOS programs that are written using "unsafe" programming techniques, you must virtualize, or imitate, the PC hardware for the DOS program, without letting the DOS program know that it isn't really working directly with the hardware. So when a DOS program "thinks" it is working directly with the serial port, actually it is working with a Windows NT-provided imitation of the port. Windows NT provides these virtual services for all the functions that a DOS program may need.

Each DOS application runs under Windows NT using a Virtual DOS Machine (VDM). The VDM is written as a Win32 application and offers the DOS program a complete virtual environment, which completely imitates a DOS-based PC for the DOS program.

> **Note** | Intel-based computers have a feature built into their processors called Virtual-86 mode. With this feature, the processor can work with Windows NT to allow the DOS program to access features in the processor directly without compromising the overall integrity of the rest of the system. RISC-based installations of Windows NT will not have this capability, and therefore emulate the Intel x86 instruction set entirely in software. For this reason, DOS programs will typically run far better on Intel-based Windows NT workstations than on RISC-based Windows NT workstations. You can still access legacy DOS applications on RISC-based machines running Windows NT; they will just operate slowly.

Windows 3.1x (Win16) Subsystem

It was critical to the design of Windows NT that it be able to run the broadest base of Windows 3.1x applications available. Windows 3.1x applications, however, are written for a very different environment, and often rely on the underlying DOS operating system for some essential services.

Windows NT runs Windows 3.1x applications through the Windows 3.1x subsystem (more commonly referred to as the Win16 subsystem). By default, the subsystem is a single VDM that runs all the Win16 applications. A crash in one Win16 application, therefore, affects other running Win16 applications; the rest of the Windows NT system will continue running.

> **Note** | It is possible to run Win16 applications in separate VDMs, but the default is to use a single VDM. Using multiple VDMs consumes a lot more system RAM than relying on a single VDM. However, by using multiple VDMs you avoid the problem of one application taking down others using the same VDM.
>
> See Chapter 18, "Running Windows Applications," for instructions on running Win16 programs in separate VDMs.

The Win16 VDM is preemptively multitasked within Windows NT. The Win16 applications running within the VDM, however, are cooperatively multitasked with respect to each other. Consequently, a Win16 application that is poorly written will inhibit other running Win16 applications but not other types of applications in the system.

> **Note** | The Win16 subsystem is sometimes called Windows on Windows, or WOW.

OS/2 Subsystem

Windows NT provides support for OS/2 1.x character-based applications on Intel-based computers only. The support for OS/2-based applications is somewhat limited in that certain types of OS/2 1.x applications won't run. The types of programs that will not run include these:

◆ Applications that need to run at the Ring 2 protection level of the processor

◆ Applications that require direct access to any ports

◆ Applications that require custom OS/2 device drivers

> **Note** When you use a Family API application (one written in such a way that a single executable file runs under either OS/2 1.x or MS-DOS), Windows NT always runs that application in the OS/2 subsystem.

POSIX Subsystem

POSIX stands for Portable Operating System Interface for Computing Environments. POSIX is a collection of standards developed by the Institute of Electrical and Electronic Engineers (IEEE). Its intention is to enable a broad set of standards for better compatibility between computer types and different operating systems. POSIX is a standard for applications written for Unix-based operating systems.

Windows NT supports POSIX-based applications through a POSIX subsystem. This subsystem requires NTFS-formatted disks to provide POSIX-required disk functions, such as case-sensitive file names.

There are three main components that make up the POSIX subsystem:

◆ **PSXSS.EXE.** The main subsystem program, which is automatically loaded the first time a POSIX program is started.

◆ **POSIX.EXE.** A Windows NT program that communicates between the subsystem and the Executive Services. Each running POSIX program uses its own copy of POSIX.EXE.

◆ **PSXDLL.DLL.** A dynamic link library file that works with each POSIX application and communicates between PSXSS.EXE and the application.

None of the POSIX subsystem components are loaded until the first POSIX-based program is started.

Win32 Subsystem

The Win32 subsystem is the main subsystem in Windows NT. It handles more than just running Win32-based applications; it also handles all user-input tasks and screen output for the entire Windows NT operating system.

The Win32 subsystem uses asynchronous input queues, in which each program has a separate input queue that takes keyboard and mouse input and passes it along to the program. This method contrasts with synchronous input queues, in which each program shares a single input queue. OS/2 Warp, for example, uses a synchronous input queue, and therefore is vulnerable to a single program "hanging" and keeping other programs from being able to accept input. Windows 3.1 and Windows 95 also use synchronous input queues. When a program hang happens on a system that uses a single, synchronous input queue, the entire system is effectively unusable, even though the other programs are still running normally; there's no way for the system to get input to those other programs. The Win32 subsystem, on the other hand, lets you gracefully continue to work with other programs even when one program hangs.

Understanding Protected Mode Operating Systems

MS-DOS and early versions of Windows for Intel platforms were *real mode* operating systems. They used the Intel family of processors in real mode, in which all running programs had full access to all of the hardware in the system. In some ways, this access was a blessing to software designers of the time because they could take control of the hardware directly when DOS programming interfaces were inadequate for getting the job they wanted done. DOS, for example, has always had relatively poor programming services for letting programs write information to the display, so virtually all DOS programs bypass the built-in DOS display functions and simply write to the video display memory hardware directly. Similar capabilities were used by some DOS programs for communications, networking, and hard disk access.

The problem with direct hardware access in real-mode operating systems occurs primarily when you move to a multitasking operating system, in which you have many programs running at the same time. Now you have a huge problem because many programs in the system are all trying to access the same hardware at the same time. Since there are no standardized signaling systems for coordinating such access in DOS, the situation quickly becomes an impossible one. In addition, a buggy program in such a system will take the entire system down, including the operating system itself.

Protected mode operating systems, such as Windows NT Workstation 4, take advantage of a special mode on the Intel 80386 and greater processors to protect parts of the system from one another. This section explores these capabilities, both in general and in how they apply to Windows NT Workstation 4.

Real Mode

The first microprocessor used in the IBM PC was the Intel 8088. It was a 16-bit, general-purpose processor that was capable of addressing 20 bits of memory, which resulted in a 1 MB memory limit using the segmented memory addressing model. The segmented memory model breaks the computer's memory up into 64 KB pieces, called segments. When a program accesses memory under this system, it specifies the appropriate segment, and then further specifies an offset, which is a 16-bit value that points to the exact byte of memory within the segment.

Real Mode is the simplest mode available; no provisions are made in how the processor works to protect programs from one another, or to protect the operating system memory space from programs that are running.

Protected Mode

When Intel introduced the 80286 microprocessor, first used in the IBM AT Personal Computer, it added a feature called Protected Mode. Protected Mode on the 80286 allowed the processor to access up to 16 MB of memory, called Extended Memory—physical memory above the 1 MB limit imposed by the 8088. The 80286 also could be run in Real Mode, where it acted just like a faster version of the 8088 processor and had the same 1 MB memory limitation of the 8088 processor.

Protected Mode offers many advantages over Real Mode:

◆ Support for virtual memory

◆ Support for multitasking operating systems that keep programs confined, or protected, within their own memory spaces

◆ Privilege levels for programs that can be used to keep non-operating system programs from corrupting the operating system

A problem in the design of the 80286 made it difficult to provide a multitasking, protected mode operating system that would also provide for easy compatibility with programs written for Real Mode (DOS programs). In order to multitask Real Mode and Protected Mode programs, the operating system had to switch the 80286 rapidly between those two modes. This switching process on the 80286 took so long that it was no longer usable for this purpose. This is why OS/2 1.x couldn't run DOS programs while OS/2 programs were running; the two modes couldn't co-exist, or even pretend to co-exist, because switching between real and protected mode simply took too long.

When Intel released the 80386 family of processors, it added an additional mode on top of the other two: Virtual 8086 (V86) mode. V86 mode was designed to allow a Protected Mode operating system to run Real Mode programs without the switching requirements of the 80286. The 80386 was also the first 32-bit processor in the x86 family, allowing it to access up to 4 GB of physical or virtual memory.

Privilege Rings

In Protected Mode, the processor can enforce different levels of protection for different parts of the system using a series of protection rings. These rings are numbered from 0 to 3 on the Intel family of processors, with lower-numbered rings having greater access to the system. Software running at ring 0, for instance, can access all memory and can preempt programs running at any higher ring. Programs running at ring 3, on the other hand, don't have the ability to directly access memory owned by lower-ring programs, nor can they preempt programs running in lower rings.

Windows NT Workstation 4 only uses two of these ring levels, ring 0 and ring 3. Ring 0 is called *kernel mode*; ring 3 is called *user mode.* Windows NT Workstation 4 only uses two rings in order to maintain compatibility with RISC-based machines, which only have two rings.

New to Windows NT Workstation 4 are the three graphics subsystems that have been moved from user mode to kernel mode. While this could, in theory, reduce the overall reliability of the system, it also provides substantially better graphics performance. The services that were moved from user to kernel mode are the Windows Manager, which provides input and output services for the screen and other devices, and the Graphics Device Interface and Graphics Device Drivers (refer to fig. 1.6).

Understanding Multitasking

Windows NT Workstation is built around a powerful preemptive multitasking, multithreaded model controlled by a task scheduler. This section examines Windows NT's multitasking abilities in detail and compares it to other possible methods.

> **Note** A single processor can only do one thing at a time. However, it does its work incredibly fast. So fast, in fact, that you can parcel out its time to multiple programs, each one doing a little bit of work before the processor moves on to the next program. It works so quickly that you won't be able to perceive that the system is rapidly switching between all these running programs. For example, right now I'm running a word processor, a graphics program, and a CD player that's playing some music. As far as I can tell, all of these programs are running simultaneously. In reality, one runs for a very short period of time, then the next one runs, and so on. This is what is meant by multitasking.

Preemptive versus Cooperative Multitasking

A computer's finite amount of processor time can be divided using one of two multitasking methods: preemptive or cooperative multitasking.

In a preemptive system, the operating system controls when and how much computer time any particular process in the system receives. The operating system can preempt a running program and give other programs a chance to run. Windows NT Workstation is a fully preemptive multitasking system.

In a cooperative system, each process has to explicitly or implicitly allow other processes to run. They can either explicitly make a call to the operating system signaling their willingness to relinquish control of the machine, or they can make a system call that implies that the operating system is free to accomplish other tasks while the call is executed (disk I/O calls are an example of this). Microsoft Windows 3.1 is a cooperative multitasker.

A cooperative system, though easier to design (because it's simpler and forces more of the work of multitasking onto the application programmers), has several problems inherent in its design:

◆ **Poorly coded applications.** Poorly coded applications might not relinquish the computer for long periods of time, potentially causing other jobs to lose information. One example is a computer that has to maintain a high-speed connection to another computer. A program written in a sloppy fashion running on the same system can cause the timing-critical application to lose its connection or data.

◆ **"Jerkiness."** Because the system relies on applications to relinquish control, and because a large number of applications running at the same time will almost certainly be guaranteed not to reliably and consistently relinquish control in regular time increments, multitasking is often "jerky" under a cooperative scheme. This jerkiness can cause productivity problems when you try to accomplish work while a background process is dominating the computer.

◆ **Programming difficulty.** Programming an application for such a system is more difficult because the programmer has to constantly insert pieces of code that will explicitly relinquish control back to the operating system, and therefore to other running programs.

A preemptive system directly addresses these problems:

◆ **Regularity/reliability.** All tasks are guaranteed to get the attention of the computer, regularly and reliably.

◆ **Centralized scheduling.** No single application, or combination of applications, can dominate the computer to the detriment of other tasks on the system.

◆ **Programming ease.** The application programmer does not have to worry about releasing control on a periodic basis in the application.

Scheduling versus Time Slicing

Two ways of actually scheduling the activity of multiple tasks running on the computer are scheduling and time slicing. A scheduling system has a component that manages the time slices—minimum units of processor time—that the tasks receive. A nonscheduling-based time slicing system divides the computer time up between all applications running in some static fashion.

Time slicing operating systems generally distribute computer time evenly to all running processes. Although this might be a good idea in certain situations, it is not optimal for most. More advanced time slicing operating systems, such as Desqview or the VDM capability in Windows 3.x, enable manual adjustment of processor time to running tasks. Although this setup is somewhat better, it still has its problems:

◆ **Inflexibility.** A process's need for processor time might be critical at some points and not at others. These needs are not easily anticipated, nor do manual time slice settings lend themselves to rapid changes.

◆ **Inaccessibility.** In most time slicing schemes, the application doesn't have the capability to directly affect its own priority levels, so it can't manage its own needs.

◆ **Changing the mix.** Adding a new program to the mix changes the relative weights of the other programs running. These changes can adversely affect an application that has minimum needs that must be met, such as a communications session.

What is needed is a fluid method for managing the computer's time, fairly and evenly, with an eye for taking especially good care of critical processes.

Windows NT Workstation 4 answers this need with a priority-based scheduling system. There are two priority classes: real-time and variable. Each priority class has 16 levels of priority. At a particular priority level, within a particular class, the system operates in a round-robin fashion; each thread at that particular priority level gets a single time slice. A thread continues to run until one of two events occurs: the time slice finishes, or an interrupt occurs that makes a thread of a higher priority class ready to run. In the second case, the running thread is preempted by the system in favor of the higher priority thread.

Threads

Under Windows NT, processes do not run; threads do all the work. Every process has at least one thread and can have many more if the programmer designs the application to use multiple threads.

Earlier multitasking operating systems, such as early versions of Unix, just had processes (also called tasks). Each running program was a process, with its own

individual assigned memory and other system resources. In a character-mode application, this type of setup is satisfactory. Graphical applications, however, can often
benefit from having multiple "sub-tasks" running.

For example, a great design for a word processor involves using a separate task to
print or repaginate a large document, enabling the user to continue working with the
document while it's being printed or repaginated. Another example: a spreadsheet
program could have a separate task that constantly recalculates a large spreadsheet
while the user is still inputting numbers and formulas. (If you've ever worked with a
large spreadsheet and had to wait for it to recalculate, you'll appreciate the second
example.)

There are two ways to accomplish this sort of multitasking within a single program.
One way involves using separate processes to do each job, and setting up a communications mechanism between the different processes that are working together.

Using the word processor example again, you would need some way for the main
program to tell the printing or repagination routines what work needs to be done,
and to receive a message back from the routines once they have finished their work.

Using the spreadsheet program example, a great deal of communication is necessary
between the main program and the recalculation process that's running so that
updated information would be passed to the calculation routine, and answers would
be received and posted into the spreadsheet. Obviously, this undertaking would be
very complex. This mechanism would also be very processor-intensive because there
would be significant overhead in just handling the interprocess communications.

Also, don't forget that each of these separate processes would all need their own
system memory assigned, and each would have to contend for devices in the computer to which they needed access.

A much simpler model involves breaking a process, or task, into threads. A thread is
the same as a separate task except that it shares all the resources of the process in
which the thread runs. (Remember that threads always belong to a process.) In the
spreadsheet example, the program with the separate recalculation module could run
in a single process, with separate threads assigned to recalculate, print, accept input
from the user, provide help, and so on. Each thread can share all of the resources of
its parent process, and the threads' individual access to the resources can be coordi-
nated with much simpler programming mechanisms, such as semaphores.

Note | A semaphore is a flag that is assigned to a resource, like a memory variable, within
a process. Different threads can manipulate the semaphore so that other threads
know whether the resource is available or busy.

On a system with one microprocessor, only one thread is running at any particular time. In a multiprocessor system, however, each processor can service a thread, so the system can handle multiple threads simultaneously (one per processor). Windows NT Workstation implements this architecture.

Understanding NT Security

Windows NT was designed from the ground up to be a secure operating system that can comply with C2-level security requirements as described by the U.S. Government National Security Agency.

Note You can learn more about C2-level security earlier in this chapter under the heading "Security."

C2-level security relies on a concept called discretionary access control, which requires that the following goals be met:

◆ Each resource owner must be able to control access to the resource. Resources can be items such as files, directories, or even ports on the computer.

◆ Every user of the system must be uniquely identified to the system by a user name and password. Additionally, the system has to be able to audit each user's actions.

◆ The administrator of the system has to be able to audit operating system events that surround the security of the system and the audit data must be accessed only by the authorized user accounts (administrators).

◆ Objects in the operating system must be managed by the operating system so that the resource cannot be randomly accessed or reused by other owners or processes, even after the resources are freed by the owning processes.

◆ The system has to be secure from outside unauthorized attempts. An outside attempt may come through a floppy disk, a network connection, a modem connection, and so on.

◆ The operating system itself must be secured so that it cannot be tampered with when running.

To meet these goals, Windows NT employs these components that work together:

◆ **Logon Process.** A logon process displays when a user logs on to a Windows NT workstation or server. It is the process that accepts a user's name and password, authenticates it, and grants entry into the system.

◆ **Local Security Authority.** The core component responsible for ensuring security within Windows NT, this process generates user access tokens, supports the logon processes, and administers the security policies defined in the system. The Local Security Authority is also responsible for auditing and logging security events.

◆ **Security Account Manager.** A database that holds all of the user information and validates users.

◆ **Security Reference Monitor.** Provides real-time services to validate every object access and action made by a user to ensure that the access or action is authorized.

In the following sections, you learn more about these components and how they work together to keep Windows NT secure.

Logon Security

Windows NT's logon process—the one you use when you enter your user name and password—is initiated by pressing Ctrl+Alt+Del. Microsoft chose this key combination to make it harder for a Trojan horse program (see the following note) to insert itself and record your user name and password. Because the Ctrl+Alt+Del keystroke is trapped at a very low level in the system, it is very difficult to intercept this keystroke and insert a Trojan horse program.

 Note In a system with sloppy security procedures or design, it can be easy to write a Trojan horse program that appears just like the system logon, but instead records user names and passwords to a log file, and then calls the real logon program transparently.

Once logged on to Windows NT, you are granted a security access token. The token contains information about your account, including your unique security ID (SID), as well as the security IDs for any groups to which you belong. The token also includes other information about your user account (the account the administrator created for you to use when accessing the system), such as your name.

Every process you invoke is automatically given a copy of your security access token. The token resides in the process, even if the application is unaware of the token. In order to allow or deny access, Windows NT automatically uses that token for all resources that the application in the process tries to access.

In some cases, other processes in the system impersonate user accounts. For instance, when a remote user makes a request of a server process, the server process takes on the security attributes of the user in order to access the resource (such as a file). This process of "borrowing" a user's security level is called impersonation.

Each account defined in Windows NT has a Security Access ID (SID) that uniquely identifies the account to the system. SIDs are guaranteed by the system to be unique and cannot be reused when an account is deleted and then reinstated. This keeps the administrator from giving accidental access to resources; all accounts must have all their accesses defined explicitly, even when adding a user who previously had an account on the system. SIDs are said to be "unique across space and time" by Microsoft.

File and Object Security

Every named object in the Windows NT system can be secured. Objects can be devices on the system or, more commonly, simple files and programs. Each object has a security descriptor that includes the owner's SID (the owner is often the creator of the object), a discretionary access control list (ACL), a system ACL, and for POSIX compatibility, a group security ID. The discretionary ACL lists all of the groups and users who can access the object; the system ACL controls the auditing level (the level of detail about accesses to the object that are recorded) that the operating system observes for accesses to the object.

Different types of objects use different types of permissions. A file object, for example, might have permissions like Read, Write, and so on; other types of objects might use different permissions.

> **Note**   You learn more about object permissions in Chapter 26, "Understanding Shared Resources."

Some objects in the system are containers (such as a directory), and others are noncontainers (such as a file in that directory). By default, objects created within a container inherit the container's permission settings. An administrator can override this function for individual objects or subcontainers if necessary.

Each object has an ACL in its security descriptor. The access control list contains a number of access control entries that list the permissions for the object.

Understanding the Workgroup Security Model

Workgroups are collections of computers on a network. Each member of a workgroup can browse other computers and resources within the workgroup. The security for each resource and user is managed on each individual computer, and each computer has its own security policies and security administration requirements.

The workgroup security model works best with small numbers of users on a network that does not have centralized security management available, such as an MIS person or department. It is a simple and convenient model for such small networks, and it is easy to implement.

Understanding the Domain Security Model

The domain security model relies on the use of the Windows NT Directory Services, a common database that manages the security and names of all the shared resources on a network. This common directory is centrally managed by someone with Administrator privileges. There is only one database per each domain, although a copy may exist on multiple computers for redundancy.

The directory services database is controlled by a Windows NT Server computer set up as a *primary domain controller*. The domain controller is contacted by other computers on the network in order to validate access to network resources. You can also create *backup domain controllers* that handle the same job if the primary domain controller is unavailable for some reason. When created, the domain directory services database is automatically synchronized (replicated) between all of the domain controllers on the network.

The domain controller controls user logon to the network and to shared resources, such as printers, files, and folders.

You should use the domain security model in larger networks (those with more than about 10 workstations), and a specific individual should be designated to maintain the security of the domain.

Understanding Windows NT File Systems

Disks are formatted using a file system. A file system defines how the data is arranged on the disk, how the system accesses data on the disk, what additional information is kept on the hard disk for each file or directory, and so on. Windows NT supports two different hard disk file systems, plus one exclusively used for CD-ROMs:

- ◆ FAT (File Access Table)
- ◆ NTFS (NT File System)
- ◆ CDFS (CD-ROM File System, used only for access to any CD-ROM drives)

FAT stems from the original MS-DOS file system. NTFS is loosely based on the HPFS designed for OS/2, but has many additional features. Both FAT and NTFS file systems can be supported simultaneously, although each partition has to be formatted to use one or the other.

FAT

All file systems in use on PCs allow files to be stored across different physical areas on the disk. A single file, for example, may have quite a few individual parts, each one stored in a different spot on the disk. The file system needs to have a way to track where all the parts of a file are in such a way that you never have to pay attention to the details of where each file is stored.

The FAT file system is named for the method with which it tracks information on the disk. Each FAT-formatted disk contains two file allocation tables (one is a redundant duplicate of the first). These tables list each of the files on the disk and their start location on the disk. The next entry contains a link to the third location on the disk, and the chain continues until the last location used by the file is defined.

FAT is most efficient for partitions under 400 MB in size, although performance worsens when many files are being stored. Also, FAT tends to be faster than NTFS for sequential file accesses, whereas NTFS tends to be faster for random file accesses.

> **Note**   The system partition on RISC-based computers running Windows NT Workstation 4 must be formatted using the FAT file system.

Understanding Clusters and Storage Efficiency

FAT file allocation units are called clusters. Clusters can be of various sizes but are always a power-of-two multiple of the sector size, which is always 512 bytes. Larger hard disk partitions require larger clusters.

FAT can only reference 16 bits of information to describe which cluster contains information on the disk. This defines the maximum number of clusters that can be used. Because 16 bits lets you count up to only 65,535, you can only have that many clusters on a single hard disk partition.

For a FAT disk with 512-byte clusters, you can support disk partitions of up to 33,553,920 bytes, or a little over 33.5 MB. You arrive at this number by multiplying the maximum number of clusters by the cluster size. In this case, you multiply 65,535 by 512 to arrive at the 33.5 MB maximum partition size.

FAT can support larger hard disk partitions than 33 MB, but it does so by increasing the cluster size. The following table shows the maximum partition size, given different cluster sizes:

continues

Cluster size	Maximum Partition Size
1024	67,107,840 (67 MB)
2048	134,215,680 (134 MB)
4096	268,431,360 (268 MB)
8192	536,862,720 (536 MB)
16384	1,073,725,440 (1.07 GB)

Every file uses at least one cluster on the hard disk. Partial clusters can't be allocated. So, on a hard disk partition that uses 16 KB clusters, every file will take up at least 16 KB on the hard disk, even when the file is only one byte long. Similarly, a file that is 16,385 bytes long will take up two clusters because it is one byte larger than a single cluster can hold. Depending on the mix of files on a FAT-formatted partition, a significant amount of hard disk space can be wasted because of this allocation method.

Because of this relative lack of efficiency, some people try to create multiple partitions of their large hard disks, each one using a small cluster size. For instance, some people carve up a 300 MB hard disk into nine different partitions, just so that each partition can use a 512-byte cluster size. The problem with this is that it becomes virtually impossible to intelligently manage the space on the hard disk. A user's out of luck when a program needs to store all of its files on a single hard disk and the program needs more space than can fit on any single partition.

The answer to finding maximum efficiency is to balance the desire to get the most storage out of your disks with the complexity of managing many different partitions. On most systems running only FAT-formatted partitions, you should generally create no more than three or four partitions. This is just a rule of thumb, but more partitions will be tougher to manage, while fewer partitions may waste too much space. Calculate the percentage of your disk that can be supported by different cluster sizes, and create your partitions so that you're getting the maximum benefit from a given cluster size without forcing FAT to use the next-larger cluster size.

The FAT file system is required by Windows 95, and therefore if you wish to run both Windows 95 and Windows NT Workstation on a given computer, at least one disk partition must be formatted with FAT. Similarly, DOS only works with FAT-formatted disk partitions.

To make the situation more complex, some versions of Windows 95 being shipped with newer computers can use an updated FAT file system called FAT32. Windows NT Workstation 4 cannot access FAT32-formatted partitions.

Under Windows NT 4, the FAT file system has the following file name features:

◆ File names can be up to 255 characters long, versus the DOS and Windows 3.x limit of eight characters followed by a three character extension.

◆ File names must start with a letter or number, but can then contain other special characters, except " / [ ] : ; | = , ^ * and ?

◆ File names can contain spaces.

◆ File names can contain more than one period; the characters following the last period are used for the file extension.

◆ File names remember the case with which you create them, but are not case-sensitive. In other words, you can create a file called MiXEd CAse.TXT and Windows NT will remember that case and display it, but you do not have to use the same case to open or access the file. (This is different from Unix systems in which the case of the file name must always match the original use.)

FAT-formatted partitions do not store security information for files or folders, and no file or FAT-formatted partition can exceed 4 GB of size.

NTFS

NTFS is the most advanced file system available for use on PCs today. Its features include the following:

◆ Support for short and long file names is included. File names can be up to 255 characters long (including extension) and short 8.3 format filenames are automatically generated for use by DOS or Windows 3.x programs being run under Windows NT Workstation 4.

◆ The Unicode character set for file names can be used. (Unicode is a character set standard that supports multiple languages.)

◆ You can store files on NTFS disks that are 2^64 bytes long (that's 18,446,744,073,709,600,000 bytes, also called *16 exabytes*).

◆ Each NTFS partition can be 2^64 bytes large.

◆ A binary-tree (B-tree) directory structure is used that provides for very fast location of file allocation units.

◆ NTFS supports lazy writing to files.

◆ NTFS supports transaction-based disk writes that make the file system recoverable from errors or sudden failures of the system; every transaction is a single unit that can be undone if it is not completed. NTFS automatically recovers from any disk errors.

◆ A feature called *lazy commit* caches the information that confirms a disk transaction was successfully completed is built in to NTFS.

◆ The system creates checkpoints of the write cache to ensure quick recovery in case of a system failure.

◆ NTFS includes built-in support for striping and mirroring disks.

◆ Support for removable media is also included.

◆ Support is built in for security information about files and folders to be stored with the file entries. This security information is used when files and folders are accessed through a network, or simply by a user on the local machine. Files on NTFS are not encrypted, however.

◆ Similar to FAT, file names "remember" the case with which you created them, but do not generally require that the same case be used to access the files. The exception is POSIX applications, which do require that the same case be used for both file creation and subsequent file access.

◆ File names under NTFS can use any characters except ? " / \ < > * | :

◆ NTFS supports compression of files and folders. This compression, while it reduces performance somewhat for those files or folders, can reduce the amount of space consumed by 40–50%.

◆ NTFS supports Macintosh files for the support of Macintosh computers over a network.

◆ On NTFS partitions, each user has his own Recycle Bin for recovering recently erased files.

◆ NTFS minimizes file fragmentation automatically, thereby keeping performance optimized.

Note | You can convert a FAT-formatted partition to NTFS easily by using Windows NT Workstation's CONVERT.EXE command. However, this is a one-way process and there is no way to return the partition to FAT except by backing up the data, reformatting the partition, and then restoring the data to the FAT drive. Understand, also, that the extra NTFS information would be lost with this approach.

The syntax for the CONVERT command is: CONVERT drive: /fs:ntfs. Substitute the appropriate drive letter for drive.

Understanding Long File Name Rules

Windows NT Workstation supports long file names on both FAT and NTFS partitions. However, you can also run DOS and Windows 3.x applications under Windows NT Workstation, and neither type of application can deal with these long file names. To get around this problem, Windows NT Workstation automatically converts its long file names to short file names that those applications can deal with. The short file names so generated follow the original DOS 8.3 naming scheme.

When converting the long file name to a short name, the first six characters of the long file name are used (without spaces) and then a tilde (~) and a number are used to make the short name unique (and use all of the eight characters available). When there are multiple files that would conflict with the resulting short names, the number is incremented to keep them unique. For instance, two files called A Letter to Mom.DOC and A Letter to Dad.DOC would be shown to a DOS or Windows 3.x program as ALETTE~1.DOC and ALETTE~2.DOC. The number is assigned when each file is created, and indicates the order in which they were created.

After the fourth such increment, however, a different conversion starts taking place. Starting with the fifth conflicting file, only the first two letters of the long file name are converted, and the remainder of the short file name is randomly generated.

Keep in mind the following guidelines when using DOS and Windows 3.x applications under Windows NT Workstation 4:

◆ When creating files using an application that understands long file names, try to keep the first six letters of files you create unique, helping you to consistently identify files when you need to access them with a DOS or Windows 3.x application.

◆ Short file names are not provided for files created by a POSIX application. Those files will be inaccessible to DOS and Windows 3.x applications.

◆ When you use the command prompt and want to refer to a file name with spaces in it, you need to surround the file name with quote marks.

◆ Many DOS and Windows 3.x applications, when saving files that they previously loaded, do not simply save on top of the existing disk file. Rather, they save to a temporary file name, delete the original file, and then rename the temporary file to the original file name. Remember, though, that this process can remove NTFS-based security entries for the original file.

◆ You can see the short file names that Windows NT Workstation assigns to long file names by typing **DIR /X** at a command prompt.

◆ On FAT partitions, long file names are stored by creating special, hidden directory entries that, taken together, make up the long file name. This is because FAT only really supports the 8.3 naming scheme from DOS, and this method circumvents that limitation. Keep in mind, however, that root directories on FAT partitions are limited to 512 entries, and these long file name entries count against that limit. Consequently, you can fill the root directory of a FAT partition with fewer than 512 actual files if there are enough long file names to fill that limit.

◆ File entries on FAT partitions can have different attributes set for each entry. The special long file name entries have the Volume, Read-Only, System, and Hidden attributes all set to true. No other files on the system will use this combination of attributes.

Choosing a File System

Objective A.3

Because Windows NT Workstation 4 has the capability to support different file systems, which one should you use when setting up your system? The simple answer is to use NTFS; it offers you the greatest number of features and performs well. However, other considerations may force you to make a different decision.

Consider using the FAT file system in the following circumstances:

◆ You need to dual-boot the computer into DOS or Windows 95; neither DOS or Windows 95 supports NTFS-formatted disks.

◆ You have applications that rely on the FAT file system.

◆ You have an important application that makes large sequential writes to files; the FAT file system is faster than NTFS for such writes.

◆ You do not require security for individual files or folders.

◆ You do not require the increased reliability of NTFS.

Consider using NTFS in these situations:

◆ You want to take advantage of Windows NT Workstation's advanced file security features, such as when networking it with other systems in a peer-to-peer network.

◆ You want the best possible performance for many random-access disk reads and writes.

◆ It is crucial that the data on the hard disk be as safe as possible from accidental data loss.

◆ You want to create striped or mirrored volume sets using multiple hard disks.

◆ You need to store files larger than FAT-formatted disks can support (FAT is limited to file and partition sizes of 2^{32} bytes).

Note   You can convert existing FAT partitions to NTFS with the CONVERT command. All data is preserved on the drive when you do so.

Understanding Fault-Tolerant Disk Systems

Windows NT Server 4 supports special fault-tolerant disk configurations that can increase both disk performance and safety. These are schemes that make use of multiple physical disks in a system in various ways. The different methods fall under the heading of RAID, which stands for Redundant Array of Inexpensive Disks. There are five main RAID levels:

◆ **RAID 1.** Supported by Windows NT Server 4, RAID 1 mirrors two disks so that they act as one disk. If one of the disks fails, the remaining disk continues to work properly and safely provide the data. Once you replace the failed disk, you can re-mirror the disks to restore the redundancy.

◆ **RAID 2.** Not supported by Windows NT Server 4, this RAID level stripes data across multiple disks using Error Correcting Code.

◆ **RAID 3.** Not supported by Windows NT Server 4, RAID 3 stripes data across multiple disks with the Error Correcting Code stored as parity information.

◆ **RAID 4.** This RAID level (not supported by Windows NT Server 4) stripes data across multiple disks using large blocks of data. Parity data used to recover from a failed disk is stored on one drive.

◆ **RAID 5.** Supported by Windows NT Server 4, this level stripes data across multiple disks with the parity data distributed equally among all of the drives.

Disk mirroring can increase performance slightly when reading data because the drive with its head closest to the data is used to retrieve the requested data, and both drives are not needed for reads. Also, disk reads can be alternated between the two drives. However, disk writes may be slower due to the requirement that both drives must write the data at the same time.

Striping distributes files automatically among multiple hard disks. This improves performance in most cases, because you have multiple drive heads all reading and writing the requested data simultaneously. While drive 1 is retrieving sector 1, drive 2 can be retrieving sector 2, and so forth.

Windows NT Server 4 supports RAID 1 and RAID 5 through software—no special hardware is required beyond the multiple hard disks. You can also achieve different RAID levels, including RAID 1 and RAID 5, through the use of special disk controllers that handle this work without involving the computer's processor. Software-based RAID approaches are generally a bit slower than dedicated hardware-based approaches.

Understanding Multiprocessor Operations

Windows NT can support systems that have more than one processor. Using symmetric multiprocessing (SMP), Windows NT evenly dispatches threads to different processors so that all processors are kept as busy as possible. Windows NT is also processed on all processors in this way; this is possible because Windows NT was designed from the ground up to be a threaded operating system, and so the operating system's threads can run on multiple processors. This compares with other operating systems in which the operating system itself can only run on one processor, and additional processors are used for applications.

End Note: Upgrading to Windows NT Workstation 4? In this chapter you've learned about the advanced features available in Windows NT Workstation 4. These features aren't free, though; computers running Windows NT Workstation require more RAM and more hard disk space than computers running Windows 3.11 or Windows 95. For different needs, you will upgrade to one operating system or the other; neither is right for all users and all needs. The following list points out the benefits and drawbacks of upgrading to either system. Consider these advantages of migrating users to Windows NT Workstation 4 from Windows 3.1 or Windows 95:

◆ "Industrial Strength" preemptive multitasking

◆ Threads

◆ Windows 95 interface

◆ Much more secure design

◆ Less prone to "crashes"

◆ NTFS-capable; important for heavy demands on disk performance

◆ Long file names (with NTFS-formatted drives)

◆ More capable file and print peer server than Windows 95

◆ Can reliably handle more intensive computing needs; runs more simultaneous tasks more reliably than Windows 95

In most organizations, you have a mixture of Windows 95 and Windows NT Workstation computers, depending on the actual needs of your users, your budget for computer upgrades, and your desire for complete consistency between computers. However, the similarities in user interface between Windows 95 and Windows NT Workstation 4 eliminate one major problem involved in supporting two operating systems: training your users is much easier.

Test Your Knowledge

1. The two different protection rings supported by Windows NT are called:
   A. User Mode
   B. Real Mode
   C. Kernel Mode
   D. Executive Service Mode

2. You should choose to use the FAT file system when:
   A. You need to control access to individual files stored on the FAT partition.
   B. Your computer only has 16 MB of RAM installed.
   C. The partition in question needs to be accessed by DOS and Windows 3.x applications running under Windows NT Workstation 4.
   D. You need to dual-boot with Windows 95 and the partition in question contains data that you need to access under Windows 95.

3. You should choose to use the NTFS file system when:
   A. The reliability and safety of the data stored on the partition is of primary importance.
   B. You need to use long file names on the partition.
   C. You need to control access to individual files or folders on the partition.
   D. You need to create files that are larger than 4 GB.

4. Preemptive multitasking is better than cooperative multitasking because:
   A. It is a simple system to implement and requires less overhead.
   B. Applications do not have to be written in such a way that they handle their own multitasking with other applications.
   C. Because the system manages the multitasking, applications cannot tie up the system unfairly.
   D. It is a newer technology.

5. You should choose Windows 95 over Windows NT Workstation 4 when which of the following are true?
   A. The computer has 8 MB of RAM.
   B. There is only 400 MB of free disk space available.
   C. Some of the hardware in the computer is not compatible with Windows NT Workstation 4.
   D. You need to run DOS applications.

6. You should choose Windows NT Workstation 4 over Windows 95 when which of the following are true?

A. There is no reason to require Windows 95; both the hardware and the applications meet all of Windows NT Workstation 4's requirements.

B. The reliability of the system is of primary importance.

C. The computer has 40 MB of free disk space available.

D. You prefer Windows 95's user interface over that of Windows NT Workstation 4.

7. Which of the following statements is true?

A. Both FAT and NTFS can store file-specific security information.

B. NTFS lets each user have his or her own Recycle Bin.

C. FAT is always slower than NTFS.

D. NTFS is always slower than FAT.

8. The paging file in Windows NT Workstation 4 is handled by which subsystem?

A. The Paging Manager

B. The Virtual Memory Manager

C. The Swap Executive

D. The Virtual Swap Supervisor

9. The following differences exist between the Windows 95 and Windows NT Workstation 4 user interfaces:

A. Windows NT Workstation's Start Menu can be larger.

B. Windows 95 incorporates more animation in the desktop than Windows NT Workstation 4.

C. The Windows 95 Recycle Bin is emptied more frequently than the Windows NT Workstation Recycle Bin.

D. There are virtually no differences between the user interfaces of the two operating systems.

10. Generally speaking, which of the following statements is true?

A. Windows 95 is the best way to run 32-bit programs on Intel-based computers.

B. Windows NT Workstation 4 is designed to be an "industrial strength" operating system that is very reliable and secure.

C. Windows NT Workstation 4 meets the Department of Defense's B-level security requirements.

D. You can run Windows 95 under Windows NT Workstation 4 in a Virtual Windows 95 Machine.

Test Your Knowledge Answers

1. A,C
2. D
3. C,D
4. B,C
5. A,C
6. A,B
7. B
8. B
9. D
10. B

Chapter Snapshot

This chapter covers the following Windows NT Workstation 4 installation topics:

Windows NT
Workstation 4

CHAPTER 2

Installing Windows NT Workstation 4

In most cases, there are no problems involved with the installation of Windows NT Workstation 4. Basically, you choose a system or components that are on the hardware compatibility list (HCL), boot to the installation disks (or CD-ROM if the system BIOS supports it), and install from the Windows NT CD. Consider, though, that if you are going to have problems, you're almost certainly going to encounter them during or shortly after installation. Several factors need to be considered in the installation process.

First, make sure that you are fully prepared with an installation plan and have the appropriate equipment. Different computers have different components, or they might have components that aren't quite up to specification. Decide on the type of installation you want to perform (for example, local via a network share, via disk replication, or other form of preinstallation) and then proceed with the installation. This chapter discusses each of these methods, beginning with an explanation of the specific changes in terms of NT installation from version 3.51.

Understanding the Specific Changes in Windows NT Workstation 4

Certain changes and requirements have been made to the installation process in Windows NT Workstation 4. These changes have made the installation different from previous versions and in some regards make the installation amenable to scripting control; in other regards, they make the process more rigid. Understanding the changes will simplify things significantly by eliminating problems before they occur, or at least helping you to understand what must occur.

Mandatory Installation Factors

Objective

B.1

In the newest revision of Windows NT Workstation 4, Microsoft included some rather stringent requirements for the installation process. These requirements include the following:

◆ Each user must see and agree to the End User License Agreement (EULA).

◆ Each user must see the Product Identification screen.

◆ Each user must see and fill in the Username/Company name screens.

These screens cannot be bypassed. Obviously, the preceding issues do not matter much to the user who buys a machine and a copy of Windows NT Workstation 4 and installs the copy onto the machine. It does make a difference to the IS manager who must install 1,000 workstations running Windows NT Workstation 4, or to a vendor who preinstalls it on a system that you purchase. Without understanding these issues, you might be surprised when you purchase a machine or get one from the IS department. When you boot the machine, for example, you find that the installation is not finished.

CD-ROM/Network Share Access

Objective

B.1

According to Microsoft, you must have access to either a CD-ROM or a network share of the necessary installation files to install Windows NT Workstation 4. In most cases, you need access to the I386 directory on the CD. Surprisingly, you can also install Windows NT Workstation 4 by using a disk replication method. This latter approach is clearly directed toward the mass distribution markets, whether original equipment manufacturer (OEM)-based or internal preinstallation.

Floppy Support

Windows NT comes in a box that contains three boot floppies and a CD-ROM. The disks are all 3.5-inch; if you use them, the 3.5-inch floppy must be the boot drive. The 5.25-inch floppy is no longer supported directly. It is possible to boot to a 5.25-inch floppy, gain access to a network share, and then install NT Workstation 4, but this is clearly not a preferred way to install the product.

Objective B.1

Processor/RAM Recommendations

Beginning with Windows NT Workstation 4, the 386 processor is no longer supported. This, of course, implies that the 486 or higher CPU is required. In reality, Windows NT installs and runs best on Pentium (or higher) processors. The minimum RAM amount that NT demands is 12 MB (16 MB on RISC machines). Although such machines are perfectly capable of running NT, a more realistic starting point is 16 MB; 24 MB is preferable, though. For serious use of NT, a Pentium Pro or comparable RISC processor is recommended. An excellent starting place for a workstation should be a Pentium 100 with 32 MB of RAM. The high-end workstation should be a Pentium Pro (or RISC equivalent) with 32 to 64 MB of RAM. These recommendations are for ideal machines. Obviously, Windows NT runs well with lesser processor/RAM combinations.

Objective B.1

Tip   Manufacturers other than Intel (such as IBM, Cyrix, or AMD) are producing CPUs that are initially seen as 386s. The logic on the CPU enables it to function at near Pentium speed. Avoid these newer processors; they do not work well with NT, and the manufacturers have done little to solve the problem. Likewise, the infamous overdrive CPU might not be such a wise purchase because the cache and RAM might not match the CPU speed.

Legacy Drivers

Although not explicitly stated as unusable, certain cards have been retired to the legacy list. They might or might not work well in Windows NT Workstation 4. Some of the older SCSI and video card drivers have been retired. These are described in the installation guide that comes with Windows NT Workstation 4. For SCSI cards, avoid using the following, if possible:

Objective B.1

Always IN-2000 (always.sys)

Data Technology Corp. 3290 (dtc329x.sys)

Maynard 16-bit SCSI Adapter (wd33c93.sys)

MediaVision Pro Audio Spectrum-16 (tmv1.sys)

Trantor T-128 (t128.sys)

Trantor T-130B (t13b.sys)

UltraStor 124f EISA Disk Array Controller (ultra124.sys)

Certain video cards have drivers in the drvlib folder. In many cases, these are drivers that Microsoft has not verified, and have come directly from the video card manufacturer. This requires you to install the video cards as VGA and then configure them after NT is installed. These cards include, but are not limited to, the following:

Compaq AVGA graphics adapter

Chips & Technologies graphics adapters

Imagine 128 graphics adapter

Imagine 128 II graphics adapter

NeoMagic graphics adapter

S3 inc. S3ViRGE graphics adapter

Trident series of graphics adapters

Unfortunately, many network cards do not have Windows NT Workstation 4-specific drivers. Surprisingly, such cards as the Intel EtherExpress PRO/10 Adapter (PCI) can be one of these cards. When you install such a card, you face the following message:

```
ANY USE BY YOU OF THE SOFTWARE IS AT YOUR OWN RISK.  THE SOFTWARE IS PROVIDED
FOR USE ONLY WITH MICROSOFT WINDOWS NT 3.XX PRODUCTS AND RELATED APPLICATION
SOFTWARE.  THE SOFTWARE IS PROVIDED FOR USE "AS IS" WITHOUT WARRANTY OF ANY
KIND.  TO THE MAXIMUM EXTENT PERMITTED BY LAW, MICROSOFT AND ITS SUPPLIERS
DISCLAIM ALL WARRANTIES OF ANY KIND, EITHER EXPRESS OR IMPLIED, INCLUDING,
WITHOUT LIMITATION, IMPLIED WARRANTIES OF MERCHANTABILITY AND FITNESS FOR A
PARTICULAR PURPOSE. MICROSOFT IS NOT OBLIGATED TO PROVIDE ANY UPDATES TO THE
SOFTWARE.
```

Certain printers and printer connections require specific sets of instructions. These include the Digital's PrintServer 17, PrintServer 17/600, turbo PrintServer 20 and PrintServer 32 plus printers, and the Lexmark Network Ports and MarkVision. Detailed instructions are in the drvlib folder under the Print folder.

Exploring Some Considerations Before You Install

Much of the performance achieved in Windows NT has to do with hardware rather than software. As such, it is essential that you consider certain factors, such as bus and drive issues.

Buying a New System

The single-most significant issue in installing NT is obtaining hardware that supports Windows NT Workstation 4. Always check out the HCL that ships with Windows NT Workstation 4. This list contains the systems and components that have been tested by Microsoft and shown to support Windows NT Workstation 4. Microsoft states emphatically that you should buy from the HCL. Some systems on the HCL might have components that have changed, and Windows NT might not run well on them. Conversely, many systems not on the list function well. Buy from a vendor that understands Windows NT and, if possible, is willing to preinstall it for you.

Bus Issues

There is no reason not to purchase a PCI system with supporting Industry Standard Architecture (ISA) or EISA slots. Most motherboards seem designed to handle seven cards: either four PCI and three ISA (EISA) or three PCI and four ISA (EISA). Newer boards are showing up with six PCI slots. These boards might be more amenable to your specific requirements.

Knowing Hard Drives

Nearly all users today choose EIDE (Enhanced Integrated Drive Electronics) drives. They are less expensive, ostensibly easier to use, and faster than SCSI drives. In reality, the only advantage that EIDE drives have is in price. They are not easier to install, nor are they faster. Instead of entering the "what drive do I use" discussion, I will simply define three levels of users:

◆ **Level 1 users.** NT is used for its stability, and its capability to run long times without the need to be rebooted. The primary applications used are word processors, spreadsheets, and a moderate use of the Internet. For such users, EIDE is the drive type of choice.

◆ **Level 2 users.** This group uses NT not only for its stability, but also for its preemptive scheduling (multitasking, multithreading). Users in this level use the same type of applications as group 1 but continually run programs in foreground/background modes. As the applications used get more complex, performance on the system improves with bus master control. This group can function well on either EIDE or SCSI, but the higher end of this group probably functions better using SCSI.

◆ **Level 3 users.** This group is comprised of the typical power user who desires maximum flexibility in the system. Such flexibility is most pronounced with SCSI devices. It is not uncommon for such a user to have two SCSI cards and combinations of drives, CD-ROMs, tape backup devices (such as DAT drives), and even a scanner. These devices work well and are easy to set up on a SCSI bus.

Understanding the Types of Installations

Objective B.1

There are two types of installations to consider. The first is a simple installation by an end-user, and the second is the large scale roll-out of Windows NT by an IS team. The rules are markedly different even though the outcome is the same. Let's start by considering the actual steps involved in the installation process.

Understanding the Installation Process

The installation process has two discrete phases. The first phase (or text phase) is comprised of hardware detection and the copying of all essential files to a hard drive. If you use the setup disks, all detection of hardware is accomplished by the files on the floppies. Following the detection, all necessary files are copied to the local hard drive into the WIN_NT.~LT temporary directory. The system then reboots into the GUI-based portion of the installation.

If you use the non-floppy based installation or upgrade, two directories or folders are created on the computer's hard drive. The first is WIN_NT.~BT, and it contains the essential files to boot into Windows NT. These files include SCSI drivers, NTLDR, and NTDETECT.COM, as well as the kernel files. The second directory is labeled WIN_NT.~LS, and it is the same as the one created with setup disks. This directory has all the necessary files for booting into the installation of Windows NT Workstation 4.

With the preceding files, a limited version of Windows NT is loaded into memory. Memory loading is used to facilitate the use of the multithreaded setup program. For Intel-based machines, NTDETECT.COM then detects specific pieces of hardware. The following in particular are detected:

◆ Bus/adapter

◆ Communication ports

◆ Floppy drive

◆ Floating point coprocessor

◆ Keyboard

◆ Mouse

◆ Parallel ports

◆ SCSI adapters

◆ Video card

◆ A mass storage device (CD-ROM)

This first phase is usually called the DOS portion of the install. As such, proprietary schemes for hard drive partitions typically are accepted. Likewise during this phase, nearly all CD-ROMs are seen and usable. This in no way dictates what will be seen in the second phase of the installation. This distinction is important because it allows Windows NT to be installed in part on hardware that is not fully supported in Windows NT. After phase one is finished, the system reboots into phase two.

| **Tip** | It is possible to change drivers between the phases. If you have a specialized or newer driver for a controller, you can copy the new drivers over the default drivers in the temporary directories (assuming that the folders are on FAT-formatted partitions). Although seemingly not important, this changing of drivers in Windows NT 3.51 was necessary when the Ultra Controllers were released by Adaptec. |

Phase two is the beginning of the specific Windows NT installation. For this process, controllers are identified, drives located, and previous versions of Windows (and Windows NT) found. You are asked if this is a new installation or an upgrade; the drives are searched for defects; and you agree to a license statement (mandatory). The following are essential for you to continue:

◆ **Hardware that supports Windows NT.** If the drives and partitions are not compliant, the installation process quits with an error message similar to "the installation process cannot continue because the drives are inaccessible."

◆ **Sufficient space for the installation.** Although an installation of Windows NT Workstation takes about 108 MB of free space, have at least 125 MB (150 for RISC) available to be on the safe side. It's actually a good idea to make sure that the partition on which you will install Windows NT has at least 300 MB of free space. (As you install applications onto the system, the Windows NT directories grow by quite a bit due to added .DLL files, larger Registry files, and so on). Also, you should reserve space (at least 20-40 MB) for any future Service Packs that become available.

◆ **Your preparation list.** This list, by providing necessary settings, will allow you to proceed with all aspects of the installation.

The system reboots a second time, and then takes you into the final aspect of the installation—the setup phase, which is under the control of setup wizards. All you need to do here is establish simple checks for the installation to finish. This is covered in the actual installation section.

Understanding the End-User Installation Process

Objective

B.1

The end-user installation is by far the most straightforward of all installations. No specific intervention needs to be done by anyone but the enduser. One step, however, is very important—the preparation of a checklist of hardware components and settings.

The first and most critical step is compiling a checklist of all the hardware components that will be used. This list will aid you dramatically in the installation, and it also forms a basis for support if an issue arises. This list will be your hardware bible for installation and support. In short, this list is a means to keep all your essential data for the installation (and keep it in order). All is not lost if you lose the list; but all becomes very inconvenient.

This checklist provides you with the necessary hardware information to complete the installation. Of particular note will be a list of cards: I/Os, DMA (if necessary), and IRQs.

Tip

If you have trouble determining the system resources on your computer, use the Microsoft utility on the CD-ROM. It is used by running the MAKEDISK.BAT file in the \support\hqtool directory on the CD. This batch file will make a DOS boot disk and application that surveys the system resources. Be aware that the application does have some serious limitations. First of all, it does not register memory above 64 MB of RAM. Second, it might not recognize new devices that are fully supported in Windows NT (for example, an Adaptec 3940uw SCSI controller).

The following facts (and reasons) should be placed on the list:

◆ **Motherboard information.** Some installation problems exist with specific motherboards or motherboard firmware. Having this information is valuable in obtaining technical support, if necessary. You can often upgrade specific motherboards so that they become compatible with Windows NT; check with the board's manufacturer.

◆ **Card information.** Knowing what IRQ, I/O, or DMA you need to assign for the installation is mandatory. If you are using a Digiboard ISA serial card, for example, you need to know what I/Os are available and not assigned to another card. Many cards have diagnostic applications that can be run from a DOS boot floppy.

 Tip   If you are using EIDE drives, make sure that you have enabled Logical Block Address (LBA) prior to doing an Fdisk or Format.

Registering Peripheral Cards

Table 2.1 is designed to help you record all the necessary information being discussed. It might seem somewhat superfluous to fill out such a list, but using the five to ten minutes to do this is well worth the effort.

Objective B.1

TABLE 2.1
Information to Keep Handy During Installation

Card	Revision	I/O	IRQ	DMA	On HCL*
Video		n/a	n/a	n/a	
Network					
Sound					
SCSI					
Misc					

* HCL means hardware compatibility list—devices and cards that have been tested by Microsoft and are still available in the Microsoft Test labs for debugging and assistance with their use.

After the lists are finished, there is one additional step: make sure that all cards are properly configured for Windows NT, and that all necessary drivers are available for the installation.

Configuring the Peripheral Cards

Objective
B.1

The peripheral cards (controllers) have to be configured in your Windows NT system. You will need to assign proper values to many components, particularly if you use ISA cards. In general, this configuration is straightforward, but some specific issues can be a problem.

The Video Card

Objective
B.1

Assuming that the video card you are using has drivers on the installation CD in the I386 directory (or appropriate RISC directory), there is little to be concerned about. If you are using specialized video cards, you should install them as VGA and then add the appropriate video driver after NT has been installed and running. With some high-end cards, you might even need to install a daughter VGA card. The latter is true for high-end CAD/CAM boards. If this is the case, be sure to obtain the proper drivers and detailed installation instructions for the high-end card. Because the Graphics Device Interface (GDI) in Windows NT 4 has been moved to Ring 0 (the kernel), the driver must be specifically designed for Windows NT version 4. Previous drivers will not work.

The Network Card

Objective
B.1

If the network card parameters are set in software (for example, newer NE2000 clones), install the card in the system, boot to a DOS floppy, and run the manufacturer's setup utility. Add the values you set to table 2.1. If there are any potential problems with the network card, do not install the card with the initial configuration of NT, but add it later. Some cards simply do not work properly with autodetection (they return a null string, and the installation hangs) but can easily be installed at a later date.

The SCSI Card

Objective
B.1

If the card is a local bus card, preferably PCI, there is usually little to worry about. One potential problem might lie with IRQ 9, which is the original rollover IRQ from IRQ2. Most new motherboards allow the use of IRQ9, but it can fail, particularly with a busmastering SCSI card. If the BIOS supports it, make IRQ9 an ISA IRQ.

If the SCSI card is ISA, be sure to record the IRQ (usually 11) and I/O of the card. Determine whether the card is a busmaster card and plan the setup accordingly.

The Network Protocols

There is one last essential task. If you are joining a domain, determine all mandated aspects of the installation. If you need to install a specialized network protocol (such as TCP/IP, for example), find out how the network handles name resolution (for instance, WINS and/or DHCP). Setting everything up properly to begin with solves many later problems. Always remember that what you can do on a domain is determined by the network administrator. On the other hand, what you do on a local boot is determined by you. These two views of Windows NT might be markedly different.

Objective B.1

> **Tip**
>
> If necessary, you can perform the installation using a Workgroup logon. After the installation completes, you can then change over to a Domain-based network logon.

Understanding the Large-Scale Roll-Out

Installation rules are the same for large scale or end-user installation. The only differences are concerned with unattended installations. In a mass scale installation, there are three types of configurations: installation via a network share, installation via disk replication, or installation via stand-alone approaches. The latter is exactly the same as the end-user installation. The first two approaches are dealt with at the end of this chapter.

Making Last-Minute Preparations for the Installation

First, remove unwanted applications and load/run statements. Specifically, the following should be done:

Objective B.1

◆ If you are running the win95 shell on 3.51, it must be uninstalled. To accomplish this, run the command \newshell\I386\shupdate.cmd /u from the Intel folder for the shell update. (Obviously, if an Alpha, run the shupdate.cmd /u from the Alpha folder.)

◆ If you are running any of the remote control applications such as Remotely Possible 32 or PCAnywhere32, remove them prior to the installation. They can be reinstalled after Windows NT is running and stable.

◆ If you are using a UPS, remove it prior to the installation. Although most systems do in fact upgrade without difficulty, many have had problems with the COM ports that have the UPS installed. Once running and stable, the UPS (including vendor applications) can be reinstalled.

◆ High Performance File System (HPFS) is no longer directly supported during installation. Data must be backed up and the drive reformatted as FAT or the files copied to a FAT drive and the partition reformatted as FAT.

◆ Drives formatted using Windows 95 OEM Service Release 2 (OSR2) often use FAT 32 instead of normal FAT. FAT 32 is not supported by Windows NT 4. You will need to backup all data on such drives and reformat them if you want to install Windows NT onto them, or use them with Windows NT after installation.

After these tasks are completed, you're ready to begin.

Performing a New Installation

Objective B.1

As stated earlier, installation has two basic phases. The first phase, sometimes called the DOS or text phase, copies all the essential files or boots components to the local hard drive. The second phase is the initiation and actual installation of a bootable Windows NT system. This component is generally called the GUI phase or, more specifically, the NT phase.

Phase 1 of Installation

Objective B.1

By far, the most straightforward approach to a new installation is to use the three installation floppies that ship with Windows NT Workstation 4. These floppies contain the necessary files to enable you to gain access to the CD-ROM attached to your computer, and automatically have the essential setup files copied to your local hard drive. In the event that you do not have the three installation floppies or you need access to a network share, you must use alternative methods, which are detailed at the end of this section.

Installation Disk 1

Place the setup disk in the computer and turn on the computer. This first disk is the system boot disk; it loads files that inspect the computer hardware, and then loads the Windows NT executive and the Hardware Abstraction Layer (HAL). These files are the key files in Windows NT. Disk 1 contains the following files:

◆ **DISK101.** The disk label.

◆ **HA486C.DLL.** The standard HAL.

◆ **HALAPIC.DLL.** The HAL for Intel Symmetrical processing motherboards.

◆ **HALMCA.DLL.** The HAL for Microchannel machines.

◆ **NTDETECT.COM.** The program that detects hardware and records this hardware in the Registry.

◆ **NTKRNLMP.EXE.** The NT kernel specifically for multiprocessor motherboards. When NT starts loading, the multiprocessor kernel loads and is displayed on the top of the screen. In Windows NT, this is named the NTOSKRNL.EXE. This file extracts the necessary boot information from the Registry.

◆ **SETUPLDR.BIN.** This file functions as the NTLOADER file for the installation procedure. In the finished installation of Windows NT, SETUPLDR is analogous to the NTLDR (NT loader) file.

◆ **TXTSETUP.SIF.** Dictates the specific files to be copied during setup and the basic modifications to be made to the Registry during the installation. This file is long, but informative if you want to examine it in Notepad or another text editor.

When asked by the installation to insert disk 2, do so and press Enter. From this point on, the installation process will cue you as to the next step.

Installation Disk 2

Disk 2 loads all the necessary files to get you into the true installation procedure. These steps might seem somewhat tedious, but each is an essential component, and each can cause an installation problem. The following files are loaded:

◆ NT configuration data

◆ Setup fonts

◆ Local-specific data

◆ Windows setup

◆ PCMCIA (PC-card) support

◆ SCSI port driver

◆ Video driver

◆ Floppy disk driver

◆ Keyboard driver

◆ File Allocation Table (FAT) file system

When these files are loaded, the system presents you with the blue screen that lists the amount of memory and multiprocessor kernel. Setup then processes setup information and loads the keyboard layout. After this, you are presented with the Welcome to Setup Screen, which gives you four options:

◆ Press F1 to learn more about NT.

◆ To set up now, press Enter.

◆ To perform a repair, press R. (This step is very important, be sure to remember it.)

◆ To quit, press F3.

For present purposes, simply press the Enter key. You are then asked if you want Setup to detect the controller card(s) for your CD-ROM and hard drives. Have the installation detect the cards. For primary hard drive controllers, you do not want to have to install specialized drivers. Simply press enter to continue. You are then asked to insert disk 3.

Installation Disk 3

Disk 3 loads the specific drivers needed to gain access to the hard drives and CD-ROMs. The specific files loaded or searched for are the sys drivers, which are loaded onto the hard drive when the /b option is used. After devices are searched for, Setup loads support for ESDI and IDE drives, and then NT File System (NTFS). At this point, if a CD-ROM has not been detected, the installation is aborted. If the installation has been successful to this point, the drivers necessary to gain access to the CD-ROM are loaded. You are then presented with the Windows NT Licensing Agreement (EULA). As stated earlier, this step is mandatory. You must scroll through the agreement and read it carefully. When you have reached the end of the agreement, press F8.

> **Note** | The three setup floppies contain the exact same files as those found in the WIN_NT.~BT directory. The only difference between the standard installation with floppies and the /b options is the latter copying boot files to the hard drive.

After accepting the terms of the EULA, Setup searches for previous versions of NT to upgrade. If none are found, you choose the drive and partition. If no partitions are found, you can then make partitions and format them. Assuming that the drive is already formatted, you are presented with a description of the drives seen along with their respective formats. At this point, you can choose to maintain the format or change the format to another file system (FAT to NTFS or NTFS to FAT). If partitions are found, you are presented with the alternatives of an exhaustive search of the hard drives or skipping the search. By all means, conduct the search.

> **Tip** | On some larger notebook drives, Setup cannot partition or format the hard drive. Boot to a DOS floppy, run FDISK and Format, and then the setup will run perfectly. You will even be able to convert the format to NTFS if you want.

Following the search, specific files are prepared for installation, and the files are copied from the CD-ROM. These files are copied to the temporary directories listed previously (WIN_NT.~LS). Finally, the basic configuration is saved (actually the default configuration), and you press Enter to reboot the computer (making sure to remove any floppy disk in the 3.5-inch drive). The system then boots into Windows NT setup (phase 2 of the installation).

| Tip | If you have a system that enables you to boot to a CD-ROM (for example, the SuperMicro Dual Pentium Pro motherboards support it), make sure to enter BIOS and disable this option before continuing. Although convenient to use in installation, if you do not disable the function in BIOS, you will be forced to remove the CD and reboot if the CD has been left in. |

Phase 2 of Installation

When the system reboots, you enter the wizard-controlled portion of the installation. The following list shows the wizards that are encountered in order of appearance:

Objective B.1

1. The first wizard you encounter simply collects information about the system. The next one presents you with the following install options:

   ◆ **Typical.** The default.

   ◆ **Portable.** Optimized for notebooks.

   ◆ **Compact.** Minimal installation.

   ◆ **Custom.** For advanced users, but the one that should be picked by default.

2. When you choose the option (Custom is highly recommended) and press Next, you see the Name Wizard.

   Enter the appropriate name and organization for the installation. Pressing Next brings up the Enter the Key Wizard.

   It is important that you save the CD case because it has the installation key on it.

3. Enter the proper key or the installation will not continue. This brings you to the Computer Name Wizard.

4. Although seemingly trivial, if you are on a network, you need a unique computer name (one that is not being used; you might need to obtain a name from the IS department). This brings you to the most important aspect of Windows NT—security.

5. The initial security of Windows NT is established by the Administrator Password Wizard. Of utmost importance is the assignment of a password

for the Administrator account. While you can choose a blank password if you like, if you do want to protect the system you should choose at least a seven-character password that has at least one nonsense character in it. Remember, passwords are case-sensitive. Bob, for example, is a poor choice for a password. The password $%bob&c* is difficult to crack but relatively easy to remember. Do not lose the password!

6. The next wizard asks if you want to make an emergency repair disk (ERD). By all means do so.

7. Assuming that you have chosen Custom, you are then presented the Component Selection dialog box. If an option is gray, this means that not all parts of the option will be installed. The accessories, for example, will be grayed out. Looking at the detail shows that the optional mouse pointers are not installed. If you want to use these options, click on them to put an x in the installation option.

8. The next few steps are critical to setting up Windows NT; they involve setting up network parameters. You are faced with several choices. The first choice is the easiest—namely, a stand-alone machine. Windows NT really functions best with a network card installed; there is an easy solution. Install the Msloopback adapter (do it after the initial installation). This adapter is a software emulation of an adapter. Simply choose the default values. The second choice is also easy; you choose not to set up the network now but will do so later. This option is clearly the safest. Finally, if you have a network interface card (NIC) that you know works well in NT, and there are no problems with it during installation, install it now. By all means, choose this and set up the necessary protocols. (See the discussion on networks for the implementation of the protocol stacks.)

The Network Wizard offers you four choices:

◆ Do not connect this computer to the network at this time

◆ This computer will participate on a network (the default)

◆ Wired directly

◆ Remote access

For present purposes, opt to not connect the computer to the network. The remaining wizards will finish the installation.

9. You will need to set the time and date. The default is Greenwich Time, but you can choose the time zone you want.

10. The final choice you have is selecting video resolution. The installation defaults to VGA and with small fonts. If you want, you can change the resolution at this time; but you can change this dynamically in Windows NT Workstation 4 so it is optional. Also, if you change settings, you must first test them by clicking the Test button and confirming that you can see a test bitmap that appears.

11. The installation finishes by copying files, finally setting security, and asking you to supply a blank formatted 3.5-inch floppy to make the emergency repair disk. If the system has been formatted as NTFS, security will finally be set.

Caution | You can set the format as NTFS during installation. It is sometimes preferable to install as FAT, and then convert to NTFS later by running the convert utility at the command prompt. To determine the appropriate parameters, type /? at the command prompt command and then press Enter.

Installing without the Installation Floppy Disks

To install without installation floppies, you need access to a local CD-ROM, to specific distribution files on the CD copied to your local hard drive, or to a network distribution share or installation CD. For this example, you will set up Windows NT Workstation 4 onto a new system that does not have direct access to a CD-ROM. Although seemingly a difficult task, the installation is actually simple. Boot to a DOS floppy that has FDISK.EXE and FORMAT.COM on it. Run FDISK and partition the drive as appropriate. After this, the system reboots. Format the drive(s) with FORMAT.COM. This makes all drives FAT; but as explained earlier, FAT can be converted to NTFS.

**Objective
B.7**

To make the necessary boot disk, you need access to a Windows NT Workstation 4 server that has been set up for client software installation (for example, Windows 95). In addition, there has to be a system on the network that has the Windows NT Workstation 4 CD in a CD-ROM that has been shared to everyone.

To make an installation disk, choose Programs, Administrator Tools, and Network Client from the Start menu on the NT Server. For simplicity's sake, choose Windows 95. Place a bootable floppy (3.5-inch) in the 3.5-inch floppy drive. Assuming that the network supports NetBEUI, choose this as your network protocol because it is the easiest to set up. Files are then copied to the floppy. (In this case, the network adapter chosen was the 3Com Etherlink lll.) After you have set all the parameters, you are presented with a standard acceptance screen.

After the files are copied, the floppy has the following standard files on it:

◆ autoexec.bat

◆ command.com

◆ config.sys

◆ msdos.sys (hidden)

◆ io.sys (hidden)

In addition, there will be a subdirectory called NET. This subdirectory contains the following files:

- ◆ emm386.exe
- ◆ himem.sys
- ◆ ifshlp.sys
- ◆ ndishlp.sys
- ◆ net.exe
- ◆ neth.msg
- ◆ ELNK3.DOS ;(3Com driver)
- ◆ protman.dos
- ◆ protman.exe
- ◆ protocol.ini
- ◆ setup.inf
- ◆ shares.pwl
- ◆ system.ini
- ◆ wcsetup.inf
- ◆ wfwsys.cfg

All you need to do is edit the AUTOEXEC.BAT so that installation CD becomes a mapped drive. Here is the default AUTOEXEC.BAT for a server named BIGCLYDE and a shared client directory called Clients:

```
path=a:\net
a:\net\net start
net use z: \\BIGCLYDE\Clients
echo Running Setup...
z:\win95\netsetup\setup.exe
Here is the autoexec.bat that is needed:
path=a:\net
a:\net\net start
net use Z: \\BIGCLYDE\SHARE_CD
Z:\
cd I386
winnt /b
```

In the changed AUTOEXEC.BAT, the system boots into the network. The user and password (added by the Network Client Administrator wizard when you supplied the proper information) are passed to the network and verified (assuming, of course, that you supplied the proper information). The network shared CD (in this case called SHARE_CD) is shared as the Z drive. This shared drive is then accessed; the I386 subdirectory is accessed; and the WINNT.EXE file is executed with the /b switch.

Alternatively, you can simply copy the I386 directory to your local drive and run the winnt /b from the local hard drive.

Note There are two means of installing Windows NT Workstation 4 from the I386 directory. These are based upon the WINNT.EXE file for DOS and the WINNT32.EXE file for existing NT installations. Various switches can be used with these files. Without any switch, the installation makes boot floppies and no WIN_NT.~BT temporary directory. This is unnecessary. Ideally, you would use the /b switch, which causes a temporary boot directory to be installed (the WIN_NT.~BT directory). This floppyless installation is the fastest and easiest.

If the system is configured to run NetBEUI, the appropriate section of PROTOCOL.INI is as follows:

```
[ms$netbeui]
drivername=netbeui$
SESSIONS=10
NCBS=12
BINDINGS=ms$elnk
LANABASE=0
```

If the system is configured to run TCP/IP, the appropriate section of PROTOCOL.INI is as follows (note that DCHP was not used and a static IP address supplied):

```
[tcpip]
NBSessions=6
DefaultGateway0=
SubNetMask0=255 255 255 0
IPAddress0=199 34 56 30
DisableDHCP=1
DriverName=TCPIP$
BINDINGS=ms$elnk3
LANABASE=0
```

If the system is configured to run IPX (NWLink IPX Compatible Protocol), the appropriate section of PROTOCOL.INI is as follows:

```
 [ms$nwlink]
drivername=nwlink$
FRAME=Ethernet_802.2
BINDINGS=ms$elnk16
LANABASE=0
```

> **Tip** | Make sure that 802.2 is the appropriate frame type for the network. Older installations might be using 802.3.

When the first part of the installation starts, files are copied from the CD to your local hard drive. As explained earlier, two temporary directories are formed—one for booting the system and one for the installation files. After the files are copied, you are asked to reboot the system. Do so. From this point on, the installation is identical to that discussed earlier.

The first part seen is the inspection of hardware. After this comes the Welcome to Setup screen, devices are found, and you are presented with the license agreement. You then choose the installation directory, and an exhaustive search of the hard drive ensues. Files are copied to the designated target and a default configuration saved. The system then has to be rebooted by pressing Enter (make sure that the floppy has been removed).

Following the reboot, you see the blue screen with the information about the system displayed at the top of the screen. From this point on, you are in phase 2 of the installation, and all is identical to that described earlier.

In this example, Windows NT Workstation 4 has been installed on a system that does not have an attached CD-ROM. Obviously, the same approach can be taken with any new workstation (including notebooks) that has been attached to the network, but not yet configured as a network PC. Remember, you need an installation sheet to have all the necessary information when the installation disk is made. Likewise, you need the cooperation of the network administrator.

If the system will be a dual system—that is, boots NT and WFWG, for example—you can join the network and simply copy the I386 directory to your local hard drive. Run winnt /b from the hard drive directory and simply state that you are going to install to a new directory rather than an existing one.

Installing without the Installation Floppy Disks but with an Attached CD-ROM

This installation is very easy. Simply make a DOS boot disk that can gain access to the system CD-ROM. In most cases, this is a standard boot floppy that loads a driver to mount the CD-ROM. The following AUTOEXEC.BAT and CONFIG.SYS will boot and connect to either a SCSI CD-ROM attached to a 2940/3940 or a Mitsumi 4x CD-ROM.

Objective B.1

```
Config.sys
DEVICE=A:\HIMEM.SYS /TESTMEM:OFF /V
DEVICE=A:\EMM386.EXE NOEMS
BUFFERS=40,0
FILES=70
DOS=UMB
LASTDRIVE=z
FCBS=4,0
SHELL=COMMAND.COM /E:4096 /p
DOS=HIGH
STACKS=9,256
DEVICE=A:\aspi8dos.sys /d
DEVICE=A:\ASPIDISK.SYS /D
DEVICE=A:\ASPICD.SYS /D:ASPICD0
DEVICE=A:\MTMCDAI.SYS /D:MTMIDE01

Autoexec.bat
ECHO OFF
Prompt $p$g
LH A:\MSCDEX.EXE /D:MTMIDE01 /D:ASPICD0 /M:12
LH A:\smartdrv.exe 4098 4098
```

Simply copy the AUTOEXEC.BAT and CONFIG.SYS and appropriate referenced files to a DOS boot floppy. Boot the system, and you can gain access to the CD-ROM. Change to the I386 directory, and run winnt /ox to create installation boot floppies or winnt /b to copy boot files and installation files to the local hard drive.

Note   Throughout this chapter, reference has been made to the switches used in winnt or winnt32. The following are most of the switches that are used:

winnt32 [/s:sourcepath] [/i:inf_file] [/t:drive_letter] [/x] [/b] [/ox] [/u[:script] [/r:directory] [/e:command]

continues

Parameters used include the following:

- **/s:sourcepath.** Specifies the location of the Windows NT files.

- **/i:inf_file.** Specifies the file name (no path) of the setup information file. The default is DOSNET.INF.

- **/t:drive_letter.** Forces Setup to place temporary files on the specified drive.

- **/x.** Prevents Setup from creating Setup boot floppies. Use this when you already have Setup boot floppies (from your administrator, for example).

- **/b.** Causes the boot files to be loaded on the system's hard drive rather than on floppy disks, so that floppy disks do not need to be loaded or removed by the user.

- **/ox.** Specifies that Setup create boot floppies for CD-ROM installation.

- **/u.** Upgrades your previous version of Windows NT in unattended mode. All user settings are taken from the previous installation, requiring no user intervention during Setup.

- **/u:script.** Similar to previous, but provides a script file for user settings instead of using the settings from the previous installation.

- **/r:directory.** Installs an additional directory within the directory tree where the Windows NT files are installed. Use additional /r switches to install additional directories.

- **/e:command.** Instructs Setup to execute a specific command after installation is complete.

For complete details on these commands, use the **winnt /?** or **winnt32 /?** commands to get on-line help.

Large-Scale Roll-Out Installations

Objective B.7

Organizations that have to roll out large numbers of machines face several hurdles. First of all, Microsoft insists that every user must go through the GUI part of the installation. This, of course, provides a serious dilemma to a task that must be done as quickly and efficiently as possible. Fortunately, Microsoft has provided tools that help dramatically in this regard.

If you are starting a large roll-out, the first essential task you face is making a reference computer that has a full version of Windows NT Workstation 4 installed. You can also set up a network share or, in the case of a large roll-out, multiple shares. Certain factors must enter the process. For an OEM installation, the following requirements must be met:

◆ All computers must have a unique name that provides a unique security descriptor (SID).

◆ All installations must immediately enter the GUI phase of installation when the system is turned on.

◆ Every user must see the EULA.

◆ All this must be done as easily and quickly as possible.

There are several ways that you can copy an installation from machine to machine: performing a stand-alone installation, installing across a network, installing through disk replication, or using a script-based installation. The first two of these approaches have already been discussed in this chapter. The third approach is unique and only recently has become economically feasible. The fourth choice is discussed later in this chapter in the section "Doing a Network Roll-Out."

In the first example you'll see, you use an approach where Windows NT is preinstalled on the master computer, replicated onto an example system, and then prepared for mass roll-out. The mass roll-out is accomplished by copying a specially-prepared set of Windows NT Workstation files onto a machine's hard disk, such that the user completes the installation when they start the machine. Although at first glance this seems to be a daunting task, it is really very simple.

Setting Up the Master Machine

The first task is to install a complete version of Windows NT Workstation 4 with the user name Administrator and a blank password. Our assumption here is that all the systems rolled out will be workstations and not servers. To summarize the procedure beforehand, you will install Windows NT, make sure that the installation temp files are present, and then run ROLLBACK.EXE to prepare the Windows NT files for roll-out. The drive will then be used for disk replication.

Objective B.7

The installation of NT has been thoroughly covered, but certain features need to be added to the list. The easiest manner of installing large numbers of NT machines (new installations) is to install everything on the master computer, run rollback to place the system at the GUI stage, and then replicate the drive. To do this, all hardware has to be the same, as do all the hard drives. Without this uniformity, the installation will not work properly. Assume that the systems being used all have the same SCSI controller and hard drive.

The Rollback Utility

There is considerable confusion as to the use of the rollback utility. First of all, it was placed on the CD-ROM by mistake. Rollback was intended to be used only by OEMs. When it is run, it renames three of the configuration files in the Registry. The normal files in the system32\config are the following:

- AppEvent.EVT
- default
- Default.log
- Default.sav
- Sam
- Sam.log
- SecEvent.Evt
- Security
- Security.log
- software
- Software.log
- software.sav
- SysEvent.Evt
- system
- system.alt
- system.sav
- userdiff

After running rollback, the default, software, and system hives are all replaced. The older versions are copied to the following:

- def$$$$$.$$$.log
- def$$$$$.del
- sof$$$$$.$$$.log
- sof$$$$$.del
- sys$$$$$.$$$.log
- sys$$$$$.del

When the hives are changed, the system indeed boots to the GUI part of the installation. Interestingly, no users see the EULA. The general consensus seems to state that handing a user a hard copy of the EULA and asking them to sign and return it will suffice.

Follow these steps to prepare the roll-out:

1. Install Windows NT by booting to a DOS floppy, accessing a CD-ROM, and running Winnt /b. Make sure to keep all disk formats FAT for now.

2. After the files are copied and you are asked to reboot, boot to a DOS floppy and copy the contents of the root directory WIN_NT.~LS to OEM_NT.~LS. This step is critical.

3. Remove the DOS boot disk and boot into setup.

4. Completely install NT, join the domain, and make sure that you can browse all resources. (Create a user called TEST, or something similar, on the PDC. Have the install create the user account TEST for you but do not use any password. Make TEST part of the admin group.)

5. If all works satisfactorily in step 4, run rollback.

6. Turn off the machine, and move the drive to a second machine that is running Windows NT Workstation 4 and has a high-speed tape device attached (a DAT drive is fine).

7. Open Explorer (or File Manager) and examine the root drive. WIN_NT.~LS is no longer present. Rename OEM_NT.~LS to WIN_NT.~LS. If desired, convert the drive to NTFS.

8. Run Barrett Edwards International's (UltraBac) or Cheyenne Software's (ArcServe) on the machine and do a sector backup of the D drive. Prepare the boot disks for the sector restore as specified for the backup software.

9. Turn off the machine and move the tape drive to a new machine, making sure that termination is set properly.

10. Boot to the restore disks you created in step 8 and restore the sector backup to the new drive (remember, the same size and preferably the same manufacturer of hard disk).

11. Remove the tape drive and you can then boot into NT, and you will start at the GUI portion of install.

Ideally, you will have users suitable to oversee the installation. These users can be trained and given the instructions necessary to complete the installation. All settings are controlled by wizards. The disadvantage of this approach is that the installation is attended. The advantage is that you will not need to have a very large number of installers because the users will accomplish most of the work.

Doing a Network Roll-Out

Doing a large scale roll-out of Windows NT via a network installation is powerful but time consuming. The process requires serious planning and documentation. Once set up, the roll-out is fast and surprisingly free of problems. The key to the roll-out is the development of the unattended answer file.

Objective B.7

Objective A.1

Unattended scripts can be made by editing a sample script or by using Setup Manager, which is on the NT Server and Workstation Resource Kit CD-ROMs. Make sure to include all answers, or the user will be asked for the missing information.

The following is a sample script:

```
[Unattended]
OemPreinstall = yes
OEMSkipEULA = Yes  ;skips end user license agreement - user needs a hard copy
Method = "express"
NoWaitAfterTextMode = 1  ;auto reboot after text phase
NoWaitAfterGUIMode = 1   ;auto reboot after GUI phase
FileSystem = ConvertNTFS  ;converts drive to NTFS
ExtendOEMPartition = 1
ConfirmHardware = no
NtUpgrade = no
Win31Upgrade = no
TargetPath = * ;defaults to C:\winnt
OverwriteOemFilesOnUpgrade = no
KeyboardLayout = "US-International"

[UserData]
FullName = "Bob Chronister"
OrgName = "Chronister Consultants"
ComputerName = BOB6
ProductId = "0123456789"

[GuiUnattended]
OemSkipWelcome = 1  ;skips welcome page
OEMBlankAdminPassword = 1 ;automatically sets admin password to blank
TimeZone="GMT-06:00 Central Time (US&Canada)"

[Display]
ConfigureAtLogon = 0
BitsPerPel = 8
XResolution = 640
YResolution = 480
VRefresh = 60
AutoConfirm = 1 ; means that no input is needed by user

[Network]
DetectAdapters = DetectAdaptersSection
```

```
InstallProtocols = ProtocolsSection
InstallServices = ServicesSection
JoinDomain = Bobsplace
CreateComputerAccount = BOBC, $BOB&C$

 [DetectAdaptersSection]
LimitTo = ELNKII
ELNKII = ELNKIIParamSection

 [ELNKIIParamSection]
InterruptNumber=5
IOBaseAddress=300
Transceiver=2
MemoryMapped=0

 [ProtocolsSection]
TC = TCParamSection

 [TCParamSection]
DHCP = yes

 [ServicesSection]
RAS = RASParamSection

 [RASParamSection]
PortSections = PortSection1
DialoutProtocols = TCP/IP
DialinProtocols = TCP/IP
TcpIpClientAccess =network
ClientCanRequestIPAddress =no

 [PortSection1]
PortName = COM2
DeviceType = "Practical Peripherals PC288LCD V.34"
PortUsage = DialInOut
```

In the preceding example, every possible request for user input was negated with a response. The example presupposes that all hardware is standard and has drivers on the installation CD. At a minimum, the I386 will be copied to a distribution server, and full access will be given to everyone. (You can use the whole CD as a share, but only if the drive is very fast. For large scale roll-outs, multiple distribution servers are needed.) With a DOS boot floppy disk, the real-time network drivers are loaded, and the distribution drive mapped for local use (see previous section on network access boot floppy disks).

Although completely functional, the preceding script has several major discrepancies. First, you could not use the script to do a mass roll-out because all machines would have the same name. One solution to this is to make a small Visual Basic (or similar) application that will change the computer name in the UNATTEND.TXT and then save the file by the computer name (for example, BOB6.TXT). If all the files were saved in the distribution share, then the unattended installation would reflect the new file name.

Because the machine is booting to DOS, the WINNT.EXE file would be run. In the original example, with the distribution share mapped to Z, the commands would be as follows to perform an installation using the script you created:

```
Z:
```

```
winnt /b /u:unattended.txt /s:Z
```

 Note You can specify more than one source of the distribution files if you use the winnt32 application. This actually enables you to install from multiple sources simultaneously because the 32-bit installation is multithreaded.

With the latter example, the commands would be:

```
winnt /b /u:bob6.txt /s:z
```

The only factors involved here are preparing unattended files for each environment. If you have various types of network cards involved, for example, you would need to have answer files for each NIC. Once more, this emphasizes the necessity of doing an inventory of all the machines onto which Windows NT Workstation 4 will be installed.

Suppose that you want to install applications with the network installation. This can be accomplished by using the OEM syntax. Assuming that you have checked yes to the OEM Preinstall option in the UNATTENDED.TXT file, you can use a setup command or use the sysdiff application also placed on the CD (presumably by accident).

Ideally, any setup commands you would use directly are installation files that need user input. As you are aware, nearly all new applications require user input; therefore, sysdiff becomes an application of great importance. To install Office 95 onto drive C via a standard setup, you would create an OEM directory in the share. The share would look as follows for an installation to an Intel machine:

I386\OEM\C\MSoffice

The drive letter specifies the target for the installation. All the Office distribution and setup files are placed in the I386\OEM\C\MSoffice folder. The setup command is placed in the CMDLINES.TXT file that is in the root of the OEM directory.

Although the preceding procedure works well, each user or installer must add all the necessary information on each installation. This is not very efficient, and the solution, as noted earlier, requires using SYSDIFF.EXE.

Sysdiff is an application that enables you to capture an image of the system, change the system, and then capture the difference between the two. Obviously, all you do is apply the difference file. In reality, the application can be used in many ways. Here you will deal primarily with the most direct use of sysdiff.

After you have the basic installation of NT in place, do not make any changes. If you installed the server resource kit, SYSDIFF.EXE was placed in the system32 folder. At the command line, type the following command:

```
sysdiff /snap [/log:log_file] drive:\folder\snapshot_file
```

where drive is the drive and folder is the folder where you want to store the snapshot file. Typically, create a folder called snap on the C drive. [/log:log_file] is optional.

Note If you have more than one drive, sysdiff makes a snapshot of all drives. Because everything has to be the same on the drive you are taking the snapshot of and the drive you are applying to, only use sysdiff on a single drive system (unless you realize the consequences).

After the snapshot has been made, you install the application in question.

In this case, you install Office 95 on your master system. (The master system must be identical to the systems on which you are going to install NT.) After the installation is complete, you run a second command:

```
sysdiff /diff [/log:log_file] drive:\folder\snapshot_file drive:\
folder\Sysdiff_file /C:"comment"
```

For the present example, all the snapshot files are placed in the C:\snap directory. The SYSDIFF_FILE is the difference between the two snapshots. Comment is the name given to the Sysdiff package—that is, MSOffice.

Note Sysdiff creates snapshots of three separate types of files. The first is the Registry; the second is of all INI files; and the last is a directory and file snapshot. All this information is included in the SYSDIFF_FILE.

Copy the SYSDIFF_FILE, SYSDIFF.EXE, and SYSDIFF.INI to the OEM folder of the distribution share. Create a file called CMDLINES.TXT and add the following line to it:

```
sysdiff /apply /m sysdiff_file
```

The sysdiff_file is the difference file you created when sysdiff was run the second time. Apply incorporates the difference file into the new system. M remaps the file changes to the default user profile so that they appear as Default User files. Move the CMDLINES.TXT file to the OEM distribution folder. During the end-user setup, the sysdiff file is incorporated into the installation. Generally, this approach is taken with small files.

You can also apply the difference during preinstallation. You need the file $$RENAME.TXT, however, to convert short to long names. With this current limitation (the file is available only on OEM kits), this preinstallation approach is not recommended.

Push Installations Upgrading via SMS

Objective

B.7

Large networks typically have a centralized management application that maintains a database of hardware, machines, software, and other related information. One such application is the System Management Server (SMS) from Microsoft. This application stores information in Standard Query Language (SQL), which is also from Microsoft. Because most large sites have SMS installed, it is easy to use SMS to push upgrades across the network.

SMS typically performs queries across the network, and thus has already found all the machines that have the appropriate hardware and are running NT 3.51. You create a job, upgrading 3.51 workstations to 4 workstations, and SMS carries out that job over the network. SMS works by running defined jobs across the network, and the installation is done automatically to selected SMS clients.

Using SMS to upgrade Windows NT 3.51 Workstation to Windows NT Workstation 4 requires several tasks. First of all, you need to determine what systems will be upgraded. You then create a PDF file (package definition file). These files form the basis of the upgrade. (Please note the proper chapters in the Microsoft SMS manual; of importance are Chapters 7, 10, and 11, dealing with queries, packages, and jobs.) The tasks are as follows:

1. Determine the machines that will be upgraded. Define these systems as a Machine group for use in the distribution phase.

2. Prepare a PDF to handle the updates. A PDF resembles an unattended text file, as discussed earlier. The following is a typical PDF:

```
[PDF]
Version=1.0
 [Automated NT (x86) Setup]
CommandLine=ntencap /NTwks winnt32.exe /U:ntupgrd.400
```

```
CommandName=Automated Upgrade of (x86) NT Client
UserInputRequired=FALSE
SynchronousSystemExitRequired=TRUE
SupportedPlatforms=Windows NT 3.51 (x86)

[Manual NT (x86) Setup]
CommandLine=ntencap /NTwks winnt32.exe /B /S:.
CommandName=Manual Upgrade of (x86) NT Client
UserInputRequired=TRUE
SynchronousSystemExitRequired=TRUE
SupportedPlatforms=Windows NT 3.51 (x86)

[Automated NT (Alpha) Setup]
CommandLine=ntencapa /NTwks winnt32.exe /U:ntupgrd.400
CommandName=Automated Upgrade of (Alpha) NT Client
UserInputRequired=FALSE
SynchronousSystemExitRequired=TRUE
SupportedPlatforms=Windows NT 3.51 (Alpha)

[Manual NT (Alpha) Setup]
CommandLine=ntencapa /NTwks winnt32.exe
CommandName=Manual Upgrade of (Alpha) NT Client
UserInputRequired=TRUE
SynchronousSystemExitRequired=TRUE
SupportedPlatforms=Windows NT 3.51 (Alpha)

[Automated NT (MIPS) Setup]
CommandLine=ntencapm /NTwks winnt32.exe /U:ntupgrd.400
CommandName=Automated Upgrade of (MIPS) NT Client
UserInputRequired=FALSE
SynchronousSystemExitRequired=TRUE
SupportedPlatforms=Windows NT 3.51 (MIPS)

[Manual NT (MIPS) Setup]
CommandLine=ntencapm /NTwks winnt32.exe
CommandName=Manual Upgrade of (MIPS) NT Client
UserInputRequired=TRUE
SynchronousSystemExitRequired=TRUE
SupportedPlatforms=Windows NT 3.51 (MIPS)

[Automated Win Setup]
CommandLine=w16ntupg winnt.exe /U:unattend.400 /W /S:.
```

continues

```
CommandName=Automated Setup of Win16 Client
UserInputRequired=FALSE
SynchronousSystemExitRequired=TRUE
SupportedPlatforms=Windows 3.1


[Manual Win Setup]
CommandLine=w16ntupg winnt.exe /B /W /S:.
CommandName=Manual Setup of Win16 Client
UserInputRequired=TRUE
SynchronousSystemExitRequired=TRUE
SupportedPlatforms=Windows 3.1


[Automated DOS Setup]
CommandLine=dosntupg.exe winnt.exe /U:unattend.400 /S:.
CommandName=Automated Setup of DOS Client
UserInputRequired=FALSE
SynchronousSystemExitRequired=TRUE
SupportedPlatforms=MS-DOS 5.0, MS-DOS 6.0, MS-DOS 6.2, MS-DOS 6.21, MS-DOS
6.22


[Manual DOS Setup]
CommandLine=dosntupg.exe winnt.exe /B /S:.
CommandName=Manual Setup of DOS Client
UserInputRequired=TRUE
SynchronousSystemExitRequired=TRUE
SupportedPlatforms=MS-DOS 5.0, MS-DOS 6.0, MS-DOS 6.2, MS-DOS 6.21, MS-DOS
6.22


[Package Definition]
Product=Windows NT Workstation
Version=4.00
Comment=Microsoft Windows NT Workstation 4.00
SetupVariations=Automated NT (x86), Manual NT (x86), Automated NT (Alpha),
_Manual NT (Alpha), Automated NT (MIPS), Manual NT (MIPS), Automated Win,
_Manual Win, Automated DOS, Manual DOS
```

3. Create a package to install the software. From the Package window in SMS, choose File, New and import the appropriate PDF, described earlier as (\\server\folder\filename). When the package is imported, the Package Properties dialog box returns. Choose Windows NT Workstation. Just as in the unattended installation, you need access to a distribution share, which you enter in the source directory. Be certain to make this an automatic setup. Click on OK, and the

package is ready to be run. This example only deals with an upgrade. Notice that in the automated scripts for installing Server in the PDF file earlier, there are references to the file ntupgrd.400. An example of NTUPGRD.400 follows.

This script file is an example script for upgrading NT. If the TCP/IP protocol stack is present on the machine being upgraded then the UpgradeEnableDhcp paramater must be correctly specified in order to fully automate the upgrade:

```
[Unattended]
;Method = custom ¦ express
Method = express
;ConfirmHardware = yes ¦ no
ConfirmHardware = no
;NtUpgrade = manual ¦ yes ¦ no ¦ single
NtUpgrade = yes
;TargetPath = manual ¦ * ¦ <path>
TargetPath = *


 [GuiUnattended]
; Specifies if TCP/IP protocol is to use Dynamic host configuration pro
;!UpgradeEnableDhcp = YES ¦ NO
!UpgradeEnableDhcp = YES
;!DetachedProgram = ""
;!Arguments = ""
!ProductId = "*** *******"
```

In this particular example, any NT Workstation (MIPS, Alpha or Intel) will be automatically upgraded to NT Server 4. In reality, making the Ntupgrade = yes should produce an automatic upgrade with settings intact.

4. To create the job, open the Jobs window and choose File, New. For the present example, define a comment similar to this: push upgrade of all NT Worksta-tions in the * machine group where * is the name defined earlier. Make sure that all necessary files, including scripts, are copied to a network share on which SMS Service Account has proper access.

5. Choose Run Command on Workstation. Click the Details command and choose the proper package in the Package window. Enter the name of the specific machine group you have defined. In the send phase, you can choose to place the files directly on the target or connect to a server to which the systems to be upgraded have access. Assuming that you have chosen to copy all files to the targets, you then issue the command you choose in the Run window (in this case, automated setup of NT client). Schedule the job and if necessary, make it mandatory. All should be automatic from now on.

6. The next time the user of a target machine logs on, the scheduled job appears. When the job is completed on the client, the upgrade will be finished. This type of "over-the-network" upgrade is called a *push upgrade* because the job is pushed onto the client instead of being initiated by the client.

Performing an Upgrade Installation

Objective

B.6

Upgrades are, in fact, the easiest of all installations, at least on the surface. In reality, all the possible mistakes of the previous version are carried over to the new installation. Currently, you can only upgrade Windows NT, Windows for Workgroups, Windows 3.1, and DOS while maintaining your current settings. This section deals with the issues of each possible upgrade. The basic means of the upgrade are the same as those discussed with new installation—namely a floppyless or a floppy-based installation.

Upgrading Windows 3.1x

Objective

B.6

This upgrade can be accomplished in two ways. You can do an upgrade into the Windows directory, or you can install NT into a new directory. The latter is preferable, but the former will work well in most cases. Doing an upgrade into the Windows directory results in most configuration information migrating to NT.

Boot into the first Setup disk. You use the same sequence as noted in the preceding installation instructions. When the installation process reaches the point of searching the hard drive for prior versions of Windows NT, the suggestion is made that you install into the Windows 3.1x directory. This enables you to migrate your applications to NT. The installation proceeds as a new installation, with the exception of the migration of applications.

When you boot into NT as a non-Administrator, you are asked if you want to migrate WIN.INI and CONTROL.INI settings, as well as groups. This works very well but can result in chaos. Many win3.1 systems have too many settings in the INI files, and some might be incorrect. If you do this type of upgrade, you might have to search the Registry to eliminate improper settings. Do so at the risk of making the machine non-bootable.

Migration Events that Occur during the Upgrade from Windows 3.1x

Objective

B.6

Migration actually occurs in two stages. First, the system settings migrate, followed by user settings. The system settings are those found in REG.DAT and sections of WIN.INI concerned with fonts, printers, and so on. The user migration occurs every time a new user logs on to the system.

You can also force a migration. Delete the Windows 3.1 migration status key from the HKEY_CURRENT_USER hive. If the user is not the administrator, the Migration dialog box will appear the next time the user logs on.

A more appropriate migration is to copy the appropriate sections of the old WIN.INI into the NT WIN.INI. Copy the DLL's from Windows into the winnt\system directory (do not overwrite any files), and copy all necessary INI files. Also copy over all GRP files and REG.DAT. If you delete the Registry key described earlier, the next time you log on you will be given the opportunity to migrate settings. If you only move over the groups and INI files you are concerned with, the migration can be kept very clean.

Upgrading Windows 95

You cannot upgrade (for example, keep the same settings) Windows 95 to Windows NT. By the same token, Microsoft recommends that you do not dual boot Windows NT and Windows 95. In reality, it is easy to dual boot Windows 95 and NT.

Objective B.6

Check to see whether all Windows 95 devices and applications are supported by Windows NT Workstation 4. (Microsoft claims that over 1,000 more devices are supported on 95 than on NT.) Simply install Windows NT Workstation 4 into a separate directory from Windows 95, creating a dual-boot system. Finally, reinstall all applications in NT. According to Microsoft, not many users are dual booting Windows 95 and NT, but the numbers are rising rapidly.

Upgrading Windows NT

Boot into the installation disks or run winnt32 /b. The installation finds the prior version of NT and asks if you want to upgrade. By all means, say yes. This carries over all (or most) of the applications and settings. Specifically, user and group accounts and network settings are brought over, as are applications. Sometimes the upgrade does not work properly. Always have a backup available in case of an upgrade problem.

Objective B.6

General Upgrade Cautions

Upgrade issues and problems are most likely to occur when you have made many customizations of the Registry or have serious alterations of the WIN.INI file. There have also been reports of loss of user information. It is always better to be prepared to fix these problems. Make sure that you know all necessary security parameters if user information needs to be repaired. If you have any doubts at all about the upgrade, do a test installation to be certain that Windows NT Workstation 4 will, in fact, install on your computer. There is no reason for the installation to fail if you have appropriate hardware.

Objective B.6

Dual Boot Options

Several applications enable you to dual boot nearly any combination of operating systems. One such application, System Commander, has enabled users to dual boot NT, Linux, NetWare, OS/2, and Windows 95 on a single system. There are NTFS readers for both Linux and DOS. It is obvious that nearly any combination of OSs can be configured on a single machine.

Removing Windows NT Workstation 4

Objective B.3

Removing Windows NT Workstation 4 from a system is quick, painless, and involves a minimum number of steps. Whether you are removing Windows NT from a system that is using FAT-formatted or NTFS-formatted drives, however, does make a difference.

To remove Windows NT Workstation 4 from a system with only FAT-formatted drives, follow these steps:

1. Boot the system from a boot disk that runs DOS or Windows 95 and that also has the SYS.COM program on it.

2. Run SYS C:. This run replaces the boot sectors on the hard disk with the DOS or Windows 95 boot sectors and also replaces the key system startup files in the root directory.

3. Remove the following files from the system using any method (that is, the DEL command, Windows 95 Explorer, or some file management program):

    ◆ C:\PAGEFILE.SYS

    ◆ C:\BOOT.INI (Use ATTRIB.EXE to remove the Hidden, System, and Read-only attributes first)

    ◆ C:\NT*.* (Use ATTRIB.EXE to remove the Hidden, System, and Read-only attributes first)

    ◆ C:\BOOTSECT.DOS (Use ATTRIB.EXE to remove the Hidden, System, and Read-only attributes first)

    ◆ The \ *winnt_root*\ folder and all subfolders

    ◆ \Program Files\Windows NT

Tip After removing Windows NT, you might want to immediately run a disk defragmentation program to optimize the disk for the new space you've created. There's no requirement that you do this, but performance might be improved.

To remove Windows NT from a system that is using NTFS-formatted disks, follow these steps:

1. Use the Windows NT Setup disk to start the setup process.

2. When you are prompted to create or choose a disk partition, select any NTFS-formatted partitions and press D to delete them.

3. Press F3 to exit the Setup program.

4. Use a DOS boot disk to boot DOS, and then run FDISK to re-create the partition. You can then format the drive with the DOS or Windows 95 FORMAT utility.

| **Tip** | You can also use the FDISK program from Windows 95 or from DOS 6 to remove the NTFS-formatted partitions. |

Troubleshooting Installation Problems

Generally the installation of Windows NT Workstation 4 proceeds without trouble. However, there are some common problems that people do run into, and simple courses of action to take to resolve them. The following bullets discuss various problems that may crop up and the course of action to take to correct the problems.

**Objective
G.3**

◆ **Error messages indicating a bad CD-ROM.** Sometimes CD-ROMs get scratched and the information cannot be accurately read from them. If this happens, try another CD-ROM, or perhaps a copy on a share prepared for a server-based installation that you know to be good. You can also request a replacement CD-ROM from Microsoft at (800) 426-9000.

◆ **Error messages indicating bad boot diskettes.** Diskette media frequently goes bad. Fortunately, you can re-create Windows NT's book diskettes by running this command from the CD-ROM (it will work under DOS or Windows 95): winnt /OX.

◆ **SCSI adapter isn't supported by Windows NT.** If the Windows NT setup program doesn't properly identify your SCSI adapter, try using DOS or Windows 95 to copy the contents of the CD-ROM to free space on your hard disk and then install from there (if you have adequate space). Next, try installing from a shared CD-ROM through Windows 95, if Windows 95 is installed on the machine onto which you are installing Windows NT. If these methods fail, first consult with the maker of the SCSI adapter you're using for advice, and if necessary replace the adapter with one listed in the HCL.

◆ **After the first boot, you get a message that "A Dependency Service Failed to Start."** This is usually caused by the network adapter not functioning properly. Ensure that all of its settings are correct and that the correct driver is installed. Note that Windows NT may make different IRQ choices than Windows 95, and so a new IRQ conflict may have developed with the network adapter. Use the Windows NT Diagnostics tool to inspect the IRQs that are assigned in the computer and ensure that no conflicts exist. You may have to run a utility supplied for your network adapter to change its IRQ or memory port address as well.

◆ **Windows NT won't install or start.** Before installing Windows NT, try running the NT Hardware Qualifier found on the Windows NT CD-ROM to ensure that all of your hardware can be properly detected by Windows NT.

◆ **During installation you cannot connect to the network domain.** First, check to ensure that the PDC is running properly. Second, ensure that you have specified the domain name, user name, and password accurately. Third, make sure that the network adapter is working correctly (check the Event Viewer and look for error messages).

End Note: Despite the complexity of this chapter, installing Windows NT is really very simple. Even the more advanced installation topics are easy once you've worked through them once to fully understand them.

You should experiment with the different installation options discussed here. Set up a computer, and use these methods to install Windows NT several times so that you really understand how server-based installations, unattended installations, and large-scale roll-out installations work in practice. Spending some time playing with Windows NT's various installation options will help solidify the information in this chapter for you.

Test Your Knowledge

1. Which of the following computer configurations make acceptable Windows NT Workstation 4 computers?

   A. 386/33, 150 MB free disk space, 16 MB RAM

   B. 486/25, 100 MB free disk space, 36 MB RAM

   C. 486/50, 300 MB free disk space, 16 MB RAM

   D. Pentium Pro/200, 1.1 GB free disk space, 64 MB RAM

2. What should you always do prior to installing Windows NT Workstation 4?

    A. Check the computer and its components against the HCL.

    B. Make a list of the installed cards and their IRQ, DMA, and port settings.

    C. Choose an installation method (that is, from CD-ROM, over a network share, and so forth).

    D. Test the computer under Windows 95.

3. When installing onto an Intel-based machine that uses a bus-mastering disk controller, what IRQ should you avoid for that disk controller when possible?

    A. IRQ 5

    B. IRQ 9

    C. IRQ 12

    D. IRQ 15

4. What step has Microsoft designed into the installation process that is mandatory and cannot be easily skipped?

    A. Installing network protocols

    B. Formatting a drive using NTFS

    C. Reading and acknowledging the EULA

    D. Installing all of the applets included with Windows NT

5. Which of the following commands lets you install Windows NT Workstation 4 without using startup disks?

    A. WINNT /OX

    B. WINNT /B

    C. WINNT /NOSTARTDISKS

    D. WINNT /BYPASS_FLOPPY

6. You are installing Windows NT Workstation 4 onto a computer that has Windows 95 already installed and working, and you want to end up with a dual-boot configuration from which you can run either operating system. To do this, you must:

    A. Install Windows NT Workstation 4 onto a different drive than the one that contains Windows 95.

    B. Start the installation with the WINNT /DUAL command.

    C. Do nothing; Windows NT Workstation 4's installation will automatically set up a dual-boot system in this case.

    D. You cannot set up a dual-boot system with Windows 95.

7. What are the main phases of the Setup Wizard?

   A. Installing Networking

   B. Setup Options

   C. Gathering Information about Your Computer

   D. Finishing Setup

8. When removing Windows NT Workstation from a system that uses only FAT-formatted disks, which of the following steps are involved?

   A. Use SYS C: to replace the boot sectors.

   B. Erase the Windows NT files manually.

   C. Run the REMOVENT.EXE program.

   D. Use ATTRIB to clear the attributes on some of the Windows NT files located in the root directory.

9. After creating an unattended setup script file, how do you use it to perform an installation?

   A. Run the Unattended Installation Wizard, and supply it the filename when it prompts you.

   B. Use the command: winnt /b /u:unattended.txt /s:Z.

   C. Run SETUP.EXE; it finds any unattended script files automatically and uses them.

   D. You cannot perform unattended installations with Windows NT Workstation 4.

10. If you create an unattended script file but fail to define some of the parameters, what happens when you use that file to install Windows NT?

   A. The installation process fails.

   B. The user is prompted for any missing information.

   C. Default choices are selected automatically.

   D. The options that are not mentioned in the file are simply not installed.

11. You can prepare a Windows NT large-scale roll-out using a reference machine and what utility?

   A. ROLLOUT.EXE

   B. ROLLFD.EXE

   C. ROLLBACK.EXE

   D. ROLL.EXE

12. When upgrading from Windows 3.x to Windows NT Workstation 4, if you want to use NTFS-formatted drives when you're done, you should:

    A. Back up the data, install Windows NT and format the drives as NTFS, then restore the data.

    B. Install Windows NT, then run CONVERT.EXE to convert the FAT drives to NTFS.

    C. Install Windows NT, then back up all the data, reformat the drives as NTFS, and restore the data.

    D. You cannot use NTFS-formatted drives under Windows NT Workstation 4 when upgrading from Windows 3.x.

13. If your CD-ROM isn't detected properly by Windows NT during installation, you cannot proceed. How can you deal with this?

    A. If you can access the CD-ROM under DOS or Windows 95, you can copy the contents of the NT CD-ROM to one of your hard drives, and from there you can then run the installation. After you're done, remove the installation files to free up the space used on the drive.

    B. You can boot Windows 95 on the system, and then access a shared CD-ROM through the network, from which you can then install Windows NT.

    C. You can upgrade or change your CD-ROM controller to one supported by Windows NT.

    D. You can purchase a diskette-only version of Windows NT Workstation 4.

Test Your Knowledge Answers

1. C,D

2. A,B,C

3. B

4. C

5. B

6. C

7. A,C,D

8. A,B,D

9. B

10. B

11. C

12. B

13. A,B,C

Chapter Snapshot

Because Windows NT Workstation 4 is designed to be a robust, secure operating system, there are many ways that you can configure Windows NT Workstation to run. This chapter covers all the important aspects of starting and stopping Windows NT Workstation 4, including the following:

Windows NT
Workstation 4

CHAPTER 3

Booting and Shutting Down Windows NT 4

O nce a workstation system is set up to log on to a network, you're pretty much home free. Getting to that point, however, can be difficult. A myriad of details are involved in getting Windows NT Workstation 4 set up to log on and start up under different circumstances and for different needs.

Understanding the Boot Process

In order to properly manage Windows NT Workstation installations and to trouble-shoot startup problems, you really need to understand *how* the operating system boots up. Knowing what happens and in what order, as well as what is required for proper system startup, is critical. This section explores how Windows NT starts, and compares how Intel-based computers boot up to how RISC-based computers (such as Digital Alpha AXP-based computers) boot up with Windows NT.

Knowing Which Files are Required for Startup

Windows NT Workstation 4 requires different files for startup on Intel-based and RISC-based workstations. Tables 3.1 and 3.2 overview these files.

TABLE 3.1
Files Required for System Boot on Intel-Based Systems

File	Description
NTLDR	This is the main loader file, a read-only, system, hidden file located in the root of your startup partition.
BOOT.INI	This file, an ASCII text file, contains information used to create the Boot Loader Operating System Selection menu that appears when multiple operating systems are installed. This file is found in the root directory of your startup partition.
BOOTSECT.DOS	This hidden system file is activated when an operating system other than Windows NT is chosen from the Boot Loader Operating System Selection menu. This file is found in the root directory of your startup partition.
NTDETECT.COM	This is a program that examines the installed hardware and creates a hardware list for Windows NT to use during the boot process. This file has the hidden, read-only, and system attributes set, and is located in the root directory of your startup partition.
NTBOOTDD.SYS	Only required for SCSI-based systems that have their BIOS disabled, this file operates SCSI devices during the boot sequence. If needed, it is found in the root directory of your startup partition.

File	Description
NTOSKRNL.EXE	The kernel of Windows NT, this file is found in the *winnt_root*\SYSTEM32 directory on your system.
HAL.DLL	The Hardware Abstraction Layer (HAL), this file communicates between the base hardware in the computer and Windows NT. It is found in *winnt_root*\SYSTEM32.
SYSTEM	Found in the *winnt_root*\SYSTEM32\CONFIG directory, this is a configuration file that specifies which device drivers and services are loaded during startup.
Device Drivers	Device drivers can be found in several directories, and vary based on the hardware installed in your computer.

TABLE 3.2
Files Required for System Boot on RISC-Based Systems

File	Description
OSLOADER.EXE	This file, equivalent to NTLDR, is the main operating system loader program.
*.PAL	Only required for Alpha-based systems, these files help interface the operating system with the Alpha processor.
NTOSKRNL.EXE	Just as on Intel-based machines, this kernel of Windows NT can be found on the *winnt root*\System 32 directory.
SYSTEM	Just as on Intel-based machines, this configuration file specifies which device drivers and services are loaded during startup. It can be found in the *winnt_root*\SYSTEM32\CONFIG directory.

Understanding the Intel-Based Boot Process

Intel-based computers go through a number of steps as they start. These steps are broken down into a pre-boot sequence, which is followed by the boot sequence. An Intel-based machine running Windows NT Workstation 4 follows these steps as it starts:

1. The computer's built-in Power-On Self-Test (POST) is run.

2. The computer's BIOS locates the boot device and loads the Master Boot Record (MBR) from that device. Inside the MBR, a program that continues the boot process is activated.

3. The Partition Boot Record is read by the MBR program to locate the active partition on the boot device. On this partition, the boot sector is loaded into memory.

4. NTLDR is then run from an entry in the boot sector. This completes the pre-boot process.

5. NTLDR puts the processor into 32-bit protected mode (Real Mode has been used up to this point).

6. An abbreviated file system driver, called a minifile system driver, is loaded by NTLDR. The minifile system driver enables NTLDR to work with both FAT and NTFS partitions to continue the boot of Windows NT.

7. The BOOT.INI file is read, and the resulting Boot Loader Operating System Selection menu is displayed for the user to choose an operating system with which to boot.

8. Depending on the operating system chosen, either NTDETECT.COM is run (if Windows NT is chosen) or BOOTSECT.DOS is run (if a different operating system is chosen). The remaining steps assume that Windows NT has been chosen.

9. NTDETECT.COM checks the computer's hardware, prepares a list of installed hardware, and returns the list to NTLDR.

10. NTLDR reads NTOSKRNL.EXE, HAL.DLL, and the System Registry hive into memory. The System hive is used to determine which device drivers need to be loaded.

11. NTOSKRNL.EXE takes over the boot process, and Windows NT starts to initialize and load into memory.

Understanding the RISC-Based Boot Process

RISC-based computers go through a simpler boot process, because they do not need to allow for the operation of other operating systems on the computer, such as Windows 95. The files and steps required on Intel-based machines, therefore, for this purpose can be skipped with RISC-based computers.

The RISC-based pre-boot and boot processes go through these steps:

1. The Read-Only Memory (ROM) in the computer chooses the boot device by reading the configuration in the computer's static parameter RAM. If no boot device is found in the parameter RAM, the user is asked to choose a boot device. On some machines, a default device may also be selected.

2. If a hard disk is being used to boot, the MBR is read into memory and the system partition is located.

3. Assuming the system partition exists, the first sector of the system partition is read into memory. The data contained in the first sector is used to determine if the file system of the boot device is supported through the computer's firmware.

4. If the firmware support exists, the firmware is used to search the root directory of the startup partition for the OSLOADER.EXE program. If found, the program is loaded, takes control of the system, and receives a list of the installed hardware from the firmware. This concludes the pre-boot phase of the boot process.

5. OSLOADER.EXE runs NTOSKRNL.EXE, HAL.DLL, any *.PAL files, and the System Registry hive.

6. OSLOADER.EXE uses the System hive to load the appropriate device drivers for the system.

7. Control is passed from OSLOADER.EXE to NTOSKRNL.EXE, and Windows NT starts loading and initializing.

Logging On to Windows NT Workstation 4

After installing Windows NT Workstation 4—after your first full startup of the system—the logon prompt appears. Press Ctrl+Alt+Del to begin the logon process. The dialog box that prompts you for your account name and password appears. Complete the fields successfully, click on OK, and you're in.

Note | Windows NT uses Ctrl+Alt+Del to begin the logon process in order to foil Trojan Horse programs that might imitate the logon screen and record your password or send it to another computer on a network. Also, while the logon process is being used, real mode programs are disabled in the system; only protected-mode programs can run. Because protected-mode programs cannot access the logon process's memory space, it is impossible for a program to be written that can "eavesdrop" on the logon process and steal the password being supplied.

Logging On to Workgroups and Domains

You can choose to use a workgroup or domain logon to gain access to your network. Typically, workgroup logons are used for smaller peer-to-peer networks, while domain logons are used to log on to your company network. You choose your type of logon with the Network Control Panel found in the Control Panel folder (open the Settings command in the Start menu and choose Control Panel). Double-click on the Network icon to open the Network dialog box. The Network dialog box appears (see fig. 3.1).

Figure 3.1

The Network dialog box enables the user to choose between a workgroup logon and a domain logon.

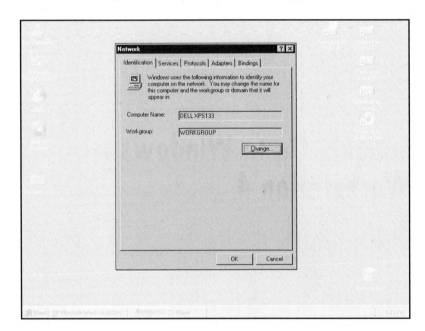

> **Tip**   You can right-click on the Network Neighborhood icon and choose Properties to call up the Network dialog box.

The dialog box shown in figure 3.1 displays the current system logon—the computer name and the workgroup to which it is logged on. To change the logon to use a domain, click on the Change button. The Identification Changes dialog box shown in figure 3.2 appears.

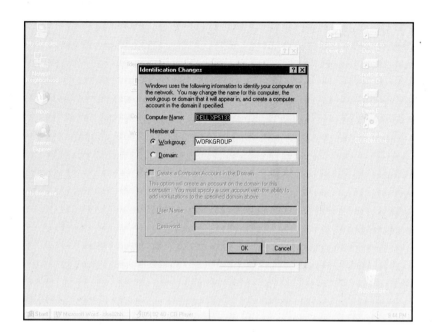

Figure 3.2

Use the Identification Changes dialog box to choose between workgroup and domain logons.

To change your system's logon so that you log on to a domain, click on the Domain option button and enter the name of the domain in the field next to the option button. Clicking on OK will search the network for the domain you specified and will attach to the domain controller in order to validate your logon. If successful, you will see a message box welcoming you to the domain. After closing the Network dialog box, you are prompted to restart your system in order to log on to the domain and make the change permanent.

When you choose a domain logon in the Identification Changes dialog box, a check box becomes available called Create a Computer Account in the Domain. All Windows NT computers in a domain must have computer accounts in the domain in order to function. If you wish to create a new computer account in the domain for the computer you're using, you can do so provided you know the account name and password of a user account in the domain authorized to create new computer accounts. Click on the Create a Computer Account in the Domain check box (refer to fig. 3.2), and then fill in the appropriate User Name and Password for an Administrator-level account in the domain. When these fields are correctly completed and you click on the OK button, a computer account is created. After closing the Network Control Panel dialog boxes and restarting the system, you can log on to the domain using an appropriate user name and password.

Reversing the process to go from a domain logon to a workgroup logon proceeds the same way and uses the same dialog boxes. Choose the Workgroup option button in the Identification Changes dialog box and enter the workgroup that you want to join. You will need to restart the system to complete the logon process for the workgroup.

Choosing Startup Options

Setting up your logon is only a small part of the battle of configuring Windows NT Workstation 4 to start the way you want. You can also control many other aspects of the system startup, such as environment variables that are set, special options for portable computers with docking stations, different hardware profiles, and so on. In this section, you learn about setting up these options.

Working with Environment Variables

Some applications rely on system-wide settings called environment variables. These settings are held in a special place called the environment and are available to all programs on your system. Sometimes, you need to view or change the environment variables in your system. Environment variables are set when the system starts. While you can change them at a Windows NT command prompt, the changes you make there are only made for that specific command prompt; they do not become system-wide until you change them properly and restart your system.

You control the environment variables with which Windows NT Workstation 4 initializes using the Environment tab of the System Properties dialog box. You can access the System Properties dialog box in one of two ways:

◆ Open the Control Panel and double-click on the System icon.

◆ Right-click on My Computer and choose Properties from the shortcut menu.

Using either method, the System Properties dialog box appears (see fig. 3.3).

There are two types of environment variables: system variables and user variables. You can only change the system variables if you are logged on with an account that is a member of the Administrators group on the system. You can always change the user variables, and the changes are stored in the system Registry so that they will always be reasserted based on which user is logged on to the computer.

Changing Environment Variables

To change any of the variables, first click on the variable name listed in either the System Variables window or the User Variables window. When a variable is selected, the variable name and its setting appear in the Variable and Value fields respectively. Type in a new value and click on the Set button to store the change.

Deleting Environment Variables

To delete a variable, first select it and then click on the Delete button.

After starting your portable computer in its undocked state, you should view the Windows NT Event Viewer to look for any errors in starting devices; it's possible that you did not remove all of the devices from your configuration that are unavailable when the computer is undocked. Use the information in the Event Viewer to resolve any lingering device configuration problems.

Sometimes as you make changes to hardware profiles, you may make a change that prevents your computer from starting properly. If you encounter a mix-up like this, the following section explains how to recover from such problems.

Reverting to the Last Known Good Profile

Any time you are changing hardware profiles and restarting your computer, you may find that Windows NT Workstation does not start successfully due to a change you made in its configuration. Perhaps you misconfigured a device that is needed for the system to start, or perhaps a Registry entry was changed that stops the system from starting. In these cases, you will need to revert to what is called the Last Known Good hardware profile in order to resolve the problem. The Last Known Good hardware profile is updated every time you successfully boot Windows NT. To do so, perform the following steps:

Objective G.1

1. Restart the computer. Because you are restarting from a stalled system boot, you might have to power the system off and then back on again.

2. The text message `Press spacebar now to invoke the Hardware Profile/Last Known Good` menu appears. Press the spacebar.

3. A text-based screen that lets you choose the hardware profile from which you want to boot appears. To use the Last Known Good profile, press the L key.

Your system should start successfully using the Last Known Good profile. You then can inspect the Windows NT Event Viewer to look for clues as to what was wrong with your new hardware profile and can also inspect the various control panels in the system to look for missing device drivers. You also may need to start from scratch with a new copy of your original configuration hardware profile, and then proceed in a step-by-step fashion by only changing one device driver at a time until you discover the change that prevented your system from starting.

Controlling Service Startup

Windows NT Workstation has a number of services, or background processes, that can start every time you boot your system. Examples of services include the Event Logger, some network services, the Alerter, and so on. These services are often crucial to the proper functioning of your computer. When you install Windows NT Workstation, the default services are selected to start automatically for you. You can change the settings for each service, and can control how a service starts for each different hardware profile you use.

There are all kinds of reasons why you might want or need to adjust service startup. You may want to control service startup to free up available memory in your system, particularly if a service isn't needed by you but is still being started at boot time. Or, if a particular service takes a while to start, you may want to force it to start at boot time so that you don't have to wait for it to start later. Finally, some services need to be stopped in order to perform certain kinds of maintenance on the system.

To control how services start on Windows NT Workstation, open the Control Panel (choose Settings from the Start menu and then Control Panel from the menu that appears) and double-click on the Services icon. The Services dialog box shown in figure 3.9 appears.

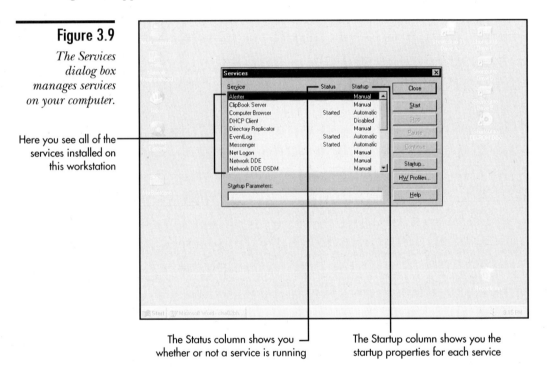

Figure 3.9

The Services dialog box manages services on your computer.

Here you see all of the services installed on this workstation

The Status column shows you whether or not a service is running

The Startup column shows you the startup properties for each service

To manually start or stop a service, click on the service in the dialog box and then use either the Start or Stop buttons. You can also control how the service starts—select the service and click on the Startup button. The Service dialog box shown in figure 3.10 appears.

Services can have one of three startup settings:

◆ **Automatic.** This setting causes the service to start each time you boot the workstation.

◆ **Manual.** You must manually start the service with the Start button in the Services dialog box (refer to fig. 3.9). Manual services are also started automatically if a dependent service (a service that requires another service) is started.

◆ **Disabled.** The service will not start, even when a dependent service is started.

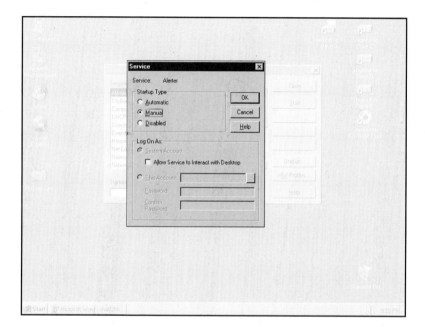

Figure 3.10

Use the Service startup dialog box to define how and when a service starts.

Service Logon

The Service dialog box also lets you control how services log on to the workstation. Each service must log on to the system (it happens automatically), and this is typically done using the system account. In fact, most of the services that come with Windows NT require that this account be used. However, you may have add-on services from third parties that should be run using a different user account. If the service in question recommends this, set the user account used by the service in the Service startup dialog box using the This Account, Password, and Confirm Password fields.

> **Tip**   If you set a service to use an account other than the system account, be sure that you create the account in the User Manager, and that you set the account's password to never expire. (User Manager is the administrative program that manages users of your computer over the network.)

Enabling a Service to Interact with a User

Some services may need to interact with the user of the workstation. When this is the case, select the Allow Service to Interact with Desktop check box. In the services that are included with Windows NT Workstation 4, only the Spooler service has this option selected.

Pausing Services

Some services can be paused. Notably, the Server and Workstation services can be paused with the Pause button in the Services dialog box. Pausing the server process, for example, keeps users from logging on to the workstation, but still allows the administrator to log on. This may be useful when carrying out maintenance work on the workstation.

Changing Service Startup Characteristics

You may wish to change the startup characteristics for some services based on the hardware profile that is selected. If you are using a portable computer with a docking station, for example, and do not have network access when the computer isn't docked, you won't want the networking services to start then. To control this, select the service for which you want to control the startup behavior (based on the selected hardware profile), and click the HW Profiles button in the Services dialog box. The Service dialog box shown in figure 3.11 appears.

Figure 3.11

The Service dialog box lets you make service startup conditional to a particular hardware profile.

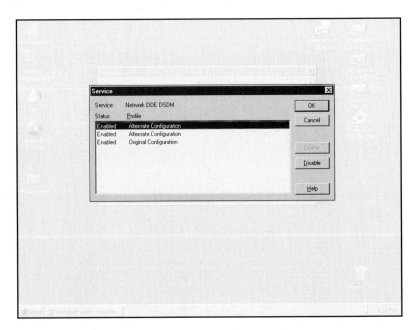

When you control service startup based on the hardware profile, you only have two choices for each hardware profile: enabled and disabled. When you disable a service for a particular hardware profile, that service won't be started when using that hardware profile.

Starting Windows NT Workstation isn't everything, though. It's also important that you shut it down gracefully. Important information about the system is saved during shutdown, and any waiting data in your disk cache is flushed before the system is shut down. You learn more about system shutdown in the following section.

Shutting Down

It is imperative that you properly shut down Windows NT Workstation every time you power down your computer. Shutting down causes the disk caches to be flushed to the disks (see Chapter 1, "Understanding Windows NT Workstation 4") and saves any changed settings for you.

There are two ways to shut down your system. First, from the Start menu, choose Shut Down. You see the Shut Down Windows dialog box shown in figure 3.12.

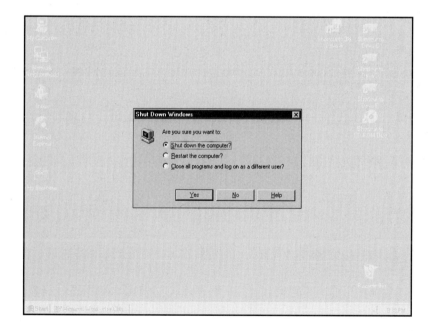

Figure 3.12

The Shut Down Windows dialog box lets you choose how the system shuts down.

There are three choices in the Shut Down Windows dialog box:

◆ **Shut Down the Computer?** prepares your computer to be turned off. Be sure to wait for the message informing you that it is safe to do so before you power down.

◆ **Restart the Computer?** causes the system to shut down and then execute a hardware reset, booting itself automatically.

◆ **Close All Programs and Log On as a Different User?** logs off the current user from the workstation, and presents the logon message for the next user who needs the workstation. This option does not restart either the computer or Windows NT Workstation.

You can also shut down the system by pressing Ctrl+Alt+Del while using the system. You see the Windows NT Security dialog box shown in figure 3.13 when you do this.

Click on the Shut Down button to proceed with shutting down the system.

Figure 3.13

The Windows NT Security dialog box provides an alternative way to shut down the system.

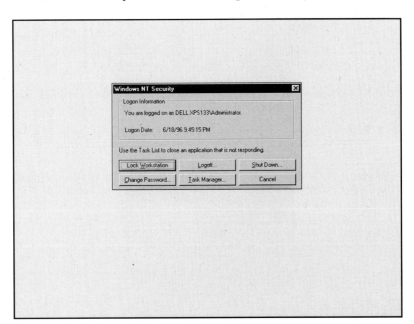

Changing Passwords

Normally, your network setup will prompt you to change your password—this is controlled by the administrator of the network domain you use. You can also control when users of the workstation are forced to change their passwords on the workstation with the User Manager application. These tasks are covered in Chapter 26, "Understanding Shared Resources."

To change your own password whenever you wish, press Ctrl+Alt+Del. The Windows NT Security dialog box appears (refer to fig. 3.13). Click on the Change Password button, which brings up the Change Password dialog box shown in figure 3.14.

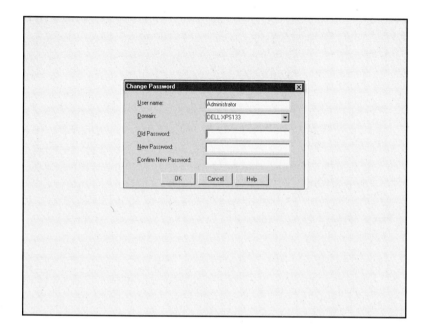

Figure 3.14

Choose a new password with the Change Password dialog box.

Fill in the Old Password, New Password, and Confirm New Password fields and click on the OK button. Make sure that you have selected the proper domain in which you want to change your password before clicking on the OK button.

Understanding Multiple Operating System Choices

Many people must use multiple operating systems on their computers. For instance, software developers often need to run multiple operating systems so that they can program for different operating system targets, or simply test their applications for different operating systems. User support personnel may need to access multiple operating systems so that they can properly support clients who use different operating systems. And, of course, many other computer professionals need to work with multiple operating systems in the course of their work for any number of reasons.

You can set up Windows NT Workstation to coexist with a variety of different operating systems on a single computer. For example, you can configure your computer to run all of the following operating systems (each one selectable from a set of menus that appears during boot):

◆ MS-DOS 6.22 (with Windows 3.11 available to be started)

◆ OS/2 Warp 3

◆ Windows 95

◆ Windows NT Server 3.51

◆ Windows NT Workstation 4

There are many different ways to set this up so that it works; this section teaches you one of these ways, as well as some tips and considerations that you'll want to take into account as you plan your own multi-OS installation.

Understanding Disk Partitions

The key to setting up a complex assortment of operating systems on a system is to understand the limitations of hard disk partitions. You should review the following terminology surrounding disks and partitions to understand more about partitions before you begin planning:

◆ **Physical hard disk.** This disk drive is installed into your computer. Some machines have multiple physical hard disks installed.

◆ **Volume.** This is the same as a physical hard disk.

◆ **Partition.** This is a subdivision of a volume. On most systems, the entire volume is assigned to a single partition, but you can have up to four partitions per volume.

◆ **Primary partition.** This special partition is bootable to most operating systems. DOS, for instance, requires a primary partition from which to boot. Only one primary partition can be active (usable) at a time when the computer is in use. So, if you have three primary partitions and one extended partition (see the next term), only one primary partition will be available at a time to be used as a C: drive, and any extended partitions will exist as drives D: through Z:. The alternative primary partitions will be "invisible" when using one of the other primary partitions.

◆ **Extended partition.** This is a type of partition that can be divided into multiple logical drives. Each of these logical drives will appear as separate drive letters on your system. You must have at least one drive assigned to an extended partition.

◆ **System Partition.** A Windows NT-specific term, this is the partition from which the system initially boots. It is the C: drive on Intel-based computers, or a firmware-designated partition on RISC-based computers.

◆ **Boot Partition.** Another Windows NT-specific term, this is the partition that contains Windows NT itself. Windows NT can be installed to run from a primary or extended partition, but whatever partition is used is referred to as the *boot partition.*

◆ **Drive.** A drive is a logical subdivision of your hard disk. Each drive appears as a separate drive letter on your system. A system can have up to 26 drives at a time, and these drives can be spread over many volumes. Primary partitions always exist as one drive, while extended partitions can be divided up into many drives.

◆ **File system.** This is the method by which you format any given drive. Under Windows NT, you may choose to format a drive using either the FAT or NTFS file systems. (You learned more about file systems in Chapter 1.)

The following sections describe how Windows NT Workstation 4 coexists with different operating systems that you may want to run. In each section, you learn about installing an alternative operating system in such a way that you can access it on a system that can also run Windows NT Workstation 4.

Coexisting with Windows 95

If you need to use both Windows NT Workstation and Windows 95 on a single machine, you need to follow these steps:

Objective

B.2

1. First, install Windows 95 onto the bootable partition of your system (a primary partition that is configured as bootable with the FDISK disk administrator program used in Windows 95).

2. Install Windows NT Workstation onto the system; you can choose to install Windows NT Workstation onto any drive or partition that exists.

When you do this, a boot menu is automatically created that lets you select which operating system you want to start each time you boot the system.

Note   Windows 95 will not be able to work with any partitions on your system that are formatted using either HPFS or NTFS. Even though those HPFS or NTFS partitions may be available to Windows NT, Windows 95 ignores them. Moreover, some recent OEM-only versions of Windows 95 include a new form of FAT file system called FAT32, which Windows NT cannot access.

Coexisting with Other Versions of Windows NT

Objective B.2

Microsoft has made it easy to install different versions of Windows NT onto the same computer. Because Windows NT does not require a primary partition for its main installation directory, you can install different versions of Windows NT onto different drives on your system, or even on the same drive but in different directories. Each time you install a new version of Windows NT, the new version is added to the Microsoft boot menu automatically so that you can select the version you want each time you start your computer.

> **Note** Different versions of Windows NT will show you the partitions on your system in different orders. For instance, Windows NT 3.51 makes its installed partition appear as the C: drive, even if that partition is an extended partition that appears to other operating systems with a different drive letter. Windows NT Workstation 4, on the other hand, maintains the drive letter mappings that you see when running Windows 95. You will want to be aware of this when installing applications onto a multi-OS computer if the applications are set up to find their files on a particular drive and directory.

Coexisting with MS-DOS

Objective B.2

MS-DOS must boot from a primary bootable partition on your first installed hard disk. If you need to access a particular version of MS-DOS and Windows NT on the same computer, first install DOS onto the primary bootable partition, and then install Windows NT to the same partition or to an extended partition. You can boot MS-DOS from the boot menu that appears after you finish installing Windows NT Workstation and restart the computer.

Keep in mind that MS-DOS cannot work with partitions formatted using HPFS or NTFS. Also, MS-DOS will not be able to work with or "see" the long file names that Windows NT can store on FAT-formatted drives, although it can see the shortened version of the file name that Windows NT Workstation 4 stores for this purpose and can access the files themselves.

Coexisting with Windows 3.1

Objective B.2

Coexisting with Windows 3.1 is fundamentally the same thing as coexisting with MS-DOS because Windows 3.1 runs on top of DOS. In order to access both Windows 3.1 and Windows NT, you first install DOS onto the primary bootable partition, and then install Windows 3.1 onto one of the FAT-formatted partitions on the system. After that's done, you can then install Windows NT to the system using any drive or directory you choose.

To access Windows 3.1, start MS-DOS with the Microsoft boot menu, change to the directory that contains Windows 3.1, and use the WIN command to start Windows 3.1.

Windows 3.1 shares the same limitations as MS-DOS with regard to coexisting with Windows NT; it cannot work with HPFS- or NTFS-formatted drives, and it will not be able to work with the Windows NT long file names stored on FAT-formatted drives.

Coexisting with OS/2 Warp

Setting up a system so that it can run the preceding operating systems and OS/2 Warp is somewhat involved. You need to do some fancy footwork to set this up so that it works properly. Part of the reason is that Microsoft has made no effort to enable OS/2 Warp to be booted from the Microsoft operating system startup menu. Also, OS/2 Warp needs some boot files in the root directory of your primary bootable partition (right where Windows 95 and Windows NT, as well as MS-DOS, want to store their files). Setting this up properly is definitely possible, however.

Objective

B.2

Consider the system mentioned previously that is able to run MS-DOS and Windows 3.11, OS/2 Warp, Windows 95, and various versions of Windows NT. There are a variety of ways to set up a system so that it can boot all of these operating systems. However, the method shown here works, is proven, is easy to use once set up, and offers a good mix of capabilities. Plus, you don't need any third-party software packages to make this work. To set this up, perform the following steps:

1. Start the OS/2 Warp installation disks, escape from the installation at the first available opportunity, and run Warp's version of FDISK from the command line.

Note | Details on performing some of the operating system-specific tasks, such as running OS/2's FDISK, are not covered here. Obtain complete documentation available for each operating system you plan to use, and refer to that documentation for details on some of these steps. Here, you're learning about the overall process that lets you run each of the different operating systems mentioned on a single machine that also runs Windows NT Workstation 4.

2. Using Warp's FDISK, create a 2 MB primary partition and install Boot Manager (OS/2's multiple operating system startup tool) onto that partition.

3. Also using Warp's FDISK, create two additional primary partitions. The first will hold MS-DOS, Windows 3.1, and OS/2 Warp; the second will hold Windows 95 and the startup files for Windows NT. You will need to plan accordingly to create enough space for these partitions. You cannot resize partitions after installing the operating systems without losing all of their data and having to start over. Name the first primary partition "Warp_DOS" and the second primary partition "Windows" or "Win95_NT."

4. Still using Warp's FDISK, mark the first primary partition (Warp_DOS) as Installable. This causes that partition to be made active when you restart the system. Exit FDISK, choosing to save changes.

5. Restart the system using the MS-DOS installation disks. Install MS-DOS onto the current primary partition (Installable), formatting the partition during the installation. Because the partition was marked Installable, you automatically install MS-DOS onto the Warp_DOS partition, and it appears as the C: drive to MS-DOS. If you want to install Windows 3.1, do that now. (Install Windows 3.1 onto the Warp_DOS partition after you've installed MS-DOS.)

6. Restart the system again, this time using OS/2 Warp's installation disks. Install OS/2 Warp onto the partition on which you just installed MS-DOS (your C: drive). This automatically creates, in that partition, a dual-boot setup for OS/2 Warp from which you can run MS-DOS or OS/2 Warp.

7. After installing OS/2, restart the system so that OS/2 starts and runs. Using OS/2's FDISK again, mark the second primary partition (perhaps named "Windows") as Installable.

8. Restart the system, using your Windows 95 startup disks. You can also use an MS-DOS system disk with your DOS CD-ROM drivers installed if you are installing using the CD-ROM version of Windows 95.

9. Install Windows 95 onto the currently active primary partition. It appears as your C drive, but is actually the second primary partition you created in step 3. The Windows 95 installation program will warn you that it will deactivate Boot Manager. Acknowledge the message and let it do so (you learn how to reenable Boot Manager in a later step).

10. Restart the computer with Windows 95. It will start automatically, and you will not see the Boot Manager menu. At this point, install Windows NT onto any available drive on your system.

11. When you finish installing Windows NT, restart the computer. You will see a menu that lets you choose to start either Windows 95 or Windows NT. Choose Windows NT and let the operating system start.

12. Access Windows NT's Disk Administrator program. It will show you a setup similar to the one you see in figure 3.15.

13. Select the OS/2 Boot Manager partition, open the Partition menu and choose Mark Active. This reenables the Boot Manager program, which you need to access the Warp_DOS partition and the operating systems installed on it.

When you boot your system normally after following these steps, you first see the Boot Manager screen that lets you choose to boot from either the Warp_DOS partition or the Windows partition. If you choose the Warp_DOS partition, whatever operating system is active on that partition starts. You toggle the operating system that is active on the Warp_DOS partition by using Warp's BOOT /DOS or

BOOT /OS2 commands. The selected operating system starts the next time you select the Warp_DOS partition from Boot Manager.

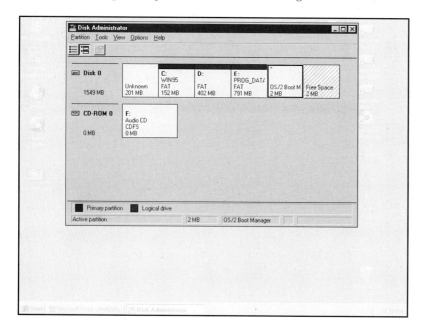

Figure 3.15

Use the Windows NT Disk Administrator to reactivate Boot Manager.

If you choose the Windows partition from Boot Manager, you immediately see the Microsoft boot menu that lets you choose to boot from Windows 95 or whatever versions of Windows NT you have installed.

> **Caution**
> Setting up your system to boot all of the operating systems discussed is time-consuming and requires that you feel comfortable with these installation issues. You should not attempt this complex of an installation if you are not experienced in performing installations of many different operating systems onto many different systems.

The next section discusses how you can manually customize the Windows portion of the startup screens that you learned about in the preceding steps.

Customizing BOOT.INI

When you install multiple Microsoft operating systems onto a computer, your primary bootable partition contains a file called BOOT.INI. This file defines all the available operating systems, indicates how to start them, and includes the default operating system choice that is made if you do not select an operating system from which to boot. You can change these settings using the System Properties dialog box in Windows NT's control panel, or you can edit it manually. In this section, you learn how to edit it manually.

| **Note** | BOOT.INI is a plain ASCII text file. You should edit it only with a non-formatting editor such as the Notepad program included with Windows NT and Windows 95. |

Figure 3.16 shows a sample BOOT.INI file from a system set up to boot Windows 95, Windows NT Workstation 4, and Windows NT Server 3.51.

Figure 3.16

A sample BOOT.INI file contains the commands needed to let you choose which operating system to start.

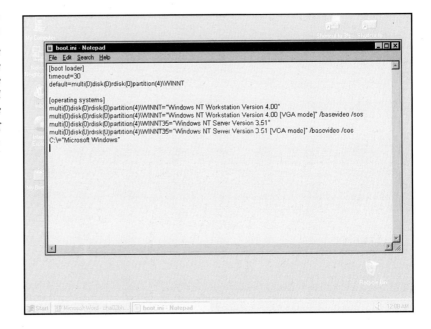

The BOOT.INI file is straightforward and easy to edit. It is broken into two sections: the first one is called [boot loader]; the second is called [operating systems].

The [boot loader] section defines how long the Microsoft boot menu waits for a selection to be made before booting the default operating system. The timeout value can be changed to any number of seconds a user wants. The [boot loader] section also defines which of the installed operating systems is started if a selection is not made from the boot menu.

The default= line in BOOT.INI defines which operating system is initially selected on the Microsoft boot menu, and which will be started if the timeout expires. To choose a different default operating system, copy one of the lines in the [operating systems] section back to the default= line. Only copy the portion of the appropriate [operating systems] line up to the equals sign. Do not copy the equals sign itself or the description listed after the equals sign. The example in figure 3.16 shows Windows NT Workstation 4 as the default operating system.

Each one of the [operating systems] lines has two parts. The leftmost part (up to the equals sign) indicates where the operating system's startup files are located. The text after the equals sign holds the name of the operating system; you see this name on the Microsoft boot menu during startup.

After changing the BOOT.INI file, save it to the root directory of your boot drive in plain ASCII text format. The changes you make will be in effect the next time you start your computer.

Handling BOOT.INI Problems

Take care when editing BOOT.INI, because incorrect changes to it can prevent Windows NT from starting. In particular, be aware of the following problems:

Objective G.1

◆ **Missing BOOT.INI.** If BOOT.INI is missing, Windows NT will try to start from the \WINNT directory. If Windows NT is installed in a different directory, however, it will not boot and you will be shown an error message indicating that *winnt_root*\ SYSTEM32\NTOSKRNL.EXE is corrupt or missing. To correct this problem, recreate BOOT.INI and ensure that you properly specify the Windows NT path using the instructions found in the preceding section.

◆ **Bad default= parameter.** If the parameter given in the default= command of BOOT.INI doesn't match up exactly with one of the operating systems listed in the [Operating Systems] section, the boot menu will simply show NT (default) as the only choice.

◆ **Bad Operating System path.** An incorrect path for Windows NT specified in the [Operating Systems] section will prevent Windows NT from booting with an error similar to the one seen when BOOT.INI is missing completely. Also, if the path to Windows NT uses an incorrect device name, you will see a different error message that indicates that there is a computer disk hardware configuration problem.

You can correct the preceding problems by editing BOOT.INI and fixing any errors, or you can use the Emergency Repair Disk to restore a working copy of the BOOT.INI file.

Troubleshooting the Bootup Process

One of the most frustrating problems that users face is dealing with a system that refuses to boot. Accessing the system to solve the problem isn't easy. There are some steps you can take, however, to make it easy to access a Windows NT system that refuses to boot for some reason, and some additional steps you can take even if you fail to prepare an Emergency Repair disk ahead of time. In the following sections, you learn how to prepare for and handle a non-booting Windows NT Workstation 4 system.

Using the Emergency Repair Disk

Objective G.1

Windows NT Workstation 4 can create an emergency repair disk (ERD) to help you solve problems on your system that prevent the computer from starting. You can create this disk during the initial installation of Windows NT, or you can run the RDISK.EXE program located in the System32 subdirectory of Windows NT's main directory (typically this is \WINNT\SYSTEM32). The ERD holds setup information from your system that you can use to more easily repair problems, such as corrupted startup files. In this section, you learn how to prepare your own ERD and how to use it to recover from system startup problems.

Preparing the Emergency Repair Disk

Objective G.1

To create or update your ERD, run the RDISK command using the Run command in your Start menu. This displays the program window shown in figure 3.17.

To create a new ERD, click on the Create Repair Disk button. You will be prompted for a blank disk that can be formatted and will hold the ERD data (key startup and configuration information about your system).

Figure 3.17

The Repair Disk Utility creates an ERD based on your current system configuration.

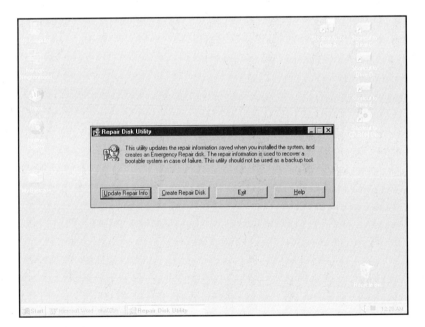

Note   You should be logged on with a user name that has administrator privileges on the system in order to create or update the ERD.

To update an existing ERD, click on the Update Repair Disk button, which transfers changed configuration data to the ERD. Do this after making changes to your system's configuration so that your ERD always contains up-to-date information with which to work.

> **Note** The key files that are placed onto the ERD can also be found in the *\winnt_root*\REPAIR directory. These files are updated whenever you run the RDISK.EXE utility.

Putting the Emergency Repair Disk to Work

If something prevents Windows NT Workstation 4 from starting or working properly, instead of reinstalling all of Windows NT, you can restore many of your important settings with the ERD and avoid having to redo all the configuration work that you've already performed.

> **Objective**
> **G.1**

To use the ERD, boot your system with Windows NT setup disks. After the second setup disk is processed, the Windows NT Setup menu appears. From this menu, choose the Repair a Damaged Installation option by pressing the R key. Another menu appears, in which you choose the repair options you want performed. By default, all options are selected and will be performed. The repair options are as follows:

◆ Inspect Registry Files

◆ Inspect Startup Environment

◆ Verify Windows NT System Files

◆ Inspect Boot Sector

You can select or deselect the options by using your arrow keys to move to an option and pressing the Enter key. Generally, however, you want to use all of the options.

> **Tip** If you cannot locate the Windows NT setup disks, but you have the Windows NT CD-ROM, you can create new disks from the CD-ROM. Insert the CD-ROM into a machine running DOS or Windows 95 and run either WINNT.EXE /ox or WINNT32.EXE /ox from the CD-ROM.

After continuing, you will be prompted for the ERD, and the specified repair tasks will be carried out. The repair process uses data stored on your ERD to carry out its tasks. When the repair process is finished, you'll be informed about what was found and whether it was able to be repaired or not.

Creating and Using an Emergency Boot Disk

Objective

G.1

You can create your own emergency boot disk for Windows NT Workstation 4. Such a disk can be invaluable in gaining access to the computer if one of the key startup files becomes corrupt or is missing.

To create such a disk, follow these steps:

1. Format a disk using Windows NT (you cannot use a disk formatted by DOS or Windows 95).

2. On that disk, place these files from your working system (or any working system): NTLDR, NTDETECT.COM, BOOT.INI and, for computers with BIOS-disabled SCSI adapters, NTBOOTDD.SYS.

3. Modify the BOOT.INI file on the disk so that it reflects the path to the system partition on the computer.

The resulting disk can be used to boot a Windows NT computer, although for Windows NT to completely boot, the rest of the operating system files located in the *\winnt_root* directory must be accessible on the system.

Setting System Recovery Options

Objective

G.1

There are some additional system recovery options available using the System object in the Control Panel. Activating this object reveals the System Properties dialog box. The Startup/Shutdown tab, shown in figure 3.18, contains these options.

A STOP event is a critical failure in the system. The Recovery area of the Startup/ Shutdown tab lets you control how the system handles STOP errors. You can choose from the following options:

◆ **Write an Event to the System Log.** When selected, the error pertaining to the STOP event will be written to the system log (*\winnt_root*\SYSTEM32\CONFIG\SYSTEM.LOG). You can subsequently view this information with the Event Viewer.

◆ **Send an Administrative Alert.** When this option is selected, an alert message is sent in a pop-up dialog box to any computer or user chosen in the Alerts dialog box within the Control Panel's Server dialog box.

◆ **Write Debugging Information To.** This option lets you dump the entire contents of memory into the paging file. This file can then be used by Microsoft to further debug the problem. For this option to work, the paging file must be located on the boot partition. After a STOP event causes the system to stop and memory to be written to the paging file, rebooting the system will cause the memory contents to be copied from the paging file into the filename specified in the field shown.

◆ **Automatically Reboot.** In certain roles, such as a server working purely as a RAS server, it is best to immediately reboot the system if an unexpected failure occurs. This action can be particularly useful with systems that can completely initialize into their normal role without intervention (for example, a Windows NT–based file and print server can do this).

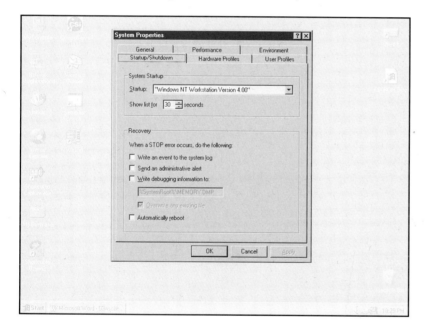

Figure 3.18

The Startup/ Shutdown tab contains several important recovery options.

End Note: If you support many users of Windows NT Workstation 4, you can do some advance planning to help recover from configuration problems caused by your users. Once you install Windows NT Workstation 4, make a copy of the hardware profile and name it something like "Backup Hardware Profile." Then, if the user of the machine mistakenly makes changes to the hardware profile that keep the system from running, choose the backup hardware profile from the Last Known Good menu to get the machine up and running again. When you do make legitimate changes to the hardware configuration, you can delete the first backup copy and create a new one, so that you always have a way of restoring a messed-up hardware configuration.

Test Your Knowledge

1. Which of the following files are *not* required for Windows NT to boot on a RISC-based system?

    A. NTLDR

    B. BOOT.INI

    C. NTDETECT.COM

    D. OSLOADER.EXE

2. During the logon process, the following type of program is not allowed to run:

    A. Real mode programs

    B. Protected mode programs

    C. Win32 programs

    D. Graphical programs

3. Which of the following environment variable settings is processed last during boot:

    A. User environment variables

    B. System environment variables

    C. CONFIG.SYS environment variables

    D. AUTOEXEC.BAT environment variables

4. When you can't start Windows NT due to an incorrect change in hardware or device driver settings, you need to invoke the hardware profile called:

    A. Initial Installation

    B. Guaranteed Working

    C. Last Known Good

    D. Last Clean Boot

5. To run both Windows 95 and Windows NT on a computer in dual-boot mode, you should do which of the following:

    A. Install Windows 95, and then install Windows NT.

    B. Start the Windows NT Installation from a DOS boot disk and create the BOOT.INI file on the C: drive.

    C. Use OS/2's Boot Manager program.

    D. You can't run both Windows 95 and Windows NT on one computer.

6. Which of the following is important in setting up a dual-boot system:
    A. Owning a ZIP drive for the special installation
    B. Choosing the appropriate file system for the primary partition
    C. Installing Windows NT onto an extended partition
    D. Having two hard disks installed in the computer

7. Which of the following statements are true:
    A. You can install multiple versions of Windows NT onto a single computer and choose any of them at boot time.
    B. Windows NT cannot coexist with OS/2 Warp on a given computer.
    C. DOS 6.22 is required for dual-boot configurations.
    D. Windows NT includes a tool that lets you choose to boot any of the Microsoft Operating Systems that are installed on your system, including DOS+Windows 3.x, Windows 95, and Windows NT.

Test Your Knowledge Answers

1. B,C
2. A
3. A
4. C
5. A
6. B
7. A,D

Chapter Snapshot

Online Help is abundant throughout Windows NT 4. The robust Help file system is easy to navigate, and specific Help functions teach you about dialog box entries and toolbar icons. This chapter discusses a variety of Help features, covering the following:

Windows NT
Workstation 4

CHAPTER 4

Getting Help

Help for using Windows NT is available through the main Help system, which is a unified group of files that are organized with a table of contents and index linked via hypertext. In addition, there are help file systems for all the applications that are part of the accessories you installed.

New to version 4 of NT is context help for dialog boxes, so you can gain a better understanding of what your entries should be as you configure hardware and software. This new feature is called What's This?, and you can use it on dialog box fields to get detailed explanations about the type of entry needed.

Understanding the Main Help System

The main Windows NT Help system is a robust, efficient way to obtain help for using the operating system and its features. You can launch Help by choosing Help from the Start menu.

> **Tip** If you are at the desktop, just press F1 to bring up the Help system. To make sure the desktop has the focus, click on any blank spot before pressing F1.

When you open Help, three tabs are displayed: Contents, Index, and Find. No matter which tab you use, you end up at the same help pages with the same contents. The decision of which to use depends on how you want to search for help:

◆ **Contents.** Use the Contents tab to get an overview of a topic, which can be helpful if you're not sure exactly which feature or function you want help for.

◆ **Index.** Use the Index tab to get information about a topic that is broad enough to have been placed in the index, such as Printers or Network Neighborhood. Actually, the index for the help files is quite abundant and includes many narrower topics, such as Network DDE service.

◆ **Find.** Use the Find tab to see all the topics that contain a specific word or phrase. When you enter the appropriate text, a listing of the index topics that contain that word is displayed.

The Help Files

Windows NT Help is comprised of a number of files that are combined and indexed to create the main Help system. A database of all the important words is also contained in the Help files so you can search the files for a word or phrase that might not be an index entry.

The individual files in the main Windows NT Help system cover the following topics:

◆ Accessibility Help

◆ Basic Tasks

◆ Control Panel Help

◆ DCOM Help

◆ Help on Help

◆ If You've Used Windows Before

◆ Mouse Help

- ◆ Network Control Panel Help

- ◆ Network Help

- ◆ System Control Panel Help

- ◆ Tape, SCSI, PCMCIA Control Panel Help

- ◆ Windows NT Command Reference

- ◆ Windows NT General Help

- ◆ Windows NT Help

There is not always a recognizable relationship between these file listings and the file names in your Windows NT System Help subfolder, although some of them are easy to figure out (for instance, it's fairly obvious that ACCESS.HLP is the file for the file listing ACCESSIBILITY).

In addition, most of the help files are unified (linked together), and opening one directly from Explorer or My Computer results in opening almost all of them. For example, if you open the file ACCESS.HLP, you will be presented with all the help topics, not just those related to the accessibility options. You will see the standard Help dialog box with three tabs, just as if you had selected Help from the Start menu.

Contents Tab

The first time you open Help, the Contents tab is in the foreground—thereafter the foreground tab will be the tab that was in the foreground the last time you closed Help.

The Contents tab displays all the major categories of Help, and each category is listed with a book icon (see fig. 4.1). You can open any book to see the topics covered in that book (think of each topic as a chapter in the book) and then open the topic of interest. Note that some books contain subcategories (identified by book icons) in addition to topics.

To open a book, double-click on it (or select it and choose Open). To close a book, double-click on it again (when the book is open, the Open button changes to Close). Find the topic you need and double-click on it (or select it and choose Display).

The Index Tab

The Index tab displays the complete index of all the help files in the main Help system (see fig. 4.2). As with all index listings, it is in alphabetic order.

Figure 4.1

The Contents tab of the Help dialog box contains a number of books, each covering a different category.

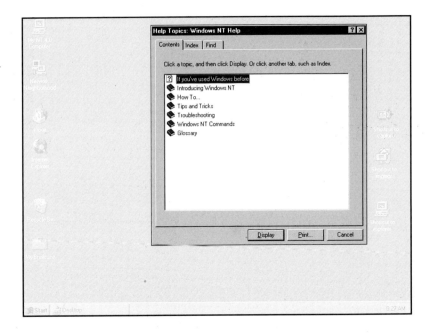

Figure 4.2

Scroll through the index to find the topic you need, or enter characters to move to a specific topic quickly.

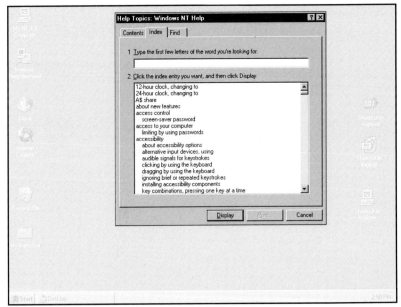

There are two boxes on the Index tab:

◆ Box 1 is an entry box in which you can enter characters to speed your search.

◆ Box 2 is the list of index entries.

Enter characters in box 1. As you type each letter, the index listing in box 2 moves to match the characters you are entering. If no index entry matches the characters you are typing, the index listing stops moving at the last match.

Scroll through the index entries in box 2, using the scroll bar to move rapidly through the alphabet.

When you find the appropriate index entry, double-click on it (or select it and choose Display).

The Find Tab

Use the Find tab to find words or phrases when you're not sure there's an index entry that matches what you're looking for (or when you're not sure which index entry contains the exact help topic you need).

Find provides a search engine for a database of all the words in the help files. You can build the database to reflect the way you use the Find tab, and you can also configure the way the Find processes work. There are three numbered boxes on the Find tab, as shown in figure 4.3.

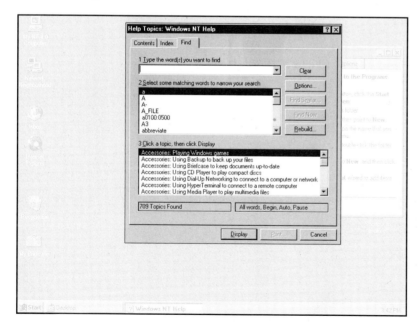

Figure 4.3

The Find tab matches the words you enter to words contained in help topics and then presents the topic choices for your selection.

The procedure for using the Find tab follows:

1. Use box 1 to Type the word(s) you want to find.

2. Use box 2 to Select some matching words to narrow your search.

3. Use box 3 to Click a topic, then click Display.

4. Choose Clear to clear box 1 and begin again.

Customizing Find

You can design the way you use the Find tab to match the way you work. The customization options include choices about building the database that's used for finding help, as well as the way the Find features work for you.

Building the Find Database

The first time you use the Find tab, you have to build the database. The Find Setup Wizard takes you through the steps (see fig. 4.4). The number of steps varies depending on the type of database you choose.

Figure 4.4

Before you can use Find, you must create a database of the words in the help files.

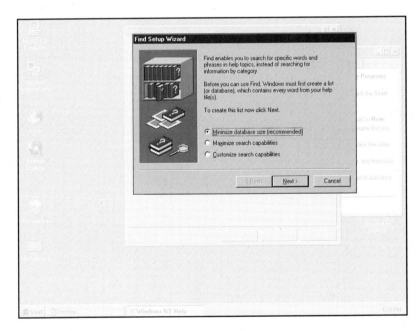

The database configuration options are as follows:

◆ **Minimize Database Size.** Select this option to create a database of all the words in the help files. This database choice provides only the ability to search for words.

◆ **Maximize Search Capabilities.** Select this option to create a database and also build in the ability to search for a topic and then ask to see similar topics without the need to enter a new word to search on. This database is larger and takes longer to load.

◆ **Customize Search Capabilities.** Select this option to add more choices concerning the way the database is built and used. This database is quite large and will be much slower to load, but you may find the following additional functions are worth the wait:

  ◆ Choosing which help files to use for the database

  ◆ Including topics that are not part of an Index entry (some definitions are not indexed)

  ◆ Gaining the ability to search for phrases in addition to words

  ◆ Having the capability to mark a section of a help topic and then search for similar sections, even if those similar sections don't contain the word you typed

 Tip   Don't worry about whether you're making the correct choice for the database because you can rebuild it at any time using a different choice. Choosing Rebuild on the Find tab starts the entire process all over again.

After you've selected a database type, choose Next to move to the next page of the wizard.

If you chose Minimize or Maximize, there is only one more wizard page. Choose Finish to build the database.

If you chose Customize, perform the following steps to complete the wizard:

1. Select the help files you want to include in the database (see fig. 4.5) and then choose Next.

2. Select Include Untitled Topics to place topics such as pop-up definitions in the database so you can search for them. Or choose Ignore Untitled Topics to omit them from the database. Then choose Next.

3. Select Include Phrase Searching to search for full phrases. Choose Don't Include Phrase Searching to omit this choice. Including phrase searching creates a much larger database, and the Find tab will probably be slower when users access it. However, it might be productive to include phrase searching if you're having trouble finding a help entry that you think should be in the database.

4. Select Display Matching Phrases or Don't Display Matching Phrases to choose whether you want to have matching phrases displayed while you are typing. Then choose Next.

5. Select Support Similarity Searches to mark help topics for later searches for related information. Select Don't Support Similarity Searches to omit this feature. Then choose Next.

6. Choose Finish to begin building the database.

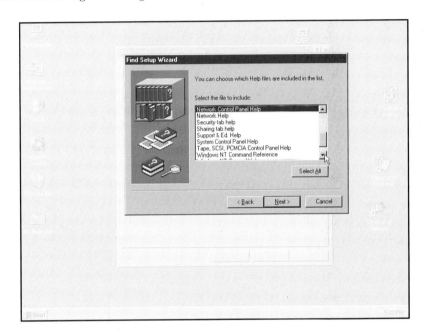

Figure 4.5

Select help files to include in the database or choose Select All to include every help file.

Working Efficiently with Help

The size of the database has an ongoing effect on your use of Help. Every time you launch Help and click on the Find tab, the database is loaded. (Microsoft has provided a cute animated icon telling you that Help is loading the word list, but after awhile, its amusement level doesn't make up for the wait.) A large database can take a while to load, even on a very fast computer.

When you close Help, the system remembers the tab that was in the foreground. The next time you open Help, that tab is selected. If the Find tab is the foreground tab, there will be a delay before you can access any of the Help tabs. To avoid the delay, train yourself to select the Contents tab or the Index tab before closing Help.

For most users, the Minimize database choice is sufficient. It's customary to use Help for a quick reminder about how to perform a task, or to get some guidance about which object in the Control Panel has the settings you need to check. It's not the norm to need an exhaustive search on all the information available about a topic.

There are some effective and productive ways to make a customized database choice available without slowing down every user who may occasionally need those advanced features. In some companies, one user in a department (usually the person people turn to for computer help) chooses the larger database. In other companies, only the Help Desk personnel configure the large database.

If there is a workstation that isn't used regularly (perhaps it belongs to a user who is frequently out in the field, it's an extra workstation, or it's mostly used as a print server), it might be the perfect place to build the large database. Keep it on the desktop all the time so all users can access it when necessary.

Regardless of the database configuration chosen, it's quite easy to set new options by choosing Rebuild on the Find tab. It might be worthwhile to experiment with various configuration options for short periods of time and listen to the reactions of users. If, in the end, the minimized configuration works, there is no reason to use the more robust, but slower, options.

Configuring Search Options for Find

You can customize the way Find works, choosing when and how the database is searched as you enter the characters and words you want Find to match. The options differ according to the choices you have made concerning the database.

To configure the Find processes, choose Options on the Find tab. The Find Options dialog box appears (see fig. 4.6).

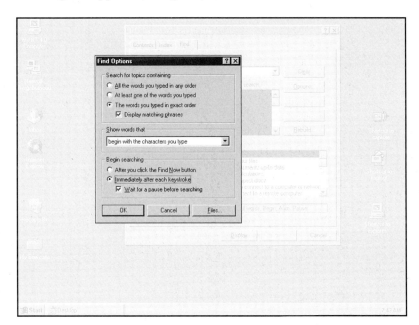

Figure 4.6

You can customize how Find uses the database to locate the help topic you need.

Make selections based on the following choices:

◆ **All the Words You Typed in Any Order.** Specifies that you want to find topics that contain all the words you enter, regardless of whether they match the order in which you entered them.

◆ **At Least One of the Words You Typed.** Specifies that if you enter multiple words, you want to find all the topics that contain at least one of those words.

◆ **The Words You Typed in Exact Order.** Specifies that you want to search for the exact phrase you entered. This choice is not available if you chose a Minimized database.

If you select this option, you can also select Display Matching Phrases, which specifies that Help will show you only those words that actually follow the phrase you entered. Otherwise, Help displays all the words in any file that contains your phrase.

◆ **Show Words That.** In this section, click on the arrow to the right of the text box to see the choices for selecting matching words. The choices are to select words that match the following criteria:

◆ Begin with the Characters You Type

◆ Contain the Characters You Type

◆ End with the Characters You Type

◆ Match the Characters you Type

◆ Have the Same Root as the Characters You Type

In the Begin searching section, specify when you want the search to start by choosing between the following options:

◆ After You Click the Find Now Button

◆ Immediately After Each Keystroke

If you choose the latter, you can also specify that Find should wait for a pause before searching.

Choose Files to see a list of all the help files and choose the ones you want to use.

When you have finished making your selections, choose OK.

Using the Help Pages

After you've selected a topic, the actual help page appears with information about that topic. The form and contents of a help page are different for different topics. A number of elements may appear on the page, but there are also some consistent elements and options.

Using the Features on Help Pages

Features are available on help pages that make it easy to accomplish a task, find additional information, or manipulate the behavior of the help pages.

Back
Choose Back to return to the previously displayed help page.

Help Topics
Choose Help Topics to return to the main help dialog box.

Definitions
Click on an underlined word or phrase to see a pop-up definition.

Move to a related topic
Click on the box next to a related topic to move directly to a help page for that topic.

Options
Choose Options to see the options submenu, or right-click anywhere on the help page to see the same menu. (See the "Help Page Options" section for more information.)

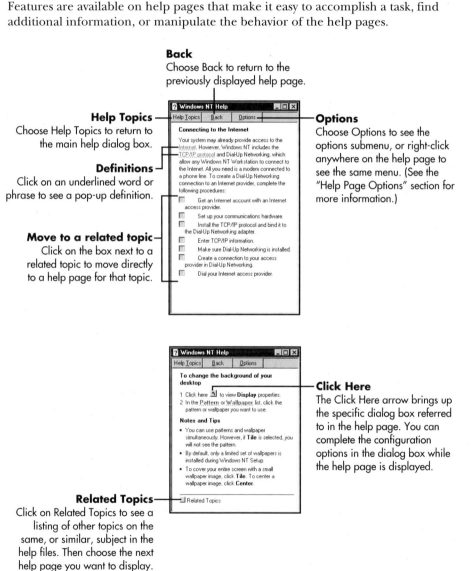

Click Here
The Click Here arrow brings up the specific dialog box referred to in the help page. You can complete the configuration options in the dialog box while the help page is displayed.

Related Topics
Click on Related Topics to see a listing of other topics on the same, or similar, subject in the help files. Then choose the next help page you want to display.

Help Page Options

On any help page, click on Options to see the options menu for the page. Some of these options control the way help pages display; others give you an opportunity to enhance the way help works for you.

Annotate

Choose Annotate to add your own notes to a help page. The Annotate dialog box appears (see fig. 4.7). Enter whatever text you wish to add to the information on the help page. Choose Save when you are finished. Hereafter, a paper clip icon appears on this help page, indicating the presence of an annotation. Click on the paper clip to see your note.

Figure 4.7

Add your own notes, reminders, or warnings to a Windows NT help page.

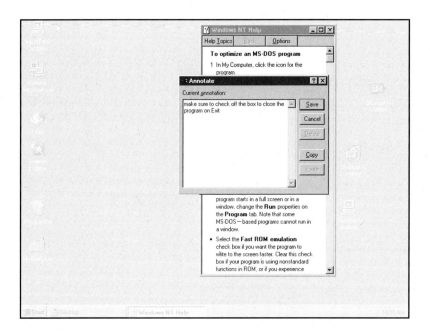

> **Note** Annotating help topics is a good way to remind people about company policies concerning configuration options or installation decisions. Perhaps a note that says "We didn't install them—don't even think about it" should be added to the help topic pages about games.

Passing along important information about installing and configuring the specific peripherals your organization uses is another productive use of annotation. Perhaps your modems or CD-ROM units require manufacturer's disks rather than the drivers on the Windows NT media. If so, you would want to make a note of that on any topic pages about installing or configuring those peripherals.

Copy

Choose Copy to copy the contents of the help page to the Clipboard. You can later paste the text into a document in any Windows application. You can select text to copy—you don't need to copy the entire page.

Print Topic

Choose Print Topic to send the contents of the help page to the printer. The Print dialog box appears so that you can choose a printer and the number of copies to print. This option only prints the entire page; you cannot opt to print selected text.

Font

Choose Font to change the size of the font used in help page text. The default font is Normal. You can change the font to Small or Large.

Keep Help on Top

Choose Keep Help on Top to change the options for keeping the help page on top of any other open windows on your screen. The choices follow:

- ◆ **Default.** Uses the default setting for the help file that was accessed for this page. Different Help files have different defaults for whether the help page is kept on top.
- ◆ **On Top.** Regardless of the default for this help file, all pages stay on top.
- ◆ **Not On Top.** Has the converse effect of On Top.

Use System Colors

Choose Use System Colors to change the color scheme for help pages. By default, help pages have a pale yellow background and use various colors for underlining and the Click Here arrow. You can change this color scheme to match the colors of application windows in your system (using the Appearance tab of Display Properties).

The System Colors choice is a toggle; you turn it off and on by selecting it. When you change system colors, the Help system and any open help pages have to be closed before the change takes effect. A dialog box informs you of this and asks if you want to close Help. After you close the Help window, the new color scheme is displayed the next time you open Help.

Using What's This?

Another source of help for Windows NT is What's This?, which provides information about a specific item.

If a dialog box has a question mark in the upper right-corner, it means that the What's This? feature is active. To learn about any section of the dialog box, click on the question mark (your pointer changes to an arrow with a question mark) and then click on any title in the dialog box to see its definition. A small box that says What's This? appears. When you click on that box, a definition appears.

 For a shortcut, the presence of the question mark in the corner of the dialog box means you can right-click on any title in the dialog box to bring up the What's This? box.

While the definition is displayed, right-click anywhere in the definition box to copy or print the definition.

Windows programs that are written for Windows NT (or for Windows 95) usually have the What's This? feature. If a What's This? question mark is on the toolbar, click on it. While your pointer has a question mark, point to any tool icon or menu item to see its definition. Dialog boxes for these programs contain the What's This? question mark.

 Most of the time, if a Windows NT dialog box does not have a question mark in the corner, there is a Help button on the dialog box.

Using Tooltips

When you open any Windows NT object that contains a toolbar, you can take advantage of tooltips. To see a tooltip, hold your pointer over any toolbar icon for a second or two. An explanation of the icon is displayed (see fig. 4.8).

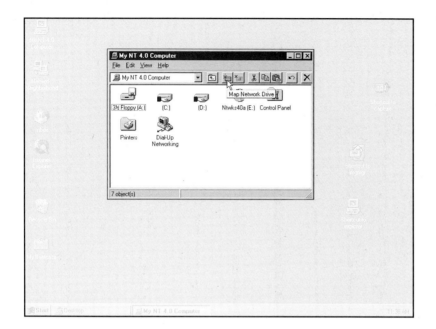

Figure 4.8

With tooltips, you don't have to guess about the function of a tool.

Getting Help for MS-DOS Commands

Your Windows NT 4 system has MS-DOS commands available for you to use in a command session. (Incidentally, the commands are located in the \system32 subfolder under your Windows NT folder.) To get help for an MS-DOS command, perform the following steps:

1. Open a command session (choose Programs, Command Prompt from the Start menu).

2. Enter *command* /? (substitute the name of the MS-DOS command you want help on for command). Information about the command is displayed (see fig 4.9).

3. If the explanation is too long to fit on one screen, add **|more** to your command line entry.

4. If you want to save the information to a text file, add **>filename** to your command line entry (substitute a meaningful name for filename). You then can bring the text file into a word processor and print it, or add it to an existing collection of MS-DOS commands.

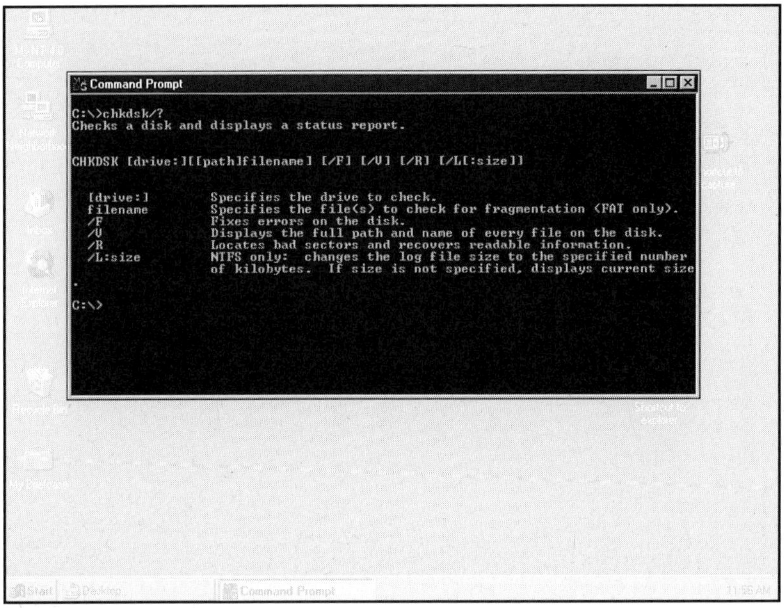

Figure 4.9

*You can get help
with an MS-DOS
command, as well
as information
about any
parameters and
switches that
apply.*

Getting Help for Applications

When you are working in a Windows NT application, or in one of the Windows NT accessory programs, choose Help from the menu bar (or press F1) to see the help files for that application. You will find the following:

◆ The format of Help is the same as it is with the Windows NT main Help system—the same three tabs are available, and they work the same way.

◆ Dialog boxes with a question mark in the corner support the What's This? feature.

◆ Tooltips are available for toolbar icons.

Using Help for Troubleshooting

The interactive troubleshooting tools built into the Help system are designed to walk you through the process of fixing problems. Troubleshooters are available for the following circumstances:

◆ Modem problems

◆ Network problems

◆ Printer problems

◆ Disk space problems

◆ Memory problems

To use a troubleshooter, open the Troubleshooting book on the Help Contents tab, and choose the troubleshooter you need.

The troubleshooter attempts to identify the specific problem (see fig. 4.10), either by guessing the problem or asking questions. Click on the box to the left of the statement or question that seems to best match your problem.

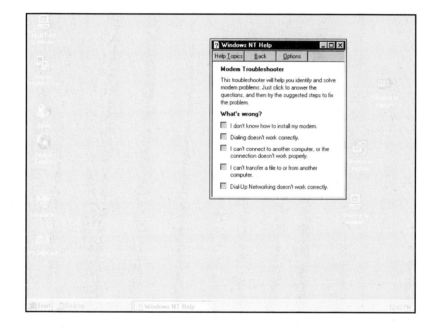

Figure 4.10

To begin the modem troubleshooting process, select the item that comes closest to describing your problem.

Depending on the statement or question you select, a variety of steps are possible. Some of these possibilities follow:

◆ An arrow appears that you can click on to bring up an installation or configuration dialog box and a list of instructions on how to use it. The troubleshooter stays on the screen while you go through all the steps.

◆ A series of questions are posed that you need to answer in order to narrow the choices about your problem; sometimes your answers lead to additional questions.

◆ A series of suggestions for remedies are given, along with the question "Did this fix the problem?" Answering yes closes the troubleshooter; answering no usually brings additional suggestions or questions.

As questions are asked and suggestions are offered, the troubleshooter moves on. The contents of each additional page depend on your responses. You can choose Back to move to the previous page.

There are, of course, times when the troubleshooter runs out of suggestions and announces you've run into a problem that it can't help you solve. This is generally accompanied by a gentle suggestion to read the documentation for the device, or contact a support person at the manufacturer.

 Tip   You can print or copy (to the Clipboard) any page of the troubleshooter using the Options menu or the shortcut menu that displays when you right-click anywhere on the page.

Getting a Tip Every Day

The first time you booted into Windows NT 4, a Welcome greeted you, and it contained a tip about using NT productively (see fig. 4.11). You may have deselected the option to Show this Welcome Screen Next Time You Start Windows NT (many users do; they're anxious to get right to work and don't want to stop to read and close this screen).

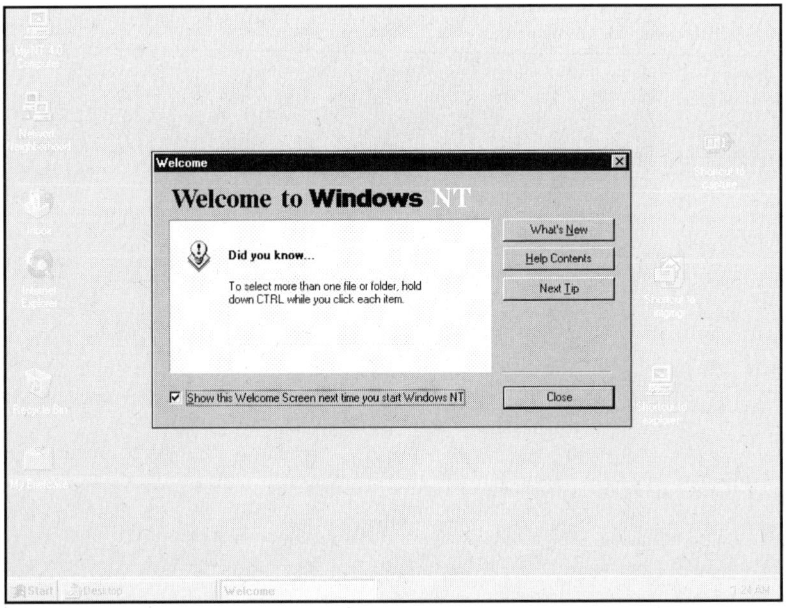

Figure 4.11

The Welcome screen has a tip to offer every time you start the operating system.

![Welcome to Windows NT screen with "Did you know..." tip reading "To select more than one file or folder, hold down CTRL while you click each item." Buttons: What's New, Help Contents, Next Tip. Checkbox: Show this Welcome Screen next time you start Windows NT. Close button.]

Sometimes, however, users want to return to the Welcome screen at startup, or administrators think it is a good idea for some users to see the startup tips.

You can launch the Welcome program at any time by double-clicking on WELCOME.EXE, which is in your Windows NT folder. After the Welcome screen is displayed, you can select the option to show it every time the system is started.

A few elements are on the Welcome screen in addition to the tip of the day:

◆ **What's New.** Choose this option to see help topics on the changes in NT since the previous version (see fig. 4.12).

◆ **Help Contents.** Choose this option to launch the Windows NT Help system.

◆ **Next Tip.** Choose this option to see another helpful hint.

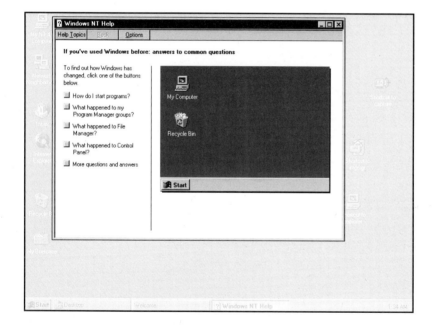

Figure 4.12

Some of the commonly asked questions about the new features of NT 4 are answered in a special help section.

Getting Help Online

There are a number of online help resources published by Microsoft on the Internet. Using these support vehicles offers you quick and easy access to the latest information, software patches, drivers, and other support information necessary to implement, support, and maintain Windows NT Workstation 4, as well as other Microsoft products.

Getting TechNet

Microsoft publishes a subscription CD-ROM service called TechNet. TechNet is the most complete technical resource available for Windows NT Workstation 4 and other Microsoft products. When you subscribe, every month you receive three CD-ROMs packed with information on Microsoft products, including the following:

◆ Over 150,000 pages of current technical information

◆ The Microsoft Knowledge Base with solutions to technical problems

◆ Service Packs for various Microsoft products

◆ Resource Kits for Microsoft products

◆ White papers on Microsoft products and technologies

For a single user, a one year's subscription is $299 (US price). You can order the TechNet subscription through a Microsoft reseller, or by calling Microsoft at 1-800-344-2121, dept. 3118 with a credit card handy.

You can also access much of the TechNet content online. Point your Web browser at http://www.microsoft.com/syspro/technet/ to access the limited online version of TechNet. Figure 4.13 shows the online TechNet main page.

Figure 4.13

The online version of TechNet enables you to access some of TechNet's information to try the service.

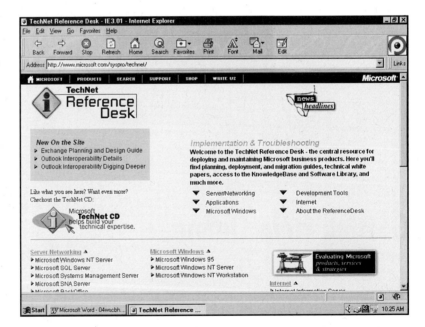

Windows NT Workstation Home Page

Most of the Windows NT Workstation support tools can be found starting at the home page of Windows NT Workstation on Microsoft's Web site. Accessing the page at http://www.microsoft.com/NTWksSupport/ lets you access these resources. Figure 4.14 shows this home page.

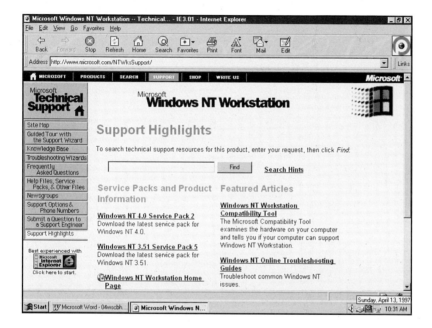

Figure 4.14

The Windows NT Workstation support home page at microsoft.com enables you to access all of the different support mechanisms at Microsoft.

Microsoft Knowledge Base

Microsoft maintains the Microsoft Knowledge Base (MSKB) with thousands of solutions to various problems. You can find work-arounds, technical advice, and solutions in the MSKB. The MSKB is searchable, which lets you find answers quickly to your problems.

Figure 4.15 shows the MSKB search page with a sample query.

Figure 4.15

You can use the Microsoft Knowledge Base to find solutions to vexing problems.

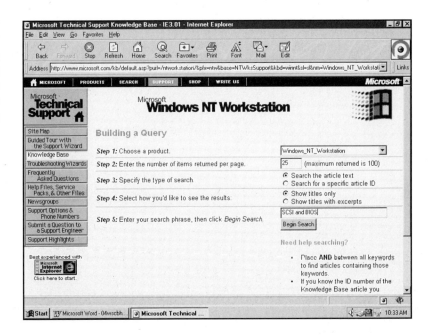

End Note: It might be useful to build your own handbooks for specific tasks, troubleshooting advice, or other help that seems to be needed on a frequent basis (either by you or others in your organization). To do this, open a Windows word processor and then open the appropriate help category in a separate window. Copy and paste the help information, using the Related Topics box selection or other similar topics found in the Index entries. If you add pictures of the screen (use the Print Screen button and then Paste into Paint, or purchase software to accomplish this function), you'll have a truly useful document.

Test Your Knowledge

1. If you build a Help database with options you don't like, such as Minimize Database Size, and later want a different database, you:

   A. Are out of luck

   B. Have to erase the help search database file and reinitialize it

   C. Can choose Rebuild on the Help system's Find tab

   D. Can choose Options on the Find tab

2. Windows NT Workstation Help is contained in:

    A. The Registry

    B. The WINNT.HLP file

    C. A collection of help files in *winnt_root*\\HELP

    D. The desktop

3. If you want to make notes about a particular help page, the easiest way to do this is to:

    A. Use a pad and paper

    B. Print the help page and mark on it

    C. Use the Annotate feature to add your notes to the help page

    D. Use memorization techniques to improve your recall

4. You can get help on specific dialog box fields by:

    A. Searching help for the list of fields and then accessing the field listing

    B. Using the What's This? feature

    C. Pressing Alt+H in a field

    D. You cannot get field-specific help in Windows NT Workstation 4

Test Your Knowledge Answers

1. C

2. C

3. C

4. B

Chapter Snapshot

Windows NT uses profiles to customize the operating system for specific conditions. There are hardware profiles to accommodate users who change peripherals (especially common for portable computers) and user profiles to furnish individual users of the same computer with a personalized interface. As users make changes to the configuration of the workstation, those changes are written to that user's profile. This chapter covers profiles, focusing on the following topics:

Windows NT
Workstation 4

CHAPTER 5

Understanding Profiles

In Windows NT, profiles provide a powerful customization tool that can be employed by users or administrators. Hardware profiles can be used to offer choices at startup that change the hardware configuration options for a workstation or a portable computer. It's a way to tell the operating system what to expect when this computer is booted for this session, avoiding error messages about hardware that can't be found. User profiles provide a method of saving a personalized setup for a workstation. For users, this means that configuration changes are saved, so every time a user logs on, he can expect to see the same desktop and configuration. For administrators, user profiles can be used to enforce the setup of a workstation in order to keep the company's desktops consistent.

Understanding Hardware Profiles

A *hardware profile* is a specific configuration that reflects the hardware that is available to the operating system during your Windows NT session. You can create multiple profiles in order to use or ignore certain hardware options.

If you have multiple hardware profiles, Windows NT asks you to select a profile during startup.

For example, you may have one profile that contains configuration options for attaching to a network with cable and a Network Interface Card, and a different profile for using your computer when no network is available. Portable computers that can switch peripherals (floppy disks versus CD-ROMs), or are sometimes portable and sometimes docked, also benefit from multiple hardware profiles.

Original Configuration

When you install Windows NT, a hardware profile is established that reflects the installation decisions you made. This profile is called the Original Configuration and is read by the operating system as Windows NT boots.

As you add hardware and install drivers, the new configuration information is added to this hardware profile. In fact, every device you add, remove, startup, or disable is reflected in your default hardware profile.

However, you can add new hardware profiles to your Windows NT system, each of which has devices configured for a particular way of working. You must be logged on as administrator to add hardware profiles.

Create a Hardware Profile

**Objective
B.5**

Creating a new hardware profile is a matter of copying an existing one, and then amending it by loading or disabling drivers to create the configuration you want when that profile is active. To begin, follow these steps:

1. In the Control Panel, double-click the system icon to open the System Properties dialog box. Select the Hardware Profiles tab (see fig. 5.1).

2. Select the existing profile you want to use as a model (if you haven't created any additional profiles, the only listing is the Original Configuration) and choose Copy.

3. The Copy Profile dialog box appears so you can enter a name for the new profile. Choose OK when you have named this profile. The new profile appears in the Available Hardware Profiles list.

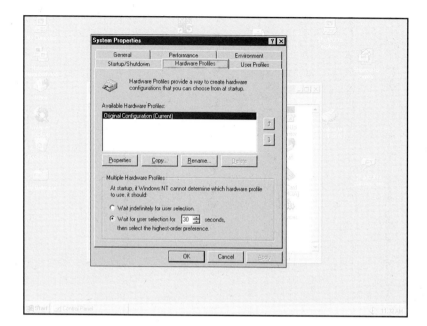

Figure 5.1

The existing hardware profiles are listed in the System Properties dialog box—copy an existing profile to create a new one.

4. The bottom of the dialog box displays the choices for choosing a profile during startup.

   Select Wait Indefinitely for User Selection to force a profile selection during startup.

   Select Wait for User Selection and specify a time in seconds, after which Windows NT chooses the profile that is first on the list.

   If you choose to let Windows NT default to a profile after a specified time, be sure the profile you want to load by default is listed first. Select a profile and use the up and down arrows to the right of the Available Hardware Profiles list to change the order in which the profiles are listed.

5. Choose OK to finish this first step in creating a new hardware profile.

The second step is to disable and enable drivers to create a driver configuration that can be assigned to this new hardware profile. This is accomplished by following these steps:

Objective B.4

1. In the Control Panel, double-click the Devices icon.

2. Scroll through the devices and select a device that will have a change in status in the new profile (for example, on my portable I have either a floppy disk or a CD-ROM, depending upon which device I've inserted).

3. When the device is selected, choose HW Profiles to see the Device dialog box (see fig. 5.2).

Figure 5.2

*The profile named
CDROM needs
the CD-ROM
device enabled.*

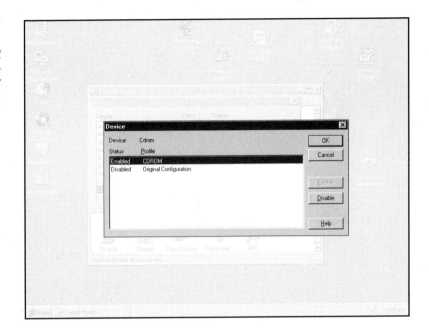

4. Select the profile you want to alter. When it is highlighted, choose Enable or Disable, and then choose OK.

5. Repeat this process for each device you want to change. When you have finished, close the Device dialog box.

You have now merged the device selection with the new profile and can choose this profile during startup if it is appropriate.

You can perform the same actions on system services as described here for devices, selecting a method of starting services, stopping services, and so on.

Disable Network Drivers

Instead of going through all the steps involved in disabling devices, if you need to create a profile that has network connection devices disabled, you can do it in one step. This is useful for portable computers that have network controllers (usually a PCMCIA device), or even for desktop computers when there is no network connection at the time of startup. If no network is running, or no working network connection exists, startup can take a very long time if network services and drivers are loading.

To disable network drivers, follow these steps:

1. In the Control Panel, double-click the System icon to open the System Properties dialog box. Select the Hardware Profiles tab.

2. Create a new profile by copying a current profile, as described earlier.

3. Select the profile and choose Properties to display the Properties dialog box for this profile.

4. Move to the Network tab of the dialog box and select the Network-Disabled Hardware Profile check box (see fig. 5.3).

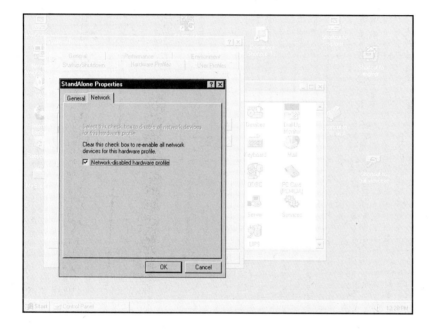

Figure 5.3

You can tell Windows NT to disable network devices when they're not needed.

5. Choose OK to return to the Hardware Profiles tab. Choose OK to finish and close the System Properties dialog box.

Note The no-network choice is a toggle; you can select and deselect it as you need to. This means you don't necessarily have to create a new profile for it; you just need to toggle the selection in your default configuration and then shut down and restart. If you do this, it's a good idea to tell Windows NT to wait indefinitely for you to make a choice about the hardware profile you want to use when starting up. Otherwise, if the profile you've changed is first, you might have a troublesome startup (unless you're infallible about remembering to change the network options back and forth to the appropriate selection for the next startup).

Portable Docking Profiles

If you are using NT on a portable computer that has a docking station available, there are quick ways to create the appropriate profiles (instead of enabling and disabling devices).

You can approach this from several directions. Either alter your default configuration for the docking state that is most common for you, and then create a second profile for the other configuration, or create two new profiles, one for each possibility.

Follow these steps to create docking profiles:

1. From the Control Panel, open the System Properties dialog box by double-clicking the System icon. Select the Hardware Profiles tab.

2. Copy an existing profile and name it to reflect the docking state you are about to configure.

3. When the new profile name appears, select it and choose Properties. The General tab of the dialog box for this profile has the docking configuration (see fig. 5.4).

Figure 5.4

You can create profiles for docking configurations without the need to disable and enable the device in another dialog box.

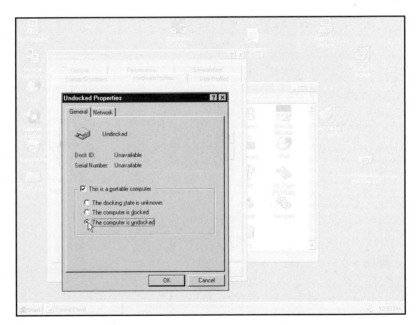

4. Select This Is a Portable Computer to make the choices accessible if they are dimmed. Then select the appropriate docking choice.

5. Choose OK. Then choose OK at the Hardware Profiles tab to close the dialog box.

You may want to expand the changes in a docked profile if the docking station gives you access to peripherals, network connections, or other drivers, all of which need to be enabled. To do that, follow the instructions earlier in this chapter about enabling and disabling devices for specific profiles.

Switching Between Hardware Profiles

After you have established multiple hardware profiles, Windows NT asks you to choose one during the operating system startup.

If you have configured Windows NT to wait a predetermined amount of time and then load the profile that is first on the list in the System Properties dialog box, you have to be careful about keeping the appropriate profile on the top of the list before shutting down.

If you don't predetermine what the next startup will need in terms of hardware profiles, you must be careful to remain at your computer during startup, so you can pick a profile. This is not the time to run for a cup of coffee.

If you tend to turn on your machine and move to the coffee pot, change your configuration to force Windows to wait until you make a decision about which profile you want to use.

Understanding Last Known Good Profile

Every time a logon is successful, the hardware profile that was used (and worked correctly) is stored in the Registry. If you make drastic, incorrect changes to hardware configuration when you are creating or changing a profile you may create a situation in which the computer will not boot properly.

You can roll back the changes you made by pressing the space bar when the boot process displays a message indicating that doing so will load the "last known good" profile. At that point the profile that permitted a successful logon is loaded. After the boot process is complete, go back and fix the errors you made.

Understanding User Profiles

Each user of a Windows NT computer has a profile that contains the configuration information that the user established while working at the computer. Some of the information that is saved includes the following:

◆ Desktop arrangement of icons

◆ Desktop colors and schemes for application and dialog box windows

◆ Screen savers

◆ Desktop shortcuts and folders

◆ Mouse settings

◆ Printer connections

◆ Network connections

◆ Program groups and programs installed by that user (called personal program groups)

As users log on and work, the information about the configuration options they choose is recorded in profiles linked to their logon names. If a number of different people use a Windows NT computer, there is a separate user profile for each of them. During the logon process, the appropriate profile is loaded.

The Default User Profile

The first time a user logs on, the desktop that is presented and the configuration options that are loaded come from a default profile that is established during the installation of the operating system.

> **Tip** You can tell a first-time logon because the Welcome to Windows NT window is displayed after the logon process is complete. This welcoming screen does not have a selection box marked Show this Welcome Screen Next Time You Start Windows NT. The same Welcome window shows up after the first logon, but the option box exists. Incidentally, if you failed to select the option to show the Welcome window and decide you do want to see it when you log on, find Welcome.exe in your Windows NT folder and double-click on it. When the window appears, check the box. The reason people opt to see this welcoming window isn't because they want to feel welcomed by Microsoft; it's because there is a button for tips about using Windows NT. You can feed yourself a tip a day (or more). When you see the same tips a couple of times, you've worn out your welcome and you can deselect the option when you log on.

The first logon creates a profile for that user name; as changes are made to configuration options and the desktop, those changes are recorded in the user's profile. Every time the user logs on, the desktop and configuration options return to the state that existed the last time the user was logged on.

After the initial installation of the operating system, the first logon name presented is Administrator, so there is a profile for Administrator established on all NT Workstations.

Thereafter, the number of profiles, and the names attached to them, depend on the number of users who log on to the workstation.

Profiles and the Registry

When users log on to a Windows NT computer, during the startup of the operating system, the Registry is read. HKEY_LOCAL_MACHINE is searched in the key \SOFTWARE\Microsoft\Windows NT\CurrentVersion\ProfileList to see if there is a profile for the user logon name (see fig. 5.5).

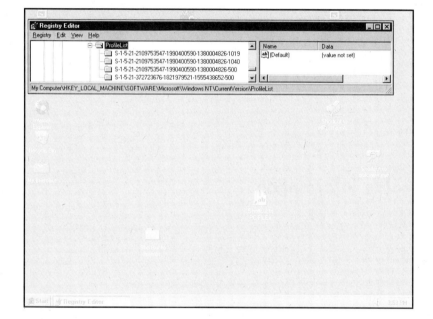

Figure 5.5

The Registry contains a list of profiles, with a folder for each user who has ever logged on to this computer.

There is a key for each user profile, although you can't tell what it is by looking at the name next to the folder icon. However, if you select folders, you will see the user name displayed in the right pane. You can also search the Registry for a user name (choose Run from the Start menu and enter regedit in the Open box; then press F3 with the Registry window opened).

When you look at user profiles in Explorer or My Computer, in addition to the subfolders in each user's profile folder, there are two files: ntuser.dat and ntuser.dat.log. Ntuser.dat is the Registry information in data file form, and ntuser.dat.log is the previously saved version of ntuser.dat (a backup is made each time a configuration change in the user's profile occurs).

The information in ntuser.dat file is the data from HKEY_CURRENT_USER in the Registry, which includes the following:

◆ Settings that were established via the icons in the Control Panel

◆ Persistent network connections and other persistent network parameters (such as redirection of printer ports)

◆ Installation locations for operating system files

◆ Application settings for applications that are Windows NT 4–aware and can write their settings to the Registry (32-bit applications that were written for Windows 95 can also usually write their settings to the Windows NT 4 Registry).

After the existence of the profile is confirmed during logon, the information about that user's environment is obtained from the information in ntuser.dat, along with the information found in the Desktop, Recent, and Start Menu folders.

If the existence of a profile for a logon name is not confirmed in the Registry, a new profile is created (in the Registry and in the Profiles subfolder of the Windows NT folder). The environment found in Default User profile is presented to the user and is initially saved in the new profile. As the user makes configuration changes, those changes are reflected in the user profile.

Viewing Profile Information

You can look at any user profile in Explorer or My Computer. To find the profiles, look in your Windows NT folder and click on the plus sign next to the Profiles folder (or open it if you are using My Computer). The Profiles folder expands to show all the profile folders on the computer (see fig. 5.6).

Extensions Added to Duplicate Folders

The profile folders in figure 5.6 show two folders for Administrator (Windows NT automatically adds extensions to duplicate folder names, starting with .000, moving to .001, and so on). The first Administrator profile belongs to the Administrator logon that occurred after the installation of the operating system. That logon was local, with Administrator logging on to the computer only.

After configuring network options, the computer became part of a domain named EASTERN, and the computer name became ADMIN. Subsequent Administrator logons were for the domain instead of the local computer. The full profile names for these seemingly duplicate logons are ADMIN\Administrator and EASTERN\Administrator.

Windows NT automatically created a new profile for the user named Administrator because the logon was not identical.

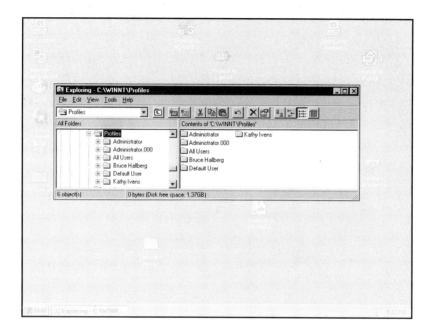

Figure 5.6

*There is a profiles
folder for each
user who has
logged on to this
computer.*

To examine an individual user profile, click on the plus sign next to the appropriate
folder in Explorer or open the folder in My Computer (see fig. 5.7).

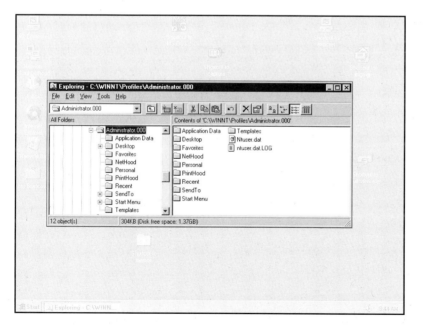

Figure 5.7

*Profiles are kept
in multiple
folders, each of
which holds
information that
plays a role in
determining
the user's
environment.*

The two profile folders of particular importance (because they contain the data that is changed most frequently) are the Desktop and Start menus.

Viewing Desktop Folders in User Profiles

If you examine the contents of the Desktop folder in any user profile, you see the elements of that user's desktop (see fig. 5.8).

Figure 5.8

This user has plenty of shortcuts on the desktop.

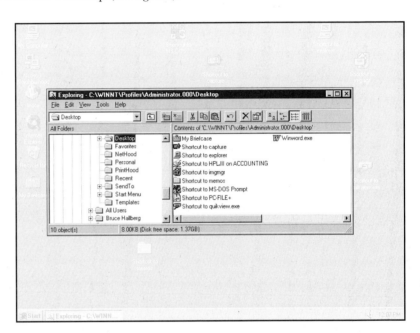

Note that listings for My Computer, Network Neighborhood, Inbox, Internet Explorer, or Recycle Bin are not in the desktop folder for any user. These desktop elements are on user desktops as a result of defaults for the operating system or specific installation options for this computer. For example, if a network adapter and network protocols are installed either during the initial installation of the operating system or afterwards, the Network Neighborhood icon is placed on all user desktops. These installation icons aren't considered desktop items that are specific to an individual user.

Other users may not have configured their desktops for shortcuts or folders (see fig. 5.9). When they log on to the workstation, the environment reflects their choices.

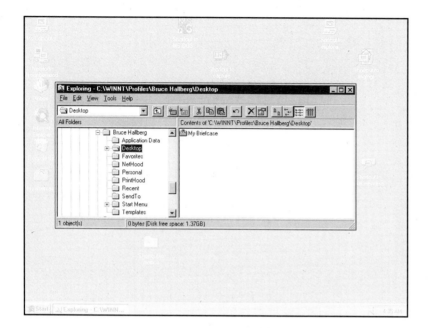

Figure 5.9

This user has opted to keep the desktop limited to My Briefcase.

Viewing Start Menu Folders in User Profiles

When you open the Start Menu folder in a user profile, you can see the menu options available to that user. The accessories and programs that were selected from the Installation Options dialog box during the installation of the operating system are automatically installed on every user's Start menu. Then, as a user installs software, that software is added to the user's Start menu.

The Start Menu folder for the Default User profile contains the items that were selected during the installation of the operating system. Figure 5.10 shows the Profile folder contents, starting at the parent folder and moving through the subfolders for Programs and Accessories for the Default User.

Start Menu Common Groups

A user who has administrator rights can add common groups to the Start menu. Common groups appear on every user's Start menu and are listed below the separator line. A common group item has the following characteristics:

◆ It is automatically placed on the Start menu of every user.

◆ It is listed below the separator line that appears at the bottom of the Programs menu (see fig. 5.11).

◆ It does not appear in the Programs subfolder of the Profiles folder for any user.

Figure 5.10

The view from the top of the Profile folder shows the programs that were selected for the Start menu when the operating system was installed.

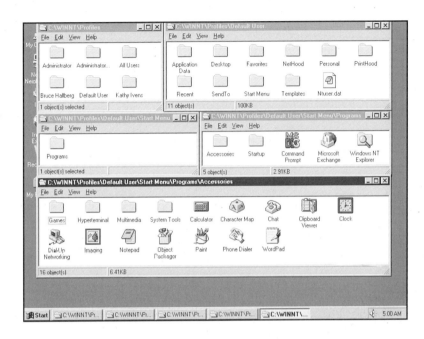

Figure 5.11

Items listed below the separator line of the Programs menu are common to all users.

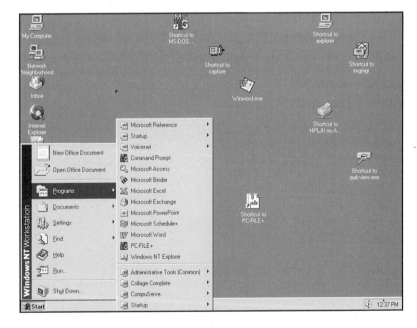

The notion of a common group is a powerful one because it's a way to make sure every user of a workstation can use the software that appears as a common group. This eliminates the need to have each user go through an installation program for a software application that everyone needs.

Add a Common Group to the Programs Menu

To add a common group application to the Programs menu, follow these steps:

1. Be sure your logon name has been given administrator rights.

2. Right-click the Start button.

3. Choose Open All Users. The WindowsNTRoot\Profiles\All Users\Start Menu subfolder opens on the desktop.

4. Install a shortcut to a program in the folder.

You can also add a Startup group to the Common section of the Programs menu.

Drag and Drop to Add Common Groups

A faster method for creating common program items is to move items directly from one folder to another. This is especially helpful if there is an installation program to get through before you can move the program into the All Users folder. Follow these steps to complete the process:

1. With administrative rights, install the software. It is added to your Programs menu.

2. In My Computer, open your user profile folder and continue to open folders until you reach the Programs folder (the path is WindowsNTRoot\Profiles\YourUserName\Start Menu\Programs).

> **Tip** I've found it easier to do this from My Computer rather than Explorer because after opening the folders I need, I can place them side-by-side.

3. Open WindowsNTRoot\Profiles\All Users\Start Menu\Programs, which is the target folder for programs that are to appear on every user's Programs menu in the Common section (below the separator line).

4. Drag the icon for the program you just installed from your Programs folder to the All Users Program folder.

5. This program menu item now appears on the Common section of every user's Programs menu.

> **Tip** You can also open Explorer and copy an executable file to the All Users Program folder to make that program available to everyone.

Making Profile Changes Quickly

You can make fast changes to the Programs menu and desktop of any user's profile by copying items into the appropriate subfolders in the user's profile folder.

Copy Another Profile Folder

Objective C.2

If one user has installed programs that you want additional users to have access to, but don't want to place those programs on the Common section of the Programs menu, you can copy items from one user's profile to another user's profile.

To accomplish this, follow these steps:

1. Open the Programs subfolder of the user who has installed the software you want to make available to other users. This is the source subfolder.

2. Open the Programs subfolder of the user who needs these programs. This is the target subfolder.

3. Open any additional target subfolders you need (for additional users you want to include in this process) and place source and target folders on the desktop so you can easily move between them (see fig. 5.12).

Figure 5.12

Line up folders to make it easy to drag items between them.

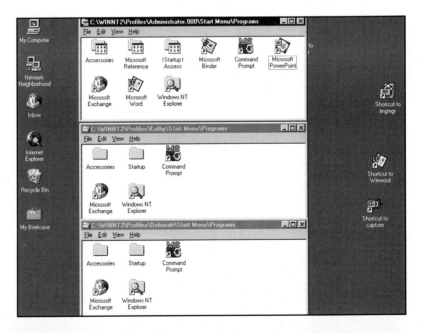

4. Right-drag items from the source folder to the target folder. Choose Copy here when you release the mouse.

You can pick and choose the programs you want to move to a target folder. Remember that you can choose multiple items by holding down the Ctrl key while you select items from the source folder.

You can do the same thing with the source user's desktop folder, copying desktop items (folders and shortcuts) to the target user profiles. Open the target Desktop subfolder and use this process to add items to the user's desktop.

Copy from Explorer

Program menu items are nothing more than shortcuts to program files. Therefore, you can add menu items to any user's profile by creating a shortcut in the user's profile (in the Programs subfolder).

You can also create shortcuts for the desktop of any user by choosing the Desktop subfolder as the target instead of the Programs subfolder.

It's easiest to do this by opening My Computer, moving to each target user's Programs or Desktop subfolder, and then opening Explorer. Just right-drag program items from Explorer to each target folder, choosing Create Shortcut(s) Here when you release the mouse (see fig. 5.13).

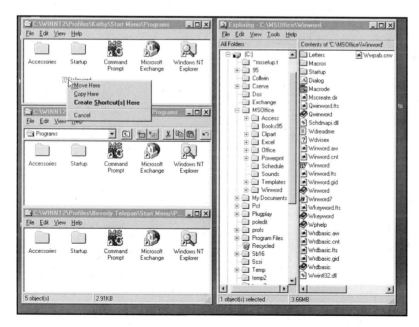

Figure 5.13

Pick and choose the program shortcuts you want to place on users' menus.

It's a good idea to change the name of the shortcut in order to eliminate the words "shortcut to." Use any of these methods to highlight the name in the title box in order to edit the name:

◆ Right-click on the item and choose Rename from the shortcut menu.

◆ Select the item and press F2.

◆ Slowly click twice on the name under the icon (do not double-click—click once, and then click again after a short pause).

It won't really change the way the software works when you select it from the Programs menu if the words "shortcut to" are on the menu; it just doesn't look as neat or professional.

Understanding Profile Policies

If connected to an NT server on the network, the network administrator can take advantage of the features available in Windows NT Server that give administrative powers over user profiles. Two of the important, and commonly used, powers available to an administrator are these:

◆ Roaming profiles so users can go to any computer and have their own desktop configuration appear at each one

◆ Mandatory profiles to make desktops consistent

Administrators can enforce rules and policies on an individual basis, a group basis, or a domain basis. As a user of NT Workstation, the results of administrative polices that affect your profile are important to know about.

The policy editor can override any values in a computer's Registry (the Local Machine key), so when a user logs on, the configuration enforced by the policy editor takes precedence.

Roaming Profiles

A *roaming profile* is a server-stored profile. Normally, your user profile is stored on the local drive. When administrative software (specifically the Policy Editor that is part of Windows NT Server) is used to enable roaming profiles, you can change the default profile storage container to the server. This means your configuration options can be brought up on any computer that is connected to the server.

This is particularly useful if you spend your work day at different computers. For example, some employees in accounting departments move between computers depending on the task at hand. Check writing may have to take place at a specific workstation because that workstation has the printer for checks attached to it, and the room in which it is located is kept locked until check writing is needed. Help desk personnel also tend to work at various computers throughout the company, as they install, tweak, or repair workstation installations. For these roaming users, logging on to a workstation produces the same desktop and other configuration options they get when they log on to their normal workstations.

This all works because when a roaming user logs on to a workstation, the profile is downloaded to that workstation from the server. If changes to the configuration are made during that work session, those changes are saved back to the server-based profile. The next logon, from any computer connected to that server, will result in the new configuration.

Creating Roaming Profiles

If you have administrative privileges on your local computer, you can change existing local profiles after you have established the necessary environment on the server through User Manager for Domains. Follow these steps to accomplish this:

Objective C.2

1. Be sure you have taken the necessary steps with the Policy Editor to invoke roaming profiles and have created the necessary shares on the server for the user you want to change. You will need to know the path of the share for each roaming profile you want to create.

2. Right-click on My Computer and choose Properties (or open the System icon from the Control Panel).

3. Move to the User Profiles tab to see a list of the profiles stored on the computer (see fig. 5.14).

4. Select the profile you want to change and choose Change Type. The Change Type dialog box appears (see fig. 5.15).

5. Change the profile type to Local Profile or Roaming Profile and, then choose OK.

Caution | If the Roaming Profile selection isn't accessible (it is grayed out), then the appropriate steps haven't been taken on the server for this user.

6. If you are changing a profile type from Local to Roaming, choose Copy To. Then enter the path to the server share for this user that was established on the server.

7. Choose OK when you have finished with the System Properties dialog box.

Mandatory Profiles

Mandatory profiles are a feature in the server-based policy editor that let the administrator deny users the right to change configuration. In actuality, users can make changes to their profiles, but they aren't saved if the mandatory profile policy is in effect, so the next time the user logs on, the changes aren't there.

Figure 5.14

The user profile list indicates the type of profile assigned to each user of this computer.

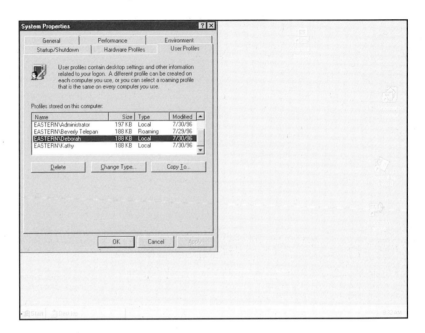

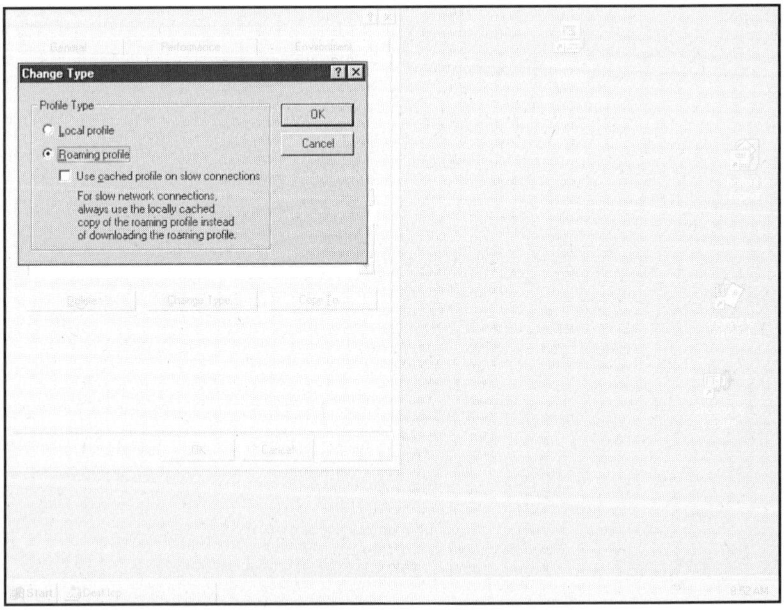

Figure 5.15

You can change the profile type of a user if the user's configuration has been changed on the server.

The power for the administrator is the ability to design and install a profile configuration on a desktop and be assured it will never be changed by configuring the profile as a mandatory one.

There are a number of reasons to use this feature, not the least of which is the obvious one—users can't mess up a configuration to the point that things don't work as they should. There is some additional benefit in the fact that because help desk personnel are called to troubleshoot problems, they know what to expect on each workstation. There is no time wasted figuring out "what's what" in the environment, and the expert can move to the problem at hand immediately.

Using the System Policy Editor

The System Policy Editor is part of Windows NT Server 4 and you can find it in the Administrative Tools section of the Start menu on your server. There are two main reasons for invoking the System Policy Editor:

Objective C.2

◆ When you want to make changes to user profiles on multiple computers, you can configure the System Policy Editor to reach out and manipulate all the computers you need to access. This is certainly faster than going to each workstation and using its Control Panel applets or its Registry to make changes.

◆ The System Policy Editor can access Registry settings that no Control Panel applet can get to, increasing the power you have over the settings of the workstations.

The rest of this chapter focuses on the System Policy Editor and what administrative tasks can be accomplished through its use.

Creating Policies

To begin the design of a new policy, open the System Policy Editor and choose New Policy from the File menu. Immediately, two icons appear in the application window, representing the default computer and the default user (see fig. 5.16). If you use these icons, the policies you design are applied to all computers and users on the domain.

If you don't plan to implement this policy across the domain, you can specify the targets through the Edit menu:

◆ Choose Add User to specify an individual user or multiple users.

◆ Choose Add Computer to specify one or more computers on the domain.

◆ Choose Add Group to specify all the users in a group or in multiple groups.

Figure 5.16

By default, the System Policy Editor assumes you want to make changes to all users and computers on the local domain.

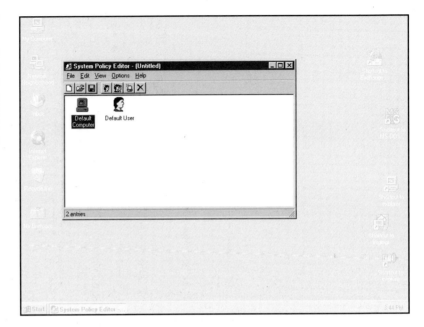

As you choose each type of target, a dialog box appears so you can name the specific units for that target type. If you don't know the exact name you can select Browse (see fig. 5.17).

Figure 5.17

If you need to browse for specific targets, the appropriate Browse dialog box opens—in this case browsing for computers displays the Network Neighborhood.

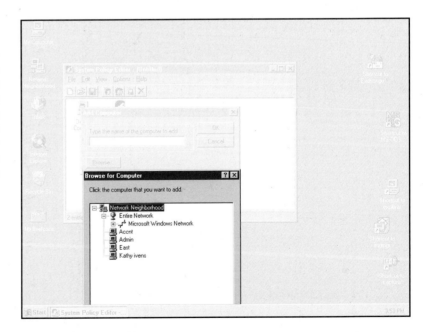

Once you've selected the specific targets you want to use, the appropriate icons appear and you can delete the Default User and Default Computer icons from the window by selecting them and pressing Del.

The targets indicate the type of policies you want to implement. If you choose a user (or a group), the Registry settings in HKEY_CURRENT_USER are affected. If you choose a computer, the Registry settings in HKEY_LOCAL_MACHINE are affected.

Once you've established your target you can begin setting policies:

1. Double-click the icon in the application window to see the settings for this target (see fig. 5.18).

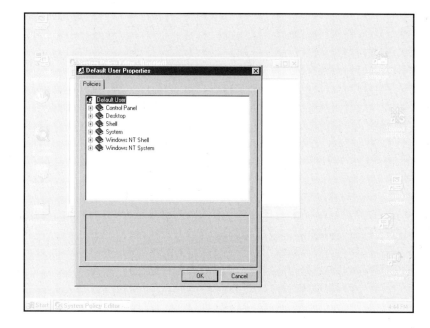

Figure 5.18

View the hierarchical display of settings for Users.

2. Open the section you want to manipulate by clicking the plus sign to display the options available for that section.

3. Make the changes you wish.

4. Save the policy (a Save dialog box appears and you must name the policy).

There's a trick to reading the policies in the hierarchical list:

◆ Checkboxes with gray shading are unspecified; no policies have been set.

◆ A checkmark indicates the policy is in effect.

◆ A checkbox without a checkmark indicates a policy is not in effect.

You can rotate through the three choices by clicking the checkbox.

Useful User Policy Restrictions

There are a few restrictions that increase your control over workstation users that you might want to consider imposing.

Restricting Shell Functions

In the Shell section of the User properties, you might want to think about restricting some functions in order to control the user's ability to make substantial changes to the workstation:

◆ **Remove Run command from Start menu.** This option prevents the user from launching applications that are not on the Start menu.

◆ **Remove folders from Settings on Start menu.** This restriction means that no folders appear when the mouse is on Settings in the Start menu. This prevents changes to system settings by the user.

◆ **Remove Taskbar from Settings on Start menu.** This leaves the Control Panel and Printers folders in the Settings submenu, but removes the Taskbar.

◆ **Hide drives in My Computer.** This action removes the drive icons from the My Computer window. Use this restriction to keep viewers away from drive tools and utilities, and also to prevent users from launching applications via the drive folders that are not on the Start menu. It also means that users cannot move or copy files from other drives to their local drives, thus eliminating their ability to use My Computer to run, install, or copy from floppy drives.

◆ **Hide Network Neighborhood.** This removes the Network Neighborhood icon from the desktop. Users cannot browse connected computers to move, copy, or delete files.

Restricting System Access

From the System Section of the User hierarchy in the System Policy Editor, you might want to think about implementing the following restrictions:

◆ **Disable Registry editing tools.** This prevents users from launching REGEDIT.EXE or REGEDT32.EXE. (I don't think I have to explain the advantages of this one.)

◆ **Run only allowed Windows applications.** This restriction prevents users from launching any Windows software except those you permit by means of a list of approved applications. If you choose this option, a dialog box opens so you can name the applications the user may run. Choose Add and enter the name of an application (for instance, WINWORD.EXE). Repeat this process for every application you want to permit. (Talk about a neat way to prevent users from playing games or using Internet software.)

Windows NT Shell Restrictions

There are several restrictions available under Windows NT Shell Restrictions, but only the first one in the following list strikes me as sensible:

◆ **Remove common program groups from Start menu.** The user is unable to run any of the administrative tools that can affect (or mess up) the workstation.

◆ **Remove right-click menu options.** The user cannot access the shortcut menu for objects.

◆ **Remove drive mapping options.** The user cannot map connected drives.

Useful Machine Policy Restrictions

You can also create policies for computers (see fig. 5.19).

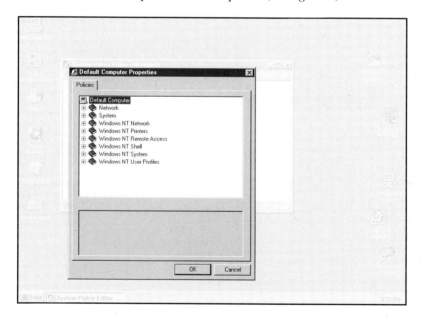

Figure 5.19

The hierarchical structure for computer policies is used for altering the configuration of machines.

There are some useful policies for machines available in the Windows NT System section of the hierarchy. In the Logon subheading, consider some of following policies:

◆ **Logon Banner.** This policy enables you to create a banner that is displayed on the computer at Logon. You get to invent the caption and the text of the message.

◆ **Do Not display last logged on user name.** This option forces a user to enter his or her name in addition to the password every time the logon process is presented.

End Note: The issue of user profiles is an extremely important and powerful one if a computer is shared by multiple users. However, after you understand the theory, you can create multiple profiles for a single user, designing the computer configuration for specific uses, and logging on depending upon the configuration needed to perform the job at hand. For example, for certain types of work, you may have a profile with certain files (documents, software, or both) in the Startup folder so that you can begin work immediately. Multiple user profiles mean you can design Programs menus that aren't so large that it's time consuming to move through them. If you know that Mondays are for writing and delivering weekly reports and this process takes at least half a day, create a user profile for a user named Monday that loads all the documents and software you need to get this task completed. Designing multiple profiles and logging on to the appropriate one is like having access to macros for startup.

And, of course, taking administrative control of user profiles by using the Policy Editor (even if there is only one user for the workstation) gives you total control of that workstation.

Test Your Knowledge

1. Which Control Panel Applet is used to create a new hardware profile?

   A. Services

   B. Devices

   C. System

   D. Server

2. When you select Last Known Good as the hardware profile, where does the NT boot loader find that profile?

   A. In the Control Panel Profile applet

   B. In the list of profile choices presented during the boot process

   C. In the boot.ini file on the root directory

   D. In the Registry

3. At what point does Windows NT establish a profile for a user?

   A. At logon

   B. When the first configuration change to the desktop is made

   C. At shutdown

   D. As soon as an application is launched

4. Where can you view the information about a user profile?
   A. In the INI files
   B. In the WindowsNTroot\Profiles folder
   C. In the WindowsNTroot\System folder
   D. In the WindowsNTroot\System\Profiles folder

5. Which is *not* saved in the user profile?
   A. Screen saver settings
   B. Network Interface Card settings
   C. Desktop Shortcuts
   D. Mapped Network drives

6. Use the System Policy Editor to create which of the following?
   A. Mandatory profiles
   B. Hardware profiles
   C. Roaming Profiles
   D. Portable Docking Profiles

7. Where are Roaming profiles stored?
   A. Only on a Windows NT server
   B. On any server for any network operating system
   C. In the local Registry
   D. In the Windows NT system root directory

Test Your Knowledge Answers

1. C
2. D
3. A
4. B
5. B
6. A,C
7. A

PART II

Exploring the Windows NT 4 Desktop

Chapter Snapshot

You spend a lot of time looking at your NT desktop, arranging it so that everything you need is right in front of you, and customizing it for ease of use is important. This chapter discusses what you can do to make your desktop the workspace you want. It covers the following topics:

Windows NT
Workstation 4

CHAPTER 6

Using the Desktop

After the installation of Windows NT 4 is complete, the first time you see the desktop, it presents the standard desktop icons. Three or more icons (depending on your installation choices) appear on the left side of the desktop screen. The taskbar is at the bottom of the screen with the Start button on the left and the clock on the right.

Understanding the Desktop

First of all, you should understand that the desktop is a folder just like any other folder in your NT system. Like other folders, it holds items, including other folders. The main difference between the desktop and all the other folders is that you cannot close the desktop folder.

The Windows NT desktop is a work area you can use as if it were a desk; you can arrange the items on it the same way. In fact, people tend to arrange their NT desktops in the same manner in which they arrange their physical workspaces.

My desk, for example, is an enormous slab of wood sitting atop two trestles. At a glance, it seems a hodgepodge of items placed in little more than a random manner. A logic to the way items on this desk are sorted prevails, however, though the logic is known only to me.

My Windows NT desktop has the same characteristics—messy but memorized (see fig. 6.1). I know instinctively where everything is, can reach for anything I want, and know that I'll find it exactly where I expect it to be.

Figure 6.1

This desktop might not look neat and trim, but the important items are there, and everything is easy to get to.

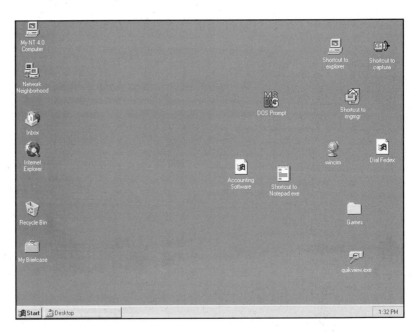

Manipulating the Desktop

If you like things neat, you can set up your desktop in that fashion (you probably also arrange your physical desk with a place for everything and everything in its place). In fact, you can be both neat and orderly, sorting the icons on the desktop by several available sorting schemes.

Arranging Icons

You can arrange your desktop icons in a way that lines them up neatly and puts them off to the side. This gives you a clean work area on the desktop.

To arrange the icons on the desktop, right-click anywhere on the desktop to display the shortcut menu. Place the mouse pointer on Arrange Icons to see the submenu (see fig. 6.2).

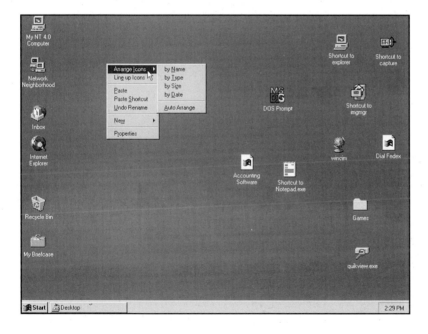

Figure 6.2

The Arrange Icons menu offers choices for placing the icons on the desktop.

The way you arrange the icons on your desktop is entirely a matter of taste. (You can experiment with various arrangements until you find one that suits your fancy.)

Sort and Arrange the Icons

If you want to sort the icons by any of the available options from the Arrange Icons menu, choose the appropriate one (Name, Type, Size, or Date). The resulting order of icon placement is determined by the Properties information for the icon. All the icons line up in neat columns, beginning in the upper-left corner of the screen.

AutoArrange the Icons

If you want to set the placement of icons according to some ordering scheme that makes sense for your own work habits, arrange them yourself, and then choose AutoArrange. The icons will line up (in the order you arranged) in columns starting with the upper-left corner of the screen (see fig. 6.3).

Figure 6.3

The icons that were free-floating on the desktop are now neatly arranged in columns because AutoArrange is turned on.

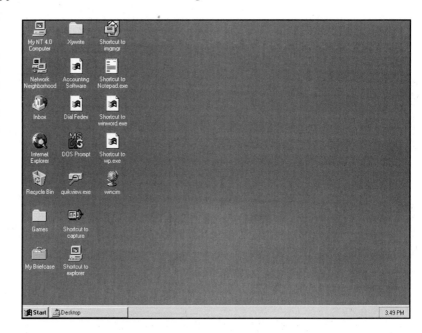

AutoArrange is a toggle that you can turn off and on. (The presence or absence of a check mark indicates its current status—the check is marked when on and unmarked when off). When it is on, no matter how you move or arrange the icons, they will pop back into their columnar placement when you release the mouse.

Line Up the Icons

There's a method of compromise that involves more order than free-floating images, but is less restrictive than the columnar alignment along the left side of the screen. You can move your icons where you want, and then choose Line up Icons from the desktop shortcut menu. The icons shift so that they are arranged in straight lines (see fig. 6.4).

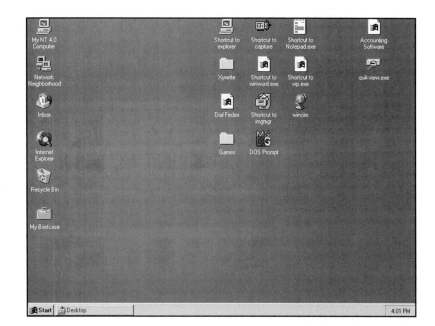

Figure 6.4

These icons are scattered around the desktop, but they are in a neat pattern and none of them overlap.

Any time you add or move an icon, choose Line Up Icons to straighten up the desktop. These icons look neat and ordered because they've been carefully placed equal distances apart in a grid.

Using the Desktop Grid

You can't see it, but there is a grid on your desktop. It creates cells through the use of horizontal and vertical lines (see fig. 6.5). The cells are measured in pixels (the smallest graphic unit that can display on your screen, usually thought of as a "dot" on the screen).

When you instruct Windows NT to line up or arrange your icons, it uses this grid to keep the icons straight.

The size of the cells depends upon the configuration of the display options. Change the spacing of the grid by performing the following steps:

1. Right-click on any blank space on the desktop, and place your pointer on Arrange Icons. Select AutoArrange from the submenu. All the icons on your desktop will line up in neat columns, starting on the left side of the desktop.

2. Right-click on any blank space on the desktop and choose Properties. Select the Appearance tab of the Properties dialog box.

Figure 6.5

The desktop grid creates cells to hold icons if you choose to Line Up or Arrange icons.

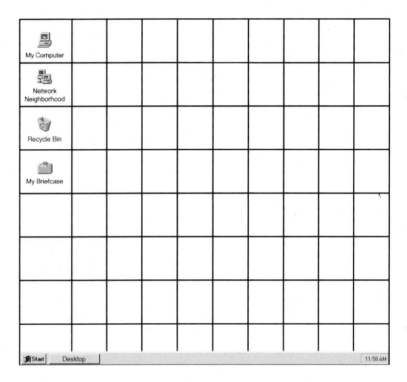

3. Click the down arrow to the right of the Item field and choose Icon Spacing (Vertical).

4. In the Size box, specify a size for this item. (You are specifying in pixels.)

5. In the Item field, choose Icon Spacing (Horizontal) and repeat step 4.

6. In the Item field, choose Icon and repeat step 4.

7. Choose Apply to make the changes without closing the dialog box. Continue to change one or more items as desired.

8. When you are happy with the appearance, choose OK to make your selections the new grid spacing formula.

Note | The math involved in figuring out the size of a cell in the invisible grid isn't difficult—it's simple addition. The size of the icon plus the size of the spacing equals the size of the cell.

By default, cells are 75 pixels high and wide. The default icon size is 32 pixels and the default spacing is 43 pixels.

Renaming Icons

The name of any desktop icon (the title under the icon) can be changed in a number of different ways. Choose one of the following methods, depending on which you find easiest:

◆ Select the icon and press F2.

◆ Right-click on the icon and choose Rename from the shortcut menu.

◆ Slowly click twice on the name of the icon (if you double-click too fast, you'll open the icon).

When a line appears around the name, and the characters in the name are highlighted, the name is ready to be edited. You can begin typing to replace the current name, or you can move your insertion point to delete or add characters (use Home or End to get to the beginning or end of a line). Press Enter or click on a blank spot on the desktop to end the editing process.

You can enter as much text as you wish, and the text will automatically be centered under the icon. To change the word-wrap, insert an extra space or two to force text to the next line—you cannot use the Enter key to move to the next line because that ends the editing process.

Caution   If you have changed the size of your grid cells and made them smaller, and you are using the grid (lining up icons or arranging icons), you'll have to keep your icon names short. Windows NT will let you enter a long name, but the name might overlap and hide an adjacent icon.

Moving the Taskbar

If you don't like having the taskbar at the bottom of your screen, you can move it to the top, or either side. Place your mouse pointer on any blank spot on the taskbar, and then drag the taskbar to a new position. When the taskbar is in its new location, all the desktop icons will shift down or over to make room for it.

If you move the taskbar to the left or right side of the screen, you'll find the taskbar buttons are hard to read because you don't have much space to spell out the words next to the icons (see fig. 6.6).

Enlarging the Taskbar

You can make the taskbar larger (deeper if it is positioned on the top or bottom; wider if it is positioned on the side) to make it easier to read the taskbar buttons. This is helpful because as the taskbar fills up with buttons, those buttons get smaller and the text becomes truncated.

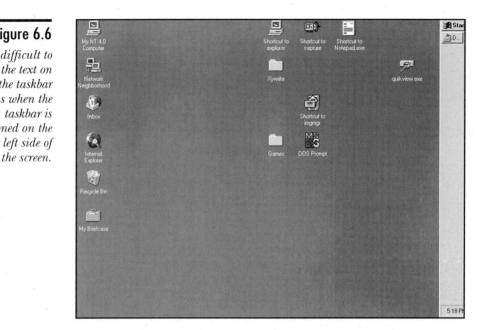

Figure 6.6

It's difficult to read the text on the taskbar buttons when the taskbar is positioned on the right or left side of the screen.

To make the taskbar larger, position your mouse pointer on the outside edge of the taskbar; the mouse pointer will change to a double arrow. Drag away from the edge of the screen.

The taskbar grows in multiples of its original size, you can't use your mouse to determine exactly the size you want. If the taskbar is on the bottom of your screen, dragging it upward results in a taskbar that's double the height of the original. Icons will appear in a double row, which gives each individual icon more room. If you continue to drag, the taskbar will triple its original height.

Note You can also configure the taskbar so that it is hidden until you need it. Instructions for hiding the taskbar are found in Chapter 7, "Understanding the Taskbar and Start Menu."

Customizing the Desktop

You can change the appearance of the desktop—making it completely unique—or just modify a few elements to make it more aesthetically pleasing.

Changes to the desktop are made through the desktop's Display Properties dialog box (see fig. 6.7). To get to this dialog box, right-click on a blank spot on the desktop and choose Properties from the shortcut menu that appears.

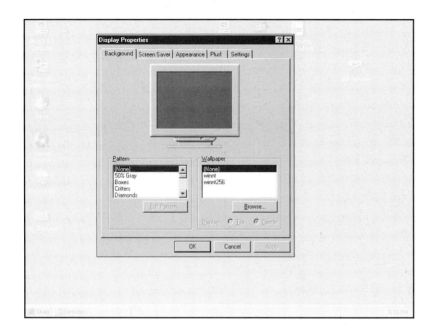

Figure 6.7

The Display Properties dialog box is the tool with which you customize your desktop.

Note   You can also reach the Properties dialog box by choosing Settings from the Start menu, choosing Control Panel, and double-clicking on the Display icon.

Desktop Backgrounds

The Background tab of the desktop Properties dialog box is in the foreground when you bring up the dialog box (refer to fig. 6.7). You can use this tab to change the basic decor of your desktop.

Patterns

A pattern is a repeating design that fills the entire desktop screen. If you want to use a pattern on your desktop, scroll through the choices in the Pattern field to see the available patterns. When you click on a pattern, it is displayed on the monitor image in the dialog box. When you find one you like, choose OK.

Tip   When you are looking at the sample display of the pattern, it is shown in black with the current color of your desktop in the background. You can change the color of the background (see the section "Desktop Appearance" later in this chapter), so don't make a final judgment on the pattern until you've seen it with different colored backgrounds.

If you find a pattern you sort of like but aren't quite sure about, you can edit it to your liking. Select the pattern and choose Edit Pattern. The Pattern Editor dialog box appears (see fig. 6.8).

Figure 6.8

You can change the shape of the repeating figure that is used to create the desktop pattern in the Pattern Editor dialog box.

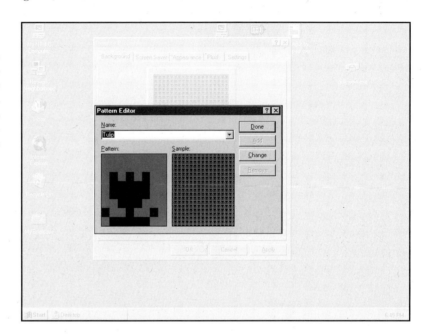

The pattern's design is merely a series of pixels that are either on or off. If a pixel is on, it appears as black; if it is off, you see the background color. Turning the color off and on is just a matter of clicking—the on/off feature is a toggle.

In figure 6.8, for example, the pattern is a tulip. To make the image less busy, you could click on the extra blobs of color on the side of the flowerpot and at the bottom of the tulip. The results are shown in figure 6.9.

The choices in the Pattern Editor dialog box are as follows:

◆ **Name.** Displays the current name, highlighted for editing. You can enter a new name for this edited pattern.

◆ **Done.** Closes the Pattern Editor. If you have made changes, you are asked if you want to save them.

◆ **Add.** Places the new pattern name (entered in the Name box) on the pattern list.

◆ **Change.** Saves the changes you have made to the pattern.

◆ **Remove.** Deletes the pattern in the Name box from the pattern list.

Once you've finished your design efforts, you can use the pattern you've changed or created.

Figure 6.9

Editing the pattern sample changes the look of the overall pattern background.

Wallpaper

Wallpaper is a picture (or image) that is displayed on the desktop. To use wallpaper for a desktop background, choose one from the list in the Wallpaper field (refer to fig. 6.7). Its image is displayed on the monitor section of the dialog box (see fig. 6.10).

By default, the Center radio button in the Display section of the dialog box is selected. This selection causes the wallpaper image to appear in the center of the desktop.

If you want to cover the desktop's entire background with the image by repeating it, choose Tile from the Display section of the dialog box (see fig. 6.11).

Almost any bitmap file can be used as wallpaper. You could scan and save a picture of your cat (or your grandchild if you're lucky enough to have one as beautiful as mine), for example, and use that as your wallpaper. (Be sure to save the image as a bitmap file.)If you have bitmap files on your drive that you'd like to use for wallpaper, choose Browse to open the Browsing for Wallpaper dialog box (see fig. 6.12). When you find the bitmap file you want to use for wallpaper, double-click on it (or select it and choose Open).

Figure 6.10

A rendition of the wallpaper graphic displays so you can see how it looks.

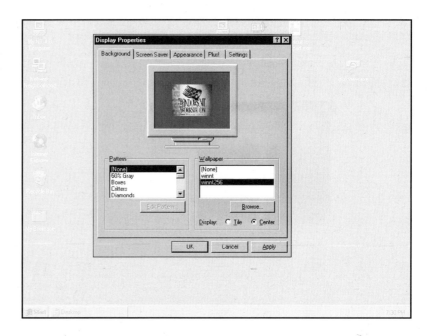

Figure 6.11

Tiling a wallpaper image repeats it across the desktop.

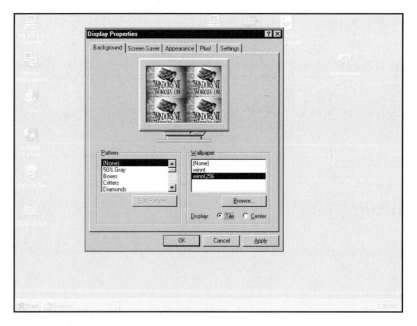

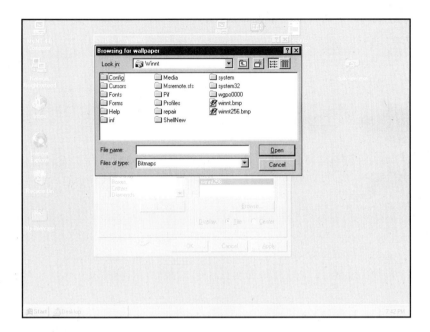

Figure 6.12

Open the appropriate folder and select the file you want to use.

If you don't know where bitmap files are stored on your hard drive and you need to look for them, you cannot do so from this dialog box; no Find function is available. You don't have to close the dialog box, however, to institute a search. Click on a blank spot on the desktop (to give the desktop the focus), and press F3. The Find dialog box appears. Using this dialog box, you can search your drive to find files with the extension .bmp.

Note   You can also get to the Find dialog box by choosing Find from the Start menu, and then choosing Files or Folders—but F3 is faster and easier.

Once you have located the bitmap file you want, close the Find dialog box and move to the appropriate folder in the Browsing dialog box to select the file.

If you find multiple files, you can save the results and try them individually as wallpaper. Further explanation on using Find and saving results is available later in this chapter, in the "Finding Files and Folders" section.

Tip   Although it almost always produces a strange effect (which you might enjoy), you can stretch a wallpaper image to fill the screen.

To stretch the image, after selecting a wallpaper image, click on the Plus! tab of the Display Properties dialog box and select Stretch desktop wallpaper to fit the screen.

Stretching the wallpaper doesn't work very well unless you are using a Pentium chip (you get bored waiting for the image to settle down).

Combining Backgrounds

You can combine a pattern and wallpaper. Choose Center for the wallpaper. It will sit in the middle of the pattern on your desktop. If you choose Tile, it will cover (and hide) any pattern you have selected.

Screen Savers

Screen savers were at one time a necessity; they saved monochrome screens from being damaged by burn-in. *Burn-in* is the term used for an image that is permanently burned into the monitor because an image was displayed for too long a time, usually over many days or weeks. It wasn't unusual in the days of amber screens to have a shadowy image of a menu haunting you as you tried to get work done.

Today's color monitors aren't susceptible to burn-in, but users continue to use screen savers, usually for one of four reasons:

◆ To provide amusement or something to look at rather than the spreadsheet or the document a user has been working on for hours.

◆ To hide the data on the screen when a user leaves the workstation and either forgets or chooses not to close down the software (very useful for when a user is playing games and doesn't want anyone to know).

◆ To hide data and lock the workstation by requiring a password to turn the screen saver off.

◆ To participate in the current fad of using screen savers as status symbols—the "my screen saver is more technically complicated than yours" syndrome is rife in the world of computer propeller heads.

To choose and configure a screen saver for your system, move to the Screen Saver tab of the Display Properties dialog box and perform the following steps:

1. From the Screen Saver box (see fig. 6.13), choose one of the available screen savers. An animated preview of the screen saver appears in the monitor portion of the box.

2. To configure the characteristics of the screen saver's graphics, choose Settings.

Note Screen saver settings are specific to the screen saver, so the elements you are able to configure differ depending on the screen saver you choose. There might be settings for color, texture, size, shape, or other elements of the screen saver's graphics.

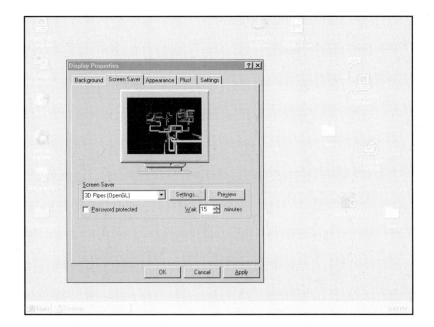

Figure 6.13

The monitor offers a preview of the shapes and animation of a screen saver you've chosen.

3. Choose Preview to see a full-screen preview of the screen saver with the settings you've selected. Move your mouse or press any key to end the preview and return to the dialog box.

4. Select Password Protected if you want to make sure nobody can turn off the screen saver and get to your screen. Choose Change to set the password.

5. In the Wait box, specify the number of minutes that must elapse without keyboard or mouse activity in order for the screen saver to kick in.

6. Choose OK when you have finished configuring the screen saver.

Once you have the screen saver configured the way you want it, you can choose the way you want to use it: let it kick in when the elapsed time is up, or force it to display whenever it's needed.

On-Demand Screen Savers

There is an undocumented method for starting your screen saver whenever you leave your desk, without waiting for the specified time to elapse or without going through a configuration change to shorten the elapsed time. The trick is to create a screen saver shortcut and a screen saver hot key. You must create the shortcut in order to create the hot key, and you can use either device to launch the screen saver. Incidentally, Microsoft calls the hot key a shortcut key, but because most of us are used to the jargon "hot key," I prefer to stick with that.

Tip | The reason you don't plan on using shortcuts is that sometimes it's difficult to get to them because open application windows are covering the desktop. Although there is a cure for that (see the section "Desktop on the Taskbar," later in this chapter), a hot key is usually the quickest way to accomplish a fast launch.

To create the shortcut and the hot key, perform the following steps:

1. Open Explorer to find the screen saver's file. It is in the \SYSTEM32 subfolder under the folder where your Windows NT files were placed during installation (usually WINNT, but you may have chosen a different name). Screen saver files start with "ss" and have an extension of .scr. For instance, if you're using the 3-D pipes screen saver, look for sspipes.scr.

2. Right-click on the file and choose Create Shortcut from the menu. The shortcut is created in the folder.

3. Drag the shortcut to the desktop and close Explorer.

4. Right-click on the shortcut and choose Properties. Select the Shortcut tab.

5. In the Shortcut Key field, enter a character to use as the hot key (Ctrl+Alt is added to the character automatically). Note that you cannot delete the current entry, None, with the Del key, but typing any character automatically replaces it. (You can use any key except Enter, Esc, Tab, spacebar, PrintScreen, or Backspace.)

6. Choose OK.

Hereafter, either double-click on the desktop shortcut or press the hot key combination to launch the screen saver.

Caution | Once you assign this combination to a shortcut, it is owned by that shortcut—no other program can use it. If you use Ctrl+Alt combinations in any of your software applications, be sure you don't use a letter that you need while running that software; it won't work for the software any longer because the screen saver owns it.

Adding Screen Savers

You can buy or download additional screen savers if the ones that come with Windows NT 4 don't provide exactly the mood, fun, or appearance you want. Either follow the instructions for installation or copy the screen saver files into the \system32 subfolder under your Windows NT folder.

Tip Screen saver files have special commands on the shortcut menu. Right click to test, configure, or install one.

Desktop Appearance

The Appearance tab of the Display Properties dialog box has a number of configuration options you can use to change the way your desktop looks. The options include the display appearance of the application windows you open (see fig. 6.14).

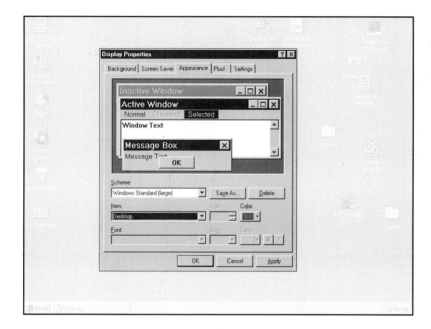

Figure 6.14

The Appearance tab displays a desktop scheme, a combination of configuration options that control— visually—the various parts of your Windows NT system.

The desktop scheme is the term used for the total look of your NT system. It combines appearance configurations for many of the elements in your Windows NT system. You can choose an existing scheme or design one of your own. The scheme you choose or design affects the way the following elements appear:

◆ Desktop background

◆ Title bars of application windows and dialog boxes

◆ Borders around windows and dialog boxes

◆ Icon spacing

- ◆ Message boxes
- ◆ Scrollbars
- ◆ Menus

There are predefined schemes available for you to examine. When you select one, the colors in the box at the top of the dialog box change to show you that scheme's configuration.

To use a predefined scheme, click the arrow to the right of the Scheme box and try schemes until you find the one you like.

Create Your Own Scheme

In the Item field, you'll find a list of all the elements that are part of a scheme. You can choose each individual element and customize it using the Color, Size, and Font fields to invent your own combination of display effects. For example, you may want to change the color of the title bars of all open windows.

Different items have different characteristics. For example, some elements have no font choices (for instance, a scroll bar) and some elements have no size choices (such as ToolTips).

Alter an Existing Scheme

You can also customize an existing scheme. Pick a scheme that comes close, and then change the individual elements that don't satisfy you.

When you have finished creating your own scheme or changing an existing one, choose Save As and then enter a name for the scheme in the Save Scheme dialog box that appears.

Desktop Graphics

Select the Plus! tab of the Display Properties dialog box to configure the graphical appearance of your desktop (see fig. 6.15).

In the Desktop icons section, you can change the icons for the following default icons:

- ◆ My Computer
- ◆ Network Neighborhood
- ◆ Recycle Bin (full)
- ◆ Recycle Bin (empty)

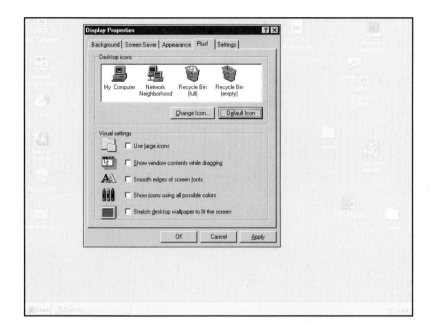

Figure 6.15

Change and enhance the graphics on your desktop with the configuration settings available on the Plus! tab.

Select the icon you want to replace, and then choose Change Icon. Scroll through the icons. When you find one you like, select it and choose OK.

> **Tip**   If there are other icon files available on your system (perhaps you created or installed some), choose Browse to add them to your range of choices.

If you change your mind later, go to the Plus! tab, select the appropriate item, and choose Default Icon to return to the original graphic.

In the Visual settings section, you can make any of the following configuration selections:

◆ **Use Large Icons.** Selecting this option changes all the icons that represent files, folders, and shortcuts on the desktop. Displaying large icons requires more memory, so if you make this change and notice that your system slows down a bit, you might want to change back.

◆ **Show Window Contents While Dragging.** This option changes the way a window looks while you are moving it or resizing it. Normally, only the outline moves and the window goes back to normal (showing contents) when you stop moving it. If you choose to have the contents move along, you may see trailing images as you move.

◆ **Smooth Edges of Screen Fonts.** Font smoothing makes fonts prettier and more readable because all the jagged edges disappear. To use it, you must have a video card and monitor that supports more than 256 colors (16-bit color).

◆ **Show Icons Using all Possible Colors.** If you do have a video card and monitor that supports 16-bit color, you can use all the colors to display your desktop icons.

◆ **Stretch Desktop Wallpaper to Fit the Screen.** If you have a Pentium, you might want to try selecting a bitmap file as a centered wallpaper, and then invoking this option (486 computers will probably see some performance degradation). The graphic stretches to cover your entire screen (the effect can be a little strange, depending on the graphic).

When you have completed all the configuration options, choose OK.

Display Settings

Objective

B.4

The look of the desktop can be changed dramatically by manipulating the basic video settings. Select the Settings tab of the Display Properties dialog box to manipulate the configuration choices for your video card (see Chapter 11, "Configuring Basic Devices," for more on video cards) and monitor (see fig. 6.16).

Figure 6.16

The Display Properties dialog box provides a preview of a screen. It changes when you alter the configuration so you can see the difference your modifications will make.

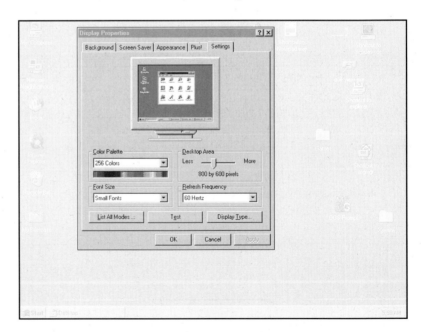

The changes you can make (whether you are installing a new video card or changing the settings for the current one) involve the following choices:

- ◆ Number of colors that appear
- ◆ Resolution
- ◆ Refresh rate
- ◆ Size of the fonts on your desktop

One of the choices on this tab of the dialog box, Display Type, is for the installation of a new video card driver, either to update a current driver or to support the installation of a new video card. Chapter 11 covers this topic in great detail. For now, assume the correct video card drivers have been installed.

Color Palette

Choose Color Palette to change the number of colors you can display. The list of choices is limited by the capabilities of your adapter.

**Objective
B.4**

Before you increase the number of colors you can display, make sure the amount of memory required to sustain that setting won't have a negative impact on the performance of your system. Many video cards come with 1 MB or 2 MB of RAM, and this may be enough if the RAM is fast. If your video card has 4 MB of RAM, you can probably run as many colors as you want without creating a major problem.

Check the documentation that accompanied your video card to see the RAM specifications. Dynamic RAM (DRAM) is not as fast as Video RAM (VRAM). However, some video cards have a type of DRAM called EDO memory (Extended Data Out), which can be almost as fast as VRAM, and is generally less expensive.

All of that said, if you're not doing a lot of complicated graphics work or desktop publishing, you probably don't need more than 256 colors. This will get the best out of any multimedia or game software you install.

Changes to the Color Palette take effect immediately; you do not have to shut down and restart your system.

Resolution

In the Desktop Area section (refer to fig. 6.16), select the number of pixels you want to use in your display. Move the slider bar to the right to increase the number of pixels (the numbers change as the slider progresses). The higher the number of pixels, the higher the resolution. This choice is actually a specification of the size of the visible screen area you use for your display. A larger desktop area makes everything look smaller on your screen, which makes it easier to fit multiple windows onscreen.

Depending upon the capabilities of your video card, you may find that specifying a higher resolution requires you to reduce the number of colors you can display (or vice versa). Resolution and colors frequently present a "trade off" type of situation.

As with colors, your ability to push the resolution is dependent upon your video card. In this case, you'll need speed. Most video cards that are sold now are accelerated. You can probably look up the acceleration rate in the documentation.

If your video card is in a VESA or PCI bus, the acceleration is enhanced because the communication between the card and the processor is much faster.

Note Cards that provide acceleration aren't equal—they perform differently, depending upon the type of acceleration they're built for. A card that has video acceleration doesn't speed up video display. Rather, it supports beefed up video sizes without slowing down the system. A card that has graphics acceleration does speed up the actual display of video.

Changes to the resolution are made immediately; you do not have to shut down and restart your computer to complete the modifications.

Font Size

You can change the fonts that appear on your screen with the Font Size option (refer to fig. 6.16). For most video adapters, there are only two choices—small or large.

 If the Font Size option is grayed-out, you cannot change this setting. This may be due to the capabilities of your video card, or the resolution setting you're using. If your Desktop area setting is 640×480, you may not be able to change the font size.

When you change this setting, you are not really changing the fonts; you are changing the magnification of the fonts. It's as if you are zooming in and out. Small fonts are a 100-percent magnification (comparable to choosing 100 percent in the zoom drop-down list in a word processing document). Large fonts are approximately a 125-percent magnification.

If you change the font size to large, it will change the display size of almost everything in your system: icon titles, title bars in windows, text in menu options, and so on. You'll even find that all the dialog boxes you bring up have grown larger (taking up more room on the desktop, which can be annoying if you have a lot of windows open).

Changes to font size take effect after you have shut down and restarted your computer.

Refresh Rate

Choose Refresh Frequency (refer to fig. 6.16) to specify the refresh rate—the rate at which your screen is re-drawn. The higher the frequency, the less flicker on-screen (*flicker* is that annoying event when the display on your screen seems unable to stay still—it jumps).

The refresh rate you choose must be consistent with the capabilities of your monitor (I set my refresh rate by walking around to the back of my monitor and looking at the label—it lists the available configuration options). Your refresh rate choice also depends on the resolution you have selected. The higher the resolution, the more complicated the refresh process (more pixels to refresh, of course). If in doubt, choose a low refresh rate.

Controlling Flicker

Flicker is a side effect of more than just the refresh frequency you choose in your display settings (the frequency rate is the number of times per second a screen is refreshed).

Monitor specifications also control flicker. Monitors are available with two refresh capabilities (these control the manner in which the screen is refreshed, rather than the rate at which the process takes place):

◆ **Interlaced monitors.** These monitors refresh the display by redrawing the odd-numbered lines, and then returning to the top of the screen to redraw the even-numbered lines.

◆ **Non-interlaced monitors.** These monitors redraw every line with each refresh pass. This process is a bit more complicated—and a non-interlaced monitor is a bit expensive—but it reduces flicker. If you are doing a lot of work with graphics software, the extra money is probably worthwhile, but if you spend almost all your time looking at text with occasional graphics (such as when word processing), it probably isn't necessary to insist on a non-interlaced monitor.

You will always see flicker if you aren't looking at a monitor straight-on. Peripheral vision always produces flicker.

Pre-loaded Combinations

You don't necessarily have to go through each of the settings one at a time; you can probably use one of the preconfigured combinations of settings.

To see them, choose List All Modes (refer to fig. 6.16). A list of combinations (colors, resolution, and refresh rate/method) appears. Highlight the one you want and choose OK (see fig. 6.17).

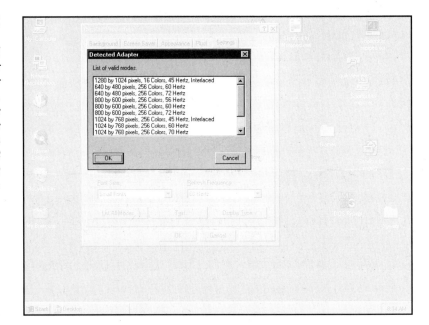

Figure 6.17

All the valid modes for your video adapter are displayed. Scroll through the list and choose the combination of settings that matches the way you want to work.

Test the New Settings

Once you've made all the configuration changes, choose Test to be sure everything works properly.

Your screen goes black for a second and then a display of colors at the specified resolution flies across your screen. Each color is labeled (if something labeled red looks green, that's an indication that something is wrong).

After a few seconds, you are asked if everything looks correct. If it does, choose Yes. If it doesn't, choose No and go back to the dialog box and start choosing settings again.

After you confirm that the new settings work properly, if you made changes that require it, shut down and restart the computer.

Using the Desktop Shortcut Menu

Thus far, this chapter has touched on some of the commands and dialog boxes available through the desktop shortcut menu (the menu that displays when you right-click on a blank spot on the desktop).

The desktop shortcut menu offers several additional items (see fig. 6.18), which this section covers in detail.

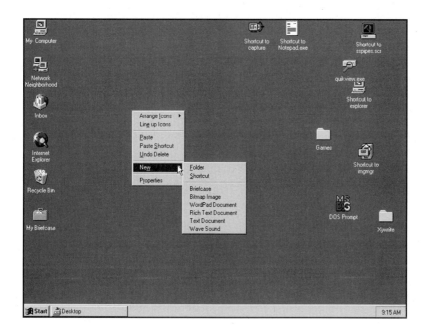

Figure 6.18

The desktop shortcut menu and submenu include the capability to place objects on the desktop in a variety of ways.

Paste to the Desktop

You can select a file or folder in Explorer, right-click and choose Copy, and then paste the item onto the desktop by choosing Paste from the shortcut menu. This is an easy way to move often-used documents or folders to the desktop so you have easy access to them.

When you move a document to the desktop, double-clicking the document launches the application that prepared it. When the application window appears, the document is open and ready for editing. This can be a very productive benefit when you work with a lot of boiler-plate documents, such as contracts, memos, or spreadsheets.

Put Scraps on the Desktop

Another handy and productive trick is to place specific paragraphs or parts of documents on the desktop. These items are called *scraps*. When you double-click on one, the application that created it launches with the scrap in the software window.

Furthermore, you can drag the scrap from the desktop into an open software window (the same software that created the scrap). This is a terrific way to retrieve often-needed text, graphics, lists, charts, or other document parts.

To create a scrap on the desktop, select the part of the document you want to save. Drag the selection from the application window to the desktop. The scrap is placed on the desktop with a title that helps you remember what it is (see fig. 6.19).

Figure 6.19

When you put a scrap on the desktop, you can use it in any document by dragging it into an open window of the software that was used to create the scrap.

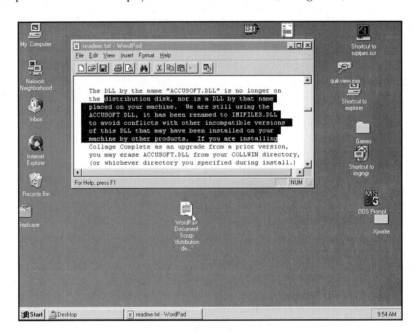

> **Tip**
>
> A couple of nifty uses for scraps are the company logo, your signature, or your standard closing for letters. To create a signature, scan one, or send yourself a fax. Use a free-standing fax machine to ship your signature to a computer-based fax machine. Clean it up with the scanner or fax software, and save it as a graphics file in a format that your software can use. Or save it several times, using different formats. Then put it on the desktop so you can drag it to an application window whenever it's needed.

Creating and using scraps works only with software that supports drag-and-drop OLE functions. Most software written for Windows can use these functions; check the software's documentation.

Create New Items

The cascading menu that appears when you put your pointer on New offers a number of choices for creating items on the desktop (refer to fig. 6.18).

New Folder

Choose Folder to put a new folder on the desktop. A folder icon is placed on the desktop, and the title area is highlighted for you to provide a name for the folder (the highlighted area reads New Folder, but as soon as you start typing, your characters replace that title).

After the folder is on the desktop, you can begin placing items in it. Remember that the folder does not have to be open to receive items; you can drag any item to the folder icon, and the item will be placed in that folder.

New Shortcut

If you want to create a shortcut—for instance, so you can double-click on a shortcut icon to open software (instead of using the Start menu)—you have a couple of choices for performing that action. Choosing Shortcut from the Desktop menu launches a shortcut wizard that uses a number of wizard pages and steps to make a shortcut. This is a long, complicated way to accomplish this task, however, so you should ignore this menu choice. It is much faster to open Explorer, find the file you need, right-drag it to the desktop, and choose Create Shortcut(s) Here. (If the file is an executable file, you can drag it to the desktop using the normal left-button drag.)

Feel free to go through the wizard process to satisfy your curiosity, but using Explorer to create a shortcut is truly much more expedient than creating one with the Desktop Shortcut menu. Detailed information about creating and using shortcuts is in Chapter 10, "Using Shortcuts."

New Briefcase

The Briefcase enables you to carry files around, so you can work on them outside the office and then bring the changed documents back to the office. It's just like a real briefcase.

If you didn't install the Briefcase when you installed the operating system, you can add it through the Add/Remove Programs applet in the Control Panel. You can also put a briefcase on the desktop by right-clicking on a blank spot on the desktop and choosing Briefcase from the cascading menu under New. (Or, create a second briefcase if you find that you need one.)

New Documents

Another productive feature is the capability to place icons representing blank documents on the desktop. When those icons are present, double-clicking on one opens the appropriate software application with this document in the application window (it doesn't have any data, but it's still a document).

By default, you can create blank document icons for the following document types:

- ◆ Bitmap Image
- ◆ WordPad
- ◆ Rich Text
- ◆ Text
- ◆ Wave Sound

To create an icon for a blank document, choose the appropriate type from the cascading menu under New.

Adding File Types to the New Menu

If you create a document type regularly that isn't listed on the New menu, you can add that type to the menu. You might regularly save from a database to a disk file reports with an extension to the file name that you invented to help you recognize those report files. This is actually a two-step process:

1. Create and register the document type.

2. Add the new document type to the menu.

This section illustrates how to do each step.

> **Note** Some of the procedures discussed in this section affect the Registry, the database that keeps the configuration of your NT system. More information about the Registry is in Chapter 31, "Using the Registry."

Creating and Registering the Document Type

Objective G.6

To create and register a new document type, perform the following steps:

1. Open My Computer (you can also open Explorer; all the remaining steps are the same for either).

2. Choose Options from the View menu. Select the File Types tab (see fig. 6.20).

3. Choose New Type to bring up the Add New File Type dialog box (see fig. 6.21).

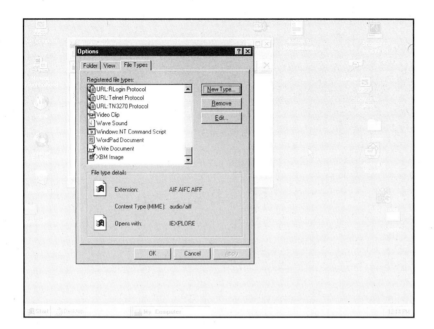

Figure 6.20

The current registered file types are displayed on the File Types tab of the Options dialog box.

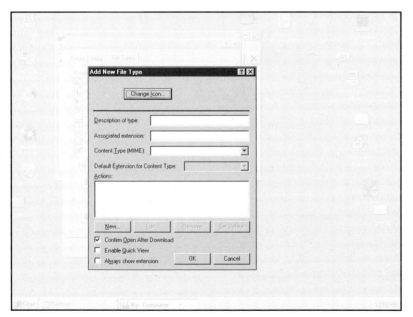

Figure 6.21

When you add a new file type, the information is added to the Registry.

4. Fill out the fields in the Add New File Type dialog box as follows:

◆ **Description of Type.** Enter text that describes the new file type. This description will appear in folder windows when details about files are shown.

◆ **Associated Extension.** Enter a three-letter extension for the new file type (just the extension—you don't have to enter the period). Any files with this extension will be displayed with the same icon and use the same commands you configure for the file type. You cannot enter an extension that already exists in the File Types listing.

◆ **Content Type (MIME).** You can use this field to indicate the MIME (Multipurpose Internet Mail Extension) type you want to associate with programs on your system. Then, your Internet browser can check the association in order to open a file over the Internet.

◆ **Actions.** When you create a new file type, there will be no actions listed in this field. Choose New to create the action in the New Action dialog box (see fig. 6.22).

Figure 6.22

*Specify the action
you want to occur
in the New Action
dialog box.*

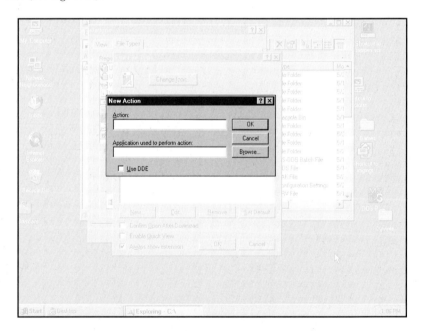

5. Fill out the fields in the New Action dialog box as follows:

◆ **Action.** Specify an Action (usually Open).

◆ **Application Used to Perform Action.** Indicate the path and executable file name for the Application used to perform the action.

◆ **Use DDE.** Select Use DDE if the application has DDE capabilities.

6. Choose OK when you have finished the New Action dialog box, and return to the previous dialog box to complete the configuration:

   ◆ **Confirm Open After Download.** Choose this option if you want your Internet program to ask before opening this file type.

   ◆ **Enable Quick View.** Choose this option if the new file type supports Quick View (see "Using Quick View" later in this chapter).

   ◆ **Always Show Extension.** Choose this option to indicate you want the extension for this file type to be displayed in folder windows.

7. Choose OK when you have completed the Add New File Type dialog box. The new File Type is listed on the File Types tab of the Options dialog box. Choose OK to close the Options dialog box.

When you complete these steps, the new file type is registered. The Options dialog box is a front end for the Registry; when you complete your work in the dialog box, the information is transferred to the Registry.

Once the file type exists and is registered, you can add it to the New menu by editing the Registry.

Caution | Working in the Registry can be dangerous if you don't understand what you're doing or don't follow instructions carefully.

Adding the New Document Type to the Menu

To change the Registry in order to place a new item on the desktop shortcut menu, perform the following steps:

Objective G.6

1. Open the Registry. You can either choose Run from the Start menu and then specify Regedit.exe; or you can open Explorer, move to the folder that contains your Windows NT software, and double-click on Regedit.exe.

2. Click on the plus sign next to HKEY_CLASSES_ROOT to expand that section of the Registry.

3. Move through the first set of listings to find the extension for the file type you just registered (the first keys in this branch of the Registry signify the file extensions). Click on the appropriate key.

4. Right-click anywhere in the right pane to bring up a shortcut menu. Choose New, Key. When the new key is inserted in the left pane, change its name from New Key #1 to ShellNew. Press Enter.

5. With the ShellNew icon highlighted, right-click on it and choose New, String Value. Type in the name NullFile.

6. Close the Registry editor.

The new entry is on the cascading New menu when you right-click on the desktop. You do not have to shut down and restart the computer to enable this change.

Desktop Tips

As you continue to use Windows NT Workstation 4 and get used to its desktop interface, you'll find (or invent) plenty of quick ways to get work done.

Finding Files and Folders

One easy-to-use feature that is available directly from the desktop is Find. You can use Find to locate files and folders anywhere on your system.

The fastest way to get to Find is to press F3 when the desktop has the focus (just click anywhere on the desktop to give it the focus).

 Tip Find is available all over the system. You can choose Find from the Start menu, or press F3 when any folder window is open (the search will start at that folder).

The Find dialog box appears so you can begin the search for the files or folders you need. There are three tabs on the Find dialog box:

- ◆ Name & Location
- ◆ Date Modified
- ◆ Advanced

You'll find that the vast majority of the time you will only have to use the Name & Location tab to locate files and folders.

Name & Location Tab

When Find launches, the Name & Location tab is in the foreground (see fig. 6.23).

In the Named field, enter the name or partial name of the file and folder you want to locate. This field offers a few different options:

- ◆ Click on the arrow to the right of the field to see the files and folders you've searched for previously (you'll probably have to look for the same thing multiple times).
- ◆ Enter multiple names or partial names, separated by commas, to search for more than one file or folder at a time. For example, to find all the batch files and all the text files on your system, enter bat,txt.

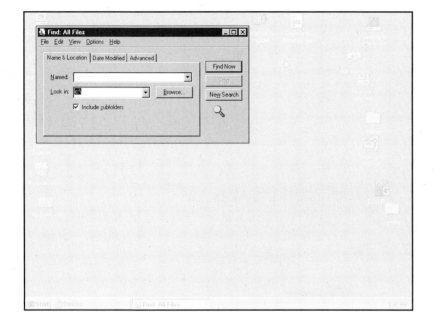

Figure 6.23

Enter the name you want Find to locate and specify where you want it to look.

Narrowing Searches with Find

One of the nicest things about Find is that you don't have to worry about file-naming conventions. Find searches for characters, not file names. You don't have to worry about wildcards, or placing a period before a file extension. It will find the string of characters you enter no matter where they fall in the word, not if the string matches the beginning of the word. If you enter the string dos, for example, Find returns results such as Dosprmpt, Aspiedos.sys, and Msdosdrv.txt, as well as all files with the extension dos.

On the other hand, you aren't prevented from using wildcards or question marks in order to help narrow the search; Find will pay attention and use the conventional search techniques for wildcards.

If you need a quick refresher: an asterisk (*) indicates that you will accept any number of characters in place of the asterisk at the point in the file name at which you placed the asterisk; a question mark (?) indicates you'll accept any individual character at the same exact place in the file name at which you entered the question mark (you can use multiple question marks to indicate a specific number of characters).

A request for Smith? would return Smith0, Smith1, and so on through Smith9, but not Smith10. A request for Smith* would produce all files that start with Smith, regardless of the number of characters after Smith. A request for Sm?th would return Smith or Smyth. A request for any of the above that included a file extension in the search criteria would narrow the search even further.

In the Look in field (refer to fig. 6.23), enter a drive or a path to begin the search. Select Include Subfolders if you want Find to search below the specified path.

The following options are available for the Look in field:

◆ You can search multiple drives or paths, separating your selections with commas.

◆ You can choose Browse to look for a specific path from which to begin the search.

◆ You can click on the down arrow to the right of the field to see a listing of the top levels of your system, and choose one to search (see fig. 6.24).

Figure 6.24

Find locates all the disk storage units in your system; you can choose one or more for this search.

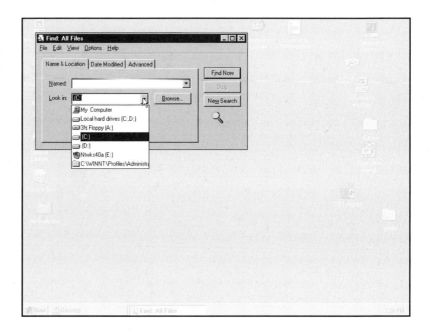

If the information in this tab is all you need to conduct your search, choose Find Now to begin the search.

Date Modified Tab

Move to the Date Modified tab to narrow the search by specifying date ranges for the files (see fig. 6.25).

Enter your specifications as follows:

◆ **All Files.** Select this option only if you had previously used this tab and set a date range that you no longer wish to use (the dates stay there until you clear them with All Files). If you have begun a new search after completing a search, don't forget to return to this page and select this option (unless you still need to qualify the search by the same date ranges).

◆ **Between.** Select this option and specify beginning and ending dates to search for files within that range.

◆ **During the Previous xx Months.** Select this option and specify a number of months to limit the search to that time period.

◆ **During the Previous xx Days.** Select this option and specify a number of days.

If completing the information on this tab is all you need to conduct your search, choose Find Now to begin the search.

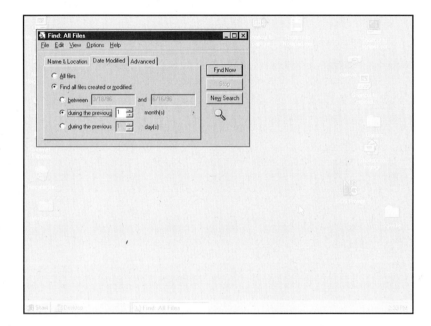

Figure 6.25

You can limit the search to files that have modification or creation dates within a range you specify.

Advanced Tab

Move to the Advanced tab to narrow the search further (see fig. 6.26).

Use the fields on the Advanced tab to enter any of the following data:

◆ **Of Type.** Choose All Files and Folders or click the arrow to the right of the field and choose a specific file type (every file type known to Windows NT 4 is listed).

◆ **Containing Text.** Enter text that can be found in the file. This is useful if you have no idea what the name of the file could be, but you know of some specific text that it contains.

◆ **Size Is.** Use the arrow to choose between At least and At most; then specify a size—in kilobytes (KB)—in the next box.

Figure 6.26

The choices on the Advanced tab enable you to hone in on the search for the files or folders you need.

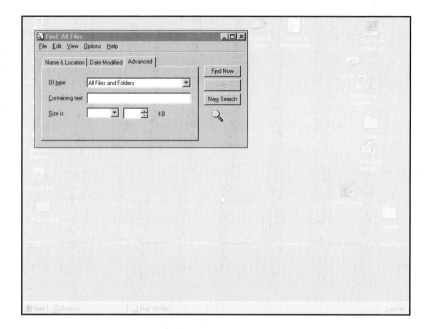

If completing the information on this tab is all you need to conduct your search, choose Find Now to begin the search.

Using the Results

When matching files or folders are located, they are listed within the Find dialog box (see fig. 6.27).

You can select any file or folder in the list of found items and manipulate it with the shortcut menu (right-click on the file to see the menu).

You can do quite a few useful things with this list, including the following:

◆ **Sort the list by any column heading.** Click on the column heading you want to use for the sort, and the entire list will be sorted in an ascending scheme by that category. Click on the same category to reverse the sort to descending.

◆ **Save the parameters you set for this search.** Choose Save Search from the File menu to save the parameters you set for this search permanently, in case you want to use them again. An icon is placed on the desktop with a title indicating the search. Double-click on it to bring up the Find dialog box with these search criteria.

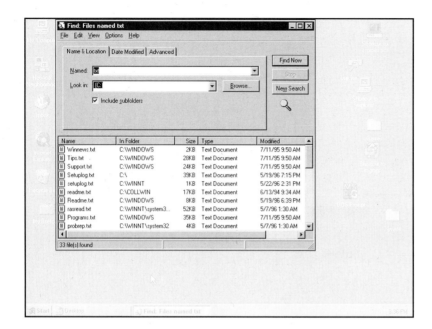

Figure 6.27

Asking Find to locate text files on Drive C results in 33 files being listed.

Tip   Saving a search is useful if you used the Date Modified or Advanced tabs and don't want to go through all the steps again. It is also advantageous to save a complicated search in case you want to search for similar criteria, because you will only need to make a couple of changes in the settings to search next time.

◆ **Save the detailed list of found files and folders.** Choose Save Results from the Options menu to save the detailed list of found files and folders. An icon is placed on the desktop and you can open it at any time to use the information.

If no files were located, or too many files were located, and you want to change or narrow the criteria, choose New Search to clear the current values and enter new ones.

Desktop on the Taskbar

Shortcuts to application software and boilerplate documents are terrific productivity aids.

However, it's very frustrating when you have application windows open on your screen because it's difficult or impossible to get to your shortcuts. Anyone used to clicking on a shortcut is terribly annoyed at having to scroll through the Start menu and submenus to launch another program.

There is a solution: put your desktop on the taskbar so that any time you want to click on a shortcut, you can get to it quickly. Read on to discover how this desktop tip works.

To put your desktop on the taskbar, perform the following steps:

1. Open My Computer and make sure the toolbar is visible (select it from the View menu if it isn't).

2. Click the arrow to the right of the toolbar list box that has My Computer listed. Although it looks as if My Computer is the topmost listing, click on the up arrow to find the listing named Desktop (see fig. 6.28).

Figure 6.28

If you move up one more level, you'll see Desktop sitting above My Computer.

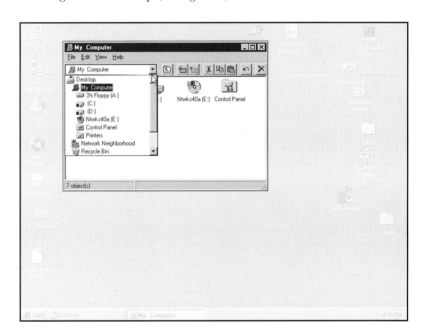

3. Select Desktop, and the window changes to reflect all the icons on your desktop (see fig. 6.29).

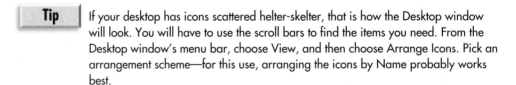

Tip   If your desktop has icons scattered helter-skelter, that is how the Desktop window will look. You will have to use the scroll bars to find the items you need. From the Desktop window's menu bar, choose View, and then choose Arrange Icons. Pick an arrangement scheme—for this use, arranging the icons by Name probably works best.

4. Minimize the window to move it to the taskbar as a button.

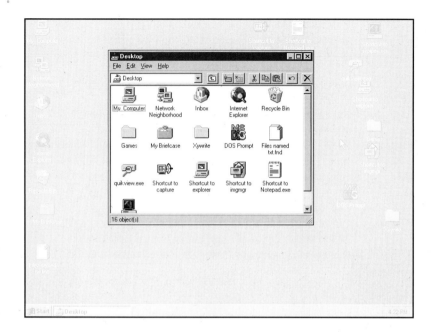

Figure 6.29

The window representing the desktop includes all the objects on the real desktop.

Hereafter, whenever you need access to a shortcut or any other icon on your desktop, you won't have to search behind open application windows. Just click on the Taskbar button, use the icon, and then minimize the Desktop window again. Remember not to close the window, only minimize it. The best thing about this trick is that when you shut down, a minimized Desktop button on the taskbar isn't closed the way minimized application buttons are. It will be there waiting for you when you restart Windows NT.

Desktop on the Start Menu

Similar to placing the desktop on the taskbar, you can also place the Desktop on the Start menu for easy access to all the icons you use regularly. The only difference is that when you follow this Start menu strategy, the desktop won't contain My Computer, Network Neighborhood, or Recycle Bin.

The secret to moving a copy of the desktop to the Start menu is that you can place folders on the Start menu—and the desktop is a folder. That is, there is a folder in your system representing your desktop (which is how Windows NT knows what to put on the desktop when you log on).

To add the desktop to the Start menu, perform the following steps:

1. Open Explorer and find the desktop folder, which is a subfolder of the folder that holds your Windows NT operating system.

2. Drag the folder to the Start button. When you drag a folder to the Start button, it is automatically copied, not moved, so you do not have to use the Ctrl key.

Note   If your Windows NT system is set up for multiple users, and there is a logon used during system boot, there is a separate desktop folder for each user. That's because each user can configure and maintain his own desktop settings. To move your desktop to the Start menu, look for the Profiles folder under the Windows NT operating system folder. Click on the plus sign to the left of the Profiles folder and find the folder with your name. One of the subfolders under your folder is the Desktop. Drag that folder to the Start button.

Hereafter, when you click on the Start menu (or use Ctrl+Esc to pop up the Start menu), the desktop folder is there and one click on it opens it (see fig. 6.30).

Figure 6.30

The desktop is now one click away.

Using Quick View

Quick View is an application that lets you view a data file without opening the application that created the file. Quick View contains viewing capabilities for most of the popular Windows programs.

To use this application, right-click on a file and then choose Quick View from the shortcut menu.

Users who learn to depend on Quick View (it's a very handy utility)
put its shortcut on the desktop and drag files to the icon to view them.
If you want to put a Quick View icon on your desktop, look in Explorer for
\WINNT\system32\viewers\quickview.exe (where WINNT is the name of the folder
holding your Windows NT software). Drag the file to the desktop to create the
shortcut.

If you don't see Quick View on the shortcut menu for Windows-based data files and
you can't find the executable file with Explorer, you have to install the software. To
do so, perform the following steps (you will need your original Windows NT disk):

1. Choose Settings from the Start menu, and then choose Control Panel.

2. Open the Add/Remove Programs object and click on the Windows NT
    Setup tab.

3. Click on Accessories and choose Details.

4. Scroll through the list in the Components box to find Quick View and select it.
    Then choose OK.

The Windows NT installation program will install Quick View.

End Note: If you are dual-booting between Windows NT 4 and Windows 95, the
desktops are much too similar for comfort. You can forget in which operating
system you're working. Even though you may have placed different shortcuts on
each desktop, there's probably no quick way to tell where you are. To make sure
you keep your sanity, your wits, and your expertise at top level, rename My Computer to My Windows NT 4 Computer and My Windows 95 Computer. Then, a
quick glance at the upper-left corner of the screen reminds you of the current
operating system.

Test Your Knowledge

1. Which of the following Control Panel applets appears when you right-click on
    the desktop and choose Properties from the shortcut menu?

    A. Display

    B. Keyboard

    C. System

    D. Regional Settings

2. Which statement about adding new file types is false?

    A. New file types must be executable files.

    B. New file types are added to the Registry automatically.

    C. New file types can be added through the menu options in the Explorer window.

    D. New file types can be added through the menu options in the My Computer window.

3. Which situation does not permit you to use F3 to invoke the Find feature?

    A. Pressing F3 on the desktop when no application windows are open

    B. Pressing F3 when working in Explorer

    C. Pressing F3 when working in an application window

    D. Pressing F3 when browsing a folder window

4. Which setting is *not* available to you when configuring a video display adapter?

    A. Resolution

    B. Number of Colors

    C. Font Size

    D. Flicker rate

5. Which video adapter setting takes effect after a reboot?

    A. Resolution

    B. Font Size

    C. Refresh rate

    D. Color Palette

6. If your video display adapter fails to display at the resolution it is supposed to, reduce _____.

7. After you have created a new file type, you can change the Registry to see the file type on:

    A. The document section of the Start menu

    B. The New section of the shortcut menu for the desktop

    C. The shortcut menu for the new file type

    D. The shortcut menu for the new file type's associated software

Test Your Knowledge Answers

1. A
2. A
3. C
4. D
5. B
6. the number of colors displayed
7. B

Chapter Snapshot

The Taskbar and the Start menu are used more than any other elements in Windows NT, and plenty of configuration options, tips, tricks, and shortcuts will help you use them more efficiently. This chapter explores these basic elements, including the following:

Windows NT
Workstation 4

CHAPTER 7

Understanding the Taskbar and Start Menu

After installation, Windows NT Workstation 4 comes into view for users in a relatively standard format. Several icons are on the desktop, and across the bottom of the screen lies an element called the Taskbar. The left side of the Taskbar displays a Start button; the right side displays a digital clock. Clicking on the Start button brings up the Start menu (see fig. 7.1). The Taskbar and the Start menu—the basic desktop elements of Windows NT Workstation —provide a great deal of the user interface's power.

Figure 7.1

The Taskbar and Start menu are the basic tools for the Windows NT 4 interface.

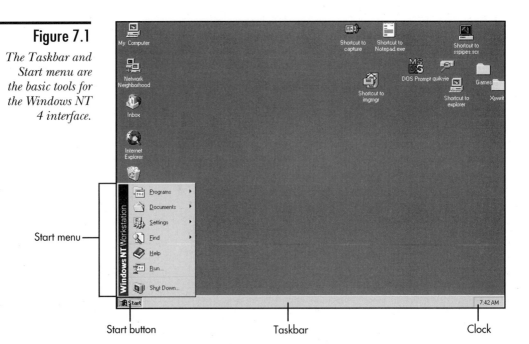

Start menu —

Start button   Taskbar   Clock

Using the Taskbar

Open applications display their presence on the Taskbar. Whenever you launch software, a button appears on the Taskbar to indicate that this software is loaded into memory. Whether the software window is active or minimized, the button stays on the Taskbar (see fig. 7.2).

This easy access to Taskbar buttons makes the Taskbar a very powerful tool. It's a one-click task switcher; there's no need to use any keyboard combinations or call up any dialog boxes. To gain access, simply click on a button.

Note Having all open programs displayed on the Taskbar provides another advantage—you can't forget programs that are open. Windows 3.x users who neglect to take a quick check of the tasklist (Ctrl+Esc) frequently shut down Windows with applications still open, sometimes causing problems with software, data, or the next launch of Windows.

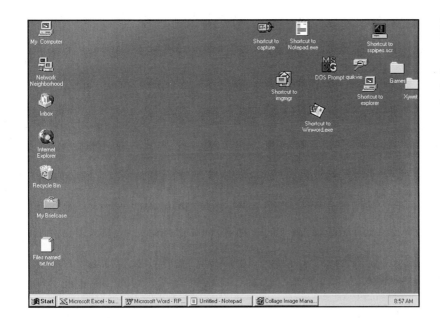

Figure 7.2

The Taskbar has a button for every application currently in use.

Switching Programs

You can move among opened multiple programs in several different ways:

◆ Switch open application windows between the background and the foreground

◆ Tile open application windows

◆ Cascade open application windows

◆ Minimize open application windows

◆ Restore minimized application windows

◆ Minimize every application window

◆ Close an application

Each of these actions can be accomplished at the Taskbar.

Switch Between Open Applications

Switching between programs in Windows 3.x or NT 3.x was sometimes quite onerous for users. If you worked full-screen, you had to use Ctrl+Tab or Ctrl+Esc to move from application to application. Even if you worked with smaller application windows so you could see (and get to) more than one application on your screen, it was some-times necessary to drag windows around in order to find the window you wanted to work in, and then click on it to bring it to the foreground.

Windows NT Workstation 4 makes application switching much easier. Click once on an open application's Taskbar button to have the application move to the fore-ground.

Tile and Cascade

When multiple applications are open, you can use the Taskbar to tile or cascade the windows easily.

Place your pointer on any blank spot on the Taskbar, right-click to see the Taskbar shortcut menu (see fig. 7.3), and choose one of the following options:

◆ Cascade Windows

◆ Tile Windows Horizontally

◆ Tile Windows Vertically

Figure 7.3

The Taskbar's shortcut menu enables you to manipulate open programs.

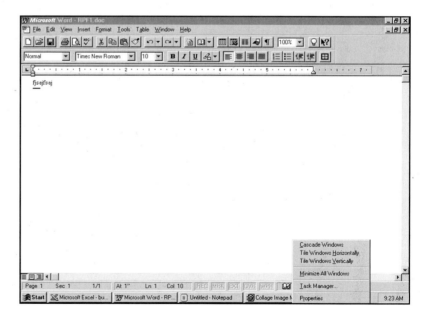

Tip If the Taskbar is packed with application buttons, it can be difficult to identify a blank spot (a spot between buttons). The space to the left of the clock usually provides enough room to place a mouse pointer without accidentally manipulating an application button.

Minimize and Restore

You can also use the Taskbar to minimize and restore application windows.

To minimize an application window, right-click on its Taskbar button and choose Minimize. Of course, if the application in question appears in the foreground, it's just as easy to click on the minimize button in the application window. If, however, it is not the foreground application (it is maximized but behind the current foreground application)—it is either hiding behind a full-screen window, or it is one of many cascaded or tiled windows—it is faster to use the Taskbar button.

Restoring minimized applications is just as easy. Click once on the Taskbar button— the application is restored and appears in the foreground. You can also right-click on the application's Taskbar button to see a menu that includes Restore, but it is much easier to left-click on the application button to accomplish the same thing.

Tip Another option on the shortcut menu that appears when you right-click on an application's Taskbar button is Maximize. If you are working with this application in a small window, and then minimize it, clicking on the Taskbar button restores the window to its previous size (small). If, instead, you right-click on the Taskbar button of a minimized application, you can choose Maximize to open it full-screen, thus saving a mouse-click (you would have had to restore the window, and then click the Maximize button on the window).

Minimize All

If you're working with multiple applications, you can minimize all of them at once. This provides a quick way to get to the desktop to find an icon and open another application. Further, if you want to minimize all but one of the open application windows, the quickest way to accomplish this task is to minimize them all at once and then click on the button of the application you want. This method is certainly easier than switching to each application, one at a time, and clicking its minimize button.

To minimize all application windows at once, right-click on a blank spot of the Taskbar and choose Minimize All Windows from the shortcut menu (refer to fig. 7.3).

After making this choice, if you were to right-click on a blank spot of the Taskbar again, you would see an alternative menu option: Undo Minimize All. Selecting this option restores the application windows that were open when you originally chose Minimize All Windows.

Close an Application

Any open application can be closed from the Taskbar—whether it is open and in the foreground, open and in the background, open along with other application windows and sharing desktop space, or even minimized. Right-click on the application's Taskbar button and choose Close from the shortcut menu. (If the application is in the foreground, it's just as easy to click the close button on the application window.)

If the document in the application window has been modified since the last time you saved it, or if you have not yet saved the document, Windows NT offers you one of two options:

◆ **Save.** If the document has already been saved, answer Yes to save it in its new, modified state.

◆ **Save As.** If the document is new, a Save As dialog box appears; name the document and save it.

If the application is running in a DOS window, the Close menu choice usually won't work (you'll be asked to force the application to close). Click on DOS application buttons to restore them, and proceed with a normal exit for that application. (If the application is merely a DOS prompt, open it and type **exit**.) There are methods for automatically closing the DOS window when you exit a program by establishing that parameter in the Properties dialog box for the DOS application file (although there may be reasons why you don't want to do that). For information about using DOS software in Windows NT 4, see Chapter 19, "Running Non-Windows Applications."

Understanding the Taskbar Buttons

There's a bit more to a Taskbar button than you might notice at first glance:

◆ **Name.** Taskbar buttons for programs written for Windows NT 4 or Windows 95 (as opposed to programs written for earlier versions of Windows or DOS programs) display the name of the current document in addition to the name of the program.

◆ **Color.** The color of the button representing the current foreground application is different from the color of all the other buttons on the Taskbar. When an application is minimized or in the background, the button is gray. The foreground application's button is white.

◆ **Size.** The more buttons on the Taskbar, the smaller the buttons get. As soon as a button size is reduced to the point that the entire title doesn't show (titles are truncated as the buttons get smaller), holding the mouse pointer over the button for a second or two displays the full title of the button. If the button is large enough to display the title, holding the pointer over the button has no effect.

Using the Keyboard

You can also use the keyboard (key combinations) for quick and efficient task-switching:

◆ **Using Alt+Tab.** Hold down the Alt key and press the Tab key to move through a series of small windows representing all the applications that have buttons on the Taskbar (see fig. 7.4). Release the keyboard when the application you want to work in is displayed, and the application window opens. This navigating method is helpful when you're working in a full-screen DOS session without mouse access.

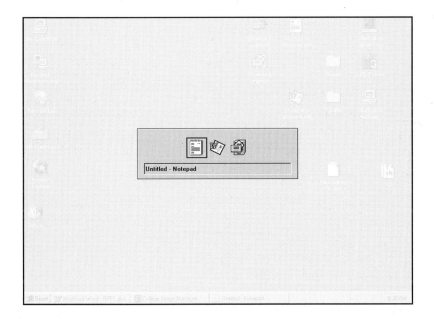

Figure 7.4

Use Alt+Tab to switch among applications.

◆ **Navigating the Start menu and Taskbar.** Press Ctrl+Esc to bring up the Start menu; then press Esc to put the focus on the Start button and get rid of the menu. Press Tab to put the focus on the Taskbar (you won't see anything change, but the focus is now on the Taskbar). Use your arrow keys to move through the Taskbar buttons. Press Enter when you get to the one you want.

◆ **Navigating the desktop icons.** To navigate through the desktop icons, follow the preceding steps, but press Tab again after you've put the focus on the Taskbar. Pressing Tab at that point puts the focus on the desktop. Use the arrow keys to move through the desktop icons, pressing Enter when you arrive at the program you want to open.

 Tip   After using Ctrl+Esc, followed by Esc to close the Start menu, the Tab key rotates among the Taskbar, the desktop, and the Start button.

◆ **Using Alt+Esc.** Use Alt+Esc to switch between applications. This key combination moves you among the applications that are open on the desktop, moving a different application to the foreground each time you press the key combination.

Applications that are minimized will not be switched to the foreground because they're not open; however, after the Alt+Esc combination has rotated through each of the open application windows, it turns its attention to the minimized applications. As you continue to press the Alt+Esc combination, you will see the Taskbar button for each minimized application change color. When a button is white, it means it has the focus of the Alt+Esc key combination. At that point, you can press Enter to restore its window.

Whether you use the mouse or the keyboard combinations, the Taskbar makes navigating easy—much easier and more efficient than the tasklist of previous Windows versions. Further, you can never forget that an application is open—it's always right there on the Taskbar.

Customizing the Taskbar

You can easily customize the Taskbar to fit the way you work. (Before you even begin the customization, you can decide where on your screen you want it—just point to a blank spot on the Taskbar and drag it to any of the four sides of your screen.)

Always on Top

You can make sure the Taskbar is always on top of any other window on your desktop. When this configuration option is selected, all the application windows will try to readjust to stay out of the Taskbar's way. This readjustment involves moving the edge of the application window that is against the Taskbar, making the application window a bit smaller to accommodate the Taskbar's location. If the Taskbar is on the bottom of your screen, the bottom of the application window is raised; if the Taskbar is on the right side of your screen, the right edge of the application window moves in a bit.

In effect, this option is an announcement that the Taskbar exists—if you turn it off, the application windows won't know the Taskbar is on your desktop.

To make sure the Taskbar is always on top, perform the following steps:

1. Right-click on any blank spot on the Taskbar and choose Properties to see the Taskbar Properties dialog box (see fig. 7.5).

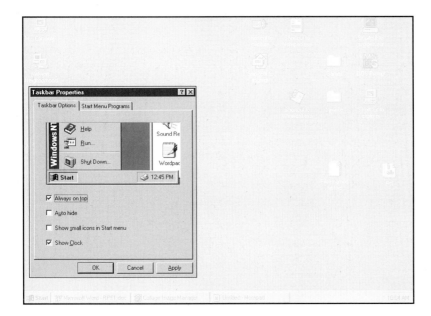

Figure 7.5

Use the Taskbar Options tab of the Taskbar Properties dialog box to configure the Taskbar's behavior.

> **Tip** If your Taskbar isn't on top and is hidden by an application window (which is why you want to get to this configuration option), you reach this dialog box by choosing Settings, Taskbar from the Start menu.

2. Select Always on top.

3. Choose OK. The configuration change takes effect immediately.

Exceptions to Always on Top

The fact that you've configured the Taskbar for Always on top doesn't mean it will be visible all the time. That's because other windows can have the same configuration option, such as Help topic windows. If two windows are competing for "always on top" status, the window that has the focus wins.

continues

It's also important to note that the only application windows that are guaranteed to respect the "always on top" status and make an effort to stay out of the way of the Taskbar are those that belong to programs written for Windows NT 4 or Windows 95. These applications actually do some quick math, measuring the number of pixels that have to be reduced from the application window in order to continue to display the Taskbar. Programs written for earlier versions of Windows may not be able to handle these evasion tactics; you may have to resize the window to see the Taskbar.

If you routinely switch between multiple open applications, having the Taskbar visible at all times is a real productivity factor.

Auto Hide

If you find the Taskbar is an annoying, busy element while you're working, or you find it covers a status bar or other part of an application window, you can make it disappear until you need it.

Follow these steps to turn on this Auto hide feature:

1. Right-click on a blank spot on the Taskbar and choose Properties.

2. Select Auto hide, and then choose OK.

While you're working in applications, the Taskbar is not visible, although if you look carefully, you can see a thin line representing the outside edge (which is the top of the Taskbar if it's on the bottom, the left edge if it's on the right, and so on).

To make the Taskbar reappear, move the mouse pointer toward the line representing the outside edge of the Taskbar. The following will occur when Auto hide is selected:

◆ After moving your pointer to the hidden Taskbar, if you move your mouse pointer away from the Taskbar, it hides again.

◆ If you click on any blank spot on the Taskbar, you will give it the focus and it will remain visible when you move your pointer away. To Auto hide it, move the focus to another item (click the desktop, an icon, or an application window).

◆ If Auto hide is on but Always on top is off, when the Taskbar pops back up, it will be behind any application window that covers the part of your screen that the Taskbar occupies. Sometimes you can still see enough of the Taskbar to figure out which button you want to click.

Note	The level of efficiency of Auto hide (versus the level of annoyance) seems to be related to the position of the Taskbar. If your Taskbar is not on the bottom, you can occasionally have some minor problems with Auto hide. Because Windows applications don't adjust the size of the window if they don't see the Taskbar, when you unhide the Taskbar, you can cover part of the window. Covering the status bar (which is what happens if the Taskbar is on the bottom) is less annoying than covering the title bar, which is where you go to use the minimize and close buttons. Covering either side of the application window can get in the way of working with the application window.

The Taskbar Clock

By default, Windows NT 4 places a digital clock on the right side of your Taskbar. If you place your pointer on the clock, a tooltip appears to show you the date.

Adjust the Date or Time

You can change the date and time, if necessary, by double-clicking on the clock to display the Date/Time Properties dialog box (see fig. 7.6). You can also right-click on the clock and choose Adjust Date/Time from the shortcut menu, but double-clicking is faster and easier.

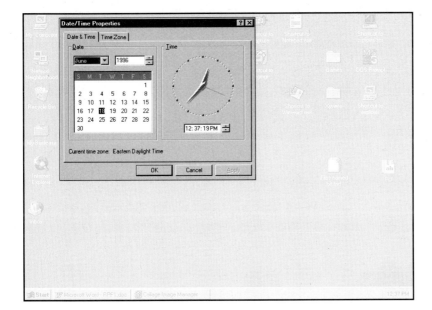

Figure 7.6

You can change the date or time that displays on the Taskbar clock by entering values or clicking the spin boxes in the Date/Time Properties dialog box.

Select the Time Zone tab to change the time zone (probably not necessary unless you're using a portable). You can also select or deselect Automatically Adjust Clock for daylight saving changes.

> **Caution** If you are dual booting between Windows NT 4 and Windows 95, only select the daylight saving option for one of them. Otherwise, they will both change your system clock on the appropriate date and you will be an hour ahead or behind.

Change the Time Format

The format for the time display may affect more than just the Taskbar clock. Some data file formats in which you insert the current time will follow the format you've configured (some software applications have a configuration option you can use when inserting time stamps). This is true for word processing documents that permit you to insert the time and date in the text and database applications, in which there are fields for the current record indicating the time and date of changes to the record.

Objective B.5

To change the format of the time display, perform the following steps:

1. Open the Start menu and choose Settings, Control Panel.

2. Open the Regional Settings Properties dialog box and select the Time tab (see fig. 7.7).

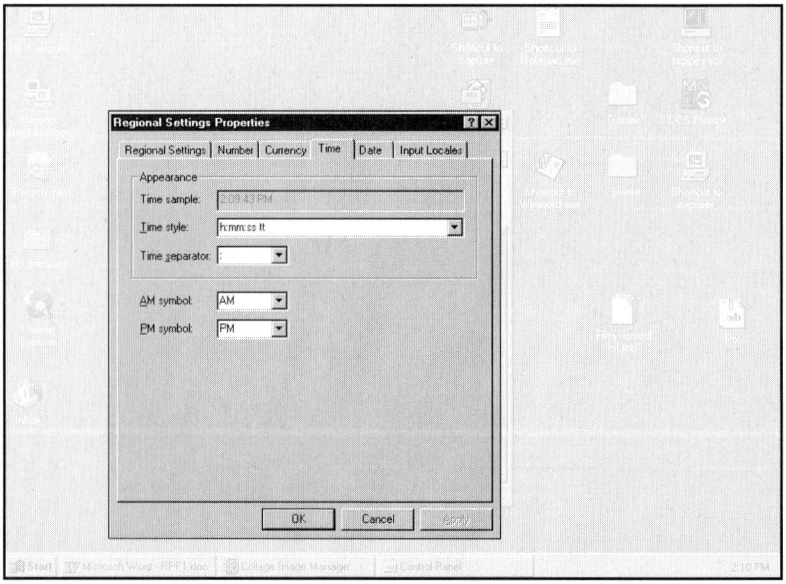

Figure 7.7

You can design your own format for the time display on your Taskbar clock and in documents.

3. Click the arrow to the right of the Time Style field to choose a new format for the time display. There are really only two format choices—whether the hour is two digits or one (if you choose two digits, a leading zero is put in single-digit hours). The format choices that begin with a capital letter indicate the same formats, but use military time (a 24-hour clock).

4. The Time Separator field displays only a colon (:) for choices, but you can enter any character you want, such as a dash, a period, or a couple of spaces.

5. The AM Symbol and PM Symbol fields do not offer additional choices, but you can enter the characters you want to use, such as am, pm, a, p, A, P, or any other preference.

6. Choose OK when you have finished making your selections. The changes take effect immediately.

Change the Date Format

Similarly, you can change how dates display by selecting the Date tab of the Regional Settings Properties dialog box (see fig. 7.8).

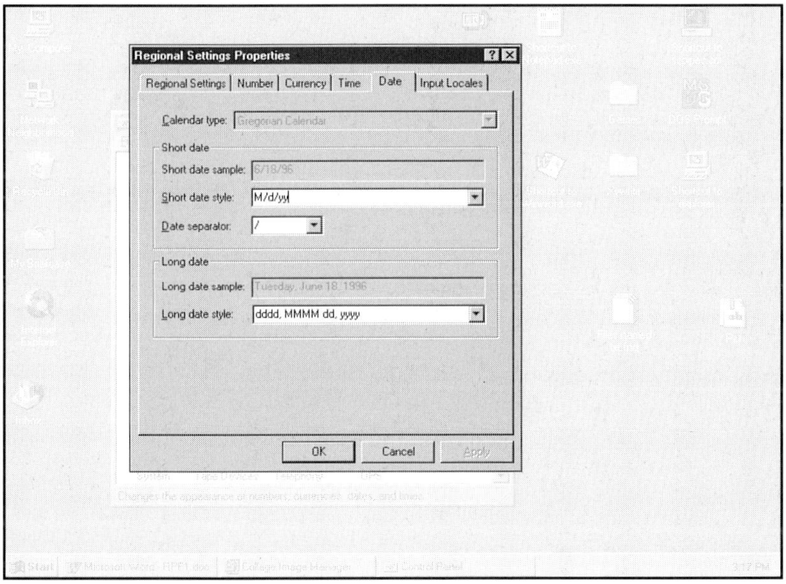

Figure 7.8

There are two different types of date formats, a short one that uses numbers and a long one that includes words.

Click the arrows to the right of the appropriate fields and choose the formats you prefer.

Change the Size of the Taskbar

If you frequently have numerous application windows open, the Taskbar gets crowded (see fig. 7.9). More important, the buttons get smaller and smaller; eventually, the only way to tell which button you want to click on for task switching is to hold the pointer over each button in order to see the complete title. This undoes all the productivity and efficiency of Taskbar switching. The solution is to make the Taskbar larger so buttons don't shrink beyond your ability to read them.

Figure 7.9

When you are seriously multitasking, the Taskbar can become almost useless—you can't tell what's what in order to switch tasks quickly.

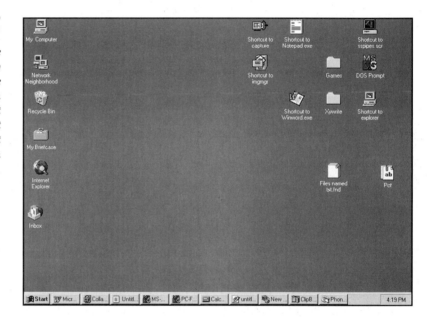

To enlarge the Taskbar, move the mouse pointer to the inside edge (the top, if the Taskbar is on the bottom; the left, if the Taskbar is on the right, and so on). When the pointer changes to a double-headed arrow, drag the edge until the Taskbar is a size that works for you.

The increment of change in the size of the Taskbar isn't dependent on how steady you are with the mouse—as you drag the edge, the Taskbar resizes itself in increments equal to the height of the buttons (if the Taskbar is on the bottom or top of the screen) or the width of the buttons (if the Taskbar is on either side of the screen).

To see how much difference it can make, look at figure 7.10, which shows a Taskbar that has been enlarged by one button size. Figure 7.11 shows the same Taskbar that has been enlarged by two button sizes. Most of the time, you won't be multitasking to this extent, but for those occasions when you have a lot of application windows open, you should realize the difference a large Taskbar can make.

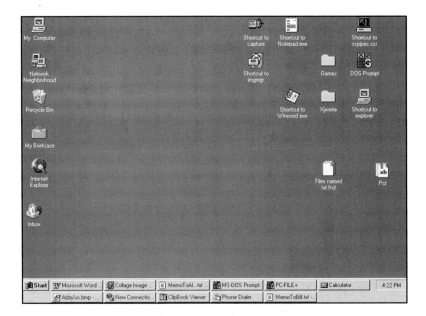

Figure 7.10

Enlarging a crowded Taskbar by the size of one button means seeing either the name of the software or the name of the current document (depending on how it's presented).

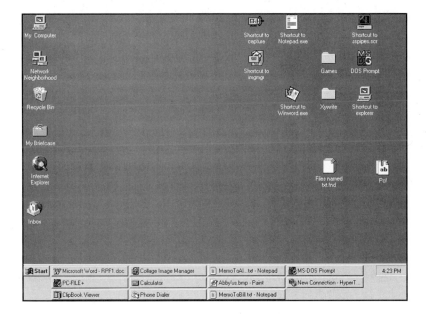

Figure 7.11

You get the most productive use of the Taskbar by enlarging it enough to see all the information on the buttons.

Understanding Task Manager

Task Manager is an application included with Windows NT 4 that monitors every program and process that is running on your computer. It is most useful when there is a problem: an application seems "stuck;" the system suddenly crawls; an application doesn't want to close; or any other mysterious, annoying problem that strikes computers every once in a while.

Even if you're not trying to resolve a difficulty, you can satisfy your curiosity about how your system works, learn what goes on behind the scenes, and even determine the resource usage of your currently open applications with Task Manager. In addition, you can make changes to the way processes and applications run in order to optimize your system's performance.

This section discusses the basic Task Manager operations, focusing on those that are similar to or enhance the functions available with the Taskbar. For information about using Task Manager to optimize your system, refer to Chapter 28, "Optimizing Performance."

Task Manager is placed in your Windows NT system root directory or in the System32 subdirectory (Taskman.exe). To open it quickly, you can right-click on any blank spot on the Taskbar and choose Task Manager. The Task Manager window looks like a dialog box with three tabs (see fig. 7.12). When the program opens, the Applications tab is in the foreground.

Figure 7.12

All the current running tasks are listed on the Task Manager Applications tab.

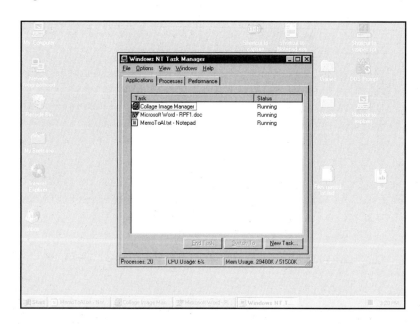

Task Manager doesn't present an application window; it displays itself in the same format as a Properties dialog box, with tabs for different tasks.

The Applications tab shows the status of the current tasks (Task Manager uses the terms task and program interchangeably). You can perform several operations from this tab:

◆ **End Task.** Choose this option to shut down the selected application when it is no longer working properly or seems frozen. If possible, you will be given an opportunity to save any changes to your document since the last time you saved. Depending on the problem (and whether the program responds properly), you may have to close down the application without saving data.

◆ **Switch To.** Choose this option to move to the selected task and put its window in the foreground.

◆ **New Task.** Choose this option to open a program not currently running. Enter the path and file name of an application you want to start and choose OK (see fig. 7.13). Browse your system to find the program if you don't know the name of the executable file.

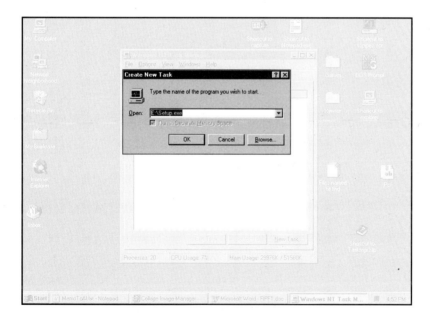

Figure 7.13

The Create New Task dialog box looks and behaves just like the Run dialog box you access by choosing Run from the Start menu.

| Tip | The Create New Task dialog box is actually the Run dialog box (with a different title); if you click on the arrow to the right of the Open field, you will see the history of programs you launched from Run on the Start menu. |

Manipulate the Applications

You can perform many of the same functions available on the Taskbar from the Task Manager dialog box. Right-click on any application in the Task list to see a shortcut menu (see fig. 7.14).

Figure 7.14

Use an application's shortcut menu to accomplish many of the same tasks provided by the Taskbar.

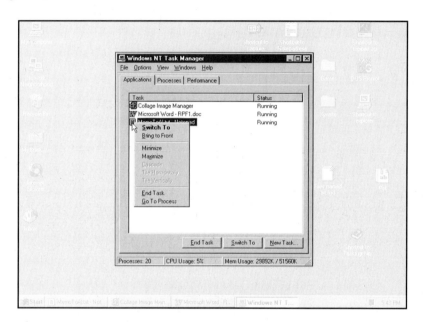

There is one choice on the shortcut menu that isn't found anywhere else—Go To Process. Choose this to move to the Processes tab. On this tab, the process connected to the selected application is highlighted so that you can view the effect of that process on your system.

> **Note** More information on interpreting and manipulating the data on the Processes tab and the Performance tab is found in Chapter 28.

Change the View

You can change the way you view the programs on the Applications tab. By default, the Task list shows small icons, with titles next to the icons (refer to fig. 7.12). A Status column (indicating the current status of a program, which means whether or not it is currently running) displays if you select Details from the View menu. You can choose one of these options from the View menu:

◆ **Large Icons.** Presents each application as an icon with a title beneath the icon (the title is the same text that appears on the application's Taskbar button).

◆ **Small Icons.** Presents each application with a small icon and a title, similar to the Details view, but without the Status column.

| Note | The choices in the menu options vary depending on the tab you are currently viewing. See Chapter 28 for more information on using the power tools in Task Manager. |

Using the Start Menu

Clicking on the Start button brings up the Start menu, the basic launch pad for everything you want to do in Windows NT 4 (see fig. 7.15).

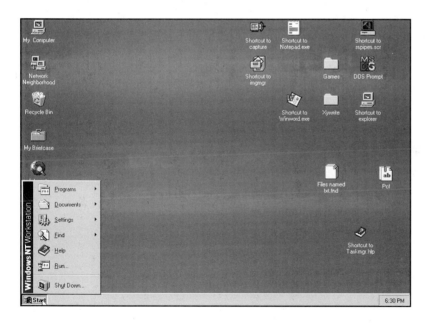

Figure 7.15

The default Start menu has seven items on it— yours may have more, depending on the software you have installed.

The Start menu replaces the Program Manager in previous versions of Windows. It is a lot faster and a great deal easier to use. The items on the Startup menu are the following:

◆ Shut Down

◆ Run

◆ Help

◆ Find

◆ Settings

◆ Documents

◆ Programs

You can use the System Policy Editor to reduce the amount of access users have to the items on the Start menu. You can also make entries directly into the Registry of a computer to reduce that access (covered in this section).

Shut Down

The first item on the Start menu is Shut Down (users generally start moving from the bottom of the menu to the top because the Start button is at the bottom). You must shut down Windows NT before turning off your computer, or else you take a risk that important system files won't be updated correctly. When you choose this menu item, the Shut Down Windows dialog box appears (see fig. 7.16).

Figure 7.16

The Shut Down Windows dialog box lets you select the type of shut down you want.

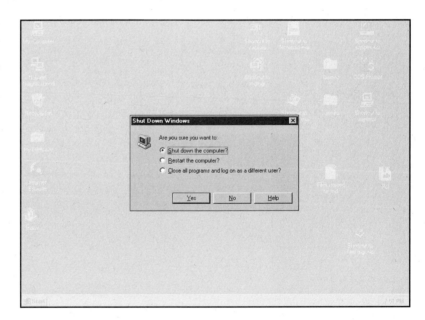

The Shut Down Windows dialog box offers three choices:

◆ **Shut Down the Computer.** Choose this option when you want to turn off your computer. This option causes the system to write all data in memory to the hard drive and update the Registry files with any configuration changes. When the work is done, a message appears telling you it is safe to turn off your computer.

◆ **Restart the Computer.** Choosing this option causes the system to perform the same file saves as a shut down, without notifying you when it is safe to turn off the computer. The system restarts the computer.

◆ **Close All Programs and Log On as a Different User.** Choosing this option causes the system to perform the same file saves as a shut down. Then the Begin Logon dialog box appears. Press Ctrl+Alt+Delete to log on and see the Logon Information dialog box, where you can log on as a different user. There is no rebooting of the system with this choice.

Restricting Shut Down

You can eliminate the Shut Down choice from a user's Start menu by changing the Registry. The user will still be able to shut down or restart the computer by accessing that option from the Logon dialog box (but the Log On as a Different User Option is not available on the Logon dialog box).

**Objective
G.6**

To perform this, or any of the Registry changes discussed, be sure to back up the Registry first. For Registry entries that restrict user access, note that the Registry entry you'll add is a negative, such as NoRun or NoClose. The value for each of these restrictive entries is Boolean, and therefore 1 (On) enforces the policy and 0 (Off) gives access back to the user.

As soon as you make the change, it takes effect (the restriction is added to the user's environment). If you remove the restriction, you have to reboot to have that change take effect (Windows NT cannot remove the restriction from the environment).

To restrict user access to the Shut Down item on the Start menu by modifying the Registry, follow these steps:

1. Open Regedit and expand the HKEY_CURRENT_USER key. Move through the key to \Software\Microsoft\Windows\CurrentVersion\Policies\Explorer.

2. Right-click on the right pane to see the menu choice New (it's the only choice on the shortcut menu).

3. Choose DWORD Value from the submenu (see fig. 7.17).

4. When the new value appears, replace the default title (New Value #1) with **NoClose**. Press Enter to complete the editing process.

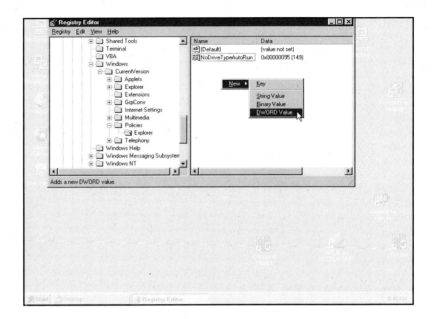

Figure 7.17

You have to know the type of value for any entry you want to add—this function requires a DWORD Value.

5. Double-click the new value entry and specify 1 as the Value data in the Value dialog box (see fig. 7.18). Then choose OK.

6. Close Regedit.

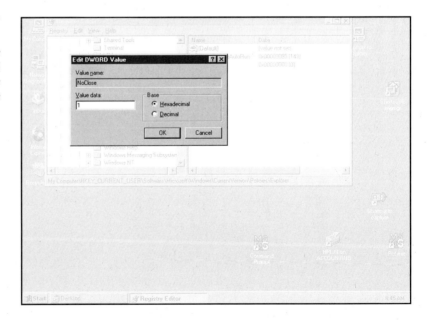

Figure 7.18

By default, the value is 0, and you must change it to 1 to turn the new setting on.

You do not have to reboot to have this Registry setting take effect. When this user clicks the Shut Down button on the Start menu, an informational dialog box displays (see fig. 7.19).

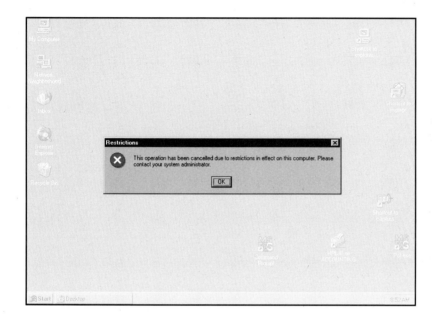

Figure 7.19

This user no longer has access to the options on the Shut Down dialog box.

To remove the restriction, go back into the Registry and delete this value. You do have to reboot to have the removal take effect.

Run

You can start an application by choosing Run from the Start menu, and then entering the name of the executable file in the Open field of the Run dialog box (see fig. 7.20).

If you're not sure of the location or name (or both) of the program you want to launch, perform the following steps:

1. Choose Browse to use the Browse dialog box to search your drives.

2. When you find the appropriate file, double-click on it (or select it and choose Open), which places the file name in the Open field of the Run dialog box.

3. Choose OK in the Run dialog box to start the application.

Figure 7.20

Use the Run dialog box to launch software applications.

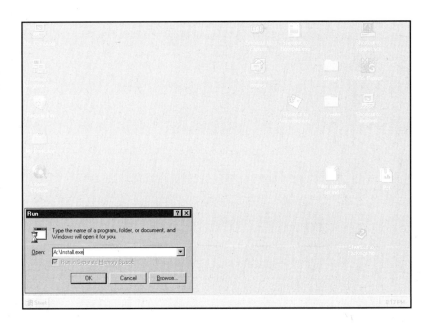

You can invoke a few functions to make the Run dialog box even more useful. They include the following:

◆ **Repeat a previous command.** Click on the down arrow to the right of the Open field to see a history of commands you have entered. If you find the same command you currently need, select it to avoid having to re-enter it. This is extremely useful for installing software, which almost always requires the same command (for example, x:\setup.exe, where x represents your CD-ROM, or a:\setup.exe for those applications that arrive on disks).

◆ **Open a document file.** Enter the path and file name of a document file in the Open field to launch the software that created it, with that file in the software window ready for editing.

Tip
If you are using the Run dialog box to open a document file and you have to use Browse to find it, don't forget to change the Files of type field to All Files. If you leave the selection at the default, Programs, you won't see data files in the Browse dialog box.

◆ **Open a folder.** Enter the name of a folder to open a folder window on the desktop. You don't need to enter the backslash (unless you're opening a subfolder, in which case you must put a backslash before the subfolder name).

◆ **Connect to another computer.** Enter the name of any computer on your network to open a folder that displays the contents of that computer. Use the UNC (place two backslash characters (\\) in front of the computer name and the share name).

◆ **Open a file on another computer.** You can open a file on a connected computer by specifying the computer name and share name, as described in the preceding paragraph, and then adding the path and file name.

> **Tip**
>
> Share names that contain spaces cannot be found by Run. You can first map the drive (by using the Map Network Drive button on the Explorer toolbar) and then enter the mapped drive letter—followed by a colon—in the Open box.

Restricting Run

You can use the Registry to eliminate the Run command from the Start menu. Follow the steps in the earlier section "Restricting Shut Down" and name the DWORD entry **NoRun**. A value of 1 hides the Run command.

Help

Click on Help to launch the Windows NT help files. For information on using the Help system, see Chapter 4, "Getting Help."

Find

Choosing Find on the Start menu activates a submenu with the following choices:

◆ Files or Folders

◆ Computer

If you choose Files or Folders, the Find dialog box appears and you can enter specifications to establish the search criteria. See Chapter 6, "Using the Desktop," for more information on using Find.

When you opt to search for a computer, the Find: Computer dialog box appears (see fig. 7.21). Enter the name (or part of the name) of the computer you want to locate. (You do not have to precede the name with two backslash characters.)

When the computer has been located, it is listed in a box that displays below the Find dialog box. Right-click on it to bring up the shortcut menu, from which you can choose to Open (open a folder window similar to the way My Computer displays the contents of a drive) or Explore (open an Explorer window) the computer.

Figure 7.21

If you know the name of the computer you want to access, use the Find: Computer search feature.

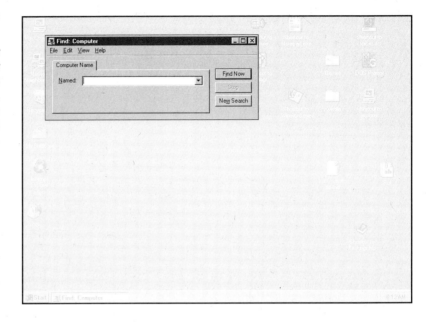

Caution When opening or exploring another computer, you can only see those objects that have been marked for sharing.

If you do not know the name of the computer (or at least a partial name), you cannot use the Find feature to find it. Open Network Neighborhood to have the system search along the cable to find connected computers. More information on using Network Neighborhood is found in Chapter 8, "Using the Default Desktop Icons."

Restricting Find

If you do not want a user to have access to the Find functions you can remove the Find option from the Start menu through the Registry. Again, follow the steps in the earlier section "Restricting Shut Down," and name the DWORD value **NoFind**. A value of 1 removes the Find command.

Settings

Pause your pointer on Settings on the Start menu to see a submenu that lists the main setting functions for Windows NT:

◆ Control Panel

◆ Printers

◆ Taskbar

Information about the various features in the Control Panel is found in Chapters 11 through 16, and information about setting up printers is found in Chapter 17, "Printing."

Restricting Access to Settings

You can restrict a user's access to all or some of the options in the Settings choices with the Registry. In fact, for some users this restriction is highly desirable (every company has at least one user with just enough knowledge to be dangerous).

Use the directions included in the earlier section "Restricting Shut Down," for changing the Registry and follow these guidelines:

◆ Use the DWORD value NoSetFolders (with a value of 1) to remove the Control Panel and Printers choices from the Settings choice on the Start menu.

◆ Use the DWORD value NoSetTaskbar (with a value of 1) to remove the Taskbar settings choice from the Start menu. This value also prevents the user from configuring the Taskbar by right-clicking on the Taskbar and choosing Properties.

Tip Removing access to the Taskbar settings also prevents users from changing the Start menu because the Start menu configuration options are on the Taskbar Properties dialog box. However, users can continue to drag objects to the Start button in order to place those items on the top of the menu.

Documents

One of the best built-in shortcuts in your Windows NT system is the Documents option of the Start menu. When you choose this option, the last 15 documents you worked on are listed, and you can click on the one you want to return to (see fig. 7.22). The appropriate software launches and the document is in the application window, ready for you to work on.

Note Not every document you create or edit makes it to the Documents list. The application that created or saved the document has to be able to send a message to Windows NT so that the Documents feature can grab the name and track the association with the application. Only application software that registers extensions with Windows NT 4 will send the appropriate information. You can force additional document types to make it to the Documents list by adding the file type to the system via Explorer or My Computer (see Chapter 6 to learn how to do that), or by registering them directly in the Registry (that process is explained later in this section).

continues

On the other hand, regardless of the application used to create or edit the document, if you started the document at any point from Explorer or from a folder window, that document will make it to the Documents list. The easiest way to accomplish this is to right-click on the document while you're in Explorer, and then choose Open from its shortcut menu.

Figure 7.22

To pick up where you left off, choose a document and go right back to work on it.

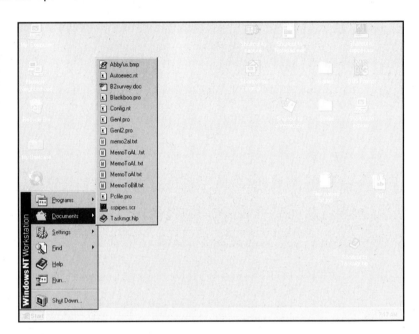

Clear the Documents List

You can clear the Documents list entirely or remove specific documents. Then, as you work, the list begins compiling again. This makes the list more useful because it contains only a short listing of your most recent documents.

To clear the entire list, right-click on a blank spot on the Taskbar and choose Properties to bring up the Taskbar Properties dialog box. Select the Start Menu Programs tab and choose Clear.

To clear specific documents from the list, perform the following steps:

1. Open Explorer. Be sure that Explorer is configured to Show all files, including hidden files and folders (choose View, Options from the menu bar).

2. Move to the folder that holds your Windows NT software and click on the plus sign to the left of the folder.

3. From the subfolders that appear, click on the plus sign to the left of the Profiles folder.

4. Find your profile subfolder (or the subfolder you want to work on if you are administering this computer) and click on its plus sign.

5. From the subfolders that appear, select the Recent folder. The contents of the Documents list appear in the Contents pane (see fig. 7.23).

6. Delete the documents you want to remove from the list. Close Explorer.

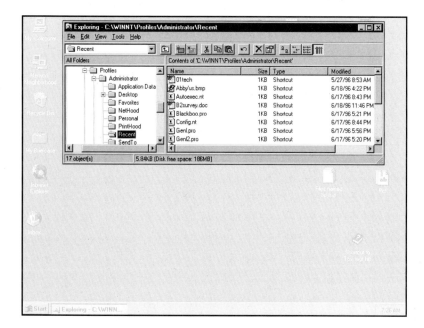

Figure 7.23

Delete the documents you want to remove from the Documents list on the Start menu.

Create a Shortcut for Clearing Documents

If you find it necessary or convenient to perform this task frequently, you can make the process easier by using the following steps:

1. Follow the preceding steps to get to your Recent folder.

2. Right-drag the Recent folder to the desktop. When you release the mouse, a shortcut menu appears (see fig. 7.24).

3. Choose Create Shortcut(s) Here; then close Explorer.

Hereafter, when you want to clear or individually delete the items on the Documents list, just open the folder and perform the necessary steps.

Figure 7.24

When you right-drag objects, you see a menu of choices for the way you want to treat the object—in this case, create a shortcut.

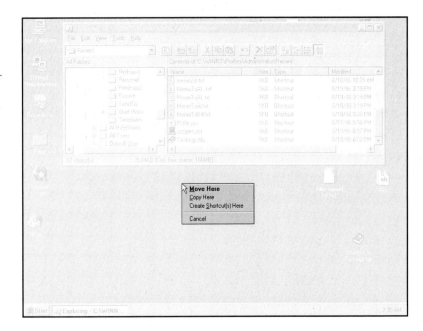

Adding Document Types to the Document List

You can use the Registry to establish additional document types that you want displayed on the Documents list. This is useful for file extensions that are not associated with applications and are not registered through application software (or by your own configuration of a new file type, as explained in Chapter 6).

This is particularly useful for files that are saved as the result of internally written software. For example, if you do database development for a variety of company needs and processes, you can name the reports or other output using extensions you invent for the purpose. For the users who frequently have to work with these files, having them available on the Document list is an aid to productivity.

Objective G.6

To add an extension to the Document list via the Registry, follow these steps:

1. Open Regedit and expand HKEY_CURRENT_USER.

2. Move to the subkey \Software\Microsoft\Windows NT\CurrentVersion\Windows.

3. Double-click the Documents entry in the right pane.

4. In the Edit String dialog box, enter the file extensions you want to show on the Documents list. Do not type a period. Separate multiple extensions with a space (see fig. 7.25).

5. Choose OK, then close Regedit.

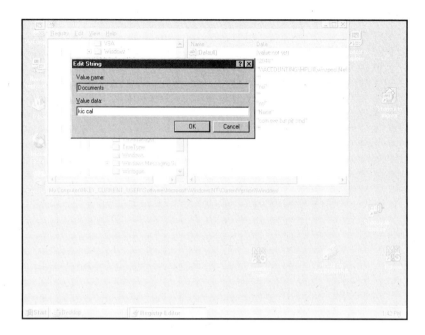

Figure 7.25

Add file extensions to the Registry to display that document type on the Documents list.

Programs

The Start menu item you'll probably access most is Programs. When you choose this menu item, the Programs submenu appears (see fig. 7.26).

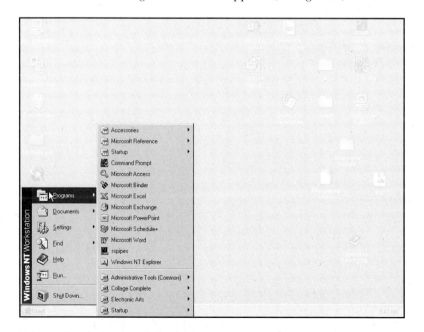

Figure 7.26

Programs and Program groups (listings with arrows) are easy to access from the Programs listing.

To launch a program, click on its listing. If there is an arrow to the right of the listing, that listing is a program group. Place your pointer on it to see the programs in that group.

How Programs Get on the List

There are several ways a program or a program group gets onto the Programs menu:

◆ Upgrading from Windows NT 3.51 moves the old program groups onto the list.

◆ Installing Windows NT 4 places certain system programs and program groups onto the list.

◆ Installing Windows software that establishes a program group or a program item places that program onto the list. (The Setup program should ask which group you want an individual program item placed in.)

If you install software that doesn't make it to the list, you can put it there yourself. In fact, you can completely customize and organize the entire Start menu. That topic is covered next.

Customizing the Start Menu

You can add, remove, and rearrange items on the Start menu quite easily, and you even have choices about how to do it.

Add Items to the Start Menu

The quickest way to add a program to the Start menu is to open Explorer, find the program's executable file, and drag it to the Start button. This places the program at the top of the Start menu (see fig. 7.27). A thin line separates such items from the rest of the Start menu.

 Note Dragging an executable file's icon from Explorer to the Start menu doesn't move it; it creates a shortcut. In fact, all the menu items on the Start menu and Programs menu are shortcuts. The menus themselves are folders; the items on them are shortcuts.

If you want to add a program to the Programs menu, perform the following steps:

1. Choose Settings, Taskbar from the Start menu to bring up the Taskbar Properties dialog box. Select the Start Menu Programs tab (see fig. 7.28).

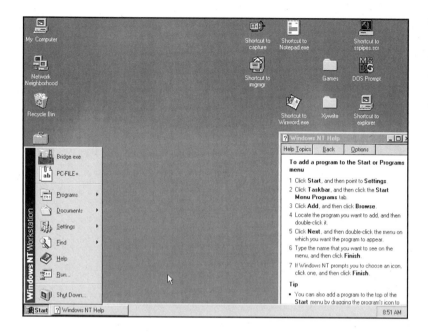

Figure 7.27

Drag a program file to the Start button to place the program at the top of the Start menu; a special section is created at the top of the menu for these added items.

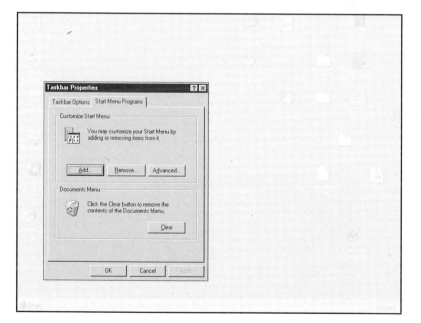

Figure 7.28

Customizing the Start menu begins with the Start Menu Programs tab of the Taskbar Properties dialog box.

2. Choose Add to launch the Create Shortcut Wizard, which will walk you through this process (see fig. 7.29). In the Command Line box, enter the path and executable file name of the program you want to add, or choose Browse to hunt for it.

Figure 7.29

*The Create
Shortcut Wizard
asks for the
location and
name of the file
you want to use to
create a Start
menu shortcut.*

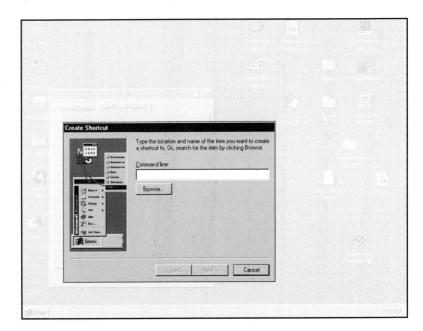

3. After filling in the Command line box, choose Next.

4. Select the Start menu folder in which you want to place the new shortcut (see fig. 7.30) and choose Next.

Figure 7.30

*You can place the
menu item
anywhere on
the Start menu or
its folders—most
of the time, you
should choose the
Programs folder.*

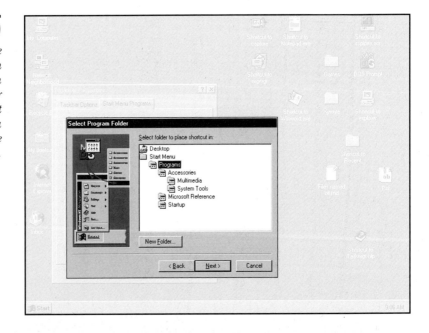

5. If you want, you can create a new folder for the Start menu and place this item in it. The folder is created below the level of the selected folder. It will appear as a listing with an arrow to the right. Choose New Folder, and then enter a name for it. Then choose Next.

6. Select a name for the shortcut item, and then choose Finish. The item is on the Start menu, in the program group you selected.

Moving and Adding Document Items

You are not restricted to moving program files onto the Start menu or its program groups. You can also move document file shortcuts. If you drag the document file to the Start button, it is placed at the top of the Start menu, which might be a useful way to handle boiler-plate documents you use frequently.

If you use the Start Menu Programs tab of the Taskbar Properties dialog box to add document items, you should probably create a program group for them during the Create Shortcut process. This is also useful for accessing boiler-plate documents you tend to return to frequently.

The difference between this method of accessing documents easily and using the Documents listing in the Start menu is that this procedure creates a permanent, unchanging list.

Remove Items from the Start Menu

You can remove an item from the Programs menu of the Start menu more easily than adding one. The items that can be removed include program listings, document listings, and program group folders (you cannot remove the Programs folder itself). To remove items, perform the following steps:

1. Choose Settings, Taskbar from the Start menu and select the Start Menu Programs tab of the Taskbar Properties dialog box.

2. Choose Remove to bring up the Remove Shortcuts/Folders dialog box (see fig. 7.31).

3. If necessary, use the plus sign to move through the appropriate menu structure to find the item you want to remove. Select it, and then choose Remove. You will be asked to confirm the removal (the item is sent to the Recycle bin).

4. Choose Close to return to the Taskbar Properties dialog box, and then choose OK to end the process.

Figure 7.31

Move through the folders and items to find the listing you want to remove from the Programs menu.

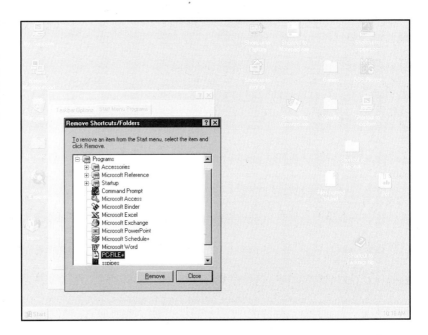

Use the Advanced Feature for Quick Add/Remove

If you choose Advanced from the Start Menu Programs tab of the Taskbar Properties dialog box, you can perform additions and deletions to the Start menu rather quickly, especially if you are comfortable working in Explorer.

When you choose Advanced, Explorer is launched and positioned so that the Start menu under your profile folder is selected in the Folders pane, and the Programs folder is displayed in the Contents pane. (Actually, although the Start Menu folder is selected and the icon is of an opened folder, it is not highlighted, so it's not found at a glance.) To work with the Start menu use one of the following methods:

◆ Use the plus sign to move through the Start menu folders.

◆ To add an item, select the parent folder and then choose New, Folder or New, Shortcut from the File menu (a new folder is a new program group).

◆ To delete an item, select it and press Delete.

Close Explorer, and then close the dialog box to complete the process.

Using the Startup Folder

As with previous versions of Windows, you can configure your system so that certain applications start up as soon as Windows NT is started. You'll find it is quite easy to configure start-up programs with Windows NT 4.

There is a folder named Startup under the Programs folder in your profile (in Explorer). To start software when Windows NT starts, place a program shortcut into that folder.

Add and Remove Startup Items

If you are comfortable navigating through Explorer or folder windows, you can get a shortcut into that Startup folder. There are a couple of quick ways you might want to consider, however.

Right-Drag Program Shortcuts

If the program you want to place in the Startup menu is listed in the Programs menu, perform the following steps:

1. Choose Settings, Taskbar from the Start menu. Then select the Start Menu Programs tab of the Taskbar Properties dialog box.

2. Choose Advanced to bring up Explorer, with the Start menu folder selected in the Folders pane.

3. In the Folders pane, select the Programs folder (directly beneath the Start menu folder) to list its contents in the Contents pane. The Contents pane lists both subfolders and program shortcuts (see fig. 7.32).

4. Right-drag the appropriate program listing up to the Startup folder and release the mouse. Then choose Create Shortcut(s) Here.

Use Create Shortcut

If the program you want to place in the Startup folder is not listed in the Programs menu, follow the steps previously outlined to add a program to the Start menu and be sure to choose the Startup folder as the target.

Regardless of the method you use to get them there, the programs in the Startup folder will launch as soon as Windows NT is started.

Figure 7.32

All the contents of the Programs folder are listed, including the subfolder for Startup programs.

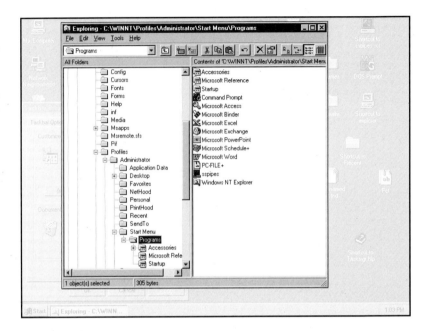

End Note: If a workstation is accessed by multiple users and you always want the same programs to start up automatically (regardless of the logon name), use the Copy and Paste commands available on the shortcut menu to duplicate one Startup folder throughout all the profiles in the system.

The quickest way to do this is to configure one Startup folder with all the programs you desire, and then right-click on that folder and choose Copy. Move to the Programs folder for each profile and right-click on it. Choose Paste. Because the Startup folder already exists, you will see a Confirm Folder Replace dialog box asking you if you want to replace the existing files with the new files. Answer Yes.

Test Your Knowledge

1. Which statements about the Taskbar are correct?

   A. Buttons for open programs look different than buttons for minimized programs.

   B. You can make the Taskbar any size you want it to be.

   C. The clock is always on the Taskbar and cannot be removed.

   D. You can configure the Taskbar by right-clicking on it and selecting properties instead of using the Taskbar entry on the Settings menu.

2. A shortcut to opening the application \WindowsNTRoot\System32\ Taskman.exe is:

3. The Start menu is the Windows NT 4 replacement for which feature in previous Windows versions?

    A. Program Manager

    B. File Manager

    C. Task List

    D. All of the above

4. Which statement(s) about Shut Down are correct?

    A. The Restart the Computer option is available by clicking on Shut Down and by pressing Ctrl+Alt+Del.

    B. The Shut Down the Computer option is available by clicking on Shut Down and by pressing Ctrl+Alt+Del.

    C. The Log On as Another User option is available by clicking on Shut Down and by pressing Ctrl+Alt+Del.

    D. All of the above.

5. User restrictions on menu options are controlled in the _____ section of the Registry.

6. Which statements about Registry restrictions on the Start menu are correct?

    A. Restricting the Run command generates an error message when the user clicks on Run.

    B. Restricting the Run command eliminates the Run choice from the menu.

    C. Restricting the Shut Down command generates an error message when the user clicks on Shut Down.

    D. Restricting the Shut Down command eliminates the Shut Down menu option from the Start menu.

7. Which statement(s) about the Document List is/are correct?

    A. It displays documents from software that registers file types during the software installation process.

    B. It displays documents from software that you register yourself by adding the software to the Registry.

    C. It displays documents from software that is launched from Explorer.

    D. It displays documents from software that is launched from the command line with a /d parameter.

Test Your Knowledge Answers

1. A,D
2. Right-click on the Taskbar
3. A
4. A,B
5. HKEY_CURRENT_USER
6. B,C
7. A,C

Chapter Snapshot

When you see the Windows NT 4 screen for the first time, you notice icons on the left side of the desktop. There could be three icons, or as many as six, depending on the installation decisions you made. This chapter covers the following default icons for the vast majority of Windows NT 4 installations:

Windows NT
Workstation 4

CHAPTER 8

Using the Default Desktop Icons

T he default icons that appear on your Windows NT 4 desktop contain some of the most powerful, and most used, functions and features in your Windows NT system. My Computer, the Recycle Bin, and My Briefcase are installed automatically on every Windows NT 4 desktop. If you are in an office and your computer is part of a network, the Network Neighborhood icon was also installed automatically (it showed up as a result of the installation of a network adapter). This chapter covers each of these default desktop icons.

Using My Computer

Although the My Computer icon doesn't look like a folder, it is. When you open it, the resulting display is a folder window just like all other folder windows (see fig. 8.1). This chapter discusses the drives that are shown in My Computer. The other folders (Printers, Control Panel, and Dial-Up Networking) are covered in various chapters throughout this book. My Computer enables you to browse and navigate through your computer, looking at and manipulating the folders and files.

Figure 8.1

The folder view of My Computer shows all the drives on your computer, as well as some special folders.

Navigate Your System with My Computer

Each of the drive icons in the My Computer window is really a folder. Open one to see a folder view of its contents. The drive folder window contains folder icons and file icons (see fig 8.2).

As you move through the contents of a drive, each folder icon can be opened to display its own window, showing the folder's contents. You can continue to open folder icons to navigate through folders, subfolders of folders, and subfolders of subfolders (see fig. 8.3).

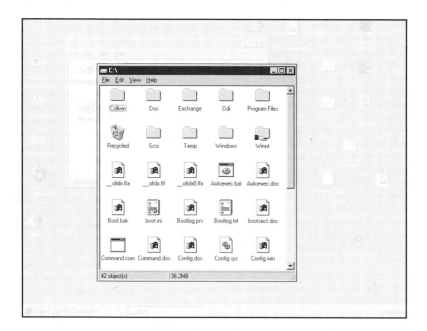

Figure 8.2

Open the C drive icon to see its contents.

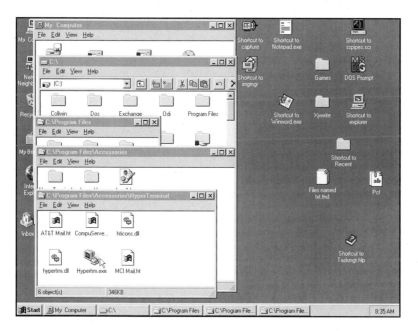

Figure 8.3

Your navigation steps can be traced on the folder title bars as you open folders to get to a target.

Navigating through the open folders is quite simple:

◆ To close a folder and move back to the previous folder, click the Close button.

◆ To move back to the previous folder and put it in the foreground, press Backspace. Each time you press the Backspace key, you move back one folder, working your way back toward the original folder.

◆ Move directly to any folder by clicking on its title bar.

◆ Close a folder and all its parent folders by holding down the Shift key while you click on the folder's close button.

> **Tip**   By default, the toolbar is not displayed on the My Computer window, nor on any windows you open from My Computer. Choosing View, Toolbar lets you move back to the previous folder by clicking the Up One Level button on the toolbar.

Find Files with My Computer

You can search for any files or folders with My Computer, using the Windows NT Find feature. With any folder you've opened in the foreground, press F3. The Find dialog box opens, prepared to start the search at the current folder (see fig. 8.4). For detailed information on using Find, see Chapter 6, "Using the Desktop."

Figure 8.4

Press F3 to search for files or folders, starting with the current folder.

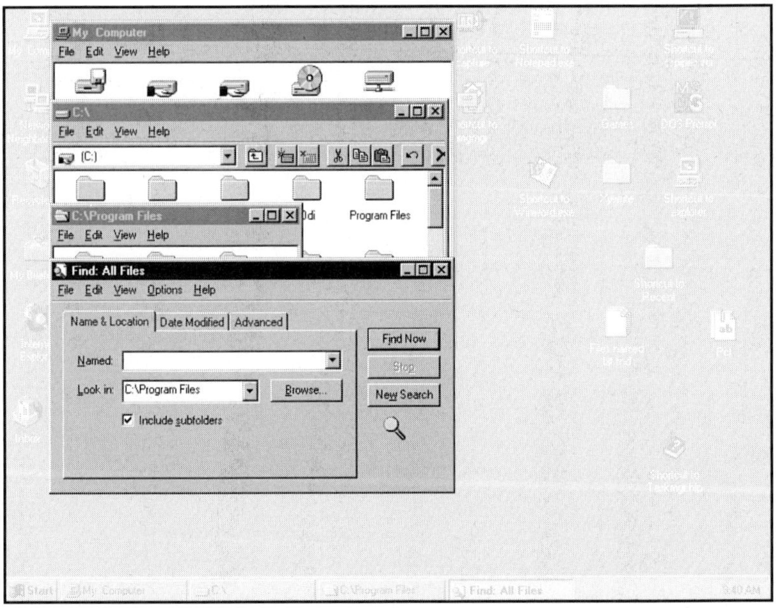

When you reach a program file, double-click on it to launch its application. You can also double-click on a document file to open the application used to create it and have that document file in the application window ready for editing.

Options for Opening Folder Windows

You can change the way windows open and the way they look to make working with My Computer suitable for the way you want to manage your system.

The default behavior for using My Computer is to open a separate, new window in addition to the existing window(s) every time you double-click on a folder.

Another option is to use the same window space each time you double-click on a folder, having the new window replace the old one. To change the behavior of opening folders, choose View, Options to bring up the Options dialog box (see fig. 8.5).

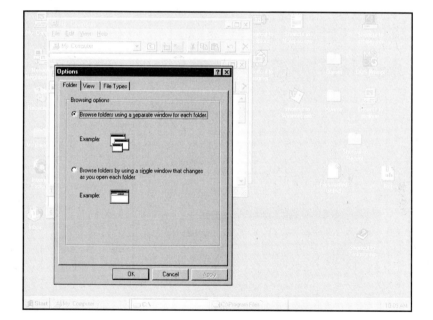

Figure 8.5

Change the way My Computer opens successive folders on the Folder tab of the Options dialog box.

| **Tip** | Any folder window's behavior can be switched at any time, regardless of the option you choose for opening windows. As you open windows to move down through your drive's folders and subfolders, find a folder that you want to open differently, and hold down the Ctrl key while you double-click. If your option is set for multiple windows, the window for that folder replaces its parent. If your option is set for replacing windows, the window for that folder is displayed in addition to any open windows. |

There are good arguments for using either of the choices for opening new windows. If you use multiple windows, you can move backward a few levels and laterally very easily. This is helpful if you are four folder levels down and want to see folders on the second level, because you just need to move to that window and select a different third and fourth level. (You can back up to the previous window, regardless of whether you're using multiple windows or replacing windows, by using the Backspace key.)

On the other hand, using multiple windows can make your desktop crowded and cluttered. The operating system doesn't always cascade them cleanly. Also, because windows are often different sizes (depending on the contents), new windows can completely obliterate previous ones. Consequently, the convenience of multiple windows isn't quite what it could (and should) be.

Tip

If you take the trouble to size and cascade the windows neatly as you open them, My Computer remembers the arrangement. The next time you browse, opening item after item, the windows are automatically arranged at the size and placement that you have established.

Configure the Files That Display

Move to the View tab of the Options dialog box to configure the elements that display when you open a folder (see fig. 8.6). You can decide whether you want to see hidden files, file extensions, and the full path of any window.

Figure 8.6

Configure the display of files and the path with the View tab of the Options dialog box.

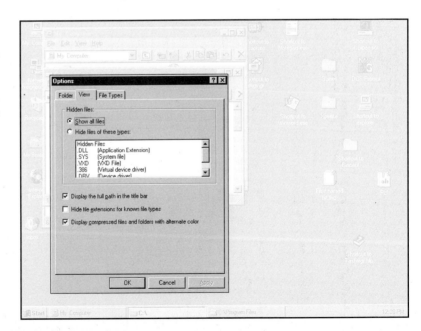

If you opt to hide the file extensions for known file types, check the File Types tab to see what those known types are. This option makes the display of file names a bit less cluttered, but it can be frustrating to look at a file name without being aware of the file type (what you really have to understand is the icon—the File Types tab lists the icons for each known file type).

Configure the Display of Items

The default display of items in a folder window consists of large icons, with the name beneath the icon. You can change the way the items display by right-clicking on a blank spot in the window and choosing View from the shortcut menu that appears (or you can choose View from the menu bar). The following three choices are available in addition to the default choice of large icons:

◆ **Small Icons.** The icon is small, and the folder or file name appears to its right. The items are sorted in rows, reading from left to right.

◆ **List.** The icon is small, and the folder or file name appears to the right of the icon. The items are sorted in columns, reading from top to bottom.

◆ **Details.** The items are listed in a display that resembles the DOS DIR display format, with information about each item (see fig. 8.7). The information includes size (for files), type of item, last modified date, and the attributes. You can click on any column title to sort the items according to the details for that column and then click again to reverse the sorting scheme from ascending to descending.

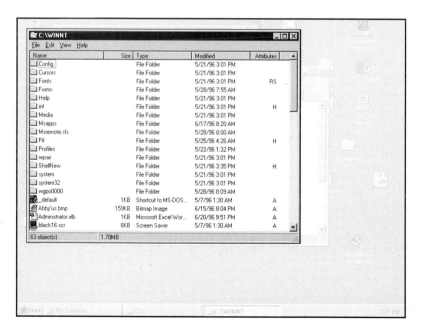

Figure 8.7

The Details view of the items in a window. You can change the column widths by dragging the vertical bars on the column title bar.

For Large Icons, Small Icons, and List, you can choose the sorting scheme by choosing Arrange Icons from the shortcut menu or the View menu. The choices are Name, Type, Size, or Date, except for the main My Computer window, which offers to sort by Drive Letter, Type, Size, or Free Space.

Folder Windows in My Computer

There are some problems with the way NT handles folder windows in My Computer.

Frequently, after neatly arranging a window, getting it just the way you like it, and making all the icons easy to access, it is messy and hard to use the next time you open it. Sometimes the window has changed its size. If you stick to the Details view, this doesn't happen.

Unfortunately, there is no parent-child inheritance for the configuration of the display. You have to go to each window and reset the options. This is true for the icon size, the display of the toolbar, and the sorting of icons.

However, one trick works to force other windows to appear the way you configure a folder window, as long as those windows have never been opened. Configure any folder window for the icon size and whether or not you want to have the toolbar displayed. Then hold down the Ctrl key and click the Close button. Any folder window you have ever accessed through My Computer duplicates that scheme when you open it. Any folder window that has been opened before you performed this action needs to be reconfigured.

Apparently, this action causes information to be written to the Registry and to be remembered.

Incidentally, the system default for folder windows is large icons, no toolbar, and sort by name.

Regardless of the configuration for displaying the items in a folder window, the status bar provides information about the folder you are viewing; press F5 to refresh the window.

Manipulate the Items

You can perform file and folder maintenance—including creating, copying, moving, renaming, and deleting them—from any folder window.

Tip As you read about the manipulation you can perform on files and folders in the following sections, remember that Windows NT 4 provides a way to undo any action you take. If you accidentally copy, move, rename, or delete an item, right-click a blank spot in the folder window in which you were working. From the shortcut menu, choose to undo the last action.

Create a New Item

If you need a new folder (actually a subfolder) when you are in a folder window, you can create one on the spot. The fastest way to do this is to right-click on a blank spot in the folder window and choose New from the shortcut menu that appears. Then choose Folder from the cascading menu (see fig. 8.8). You can also create files and shortcuts in the same manner. Information about creating and using shortcuts is found in Chapter 10, "Using Shortcuts."

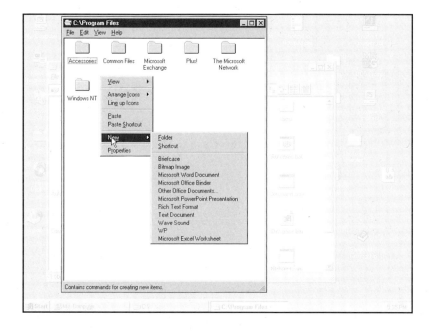

Figure 8.8

You can create a new folder, shortcut, or file in the current folder window.

Copy or Move a File or Folder

There are a number of different ways to move a file or a folder from one folder window to another.

The fastest way to accomplish this is to have both the source and target folder windows open so you can drag the item. After both windows are open, arrange them so you can easily get to both of them.

Note You cannot move or copy the items in the My Computer window (the window you see when you first open My Computer); you can only create shortcuts.

Copy or Move by Right-Dragging

If you drag the file or folder with the right mouse button, and then release the mouse in the target folder, a menu appears with the following options:

◆ Move Here

◆ Copy Here

◆ Create Shortcut(s) Here

◆ Cancel

This is the safest way to move or copy because you are always sure of the action you're performing.

Copy or Move by Left-Dragging

Using the left mouse button to drag and drop is a little more complicated because you don't get a menu choice when you drop the item. A left drag, therefore, is a little more dangerous. If you understand the following rules, however, you should be able to accomplish the move safely:

◆ Dragging an item to another folder window on the same drive moves the item. To copy the item instead of moving it, hold down the Ctrl key before you begin dragging the item.

◆ Dragging an item to the folder window on another drive copies the item. To move the item instead of copying it, hold down the Shift key after you have selected the item (but before you begin dragging it).

◆ Dragging an executable file to another folder window (regardless of the drive) creates a shortcut. To move an item instead of creating a shortcut, hold down the Shift key while you are dragging the file. To copy the item instead of creating a shortcut, hold down the Ctrl key while dragging.

◆ If you change your mind while dragging, either drag the item back to its original location before releasing the mouse button, or press Esc while you are dragging and then release the mouse button.

Tip When you drag an item to a target folder, be sure you don't drop it on an existing folder icon (unless you want to deposit the item in that subfolder). The safe places to drop the item are on a blank space in the folder window, the menu bar, or the toolbar.

Cut or Copy and Paste

You can also use Cut and Paste or Copy and Paste to move or copy items between folders. This works whether or not you have both folders open at the same time.

Select the item you want to cut or copy, and then right-click and choose Cut or Copy from the shortcut menu that appears (you can also select the file and use those same choices from the Edit menu). Open the folder window that you want to use as the target for this operation and right-click on a blank spot; then choose Paste.

To use this method to create a shortcut to a program file in a different folder, choose Copy, and then choose Paste Shortcut in the target folder.

Rename an Item

You can rename an item (don't try to rename items in the main My Computer window; move to the drive folders) quite easily by using one of these methods:

◆ Select the item and press F2.

◆ Right-click on the item and choose Rename from the shortcut menu.

◆ Slowly click twice on the item name, being sure to pause about two seconds between the first and second click (otherwise, you will open the item).

Any of these actions highlights the name in reverse colors and puts a box around the name. This means you are in edit mode.

You can begin typing characters to create a new name, or use the arrow keys to move through the existing name and make minor changes. Press Enter or click on a blank spot in the folder window to end the process.

Delete an Item

Except for the items in the main My Computer window, you can delete files and folders by selecting them and pressing the Del key. You can also right-click on the item and choose Delete from the shortcut menu, or select the item and choose Delete from the File menu.

The files and folders you delete aren't really deleted yet; they are moved to the Recycle Bin (see "Using the Recycle Bin," later in this chapter).

Select Items

You can select multiple items to move, copy, or delete. Then, whatever you do to one, you do to all. If you select five files to move, for example, you can drag one and the rest move too. Also, you can right-click any one of a group of selected items and choose an action from the shortcut menu. Whatever action you choose, it is performed on all selected items.

To select more than one file or folder, click on the first one, hold down the Ctrl key, and click all the other items you want to include in this manipulation.

To select contiguous items, click on the first item, move to the last item you want to select, and hold down the Shift key. When you click on the last item, all the items between the first and last ones are selected.

If icons are displayed with the Details view, it is easy to figure out what contiguous means because you are looking at a vertical list.

The List view displays items in columns, and works the way newspaper columns work. When you select the first item, move down the column, up to the top of the next column, and then down again, until you find the last item in the group you want to select (see fig. 8.9).

Figure 8.9

To select multiple items in List view, follow the snaking columns.

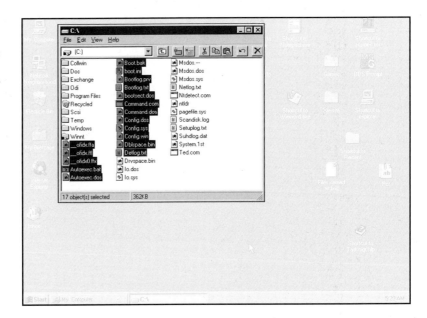

The icon views, both large and small, are a bit less straightforward. In effect, when you select a file and then select the last file, everything in a rectangle between those items is also selected (see fig. 8.10). The easiest way to picture this is to think about how graphics programs work when you draw. As you drag your mouse to the right and down, a rectangular shape appears.

In fact, you can actually draw the rectangle to select multiple items in an icon view. Click the mouse anywhere to the left of the first item and then drag right and down until you've included all the items you need (see fig. 8.11). Release the mouse, and all the items are selected.

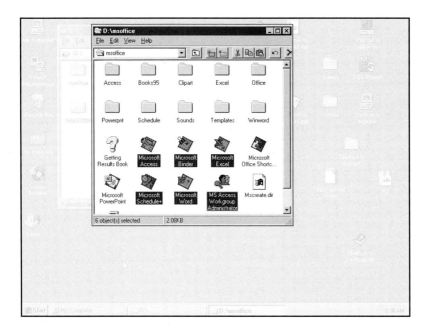

Figure 8.10

Select multiple items by choosing the beginning and end points of a rectangle.

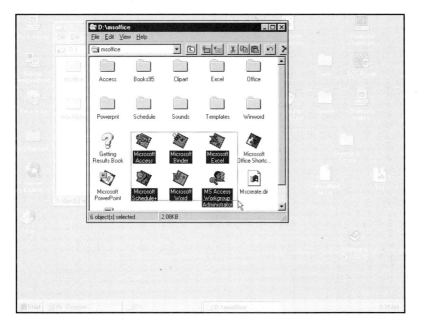

Figure 8.11

Drag and draw a rectangle to grab contiguous items you want to select.

When you need to select multiple items, that are not contiguous, there are some shortcuts that might be helpful:

◆ Ctrl+A selects all the items in a folder window (this is the same as choosing Edit, Select All).

◆ To select all but a few items, use Ctrl+A to select everything and then deselect the items you don't need by holding down the Ctrl key while you click on them.

◆ Select contiguous items as described above and then select additional blocks of contiguous items by holding down the Ctrl key while you work (that is, use Ctrl+click for the first item and then Ctrl+Shift+click for the last item).

Map and Disconnect Network Drives Using My Computer

Mapping is assigning a drive letter to a shared resource. Usually that resource is a drive, but it could be a folder. The resource is on another computer on your network and, in effect, you are treating that shared resource like an additional drive. After a shared resource is mapped, it appears in the My Computer window.

Mapping also means that you can use the drive letter to manipulate these drives as if they were on your local computer. For example, you can use the letter in a DOS command prompt to copy files, look at a directory listing, or use any command you would use with a local drive.

To map a share (the popular jargon for a shared resource is "share"), the computer must be configured to share resources and you must have the appropriate permissions to access them.

To map a network share as a drive, follow these steps:

1. Open My Computer and make sure the toolbar is visible (choose View, Toolbar if it isn't).

2. Click on the Map Network Drive icon on the toolbar to display the Map Network Drive dialog box (see fig. 8.12).

3. Enter a letter in the Drive field (the next available drive letter is displayed, but you can change it).

4. Enter the Path to the computer, using the UNC format.

5. Use the Connect As field to connect to this computer using a different name than you used to log on to your computer. This is rarely necessary and should only be done if there are serious security issues. For instance, if multiple users access this particular workstation, and some of the shares on the network have specific users listed for permissions (instead of anyone who sits in front of this workstation), you need to make sure the share is accessed with a user name that has the appropriate permissions.

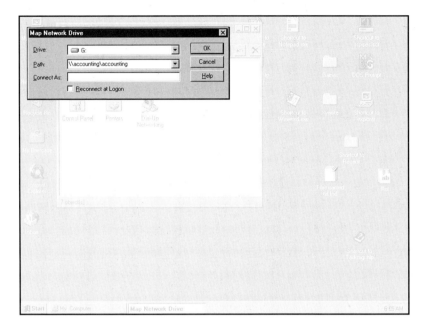

Figure 8.12

Map a network computer as a drive in order to see it in My Computer.

6. If you want to reconnect and re-map this computer the next time you start Windows NT, select Reconnect at Logon.

7. Choose OK. When the computer is mapped, a window opens to display its contents. It may take a few seconds for your computer to find and map the computer.

After the drive is mapped, it appears in My Computer along with the drives on your computer (see fig. 8.13).

 Tip   If you don't know the name of the computer or the name of its shared directory, you can use Network Neighborhood to locate all the computers on the network. Information about using Network Neighborhood is found later in this chapter.

After a network drive is mapped, you can open it from My Computer and work with it. The manipulations and functions discussed in this chapter can be applied.

To disconnect a mapped drive, right-click on it and choose Disconnect from the shortcut menu, or highlight it and click the Disconnect Net Drive button on the toolbar. To disconnect multiple mapped drives, select the first drive and then select the others by holding down the Ctrl key as you click on them. Choose Disconnect Network Drive from the toolbar. A Disconnect Network Drive dialog box appears, listing all the drives you selected. Confirm the disconnection for each drive by choosing OK.

Figure 8.13

The mapped drives appear in My Computer and can be accessed as if they were physical drives on your computer.

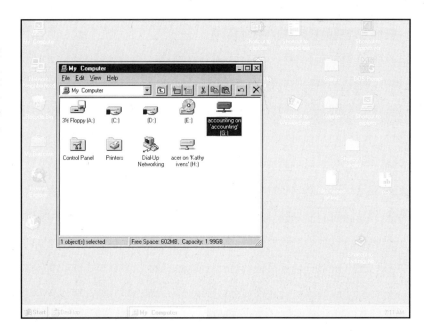

Share Folders and Files

You can configure your computer so that other users on the network can share it (and map it as a drive). Actually, you are not sharing your computer; you are sharing the folders and files on your hard drive(s). You can share all the folders and files or choose specific folders. In fact, you can create different sharing schemes (each configuration of shared folders you create is called a share), giving specific users access to folders depending on the share for which they're given permissions.

Share a Drive

Objective C.3

To share all the folders and files on a drive, follow these steps:

1. Right-click on the drive's icon in My Computer and choose Sharing. This brings up the Sharing tab of the drive's Properties dialog box (see fig. 8.14).

2. Choose Shared As and then enter a Share Name. It's usually a good idea to enter a share name that other users will recognize (so they know which computer they are accessing). Use your initials or some other descriptive name, such as your division or department (accounting or personnel, for example).

3. Enter an optional comment about this share. When users access your computer, the comment is viewed if they choose the Details view.

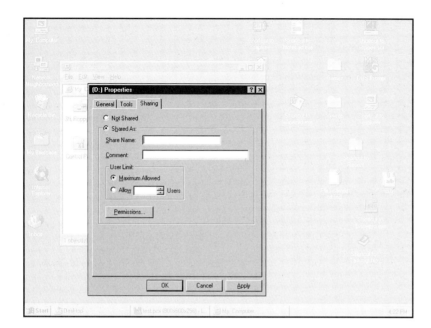

Figure 8.14

Use the Sharing tab to configure a drive for shared access.

4. Choose the number of simultaneous users who can access this share. Maximum Allowed means unlimited users. If you want to limit the number of simultaneous users, choose Allow and then specify a number.

5. Choose Permissions to provide access to other users. The Access Through Share Permissions dialog box is displayed so you can begin adding names for this share. Choose Add to begin adding permissions. This brings up the Add Users and Groups dialog box (see fig. 8.15).

6. Select a group or user (or Everyone) and choose Add. Then click the arrow on the Type of Access box and choose an Access level for this user (see the section "Access Levels" later in this chapter). Continue to do this until all the permissions for this share are given.

7. Choose OK when you are finished and then choose OK two more times to close all the dialog boxes.

Tip

The whole issue of naming shares is very subjective. In this case, the share has the same name as the computer to indicate that every file and folder is included in the share. If there were additional shares with specific folders included, they would have been named to reflect their scope. Your company may use a similar naming policy, or invent something different. It is, however, a good idea to come up with a share naming policy that gives users a hint about the scope or intent of the share.

Figure 8.15

You can add users, groups, or everyone to the list of people who can access this share.

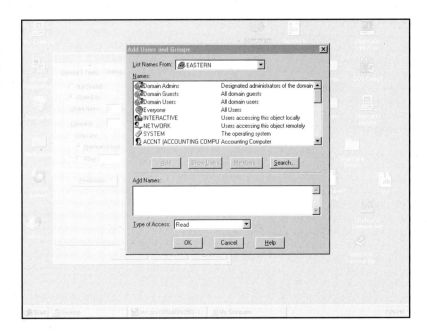

Share Specific Folders

You can open a drive in My Computer and find a folder that you want to share with other users. Perhaps the files in that folder are of interest to specific users or all users.

Right-click on the folder and choose Sharing. Then follow the previous steps to create a new share for this folder. Remember to give this share a name that reflects the folder.

Note   When you create a share, all subfolders under that share are also shared. That means if you create a drive share, all the folders on that drive are automatically shared. If you create a folder share, any subfolders are automatically shared.

Multiple Shares for the Same Drive or Folders

You can create multiple shares for the same drive or folder, so that different groups of people access them with different access levels. For example, if you keep spreadsheet files in a shared folder, you may want some users to be able to change them, and others to only be able to read them.

Objective C.3   To create multiple shares, follow the same steps as previously outlined. When you right-click on a shared drive or folder and choose Sharing, however, the dialog box includes a button named New Share. Choosing that option gives you the opportunity to invent a new share name in addition to the established share name. The new share has its own user limit, permissions list, and access levels. Users who match the criteria for the permissions you select are given access to the share name that matches your permissions.

Access Levels

Access levels are the levels of permission extended to users who have shared directory permissions. The Add Users and Groups dialog box provides a way to set an access level for each user or group you give permission to when you are creating a share. This section describes the three levels.

Read

Giving a Read access level to a user allows these actions in the share:

◆ View file names and subfolder names

◆ Move to the subfolders of the shared folder

◆ View the contents of data files

Change

Giving a Change access level permits these actions in the share:

◆ All the permissions given for Read access

◆ Add files and subfolders to the shared folders

◆ Delete files and subfolders from the shared folders

◆ Change the contents of data files

Full Control

Giving a Full Control access level permits these actions in the share:

◆ All the permissions given for Change access

◆ Changing permissions in NTFS files and directories

◆ Taking ownership of NTFS files and directories

Manage Shares

When users access your computer, your shared drives, folders, and files are host computers, or servers. You can view and manage the access to your computer by opening the Server dialog box in the Control Panel (see fig. 8.16).

Figure 8.16

Use the Server dialog box to keep an eye on the activities of users who are accessing your computer.

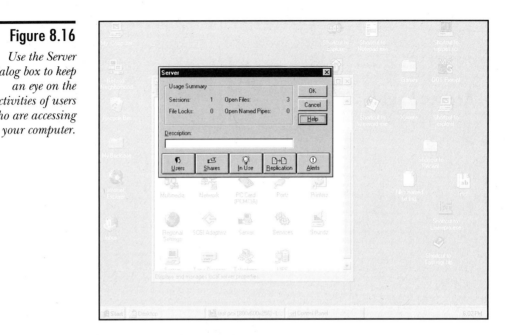

When you view the Server dialog box, you can see how many users are currently connected to your computer (Sessions) and the file activity the connected users are generating.

User Information

Click on Users to activate the User Sessions dialog box, which lists the currently connected users and statistics about each user's connection (see fig. 8.17).

To break the connection, select a user and choose Disconnect, or choose Disconnect All to break all connections.

 Caution If connected users have files open, disconnecting them could result in a loss of data. If you need to disconnect one or all users, you should contact them so they can close any open files. If a connected user does not have any files open, there is no danger of data loss, but it is certainly polite to contact the user before disconnecting.

Shares Information

Choose Shares (refer to fig. 8.16) to see connection information arranged by share (see fig. 8.18). This, of course, is valuable information only if you've configured more than one share for your computer. You can also disconnect one or all users from this dialog box.

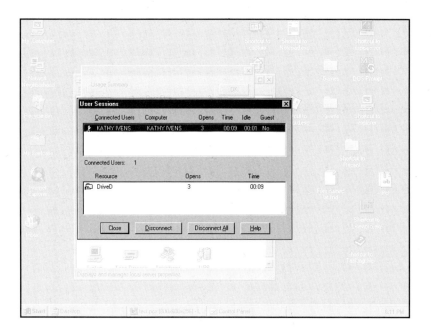

Figure 8.17

Everything you need to know about each connected user is in the User Sessions dialog box.

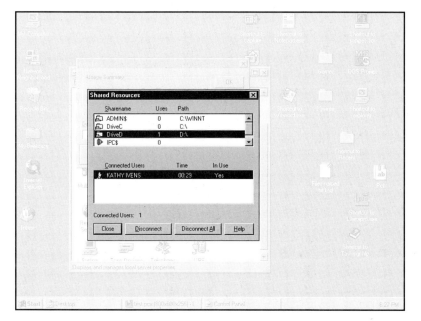

Figure 8.18

Information about connections for each individual share is available in the Shared Resources dialog box.

Resources Information

Click on In Use (refer to fig. 8.16) to see information about the resources being accessed and used (see fig. 8.19). You can close one or all of those resources, but it may be dangerous to close files because you could lose or corrupt data.

Figure 8.19

The Open Resources dialog box lists the shared resources that are currently open.

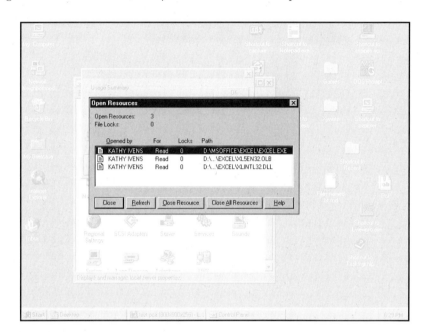

My Computer Properties

It is possible to view the properties for all the folders and files on your computer, but there are some special drive property features in the My Computer folder. This section focuses on the hard drive properties.

Right-click on a drive icon and choose Properties from the shortcut menu to see the drives Properties dialog box (see fig. 8.20).

The General tab is mostly for viewing information, but you can enter a label for the drive (or change the existing label) here.

Click on the Tools tab to use these Windows NT tools available for your hard drive(s):

◆ **Error Checking (Scandisk).** You can choose to check the file system (and optionally choose whether or not to fix errors automatically) or perform a physical scan of the disk to check for bad sectors (or both).

◆ **Backup.** This choice launches Windows NT Backup. See Chapter 27, "Protecting Your Workstation," for more information about Backup.

◆ **Defragmentation.** This choice rearranges files to make them contiguous, speeding up the process of accessing files. There is no defragmentation tool in the Windows NT 4 operating system, but you can purchase and install any one that is supported by NT.

For the Floppy disk(s) that appear in My Computer, you can perform a number of tasks through the shortcut menu that appears when you right-click the icon. For example, you can format or copy a disk.

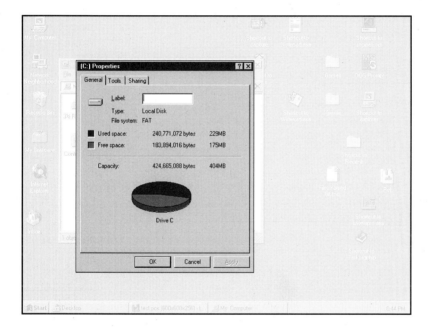

Figure 8.20

The General tab of the drive Properties dialog box displays all the basic information about the drive.

Using Network Neighborhood

Network Neighborhood is the My Computer for other computers on the network. It looks and works similarly to My Computer, except the folders and files you work with are located on other computers. Servers, shared resources, and peer-networked computers are all visible in the Network Neighborhood (see fig. 8.21). To open it, double-click on the Network Neighborhood icon.

Figure 8.21

Open Network Neighborhood to browse the network connections.

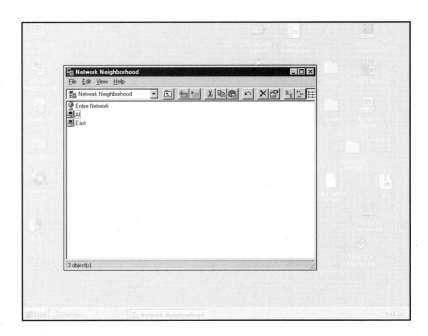

Navigate the Network

Browsing with Network Neighborhood is very much like browsing your computer with My Computer. When you first open Network Neighborhood, the window displays the top level of your network (figure 8.21 shows icons for the Entire Network, the local computer, and the domain server to which the local computer is logged on). This, of course, varies depending on your organization's setup. As you double-click on icons, you open additional windows to move deeper into the structure.

> **Tip**   Your computer is displayed in the Network Neighborhood window, but you can't access it. If you want to open folders in your own computer, use My Computer.

Click on Entire Network to open a new window. From this point on, the icons and windows you see depend on the configuration of your network and shared resources. For example, you may see an icon named Microsoft Windows Network, or you may see an icon representing the name of the domain or server to which you log on (see fig. 8.22).

Objective D.2

Browse through Network Neighborhood until you find a computer to which you want to connect. Figure 8.23 shows the windows that were opened for one computer to browse its Network Neighborhood in order to locate the computer named Accounting. Double-clicking on it displays a share named Accounting.

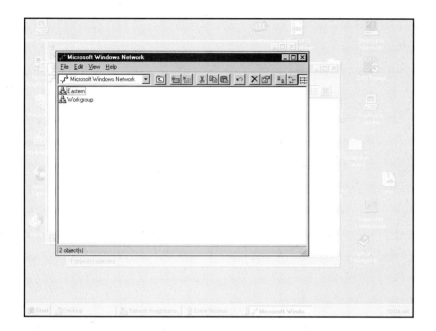

Figure 8.22

This computer is part of a Microsoft Windows Network that permits access to both a domain and a local workgroup.

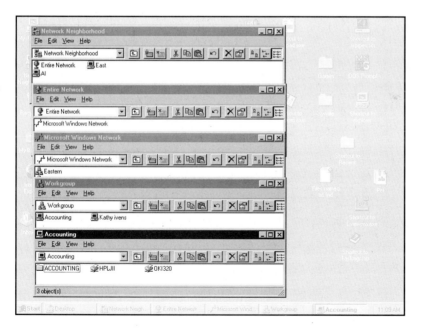

Figure 8.23

Browse the Network Neighborhood by opening one icon after another to get to a specific target; you can see the steps by reading the title bars.

Using Shared Resources

When you get to the computer share and/or resources you want to access, you can manipulate them. The icon name is the share that has been established at that computer.

> **Tip** If you take the trouble to size and cascade the windows neatly, Network Neighborhood remembers the arrangement. The next time you browse, opening item after item, the windows will arrange themselves as you arranged them the last time you browsed.

Open a Network Computer

When you open the share, you see its contents. The folders and files that appear are the result of the share that is configured. Double-clicking on the share folder opens a window that is similar to the window you see in My Computer (see fig. 8.24).

Figure 8.24

The folder for this computer displays folders and files for the share named Accounting on the computer named Accounting.

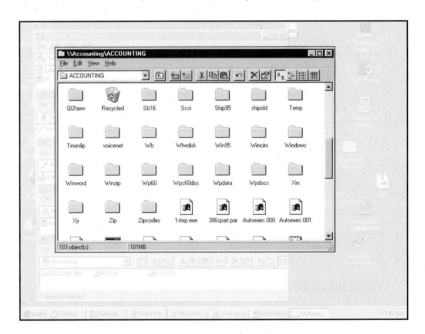

> **Tip** The folder windows in Network Neighborhood look just like the folder windows in My Computer. That is not a coincidence. Network Neighborhood is really My Computer for the other computers on your network. It is deliberately designed to make working with networked computers the same as working with your local computer.

If you have the appropriate permissions, you can open and manipulate any folder or file the same way you open folders and files in your own computer.

Use the Resources

When you open a computer in the Network Neighborhood, any shared resources attached to that computer are displayed in addition to the folder share(s).

Objective D.2

The most common shared resource is a printer. If you refer to figure 8.23, you see that the window for the computer named Accounting displays two printers. These printers are configured for sharing with other users and you can use them as your system printers. Other computers on the network may have a CD-ROM drive as a shared resource, which you can access if you have the appropriate permissions.

In fact, for printers, there's a nifty shortcut for installation. If you find a remote printer that you haven't already installed in your system and want to use it for printing, you can install it by right-clicking on the printer's icon and choosing Install.

Objective C.5

Caution   If you do not have administrative permissions on your local workstation, you will not be able to install a printer.

If the computer to which this printer is attached is not running Windows NT 4, you will be notified that the printer driver is not suitable for use on your NT system. You will have to install a local Windows NT 4 driver to use the printer. Be sure you have your original Windows NT media and then choose OK to install the printer driver. The Add Printer Wizard will walk you through the installation routine for the printer.

Tip   Just as with a local printer, you can create a shortcut for a remote printer. Put the shortcut on your desktop and drag documents to it in order to print them (the creating application is launched, the document is loaded, and printing begins).

Set Options

You can configure Network Neighborhood to control the way items are displayed when you browse the network computers.

As you open computer windows and folder windows, the items are displayed in a list by default. You can choose a different view, however, by selecting one of these choices:

◆ **Large Icons.** The icons are large and the folder or file name appears below the icon. The items are sorted in horizontal rows, reading from left to right.

◆ **Small Icons.** The icons are small and the folder or file name is to the right of the icon. The items are sorted in rows, reading horizontally.

◆ **List.** The icons are small and the folder or file name is to the right of the icon. The items are sorted in columns, reading vertically.

◆ **Details.** The items are listed in a single vertical column with information about each item in columns to the right of the item name.

> **Note**
>
> If you choose Details, the column information differs depending on the items being displayed. If you are looking at a computer, a share, or a resource, the only details are the comments about the item. Details about folders and files include size (for files), type of item, last modified data, and attributes.
>
> Click on any column title to sort the items according to the criteria of that column. Click again to reverse the sorting scheme from ascending to descending.

Find Computers from the Start Menu

If you want to connect to another computer in a very large network, it can take a long time to search through Network Neighborhood (the more connections there are, the slower Network Neighborhood works as you browse through it). Windows NT offers a feature called Find that is a more direct, faster method of connecting to a specific computer.

Objective D.2

To move directly to another computer, follow these steps:

1. Open the Start menu and choose Find. There are two choices on the Find menu: Files or Folders, and Computer.

2. Choose Computer to bring up the Find: Computer dialog box. Enter the name of the computer you want to connect to in the Named box.

> **Tip**
>
> The Find feature does not insist on the Universal Naming Convention (preceding the computer name with two backslash characters).

3. Choose Find Now. The animated magnifying glass moves around for a few seconds, and then the computer you're looking for is listed at the bottom of the Find: Computer dialog box (see fig. 8.25).

4. Double-click on the computer listing to move to the shared folders and files you need to access.

There's another advantage to using Find that saves you even more time—the system saves the recent computer names you entered in the Named field of the dialog box. After you've accessed a computer once, you can press the arrow to the right of the Named field and click on that computer name instead of re-entering it.

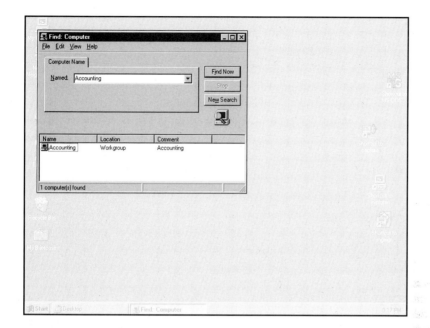

Figure 8.25

Move quickly and directly to any computer using the Find: Computer dialog box.

Map Network Drives Using Network Neighborhood

You can use Network Neighborhood to map a network share as a drive. Read the section on mapping network drives in the earlier "Using My Computer" section of this chapter for the reasons why you should do this.

To map a network drive from Network Neighborhood, follow these steps:

Objective
D.2

1. Right-click on the Network Neighborhood icon and choose Map Network Drive from the shortcut menu. The Map Network Drive dialog box appears, showing the computers contained in the Network Neighborhood folder (see fig. 8.26).

Tip | If you have already opened Network Neighborhood, you can also map a drive from the Network Neighborhood window by selecting the Map Network Drive button on the toolbar.

2. Double-click on the domain, workgroup, or computer that contains the share to which you want to connect. When you find the share you want to map as a drive letter, click on it. The computer and the share are displayed in the Path field. (see fig. 8.27).

Figure 8.26

The Map Network Drive dialog box displays the computers found in Network Neighborhood. Browse them to find a shared resource to map as a drive.

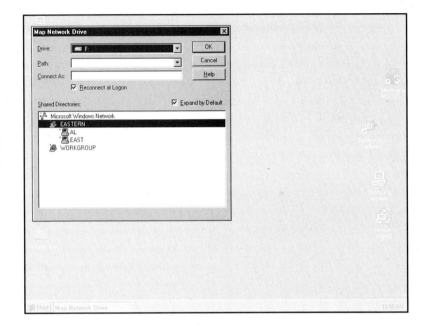

Figure 8.27

The General Ledger Data share is selected and appears in the Path field.

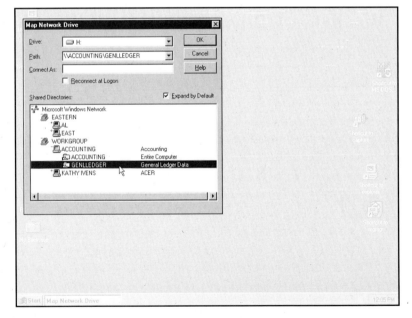

| Tip | To place the computer and share in the path, be sure to single-click on your selection. Double-clicking opens a folder window that displays the contents of that share. Also, note that the Path field does not automatically fill in until you have clicked on a valid share—clicking on a computer name doesn't do it. |

3. Repeat this process for all the computer shares you want to map as drives.

After a share is mapped, it's easier to get to and use. The share appears in My Computer, is listed in the hierarchical display in Explorer, and can be accessed from the command line.

Using the Recycle Bin

By default, the files and folders you delete while working in Windows NT 4 are sent to the Recycle Bin instead of being sent to oblivion. When you delete the file from the Recycle Bin, the deletion is complete. This can be a lifesaver if you accidentally delete a needed file, but it also means that you're not gaining any disk space when you delete files. Therefore, you must be conscientious about emptying the Recycle Bin frequently.

Deleting Files and Folders

When you are working in Explorer, a folder window, or the desktop, files you delete are sent to the Recycle Bin. You can delete a file or folder by selecting it and pressing Del, by right-clicking on it and choosing Delete from the shortcut menu, or by selecting it and choosing Delete from the File menu. The Confirm File Delete dialog box asks if you are sure you want to send the file to the Recycle Bin (see fig. 8.28).

You should be aware of some other features when you want to delete files or folders:

◆ You can drag a file or folder to the Recycle Bin to delete it.

◆ When you delete a folder, all the files and subfolders in the folder are also deleted.

◆ When you are working in software written specifically for Windows NT 4 (or Windows 95), the Open and Save As dialog boxes usually provide the capability to delete files (as well as perform other manipulations on files)—a feature that is long overdue.

◆ When you select multiple files for deletion, the Confirm Delete dialog box doesn't name them; it asks if you are sure you want to send these xx files to the Recycle Bin (where xx is the number of files you selected).

◆ When you delete a program file, the Confirm Delete dialog box informs you that the file is a program file and you will no longer be able to run the program.

◆ When you delete a shortcut, only the shortcut is deleted. The original file remains untouched.

◆ There is a warning displayed when you attempt to delete a system or hidden file—most of the time, you should pay attention to the warning and choose No on the Confirm File Delete dialog box (see fig. 8.28).

Figure 8.28

The Confirm File Delete dialog box doesn't ask if you are sure you want to delete the file; it asks if you want to send it to the Recycle Bin.

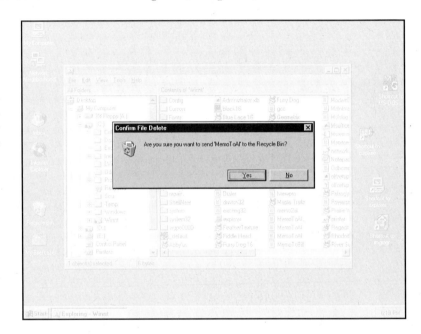

Files Not Sent to the Recycle Bin

Not all the files you delete are sent to the Recycle Bin; some are really deleted. If you delete any files under the following circumstances, they are not recoverable through the Recycle Bin:

◆ Files deleted at an MS-DOS command prompt

◆ Files deleted by DOS software that runs in a DOS window

◆ Files deleted from floppy disks

◆ Files deleted on connected network drives

Unless you have a third-party utility that can recover these deleted items, they are gone forever.

Viewing the Recycle Bin Contents

The Recycle Bin announces when it contains deleted files by changing its icon from an empty waste basket to a waste basket stuffed with papers. You can't determine how many files are in the Recycle Bin by looking at the volume of paper rising from it—as soon as one file is deleted, the icon becomes an overflowing receptacle.

To view the contents of the Recycle Bin, double-click on it. When the Recycle Bin window opens, it displays information about the deleted items (see fig. 8.29).

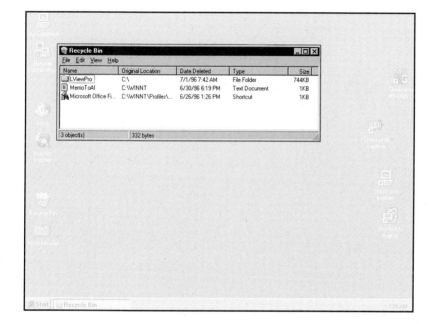

Figure 8.29

The column titles for deleted items are appropriate for this folder.

You can also see the Recycle Bin in Explorer and My Computer. In Explorer, select the Recycle Bin to see the contents in the Contents window. In My Computer, double-click the Recycle Bin to see the same window that is shown in figure 8.29.

Viewing the Recycle Bins on Other Drives

There is one unusual aspect to the Recycle Bin when you have multiple drives (either in your computer or across the network): the Recycle Bin is a one-to-a-customer commodity.

Regardless of how many drives are in your computer, when you delete files or folders from any drive, they go to one Recycle Bin. Open any Recycle Bin on any drive and you see the same items. In effect, the Recycle Bin icon on any drive is a mirror of the Recycle Bin icon on every other drive.

When you access the Recycle Bin on a network drive, you are again looking at a mirror of your own Recycle Bin. Even if files and folders are deleted from that drive and placed in the Recycle Bin, you can't see that drive's Recycle Bin; you only see your own. The user at that computer sees the appropriate Recycle Bin for that drive, but you can't (and that user can't connect to your drive and see the contents of your Recycle Bin).

Viewing the Hidden Recycle Bin

The Recycle Bin icon doesn't look like a folder, but it is. In fact, it is a folder that is placed on the root directory of your boot drive during the installation of Windows NT 4. It is a hidden directory named RECYCLED that does not appear in Explorer, even if you have configured Explorer to show all files (which causes hidden files to be displayed, but not hidden directories). You can confirm the existence of this directory from a command prompt by entering dir/a at the C:\ prompt.

If you're interested in seeing the way Windows NT 4 handles deleted, but-not-really-deleted files, go to the directory by entering cd\recycled. When you are at the \RE-CYCLED prompt, enter dir. You see a file entry for each item in the Recycled Bin that was originally deleted from this drive. You may not recognize the listing, however, because Windows NT has changed the name of the files (see fig. 8.30).

Figure 8.30

The right number of deleted files is listed, but the names are different.

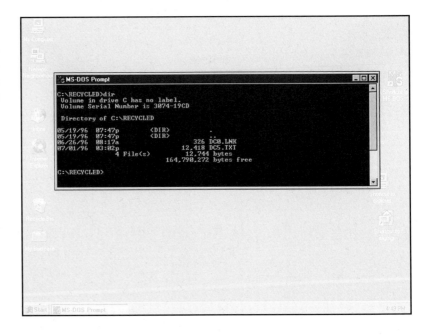

The date and time listed for each file refers to the point at which the original file was deleted.

You can tell what type of file each entry is because the file extension matches the file type (for instance, an extension of .LNK means a deleted shortcut, .TXT is a text file, and so on).

If you are in Explorer and select the Recycle Bin, the file names that appear in the Contents window match the names in the Recycle Bin window. While there is a link between the Recycle Bin folder that is displayed in Explorer and the hidden \RECYCLED directory you see from the command prompt, the file names aren't the same.

The operating system resolves the difference in names with a special file named INFO. This file exists in the \RECYCLED directory, but it is hidden. Enter dir/a at the C:\RECYCLED prompt to see all the files in the directory, including hidden files (see fig. 8.31).

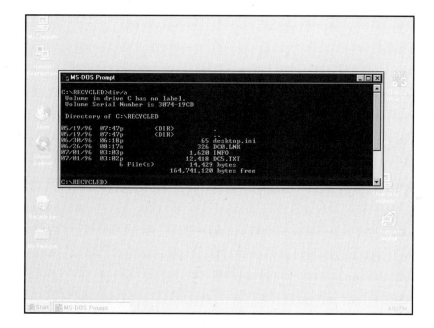

Figure 8.31

Two hidden files link this hidden directory to the Recycle Bin and its contents.

In addition, there is a file called desktop.ini that references the Recycled Bin on the desktop.

These listings for deleted files are for those files that were deleted from the current drive only. Even though the Recycle Bin combines the deleted files from all local drives, the drives themselves only track their own deleted files. The Recycle Bin collects information from each \RECYCLED directory on your computer in order to present the unified list of deleted files.

You can delete the deleted files from the Recycle Bin by deleting them at the command prompt. Because you can't see your file names, however, you may not really be sure what it is that you are deleting.

There is, however, one set of circumstances in which it might be advantageous to use the command line to empty the Recycle Bin (especially if many files are waiting for final deletion). This is the case if you want to empty all the files of a certain type. For example, if you know it's perfectly safe to empty the Recycle Bin of all the text files or all the document files from WordPerfect, it's faster to enter del *.txt or del *.wpd than to navigate through the Recycle Bin to find them.

Emptying the Recycle Bin

You can empty the entire contents of the Recycle Bin or choose individual items, saving those items you're not sure you want to delete yet.

To delete the entire contents of the Recycle Bin, right-click on it and choose Empty Recycle Bin. (It doesn't matter whether you use the Recycle Bin icon on the desktop, in Explorer, or in My Computer.) A dialog box asks you to confirm your action.

To delete an individual item in the Recycle Bin, use one of the same methods you would use to delete regular files and folders:

- ◆ Select the item and press Del.
- ◆ Select the item and choose Delete from the File menu.
- ◆ Right-click on the item and choose Delete from the shortcut menu.

You are asked to confirm the deletion. This time Windows NT means it; the files are really gone, and you have the disk space back.

Restoring Files

Restoring deleted files from the Recycle Bin is very easy. There are several ways to accomplish this:

- ◆ Open the Recycle Bin and right-click on the item you want to restore. Choose Restore from the shortcut menu. The item is restored to its original location.
- ◆ Select multiple items by holding down the Ctrl key while you click on each item. When you choose Restore, all items are restored to their original locations.
- ◆ Select an item (or multiple items) and choose Cut from the File menu. Then open Explorer and choose Paste on the folder in which you want to restore the item. The target folder does not have to be the item's original location.
- ◆ Drag an item out of the Recycle Bin window to any folder. You do not have to drag it to its original location.

If you restore a file for which the original location has disappeared (the folder was deleted), the folder will be recreated to hold the restored file.

Empty folders that were deleted and placed in the Recycle Bin cannot be restored.

> **Tip** If you rush to open the Recycle Bin and restore a file because you just deleted one you shouldn't have, there is a shortcut to restoring that file to its original location. Right-click on any blank spot in the Recycle Bin window and choose Undo Delete from the shortcut menu. The last file you deleted is removed from the Recycle Bin and placed in its original location. The Undo Delete choice is only available on the shortcut menu if the last thing you did in Windows NT was delete a file. Undo Delete does not undo the deletion of a file from the Recycle Bin; it only reverses the action of deleting a file or folder from your hard drive.

Working with Files in the Recycle Bin

In effect, the Recycle Bin is just another folder. The files and folders it contains are still in existence. That means you can work with them, although you can't just open an application and load a file from the Recycle Bin.

However, you can drag a file from the Recycle Bin to the icon of the program file in which is was created. The software launches and the deleted file opens. You can look at it and decide whether or not it should have been deleted. If you decide that deleting it was a good idea, just close the file or close the software. You don't have to delete the file; it already is deleted.

> **Tip** Double-clicking on a document file doesn't launch its associated software the way it does in Explorer. Double-clicking on a file when you are working in the Recycle Bin window opens the file's Properties dialog box.

You can even edit the file after it's in the software window. Don't use Save to save the changes, however, because it will be saved to its original location—Recycle Bin. Make sure you choose Save As from the software window and change the folder to which you are saving the file.

Skip the Recycle Bin

You can, if you want, delete a file without sending it to the Recycle Bin. It's not as safe, of course, because if you make a mistake and delete a file you need, it can be difficult or impossible to undo your action. If you're confident about managing your files and folders, however, you might occasionally want to skip the extra step involved in deleting files (and it does save disk space).

To delete a file without sending it to the Recycle Bin, hold down the Shift key as you delete it. That means you must perform one of these actions:

◆ Select the file or folder and press Shift+Del.

◆ Select the file or folder and hold down the Shift key as you choose File, Delete from the menu bar.

◆ Right-click the file or folder and then hold down the Shift key as you choose Delete from the shortcut menu.

The Confirm File Delete dialog box asks if you are sure you want to delete the file; it does not ask if you are sure you want to send the file to the Recycle Bin. Answer Yes if you know it is safe to delete this item.

Configuring the Recycle Bin

You can configure the way the Recycle Bin works. In fact, you can even decide to turn off this feature and just delete files the old-fashioned way—they're gone.

Note Some of the configuration options are connected to the amount of disk space used by the Recycle Bin to hold deleted files. By default, 10 percent of each local hard drive is established as the maximum portion of your drive that can be used for this purpose. This means that if you fill 10 percent of your drive with deleted files and don't empty the Recycle Bin, the system will automatically begin removing files in order to accept newly deleted files without exceeding the 10 percent limit. This flushing out of the Recycle Bin is accomplished by purging the oldest files first (oldest is measured by the date the file was deleted, not the original file's creation or last-modified date).

To set the configuration options for the Recycle Bin, right-click on its icon (either on the desktop or in Explorer) and choose Properties. The Recycle Bin Properties dialog box appears (see fig. 8.32).

The Global tab of the Recycle Bin Properties dialog box contains the configuration options. In addition, there are tabs for each local hard drive that can be configured only if you use the Global tab to indicate you want to configure drives separately. Use the Global tab to set the following options:

◆ **Configure Drives Independently.** Choose this option if you have more than one local hard drive and want to set separate maximum sizes for the \RECYCLED directory.

If you choose this option, click on the Drive tab for each of those drives and specify a percentage by moving the slider bar.

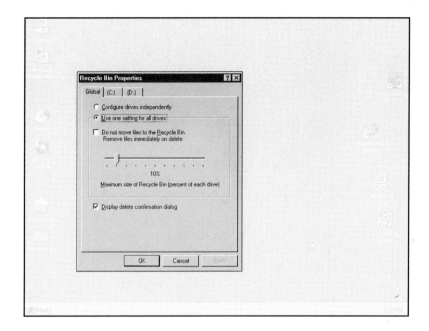

Figure 8.32

The changes you make in the Recycling Bin's configuration can have a very large impact on your work habits— think carefully before giving up the use of the Recycle Bin.

| **Tip** | There are some practical reasons for configuring drives separately. For example, you may have a very large drive that holds most of your application software. As you work in that software, it is likely that you will be deleting files and folders that have become obsolete or no longer useful. Creating a large Recycle Bin means you don't risk losing files to automatic purges before you have a chance to examine the deleted files and either restore them or archive them to another location. |

◆ **Use One Setting for All Drives.** Choose this option to establish a maximum size that applies to every drive on your computer.

◆ **Do Not Move Files to the Recycle Bin.** Choose this option to skip the transfer of deleted files to the Recycle Bin. Files are deleted as if you do not have a Recycle Bin.

◆ **Display Delete Confirmation Dialog.** Choose this option to instruct Windows NT to present a Confirm File Delete dialog box so you have a chance to say Yes or No when asked if you want to move this file to the Recycle Bin (or delete the file if you are not using the Recycle Bin).

| **Note** | The confirmation dialog option is available whether you are using the Recycle Bin or have opted to delete files permanently. After you choose whether or not to display a confirmation dialog, that choice is locked in if you have chosen to skip the Recycle Bin. The only way to change whether or not you want to display a confirmation dialog box is to deselect the choice Do Not Move Files to the Recycle Bin. |

If you choose not to use the Recycle Bin to hold deleted files, you can still drag files to it (either on the desktop or in Explorer) to delete the files. They just won't be held in the Recycle Bin.

Using My Briefcase

If you use a portable computer to work outside the office or take work from the office to your home computer, you can keep all your files synchronized by using My Briefcase. My Briefcase matches the contents of your data files, and the latest versions exist in all the computers on which you work.

 Tip   The My Briefcase icon (which looks just like a briefcase) is on your desktop if you chose it during installation of the operating system. If it isn't installed, you can add it to your system with the Add/Remove Programs feature in the Control Panel.

You can move folders as well as files into the Briefcase. The process is quick and easy.

Transfer the Files to My Briefcase

You can move data files into My Briefcase in two ways:

◆ You can move the files from your computer to the My Briefcase folder on a connected portable computer.

◆ You can move the files from your data folders to your computer's My Briefcase folder and then move the Briefcase to a floppy disk.

Use the second method for portable computers that have no docking stations or network connectors and for off-site computers, such as your home computer or an office computer at a remote location.

Use a Connected Portable Computer

If you install Windows NT 4 onto a portable computer, My Briefcase is placed on the desktop automatically (assuming you choose the Portable Computer installation option). You can move files directly from your office computer to the portable computer if the portable is connected to the network. Your portable computer, therefore, has a docking station with a network card, a PCMCIA network card, or a network card that works through the parallel port.

Note Unlike the Windows 95 Briefcase features, Windows NT 4 does not support direct cable connection between your computer and a portable computer.

To move files between your office workstation and the connected portable, follow these steps:

1. From the portable computer, open Explorer and move to the Network Neighborhood object.

2. Use the plus sign next to the Network Neighborhood folders to find the folders on your office computer that contain the files on which you want to work.

3. Select the files you want to send to My Briefcase.

4. Move the files from the Contents window of Explorer to the My Briefcase folder on the portable computer's desktop using one of these methods:

   ◆ Drag the files to the My Briefcase icon (the Briefcase does not have to be open to receive the files).

   ◆ Right-click on a file, choose Send To from the shortcut menu, and then choose My Briefcase as the target.

After the files are in the portable computer's Briefcase, you can disconnect the portable and take it on the road.

Move the Briefcase to a Floppy Disk

If you aren't connected to a portable, you have to use a floppy disk to move the Briefcase. This is a two-step process:

1. Select the files and folders on which you want to work and move them to the My Briefcase folder, either by dragging or using Send To.

2. Right-click on the My Briefcase icon, choose Send To, and then choose the floppy drive.

The Briefcase is sent to the floppy disk. Actually, a Briefcase is created on the floppy disk and the contents of the desktop computer's Briefcase are copied to the floppy disk's Briefcase.

If you view the contents of the floppy drive in Explorer, you'll see My Briefcase in the right pane (see fig. 8.33).

This is not the same as a file copy operation because replicating the Briefcase takes advantage of special functions and features to track Briefcase contents against the original contents.

Figure 8.33

A Briefcase was created on the floppy disk to transfer the desktop computer's Briefcase.

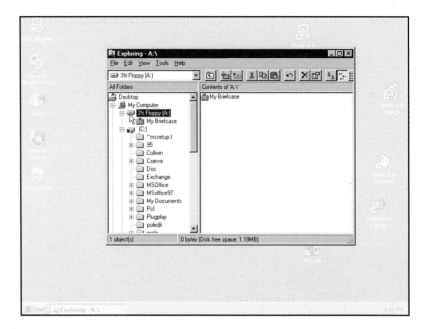

Work on the Files Off-Site

You can take the floppy disk briefcase to any computer that has the software necessary to manipulate the files within it. Therefore, you do not have to have Windows NT 4 running on the off-site computer. In fact, you can move documents via the Briefcase between a Windows NT 4 computer and a computer running Windows 3.1.

Open the Briefcase and then open the file(s) on which you want to work. (Open them from the Briefcase and save your modifications back in the Briefcase.) When you return to the original computer, put the floppy disk with the Briefcase into the floppy disk drive. At this point, you can begin updating your files.

Synchronizing Changed Files

When you are ready to synchronize the files in your Briefcase with the original files on your desktop computer, open the Briefcase (the easiest way to open My Computer is to open the floppy drive and then open My Briefcase). When the My Briefcase window opens (see fig. 8.34), any files that were changed display Needs Updating in the Status column.

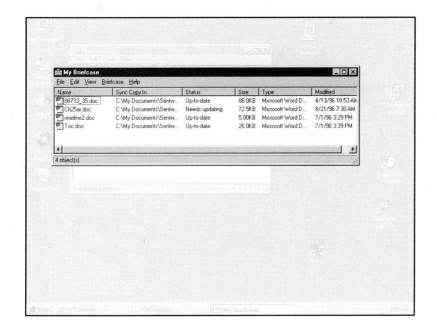

Figure 8.34

The Status column of My Briefcase indicates whether or not a file needs to be synchronized with the original document.

You have several options for updating the files that you changed while you were off-site:

◆ Select the file(s), right-click, and choose Update from the shortcut menu.

◆ Select the file(s) and choose Update Selection from the Briefcase menu.

◆ Choose Update All from the Briefcase menu.

When you initiate the Update action, the Update My Briefcase dialog box opens (see fig. 8.35).

By default, updates are performed to replace older files with new versions. You can change this action by right-clicking on a file and choosing an option from the shortcut menu (see fig. 8.36).

When you have configured the action for each file, choose Update from the dialog box.

When the update process is complete, the original files are modified to match the condition of the files in the Briefcase.

Split Files

There may be occasions when you want to separate files in the Briefcase from their original files (which is called splitting). For example, you may want to have both versions of the file, or you may return to the desktop to find that the original file has been modified and you don't want to replace the modifications with the work you did off-site.

Figure 8.35

The status of both copies of the file is displayed, as well as the update action that is about to be performed.

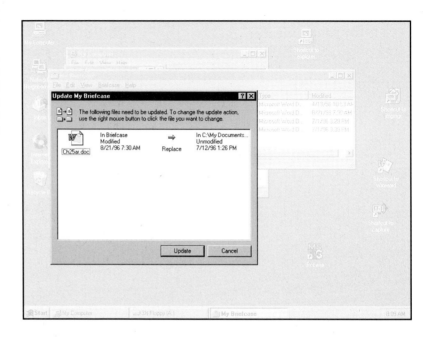

Figure 8.36

You can change the update pattern or skip the update for any file.

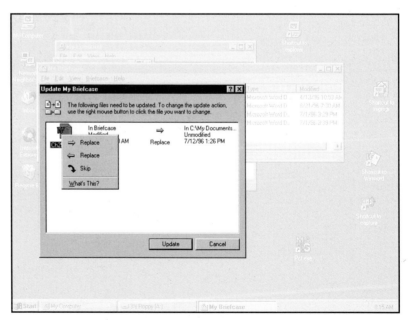

After a file is split, it can no longer be part of the update process (which is fine, because you won't have to keep changing the update window to skip this file). In fact, its status changes to Orphan.

To split a file, select it in My Briefcase and choose Split from the Briefcase menu. You will be asked to confirm the fact that you want to prevent future updates of this file.

You can continue to work on orphan files in the Briefcase. Eventually, you may want to copy them back to the original computer. Either copy the file to a different directory than the original file or rename the file and then copy it to its original directory.

End Note: If disk space is a problem, it is probably a good idea to make the Recycle Bin's maximum size extremely small (perhaps as little as three or four percent), or not to use it at all. However, you should give serious consideration to installing a reliable undelete program, such as Norton Utilities. You might even want to look at shareware applications available from BBS systems or the Internet. You don't have to install every feature of the utility application because most of them provide a way to install specific features (installing the entire application frequently uses a lot of disk space, which is the problem you're trying to solve).

Test Your Knowledge

1. The Universal Naming Convention for computers that you access over the network uses which format?

    A. //:computer name

    B. \computer name

    C. \\computer name

    D. //computer name

2. Which object on a connected computer cannot be mapped as a shared resource?

    A. Floppy drive

    B. Executable file

    C. CD-ROM

    D. Printer

3. Double-clicking on a file in the Recycle Bin results in which action?

    A. The file's Properties dialog box is displayed.

    B. The file is restored to its original folder.

    C. The file is restored to your Windows temp folder.

    D. The file is permantely deleted.

4. Which of the following is correct when you install and configure a printer that is connected to another computer?

   A. You must install a Windows NT 4 printer driver locally no matter what driver is used on the other computer.

   B. You must install a Windows NT 4 printer driver only if the other computer is not using a Windows NT 4 driver.

   C. You must use the driver on the other computer by creating a shared resource for the driver files.

   D. The remote printer handles the printing with its own driver, and you do not have to do anything regarding drivers.

5. Assigning a drive letter to a shared resource on another computer is a process known as _____.

6. Indicate the correct statement(s) about the initial view when you open Network Neighborhood.

   A. Opening Network Neighborhood displays all computers on the network, regardless of the status of shared drives and folders.

   B. Opening Network Neighborhood displays only computers that have established a share for Drive C.

   C. Opening Network Neighborhood displays only computers that have established a share for drives, folders, or resources such as printers.

   D. Opening Network Neighborhood displays all computers except your computer.

7. To view the current activity by users on shares that are established on your computer, open the _____ dialog box in the Control Panel.

Test Your Knowledge Answers

1. C
2. B
3. A
4. B
5. mapping
6. A
7. Server

Chapter Snapshot

Explorer is a filing cabinet that displays
the elements of your computer in a
hierarchical format. In addition to
viewing all the files and folders on your
drives, you can manipulate them by
using the features and functions built
in to Explorer. This chapter looks at
the power of Explorer, focusing on the
following topics:

Windows NT
Workstation 4

CHAPTER 9

Using Explorer

Explorer opens with a hierarchical view of your computer, which is in fact a hierarchical view of the My Computer folder. Because the objects are all displayed in one place, however, you can scroll through the objects to find what you need instead of opening folders and subfolders as you generally do with My Computer.

Introducing Explorer's Display

There are two panes to Explorer: the left pane shows the tree (directory structure) for your system; the right pane shows the contents of the selected item in the left pane.

Incidentally, the name of the left pane is the All Folders pane; the right pane is named Contents of. For convenience and clarity, this discussion will continue to use left and right (since the right pane often displays folders).

In the left pane, Explorer displays the contents of your computer in outline form. Just like an outline, each sublevel is indented. To make it easier to follow the way in which each level is connected, Explorer draws vertical and horizontal lines in the left panel (see fig. 9.1).

Figure 9.1

The Explorer view of a computer shows the directory structure in a hierarchical view.

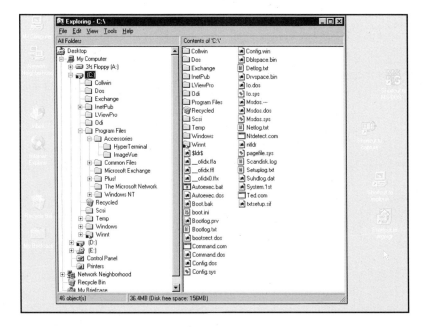

> **Note**   Just as a passing note of interest, if you follow the vertical lines, there are some mysterious connections made, or, if not mysterious, certainly whimsical and without any apparent logic. For example, Explorer puts My Computer, Network Neighborhood, Recycle Bin, and My Briefcase on the same level. While I can understand connecting My Computer and Network Neighborhood (which I can think of as "their computers"), the placement of the other two objects on the same level seems less logical. There's also the question of why the drives are on the same level as the folders for Control Panel and Printers.

Profiling Explorer versus File Manager

If you've used an earlier version of Windows (either 3.x or an earlier version of NT), you probably spent a lot of time in File Manager. There are some differences between the way Explorer and File Manager work.

To view subfolders in Explorer's left pane, click on the plus sign next to the parent folder. This action does not select that folder and the right pane does not display the folder's contents (because you didn't select the folder, you only expanded it). In File Manager, you expand a folder by double-clicking on it, which also selects it, changing the display in the right pane to reflect the contents of that folder.

In File Manager, to view the contents of two folders or two drives, you can open another window. You cannot open multiple windows in Explorer, but you can open multiple instances of Explorer, which has the same effect (or you can open Explorer and My Computer).

In addition to these differences in how you view contents, there are also some differences in the way you accomplish tasks. The differences are discussed in this section. More detailed information on accomplishing these tasks (and others) in Explorer is found throughout this chapter.

Move, Copy, Open, and Delete

The File menu in File Manager offers Move, Copy, Open, and Delete commands for any selected file(s).

Explorer carries out these tasks through the right-click shortcut menu. Open and Delete are menu choices, Cut and Paste is used to move a file, and Copy and Paste copies a file.

File Manager supports drag and drop for moving and copying files, but you have to remember to hold the Ctrl key to copy a file instead of moving it (unless you are copying across drives). The right-drag maneuver, available in Explorer, eliminates the guesswork by providing a menu that gives you the choice to move or copy. You can also left-drag files in Explorer to move them, or hold down the Ctrl key while left-dragging to copy instead of move files.

Rename

File Manager lets you rename files and folders through a dialog box that also supports wildcard file renames. Renaming a group of files or changing extensions is quite easy.

Explorer permits you to rename one file or folder at a time. There is no dialog box; you rename directly on the file or folder's listing in the right pane.

Create a Directory/Folder

In File Manager, you create a directory/folder by selecting the folder in which you want to place this new subfolder and choosing Create Directory from the File menu. A dialog box opens so you can enter the name of the new directory.

In Explorer, you create new folders in the Contents pane of the parent folder (which can be a drive if the folder is being placed on the root directory).

Disk Management

File Manager has a Disk menu that includes commands for Diskcopy, Label, and Format.

In Explorer, managing disks is accomplished by right-clicking the disk icon to bring up the shortcut menu. You can choose Copy Disk or Format.

Viewing the Explorer Panes

Your view of the contents of either pane is dependent on the size of the Explorer window. Also, in the left pane, the more you expand folders, the further the display moves to the right. In the right pane, the number of items and the way you choose to view them determines the way you have to scroll through the display to see all the items.

Change the Width of the Panes

You can change the width of the panes by moving the mouse pointer onto the vertical bar that divides the panes. When the pointer turns into a double-headed arrow, hold the left mouse button and drag the bar left or right (depending on which pane you need to expand).

> **Note** Unlike in File Manager, you cannot drag the separator all the way to one side in order to see only one pane, nor is there a menu choice to provide a view of only one pane.

New Feature for Viewing Folder Names

Kudos to the Microsoft programmers for a great feature in the left Explorer pane— ToolTips (small pop-up text boxes) for folder names. As you expand the folders in the left pane, each level of subfolders moves to the right. To see the names of second- and third-level subfolders, you can expand the pane, but that makes the right pane smaller, which means you have to scroll more frequently to see its contents.

ToolTips for left pane objects work by showing the name of any left pane object that has its name truncated by the separator bar. Just hold your pointer on the object to see a ToolTip that displays the entire name (see fig. 9.2). If the entire name is visible, the ToolTip doesn't appear.

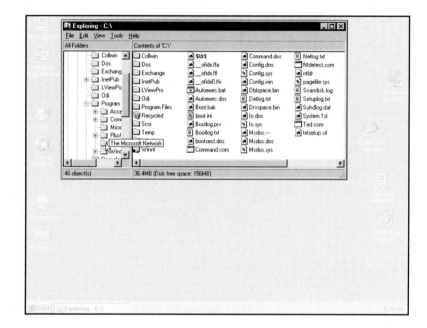

Figure 9.2

Pause the mouse pointer on a folder to see its name when that name is obscured by the separator bar.

Viewing the Contents Pane

The manner in which you scroll through the contents of the right pane varies depending on the view you've chosen. There are four different choices for displaying the right pane contents. You can select any of them from the View menu by right-clicking on a blank spot on the right pane and choosing View, or by selecting a view button from the toolbar. These are the choices:

◆ **Large Icons.** The icons are large with names placed under the icons. The display is arranged from left to right across the top row, left to right on the next row, and so on. Folders are displayed first, and then files.

◆ **Small Icons.** The icons are small with names to the right of the icon. The display is arranged from left to right across the top row, left to right on the next row, and so on. Folders are displayed first, and then files.

◆ **List.** The display looks just like small icons, but the contents are arranged by columns rather than rows (this is the default view).

◆ **Details.** The display is arranged in columns that provide information about each item (see fig. 9.3).

Figure 9.3

The Details view of the contents pane presents information about each item.

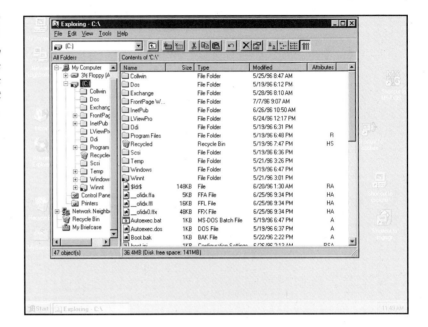

Arranging Contents

The contents in the right pane are arranged in a distinct order. By default, the order is alphabetical by name, with folders listed before files. You can change the way contents are arranged by choosing Arrange Icons from the View menu (either on the menu bar or the shortcut menu you get when you right-click on a blank spot of the right pane). The choices follow:

◆ by Name

◆ by Type

◆ by Size

◆ by Date

In addition, if you have selected large icons or small icons, the Auto Arrange option is available. This is a toggle; you select it to turn it off and on (when it is on, there is a check mark next to the option). When it is on, icons snap to the left side of the pane and line up neatly.

There is an additional menu item under View called Line Up Icons (it is also available on the shortcut menu that appears if you right-click on a blank spot of the right pane). Available only for the large or small icons view, click this menu item to force the icons in the right pane to line up neatly (they line up inside an invisible grid).

When you display the contents pane with details, you can rearrange and configure the pane with a number of different options:

◆ To enlarge any column so that every line item can be read easily, place the mouse pointer on the column separator on the title bar, using the column separator to the right of the column title. When the pointer changes to a double-headed arrow, double-click to force the column to widen to a size that includes the widest item listed in the column.

◆ Manually change the width of a column by positioning the pointer on the column separator and dragging when the pointer changes to a double-headed arrow.

◆ To sort the items by any of the criteria, click on the appropriate column title. The list is sorted by the criteria used by that column. Click again to reverse the sort order.

Note that if you sort by Name, the folders are listed first (sorted by name), followed by the files (sorted by name). If you reverse the sort by clicking again on the Name column title, the folders are listed last.

Managing Files and Folders

You can do more with Explorer than browse your computer; you can add, move, copy, delete, and rename files and folders. This means that as you manipulate your files and folders, you continue to see where they are in the system's hierarchy. Everything is done in Explorer; there are no dialog boxes requiring the entry of paths.

Add Folders

Adding a folder is an easy process that is completed right in Explorer. Folders are added as children of parent folders, although the parent can be a drive if you're creating a folder on the root directory of that drive. To add a folder, follow these steps:

1. In the left pane, select the parent folder. The current contents of that folder are displayed in the right pane.

2. Right-click on any blank spot of the right pane and choose New, Folder from the shortcut menu. A folder appears in the right pane with the temporary name New Folder. The name is surrounded by a box and highlighted (see fig. 9.4).

3. Enter the permanent name for the folder and press Enter to end the process.

The new folder is in its right place in the hierarchy and is ready to use.

Figure 9.4

New folders are placed right where you want them in the system's hierarchy.

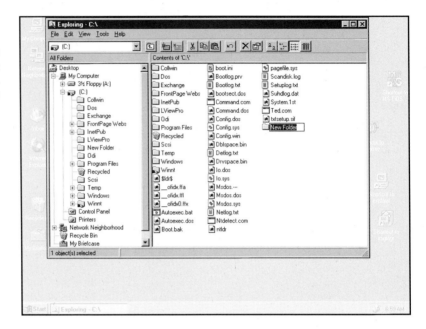

Add Files

You can also add a new file to any folder while you are working in Explorer. The process is similar to adding a folder. Follow these steps to add a file to any folder you select in the left pane:

1. Right-click on any blank spot of the right pane and hold your pointer over New on the shortcut menu to see the cascading menu shown in figure 9.5. (The choices on your menu vary depending on the resources and applications installed in your computer.)

2. Choose a file type (from the menu) to create a new file icon that is associated with the application type you selected.

3. The file name is highlighted and has a box around it, indicating it is ready for editing. Enter characters to replace the default name with a name of your own choosing (don't forget the extension).

The new file is in the correct folder. The file is empty, acting more or less as a placeholder.

Double-click on this file to open its associated application. The application window is empty but the title bar displays the name you gave this new file. After you enter data, you can save the file again (no dialog box appears when you choose Save—the file name is already determined; use Save As if you want to use a different name).

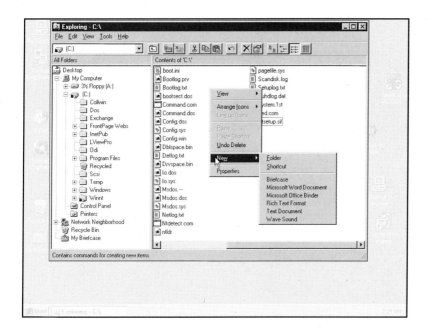

Figure 9.5

From the right pane of Explorer, you can add a new file to any folder.

Note There are not a lot of reasons to use this feature. You can accomplish the same task by creating the file while in an application—which is where you end up anyway. This might be a good way to place a file in a folder that is not the normal, default folder for its associated application's data files. For example, you might want to keep certain Word files in a different folder for some specific reason. But working with this file becomes more difficult because you have to hunt it down when you launch Word (the Open dialog box defaults to your preset folder). The feature does exist, however; therefore its coverage is necessary.

Rename Files and Folders

In Explorer, you rename a file or folder in the Explorer pane; there is no dialog box. Choosing the Rename option (discussed in following paragraph) highlights and places a small box around the file name (see fig. 9.6). You can enter characters to replace the highlighted name, or you can use the arrow keys to move through the file name and make minor changes.

There are several ways to invoke rename and cause the rename box to appear around a file name:

◆ Select the file and press F2.

◆ Click twice on the file name slowly (not fast enough to qualify as a double-click).

◆ Right-click on the file and choose Rename from the shortcut menu.

◆ Select the file and choose Rename from the File menu.

No matter which method you use, the file name is ready to be renamed.

Figure 9.6

After the file name is highlighted and boxed, you can rename it.

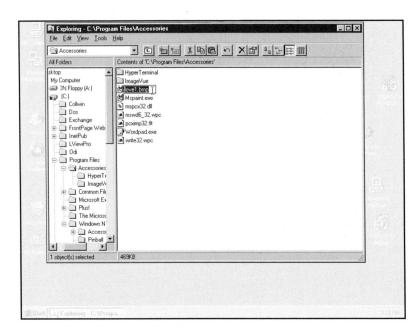

Renaming Multiple Files

Explorer does not provide any way to rename multiple files (that is one advantage of the File Manager dialog box approach). If you need to rename multiple files and want to do it quickly (instead of working in Explorer one file at a time), go to an MS-DOS prompt and use the ren command. (You can also use File Manager by choosing Run from the Start menu and entering **winfile** in the Open box, but be careful if you have long file names, because they can be destroyed by winfile.)

You can use wildcards (both the asterisk and question mark) to accomplish the chore.

The syntax is ren \path\originalnames newnames.

If you are at the prompt for the directory in which the files reside, you do not need to enter the path in the command. Actually, it's easier to do this if you move to the appropriate directory so you don't have to enter long path names when you use the command.

Note that you do not repeat the path with the new names. In fact, it's not permitted—you cannot repeat the path in the target file name; you will get an error message. This means you cannot use ren to move files to a different directory.

> You cannot rename files across drives.
>
> There is no rendir (rename directory) command, but you can use ren to change the name of a directory.

Delete Files and Folders

Deleting files and folders in the Explorer window is quite simple. You can delete a file, a group of files, all the files in a folder, or all the files in a folder and the folder itself.

Delete a File

To delete a file, select the folder in which that file is contained in the left pane to display the folder's contents in the right pane. Select the file you want to delete and use one of these actions:

◆ Press the Del key.

◆ Right-click on the file's listing and choose Delete from the shortcut menu.

◆ Drag the file to the Recycle Bin (either the desktop or Explorer Recycle Bin folder).

◆ Choose Delete from the File menu.

Delete Multiple Files

You can select multiple files for deletion (or for any other manipulation) by using one of these methods:

◆ Hold down the Ctrl key as you click on files to select them. The use of the Ctrl key prevents the second selection from replacing the first.

◆ If the files are contiguous, select the first file and then select the last file while holding down the Shift key. All the files between the first and last are also selected.

◆ If the files are contiguous, enclose them in a box by clicking just to the right of the first file and dragging the mouse right and down, until you reach the last file (see fig. 9.7). When you release the mouse, all the files along the left edge of the box are selected.

Figure 9.7

Click and drag to draw a box that will enclose and select the files along its length.

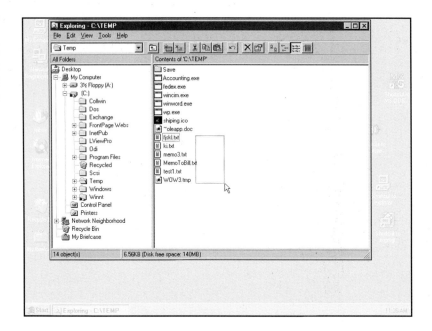

After you have selected all the files you want to delete, use one of the methods described previously to accomplish the multiple deletion.

Delete All Files in a Folder

You can delete all the contents of a folder and retain the empty folder on your system. Just select the folder in the left pane to display its contents in the right pane. Then press Ctrl+A (or choose Edit, Select All). All the files are selected and you can delete them using one of the methods described previously.

 Tip   The reasons for saving empty directories vary according to your setup and computing habits. Your temporary directory (\temp) is one good example of a directory that frequently is empty but should remain on your system. Temporary directories can also be used to unzip files, transfer files for zipping, and so on. Once the work is done and the resulting files are moved where they belong, you can delete the contents but hold on to the directories for the next time you have to perform those tasks.

Delete a Folder and All Its Files

The easiest thing to do is delete a folder (in fact, it's so easy it's dangerous). Select the folder (if it's a subfolder, you can select it in either pane), and then use one of the deletion methods mentioned previously. It's gone.

This is also the method you use to delete an empty folder. Be aware that empty folders aren't tracked in the Recycle Bin (but it's so easy to create a folder, it doesn't really matter).

No matter what you're deleting or how you're deleting it, you will see a confirmation dialog box, so there's a last minute chance to change your mind (unless you have turned off the confirmation feature in the Properties dialog box for the Recycle Bin).

Move and Copy Files and Folders

You can move or copy files and folders throughout your system from within Explorer. As with most Explorer manipulations, you have several methods to choose from when you want to perform these tasks.

Move Files and Folders

There is no Move command in Explorer. You can drag items to move them or use Cut and Paste from the shortcut menu.

To move files or folders, drag them to the new location (if you have selected multiple files, drag any one of them and all the rest come along for the ride).

The best (and safest) way to drag files is to use the right mouse button (this is called a right-drag). When you release the mouse at the target location, a menu appears so you can choose the action you want to complete (see fig. 9.8).

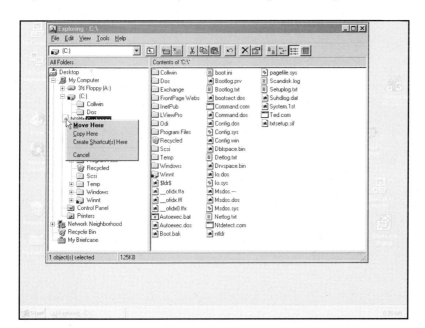

Figure 9.8

The right-drag menu makes it easy to accomplish tasks when you are manipulating files and folders.

If you can see both the source and target folders at the same time in Explorer, drag the items. If you cannot see both folders, choose one of these methods:

◆ Right-click on the item you want to move (if you have selected multiple files, right-click on any one of them and whatever you do to one you do to all). Choose Cut from the shortcut menu. Right-click on the target location and choose Paste.

◆ Open a second copy of Explorer and make sure the target folder is visible in the left pane. Then drag between the Explorer windows.

◆ Open My Computer and open folders to move to the target folder. Drag between Explorer and My Computer.

 Tip   If you prefer to left-drag items, remember that dragging moves (not copies) the items. However, if you are dragging between drives, the default is to copy the items when you drag—if you want to move those items, hold down the Shift key while you are dragging.

Copy Files and Folders

Copying items is accomplished in much the same way as moving items, and right-dragging is the easiest and safest way to copy. If you do not right-drag (or forget it's available, which is a common problem for users who are new to NT 4), follow the earlier instructions for moving items, bearing in mind these facts:

◆ If you left-drag, hold down the Ctrl key to copy instead of move.

◆ If you right-click on the item and use the shortcut menu, choose Copy and then choose Paste at the target location.

Of course, just as with moving or deleting files, you can follow the old-fashioned route of using the menu bar—the selections are Edit, Copy, and then Edit, Paste.

Understanding File Types

A file type is exactly what that term implies—it is the definition of a type of file (and its type is indicated by its filename extension). A great many file types are available in the computer world, and those that are recognized by Windows NT are defined in the Registry. (Briefly, the Registry is a database that stores all the information about a computer's configuration.)

You can see the list of registered file types in Explorer or My Computer by choosing View, Options to bring up the Options dialog box and then selecting the File Types tab (see fig. 9.9).

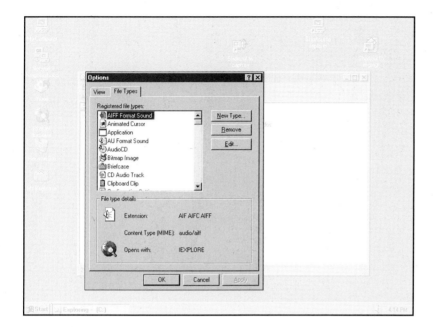

Figure 9.9

Every registered file type is listed in the File Types tab of the Options dialog box.

You can add, remove, change, or manipulate file types in Explorer or My Computer. The results are then transferred to the Registry. (Technically, you could do it the other way around, manipulating data in the Registry, which would then become the configuration displayed in Explorer, but Explorer is easier to work with for this task.)

As you scroll through the registered file types, you can select any type to see more information in the dialog box.

File Type Associations

If a file type is registered (known to your NT system), you can associate it with a software application. This means that if you double-click on a data file, the associated software opens automatically, and the data file appears in the software window, ready for you to work on. You can even associate multiple applications with a file type so you can have a choice about which application opens, or you can specify actions to be taken when you double-click on a file of a certain type.

Most of the file types listed in the Options dialog box are already associated with a program. To see the association, select the file type and see the program listed at the bottom of the dialog box (it says Opens With).

Create a File Type

You can create a file type so that when you double-click on any file of that type a software application of your choosing opens. This is useful for the applications you use that don't have file types registered by default. For example, if you use a software application that doesn't register its extensions when you install it, you will have to create the file type. This frequently happens with software that is developed in-house.

For example, you might have a software application in which all data files have an extension of rep. Or, you might have a database program in which text-based reports that are saved to disk have that extension (either by default or because you entered that extension when you named the report file). If you right-click on any file with that extension in Explorer, the shortcut menu looks different from those of files that are registered—it lacks an Open command (see fig. 9.10).

Figure 9.10

This file has no Open command, so double-clicking on it doesn't work; nothing happens.

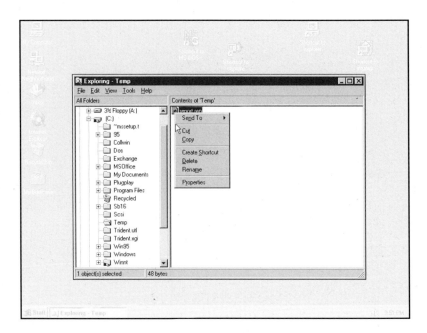

If you want to be able to open that file into WordPad or Notepad, you have to create the association. Or, you can create an association to the software package that created it. In order to do this, you first have to create a new file type for files that have this origin.

Tip   In order to make the association work, you have to be sure to save your document files in the appropriate software with the same three letter extension you specify when you establish the new file type.

New file types can be created from the File Types tab of the Options dialog box (refer to fig. 9.9) and the modifications you make also modify the Registry. Choose New Type to display the Add New File Type dialog box (see fig. 9.11).

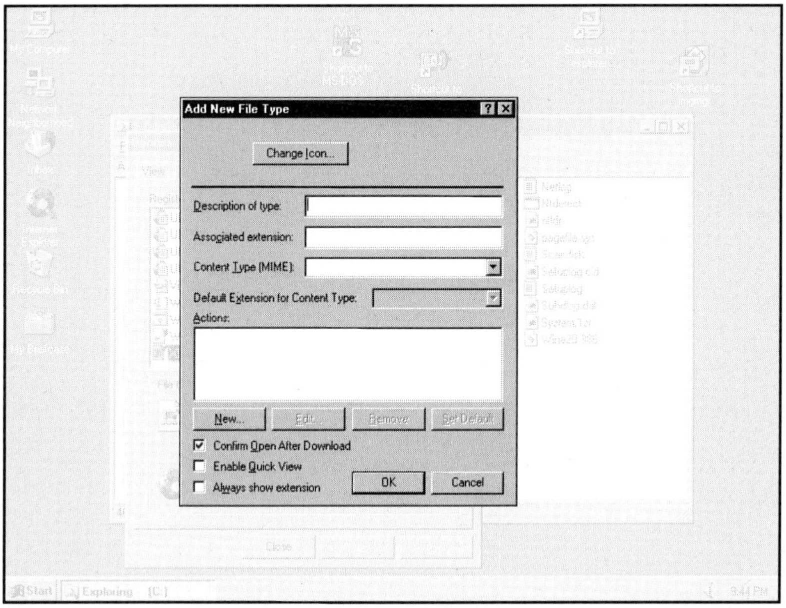

Figure 9.11

You can add a new file type to your system and specify the way it can be used and manipulated.

The fields available in the top of this dialog box are for the following configuration options:

◆ **Description of Type.** Describes this file type. This description is displayed in Explorer and My Computer when you use the Details view.

◆ **Associated Extension.** The three-letter file name extension that appears with this file type. Every file that has this extension uses the configuration options you establish.

◆ **Content Type (MIME).** The MIME type (see the following note) you want to associate with this file type. Click the arrow to the right of the field to see the available choices. This field is optional.

◆ **Default Extension for Content Type.** The file name extension for the MIME type. Some MIME types permit more than one extension and this field is the place to establish a default. This field is optional.

Note   MIME (Multipurpose Internet Mail Extension) types permit Internet browsers to link a MIME type with a file type. This means if you want to open a file of this type over the Internet, the appropriate software launches.

After you've configured file types, you can move to the next step, which is defining the action that takes place for this association. You can even choose multiple actions, all of which is explained in the next section.

Specifying Actions for the File Type

The Actions field of the Add New File Type dialog box is the place to configure the commands you want to run for this file type. To create an action, follow these steps:

1. Choose New to open the New Action dialog box (see fig. 9.12).

Figure 9.12

Add and configure an action to place on the shortcut menu for any file of this type.

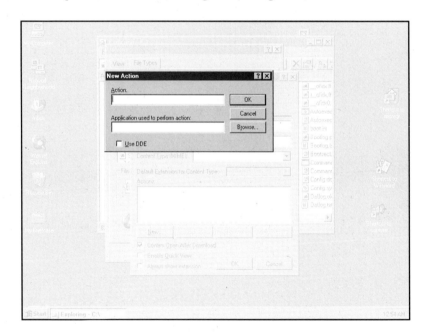

2. In the Action field, enter the command you want to appear on the shortcut menu (most of the time, this command is Open).

Tip   If you want the command you place on the shortcut menu to have a *hot key* (an underlined letter that you can press instead of clicking on the item), precede that letter with an ampersand (&). Do not use any letter that is already used by items on the shortcut menu.

3. In the Application Used to Perform Action field, enter the path and name of the software you want to associate with this file type. You can choose Browse to search your drive for the application's executable file.

4. If the application uses DDE, select the Use DDE box.

> **Tip** Selecting the DDE option opens additional dialog box options that permit you to customize the way DDE will work with this application. This assumes you know how to program DDE statements.

5. Choose OK to finish configuring the New Action dialog box and return to the Add New File Type dialog box.

6. At the bottom of the dialog box, select or deselect the available options, as follows:

   ◆ **Confirm Open After Download.** Indicates you want a confirmation dialog box before this file type is opened following a download (the dialog box asks whether or not you want to open the file).

   ◆ **Enable Quick View.** This option is only available if the file type supports the Quick View feature. (See Chapter 6, "Using the Desktop.")

   ◆ **Always Show Extension.** Displays this file type's extension in folder windows.

7. At the top of the dialog box is a Change Icon button. This button calls up a display of icons. Choose the icon that you want to appear with any files of this type.

> **Tip** Many applications automatically assign their own icons to data files so you need to choose an icon only if you know the associated application does not perform this action.

8. Choose Close when you have finished configuring this new file type.

The new file type is registered and appears in the File Types tab of the Explorer and My Computer Options dialog box (see fig. 9.13). Close the dialog box. Find a file of this type and right-click it to see the new command on the shortcut menu.

Multiple Actions for a File Type

You can assign more than one action to a file type and each of them will be listed on the shortcut menu.

To assign additional actions while you are adding a file type, when you return to the Add New File Type dialog box previously shown in step 6, repeat the steps to add an action.

Figure 9.13

The new file type, its icon, and other information are displayed.

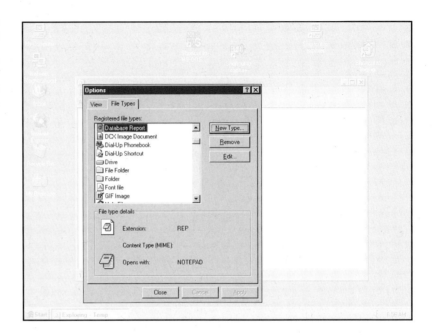

To assign additional actions later, edit the file type as described in the next section.

When you have multiple actions listed in the Actions box for a file type, you have to choose a default action to determine what happens when you double-click on the file listing.

Edit a File Type

To change the configuration of a file type, select it in the File Types tab of the Options dialog box and then choose Edit. The Edit File Type dialog box, which looks like the Add File Type dialog box, appears (see fig. 9.14).

You can add a New action or Edit an existing action. For example, you might want to change the application that is associated with the Open command. You can also select or deselect options to change the current configuration.

Adding Open Commands

You can even add additional Open commands if you wish, as long as the command is specific. For example, the report data file you've been looking at as an example during this explanation of file types is a text file. The first action added was Open, and the associated application was Notepad.

However, you might have a template or a macro in a word processor that takes text files like this and formats them in some special way. You can add an action named Open With xxx (substitute the name of the application for xxx).

Or, you may have saved this database report file with delimiters included in the file. You might want to choose to open this file in an application for which you can include a startup parameter to import text files and use the delimiters to separate items.

As an example, in WordPerfect you might have a macro that launches the import delimited text feature. You can add a command named Open in WP to this file's Actions list. When you configure the associated application (WordPerfect), you just have to add the switch that opens WordPerfect with a macro (/m-macroname).

As you become familiar with the ways to open your software applications by using switches and parameters, you'll think of inventive ways to use this Actions feature on file types.

You can also choose other actions besides Open, such as Print or Export, depending on the features of the associated application.

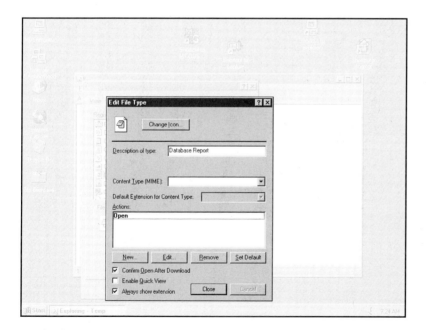

Figure 9.14

Change a file type configuration by adding actions or changing existing options.

Once there are multiple actions in the Actions box, select the one that should be invoked when you double-click on the file and then choose Set Default (see fig. 9.15).

Figure 9.15

Choose the action that occurs when you double-click on any file of this type; this is called the default action.

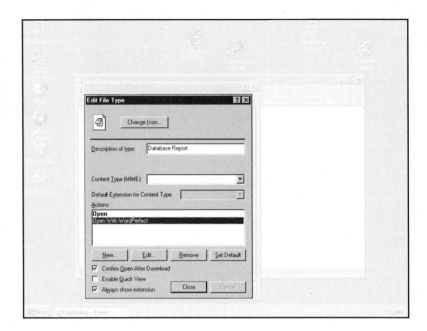

Remove a File Type

You can remove an existing file type through the File Types tab of the Options dialog box. Select the file type and then choose Remove. This means there is no longer an application association with this file type and nothing will happen if you double-click on any file of this type.

Using Find in Explorer

While you are working in Explorer, the Windows NT Find feature is available so you can find any file, folder, or computer quickly.

Find a Computer

You can view all the computers to which you are attached by clicking the plus sign next to the Network Neighborhood folder in the left Explorer pane. However, if there are a lot of entries to scroll through, it is faster to go right for the computer you need by using Find.

Choose Tools, Find, Computer from the menu bar to bring up the Find: Computer dialog box (see fig. 9.16).

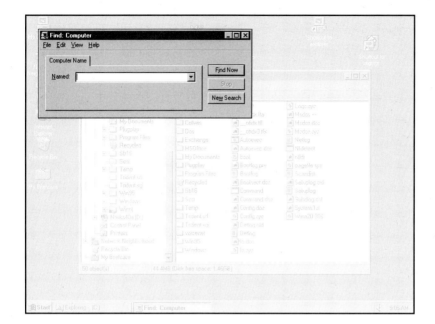

Figure 9.16

You can search for any connected computer with Find.

Enter the name of the computer you need to access in the Named box (you do not have to use the UNC format in a Find box; just the name will do).

When the computer is located, it is displayed in a box that appears in the lower portion of the Find dialog box (see fig. 9.17). Double-click on it to see the shares you have access to and then proceed with whatever tasks you need to perform.

Find Files and Folders

You can search for files and folders in Explorer by pressing F3 (or from the menu bar, choose Tools, Find, Files or Folders).

Find works by starting at a specific point in your system and through subfolders from that point. You can speed the search by selecting the folder at which you want to start your search, and then pressing F3. The selected folder becomes the starting point (see fig. 9.18).

If you change your mind about the starting point, click the arrow to the right of the Look In box and choose a new starting point.

Tip

If you map drives for a connected computer and select My Computer as the starting point, Find will include those connected drives in the search for files and folders.

Figure 9.17

The computer is found and can be manipulated from the dialog box.

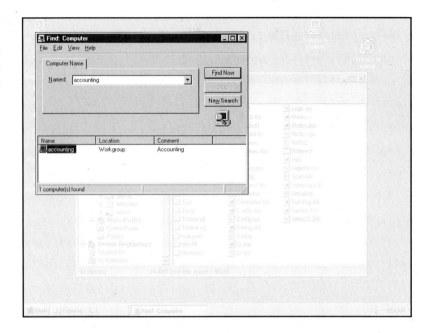

Figure 9.18

Start a search for a file or a folder at any point you want.

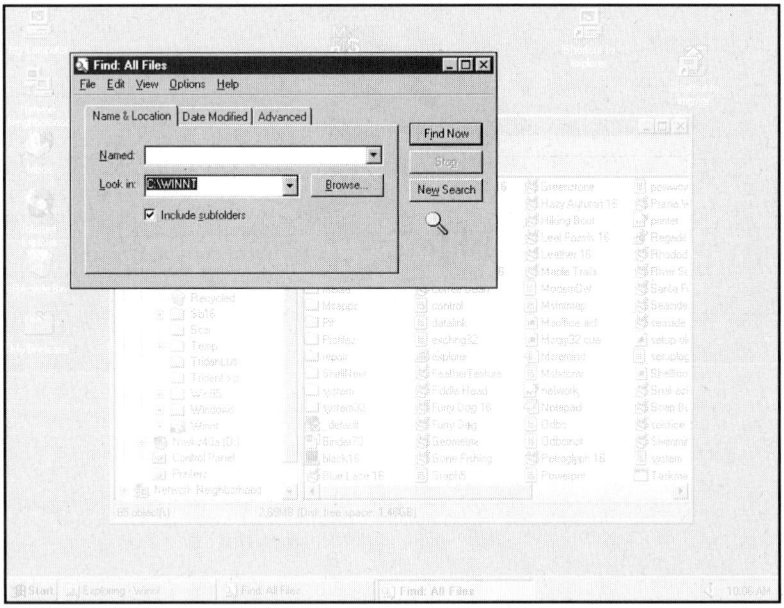

For detailed information on using Find, see Chapter 6.

Setting Explorer Options

You can customize Explorer to suit your needs and work habits. The configuration options affect the appearance of Explorer as well as the display of files and folders.

By default, the toolbar is not on the Explorer window. You can add it by choosing View, Toolbar.

The remaining configuration choices are found in the Options dialog box (see fig. 9.19), which is reached by choosing View, Options.

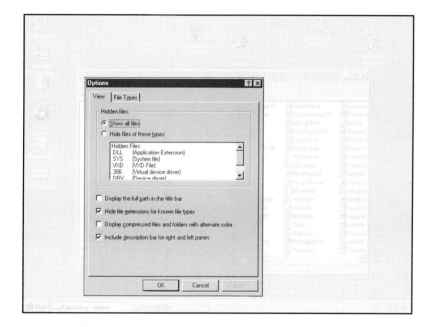

Figure 9.19

Configure the way Explorer displays files on the View tab of the Options dialog box.

The following options can be selected or deselected (choose OK when you have finished making changes):

◆ **Show All Files.** Choose this option to have Explorer display every file in your system. This includes hidden and system files, as well as hidden folders.

◆ **Hide Files of these Types.** Choose this option to eliminate the display of any file types in that list. These are hidden, system, and DLL (Dynamic Link Libraries) files.

◆ **Display the Full Path in the Title Bar.** Choose this option to see detailed path information on selected items.

◆ **Hide File Extensions for Known File Types.** Choose this option to eliminate the extensions for file types that are listed in the File Types tab. This makes the display less cluttered.

◆ **Display Compressed Files and Folders with Alternate Color.** Choose this option if you have disk compression enabled.

◆ **Include Description Bar for Right and Left Panes.** Choose this option to see labels on both panes. If you turn this off, you have a bit more room to display items.

> **Tip**
>
> There are advantages to hiding the system, hidden, and DLL files. First of all, there's less chance they will be deleted or moved accidentally. Secondly, because you almost never have to access or manipulate them, you won't have to wade through those listings to get to the files you do need to manipulate.

Understanding Send To

The shortcut menu that appears when you right-click a listing includes a menu item called Send To. Although it depends on the installation configuration for your system, your default Send To menu probably includes a disk drive, the Briefcase, and Mail Recipient.

In practice, using Send To is similar to dragging an item and dropping it on the Send To target. If the target is a container, such as the Briefcase or a disk drive, it is parked there. If the target is a program, the program opens.

The Send To Folder

The items that are displayed in the Send To list are a reflection of the items that have been placed in your Send To folder. Notice the use of the word "your"—each user of your computer has a Send To folder and, therefore, each user can have a different list of Send To items. (See the discussion on profiles in Chapter 5, "Understanding Profiles.")

To find your Send To folder, follow these steps in Explorer:

1. Click on the plus sign next to your Windows NT folder.

2. Click on the plus sign next to the Profiles folder.

3. Search for your profile folder (your logon name) and click on the plus sign.

4. Select the Send To folder.

The right pane of Explorer shows shortcuts that match the menu items you see when you choose Send To from a file's shortcut menu (see fig. 9.20).

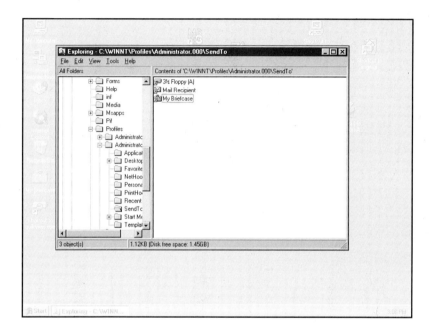

Figure 9.20

Shortcuts in the Send To folder create the menu items in the Send To selection of the shortcut menu.

Note that the contents of the Send To folder are all shortcuts.

Adding to the Send To Folder

You can add items to the Send To folder (and thereby add to the menu choices) by following these steps:

1. Follow the previous steps to expand folders so that your Send To folder is accessible in the left pane.

2. Open the folder that contains the item you want to add to the Send To menu.

3. Right-drag the item to the Send To folder. Release the mouse and choose Create Shortcut(s) Here.

Tip

If you cannot drag the item to the Send To folder easily (perhaps the items are widely separated and you cannot view both at the same time), highlight the item and then scroll through the left pane to put the Send To folder into position.

You can repeat this process for every item you want to move to the Send To folder (and place on the Send To menu). Some of the items you might want to consider for the Send To folder follow:

◆ Shortcuts to printers. The file must have an application associated with it if you want to send it to a printer (the application opens, prints the item, and then closes).

◆ Shortcuts to connected, mapped drives.

◆ Shortcuts to folders that hold documents for special uses.

◆ Shortcut to the Recycle Bin (using Send To to send a file to the Recycle Bin eliminates the confirmation dialog box).

Creating Shortcuts to Folders

Creating shortcuts to folders can be extremely productive. For example, if you have created files in various applications for a project, you might want to create a project folder and then put a shortcut to it in Send To. When you see a file in Explorer that belongs there, you can send it.

This is also a wonderful way to archive files that you don't need, but don't want to delete. Create a folder for this purpose and put a shortcut to it in the Send To folder. Then, as you come across files you want to archive, send them to this folder. Eventually, you can move the folder to a floppy disk and store the files without using hard disk space.

The same theory works for a shortcut to a folder that contains software to compress files. You can send files to the folder, zip them, and then send them to a floppy.

Remember that applications written for Windows NT 4 (or Windows 95) provide right-click functions for document files in the Open and Save As dialog boxes. This makes it easy to do housekeeping on your drive, sending old files to floppy disks or special folders via the Send To menu item on the shortcut menu.

Shortcut Menu Tips

There are some productive additions you can make to the shortcut menu that are easy to do. This section discusses a couple, which should stimulate you to think of some that are relevant to your work habits.

Multiple Choices for Open

You can have more than one choice for opening a file. For example, some graphics files (.pcx or .tif) can be opened in a host of different programs. To create a second choice for opening a document file, follow these steps:

1. Choose View, Options from the menu bar and move to the File Types tab of the Options dialog box.

2. Select the file type to which you want to add this command and choose Edit to bring up the Edit File Type dialog box (see fig. 9.21).

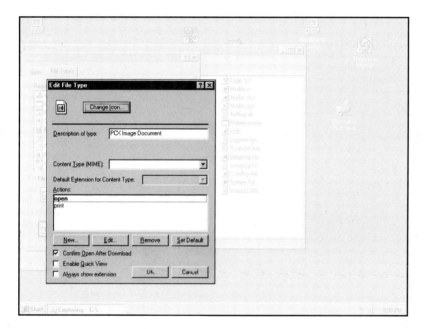

3. Choose New to enter the New Action dialog box. Enter the new Open command in the Action box. Then enter the Application you want to use for this command (see fig. 9.22).

4. Choose OK to return to the Edit File Type dialog box.

5. Select one of the Open commands and choose Set Default to make that application the one that launches when you double-click on the file listing. To use the other application, you will have to choose it from the shortcut menu.

6. Choose Close when you are finished. Then choose Close again to close the dialog box.

Hereafter, when you right-click a file of this type, the new choice is on the shortcut menu (see fig. 9.23).

Figure 9.22

Enter an action and the application you want to use to perform the action.

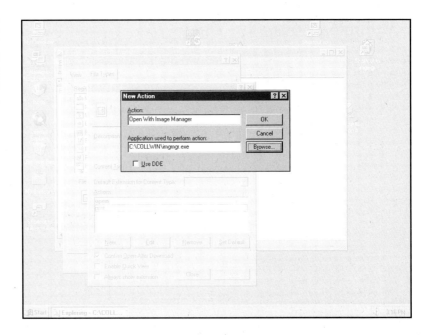

Figure 9.23

The new menu item gives an additional choice for opening this file.

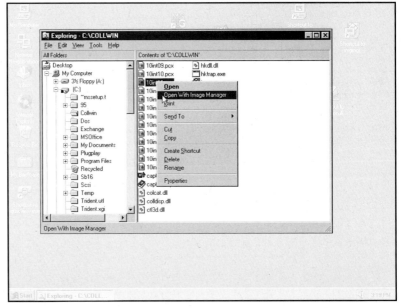

You can repeat this process for as many programs as will work for this file type. For example, most word processors will open a text file, so it might be a good idea to add your word processor as an optional open command. Then you can add fancy formatting and other goodies to the document, which are not available in the default application for opening the file.

Create Submenus

As you get comfortable working with file types, changing menu options, and adding new commands to the shortcut menu, you might want to think about making the shortcut menu more efficient as it presents all the commands you've added.

For example, if you add a number of items to Send To, you might find it easier to maneuver if you group items that are similar and then create a submenu.

To do this, just create the necessary items in your Send To folder (see the section earlier in this chapter on using this folder).

As you go through this procedure, it's important to remember that you can only perform a Send To operation to a shortcut. However, if you have a subfolder (a real one, not a shortcut to a subfolder) in your Send To folder, it will act as a menu item that points to shortcuts.

Create a folder or multiple folders in your Send To folder, assigning a category to each folder.

In each folder, place a shortcut to a folder that you use to hold files of a particular type or files that need particular manipulation.

The folders are menu items that have arrows to the right of their entries to indicate submenus. Hold the pointer on a menu item to see its submenu.

Using Subfolders

The best way to illustrate this is to use a real-life example. I have a number of folders in my system that hold specific types of documents or act as a holding bin for documents that I need to work on. For example, I have a number of subfolders under the folder that holds my file-zipping software. These subfolders are divided by topic because as I unzip files I've downloaded or zip files I need to upload, I like to keep each project together (for me, a project is a book; for you, it might be something else).

All the documents and messages I receive from online services and the Internet get downloaded to the same folder. I move through that folder, selecting files and sending them to the appropriate folders for later manipulation. Before I came up with this scheme, I would send files to a folder and then later have to cut and paste my way around a number of subfolders until everything was where it should be.

I tried adding all those subfolders to the Send To menu item, but it made the menu busy and hard to read.

Finally, by using the cascading menus in my Send To menu system, I can either send each file directly where it belongs, or send it to a holding directory and then go back to the Send To menu to make the final decision. No matter which method I choose, it is a one-click action to move a file that enables me to avoid using cut, paste, or drag.

To see a graphical representation of this system, examine figures 9.24 through 9.26. Figure 9.24 shows the contents of a Send To folder. Figure 9.25 shows the contents of one of those folders. Figure 9.26 shows how the shortcut menu works.

Figure 9.24

The folders in the Send To folder are menu items, not targets for the Send To command.

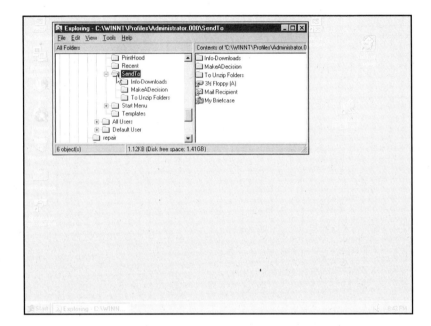

Figure 9.25

The shortcuts in the folders represent the target folders available for the Send To command.

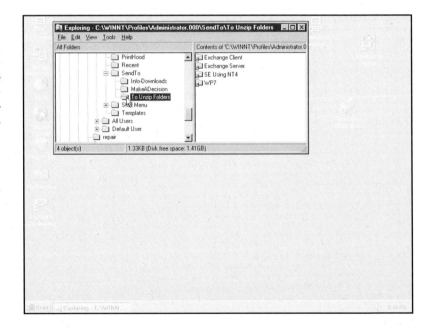

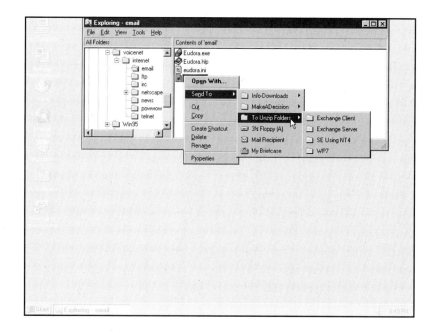

Figure 9.26

The shortcut menu now has everything necessary to handle all sorts of files.

Open a New Window

There are times when you are working with files and folders in Explorer and you realize that if you had an additional window, your task would be accomplished faster. And, to make the process of opening a new window easier, it would be handy to have the window as an item on the shortcut menu.

You can accomplish this by adding that feature to the Registry. Follow these steps to add this command to the shortcut menu for folders:

Objective

G.6

1. From the Start menu, choose Run and enter regedit in the Open box. Press OK to bring up the Registry.

2. Click the plus sign next to the HKEY_CLASSES_ROOT folder to expand it.

3. Scroll through the first set of entries (file extensions are arranged alphabetically) to the second set of entries. Find the folder named Directory.

4. Click the plus sign next to the Directory folder to expand it.

5. Select the Shell folder and right-click on any blank spot in the right pane. Choose New, Key to create a new subfolder under the Shell folder.

6. Name the new folder OpenWindow, OpenNew, or some other name that indicates the purpose of this command. Press Enter when you have entered the name.

7. Select the new folder to display its contents in the right pane. The only listing is a Default entry with no value set for the data.

8. Double-click on the Default entry to bring up the Edit String dialog box. Enter **Open New &Window** in the Value data entry box (the ampersand means that the letter W will be the hot key for this menu choice and will be underlined when it appears on the shortcut menu). Choose OK.

9. Right-click on a blank spot in your new folder and again choose New, Key. A subfolder is created under your new folder. Name this subfolder **Command** and hit Enter. A Default entry appears in the right pane for this Command folder.

10. Double-click on the Command folder's Default entry and enter **Explorer %1**. Choose OK.

11. Close the Registry Editor.

Hereafter, when you right-click on a folder in either pane of Explorer, the command Open New Window appears on the shortcut menu.

When you choose the Open New Window command from the shortcut menu, a folder window opens that displays the contents of the current folder (the folder you right-clicked). You can move through your system from this window until you find the folder or file you need. Then you can drag files between the Explorer window to the folder window.

End Note: With all the explanations of how to use Explorer to manipulate files, it should be mentioned that when you're searching the left pane for a folder or scrolling the right pane to find a file, the quickest way to get to the object you want is to type its name. As you type, Explorer moves you to the next instance of an object with a name that matches the characters you're typing.

Explorer is easy to use and is full of power. The best part of that power is that you can use your imagination (and your knowledge of the way Explorer works) to create a system that works exactly the way you want it to. The configuration options and the ability to add on the features you need combine to make Explorer much more useful than File Manager.

The first desktop shortcut you should create is the one for Explorer. Just find Explorer's executable file in your Windows NT folder and drag it to the desktop.

If all this didn't convince you of the advantages of Explorer compared to File Manager, and there are times when you think that working in File Manager would be easier, you still can. Windows NT 4 includes File Manager in the operating system.

To use File Manager, choose Run from the Start menu and enter **winfile** in the Open box. When File Manager launches, it looks and acts exactly as it did in your earlier version of Windows.

Test Your Knowledge

1. To delete all the files in a folder from Explorer:
   A. Click the folder, then click Delete.
   B. Click the folder, press Ctrl+A, then click Del.
   C. Right-click the folder, then choose Delete_Contents from the shortcut menu.
   D. Right-click the folder, then choose Cut from the shortcut menu.

2. Choose the correct statement(s) about file types:
   A. If a file type is registered, it is associated with a software application.
   B. If a file type is registered, it means its filename extension is contained in the Registry.
   C. If a file type is not registered, you cannot display the filename extension in Explorer.
   D. If a file type is not registered, you cannot open it from Explorer.

3. What are the three Windows NT locations you can access in order to register a file type?

4. Choose the correct statement(s) about the Send To item on the shortcut menu:
   A. Each user can have a separate list of choices under Send To.
   B. All users must have the same list of choices under Send To.
   C. The Send To choices are listed on the File Types tab of the Options dialog box in Explorer and My Computer.
   D. The Send To choices are shortcuts in user profile folders.

5. To add items to the shortcut menu, open _____.

6. Choose the correct statement(s) about specifying actions for file types:
   A. Multiple file types can be associated with the same software application.
   B. Multiple software applications can be associated with the same file type.
   C. You cannot change the association for a file type once it is set.
   D. If you have multiple associations on one file type, you can choose one association to be the default action.

Test Your Knowledge Answers

1. B
2. B
3. Registry, Explorer, and My Computer
4. A,D
5. the Registry
6. A,B,D

Chapter Snapshot

One of the most powerful elements of Windows NT 4 is the shortcut, an icon you create that acts as a substitute for a file. You can place shortcuts in handy locations, such as directly on the desktop or in a folder, and manipulate them without the need to scroll through listings or menus. This chapter discusses creating, configuring, and using shortcuts, focusing on the following topics:

Windows NT
Workstation 4

CHAPTER 10

Using Shortcuts

A shortcut is a quick way to access a file. Shortcuts make work easier, faster, and more productive because instead of searching for the files you need in the folders or on the Start menu, you use the shortcut.

Understanding Shortcuts

A *shortcut* is an icon that represents (and is linked to) a file or resource in your system. The file can be an executable file or a document, and the resource can be a printer, a drive, or any peripheral. Manipulating the shortcut is the same as manipulating the linked object.

When you install software, most of the time all the files associated with that software are placed in a folder or subfolder. And when you use software, the documents you create are also placed in a particular folder that is linked somehow to the software (or perhaps several folders are configured for specific document types connected to the software). You can end up with a great many folders and subfolders on your system.

As hard drives continue to drop in price, purchases of 1 GB or 2 GB hard drives are common (in fact, if you want to buy a small hard drive, you'll have a hard time finding one). That makes it easy to decide to add even more software to your system.

Today's software is written with the knowledge that hard drives are large; it isn't uncommon to purchase a software application that fills double-digit megabytes of space even before you produce the first document. Integrated software applications (suites) commonly use triple-digit megabytes. After a while, with a couple hundred megs here and a couple hundred megs there, it starts to add up to real disk space.

The Start menu's Programs group gets very long when you've installed a lot of software. Scrolling through the list to find the program you need can become bothersome. Of course, think about what it would be like working in previous versions of Windows, with all those program groups filling your screen, and all those mouse clicks as you opened groups, and then opened programs.

The answer to all of this is shortcuts, either on the desktop or in folders on the desktop. Shortcuts eliminate much of the time you spend searching for files.

Shortcut Uses

Several approaches are available for creating and using shortcuts. As you work with Windows NT Workstation 4 and get used to these shortcuts, you'll invent your own system for using them. Following are some common uses:

◆ Put shortcuts to frequently used software applications on the desktop to make it easy to launch the software.

◆ Put shortcuts to documents you're currently working on right on the desktop. Double-clicking the document opens the software it was created in (with the document in the software window, ready for editing).

◆ Put multiple shortcuts to your favorite software applications in a desktop folder.

◆ Put multiple document shortcuts into a desktop folder.

◆ Put a shortcut to your printer on the desktop so that you can drag files from Explorer or My Computer to the shortcut for quick printing.

◆ If the documents you work on frequently are all located in a folder on your system, put a shortcut to that folder on the desktop. Again, opening any of those documents opens the application in which they were created.

The ability to create shortcuts to files and folders along with the ability to put folders on the desktop is a terrific combination for productivity.

Relationship to Source Files

Each shortcut is linked to a source—a file, a folder, or a resource such as a printer or a connected drive. The link, however, isn't absolute because you can delete the shortcut without deleting the linked source. In fact, if you delete the source file, the shortcut isn't deleted—it just won't work.

You can view information about the link by right-clicking on the shortcut icon and choosing Properties from the pop-up menu. Move to the Shortcut tab to see the information about the target.

Shortcut Properties

All the information about the linked file or resource is available on the Shortcut tab of a shortcut's Properties dialog box.

Target Type
The item type of the linked file or resource. The UNC (Universal Naming Convention, which includes double backslashes in front of the computer name) for files or resources on connected computers is included if the linked item is not on the local computer.

Target
The path and filename for the linked item. You must change this if you move the linked item (the shortcut does not change automatically if you do move the linked item).

Icon and Name
The shortcut's icon and name. Notice the little curved arrow on the icon. This indicates a shortcut.

Start In
For program items, the folder in which the program should be launched, usually the program's home folder. You can think of this item as the working folder.

Target Location
The folder in which the linked item resides.

Change Icon
Click here to choose a new icon for the shortcut. You can choose one of the default icons that comes with Windows NT or install one from another source.

Run
The type of window that opens when you open the linked file by manipulating the shortcut. The choices are Normal window (the size you created when you first worked in the software), Minimized, or Maximized.

Shortcut Key
A Ctrl+Shift key combination you can use to manipulate this shortcut instead of double-clicking on it. Just enter the key you want to use and the system adds Ctrl+Shift automatically.

Find Target
Click here to open the folder window for the folder that contains the linked file. When the window opens, the linked object is selected.

Creating Program Shortcuts

The most common shortcut is one that is linked to a program. This makes it easy to launch the program because you can double-click on the shortcut instead of scrolling through the Start menu (or searching through Explorer or My Computer if the program is not on the Start menu). You can create a program shortcut in a number of ways and choose the method that feels the most comfortable.

Drag and Drop Shortcuts

The fastest way to create a program shortcut is to drag an executable file (one with a filename extension of .exe or .com) from Explorer or My Computer to the desktop. As soon as you release the mouse, a shortcut icon appears.

In any other situation, dragging and dropping moves a file. Windows NT 4, however, is intuitive enough to know you wouldn't be moving an executable file out of its working directory to your desktop, so it assumes a shortcut.

Caution While batch files and command files are executable, Windows NT loses its intuition with them. If you drag and drop a file with the extension .bat or .cmd to the desktop, you will move the file instead of creating a shortcut. Instead, use a right-drag and choose Create Shortcut(s) Here when you drop the file in the target location.

You can also right-drag an item from Explorer or My Computer. When you release the mouse after a right-drag operation, a menu appears offering several choices (see fig. 10.1). You can move or copy the file, create a shortcut, or cancel the task.

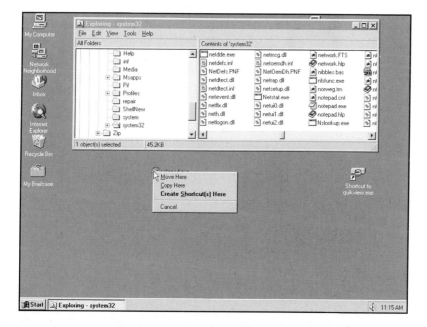

Figure 10.1

Right-dragging is safe and easy because you can choose the operation you want to perform.

Creating a shortcut by right-dragging works for any file type, including batch and command files, or document files.

 Tip   You can select multiple program files and drag or right-drag them to the desktop to create multiple shortcuts.

The Create Shortcut Wizard

Windows NT provides a shortcut wizard to walk you through the process of creating a shortcut. This method doesn't provide any particular advantage over any other method of creating a shortcut, but it is available and therefore covered in this discussion.

To create a shortcut with the shortcut wizard, follow these steps:

1. Right-click on a blank spot on the desktop and choose New, Shortcut from the menu to bring up the Create Shortcut Wizard (see fig. 10.2).

Figure 10.2

The wizard needs the path and filename of the program file you want to create a shortcut for.

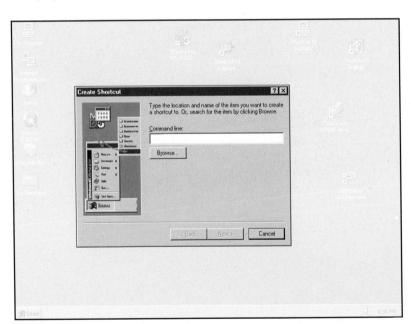

2. In the Command Line box, enter the path and file name of the program you want to create a shortcut for. Choose Browse to open a Browse window and move through the folders on your system to find the file. When you find it, double-click on it to insert the path and name into the Command Line box.

3. Choose Next to move to the next page, and enter the name you want to use for the shortcut.

4. Choose Finish. The shortcut is on the desktop.

Note that the shortcut wizard looks for a command line, so you can't use it for any shortcut other than a program file.

Shortcuts from a Menu

If you are working in Explorer or My Computer, you can create a shortcut by using menu options, as follows:

1. Find the file you want to have a shortcut to and select it.

2. Choose File, Create Shortcut from the menu bar, or right-click on the file listing and choose Create Shortcut from the shortcut menu.

3. A shortcut icon is placed in the current folder at the end of all the listings in the right pane (see fig. 10.3). A default name (Shortcut to file name) is assigned.

Now that the shortcut has been created, it has to be moved to a more convenient location, usually the desktop (having a shortcut in the same folder as the linked program file doesn't save any keystrokes at all). You have several choices for moving this shortcut:

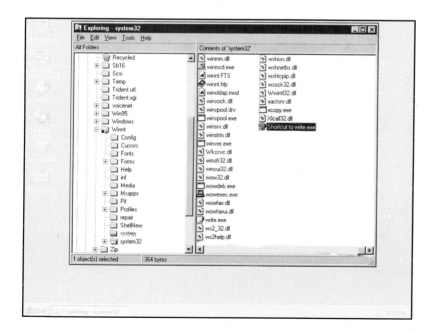

Figure 10.3

When you create a shortcut by using a menu command, the shortcut is placed in the same folder as the original file.

◆ Drag the shortcut to the desktop.

◆ Right-drag the shortcut to the desktop and choose Move Here. (Don't choose Create Shortcut because you aren't creating a shortcut to a shortcut; if you do, the original shortcut will remain in the folder.)

◆ Right-click on the shortcut and choose Cut from the shortcut menu. Then right-click on the desktop and choose Paste.

◆ Select the shortcut and choose Cut from the Edit menu. Then right-click on the desktop and choose Paste.

Shortcuts in Folders

Most of the time, the desktop is the target location for shortcuts. It makes them easy to find and handy to access. If you like the idea of having an icon handy for double-clicking to open all the programs you use frequently, the desktop seems like a natural location. But there's always the danger that the desktop can get a little busy (see fig. 10.4).

The solution is to organize your work in some fashion; the easiest method is to create folders and place similar shortcuts together in a folder. Most people find that even the extra mouse movements involved in opening a folder to access a shortcut are faster than maneuvering through the Start menu and its submenus.

Figure 10.4

Too many shortcuts can be so confusing that the efficiency is lost.

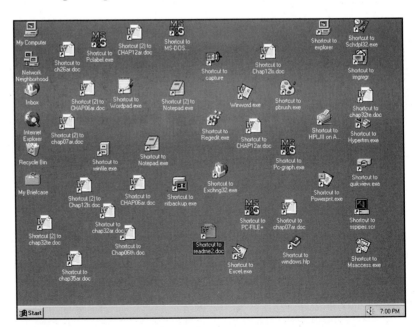

To create a folder on the desktop, follow these steps:

1. Right-click on any blank spot on the desktop and choose New, Folder. A folder icon is placed on the desktop with the title "New Folder." The title box under the folder is highlighted and ready for editing.

2. Entering any character deletes the original title. Name the folder by using a title that matches the use the folder will have. Press Enter to end the name entry process.

3. Repeat these steps for each folder you need in order to organize your icons.

There is, of course, no standard approach to the way you organize shortcuts in folders. It is totally subjective. You can organize by shortcut type (programs in one folder, documents in another folder) or by program type.

Many people leave one or two program shortcuts on the desktop, if those programs are accessed constantly.

Moving the shortcuts into folders is extremely easy. The best approach is to select multiple shortcuts by holding down the Ctrl key while you click on each shortcut you want to move into a specific folder. Then drag one of the shortcuts to the folder; they all come along. The best part is that the folder does not have to be opened; dropping shortcuts onto a closed folder moves all of them into that folder.

Configuring Program Shortcuts

You can modify the way a program works by changing some of the configuration options in its shortcut. For Windows programs, this means you can use parameters and switches to alter the way the program launches. For DOS programs, you can also control the environment in which the program runs.

While you can make the same configuration changes to the program itself, there are some cogent reasons to manipulate the shortcut instead of the program file:

◆ The changes made to a shortcut aren't permanent changes to the program (if they don't work, you don't have to remember what the original configuration was; you just delete the shortcut and then re-create it).

◆ You can create multiple shortcuts for the same program, using different startup parameters in each shortcut.

Note   You can also apply this technique to shortcuts to documents, creating a second shortcut that opens the document with a different application.

All of this manipulation is accomplished through the Shortcut tab of the Properties dialog box. Right-click on the shortcut icon and choose Properties, and then move to the Shortcut tab.

Modify a Windows Program Shortcut

If the Windows program linked to the shortcut has the ability to accept parameters on the command line, you can add those parameters to the shortcut instead of modifying the original program file. When you double-click the shortcut to launch the program, the parameters are passed to the program.

The place to accomplish this is in the Target field of the Shortcut tab of the Properties dialog box (see fig. 10.5).

Figure 10.5

Adding a startup parameter to the command line in the shortcut passes the parameter to the linked program— this shortcut to MS Word will load the MS Graph add-in when Word loads.

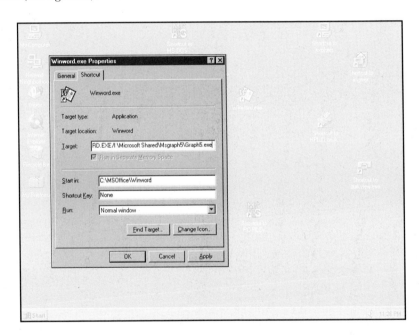

> **Tip**   If you create multiple shortcuts in order to start a program in a variety of ways, be sure you name the shortcuts appropriately (so you remember what they do and you don't have to open the Properties dialog box to figure it out).

Modify a DOS Program Shortcut

The configuration options for shortcuts to DOS programs are plentiful, and are available by right-clicking on the shortcut and choosing Properties. The Properties dialog box of a DOS program has more tabs than that of a Windows program shortcut (see fig. 10.6). Incidentally, the same Properties dialog box is available for the actual program file.

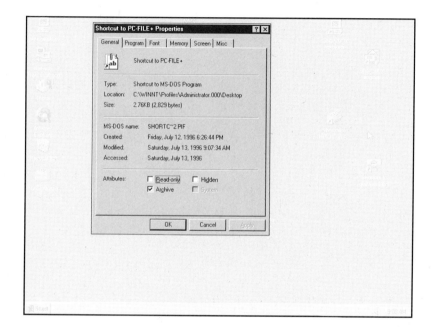

Figure 10.6

A host of configuration choices are available for running DOS programs.

Several tabs on the Properties dialog box provide methods for configuring the way DOS programs run in Windows NT 4:

◆ **Program.** Move to this tab to modify the executable command in the same way that was described in the previous section for Windows program shortcuts.

◆ **Font.** Move to this tab to change the default font size used for this program. Your Windows NT 4 system has a default font setup for MS-DOS sessions, which you can change for this program.

◆ **Memory.** This tab (see fig. 10.7) provides methods of controlling the memory environment for this DOS program.

Figure 10.7

Configure the memory usage options to get maximum productivity when you run this program.

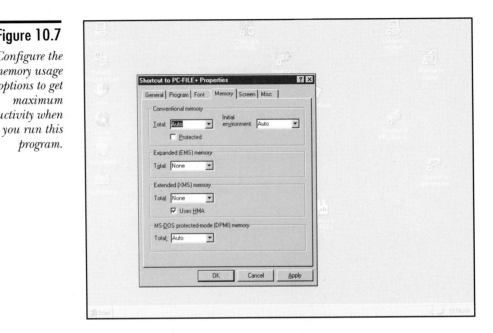

To configure the memory options, follow these guidelines:

◆ Conventional memory can be specifically allocated in kilobytes—check the specifications for the program to be accurate. Click the arrow to the right of the Total box to select a choice. You can also select Auto to let the operating system determine the allocation.

◆ If the program is capable of modifying system memory when it runs, you can protect against that by selecting the Protected check box.

◆ Choose the amount of Expanded and Extended memory you want to allocate to this program. Many DOS programs use one or the other, so check the specifications.

◆ Initial environment specifies the amount of memory (in KB) allocated for the command interpreter. (It's also the memory reserved for running batch files.) This memory option is set at the default setting in Config.NT unless you change it.

◆ **Screen.** The Screen tab of the Properties dialog box is the place to configure the program window (see fig. 10.8).

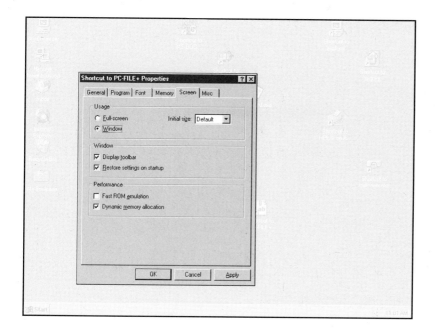

Figure 10.8

Configure the application window behavior with the Screen tab of the Properties dialog box.

You can make changes to the default configuration with these guidelines:

◆ Configure the Usage section of the dialog box for Full-screen or a Window. You can set an initial size of 25, 43, or 50 lines or use the default size for this program. If the program has a built-in configuration setting for the number of lines on the screen, anything you enter will be ignored.

Tip Full-screen usage is the most productive because it uses the least amount of memory. Pick this option for DOS games, which generally need a lot of memory. The advantage of using a window is that you can see and access other application windows that are open at the same time. Of course, a number of games just won't work properly in NT because of the hardware access calls they make, which NT does not permit.

◆ Configure the window by specifying whether or not you want to display the MS-DOS toolbar, and whether or not you want to restore the program settings for the window when you startup.

◆ Configure screen performance by choosing Fast ROM Emulation or Dynamic Memory Allocation. ROM emulation instructs your video driver to emulate any video functions it finds in ROM (read only memory). Dynamic allocation changes the amount of video memory being used as you run the program—graphics displays use more memory; when you switch to text, some of that memory is released to other running software.

◆ **Misc.** The Misc tab of the Properties dialog box has a number of additional configuration options for DOS programs (see fig. 10.9).

Figure 10.9

Use the Misc tab to set configuration options for the way the program uses the Windows environment.

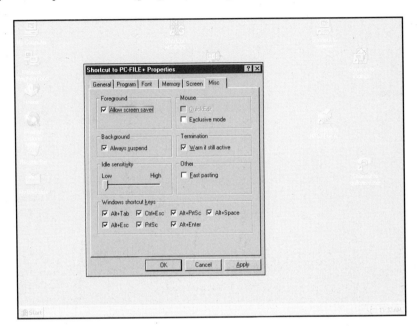

Use these guidelines to make any changes to the configuration options on this tab:

◆ Choose Allow Screen Saver to permit your screen saver to kick in while this program is in the foreground.

◆ Choose Always Suspend to stop the program from performing any tasks (and using system resources) when it is minimized.

◆ The Idle Sensitivity level is a measurement of the amount of time this program has to be idle before the resources allotted to it are reduced. Set the sensitivity to Low to permit the program to run for a longer time before the resources are re-allotted.

◆ Set the mouse for Exclusive Mode to assign the mouse to this program exclusively while it is running. Don't select this option unless the program requires it or you won't have the use of the mouse for other tasks while this program runs.

◆ Choose Warn If Still Active to have the operating system give you an alert if you attempt to close the DOS window while this program is still active.

◆ Select Fast Pasting to use a quick way of pasting information into the program (the operating system provides this Fast Pasting feature). This does not always work with DOS programs, so if you select this option and then have difficulty pasting accurately, return to this dialog box and deselect it.

◆ At the bottom of this tab are the Windows shortcut keys. If this program uses any of these key combinations to perform tasks, you can take the key combination away from Windows and give it to the program by deselecting it.

The ability to configure application behavior by manipulating shortcuts is a powerful tool.

Creating Other Shortcuts

Besides shortcuts for programs, you can create shortcuts that provide fast access to other elements in your system. As you create and configure them, remember that it might be more convenient to group them and place them in folders than to fill your desktop with icons. If you don't want to give up the ease of having them right on the desktop, you should think about using the Arrange feature for the desktop to put the shortcut icons into some kind of order so they're easier to find when you need them.

Folder Shortcuts

If there are folders in your system that you access frequently, you can create folder shortcuts and place them on the desktop. Then you won't have to move through Explorer or My Computer whenever you need to copy or move a document into that folder.

For instance, if you download files from CompuServe, the Internet, or another online service, you usually have to move those files into another folder in order to make use of them. You can drag them from the download folder to the appropriate target folder or use Cut and Paste, but it's almost always faster to drag them to a desktop folder shortcut.

Tip You can also create shortcuts for the important system folders, such as Control Panel and Printers. In fact, you can open Control Panel and right-drag any of the icons to the desktop. Choose Create Shortcut(s) Here to place a shortcut to the Control Panel application on the desktop.

To create a folder shortcut on the desktop, locate the folder in Explorer or My Computer and right-drag it to the desktop. Then choose Create Shortcut(s) Here. A shortcut to that folder, and its contents, is placed on the desktop.

You can also create a folder shortcut for a folder on a connected computer. You don't have to map the drive or share; just locate the folder in Network Neighborhood or Explorer and right-drag it to the desktop.

Folder Shortcuts

A folder shortcut acts like a pipe through which the item in the shortcut is sent to the real folder. Placing an item in the shortcut to the folder is like placing it in the real folder.

After you get used to the convenience of folder shortcuts, you can't live without them. In my case, downloaded files almost certainly will end up in one of four folders. I put shortcuts to all four folders on my desktop, and then found it less messy to create a folder on the desktop to hold those folder shortcuts. After I finish downloading files, I open Explorer and open that desktop folder to reveal the folder shortcuts. I can then drag files to the appropriate folder shortcut (remember, the folder shortcut doesn't have to be opened to accept files; just drag the files to the folder icon).

Drive Shortcuts

You can create a desktop shortcut to a drive on your computer or on a connected computer. This is most useful for connected computer drives because it eliminates the need to open Network Neighborhood or expand the Explorer folder for Network Neighborhood.

The definition of drive doesn't necessarily refer to a physical hard drive. It can be a mapped drive that represents the connected computer's physical hard drive or a share that was established on that drive. That share can be a folder (along with subfolders). After the share is mapped to a drive letter, it is considered to be a drive and you can create a drive shortcut to it.

After drives are mapped, go to Explorer or My Computer, right-drag a drive to the desktop, and choose Create Shortcut(s) Here. A shortcut to the drive is on the desktop. Now, when you want to access files, you can use the shortcut instead of browsing through My Computer, Network Neighborhood, or Explorer.

Tip   You can also create a shortcut for a connected computer. The computer does not have to be mapped to a drive; you can browse Network Neighborhood or Explorer to locate a computer and then create a shortcut to it.

Document Shortcuts

Document shortcuts on the desktop can be extremely handy if you have documents you access frequently. Boilerplate documents, such as fax covers, contracts, and other similar files, fit into this category.

To create a document shortcut, find the document file in Explorer or My Computer and right-drag it to the desktop. Then choose Create Shortcut(s) Here.

If the document was created in a software application, it is automatically linked to that application. If the document was downloaded or copied to your drive, you will have to associate it with an application. To do this, right-click on the document listing and choose Open. If there is no associated software, a list of available applications is presented and you can choose the appropriate program.

Double-clicking on a document shortcut launches its associated software; when the software window opens, the document is loaded and ready for editing.

Printer Shortcuts

Putting a shortcut to a printer on the desktop saves a lot of keystrokes when you want to print an existing document. Just drag the document listing from Explorer or My Computer to the printer shortcut. The application associated with the document opens, prints the document, and closes. Compare that to the steps involved in choosing the application from the Start menu (or opening it from a desktop short-cut), going through the keystrokes and mouse movements involved to open the document, going through the keystrokes need to print it, and then closing the application.

To put a printer shortcut on the desktop, open the Printers folder in My Computer and right-drag the printer(s) to the desktop. Then choose Create Shortcut(s) Here.

Text Shortcuts

A neat feature is the ability to grab text from a document and make it a desktop shortcut. The shortcut is called a *scrap*.

Think about the time this could save if you spend a large part of your workday typing the same (or very similar) paragraphs over and over—such as the closing paragraphs to a letter, the heading for a letter or a report, or clauses that are inserted into contracts.

Create the Scrap

To create a scrap, highlight the text you need while you are working in the application, and choose Copy from the Edit menu. Switch to the desktop and right-click on any blank spot. Then choose Paste Shortcut. The scrap is placed on the desktop.

| Caution | There are two caveats to be aware of when you create a scrap. First, the application software in which the text is created must be OLE (object linking and embedding)-enabled for drag-and-drop. Second, you must paste the scrap on the desktop while the application is running. For some reason, this doesn't work if you exit the software before pasting the shortcut on the desktop. If you work in the application in full-screen mode, either minimize the window or reduce the screen enough to see a piece of desktop real estate.

Use the Scrap

To insert the scrap into a document you're preparing, drag it from the desktop into the application window. Dragging the scrap doesn't move the scrap, but rather copies it (the operating system is intuitive enough to figure out what you're doing).

Tricks and Tips for Shortcuts

You can do a few things with shortcuts to make using them easier, or just make your desktop neater after you've begun filling it with shortcuts.

Assign a Shortcut Hot Key

If you need to open a shortcut and either don't want to bother with the effort of double-clicking on it, or you can't see it because the desktop is covered with application windows, you can use a hot key combination to open it.

To assign a hot key to a shortcut, follow these steps:

1. Right-click on the shortcut icon to display the shortcut menu, and then choose Properties.

2. In the Properties dialog box, select the Shortcut tab and move to the Shortcut Key box.

3. Enter the letter you want to use as a hot key (the Ctrl+Alt keys will be added automatically).

Caution After you assign a Ctrl+Alt+letter sequence, no other Windows program can use that combination. If you have software that is using Ctrl+Alt+key combinations, be careful not to use the same letter for a hot key that you need for your software.

4. Choose OK.

Now, whenever you want to open that shortcut, press Ctrl+Alt+the letter you chose.

Clean Up Shortcut Names

If you don't like the words "Shortcut to" in the title of every shortcut icon, you can get rid of them by editing the title. If you don't mind spending a few minutes, you can train Windows NT to do it for you.

Create a number of shortcuts, one after the other. As soon as you create each shortcut, edit its name to remove the words "Shortcut to." It doesn't matter what type of file you use to create these shortcuts and it doesn't matter how crowded your desktop gets because you're going to delete them after you've taught Windows NT to stop putting those words in the title.

Right-drag a file to the desktop, choose Create Shortcut(s) Here, click on the name while it is still highlighted to get to edit mode, move the arrow keys to the beginning of the name, and delete the words "Shortcut to." After performing this task about eight times, Windows NT will stop putting those words in the name. Hereafter, when you create a shortcut, only the file name will be used for the shortcut name.

Get Rid of Shortcut Arrows

You can also get rid of the curved arrow that appears in every shortcut icon. This involves editing the Registry, which can be dangerous if you don't follow directions exactly. Follow these steps to get rid of the arrows in shortcut icons:

Objective G.6

1. Choose Run from the Start menu, and then type REGEDIT.
2. Click on the plus sign (+) by HKEY_CLASSES_ROOT.
3. Find the folder lnkfile (this removes the arrows from the shortcuts for Windows files).
4. Click on it to show its contents in the right pane.
5. Right-click on the IsShortcut item.
6. Select Rename from the shortcut menu and put a character in front of the item (for instance, make it xIsShortcut). Press Enter to save the new name.
7. Find the folder piffile (for DOS shortcuts) and repeat steps 4–6.
8. Close the Registry.

When you reboot your system, you'll notice that the arrows are gone. To restore them, go back and remove the character you added in step 6.

Train Windows NT to Omit "Shortcut To"

If you find the words "Shortcut to" before the name of the shortcut's file esthetically annoying, or have any other objection to it, you can teach Windows NT to stop using it.

Windows NT is a slow learner; it takes some repetition before it catches on. When you have a few moments with nothing to do (perhaps during a boring telephone call or while you're having lunch at your desk), take these steps to re-train Windows:

1. Drag any executable file from Explorer to the desktop—executable files are quicker because you can left-drag them to create a shortcut without having to use a menu selection. It doesn't matter which file you use—you're going to get rid of the shortcut after school is out.

2. As soon as the shortcut is on the desktop, press F2 to edit the name.

3. Move the cursor and use the Backspace or Delete key to eliminate the words "Shortcut to" (do not simply retype the filename when the original name is highlighted—you must edit out the words "Shortcut to" and leave the filename).

4. Drag a different executable file to the desktop and repeat step 2.

5. Continue to do this until a shortcut appears without the words "Shortcut to." It should take about seven tries (some systems require a few more and I've never figured out why).

Of course, now you can delete all those shortcuts you used as training aids.

> **Caution** | Changing the appearance of shortcuts can be dangerous if you also put file icons on your desktop, because you won't be able to tell the difference between a file and a shortcut by looking at the icon. Deleting a shortcut isn't dangerous; you can always re-create it. Deleting a file is extremely dangerous (although you're warned when you are about to delete a program file).

End Note: Shortcuts are productive, efficient, interesting to play with, and fun to use. The most important thing to remember is that right-dragging any object produces a menu with a choice of Create Shortcut(s) Here. With that in mind, you can right-drag objects to any location in your system, not just to the desktop. Think about the power of placing or opening shortcuts between connected drives. The work you do on your computer, combined with your imagination, will guide you to intelligent and productive use of shortcuts.

Test Your Knowledge

1. Shortcuts are only available for executable files.

   A. True

   B. False

2. A shortcut is created by left-dragging any file icon from Explorer to the Desktop.

   A. True

   B. False

3. You can configure a shortcut so that it changes the way its associated software file opens.

   A. True

   B. False

4. Deleting a program file also deletes any shortcuts to that program file.

   A. True

   B. False

5. To eliminate the curved arrow in the shortcut icon, use which of these actions?

   A. Change the Registry.

   B. Change the Options Properties for file types in Explorer.

   C. Change the Properties in the shortcut Properties dialog box.

   D. Choose a different icon.

6. Which Windows NT element(s) can have shortcuts?

   A. Printers

   B. Executable files

   C. Document files

   D. Subfolders

7. You cannot create a shortcut to a file in the folder that contains the file.

   A. True

   B. False

Test Your Knowledge Answers

1. B
2. B
3. A
4. B
5. A
6. A,B,C,D
7. B

PART III

Configuring Devices for NT 4

Chapter Snapshot

This chapter covers the configuration of basic devices such as the mouse, monitor, and keyboard. Additionally, it discusses date, time, and location settings. Among the topics covered are the following:

Windows NT
Workstation 4

CHAPTER 11

Configuring Basic Devices

T his chapter examines some of the options available to you in setting up your computer's peripheral devices to suit your working style. The Control Panel is shown in figure 11.1. The following Properties dialog boxes are described in this chapter:

♦ **Display.** Enables you to change a monitor's resolution; set up wallpaper, color schemes, and other appearance attributes; and turn on a screen saver.

♦ **Mouse.** Lets you set up your mouse as left- or right-handed, control pointers, and set the motion characteristics of your mouse.

♦ **Keyboard.** Provides settings for keyboard layout, repeat rate, and cursor blink rate.

♦ **Date/Time.** Lets you set your system clock and time zone. You can also have the system adjust automatically for daylight savings time.

♦ **Regional Settings.** Stores a number of formats for dates, time, numbers, and currency that you can select and use.

Figure 11.1

The Control Panel contains various applets for modifying system settings.

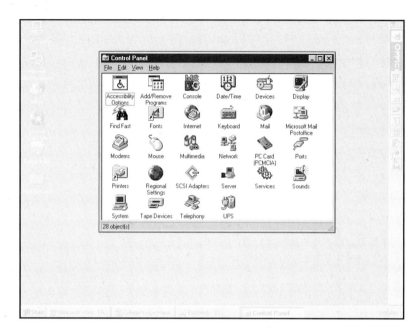

Additionally, the Accessibility Options icon in the Control Panel lets you set some special features that people with special needs require to work with computers.

Settings you make from the Control Panel are stored in the Registry and are part of your user profile. These settings are recalled when you log on to a computer with your user name. Some settings you make take effect immediately; other settings require that the Control Panel dialog box be closed to take effect. In a few cases, changes may require that Windows NT be restarted.

When your mouse (or other pointing device), keyboard, and monitor are properly configured, you can work longer and in greater comfort and are less prone to make errors. Windows NT Workstation 4 is more sophisticated in its handling of peripherals than its predecessor was, and contains features such as multiple monitor support, in-session resolution switching, and other features that you will come to appreciate.

Configuring Video

In the Control Panel, double-click on the Display icon. The Display Properties dialog box appears (see fig. 11.2). The Display Properties dialog box lets you change your video's resolution and color depth, set screen colors and fonts, and enable a screen saver. Depending on your monitor type and video card, some or all of these options are enabled. Because Windows NT Workstation 4 requires a minimum VGA video controller, you will probably find that these settings are available to you.

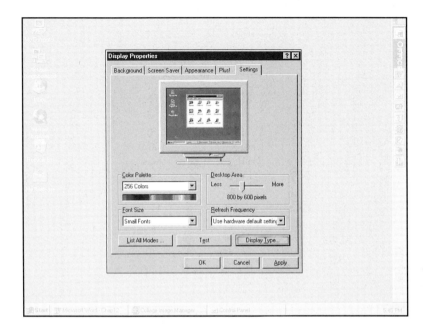

Figure 11.2

The Display Properties dialog box changes the characteristics of your display monitor.

> **Tip** To quickly open the Display Properties dialog box, right-click on a blank area of the desktop and select the Properties command from the pop-up shortcut menu.

Changing Video Drivers

The Settings tab of the Display Properties dialog box (refer to fig. 11.2) is where you install and select new video drivers. Your monitor may be operating correctly using a generic VGA driver that Windows supplies, but a proper (the most up-to-date version) video driver can display all of the high-resolution and color depth that you purchased with your adapter. The video driver is a piece of software that interprets the output from your system software's graphics display subsystem and translates it to a signal that your adapter can use to write the image to the screen.

Objective B.4

> **Note** You do not remove video drivers, but rather simply select a new one using the Display Properties dialog box. The video driver you select using the steps shown replaces the previously selected video driver.

To install a new video driver, follow these steps:

1. Insert the Windows NT 4 installation CD-ROM (or any disk containing the video driver you want to install) into your drive.

2. Click on the Display Type button on the Settings tab of the Display Properties dialog box to view the Display Type dialog box (see fig. 11.3).

3. Click on the Change button to view the Change Display dialog box (see fig. 11.4).

4. Select the manufacturer and video card model from the Manufacturers and Display lists.

   Or, click the Have Disk button and select the driver from a standard file dialog box.

5. Click on OK to return to the Display Type dialog box. Click on OK again to return to the Settings tab of the Display Properties dialog box.

6. Click on the Test button to see if your new video adapter works. Windows switches to the new adapter and settings and momentarily displays a test pattern.

7. If the pattern is correctly observed, click the Yes button to enable the driver. If not, revert back to your previous settings.

8. Press the OK button to close the Display Properties dialog box.

Figure 11.3

The Display Type dialog box enables you to modify your video driver.

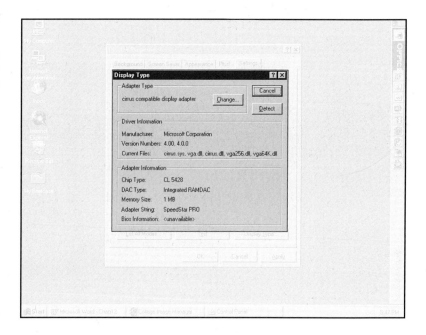

| Tip | You can often find the most current driver for your specific adapter by visiting the home page of the manufacturer of your video board. |

Windows NT Workstation's Setup program ships with many of the most popular adapters' video drivers, and is generally the most up-to-date source of video drivers available. This is particularly true when you are installing your display driver recently after a system software release.

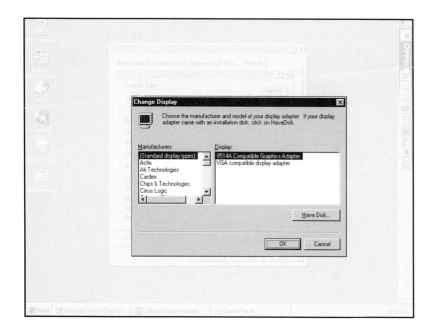

Figure 11.4

The Change Display dialog box enables you to select a driver for your particular video card.

Caution	If there is a problem with your video settings and you install an improper driver (one that doesn't display correctly on your monitor), you can run into trouble. Windows NT Workstation requires a properly operating graphics adapter and may not start up if one isn't selected.

To circumvent this problem during the startup, choose Windows NT (VGA mode) from the Boot Menu. Also, you can press the spacebar during startup when the message to go back to the Last Known Good startup configuration appears. If neither of these choices works for you, you will unfortunately have to reinstall the operating system.

Changing Video Settings

Windows lets you alter different characteristics of your display adapter. For example, you can change colors, the size of text on your screen, and other aspects of your operating system's appearance. This can be very useful if you have difficulty seeing your monitor, or for aesthetic reasons. The sections that follow detail some of your options.

Objective

B.4

The Settings Tab

Objective B.4

The Settings tab (refer to fig. 11.2) enables you to change other aspects of your adapter's display characteristics. You can select the following characteristics on that tab:

◆ **Color Palette.** Use this drop-down list to select the color level. Your adapter, its installed memory, and the display driver determine what color depth can be supported. A color text ramp shows the range.

◆ **Font Size.** Use this drop-down list to select Small Fonts or Large Fonts. Windows uses these fonts in system dialog boxes.

◆ **Desktop Area.** Select the resolution in this section by moving the slider left or right.

◆ **Refresh Frequency.** Select a frequency from this drop-down list.

Tip   Minimize perceptible flicker on your screen by choosing the highest refresh frequency that your monitor supports. 72 MHz or higher is the best bet to minimize eye strain when using the system.

The Background Tab

Objective B.4

Figure 11.5 shows the Background tab of the Display Properties dialog box. On that tab, you can select a background from the Pattern list. You can also select a bitmap to use in the Wallpaper list.

Wallpaper is a .BMP, or *bitmapped*, paint file. You can create your own wallpaper using Microsoft Paint, or by saving a scanned image at the desired size using your monitor's resolution (typically about 75 dpi). If the wallpaper is screen sized, it will fill the screen when you click the Center radio button. You can also tile small bitmaps using the Tile radio button.

Note   Wallpaper can require several hundred kilobytes of video RAM and can slow screen refresh significantly. You can improve performance by lowering the wallpaper color depth (to black and white, for example) or by foregoing the wallpaper option entirely.

The Appearance Tab

Objective B.4

On the Appearance tab, shown in figure 11.6, you can change the colors of various interface elements like window title bars, menus, scroll bars, and so on. You also have control over the fonts used. Windows can store a set of appearance settings as a named set (or scheme), and you can switch over to some predefined set by name or create your own. Items like Eggplant, Pumpkin, Rose, Steel, Slate, Wheat, and others are yours for the asking. They represent a collection of colors used for different interface elements stored as a set.

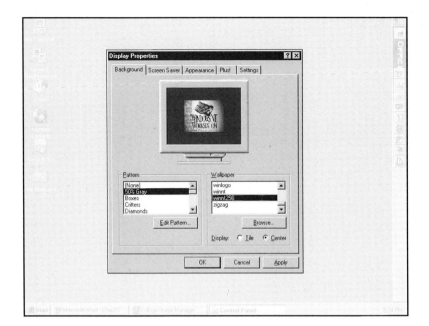

Figure 11.5

The Background tab of the Display Properties dialog box enables you to set a pattern or wallpaper, effects that can make your view more pleasant.

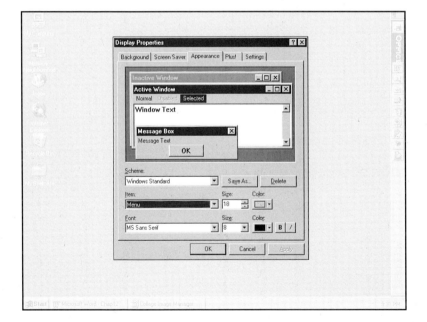

Figure 11.6

The Appearance tab of the Display Properties dialog box enables you to control different elements of your operating system's interface.

The Screen Saver Tab

You should also consider visiting the Screen Saver tab of the Display Properties dialog box (see fig. 11.7) to set the screen saver. In the past, images burned into the phosphorescent dyes on the screens of older models of CRTs (cathode ray tubes) when a static display was left on the screen for long periods of time, usually over weeks or months of time. These days (and with GUI interfaces), CRTs are much less susceptible to the problem. Still this feature is useful for its amusement value (spawning a whole little industry) and to set password protection. If you select the Password Protected check box, other users are locked out of your computer during your sessions. They must reboot and log in under their own password to access your computer. This scheme works well with the NT Security scheme.

Figure 11.7

The Screen Saver tab of the Display Properties dialog box enables you to turn on a screen saver during periods of inactivity to prevent screen burn-in.

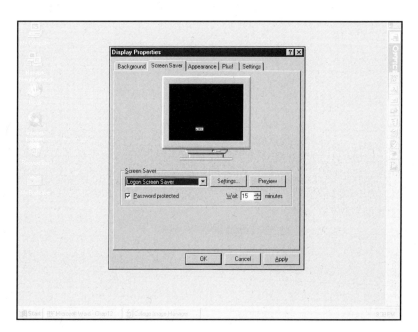

The Plus! Tab

Finally, you can visit the Plus! tab of the Display Properties dialog box (see fig. 11.8) to set interface options. These items were part of the very popular Microsoft Plus! package for Windows 95 and include a potpourri of settings. You can alter desktop icons and their colors, wallpaper, or smooth system fonts.

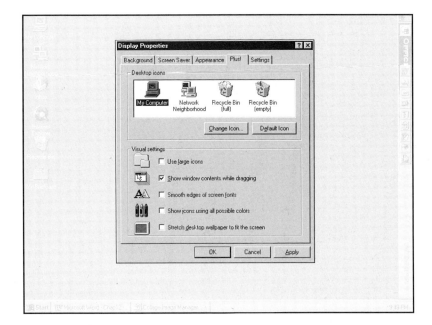

Figure 11.8

The Plus! tab of the Display Properties dialog box offers some settings for modifying the appearance of your computer's interface.

Configuring the Mouse

Most mouse devices in use today emulate the Microsoft mouse and can use the driver that Microsoft provides for that rodent. Other supported mouse types are an InPort adapter mouse, a standard bus adapter mouse, and a PS/2 Port mouse. During setup, Windows can detect a Microsoft, Logitech, or Microsoft Mouse-compatible mouse, which represents about 95 percent of the mouse devices sold. Setup installs a virtual mouse driver that provides both MS-DOS and Windows support so that separate drivers are no longer required for both of those operating systems. Without this kind of support, Windows used to require that you switch drivers when you opened an MS-DOS session. Often, the mouse froze and could not be reactivated during the switch. Under this new scheme, the driver can detect which operating system is in use and support it.

Objective
B.4

The VMOUSE (virtual mouse) driver provides the following advantages:

◆ Provides for some fault tolerance when a mouse error occurs. For example, you can press the Esc key to prevent your mouse from freezing.

◆ Allows better memory management because the drivers run in extended memory.

◆ Supports the use of any serial port and two or more serial pointing devices at the same time. A serial port is a slow speed port connecting your mouse, keyboard, or other input device.

With the appropriate mouse driver installed in your computer, the Mouse Properties dialog box enables you to change the settings of your mouse. Changes you make are immediately put into effect when you close this dialog box.

Defining Buttons

Objective

B.4

The Buttons tab of the Mouse Properties dialog box (see fig. 11.9) provides two important settings: Button Configuration and Double-Click Speed. This section covers button configuration; the next section covers double-click speed. In the default configuration, a mouse is set up for a right-handed person. The left mouse button of a two- or three-button mouse is used to select and drag objects on your screen. The right mouse button of a two- or three-button mouse is used for context-sensitive actions such as opening a context menu, or special drag operations such as copying an object or creating a shortcut.

Figure 11.9

The Buttons tab of the Mouse Properties dialog box enables you to assign which buttons are for clicks and which activate the context-sensitive menu in the operating system.

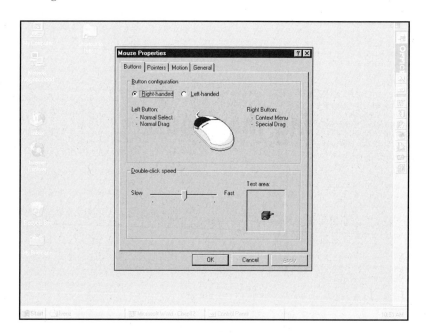

If you are left-handed, you may want to switch button settings. Click on the Left-Handed radio button in the Button Configuration section to perform the switch.

The Buttons tab you see is for the Microsoft Mouse. Another input device (such as a mouse or trackball) may show a different Mouse dialog box or provide a special program with its own dialog box that offers additional settings. For example, with a three-button mouse that many vendors (such as Logitech) provide, pressing the middle button or the middle button together with the left or right button can be assigned to common operations like a double-click or keystrokes like Ctrl+S for the Save command in common programs.

Setting the Double-Click Speed

In the Windows interface, a double-click provides special object actions like launching executable programs, restoring windows from an icon, and performing myriad other tasks. Many users have difficulty performing a double-click, either clicking twice quickly when they meant to click once, or not being able to click quickly enough to have the action recognized as a double-click. The Double-Click Speed section lets you set a slider to adjust the double-click speed. Drag the slider to the right for a slower action to be recognized as a double-click, or to the left for a faster double-click speed.

Objective B.4

To test the double-click speed you set, click twice in the Test Area. The Jack-in-the-Box (refer to fig. 11.9) will pop out of the box and disappear into the box when the double-click action is recognized.

Working with Pointers

In Windows, the pointers that you see indicate the condition of your computer at the moment. For example, during processing you see an hourglass cursor. When selection is possible, you see an arrow cursor. You change and set pointers on the Pointers tab of the Mouse Properties dialog box, as shown in figure 11.10.

Objective B.4

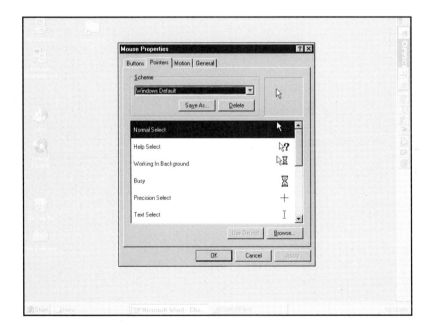

Figure 11.10

The Pointers tab of the Mouse Properties dialog box lets you assign cursors.

Note Windows 95 ships with a feature called Pointer trails, which is quite useful for laptop users. Pointer trails leaves a fading set of pointers along the path your pointer moves, thus allowing you to locate the new position of your pointer on the screen more easily. As Windows NT Workstation is adopted by more mobile computer users, this feature will undoubtedly be added to the operating system.

The standard pointer conditions are the following:

◆ Normal Select

◆ Help Select

◆ Working in Background

◆ Busy

◆ Precision Select

◆ Text Select

◆ Handwriting

◆ Unavailable

◆ Vertical Resize

◆ Horizontal Resize

◆ Diagonal Resize 1

◆ Diagonal Resize 2

◆ Alternate Select

You have individual control over each pointer and can load a variety of pointer sets. A pointer set is a collection of cursors in a style saved as a unit. Some of these pointer sets are 3D, and others are animated. Select a scheme from the Scheme drop-down list to view the different sets. Users of the Microsoft Plus! package in Windows 95 will recognize some of these pointer sets from the various schemes that that program offered. You can use the Save As button to save a scheme or delete a scheme with the Delete button.

Tip Pointer schemes can be particularly valuable for users who have impaired vision, or users whose laptop screens are difficult to see in bright light. Consider using the Magnified scheme in these instances.

To view a particular pointer, click on that cursor in the large scrolling list in the center of the Pointers tab. The Preview section to the right of the Scheme drop-down list shows the pointer and displays any animation that your video can support.

To change a pointer in a set, follow these steps:

1. Double-click on the pointer you want to modify, or click once on the pointer and click the Browse button.

2. In the standard file Browse dialog box, navigate to the Cursors folder in WINNT folder (if required).

3. Click on the .CUR or .ANI file desired; a Preview can be viewed at the bottom of the Browse dialog box.

4. Click on the Open button to change the pointer.

You can add additional static pointers or cursors (.CUR files) and animated pointer (.ANI) files by using the Add/Remove Program dialog box to add more files from your Windows NT Workstation 4 installation disks. Also, you can use several third-party programs, like DeltaPoint's FreezeFrame for Windows, to create these kinds of files. Collections of pointers are also floating about in the public domain that you can purchase.

Use the Use Default button to return any cursor in a scheme to the standard Windows pointer.

Setting Motion Speed

The mouse is a relative pointing device. That means in order to move on the screen, you must move the mouse on your desk. The movement of the rollers in the mouse provides motion on your screen. If you pick up the mouse and move it to another location on your desk, the pointer on your screen stays put.

**Objective
B.4**

If you find that you are running off the mouse pad too quickly, or that your mouse motions are too fast and jerky on the screen, you can adjust the amount of motion required to move a distance across the screen on the Motion tab (see fig. 11.11) of the Mouse Properties dialog box. Drag the slider left toward the Slow side to increase the amount of motion required to move a distance across the screen. Or drag the slider right toward the Fast side to increase the sensitivity of the pointer to the motion of the mouse. In either instance, you can test your setting by clicking the Apply button and then moving the mouse.

A graphics tablet is an example of an absolute pointing device. In a graphics tablet, the tablet maps directly to the screen. When you touch the pointing device (pen or whatever) to some point on the tablet, the point that that corresponds to on the screen is activated. Many users prefer tablets for precise graphics work for this reason. Absolute pointing devices also tend to have higher sensitivities.

A second setting also appears on the Motion tab: the Snap mouse to the default button in dialogs check box. This setting puts the pointer on top of an OK or Apply button—any button that is outlined in the dialog box and activated by pressing the Enter key—that is, the default action.

Figure 11.11

The Motion tab of the Mouse Properties dialog box enables you to control the sensitivity of your mouse to movement.

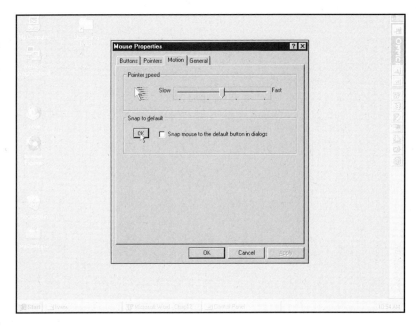

Changing Mouse Drivers

Objective B.4

The Mouse Properties dialog box is appropriate to the Microsoft Mouse and can support many other Microsoft Mouse-compatible mouse devices. Other pointing devices may, and probably will, require their own dialog boxes. They are installed from setup disks that the manufacturers provide. However, in order to use the specific features of other mouse devices (for example, those mouse devices that contain three buttons, cordless mouse devices, and so on), you will need to install another mouse driver. The General tab of the Mouse Properties dialog box (see fig. 11.12) provides a method for installing new device drivers.

To change mouse drivers, perform the following steps:

1. Click on the Change button on the General tab to view compatible device drivers (see fig. 11.13).

2. Click on Manufacturers and Models in the Select Device dialog box.

3. If you don't see the device you want to install, click on the Show All Devices radio button.

4. Or click on the Have Disk button to open the Install from Disk dialog box; then select the device driver file desired.

5. Click on the OK button in both dialog boxes to return to the Mouse Properties dialog box and make your selection.

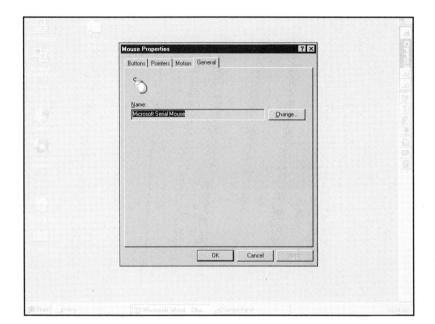

Figure 11.12

The General tab of the Mouse Properties dialog box enables you to install new mouse device drivers.

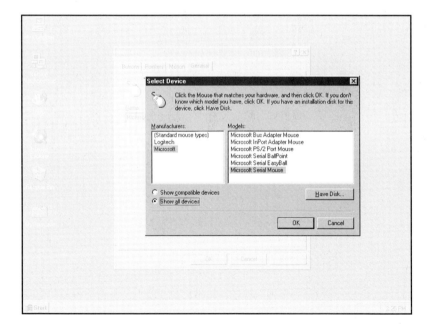

Figure 11.13

The Select Device dialog box lets you choose a new mouse driver.

> **Tip** If you don't find the desired device driver, or if your current driver is operating incorrectly in Windows NT Workstation 4, all is not lost. Although most vendors work hard to ensure that a compatible driver ships with each operating system version, you can download the latest drivers from a number of sources. Most vendors maintain a BBS with free access, a section on an online service such as CompuServe or America Online, or an Internet Web site with downloadable file libraries (usually as an FTP service).

Configuring the Keyboard

Objective B.5

Most computer keyboards are based on the IBM PC AT keyboard layout, which is the industry standard. That keyboard came with 101 keys, and included features such as an inverted T cursor key set, a numeric keypad, 15 function keys along the top row, and a set of six special keys for Insert, Delete, and navigation (Home, End, Page Up, and Page Down). Apart from the convenience that this keyboard configuration offered, the general tactile click, touch, and sound of the original AT keyboard had users holding onto obsolete computers just to retain the keyboard. IBM learned a lot from its typewriter business, and the results showed in this keyboard.

The Keyboard Properties dialog box lets you change some of the characteristics of your keyboard, or install a new keyboard driver for a new mechanical keyboard, if required. Given how much can be assigned on a keyboard, what you can do with the Keyboard Properties dialog box is really rather limited. For example, you will find no remapping or keyboard macro feature in NT Workstation, which really should be part of any user's utility arsenal.

Among the aspects of your keyboard that you can control are the speed with which keys repeat, any local configurations required by your country, different keyboard layouts, and different character sets.

Adjusting Speed

Objective B.5

You can change the repeat rate of the keyboard character keys (the typematic feature) on the Speed tab of the Keyboard Properties dialog box (see fig. 11.14). As before, adjust the sliders for Repeat Delay and Repeat Rate. Click the Apply button to put your new settings into effect. To test the repeat rate, click in the Click Here and Hold Down a Key to Test Repeat Rate text box, and press and hold any character key.

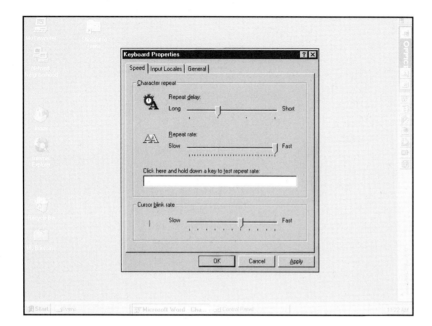

Figure 11.14

The Speed tab of the Keyboard Properties dialog box enables you to assign the sensitivity of the keyboard to repeated keystrokes.

Defining Cursor Rate

You can adjust the blink rate of the cursor (or insertion point) on your screen (refer to fig. 11.14). Adjust the Cursor Blink Rate slider to your taste. Click the Apply button to put your new settings into effect. A blinking cursor in the Cursor Blink Rate section illustrates your new cursor blink rate setting.

Objective B.5

Setting Input Locales

Keyboards are often language-specific. Some countries (even those with the same language) use special symbols that others don't. For example, there are different versions of Spanish keyboards depending on which country it is being used in. In some instances (Latin-based languages), a keyboard is simply remapped by a keyboard layout, and you can switch between the supported input locales. In most instances where a non-Latin-based language is used, a keyboard manufactured specifically for that language is required. For example, Hindu, Hebrew, Arabic, Han, and other languages do best with their own keyboards. Even some Latin-based languages use so many special accented characters that they work best with their own keyboards.

Objective B.5

You tell NT Workstation which layout you want to use with your keyboard by selecting that layout on the Input Locales tab of the Keyboard Properties dialog box (see fig. 11.15). If you are working in multiple languages, you can switch between these languages at any time while you work in your applications.

Figure 11.15

The Input Locales tab of the Keyboard Properties dialog box enables you to choose keyboard layouts of different countries.

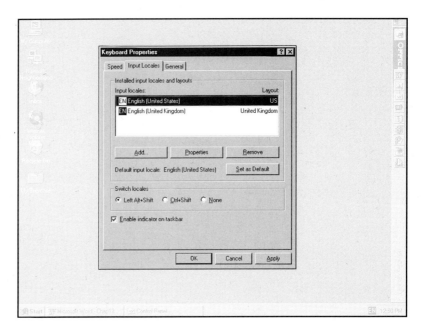

You can switch keyboard layouts to accomplish the following things:

◆ Change layouts based on the internally held keyboard map.

◆ Change the sorting order for that language based on the character set used by that country. You should note that even countries supposedly sharing the same language (the U.S. and England, for example) use different character sets that sort differently. Character sets are a collection of the allowed symbols for that language or location.

◆ Perform automatic font substitution.

To change a keyboard layout, follow these steps:

1. Click on the Input Locales tab of the Keyboard Properties dialog box.

2. Select the layout from the Layout list, and click the Apply button.

You can have as many layouts as you desire, and because these drivers take up minimal space, there is little penalty for storing any number of them. If you don't see the appropriate keyboard layout, you will need to install it.

To install an additional keyboard layout, follow these steps:

1. Retrieve your installation CD-ROM and insert it into your CD-ROM drive.

2. Click the Add button on the Input Locales tab of the Keyboard Properties dialog box.

Note An administrator's privilege level is required to install new keyboard layouts.

3. In the Add Input Locale dialog box (see fig. 11.16), select the layout from the list and press the OK button. The keyboard driver files are copied to your system.

   (If the appropriate driver isn't found, you will be requested to locate it or supply the file on disk.)

4. Click the Apply button to switch to the new layout or the OK button to close the Keyboard Properties dialog box.

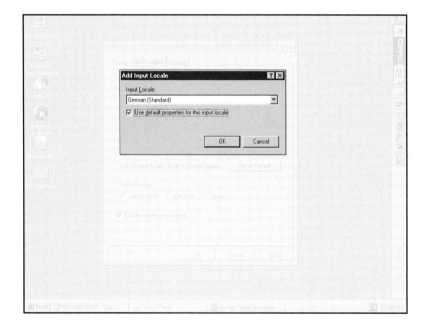

Figure 11.16

The Add Input Locale dialog box enables you to change your keyboard's layout.

If you typically use two or more keyboard layouts, the Input Locales tab offers you some convenient features that you should know about. You can set a default keyboard by clicking the Set as Default button and selecting the desired layout.

You can also set a keyboard shortcut by clicking the appropriate radio button in the Switch locales section. When working in one layout, you can switch between that layout and another layout by pressing the shortcut keys using these keyboard modifiers. A pop-up menu with installed layouts appear. The None choice disables this option.

Another method for switching between different language layouts is to use the Enable indicator on taskbar check box. With this option set to on, an icon for the current locale appears in the right section of the taskbar. For example, you see a blue box with the letters EN in it next to the time indicator. When you click on this icon, a pop-up menu of installed locales appear, enabling you to select between them.

As you work in a word processor, you can select from the various languages on the fly using the operating system. If the word processor supports the Win32 NLS API (National Language Support Application Program Interface), the text you type is recorded as belonging to that language. Word versions 6 and greater support this feature. Language is considered to be a format attribute of text in that wordprocessor.

Changing Keyboard Types

Each keyboard locale offers one or more keyboard types. For English (United States), you can switch between the following keyboard types: US (standard), Dvorak, Dvorak for left hand, Dvorak for right hand, and US International.

To switch between keyboard types, follow these steps:

1. Click on the Properties button on the Input Locales tab of the Keyboard Properties dialog box.

2. Select the keyboard type from the Input Locale Properties dialog box, as shown in figure 11.17.

3. Click the OK button to close the Input Locale Properties dialog box.

4. Click the Apply button or OK button to set the new keyboard type.

Figure 11.17

The Input Locale Properties dialog box enables you to change keyboard types.

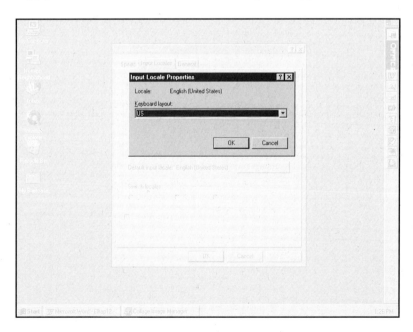

Using the General Tab

As with the Mouse Properties dialog box's General tab, the General tab of the Keyboard Properties dialog box lets you install a new keyboard driver. Typically, you install a new keyboard driver when you are using a different keyboard than the standard AT driver. This driver is often supplied on disk when you purchase the keyboard. For details on installing a keyboard driver, refer to the instructions for installing a mouse driver described earlier in this chapter.

Objective

B.4

Configuring Date and Time

Windows lets you configure your computer's date and time in the Date/Time Properties dialog box, shown in figure 11.18. The date and time you set is a system-wide setting that is used for purposes such as the date and time stamp file attributes. Date and time stamps are properties that the operating system applies to any file it creates based on the current setting of your system clock. Therefore, this is an important setting—but one you infrequently change. Date and time stamps are used for a variety of essential purposes such as backups, software upgrades, and many other system modifications. It appears in programs such as the NT Windows Explorer.

Objective

B.5

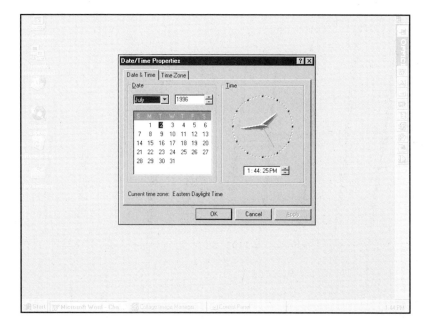

Figure 11.18

The Date & Time tab of the Date/ Time Properties dialog box enables you to change your system clock's setting.

Note An administrator's privilege level, or membership in the Power User group, is required in order to change Date/Time settings.

To set a system date and time, follow these steps:

1. Open the Date/Time Properties dialog box and select the Date & Time tab.

2. Select the month and year from the drop-down list and spinner box in the Date section.

3. Click on the date in the month panel.

4. Enter the time in the spinner box in the Time section.

5. Click on the Apply button or the OK button to set the date and time desired.

Tip If you find that your computer is not keeping time accurately, chances are that your battery is failing. The life of a battery can be a couple of years or more, but eventually they do fail and require replacement.

While in the Date/Time Properties dialog box, set your time zone on the Time Zone tab (see fig. 11.19). Select the time zone from the drop-down list. In many cases, representative cities are offered to help you determine which time zone to select. The difference from Greenwich Mean Time (GMT) is also indicated. For example, Eastern Standard Time (EST) is –5, or five hours earlier than GMT.

Figure 11.19

The Time Zone tab of the Date/Time Properties dialog box enables you to set your computer's location—a very useful feature for mobile computer users.

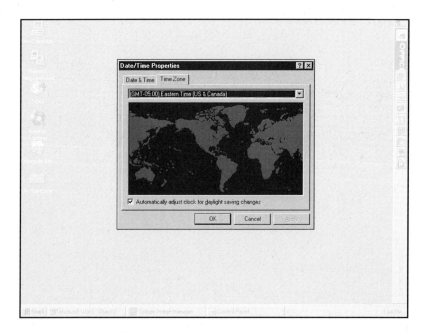

You should also enable the Automatically Adjust Clock for Daylight Saving Changes check box if your locale uses Daylight Savings Time. It is a great convenience.

Configuring Regional Settings

The Regional Settings Properties dialog box enables you to select from standard formats for dates, time, numbers, and currencies that are appropriate to your region. This is a system-wide setting that appears in standard Windows dialog boxes. Many Windows programs have specific format settings that override the system settings whenever a session with that application is running. Figure 11.20 shows you the Regional Settings tab of the Regional Settings Properties dialog box. On that tab, select a country by region name.

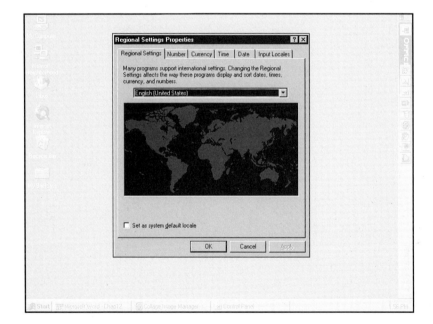

Figure 11.20

The Regional Settings tab of the Regional Settings Properties dialog box enables you to format dates and time according to your location.

Each of the remaining tabs in the Regional Settings Properties dialog box—Number, Currency, Time, Date, and Input Locales—present you with a template that defines how that data type is handled. As an example, the Number tab is shown in figure 11.21. You can alter the characteristics of number formats by selecting a new format from the various drop-down lists. Each data format applies to a specific input locale, so the Regional Settings Properties dialog box enables you to switch between your installed input locales as you apply these changes. Each format set applies to a specific input locale. Click the Apply button or the OK button to put your changes into effect.

Figure 11.21

The Number tab of the Regional Settings Properties dialog box enables you to format numbers according to your location.

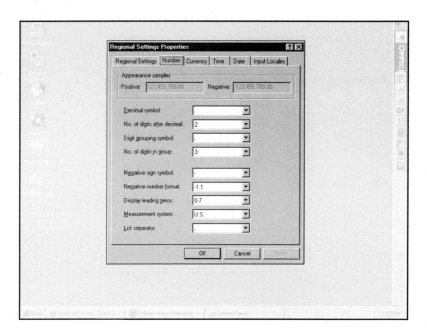

End Note: You can assign system settings in a friendly and obvious way. You can assign properties to your mouse, keyboard, and display. You can assign system-wide properties, such as date, time, and regional settings. These settings are important characteristics of your working environment that can have an important impact on a user's productivity.

The settings you make are stored in the Windows Registry as part of a user's profile. When you log on at an NT Workstation, your settings are restored based on your user name and are validated by your password.

Test Your Knowledge

1. Which of the following are settings that you can change in Windows NT Workstation 4?

    A. Keyboard repeat rate

    B. Display monitor refresh rate

    C. Colors of different screen elements

    D. Voice command language

2. Changes you make to basic device settings are stored in:

    A. The Registry

    B. The CONFIG.NT file

    C. The SETTINGS.INI file

    D. The DESKTOP directory

3. If you change your video driver and your display doesn't function properly, you can:

    A. Revert to the Last Known Good settings.

    B. Choose Windows NT Workstation [VGA Mode] from the Boot Menu.

    C. Check the brightness and contrast settings on your monitor.

    D. Reinstall your mouse driver.

4. The screen savers built into Windows NT Workstation are useful for:

    A. Avoiding burning images into older monitors.

    B. Providing additional password protection of the system.

    C. Hypnotizing yourself or your users into eating lots of buttered, flying toast.

    D. Speeding up your computer.

Test Your Knowledge Answers

1. A,B,C

2. A

3. A,B

4. A,B

Chapter Snapshot

This chapter covers the installation and configuration of some important peripheral devices that you need to operate your computer. The following topics are covered:

Windows NT
Workstation 4

CHAPTER 12

Installing and Configuring Basic Hardware

Windows NT Workstation 4 is notable in its improvement over its predecessors in supporting a wide variety of legacy peripherals and new classes of devices and computers. You can view a list of running devices in the Devices dialog box, described later in this chapter.

When installing peripheral devices, you must assume the role of mediator and make sure that there are no interrupt address conflicts or base I/O address conflicts. For a loaded multimedia computer, installing sound boards, juggling network cards, and adding boards for SCSI adapters and scanners can be a formidable task that has turned many into weekend warriors.

Introducing the Devices Dialog Box

The Devices icon, shown in figure 12.1, enables you to view and manipulate device drivers running on your computer. The Devices dialog box gives you an overview of installed devices and lets you start them, stop them, or make the device driver load them at startup. Additionally, you can use this dialog box to enable or disable the driver as part of a hardware profile. (See Chapter 5, "Understanding Profiles," for more on hardware profiles.)

Devices icon

Figure 12.1

The Devices icon can be found in Control Panel.

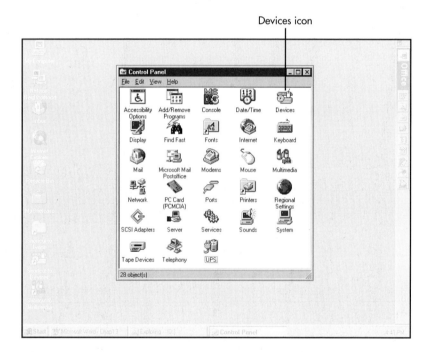

| Note | A device driver is a piece of software that takes instructions (usually input/output instructions) from the operating system and translates them into a form that the peripheral device can understand and use. |

Objective B.5

Double-click on the Devices icon. The Devices dialog box appears (see fig. 12.2).

The actions of the Start and Stop buttons are obvious. If you click the Startup button, you are offered several different startup actions in the startup Device dialog box (see fig. 12.3): Boot, System, or Automatic starts up the driver whenever the system starts up; Manual forces a user to start the driver; and Disabled cannot be started up by a user but can be started by the system.

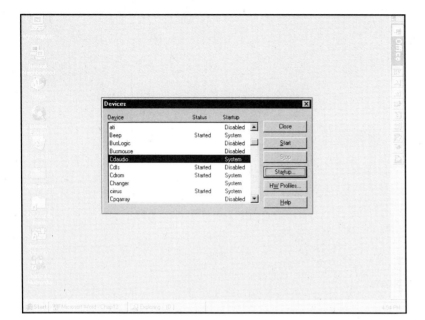

Figure 12.2

The Devices dialog box gives you an overview of your installed devices.

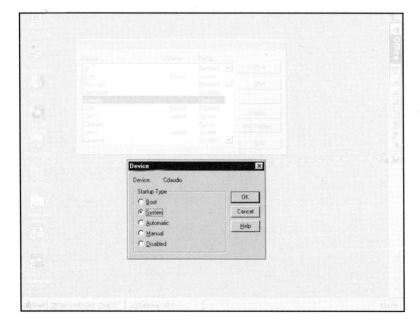

Figure 12.3

The startup Device dialog box lets you set up different devices to run automatically.

Note You must be part of an Administrator local group and have that privilege level in order to change startup services.

The collection of devices and device drivers running at any one time can be part of a user's hardware profile. To enable or disable a driver as part of the hardware profile, click on the HW Profiles button and make those changes in the HW Profile dialog box. You can view and work with the current hardware profile (as well as any other defined) by selecting the Hardware Profile tab of the System Properties dialog box.

Installing and Configuring Ports

A port is a channel—either into your computer or out of your computer. A computer can have a number of different ports, but the two types of ports commonly encountered are the following:

◆ **Serial ports.** Also called COM ports, these ports are typically RS-232 (an interface standard) compatible connections to low input/output speed devices such as modems and mice. This connector uses 9- or 25-pin plugs.

◆ **Parallel ports.** Also called printer ports or LPT ports, these ports are medium-speed connections to printers, scanners, and other devices.

The number of physical ports into which you can plug external devices or peripherals is usually four COM (serial) ports and two printer (parallel) ports. However, depending on the model and make of your computer, you can have fewer or more COM and printer ports. You may find that your computer comes with as many as three LPT ports and as few as two COM ports. Many laptop computers that allow PCMCIA modem cards are assigned a COM port. Built-in modems in desktop models also take a COM port. If you have a laptop computer with a PCMCIA device, double-click the PC Card icon (see fig. 12.4) to enable PCMCIA sockets and to configure that device.

From an operating system point of view, a channel (communications path) to a peripheral device or logical device (a hardware device created in software) is an asynchronous data stream (two-way data communication) that is managed as a virtual device by a port driver of the VCOMM VxD. Windows supports many more assignable communication channels than there are physical connections on your computer. You can select from any of the 256 possible COM ports and assign the I/O base address of choice.

> **Caution** If two COM ports share the same I/O base address, there will be a device conflict that prevents your serial devices from operating correctly.

When you install a communications device on your computer, Windows assigns COM1, COM2, COM3, or COM4 to it if that device has a standard base I/O port address (as most do). Non-standard addresses result in the assignment of COM5 to those devices. For COM5 assignments or to resolve conflicts, you can reassign COM port assignments in software. You can assign logical COM ports (addresses) to your serial ports after they become available.

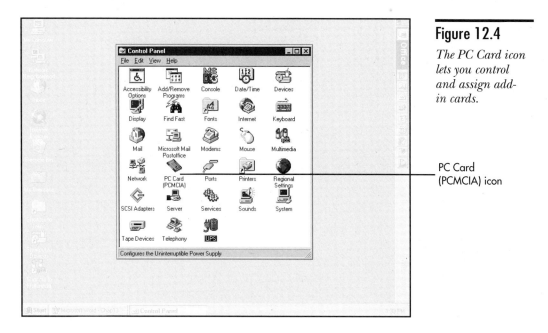

Figure 12.4

The PC Card icon lets you control and assign add-in cards.

PC Card (PCMCIA) icon

Adding and Deleting Serial Ports

Go to the Ports dialog box to change the communications setting for a serial or COM port. In this dialog box, you can also add and delete ports.

Objective

B.5

To add a new port, perform the following tasks:

1. Select the Control Panel command from the Settings submenu of the Start menu.

2. Double-click on the Ports icon (see fig. 12.5) to open the Ports dialog box (see fig. 12.6).

3. Click on the Add button.

4. Enter the settings for the new COM port in the Advanced Settings for New Port dialog box (see fig. 12.7). These settings are described in the next section.

Figure 12.5

The Ports icon appears in the Control Panel.

Ports icon —

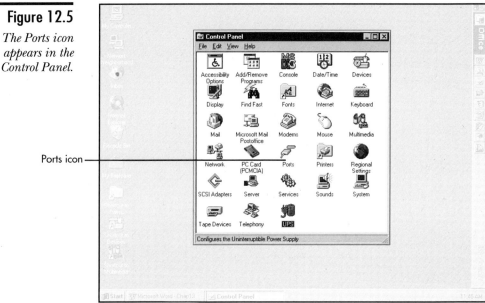

Figure 12.6

The Ports dialog box lets you assign communication speeds and other characteristics to your input/ output connections.

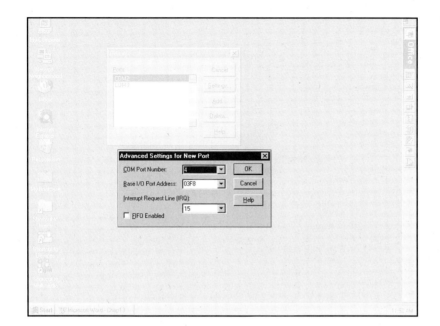

Figure 12.7

Assign port configurations with the Advanced Settings for New Port dialog box.

5. Click on the OK button.

You must restart your computer to activate the newly assigned COM port.

To delete a serial port, perform the following tasks:

1. Select the Control Panel command from the Settings submenu of the Start menu.

2. Double-click on the Ports icon to open the Ports dialog box.

3. Click on the port name in the Ports list to select it.

4. Click on the Delete button to delete the port and the OK button to confirm your deletion.

Changing Serial Port Settings

You can also use the Ports dialog box to view and change basic port settings. To change basic settings, follow these steps:

1. Select a port in the Ports list of the Ports dialog box.

2. Click on the Settings button to open the basic Settings dialog box (see fig. 12.8).

Figure 12.8

The Settings dialog box provides access to characteristics of your input/ output connections.

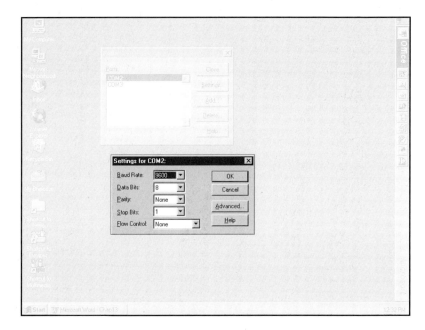

3. Enter your new settings in the various setting drop-down lists. (Continue reading for specific explanations of each of the settings.)

4. Click on OK.

If you have used communications programs before, these settings should be familiar to you. A brief summary of their definitions follows:

◆ **Baud Rate.** This setting controls the speed at which data is transferred.

Tip If a device can't perform at your assigned baud rate, typically the device will perform *handshaking* (a method for agreeing on a common communications scheme) and drop down to a lower transfer rate that both modems can support (the rate of the slower modem). You should set the baud rate as high or higher than the device you plan to use on this port.

◆ **Data Bits.** The size of the "words" being communicated. Either 7- or 8-bit communications are typically used.

◆ **Parity.** An error-checking method that validates data communication based on the value of a check byte used to determine if the preceding information transferred was correct. Parity can be None, Odd, Even, Space, or Mark.

◆ **Stop Bits.** Stop bits represents the timing unit used between transmitted bits in a data stream—1, 1.5, and 2 are the choices offered.

◆ **Flow Control.** This is the method for controlling the flow of data. The choices are None, Xon/Xoff for software control, and Hardware for hardware control.

Use the Advanced button to open the Advanced Settings dialog box (refer to fig. 12.7). In the Advanced Settings dialog box, you can assign I/O base addresses, interrupt requests (IRQ), the port number, and buffering of incoming data to increase performance.

A short summary of the advanced port options follows:

◆ **COM Port Number.** Select from any of the 265 serial port assignments. Standard computer BIOS recognizes COM1 and COM2 automatically. Thus assigned values are from 3–256.

◆ **Base I/O Port Address.** You can change the base I/O address for a serial port if your device uses addresses other than the standard values that Windows NT Workstation 4 automatically detects. The addresses 3F8 and 2F8 are usually assigned to COM1 and COM2. Using these addresses on another COM port may cause COM1 or COM2 to malfunction.

◆ **Interrupt Request Line (IRQ).** For any computer that cannot access COM1/COM3 or COM2/COM4 simultaneously, a unique IRQ number for each port lets you use these common port assignments.

◆ **FIFO Enabled.** With the FIFO Enabled check box selected, the serial port uses a buffering scheme for incoming data.

Remember, any changes you make to serial port settings require that Windows NT Workstation 4 be rebooted to take effect.

When a device is attached to a port, the port doesn't appear in the Ports dialog box in Control Panel. This means you can't accidentally attach a device to a port that already has a device.

However, a port won't appear in the dialog box if another device on your computer is using the same interrupt as that port.

If you can't figure out why a port fails to appear in the dialog box, you can check to see what device is using an unlisted serial port in the Registry. This is sometimes the only way to solve missing port mysteries.

To check a port's device status in order to troubleshoot this problem, follow these steps:

Objective G.7

1. Run Regedit and expand HKEY_LOCAL_MACHINE.

2. Move to \Hardware\Description\System\MultifunctionAdapter (or \Hardware\Description\System\EisaAdapter for EISA machines).

3. Move through the subfolders that display a plus sign (they vary in number depending upon the adapter devices in your machine) to find Serial Controller.

4. There is a subkey under Serial Controller for each port in your computer (port 1 is assigned to the subkey 0, port 2 is assigned to subkey 1, and so on).

5. Every port that is used has a plus sign and you can expand it to see its subkey.

6. If a mouse is attached to the port you will see a subkey named \PointerPeripheral.

7. If there is an existing subkey (folder) and it is not named \PointerPeripheral, it means another device is attached to the port, or another device is using the same interrupt as the port.

Armed with this information, you can begin to unravel the mystery. Of course, the first step is to walk around to the back of your computer and check the serial ports. If they are empty (except for the mouse), you have an interrupt conflict. If there is a cable attached to a port, follow the cable to see what's at the other end (probably a scanner or serial printer or modem). You will have to go through the settings for all of your devices in order to determine which device is using the interrupt normally assigned to the missing port.

Exploring Parallel Ports

When you are connected to a network printer, the configuration of your printer ports are probably not of great concern. However, if you use NT Workstation 4 as a stand-alone computer or take a laptop running this operating system on the road, then you will have to print through one of your communication ports. Some printers connect to COM ports, and the discussion in the previous sections applies to those printers as it would to any serial devices. Other printers, like the IBM Personal Page Printer, use an add-in board referred to as an EPT port. However, the vast majority of printers use one of the one, two, or three LPT ports on your computer for printing.

The three LPT ports are referred to as LPT1, LPT2, and LPT3. You are free to assign or reassign printers to any one of these addresses, and attach those printers to any one of the physical ports that were assigned to that logical port on your computer.

In Windows NT Workstation 4, the appropriate method for adding a printer to your computer is to run the Add Printer Wizard in the Printers window. (A *wizard* steps you through a setup process using graphics and suggestions.) You can open the Printers window in one of two ways:

◆ Select the Printers command on the Settings menu of the Start menu.

◆ Double-click on the Printers shortcut icon in the Control Panel.

To install and configure a printer that is connected to your computer, follow these steps:

Objective

C.5

1. Double-click on the Add Printer icon shown in figure 12.9.

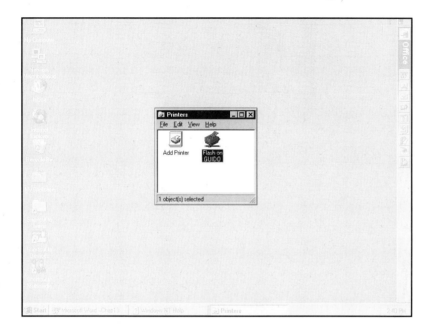

Figure 12.9

The Add Printer icon is found in the Printers window.

2. Select the My Computer radio button in the first screen of the wizard, as shown in figure 12.10 and then click the Next button.

3. Clicking on Next causes the second screen of the Add Printer Wizard to appear (see fig. 12.11). Select from any one of the available ports and then click the Next button.

4. Click the Add Port button to view the Printer Ports dialog box (see fig. 12.12) and change the type of printer port (optional). Select that port in the Available Printer Ports list.

5. If your printing setup requires a print monitor (optional), click on the New Monitor button to install a print monitor for that printer port type in the Install Print Monitor dialog box.

6. Click the OK button(s) to return to the Add Printer Wizard.

7. Click the Configure Port button to open the Configure LPT Port dialog box (see fig. 12.13). Enter a new Transmission Retry value into that text box, if desired (optional). Then click the OK button.

Figure 12.10

The Add Printer Wizard enables you to select your printer type.

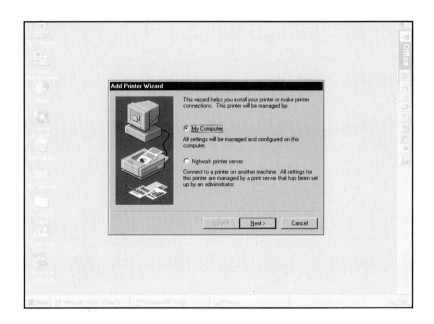

Figure 12.11

The Add Printer Wizard enables you to select a port for your printer.

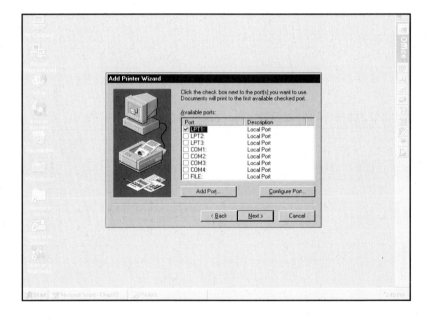

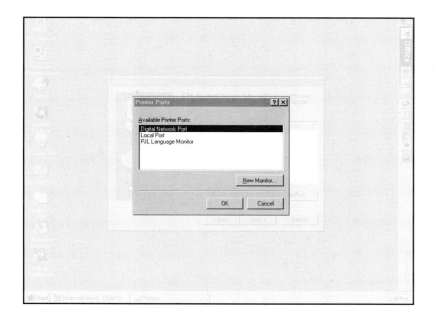

Figure 12.12

The Printer Ports dialog box enables you to modify the type of printer port.

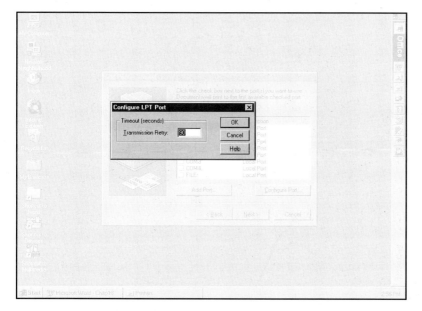

Figure 12.13

The Configure LPT Port dialog box enables you to enter a timeout value.

8. Click the Next button to view the list of available manufacturers and printers shown in Step 3 of the wizard (see fig. 12.14). Select a manufacturer and printer, and then click the Next button.

Figure 12.14

The Add Printer Wizard enables you to select your specific printer.

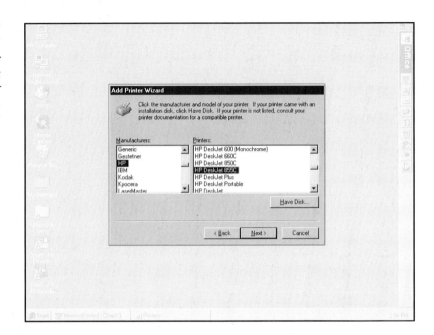

9. Name your printer in Step 4 (see fig. 12.15) and specify whether it is your default printer; then click the Next button.

Figure 12.15

The Add Printer Wizard enables you to name your printer and set it as the default printer.

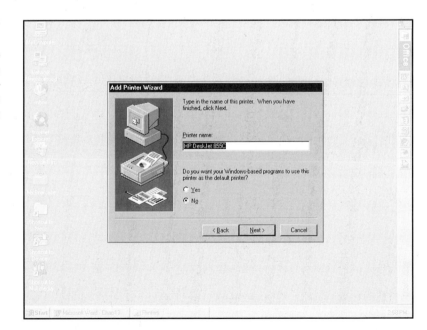

10. Select the Shared radio button to set up your printer as a printer share in Step 5 of the Add Printer Wizard (see fig. 12.16) and specify the operating system of all connecting computers. After you have specified this information, click on Next.

    Or, select the Not Shared radio button to prevent other users from accessing the printer. Then click on the Next button.

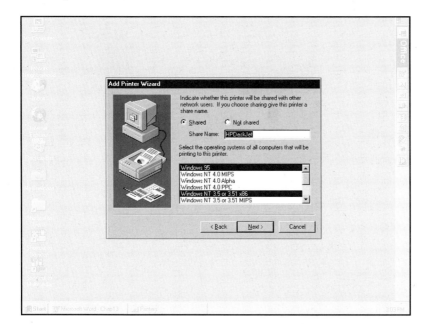

Figure 12.16

The Add Printer Wizard enables you to create a shared printer.

11. On the last page of the Add Printer Wizard, select Yes (Recommended) to print a test page or No and then click on the Finish button.

Windows will install your printer and copy the required files from your NT Workstation 4 installation disk. If you set up a printer share, you will be required to locate the installation disk(s) of the various operating systems to which you chose to give access to the printer. Then the text page is printed to your new printer.

> **Tip** If your printer is shared by other users, Windows NT provides the drivers for those users (earlier Windows operating systems do not perform this service). That means that a Windows 95 computer can use your printer without installing printer drivers locally. This is a nifty, productive feature.

Windows creates the virtual printer (a software device that controls the communication between your computer and the physical printer) and adds it to your printer folder as an icon with the name you assigned it in the wizard. If you created the printer (and printer share), you are the owner of that network resource. A printer share shows an icon of a printer with a hand holding it. A non-shared printer shows a printer without a hand. (A network printer icon displays wires attached and represents a printer attached to another computer.) In the Printers window (see fig. 12.17), you see the three different printer types.

Figure 12.17

This system displays three printer icon types because there is a network printer, a shared printer, and a non-shared printer.

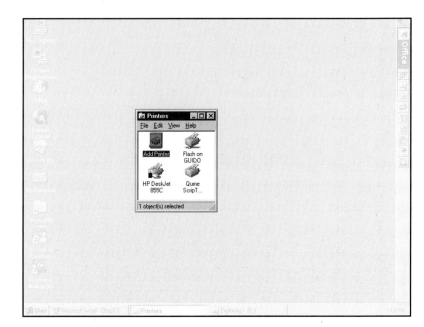

Exploring Printer Properties

If you right-click on a printer icon, the shortcut menu for that printer appears (see fig. 12.18). This menu enables you to perform a number of important printer functions.

These commands are briefly described in the following list (for more detailed information, see Chapter 17, "Printing"):

◆ **Open.** Opens the Printer window to view the print queue.

◆ **Pause Printing.** Pauses a queued document, printing the last page in the document before the command was given. This command changes to Resume Printing for a paused printer.

◆ **Purge Print Documents.** Deletes spooled documents in the print queue.

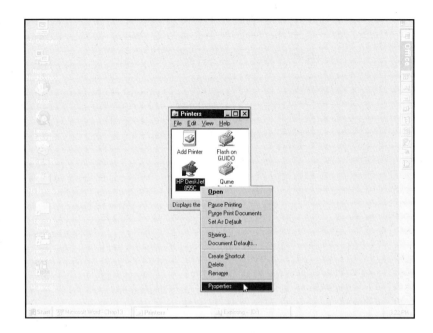

Figure 12.18

A printer's context-sensitive menu is a quick way to configure a printer, the printer's print queue, and a printer's properties.

◆ **Set As Default.** Makes the selected printer the default printer for any session. You can switch to another printer, but the default printer always comes up (by default) in application Print dialog boxes.

◆ **Sharing.** Sets up or configures a printer share.

◆ **Document Defaults.** Sets defaults such as paper size, printer tray, orientation, and number of copies.

◆ **Create Shortcut.** Creates a shortcut in the Printers window for that printer.

◆ **Delete.** Deletes the printer.

◆ **Rename.** Activates the name of the icon and lets you rename the printer (which you can also do by clicking twice slowly on the name).

◆ **Properties.** Opens the Properties dialog box for that printer.

From the standpoint of port assignment, the Properties dialog box of the printer provides you with the ability to reassign the port. Figure 12.19 shows you the Ports tab of the Properties dialog box. You can also change drivers, scheduling, sharing, security, and other settings from within this dialog box.

Remember, you must either be the owner of the printer or have Full Control access permission for that resource to make changes to the printer. In the NT security scheme, members of the Administrators, Server Operators, Print Operators, or Power Users groups have Full Control permission by default.

Figure 12.19

The Ports tab of a printer's Properties dialog box enables you to modify port assignments.

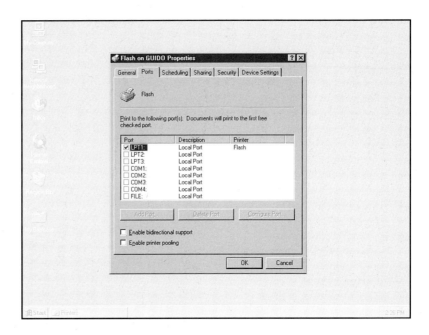

Installing and Configuring SCSI Adapters

The Small Computer Standard Interface, or *SCSI,* specification is an industry-wide bus architecture standard. Older devices conform to SCSI-1 (the original specification), while newer devices support the improved faster version, SCSI-2. SCSI was popularized in desktop computers by the Apple Macintosh, but has many proponents in the PC market. SCSI is used to connect devices like hard drives, CD-ROM drives, scanners, and other input or output devices that require good data transfer rates.

The SCSI Adapters Dialog Box

Objective B.5

SCSI is notable in that it is a self-mastered bus. It senses the devices attached to a SCSI chain and the bus master adjusts data I/O accordingly. To view and configure SCSI devices in Windows NT Workstation 4, open the SCSI Adapters dialog box by double-clicking on its icon (see fig. 12.20). Two tabs are in this dialog box, one for viewing SCSI adapter devices and another for viewing and installing SCSI device drivers. Figures 12.21 and 12.22 show you the Devices and Drivers tabs of the SCSI Adapters dialog box, respectively.

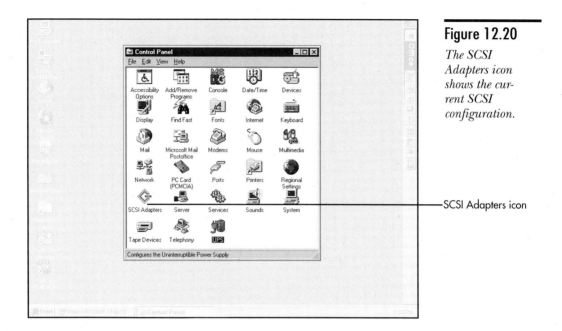

Figure 12.20

The SCSI Adapters icon shows the current SCSI configuration.

SCSI Adapters icon

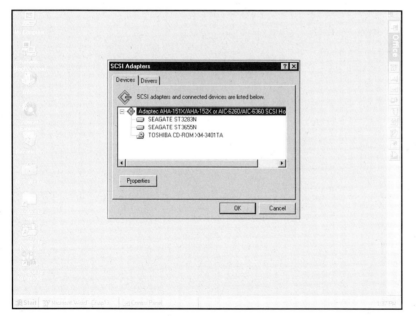

Figure 12.21

The Devices tab of the SCSI Adapters dialog box shows what devices are currently on your SCSI chain.

You can view the properties of a SCSI host adapter and the various SCSI devices on a SCSI chain to get information on those devices. Among the useful pieces of information to be found are the SCSI ID address assignments, the manufacturer and device type, device drivers, IRQ assignment, memory and I/O address ranges, and other hardware specific properties. Figure 12.23 shows you the Properties dialog box for a SCSI host adapter.

Figure 12.22

The Drivers tab of the SCSI Adapters dialog box enables you to install new drivers for your SCSI devices.

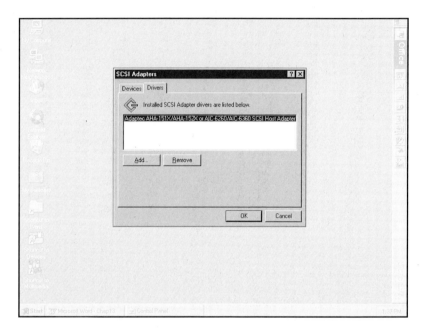

Figure 12.23

The Properties dialog box for a SCSI host adapter gives you information about your SCSI bus.

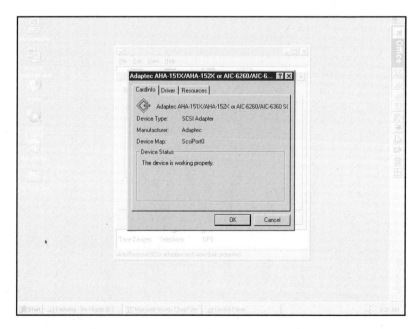

Installing SCSI Device Drivers

Use the Drivers tab of the SCSI Adapters dialog box to install new SCSI device drivers for your SCSI bus or host adapter. This is most useful when you switch SCSI boards, or when you get an updated driver from the manufacturing vendor of the board.

Objective B.4

To install a new SCSI device driver, follow these steps:

1. Open the SCSI Adapters dialog box and select the Drivers tab.

2. Click on the Add button to open the Install Driver dialog box shown in figure 12.24. Windows builds a list of available drivers.

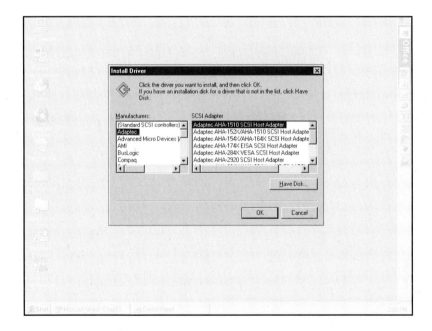

Figure 12.24

The Install Driver dialog box enables you to install a new SCSI driver for your SCSI devices.

3. Click on the vendor name in the Manufacturers list.

4. Click on the model number in the SCSI Adapter list.

   Or, if you don't see your model, click on the Have Disk button and install the device driver from a disk your vendor provides.

5. Click the OK button to return to the SCSI Adapters dialog box, and click OK again to assign the new device driver.

6. Reboot Windows NT Workstation 4 to enable the driver.

Note | SCSI device vendors work very hard to include the latest device driver on the first shipping copy of a Windows operating system. (This cuts down enormously on technical support calls.) Your best bet for the latest driver is to use the one that comes with Windows NT Workstation 4. However, sometimes vendors don't make the operating system release-to-manufacturing date so you must get the driver directly from the vendor. You can often find the latest drivers on a company's BBS, its online services' forum, its Internet web site, or a variety of NT FTP sites.

Configuring SCSI Chains

You can daisy chain up to seven SCSI devices, provided that no two devices have the same SCSI address (0–6) or Device ID. When you daisy chain devices together, you connect them in a line, one to the next. You can change the SCSI address of a device in hardware on the device itself or, more rarely, in software. A SCSI chain that has two devices with the same SCSI address will not start up properly.

SCSI uses a parallel communications wiring, with 50-pin plugs as a standard. Some variations of SCSI use 25 pins. SCSI couples through male and female connectors. There are limitations to the length of SCSI chains: they should be no more than 50 feet in total length. You should try to keep your SCSI chains as short as possible, with two to three feet being optimal. (Among many consultants, there is also a theory about performance that says that no two sections of cable should be the exact same length).

Caution | SCSI cables are expensive and notoriously unreliable. These thick cables cannot be viewed for breaks and are subject to malfunctions. Buy the best SCSI cables you can get because it's common to have SCSI cables fail right out of the box. If your SCSI chain doesn't function properly, and you have checked ID addresses and termination, start rearranging your SCSI cables and building the chain one SCSI device at a time.

SCSI chains also require that the first and last devices in a SCSI chain be terminated, which means that a resistor is added to prevent additional reflections of data back through the chain when data reaches the end of the SCSI chain. A SCSI device can be internally terminated and sense when it is the first or last device; but, most often, you terminate a SCSI device by adding a plug to the device. Some SCSI terminators are a pass-through connection, allowing a single connection on a device to serve a single role. When improperly terminated, you will often be able to start your computer, but you may get many spurious errors.

You can purchase computers that have SCSI built into the motherboard directly, or add an add-in board to your computer that is a SCSI bus master. Adaptec is one well-known manufacturer of high-quality SCSI host adapter boards. The newer SCSI boards (manufactured since early 1995) are all Plug and Play compatible. Chances are that unless you are dealing with a legacy system, your SCSI adapter will be of this type.

To install and configure a SCSI adapter, follow these steps:

1. Install the board in your computer.

2. Set the IRQ channel, base I/O address, and DMA channel as required so that your computer starts up correctly with a single SCSI device (like an internal hard drive). Most SCSI host adapters use IRQ 11 and start up with few hardware conflicts.

3. Turn the computer off.

4. Attach the different devices in the SCSI chain as desired.

5. Terminate the first and last device in the SCSI chain.

6. Set and check the SCSI device IDs for each device to see that no two are the same.

7. Restart the computer and check for conflicts.

If you need to install an older SCSI bus adapter, check SCSI parity, command sets, disk geometry, and software. When one SCSI host adapter is replaced with another, you may encounter problems due to disk geometry and device mapping through INT 11 (interrupt address 11). Interrupts are a method for allowing your operating system to address different peripheral devices in turn.

One of SCSI's many advantages is that it is a full 32-bit I/O bus that permits easy reconfiguration. SCSI adapters can handle several hard drives so you can take full advantage of NT Workstation 4's capability to create fault-tolerant mirrored drive sets and other RAID levels that the Disk Administrator permits. When Windows NT Workstation 4 starts up, it loads any SCSI disks it finds as the startup or boot disk in preference to any other hard drives (like IDE) that might be in the system.

Exploring Multimedia Devices and Drivers

The Media Control Interface (MCI) lets applications communicate with the Windows operating system through a set of standard drivers so that a standard set of commands can control multimedia devices such as MIDI devices—a music standard for the recording and playback of notes (not sounds)—sound boards, video disc players, and

**Objective
B.4**

so on. These devices show up in the Devices dialog box, described earlier in this chapter, and appear in the Devices tab of the Multimedia Properties dialog box, described in the next section.

Among the MCI device drivers you may find running on your computer are the following:

◆ **Animation.** An animation device.

◆ **CDaudio.** A compact disc (CD) audio player.

◆ **DAT.** A digital audio tape device.

◆ **Digital Video.** Digital video in a Windows window on the desktop—one that isn't controlled using the Windows GDI graphics drawing interface.

◆ **Other.** An undefined MCI device.

◆ **Overlay.** Overlay device (an analog video in a window).

◆ **Scanner.** An image scanner or video digitizer.

◆ **Sequencer.** A MIDI sequencer.

◆ **VCR.** A videocassette recorder or video tape player.

◆ **Video Disc.** A video disc player.

◆ **Waveaudio.** An audio device that plays sound (digitized waveform audio) files.

What you see in the Devices dialog box depends on the peripheral devices you have installed and configured.

Regardless of the drivers running, Windows writes multimedia files in three principle formats: .AVI (for digital video), .WAV (for sound or waveform audio files), and .MID (for Musical Instrument Digital Interface). As you read and write these media forms or change various system events, these are the file types you should be looking for.

Click on the Multimedia icon in the Control Panel (see fig. 12.25) to activate the Multimedia Properties dialog box (see fig. 12.26). The Multimedia Properties dialog box provides a central location from which to configure multimedia devices.

The five tabs in the Multimedia Properties dialog box provide access to the following settings:

◆ **Audio.** This tab lets you set input and output sound levels and specify the sound board that you wish to use. It is described more fully later in this chapter.

◆ **Video.** This tab lets you configure video playback for full screen or in a window. You can choose to run the video at the Original size, Double, $1/2$, $1/4$, $1/16$, or in a Maximized window.

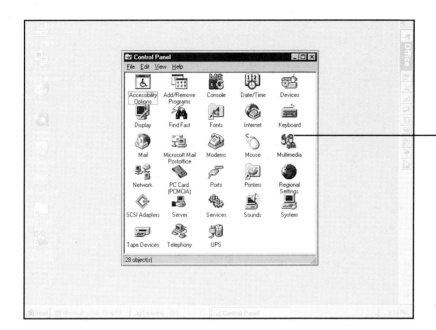

Figure 12.25

The Multimedia icon is found in the Control Panel.

Multimedia icon

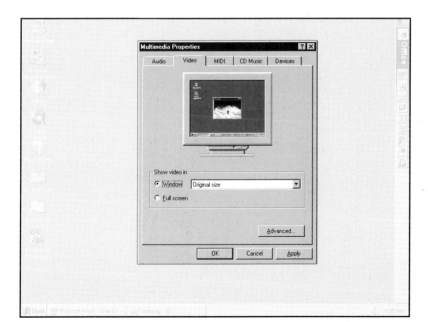

Figure 12.26

The Multimedia Properties dialog box enables you to configure various multimedia devices.

◆ **MIDI.** The MIDI tab lets you assign instrument(s) to the channels of your sound card. MIDI devices and this tab are discussed later in this chapter.

◆ **CD Music.** This simple tab, shown in figure 12.27, lets you change the default drive the other multimedia applets use, as well as change the headphone output level.

Figure 12.27

The CD Music tab of the Multimedia Properties dialog box enables you to change the default drive used by your multimedia applets.

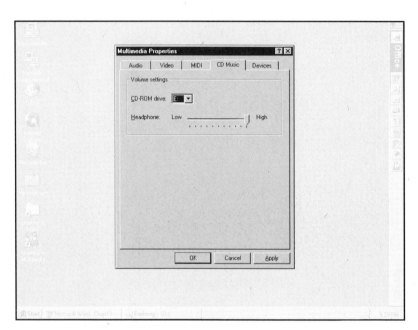

◆ **Devices.** This tab lets you view the properties of the various multimedia devices on your computer. It lets you change defaults, change (add or delete) devices, and change (add or delete) device drivers in many cases.

For configuration issues of multimedia devices, the Multimedia Properties dialog box is a good place to start to look for help.

Installing and Configuring a CD-ROM

CD-ROM drives come in internal and external models. Many CD-ROM drives connect to a CD-ROM controller on a sound board. Your sound card may support some CD-ROM drives, but not others. For CD-ROM drives not supported by your sound card, you can purchase a CD-ROM controller card.

More recently, IDE CD-ROM drives have been supported, a few of which are on the market and are good choices. A SCSI drive is likely to be faster, more reliable, easier to install, and a little more expensive.

Regardless of the model you choose, you will want to connect your sound output from the CD-ROM to your sound board for better sound. There are also headphone jacks on most models that provide adequate sound, but generally not as good as the amplified sound from the sound board itself.

After the physical installation of a CD-ROM is completed, NT Workstation 4 should recognize the device. Use the Devices tab of the Multimedia Properties dialog box to add a new device driver—provided, of course, that the driver for that CD-ROM shipped with the NT Workstation 4 installation disks and is found in the List of Drivers in the Add Driver dialog box. The following section, "Installing and Configuring Scanners," details the steps for adding device drivers with the Multimedia Properties dialog box.

If your CD-ROM's device driver is not on the list, the driver may be installed with a special installation disk that your CD-ROM vendor supplies. You should contact the hardware vendor to obtain the necessary disk or files if you don't have it (them) in your possession. Place the floppy disk for the CD-ROM drive into your floppy disk drive and use the Run command on the Start menu to run the Install or Setup program that is on that disk.

Once the drivers are installed, CD-ROM drives behave like any other volume. A new file system called CDFS, or CD File System, first introduced in Windows 95, is supported in NT Workstation 4.

If you are connected to a network and CD-ROM drives either are a rare resource or are configured to provide some service (like access to an encyclopedia), you can set up a network share using that CD-ROM.

Unlike a volume share on a hard drive (which is a read/write device), a CD-ROM is read only. Therefore, that is the highest access any user can have. Additionally, your request may be queued until the CD-ROM becomes available because CD-ROMs are slow devices.

Installing and Configuring Scanners

Scanners are much like CD-ROM drives in that a large amount of information must be transferred from them to your computer in a short amount of time. Therefore, you will find that many scanners are SCSI devices or come with their own controller boards. In rare instances, you will find that scanners attach to parallel ports.

In nearly all cases, scanners come with their own software installation disks. You should use the Run command on the Start menu to run the Setup or Install program that comes on those disks. Not only will that program install the device driver, but it will also install a controller program. For example, the popular Hewlett-Packard ScanJet II (a SCSI device) installs DeskScan II software. Additionally, paint or image editing software may be installed along with your device driver and scanner controller software.

Installing and Configuring Sound

To have your computer play anything other than a beep or alert sound, you need a sound board. Sound boards come in 8-bit (obsolete), 16-bit, and 32-bit varieties. Some 16-bit models cost less than $100, and the 32-bit models cost between $250 and $500.

The quality of your sound board can be heard through even modest speakers. Most come with a portfolio of applets for recording sound, CD-ROM playback, MIDI, sound mixers, voice recognition, and many other functions.

Sound boards (or audio boards) are add-in boards that usually take IRQ 5, and often conflict with other devices. Later models are configurable in software, and many now are PnP (Plug and Play) devices. Once installed, you will need to set up the device driver for your sound board.

Caution | Installing some sound boards can be difficult due to IRQ and base I/O address conflicts. When purchasing a sound board, make sure that its settings can be changed if they conflict with other boards in your system. Many sound boards and network boards use IRQ 5 as one of their default settings.

Objective B.4

To add or change your sound board's device driver, follow these steps:

1. Double-click on the Multimedia icon. The Multimedia Properties dialog box appears.

2. Select the Devices tab, and then click on the Audio Devices category, as shown in figure 12.28.

3. Click the Add button to view the Add dialog box (see fig. 12.29).

4. Select the driver from the List of Drivers.

5. Click the OK button; the Base I/O Address dialog box shown in figure 12.30 appears.

6. Click the Continue button to test your sound board (make sure your speakers are on).

7. The Configuration dialog box shown in figure 12.31 appears. Check your settings (to make sure they match the actual settings on the hardware, of course) and then click the OK button.

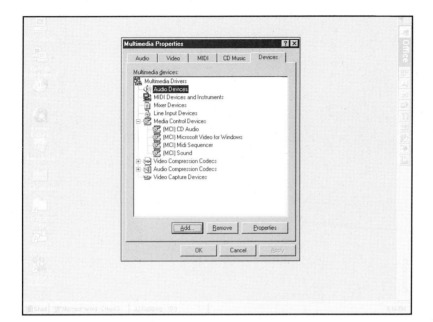

Figure 12.28

The Devices tab of the Multimedia Properties dialog box lets you add new devices to your system.

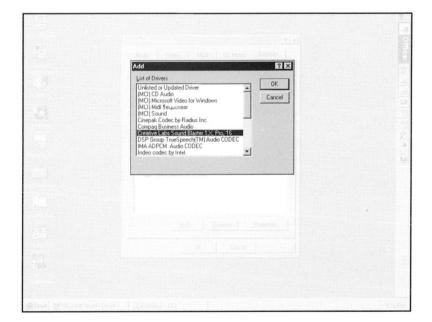

Figure 12.29

The Add dialog box is where you specify the actual driver.

Figure 12.30

The Base I/O Address dialog box is where you set the hardware address for a multimedia device.

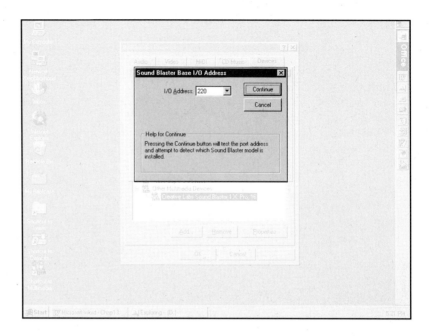

Figure 12.31

The Configuration dialog box shows your current settings.

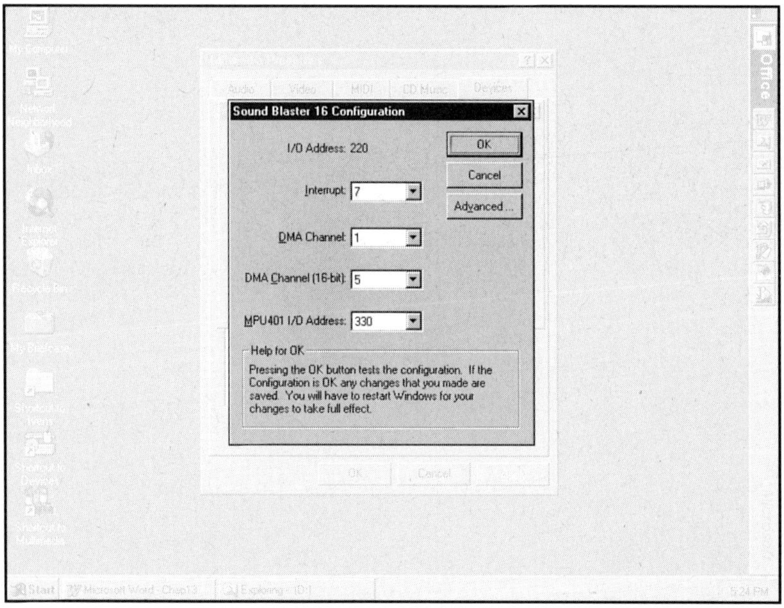

8. If the driver is successfully tested, you will be prompted to restart Windows to install the driver.

After you have installed your sound board and restarted the computer, go to the Audio tab of the Multimedia Properties dialog box, shown in figure 12.32. On this tab are some of the additional settings required to complete your sound board's configuration. Two main classes of settings can be found on the Audio tab: Playback and Recording. In addition to setting the volume sliders, if you intend to record sound by using your sound board, make sure you set the sound quality in the Preferred Quality drop-down list. The choices Telephone Quality, Radio Quality, and CD Quality affect both the quality and the file sizes (dramatically) of the .WAV files you create.

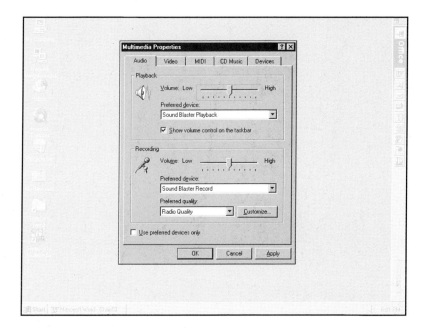

Figure 12.32

The Audio tab of the Multimedia Properties dialog box enables you to modify your sound board configuration.

Assigning Sounds

You can assign sounds to the various system events by using the Sounds icon (see fig. 12.33). In order to preview these sounds, you must have a working sound board installed and the proper driver running.

Sounds are useful interface items and great whimsical fun. If you haven't heard your computer roar off "Tada!", the Sounds Properties dialog box shown in figure 12.34 is the place to go. Double-click on the Sounds icon to get there.

Figure 12.33

The Sounds icon is found in the Control Panel.

Sounds icon————

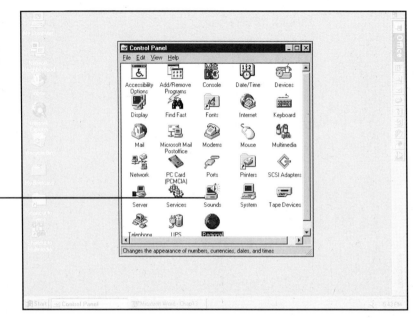

Figure 12.34

The Sounds Properties dialog box enables you to add sounds to system events.

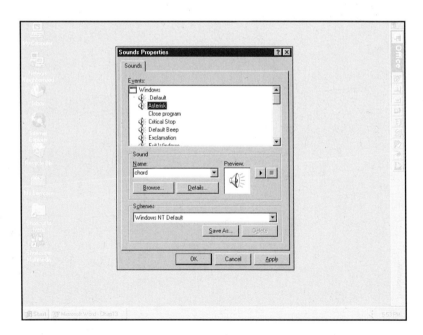

You can assign a sound to an event by clicking on that event in the Name list in the Sound section. You can also click Browse and assign any .WAV sound to an event. (There's a universe of .WAV sounds available, and you can easily record your own.)

Events with an assigned sound have a speaker next to them. Click on the play button (the right-facing triangle) next to the Preview icon to hear the sound.

You should note that the Sounds Properties dialog box lets you assign sounds to the following programs: Windows, the Windows Explorer, Media Player, and the Sound Recorder. Also, the Sounds Properties dialog box supports the saving of sounds as sound sets. Some of the sets you can switch to in the Schemes drop-down list are these: Windows NT Default, Jungle Sound Scheme, Musica Sound Scheme, No Scheme, Robotz Sound Scheme, and Utopia Sound Scheme. Changes you make can be saved to the sound set.

MIDI Settings

The *Musical Instrument Digital Interface (MIDI)* is a serial device interface standard. MIDI devices include all sound boards, musical synthesizers, and many musical instruments. Windows conforms to the *General MIDI Specification (GMS)*, an industry standard. NT Workstation 4 uses the advanced MIDI streams technology that allows for greater throughput.

MIDI is a system for music recording and playback. Instead of storing a copy of the actual sound, MIDI stores the musical note and information about duration and other factors. Then, during playback, this information is transmitted to the musical instrument for playback. The information is often encoded and compressed. MIDI is a favored method in the music recording industry to capture and manipulate a soundtrack.

Chances are that when you install your sound board's driver, you will also install your MIDI driver for the sound board at the same time. If this isn't the case, or if you want to install a new, updated, or different MIDI driver, go to the Devices tab of the Multimedia Properties dialog box.

To install or change a MIDI device driver, follow these steps:

1. In Control Panel, open the Multimedia Properties dialog box and select the Devices tab.

2. Click on the MIDI Devices and Instruments selection to highlight it.

3. Click on the Add button and select the appropriate driver from the List of Drivers in the Add Driver dialog box (refer to fig. 12.29).

4. Click the OK button and close the Multimedia Properties dialog box.

5. Restart Windows to install your device driver.

Objective B.5

Objective B.4

After installing your sound board and MIDI driver, you need to attach your MIDI device or instrument to your sound board's input and/or output channels. Then you should select the MIDI tab of the Multimedia Properties dialog box (see fig. 12.35).

Figure 12.35

Configure your devices with the MIDI tab of the Multimedia Properties dialog box.

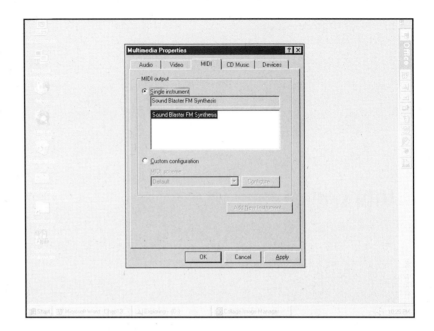

You can have a single instrument or two or more instruments attached to a serial port through a MIDI connection box. The MIDI tab lets you add and remove MIDI devices to and from your sound board. You can create and manage instrument schemes to provide groups of instruments support to MIDI, thus providing for full sound, even up to the orchestral level.

End Note: Basic peripheral hardware requires an input/output bus to operate. This chapter describes the configuration of serial and parallel ports and several devices like MIDI. Other higher-speed buses, like SCSI, are available and are useful for installing scanners, hard drives, and CD-ROM drives. The chapter also describes the installation of other multimedia devices, such as sound boards.

Several dialog boxes help you install device drivers, configure ports, and assign a variety of device settings. Among those described in this chapter were the following: the Devices, Ports, Multimedia, PC Card, SCSI Adapters, and Sounds Properties dialog boxes.

Test Your Knowledge

1. Choose the correct statement(s) about device drivers:

   A. Device drivers are transferred to your computer from the Windows NT 4 installation disk.

   B. Device drivers are on disks that are packaged along with peripherals.

   C. Device drivers can only be installed with the devices applet in Control Panel.

   D. Only peripherals attached to serial ports need device drivers.

2. For which serial port settings do you use the Advanced Settings dialog box?

   A. Baud Rate

   B. Flow Control

   C. COM Port Number

   D. Parity

3. Which type of user cannot change the settings of a printer attached to the computer?

   A. Administrator

   B. Replicator

   C. Power user

   D. Owner

4. Which action(s) can be performed in the Multimedia applet in Control Panel?

   A. Assigning sounds to events

   B. Adjustment of volume for sound playback

   C. Installation of animated video files

   D. Selection of a MIDI instrument to be used while running software programs

5. An asynchronous device sends data:

   A. From the computer to the peripheral

   B. From the peripheral to the computer

   C. In both directions between the peripheral and the computer

   D. Between any two peripherals

6. An RS-232 port is also called a _____.

7. Fill in the correct Control Panel applet:

    A. Use _____ to stop and start hardware devices.

    B. Use _____ to assign .WAV files to Windows events.

    C. Use _____ to see the IRQ assignment for a COM port.

Test Your Knowledge Answers

1. A,B

2. A,C

3. B

4. B,D

5. C

6. serial port, COM port

7. A. Devices, B. Sounds, C. Ports

Chapter Snapshot

This chapter covers the installation and configuration of communication devices. It expands on the discussion of serial ports and their devices from the previous chapter. Topics covered include:

Windows NT
Workstation 4

CHAPTER 13

Installing Communication Devices

This chapter covers the installation and configuration of basic communication hardware. Among the devices covered here are modems, fax/modems, and voice/fax/modems; X.25 and ISDN card connections for high-speed data access; and telephony services. For many, modem connections are old hat, but even your garden variety modem sprouts fax and, sometimes, voice services.

It's definitely a brave new world when it comes to communication services. Many, if not most, users require high-speed services to provide them with satisfactory online and Internet access connection rates. Many of the connection capabilities described in this chapter are rather new to the Windows operating systems and deserve a concentrated reading.

Windows Communications Architecture

With the release of Windows 95, Microsoft rewrote the older communications drivers found in Windows 3.1, and separated many functions. Figure 13.1 shows you a simple schema of the Windows communications architecture.

Figure 13.1

The Windows communications architecture shows you how communication is organized. Adapted from the "Windows 95 Resource Guide."

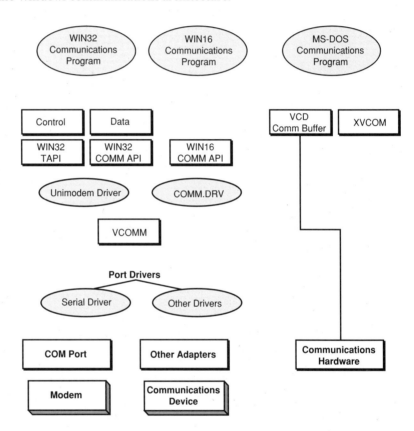

The new model, which replaces the COMM.DRV communications driver, is based on three components:

◆ **The WIN32 communications API and the Windows Telephony API (TAPI).** A device-independent interface that provides a command set for communication devices on one side and applications on the other.

Note   An API is an application programming interface that allows your program to perform complex system functions by calling them by name. As the operating system changes, the code might change, but the name and any parameters that it takes don't; therefore, your program continues to operate correctly.

◆ **Unimodem, or universal modem driver.** Provides services for modems of all types, and is a TAPI service provider. The Unimodem Driver is extensible, and can use small drivers written for various communication devices to provide services.

◆ **Communication port drivers.** Translate communications between the operating system on one side and serial and parallel ports on the other.

The VCOMM device driver is a new communications driver that communicates between the 32-bit Unimodem driver and the older 16-bit COMM.DRV driver on one side, and the Port drivers on the other side.

Installing and Configuring Modems

Once a modem on a computer was an option; today it's a necessity. Whether the modem is used to access the Internet, to fax your correspondence with fax software, or for dial-up registration of your software, a computer is rarely found without a modem these days.

Modems take digital computer data (a series of on and off pulses) and translate (modulate) them into analog data so that they can be transmitted through phone lines. At the receiving end, another modem demodulates the incoming data to translate the analog data back into digital signals that digital computers can understand.

In the wire, signals can be lost or garbled, and it is the job of the modem and modem software to perform an error check and get the correct data from one computer to another. If there's an error, the data is resent.

Modems are now very capable devices, most coming with fax capabilities offering relatively high-speed data transport. There's a lot to know about modems; this section focuses on some of the basic details, aiming to communicate an understanding of how the Windows NT Workstation 4 operating system interacts with your modem.

Modems fall into the following classes:

◆ **Data modems.** These modems are very basic and don't offer other services, such as voice or digital data transfer.

◆ **Fax modems.** Most modern modems offer fax capabilities (the capability to communicate with any fax machine, whether stand-alone or modem-based) burned into the modem chip set. Currently, there is little or no price differential between fax and data modems.

◆ **Multichannel modems.** These modems can handle voice, answering machine, mailbox capabilities, fax, and data all rolled up into one. These modems use the UNIMODEM2.DRV driver. NT 4 supports many variants of these modems, including DSVD (Digital Simultaneous Voice & Data).

◆ **Auto-answer modems.** Using an auto-answer modem, you can dial up a network and have your modem accept return phone calls that validate you as a user as part of the security scheme.

◆ **Cellular modems.** A cellular modem attaches to a cellular phone and permits data or fax transmission. In laptop computers, cellular modems are typically packaged as PCMCIA cards.

◆ **Telephony boards.** A telephony board offers data/fax and sound capabilities. Using a telephony board, you can set up your computer as a phone answering machine or as a voice and e-mail system. Telephony is relatively new, but is expected to undergo rapid growth. Because telephony doesn't require considerable processing power (it's input/output limited), it represents a good use for an aging computer. The section "Understanding Telephony Drivers," located toward the end of this chapter, describes Windows telephony services in detail.

Modems come as external or internal devices, or as PCMCIA cards of several packaging types. Some modern modems are amazingly small in size, especially in the PC card format. Modems are serial devices, so installation of a modem uses up one of your serial ports.

These days 19.2 Kbps (the throughput speed) is considered a slow modem speed, with 28.8 Kbps v.34 (v.34 is a data compression standard that improves throughput) emerging as the average speed. Modems that offer 33.6 Kbps are now reasonably priced and are popular items. You don't want to connect to the Internet with less than 28.8 Kbps, and fast modems generally pay for themselves in reduced connect time.

Windows NT Workstation 4 ships with many modem drivers. Check the hardware compatibility list that came with your operating system CD.

Installing a Modem

The procedure for installing a modem depends on whether you have previously installed a modem or not. For an initial installation, the Install New Modem Wizard runs. This section begins with a look at the procedure for an initial installation. If you are replacing a modem or changing the driver for a modem, you can move right to the section "Configuring Modems" later in this chapter.

To install a modem:

1. Follow the manufacturer's instructions using one of the following methods:

    ◆ Attach an external modem to the desired serial port using an RS-232 connection (in the store it might be called a modem serial cable). Normally, this connector does not come with the modem.

◆ Install the internal modem, being certain that there are no IRQ or base I/O address conflicts with other boards.

◆ Insert the PCMCIA modem card into your PCMCIA slot.

2. Plug the telephone wire into the modem and desired phone or surge suppressor.

> **Caution** It's not a great idea to plug a modem directly into a telephone socket. Modems are sensitive to power surges through the phone lines, and a power surge can make your computer's motherboard inoperable. Plug a modem into a telephone or a surge suppressor that comes with a modem plug. Many manufacturers offer special modem surge suppressors.

3. Plug the power line from the modem into an appropriate power source.

Windows automatically detects most PCMCIA card modems when they are inserted. The Install New Modem Wizard will run if the modem hasn't been installed before. If the modem isn't detected, run the PC Card control panel and check the configuration of the PCMCIA socket driver.

To install a modem, use the Install New Modem Wizard, as follows:

1. Double-click on the Modems control panel icon (see fig. 13.2) in the Control Panel folder.

Objective B.5

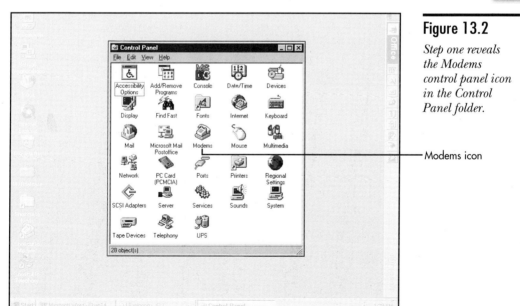

Figure 13.2

Step one reveals the Modems control panel icon in the Control Panel folder.

Modems icon

Assuming that this is an initial installation, the first step of the Install New Modem Wizard appears (see fig. 13.3). (If this were not an initial installation, at this point the Modems control panel would appear.)

Figure 13.3

The first screen of the Install New Modem Wizard sets up autodetection or manual selection.

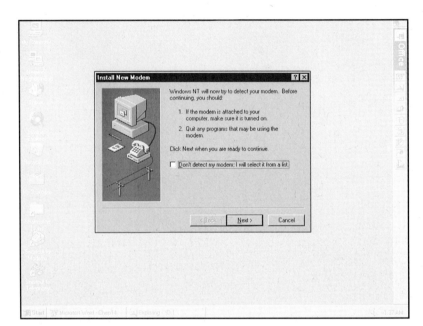

2. To select your modem from a list, enable the check box that says Don't Detect My Modem; I Will Select It from a List. Don't click the checkbox (in other words, leave it disabled) if you want the wizard to autodetect your modem.

   Windows almost always successfully autodetects modems, so you might want to try leaving the option unchecked first. If you do, then each COM port is queried and the identified modem is returned in a dialog box. If the autodetection is not correct, you can select the correct modem from the list you see in figure 13.4.

3. Click the Next button to view Step 2 (see fig. 13.4), a list of manufacturers and models (this is the same list that displays when you use the Don't Detect My Modem option).

4. Select the manufacturer and the model from the Manufacturers and Models lists, respectively, then click the Next button to view Step 3 of the wizard. Choose Selected Ports (see fig. 13.5).

   If your modem is not listed, click on the Have Disk button, and install the appropriate driver from disk or from file(s) obtained from the vendor (be sure it is an NT 4 driver).

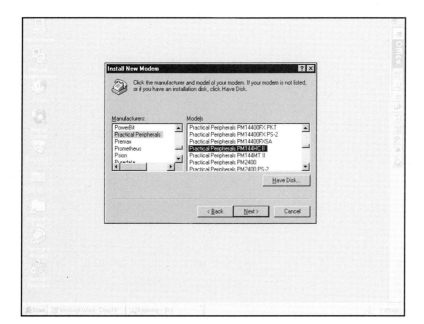

Figure 13.4

The next screen of the Install New Modem Wizard enables you to select your modem from a long list of supported modems.

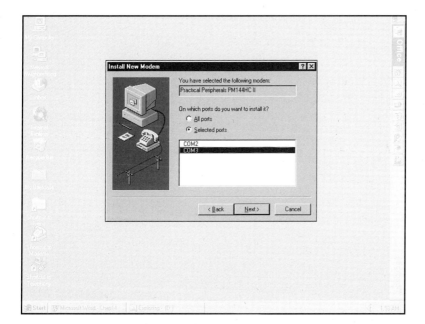

Figure 13.5

Step 3 of the Install New Modem Wizard enables you to specify your modem's port.

5. Select the port for your modem by clicking on that port with the Selected Ports radio button enabled, or click the All Ports radio button if you want to communicate on two or more ports (useful for a multimodem or a shared network modem for faster throughput).

You see Ports list only when you manually select your modem from the list. If the wizard autodetects your modem, it assumes (okay, it insists) that the port assignment is the one it found.

6. Click on the Next button to view Step 4 of the wizard, Location Information.

7. Fill in the text boxes for your country, area code, and outside line dialing prefix, and click on a radio button for Tone or Pulse dialing; then click the Next button.

Note This dialog box only appears for a first installation.

8. Click on the Finish button to complete the installation; Windows opens up the Modems Properties dialog box for viewing (see fig. 13.6).

Figure 13.6

The Modems Properties dialog box enables you to view the configuration of your installed modem.

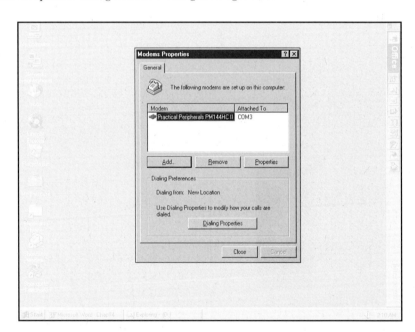

The Install Modem Wizard isn't always a perfect installation. If you have a telephony modem, it might not detect the additional services. You might have to activate the telephony services manually, as described in "Understanding Telephony Drivers," later in this chapter.

Configuring Modems

The key to configuring modems is to open up their Properties dialog box and adjust the settings there. Unlike printers, which create virtual devices with their own icons, Windows NT Workstation 4 doesn't create modem icons. Instead, you work with the Modems applet in the Control Panel.

This section takes you through the different settings that you can apply to your modems to make them operate correctly and optimally.

To configure a modem after it is installed, follow these steps:

> **Objective**
>
> **B.5**

1. Choose the Control Panel command from the Settings submenu of the Start menu.

2. Double-click on the Modems icon to open the Modems Properties dialog box (refer to fig. 13.6).

3. Select the installed modem you wish to configure. Then, click on the Properties button to display the Properties dialog box.

General Properties

The Properties dialog box opens with the General tab (see fig. 13.7).

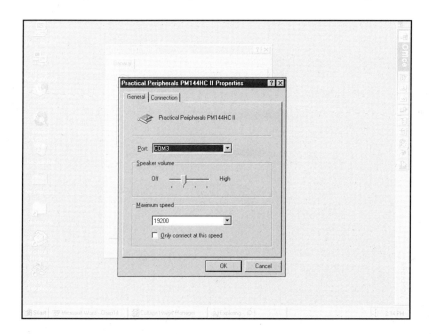

Figure 13.7

The General tab of the modem's Properties dialog box shows you important modem settings.

The General tab is concerned with the following items:

◆ The port to which the modem is connected.

◆ Speaker Volume slider. Turn those squelches up or down to suit your mood.

◆ Maximum Speed drop-down list. Select the speed of your modem, or a speed somewhat above it.

◆ Only Connect at this Speed checkbox. This checkbox disables the drop-down list, enabling your modem to connect only at the speed you entered in the Maximum Speed drop-down list.

 Tip Setting your modem speed higher than its rated speed is usually a good idea. If you have a 14.4 Kbps modem, for example, set your speed to 19.2 Kbps; if you have a 28.8 Kbps modem, set your modem's maximum speed to 38.4 Kbps. If your modem supports advanced data compression routines, you can frequently get the better throughput that those standards allow.

Connection Properties

The connection properties for a modem are the settings that are used, by default, as your modem and the host computer are getting to know each other. They have to agree on the way they'll communicate, and this is where you establish those options. Figure 13.8 illustrates the Connection tab of the Properties dialog box.

Figure 13.8

The Connection tab of the modem's Properties dialog box displays your connection properties.

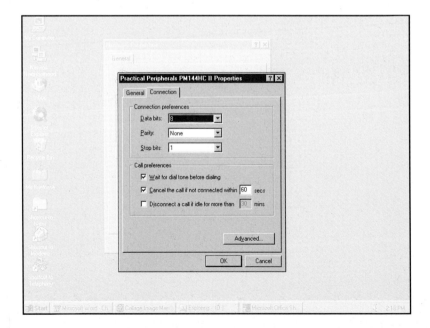

The configuration options with this tab are the following:

◆ **Data Bits.** The size of the "words" transmitted—8 bits is the most common size; a 7-bit byte is less commonly encountered than an 8-bit byte. The word *byte* here refers to the word size.

◆ **Parity.** *Parity* is an error-checking bit that determines if data should be retransmitted. Choices are None, Even, Odd, Mark, and Space. None is common; occasionally, Even and Odd are encountered.

◆ **Stop Bits.** *Stop bits* are the timing units used between transmitted bits in a data stream: 1, 1.5, and 2 are the choices offered. 1 is the most common setting, and 1.5 is occasionally encountered. A stop bit helps determine when a bit has ended, validates data communication, and enables parameters such as the amount of data transferred to be calculated.

Note Data bits, parity, and stop bits are assigned in the Ports control panel. They are default settings. The settings you make here override the default settings for the port during any session that your modem is active.

◆ **Wait for Dial Tone Before Dialing.** This option is set by default (recommended). If your modem starts to dial before the tone is available, you may lose some of the numbers and end up misdialing. Also, if someone is on the line (faxing, for example), this prevents a broken connecton.

◆ **Cancel the Call if not Connected Within xx Secs.** The default setting is 60. (This is a good default because any setting of less than 60 seconds can result in constant and often unnecessary redialing. If you haven't connected within 60 seconds, you are probably not going to connect and should redial.)

◆ **Disconnect a Call if Idle for More than xx Mins.** Unchecked by default, this option should be left that way for permanent modem connections (such as a dedicated Internet connection). If you dial in to an Internet service that charges for your time online, or you dial a number that has toll call charges, enter a reasonable time period so you won't get massive bills if you forget that you are connected.

Advanced Connection Properties

Click on the Advanced button to view additional modem settings in the Advanced Connection Settings dialog box (see fig. 13.9).

Figure 13.9

The Advanced Connection Settings dialog box contains additional connection settings.

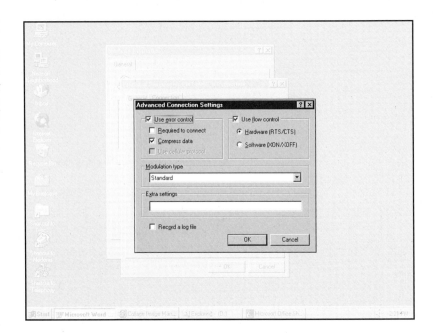

You can make changes as needed to the following configuration options:

◆ **Use Error Control.** The Error Control setting turns on any error control protocols that your modem supports. If you leave it on (it's selected by default), you get improved transmission accuracy, but a slightly diminished data transfer speed.

◆ **Required to Connect.** Because error control must be supported by both connected modems, leaving this option off (the default setting) allows a session to proceed even if the other modem doesn't support your modem's error correction protocols.

◆ **Compress Data.** Checking this option enables any data compression protocols your modem supports. Because these protocols are established (but not required) during *handshaking* (agreement between two modems on the communications methods), it is recommended that you select this option (it's unchecked by default).

◆ **Use Cellular Protocol.** This check box is enabled and should be selected for use with cellular modems.

◆ **Use Flow Control.** *Flow control* is a process by which devices make a determination of how data is transferred when the two communication devices don't transmit data at the same speed. This setting is on by default (recommended).

◆ **Hardware (RTS/CTS).** Most modems support flow control in ROM. Unless you have reasons to choose otherwise (for instance, you've received specific instructions from a host system), leave this option checked (its default) because hardware flow control is faster than software flow control.

◆ **Software (XON/XOFF).** You usually won't need this service from your operating system configuration because many communication programs provide the capability to perform flow control using software.

◆ **Modulation Type.** This option refers to the modem signals that are delivered to computers. Select Standard (the default) for Hayes type modems; otherwise, select Non-Standard (Bell, HST).

◆ **Extra Settings.** If you want to enter a modem string to alter the operation of your modem or to set it up for a session, enter it here. Under certain circumstances (for specific connections), these modem strings will eliminate connection problems. If you do specify additional modem strings in this box, those strings will be sent last, overriding all previous settings.

◆ **Record a Log File.** When selected, this option creates a text file (MEMOLOG.TXT) of all modem commands that are sent and received by your modem. It can be useful for troubleshooting and is generally not selected unless you've been having problems.

Dialing Properties

When you finish with the Advanced Connection configuration, click on the OK button to return to the basic Properties dialog box and click OK again to return to the Modems Properties dialog box.

Click on the Dialing Properties button to view the Dialing Properties dialog box (see fig. 13.10), and make desired adjustments.

Many of the dialing properties you can set are self-explanatory. A few of them show up in the Install New Modem Wizard. However, the Dialing Properties dialog box of your modem contains several options that you haven't previously seen. These are worthy of a brief explanation.

Note The Dialing Properties tab shows up in any application that uses the TAPI interface. If you open the Telephony control panel (described later in chapter), you can view the default dialing properties settings for any telephony application.

Figure 13.10

*The Dialing
Properties dialog
box enables you to
set up your
modem's default
dialing
configuration.*

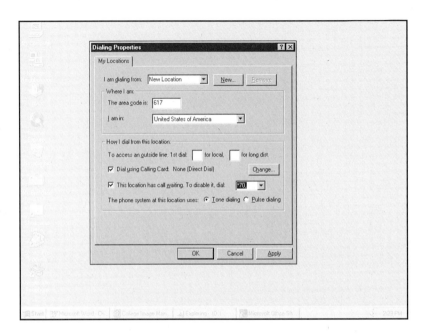

The Dialing Properties dialog box offers the following options:

- ◆ **I Am Dialing From.** You can create additional locations, which is a feature of interest to mobile computer users. Each location supports its own set of options.

- ◆ **The Area Code Is.** Enter your area code here.

- ◆ **I Am In.** Enter your country of residence here.

- ◆ **To Access an Outside Line, 1st Dial.** Enter the prefix required to get to an outside line. Typically, the number 9 is used on many business phone systems for local calls. If your company's telephone system uses a different outside line for long distance calls, specify that number in the Long Distance box.

- ◆ **Dial Using Calling Card: None (Direct Dial).** Select for None, or click the Change button to select a calling card access number and enter your calling card number in the Change Calling Card dialog box (see fig. 13.11).

- ◆ **This Location Has Call Waiting.** Set to on to activate call waiting suppression.

- ◆ **To Disable It, Dial.** Select the sequence required to dial in a connection to disable call waiting (recommended). The value *70 is common, but you need to know what your telephone company expects (check the front of your telephone book or call the telephone company).

- ◆ **The Phone System at this Location Uses Tone Dialing/Pulse Dialing.** Set the radio button for the type of phone connection you have.

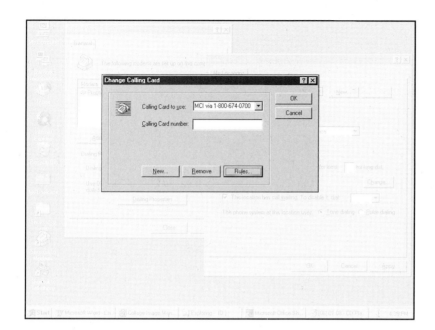

Figure 13.11

The Change Calling Card dialog box enables you to reassign the phone calling card that you wish to use.

Using Calling Cards

When using a calling card, you are specifying a set of numbers that are entered after your connection is made. The Change Calling Card dialog box not only lets you enter an access number, but the calling card number itself. You are offered standard calling cards, including AT&T, AT&T Direct Dial, British Telecom, Calling Card 0, Carte France Telecom, CLEAR Communications, Global Card, Mercury, MCI, None, Optus, (Australia), Telecom Australia, Telecom New Zealand, and US Sprint. You can create and name a calling card service to match your own situation. From the Dialing Properties tab, you can add, delete, and edit calling card information.

You can click on the Rules button in the Change Calling Card dialog box to open the Dialing Rules dialog box (see fig. 13.12) and specify additional dialing rules. There are three different codes you should fill in: local, long distance, and international.

The following codes are used in various Dialing Rules text boxes:

◆ **0–9.** A number dialed.

◆ **#.** Touch-tone pound sign.

◆ ***.** Touch-tone star.

◆ **!.** Hook flash.

◆ **, (comma).** Two-second pause.

- ◆ **E.** Country code.

- ◆ **F.** Area code.

- ◆ **G.** Destination local number.

- ◆ **H.** Calling card number.

- ◆ **T.** Dial the following number using touch tone.

- ◆ **P.** Dial numbers using pulse tone.

- ◆ **W.** Wait for a second dialing tone.

- ◆ **@.** Wait for a ringing tone followed by five seconds of silence.

- ◆ **$.** Wait for a calling card prompt code (requires modem support).

- ◆ **?.** Display an on-screen prompt to the user to continue dialing.

Figure 13.12

The Dialing Rules dialog box enables you to set up types of calling services.

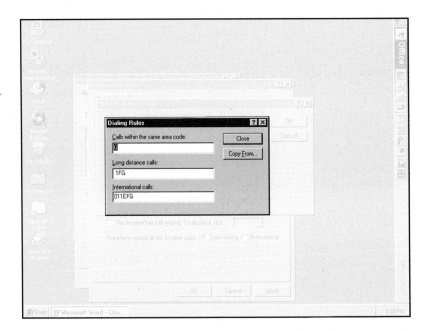

Click on the OK button to return to the modem's Properties dialog box; then click on the Close button to close the dialog box.

Your property settings take effect immediately upon closing the modem's Properties dialog box.

An Overview of ISDN Connections

ISDN, or *Integrated Services Digital Network,* is a telecommunications standard codified by the CCITT (a communications standards committee) that sends digital and electric signals with voice, data, and video on a line. ISDN is a higher speed alternative to modem access; therefore, ISDN is favored by users who require large amounts of data to be transferred quickly. Many people using the Internet, for example, or those running intranets use ISDN for outside connections or remote dial-in services.

Three basic service components comprise ISDN:

◆ **Teleservices.** ISDN supports fax, text and fax, speech or telephony, teletex, and videotext.

◆ **Bearer services.** Among the common protocols that ISDN provides are Frame Relay, X.25, and circuit-switched connections. Frame relay and X.25 provide packet switching. Using Frame Relay, you can obtain throughput of up to 2 Mbps. X.25 is a lower-speed service, but offers quality error-handling capabilities and can work with many internetworking protocols. Circuit-switched connections offer voice or data transmission speeds of up to 64, 128, and higher Kbps.

◆ **Supplementary services.** Supplementary services provide capabilities such as call forwarding, call hold, call transfer, call waiting, conference calling, direct dial-in, line hunting, three-party services, and user-to-user signaling.

ISDN is a widely accepted protocol, and many countries install the special lines it requires. To install ISDN, you must have access to an ISDN line and an ISDN card installed in your computer. Not every area of the United States is currently wired for ISDN (although many are). Check with your local phone company, or with independent service providers (like your Internet service provider), to see if they can offer you ISDN line access.

ISDN typically operates at speeds of 128 Kbps, which is roughly six times the speed of 28.8 Kbps modems. There are faster communication media available via wide band methods (coming soon from a television cable company in your neighborhood), and in the world of fast communications, ISDN is considered a medium-speed method. Modem access is a low-speed method in terms of communication media.

ISDN add-in adapter boards typically cost in excess of $1,000. Their cost is dropping, however, and the technology is becoming more prevalent. Their current cost makes these boards impractical for connecting the nodes of LANs on a network. The speed of ISDN boards makes them practical for internetworking applications. When using ISDN in an internetworking application, you should use the same type of manufacturer's boards on both ends.

To install ISDN cards (also called ISDN modems) and multiport adapter cards, use software drivers supplied by their manufacturers. You should follow the instructions that come with the card, and use the Setup or Install program if one is supplied on disk. If only drivers are included on disk, then use the Add/Remove Programs control panel or the Telephony Drivers tab of the Telephony control panel to add the driver(s) to your system. (The Telephony control panel is described in more detail in the following section.) Once the driver is installed, you should continue to configure your ISDN modem's connection settings and dialing properties.

Understanding Telephony Drivers

Telephony is a set of services that your computer provides to enable phone and voice communications between your computer and the outside world. Windows provides a telephony application programming interface (API) called TAPI that enables a range of communication services to be easily created by hardware and software vendors.

TAPI controls signaling, dialing, answering, and hang-ups. It also supports the telephone system functions found in PBX and ISDN phone systems such as hold, transfer, and call park. Developers can write add-in modules or plug-ins to provide TAPI with additional capabilities not found in the native API. Therefore, TAPI can provide specific services for manufacturers and service providers and can be easily upgraded by Microsoft, based on future developments.

These are among the common services considered to be part of telephony:

◆ **Voice mail.** This service occurs when a person calls into your phone system and is connected to your computer through a modem that supports telephony. Spoken messages can be sent to that person, and his messages can be recorded.

| Note | Voice mail was once only available to those willing to spend tens of thousands of dollars on very expensive phone systems. These days, complete telephony systems can be purchased for less than $5,000. Before you can enable a telephony system, you need a voice modem. |

◆ **On-demand fax.** An on-demand fax system enables someone to call into your system, make menu selections, indicate his fax number, and have information faxed back to him. Many companies use this system for technical support.

Telephony boards also are known as modem-voice boards. They are a combination modem sound card with record and playback capabilities, and headphone or speaker access. A telephony board has the capability to replace not only your answering machine, but also your fax machine and your telephone.

We are only at the beginning of a telephony revolution in the personal computer industry. Because adding these capabilities is inexpensive, many vendors are bundling this capability into multimedia computers.

Installing TAPI

TAPI is installed automatically in your computer when you install Windows NT Workstation 4, provided you don't omit communication services in a Custom installation. If you want to determine which drivers are installed for communications, double-click on the Telephony icon in the Control Panel (see fig. 13.13). In the telephony Properties dialog box, select the Telephony Drivers tab (see fig. 13.14). Chances are that you will see the TAPI Kernel-Mode Service Provider and Unimodem Service Provider installed.

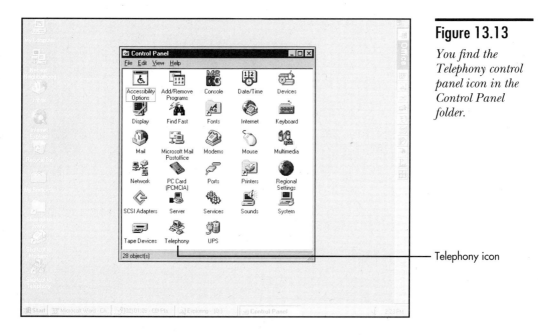

Figure 13.13

You find the Telephony control panel icon in the Control Panel folder.

Telephony icon

You can install either of these services, or other drivers required, from the Telephony Drivers tab. You can also use the My Locations tab in the telephony Properties dialog box to set up default dialing characteristics of any application that uses the telephony interface.

You can use the Add/Remove Programs control panel to install the telephony drivers on your computer or another computer over the network. Software driver installations work fine when the TAPI devices use only software drivers.

Figure 13.14

*The Telephony
Drivers tab of the
telephony
Properties dialog
box enables you to
configure voice
answering and
mailbox services
on your computer.*

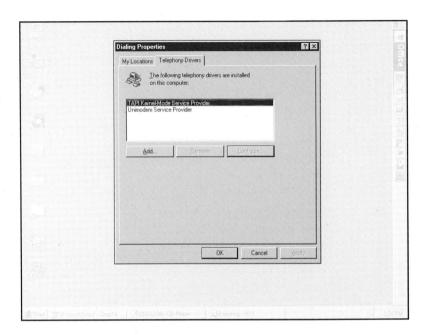

Some TAPI devices have TAPI encoded in ROM on add-in boards. For that class of
hardware, you should follow the installation instructions that came with the board
and use the Setup program supplied by the vendor, provided an installation disk was
included.

TAPI Kernel Services

TAPI is the control portion of the 32-bit Windows communications architecture.
It takes commands from an application and translates them into a form that the
Unimodem can use. TAPI is multithreaded, enabling one process to start up while
another is running. A TAPI application can place and accept phone calls simultaneously because it is part of a telephone answering system. However, only one call at
a time can be placed using a single COM port.

TAPI is composed of both an API for applications and a service provider interface
(SPI) accessed by applications to connect to a network. Typically, vendors write the
TAPI communications drivers for their device or system for the SPI, and developers
develop TAPI applications using the API. A simple schema of a TAPI application
appears in figure 13.15.

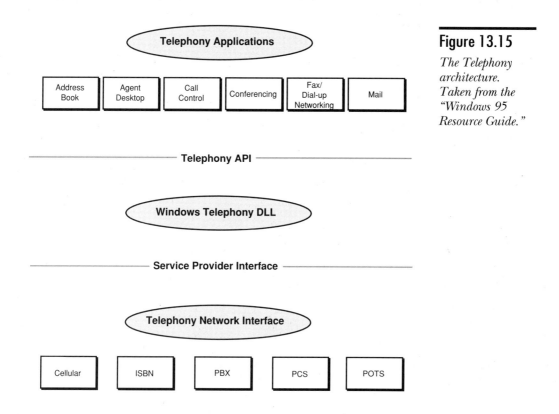

Figure 13.15

The Telephony architecture. Taken from the "Windows 95 Resource Guide."

End Note: Windows NT Workstation 4 offers a common interface for communication devices and communication services. In this chapter, you learned about the Windows communications architecture, communication drivers, and the telephony services provided by Windows. You also learned how to install and configure a modem. You can control the various settings of a modem from the Modems control panel. Among the various settings are connection and dialing properties. Other TAPI or telephone devices use similar settings.

Test Your Knowledge

1. You control a modem's configuration with:

    A. The virtual modem icon that appears for each modem you install

    B. The Properties dialog boxes in the Modem applet of the Control Panel

    C. The TAPI applet in the Control Panel

    D. The TAPI properties in the Devices applet in the Control Panel

2. Choose the correct statement(s) about using ISDN:

    A. You must connect your modem to an ISDN line.

    B. You must install a separate physical ISDN device in your computer.

    C. You must connect an ISDN board or PC Card to your telephone line.

    D. You cannot use modems and ISDN devices in the same computer.

3. Choose the correct statement(s) about Telephony Communications:

    A. TAPI provides the dialing information for any device on your system that dials out.

    B. TAPI provides the interface between a physical device and software, and you cannot configure it.

    C. TAPI is a driver that is installed when you install a modem or other device.

    D. TAPI services are provided by the operating system.

4. When you install a modem supported by the operating system, the device driver you select for the modem is named_____.

5. Which service does not use the Telephony API and, therefore, cannot use your TAPI configuration setup?

    A. Voice mail services

    B. ISDN services

    C. Fax services

    D. None of the above

6. Setting the modem configuration for a higher baud rate than the modem has the following effect:

    A. May hamper error correction

    B. May improve line noise problems

    C. May make the modem perform faster

    D. Has no effect

7. The maximum number of setups for different dialing properties in NT 4 is:

    A. 10

    B. 26

    C. Unlimited

    D. One for each port

Test Your Knowledge Answers

1. B
2. B
3. A,D
4. Unimodem
5. D
6. C
7. C

Chapter Snapshot

Windows NT Workstation 4 includes built-in multimedia capabilities that enable you to play back audio and video multimedia files. Using these tools, you can directly access multimedia files and include them in documents of OLE-aware applications (OLE stands for Object Linking and Embedding). This chapter explores:

CHAPTER 14

Working with Multimedia

Some people used to sneer at multimedia capabilities. "Real computing doesn't require that your computer talk to you and make all kinds of bizarre noises every time you turn around," they would say.

Today's applications, however, are making more and more use of the multimedia capabilities of newer computers, and for a very simple reason: taking advantage of more sensory modalities enables computers to interact more effectively with the people using them. The concept of "a picture being worth a thousand words" extends to other areas of multimedia. Sometimes, a sound can be worth a thousand words. Try writing down, for instance, exactly how the call of a particular bird sounds. Other examples abound in the areas of education—animation on the screen can rapidly illustrate how something works better than a picture with callouts. Further, the day isn't far off when you will interact with your computer by simply speaking to it—yet another form of multimedia.

Installing Multimedia Devices

Before taking advantage of all these cool multimedia capabilities, though, you need to configure your computer's multimedia hardware properly. Multimedia hardware are the installed components that give your computer multimedia capabilities. Examples include sound boards (that play sound files or music files), CD-ROM drives and interface cards, special video boards for working with movies and videotape, and so on. Depending on the equipment you own, you may have several types of these multimedia devices, such as the following:

♦ **Sound board.** Plays back and records sounds, and acts as an amplifier for audio CDs in your CD-ROM reader.

♦ **CD-ROM readers.** These are special disc drives that play CD-ROMs and music CDs. They come in different speeds, expressed as 2x, 4x, 6x, 12x, and so on. A 2x CD-ROM reader is twice as fast as the original CD-ROM standards, a 12x reader is twelve times as fast, and so on.

♦ **MIDI interface (Musical Instrument Digital Interface).** Enables you to interface with musical instruments that are MIDI-capable.

♦ **Special video board (or simply a special driver).** Enables you to play MPEG or other animation files optimally.

♦ **Video Capture Board.** Enables you to convert video data, perhaps from a video camera or a video tape player, into a playable computer file.

The preceding list covers the most common possibilities. There may be other devices connected to multimedia that will be developed in the future or that come into wider use over time, but these are the most common choices that you see in use.

Windows NT Workstation includes drivers (operating system programs that control hardware devices) for the most popular devices available; in fact, the devices you have should have been automatically recognized and installed during the installation of Windows NT Workstation. At some time, however, you will want to add or remove a device, and you will need to know how to accomplish that. In the following sections, you will learn how to add or remove a device.

When you want to add any multimedia device to your system, you first need to install the device, following the manufacturer's instructions. Then you need to configure Windows NT Workstation to work with the device properly.

Caution When purchasing any multimedia device for your computer, ensure that a driver for Windows NT 4 is included or available for the device. Sometimes device drivers are not included in the package, but are available from online sources. In any event, ensure that the device drivers are available; some manufacturers may not have Windows NT drivers written for their devices.

Note Before purchasing a multimedia device, you can consult the Hardware Compatibility List for Windows NT Workstation 4. In the list, you find all devices that have been tested with Windows NT Workstation 4. You can download the latest version of this file from Microsoft's Web site at http://www.microsoft.com/. You can also find a copy on the *Windows NT Workstation 4* CD-ROM as *\SUPPORT\HCL.HLP*.

To configure Windows NT Workstation for a multimedia device, follow these steps:

1. Use the Multimedia icon in the Control Panel (see fig. 14.1). In the Start menu, choose Settings, and then choose Control Panel.

2. Open the Multimedia icon by double-clicking on it to reveal the Multimedia Properties dialog box shown in figure 14.2.

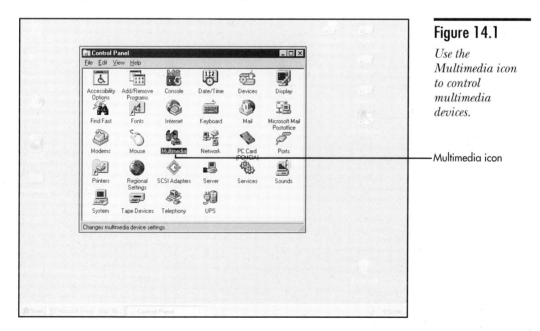

Figure 14.1

Use the Multimedia icon to control multimedia devices.

Multimedia icon

Figure 14.2

The Multimedia Properties dialog box contains tabs that enable you to control different types of devices.

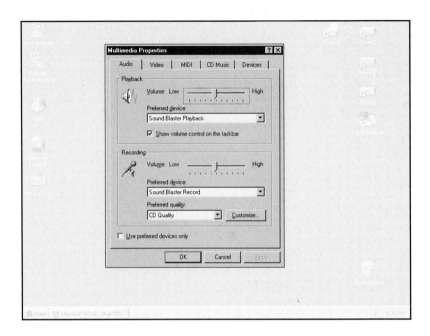

To add or remove multimedia devices from Windows NT Workstation, select the Devices tab of the Multimedia Properties dialog box (see fig. 14.3).

Figure 14.3

The Devices tab of the Multimedia Properties dialog box shows all installed multimedia devices.

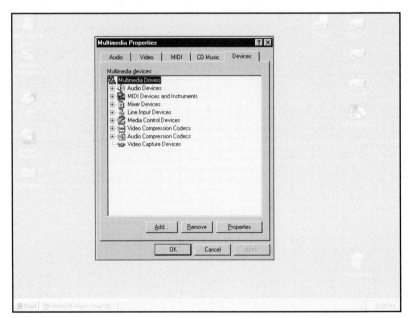

The Devices tab of the Multimedia Properties dialog box lists the classes of multimedia device drivers installed on your system. Expanding any of the classes displays a list of the actual device drivers of that type installed. Expand each class by clicking on the small plus (+) button to the left of the class. Figure 14.4 shows the display with all classes expanded.

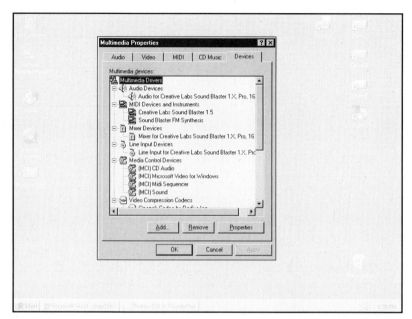

Figure 14.4

Use the expanded listing to see all the installed multimedia devices.

| Tip | You can expand all the classes at once by selecting the top entry (Multimedia Drivers) and pressing the asterisk key (*) on your numeric keypad. |

The Devices tab enables you to add and remove multimedia device drivers. Follow these steps to add a new device driver:

1. Click on the Add button at the bottom of the Devices tab. This displays the Add dialog box shown in figure 14.5.

2. Select the device you want to add from the list and click on the OK button. You will be then prompted through the installation process for the driver (each driver may have different steps at this point).

If the device driver you want to add is not included in this list (the Add dialog box list includes all the device drivers offered through Windows NT Workstation), you can add it to the list (if the driver is provided by the manufacturer of the device).

To add a driver not listed, follow these steps:

1. Select the Unlisted or Updated Driver entry (located at the top of the list) and then click on the OK button.

2. You are then prompted for the location of the device driver file you want to add (it may be on a floppy disk, a CD-ROM disc, or on your hard disk). Use the dialog box to locate the driver file and click on the OK button to install that driver.

Figure 14.5

The Add dialog box lets you add new multimedia devices.

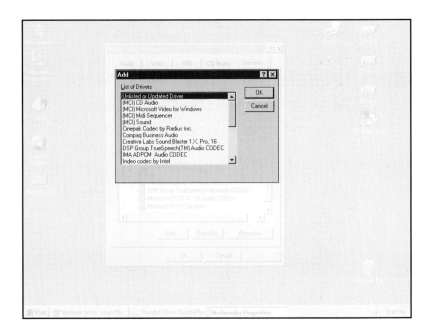

Figure 14.6 shows the Install Driver dialog box that appears when you select Unlisted or Updated Driver.

Figure 14.6

The Install Driver dialog box for Unlisted or Updated Drivers lets you add an unlisted device for which you have a Windows NT device driver file.

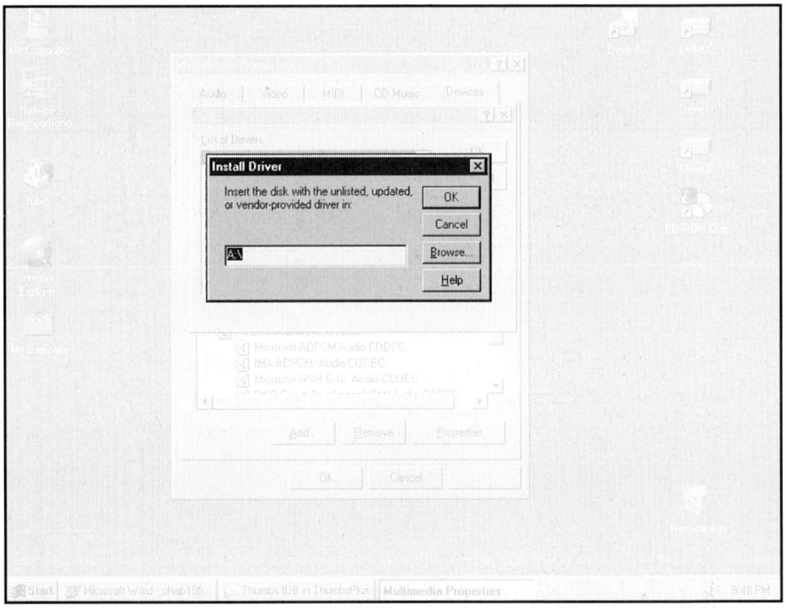

| Tip | Use the Browse button to graphically locate the drive and directory that contains the driver you want to install. |

Removing Multimedia Devices

Removing multimedia devices is even easier than adding them. Follow these steps to remove a multimedia device:

1. Start by opening the Multimedia icon in the Control Panel.

2. Move to the Devices tab of the Multimedia Properties dialog box.

3. Expand the appropriate entry in the display by clicking on the appropriate plus button.

4. Select the device you want to remove and click on the Remove button.

The multimedia device driver is now removed from the system. If appropriate, you can then shut down the system and remove the hardware device that was supported by the driver.

| Caution | If you remove a multimedia device driver to remove the physical device, you will want to carefully inspect all the multimedia device driver entries. Some devices have multiple drivers associated with them. A sound card, for example, may have an Audio Device driver, a MIDI driver, a Mixer driver, and other associated drivers. |

Configuring Audio Devices

The Multimedia Properties for audio devices let you configure some of the properties of the devices, or even select which device to use for different jobs if you have more than one possible device for a particular job—such as playing a MIDI file. To access these functions, start with the Audio tab shown in figure 14.7.

The Audio tab is divided into two sections: Playback and Recording. In each section, you control the volume for those actions with the Volume slide control. If multiple device drivers are available to play or record sounds, you can choose which Device you want to use with the Preferred Device field.

Objective B.4

Objective B.5

Objective B.4

Objective B.5

Figure 14.7

The Audio tab of the Multimedia Properties dialog box lets you configure aspects of your sound board.

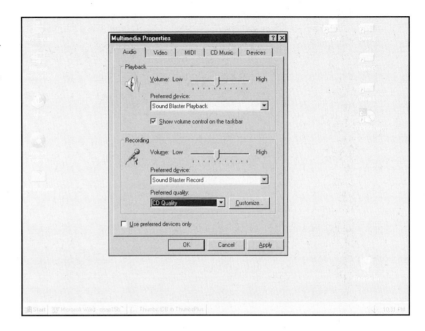

Selecting the Show Volume Control on the Taskbar option in the Playback section causes the speaker icon to appear (to the left of the time at the lower-right corner of the screen). You can then click on the volume control icon to bring up the control shown in figure 14.8.

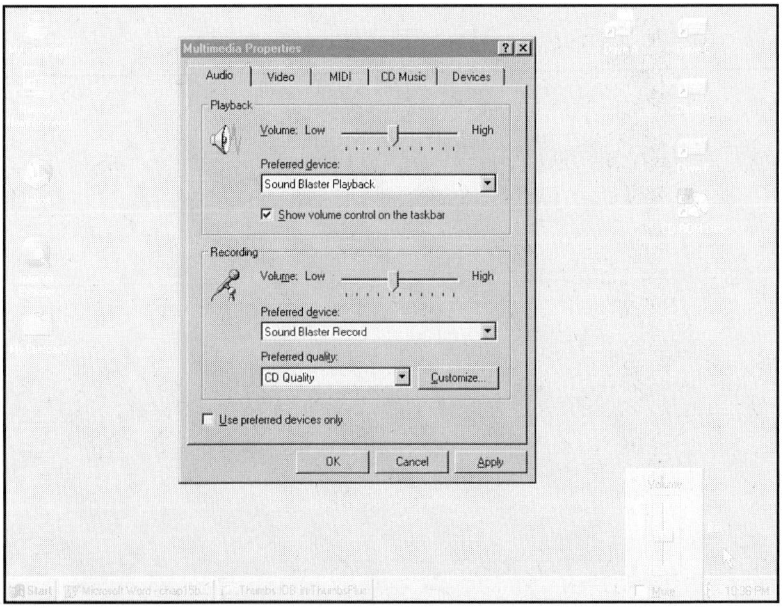

Figure 14.8

The simple volume control is easy to use in a pinch.

Another important setting on the Audio tab is the drop-down list called Preferred Quality (in the Recording section of the tab). You can choose from these settings:

◆ Telephone Quality

◆ Radio Quality

◆ CD Quality

The quality settings control how often the sound coming into the sound card from an attached microphone, or recorded into a file from a music CD, is sampled when you use the Sound Recorder. *Sample rates* determine how often the sound coming in is recorded into the file you're creating. Higher sampling rates mean better quality sound (CD Quality). Lower sampling rates mean lower quality sound (Radio Quality or the lowest, Telephone Quality). Sampling rates also directly impact the amount of disk space that a recorded sound takes up. Table 14.1 displays the different settings and their storage requirements. As you can see, storing CD Quality sound recordings with 16-bit stereo consumes significantly more disk space than the other two qualities. To put it another way, you can record 100 seconds (1⅔ minutes) of Telephone Quality sound in 1 MB, whereas you can only store less than six seconds of CD Quality sound in the same 1 MB.

TABLE 14.1
Sampling Rates (Quality) versus Storage

Quality Setting	Sampling Frequency	Bits	Stereo?	Space Required
Telephone Quality	11.025 kHz	8	No	10 KB/second
Radio Quality	22.050 kHz	8	No	21 KB/second
CD Quality	44.100 kHz	16	Yes	172 KB/second

Using the Media Player

You often will want to play back multimedia files on your computer. These files may be video (movie) files or sound files. The Media Player application included with Windows NT Workstation (see fig. 14.9) can be used to play these types of multimedia files:

◆ Sound files (WAV files)

◆ MIDI sequencer files (RMI or MID files)

◆ CD music discs

◆ Video for Windows files (AVI files)

Figure 14.9

The Media Player application offers a simple interface with which to work.

The slider indicates the location in the file that is currently playing. Drag the slider to select a spot.

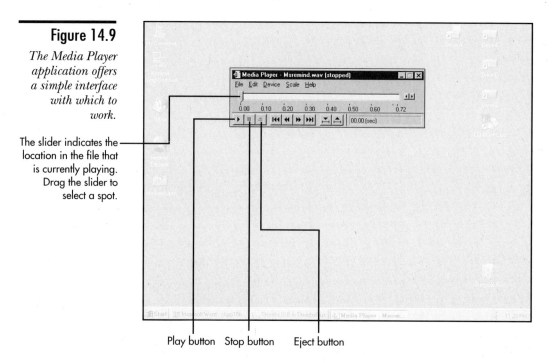

Play button   Stop button   Eject button

To use the Media Player, first open one of the accepted multimedia files by opening the File menu and choosing Open. In the Open dialog box that appears (see fig. 14.10), select a file type in the Files of type drop-down list and then locate the exact file you want. After opening a file, the Media Player controls become usable.

Tip You often can simply double-click on media files to open them in the appropriate media playback program.

When you use Media Player to play a movie file, the movie appears in a separate window on your desktop, as shown in figure 14.11.

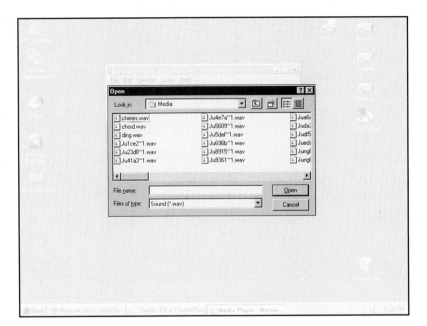

Figure 14.10

The Open dialog box in Media Player enables you to load media files in preparation to play them.

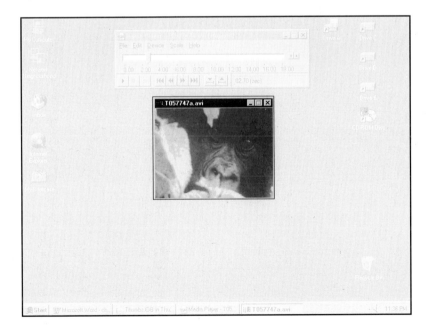

Figure 14.11

A Video for Windows file plays in a separate window on your desktop.

Setting Media Player Options

A variety of options are available in Media Player that let you fine-tune how it behaves. The first place in which you control options is with the Options command in the Edit menu, which displays the Options dialog box shown in figure 14.12.

Figure 14.12

Control Media Player settings with the Options dialog box.

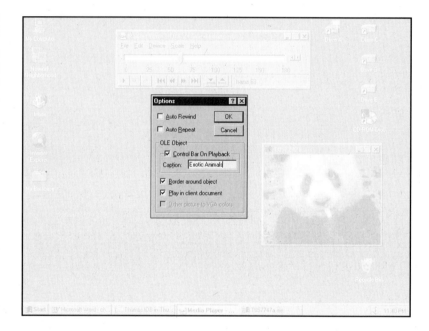

You can choose to have Media Player automatically rewind loaded files after they play with the Auto Rewind check box. You can also set a file to constantly keep playing with the Auto Repeat check box.

The lower half of the Options dialog box controls how the loaded file behaves when linked into another application's document (for instance, you can embed a media file into a Word, Excel, or PowerPoint document).

Selecting Control Bar On Playback causes the control bar (the set of icons that let you play, stop, rewind, and fast-forward) to appear on top of the application when the embedded media object is played.

When you embed a media file into another application, it appears in a box inside that application, and that box has a caption. The Caption field controls the displayed caption.

You can also control whether or not a border appears around the embedded object with the Border Around Object check box.

If the Play in Client Document option is checked, the media file you link is automatically played when its icon is double-clicked in the client document. If Play in Client Document is not selected, Media Player is started when you double-click on the icon, and you must then manually click on the Play button.

Finally, you may choose the Dither Picture to VGA Colors option. If selected, an embedded picture is modified automatically to use standard VGA colors. If not selected, the picture uses the color settings in the attached file. On some systems, using the color settings in the file may result in distorted colors being displayed.

> **Tip**
>
> If pictures are grainy and display poorly on your screen, even when you try many different picture files, you may not have enough colors or a high-enough resolution set in your display properties. To get photo-quality image display (assuming the underlying image file is of high-enough quality) use at least 800×600 screen resolution and at least 16-bit color.

Depending on what kind of media file you have loaded, you can change the scale displayed on Media Player's slide bar. Use the Scale menu (see fig. 14.13) to choose from the available scales.

Figure 14.13

The Scale menu chooses measurement display options for Media Player.

Embedding Media Files into Applications

Most applications capable of OLE can accept embedded multimedia files. You can easily embed, for instance, a sound file into a Word or PowerPoint document. You can even use WordPad (the simple word processor included with Windows NT Workstation 4) as the containing application, which is demonstrated in this section.

> **Note** OLE lets you link and embed objects into a document. You can embed, for instance, a sound file into a spreadsheet, or a movie file into a presentation. When you do link or embed objects, the document that holds the embedded object is called the *container document;* it contains the object. The application that generates or plays the embedded object is called the *server application,* and the application that owns the container document is called the *client application.*

Generally, two ways exist to embed multimedia files into applications. The first, most common way, is to open the multimedia file with Media Player and copy it to the Clipboard. Then in the container application, choose Paste Special from its Edit menu. A link will then be formed between the actual file and the container document.

The second method depends on the specific application in which you want to embed a file. Most of the Office applications, for instance, have an Insert menu with an Object command. This command can be used to embed media files (as well as other types of embedded objects). Other applications might have other methods that embed external files (objects) into their documents.

The most common way to embed a media file into an application involves using the Copy command in Media Player, and then using the application's Paste Special command. To see how the Copy command works in the Media Player, follow these steps:

1. First, open a media file in Media Player.

2. In Media Player, use the Copy Object command in the Edit menu (see fig. 14.14).

3. In the destination application, choose the Paste Special command in its Edit menu. (For this example, WordPad is used as the destination application.)

4. You see a Paste Special dialog box that asks you how you want the object to be treated by the application (see fig. 14.15). Choose the name of the media file you copied (MSREMIND.WAV in figure 14.15) and click on the OK button.

5. The object is now embedded into the open document and appears as an icon, as shown in figure 14.16.

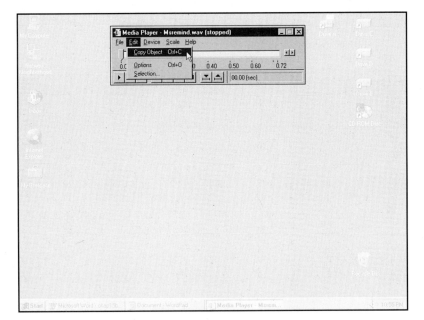

Figure 14.14

The Copy Object command in Media Player copies the opened file onto the Clipboard.

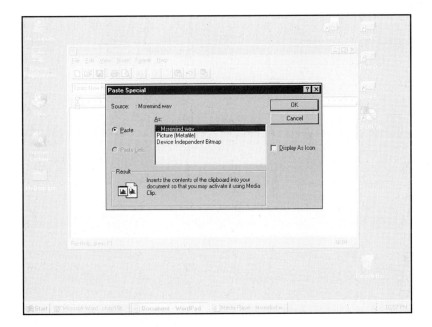

Figure 14.15

The Paste Special dialog box controls how the object is pasted into the document.

Figure 14.16

The icon of an embedded object represents the object and can be double-clicked to open the object.

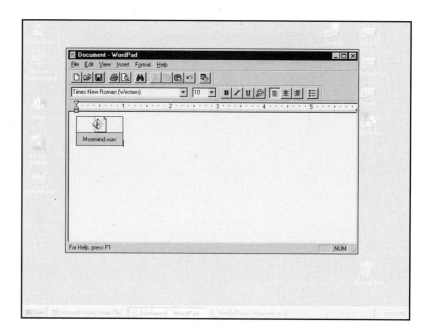

To play the object in the container document, just double-click on it. This automatically causes Media Player to be invoked (even if it's not running) and play the file. You can also right-click on the icon to access its pop-up menu, which contains some commands that let you control it (see fig. 14.17).

Figure 14.17

An embedded object's pop-up menu gives you commands to control the object.

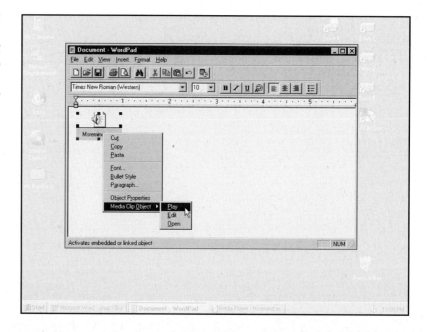

Introducing the Sound Recorder

Windows NT Workstation includes an application that lets you record sounds into files that can be played back later. The application, Sound Recorder, is shown in figure 14.18.

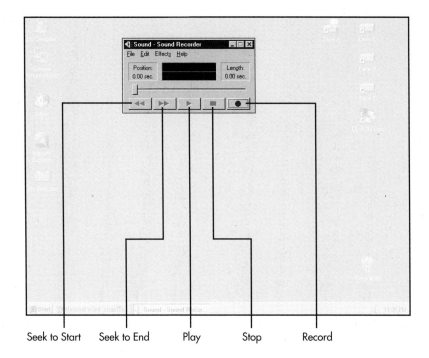

Seek to Start   Seek to End   Play   Stop   Record

Figure 14.18

The Sound Recorder application is used to record sounds from another source, such as a microphone or CD player.

To use Sound Recorder, you need to have some sort of audio input device connected to your computer. Sound Recorder can accept input from a microphone attached to a sound card, or from an audio CD-ROM attached to a sound card.

Note The Sound Recorder that comes with Windows NT Workstation is limited to 60 seconds of recorded sound.

To record from either source, click on the Record button. (To record from a CD, you need to play the CD with CD Player.) You will see the waveform of the recorded sound appear in the window as the recording is performed. When you want to stop recording, click on the Stop button.

If both the microphone and CD player are active, both sources are recorded from simultaneously, and the resulting recording is a "blended" sound from both sources. To record from only the CD player, you need to disable the microphone first. You can disable the microphone by unplugging it, or by using a switch installed on the microphone designed for that purpose. Many sound cards also come with a mixer application (a program that lets you choose the sound levels for different sound inputs and outputs) that lets you control whether the microphone is active or not.

You can listen to your recorded sound with the Play button. Once you're happy with it, use the File menu's Save As command to store the file on your hard disk. If you would like to rerecord the sound, use the New command in the File menu to start with a blank recording file. Also, if you want to rerecord only a portion, you can position the slider control to the point at which you want to start recording again and then click on the Record button.

Using Advanced Sound Recorder Features

Sound Recorder, although a fairly simple application, contains a number of capabilities that extend its usefulness. Using various commands, you can do the following:

◆ **Convert a recorded sound file into another audio format.** Choose the Properties command in the File menu. In the resulting dialog box, use the Convert button to choose a different audio file format.

◆ **Mix an existing sound file with the one that's currently open in Sound Recorder.** Choose the Mix with File command in the Edit menu. *Mixing* means that the two files are combined so that the mixed file's sound is overlaid onto the open file's sound.

◆ **Insert an existing sound file.** First choose a position in the open sound file with the slider control in Sound Recorder. Then choose Insert File from the Edit menu.

◆ **Delete portions of the open file.** Position the file to either the end or beginning of the section you want to delete. Then using the Edit menu, choose either Delete Before Current Position or Delete After Current Position.

◆ **Increase or decrease (in 25% increments) the stored volume of the file.** Use the Increase Volume (by 25%) and Decrease Volume commands in the Effects menu.

◆ **Control how quickly the sound plays.** Use the Increase Speed (by 100%) and Decrease Speed commands in the Effects menu. Increasing the speed cuts the playback time in half each time you use the command; decreasing the speed doubles the playback time each time you use the command.

◆ **Add an echo effect to the sound.** Use the Add Echo command in the Effects menu.

◆ **Reverse the file (so that it plays from end to front).** Use the Reverse command in the Effects menu.

> **Tip** Use the Reverse command to search for hidden messages in your music CDs; record songs into Sound Recorder, and then reverse the file and play it. Use the Decrease Speed command to make finding those pesky hidden messages even easier.

◆ **Control the quality of the recordings you make.** Use the Audio Properties command in the Edit menu. This command brings up a settings dialog box that lets you choose the recording and playback volume, as well as the sampling rate for recordings.

> **Tip** Many sound cards come with packaged utilities that are more powerful than the utilities included with Windows NT Workstation.

Sound Recorder can be a useful utility when you want to record your own sounds for playback. You can record, for instance, your own WAV files and attach them to Windows events with the Sounds icon in the Control Panel. (If you share a home computer with someone else, you can have some fun with this one.)

Using Volume Control

Two ways to control the volume of playback from your audio card are the volume control on the Taskbar and the Volume Control application. The Volume Control application has more settings and lets you control more than the playback volume.

Using the Taskbar to Control Volume

To use the Taskbar's volume control, you first must ensure that it is activated. Open the Control Panel and then double-click on the Multimedia icon to access the Multimedia Properties dialog box. Make sure that the Show Volume Control on the Taskbar check box is selected (see fig. 14.19).

To use the Taskbar's control, simply click on the small speaker icon next to the time display at the far right end of your Taskbar. This brings up the simple volume control shown in figure 14.20. Drag the slider to adjust the playback volume from your sound card's amplifier.

Figure 14.19

Use the Multimedia Properties dialog box to enable the Taskbar's volume control.

Check this box...

...to enable this control

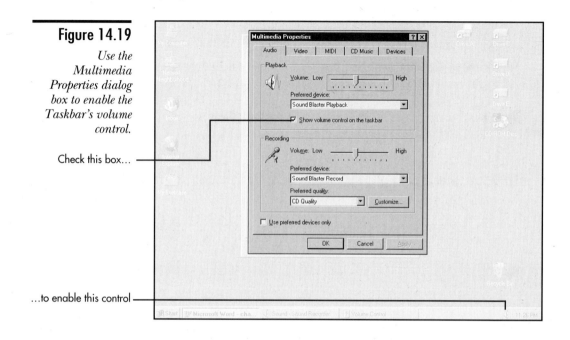

Figure 14.20

Use the Taskbar's volume control to quickly change playback volume, or to turn sound off entirely.

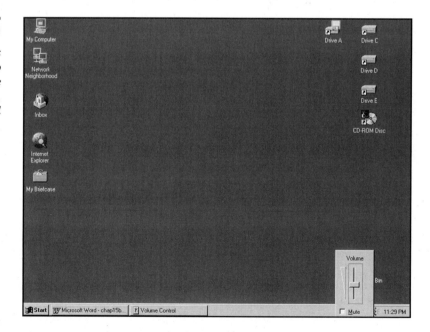

Tip   You can instantly turn off your sound card's sound by selecting the Mute check box shown in figure 14.20.

Using the Volume Control Application

Far more comprehensive than the Taskbar's volume control is the Volume Control application, which lets you adjust volume levels for different sound inputs and outputs. Figure 14.21 shows the Volume Control application with all volume settings enabled.

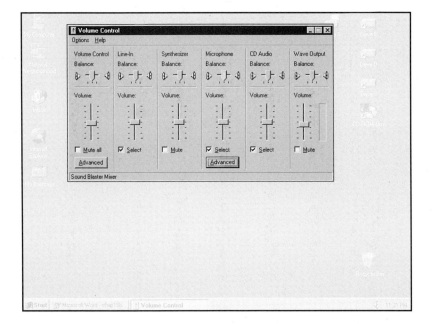

Figure 14.21

The Volume Control application lets you exert more control over volumes in your system.

By default, the Volume Control application displays the different controllable volumes for playback. You can also configure it, however, to show the controls relevant to Recording or for Voice Commands (you would use Voice Commands if you had appropriate voice command software installed in your computer). To view input controls, open the Options menu and choose the Properties command. You will see the dialog box shown in figure 14.22.

In the Properties dialog box, you first choose which available mixing device you want to control (most computers will only have one installed), and then select the appropriate option button in the Adjust volume for box (choose from Playback, Recording, or Other). Once you have selected a mode, you can further choose which controls will be available with the check boxes in the Show the Following Volume Controls list.

After choosing the mode with which you want to use Volume Control, you can affect the volume for each volume control on the main display by simply using the appropriate slider controls. You can also control the balance (how much sound comes from the right versus left speaker channels) with the various Balance commands (refer to fig. 14.21).

Some of the volume controls also have an Advanced button. This button lets you make changes to the tone of a particular volume control. Choosing the Advanced button of the Microphone control, for instance, displays the dialog box shown in figure 14.23. The exact controls and how they are used vary depending on the specific volume control and the capabilities of your installed sound hardware.

Figure 14.22

Volume Control's Properties dialog box lets you choose which controls you can see and change.

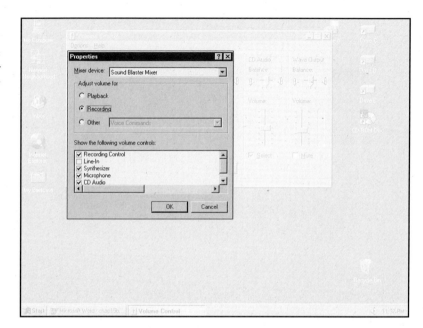

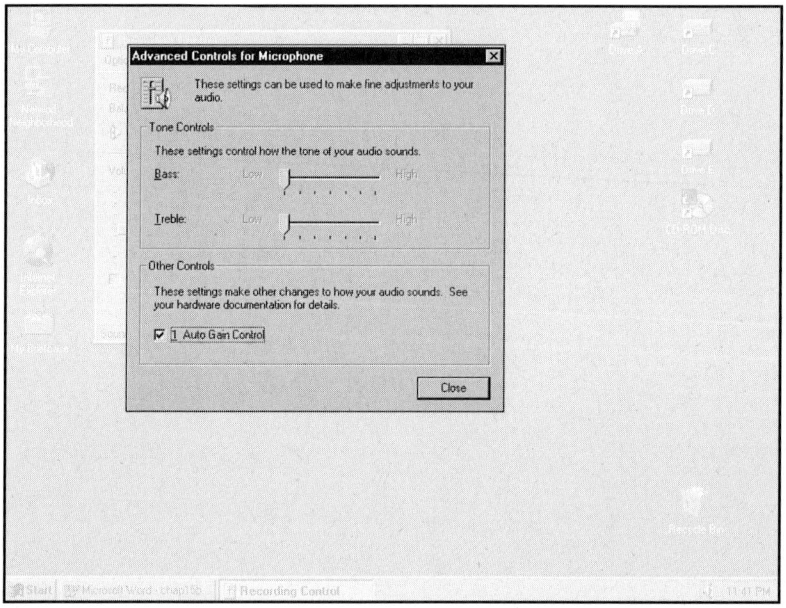

Figure 14.23

The Advanced Controls for Microphone dialog box lets you control sound card-specific settings that are available.

Using the CD Player

When you hear computers play audio CDs, the computer is not actually processing the sound you hear. Instead, a patch (connection) cable runs from an audio output jack on your CD-ROM drive to an audio input jack on your sound card. This cable is inside your computer. When you play an audio CD, the sound output from the CD is routed to your sound card, which then simply routes the sound through its amplifier and out to your speakers. Because this is the case, you can play audio CDs in your computer while doing other work without affecting your computer's performance. The computer is not processing the actual sounds you hear from the CD; the sound board is just "passing them along."

Windows NT Workstation includes a CD Player application that lets you play audio CDs. You can access the program using either of two methods:

◆ When an audio CD is inserted into your CD-ROM drive, you can simply double-click on the CD-ROM's drive icon in My Computer. This automatically starts the CD Player application (see fig. 14.24).

◆ Choose Start, Programs, Accessories, Multimedia to locate the CD Player program icon.

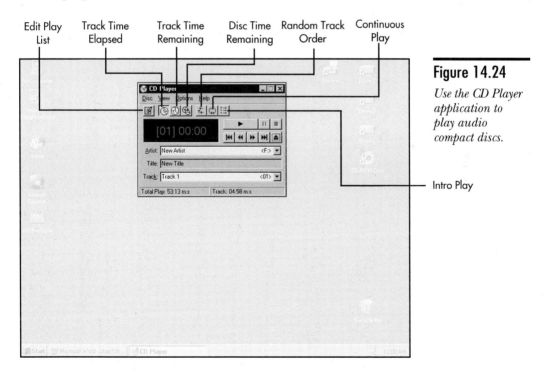

Figure 14.24

Use the CD Player application to play audio compact discs.

Note	A bit of trivia: computer disks are correctly spelled with the letter "K," while music discs use the letter "C." Also, "CD" always refers to audio CDs, while "CD-ROM" is always used for the variety that holds data.

The CD Player is actually a fairly sophisticated application that lets you control exactly how your CDs play. You have the following capabilities with the program:

◆ **Input text for the CD's artist, title, and the names of each song.** Select the Edit Play List button on the toolbar. The CD Player: Disc Settings dialog box appears (see fig. 14.25). The data you enter is automatically stored on your hard disk, and the CD Player automatically recalls it when you reinsert that particular audio CD in the future.

Figure 14.25

Control exactly which songs play when with the Edit Play List feature.

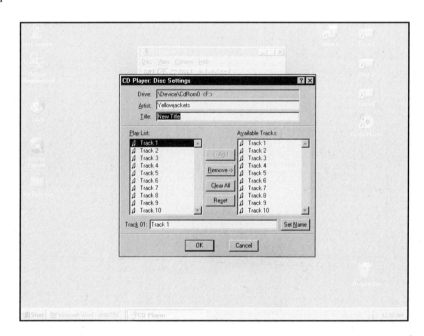

◆ **Name each of the tracks on the CD.** First select the track in the Available Tracks list, and then type the name of the track in the Track field. Click on the Set Name button to store the name of the track.

◆ **Control which tracks are played.** Select them in the Play List list, and then select either the Add or Remove button.

◆ **Control order of tracks by removing and re-adding.** If you remove and then re-add tracks, the track is added at the end of the list instead of to its original position.

◆ **Instantly select a track by name.** On the main CD Player screen, use the Track drop-down list.

◆ **Play just 10 seconds of each of the tracks.** Use the Intro Play button on the toolbar.

◆ **Access the Volume Control application easily.** Use the Volume Control command in the View menu.

◆ **Control how CD Player works and appears.** Choose the Properties command in the Options menu. The Preferences dialog box appears (see fig. 14.26). Use the options in this dialog box to accomplish this task.

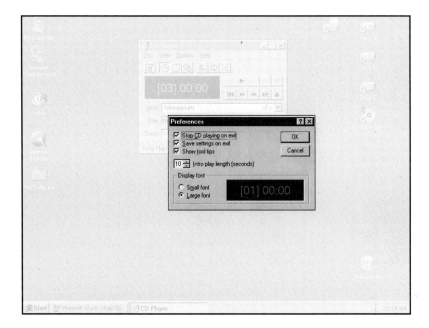

Figure 14.26

Control some of the finer points of the CD Player with its Preferences dialog box.

End Note: Most computer audio setups let you control the volume output from the sound card, but also have a volume control knob for the speakers. Sometimes the amplifier in either the sound card or the speakers is of a higher quality than the other. When you want to really crank up the volume coming from your computer, you may find that you have better luck (less static) leaving the sound card volume low (using the Windows NT Workstation volume controls) and relying on the speaker's amplifier to raise the volume. Or perhaps you may find that you get better sound by leaving the speakers set relatively low and turning up the sound card's volume. It all depends on the relative quality of the amplifiers in your sound card and speakers; you should experiment with your particular equipment to find out what works best.

Test Your Knowledge

1. The following are types of multimedia devices:

   A. Keyboard

   B. CD-ROM drive

   C. Sound card

   D. Video capture board

2. Before purchasing a multimedia device for a Windows NT Workstation 4 computer, you should:

   A. Open the package and read the instructions.

   B. Consult the Hardware Compatibility List to see if the device is listed or get the manufacturer's assurance of Windows NT-compatibility and driver availability.

   C. Find out if the device works under Windows 95.

   D. Ensure that the device supports Plug and Play.

3. To add or remove multimedia device drivers from Windows NT, you:

   A. Use the INSTALL program.

   B. Access the Multimedia Properties icon in the Control Panel.

   C. Access the Devices Properties icon in the Control Panel.

   D. Access the Services Properties icon in the Control Panel.

4. You can configure which driver is responsible for playing sounds in Windows NT Workstation 4 by using:

   A. The Multimedia Properties icon in the Control Panel

   B. The Sound Properties icon in the Control Panel

   C. The SOUNDSET utility program

   D. The Creative Labs web page

5. Which of the following sound qualities are available in Windows NT Workstation:

   A. Telephone Quality

   B. Radio Quality

   C. Laser Disc Quality

   D. CD Quality

6. To play a WAV file on Windows NT Workstation, use:

    A. The Multimedia Properties icon in the Control Panel

    B. The Media Player program included with Windows NT Workstation 4

    C. The Sound Player program included with Windows NT Workstation 4

    D. The WAV Player program downloadable from Microsoft's web site

7. You use which of the following technologies to embed media files into applications:

    A. DDE

    B. OLE

    C. MediaEmbed

    D. Common Object Model (COM)

8. You can adjust the playback volume of an installed sound card by using:

    A. Media Recorder.

    B. Sound Recorder.

    C. Audio Note Taker.

    D. You can't record sounds in Windows NT Workstation with any included applications.

9. You can adjust the playback volume of an installed sound card by using:

    A. By using the Volume Control application.

    B. Only with knobs on your speakers.

    C. Only with a program that comes with your sound card.

    D. You can't control the volume of sounds in Windows NT Workstation 4.

Test Your Knowledge Answers

1. B,C,D
2. B
3. B
4. A
5. A,B,D
6. B
7. B
8. A
9. A

Chapter Snapshot

Windows NT Workstation 4 is a virtual memory-based operating system—space in a disk-based paging file is automatically used when the demands of your programs exceed the available amount of Random Access Memory (RAM) installed in the computer. By using the paging file, the system can perform more work than if it were strictly limited to the installed RAM. Managing the virtual memory in your system is important to achieve maximum performance, and this chapter shows you how to do just that. It covers the following topics:

Windows NT
Workstation 4

CHAPTER 15

Configuring Memory Usage

R AM in your computer is a very precious commodity. (In fact, the way RAM prices keep changing on a day-to-day basis, it wouldn't be surprising to actually see RAM traded on the commodity markets soon!) Most systems today do not have all the RAM installed that they could actually use. Not only are operating systems growing increasingly complex, but applications are becoming more and more sophisticated; with this complexity and sophistication come higher RAM requirements.

Windows NT Workstation makes use of sophisticated techniques to extend the amount of memory your programs can use, and therefore extends the amount of work you can accomplish with your system. In this chapter, you learn how virtual memory works and how to manage it.

Understanding Virtual Memory

In the days of DOS-only computers, a computer only had so much RAM installed; if a program needed more RAM than your computer had, well, tough luck. A user either had to buy more or find some other way to get the job done using less memory.

Modern operating systems—such as Windows NT Workstation—have changed, so you're not stuck when your programs need more RAM than you have installed. They do this by using something called *virtual memory*. The memory is called virtual because it's simulated memory; it's not actual RAM installed in your computer. Instead, the operating system uses space on your hard disk to simulate RAM for your running programs. This is all well and good, but remember that hard disks operate much slower than RAM does—in fact, hard disks are several orders of magnitude slower than RAM. Not only do hard disks access stored data more slowly than RAM, but they also transfer the data to the processor much more slowly.

This may have you thinking that virtual memory is a bad thing. After all, who wants to slow their computer down by using virtual memory? Most of the time your programs are running, they're not using all of their loaded programming instructions. In fact, most programs spend most of their time running just 20 percent of their programming code. For instance, if you're using a word processor and you're not using its outlining feature at the moment, you're not actually using all those loaded programming instructions for the outlining feature. In fact, if you think of all the features of all the programs you use, you'll quickly come to the conclusion that you rarely use most of the available features. When you want them, you need them to be available, but you don't use them all the time. Here's where virtual memory pays off: all those features that you're not currently using can be safely moved into virtual memory without impacting the performance of the program you're using. When you access those features, the code is moved from virtual memory back into RAM, where it can then be run. Moving memory from physical RAM to the paging file is called *paging out memory*, while moving it from the paging file back into RAM is called *paging in memory*.

Similarly, if you have 10 programs open and running at once, but you're only using one of them, those other programs can be safely kept in virtual memory, ready to be called back into RAM when you need them. They are not otherwise consuming precious RAM resources, which might adversely affect the program that you are using.

Moving the code back and forth from virtual memory does take a little extra time. The benefit is that your computer can keep more working code in memory at any given time and can get more work done within the constraints of the amount of RAM that is installed.

Keep in mind that virtual memory—under Windows NT Workstation—only comes into play when your system needs it. If you are using programs that fit entirely into RAM, then your virtual memory will not be used. When it is used, Windows NT Workstation moves pieces of memory that are least used into virtual memory. Because the system keeps track of how often different parts of memory are needed while it is running, good choices are made about what is moved into virtual memory and what should be kept in RAM. The system automatically adjusts for different usage, too. If you start using parts of memory that have previously been moved into virtual memory, those parts are preferentially kept in physical memory, and other, less used parts of memory are moved into virtual memory.

Paging

Windows NT Workstation breaks up all memory in your computer into *pages*. A page of memory is exactly 4 KB large, except when Windows NT Workstation is running on a DEC Alpha AXP-based machine, in which case a page is 8 KB large. The process of moving memory contents from physical memory to the virtual memory on your hard disk is called *paging*. When the system allocates memory for a program, it does so in pages. Even if a program only requests one byte of memory from the system, the system gives it an entire page.

Every running program in the system has its own *virtual address space*. The virtual address space is a series of memory addresses that map into RAM or virtual memory. The address space is 4 GB large for each program, with 2 GB available for program storage and 2 GB available for system storage. Programs allocate memory from within their virtual address space, and the system takes care of allocating memory pages from the available pool of RAM and virtual memory to satisfy each program's requirements.

Windows NT Workstation uses *demand paging*, whereby pages of memory are kept in RAM versus virtual memory, based on the current demand for those pages.

Virtual memory is stored in a file called the *paging file*. The actual file name is PAGEFILE.SYS. Windows NT Workstation can have multiple paging files (one per disk partition), and each can be of varying size. The system uses all of the paging files collectively, so that they all constitute a single resource for the system. You can determine which drives contain paging files and how large each one can be.

Working with the Paging File

You can control a number of settings for your system's paging file. You can choose on which disks to store the paging file, what its initial size should be, and to what size it can grow.

You locate paging files onto different disks to maximize performance. As a rule of thumb, locate your paging file on the most active partition of the least busy disk. Doing so means that the disk's read and write heads can access the paging file more quickly than they otherwise could (the paging file has to be accessed very frequently, especially when the system is very busy). Putting the paging file on a disk that is less busy than other disks reduces contention for the disk between the system's paging needs and running programs.

You choose different initial sizes for your paging file based on its activity. For instance, if the paging file's initial size is 20 MB, but it grows to 60 MB when the system is in use, you can improve the performance of the system by making the paging file's initial size 60 MB. Doing so lets the system spend less time expanding the paging file as needs develop.

You control the maximum size of the paging file based purely on what other needs you have for the disk or disks that hold the paging file. If you let the paging file grow until it consumes all but 2 MB of disk space, and a program tries to save a file larger than that to the disk, it will be unable to do so. You choose a maximum size for the paging file based on other storage needs that you have.

<table>
<tr><td>**Objective**
B.5</td><td>To change the paging file's settings, double-click the System icon in the Control Panel and select the Performance tab in the System Properties dialog box (see fig. 15.1).</td></tr>
</table>

The Performance tab has a section that tells you how large the paging file is and contains a button called Change that lets you control the file. Figure 15.2 shows the Virtual Memory dialog box that appears when you click on the Change button.

Figure 15.1

The Performance tab of the System Properties dialog box lets you see the size of the paging file and contains a button that lets you change it.

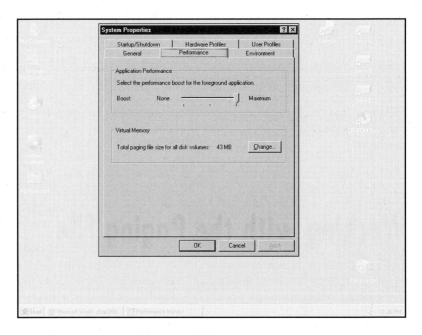

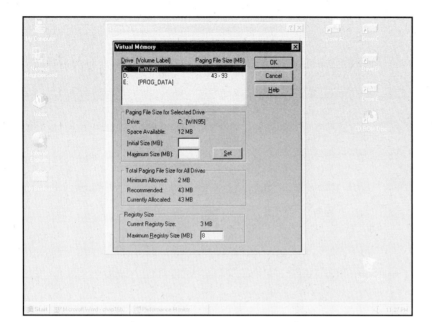

Figure 15.2

The Virtual Memory dialog box lets you change the settings for your paging file.

The Drive window shows you all of the available drives that can contain portions of the paging file, as well as the minimum and maximum sizes for the paging file on each drive. In figure 15.2, you can see that only a single paging file exists on drive D, and that it will be between 42 MB and 93 MB in size.

Adding a Paging File

You can easily add a new paging file to another drive on your system to increase the maximum amount of memory the paging file holds. You want to do this if your system runs out of virtual memory space when you use it. There are two strategies you can follow to increase the size of the paging file: you can simply increase its size on whatever drive contains it, or you can add a second paging file on a different partition of your system.

Objective B.5

To add another paging file, follow these steps:

1. Click on the drive on which you want to create the new paging file in the Drive window of the System Control Panel.

2. The Paging File Size for Selected Drive box will show you the drive name and the available space on the drive once you click on the drive.

3. Fill in the Initial Size and Maximum Size fields to indicate the desired size of the paging file on the selected drive.

Figure 15.3 shows a new paging file being created on drive E that will be between 25 MB and 50 MB in size.

Figure 15.3

Select a drive, fill in the fields, and then click on the Set button to create a new paging file on that drive.

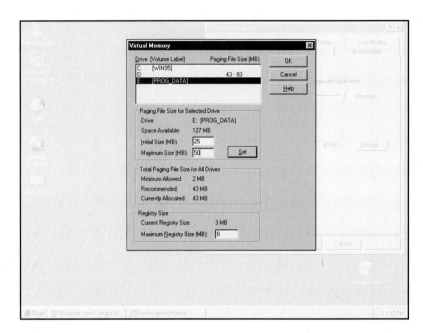

When choosing to create an additional paging file, pay attention to the limits shown in the Total Paging File Size for All Drives box. In it, you see the Minimum Allowed, Recommended, and Currently Allocated sizes for the virtual memory on your system. You should always set the Initial Size of your paging file to be equal to the recommended size (if not greater) because it takes the system time to expand the size of the paging files, which is done when demands exceed the available size of the file. You should set the minimum size of the paging file to be at least equal to the size you typically need.

Tip If you run multiple operating systems on your computer, you can safely delete Windows NT Workstation's paging file when running other operating systems in order to get back the disk space consumed. Windows NT Workstation automatically re-creates the paging file when it is restarted. The system will take more time to start while it does so.

Clicking on the Set button does not create the new paging file. After changing your virtual memory settings, close the Virtual Memory dialog box, and then the System Properties dialog box. Then you are prompted to restart your system. The new paging file choices are implemented during the restart.

Relocating the Paging File

By default, your paging file is created on the same partition that contains Windows NT Workstation. You can relocate it to another partition on your system, though. Sometimes you want to do this to better manage disk space, or because you can realize performance benefits from having the paging file located on the fastest disk on your system (or on a disk that's less busy than your main disk).

Objective
B.5

To relocate the paging file, create a new paging file on a different drive by setting the initial and maximum paging file sizes for that drive in the System Control Panel dialog box (see the preceding section for instructions). Then select the drive from which you want to remove the paging file and set both its values to 0. Remember to Set each of these choices. When you restart the system, the old paging file will be removed, and the new one created.

> **Note**
>
> You must maintain a 2-MB paging file on the partition that contains Windows NT Workstation if you want STOP events (critical errors in Windows NT itself) to be logged to disk. If you allocate a paging file smaller than this on the Windows NT Workstation drive, the system warns you and deactivates this emergency logging feature. The logging feature can help Microsoft diagnose the cause of the STOP event.
>
> The system's handling of STOP events is configured on the Startup/Shutdown tab of the System Control Panel dialog box.

Examining Memory Usage

When your program's use of memory exceeds the installed physical RAM by a little bit, virtual memory comes to the rescue, and your system continues running fine. Most running processes have some unused pages associated with them that can be easily paged to disk to create more room for running programs.

Thrashing

When your program's use of memory exceeds physical RAM by a lot, however, the system becomes so busy paging memory to and from disk that your system slows to a creeping halt. This phenomena is called *thrashing* because your hard disk thrashes around like mad trying to keep up with all of the paging activity required. If you continue pushing things to the limit of your paging files, you'll eventually see the dreaded Out of Virtual Memory dialog box shown in figure 15.4.

Objective
F.2

Figure 15.4

You see this message when you try to use more virtual memory than your system can access.

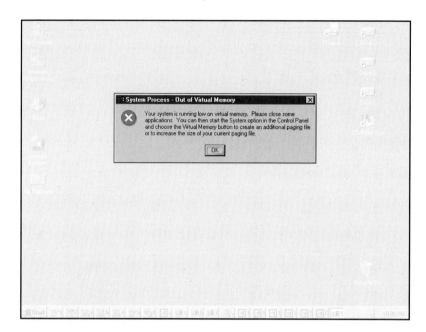

When you get into a thrashing situation, your first impulse will probably be to blame the disk as the bottleneck. Just looking at its indicator light and listening to it shows you how busy it is and how much it's slowing the speedy operation of your computer. You might even think that one of your programs is making excessive use of the disk. Although this can be the case with very disk-intensive applications, the problem is usually due to inadequate RAM.

In order to learn whether your system's performance is suffering due to inadequate RAM, you want to look at some key indicators in the Windows NT Performance Monitor, which you find in the Administrative Tools menu. The Performance Monitor is shown in figure 15.5.

One indicator of inadequate memory is too much paging activity, specifically the Performance Monitor measurement Page Writes/sec. Page Writes/sec. shows you how many pages of memory had to be written to your paging file, which only occurs when the system needs to make room for memory demands by running processes. Figure 15.5 shows a system that has temporarily had its available RAM exhausted.

Performance Monitor has been set up in these figures to show the amount of available memory (Available Bytes) in the system, as well as the number of Page Writes/sec. and Page Reads/sec. Available Bytes is the memory available for use at any given time. Generally, the system preferentially tries to keep more than 4 MB of RAM free at any given time. Page Writes/sec. shows you pages being swapped out of physical RAM to virtual memory, while Page Reads/sec. shows you pages being brought back into physical RAM from virtual memory.

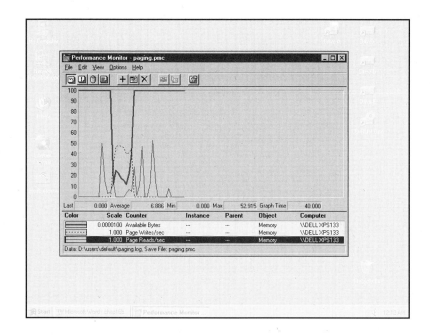

Figure 15.5

The Windows NT Performance Monitor is a crucial tool in finding out whether your system has enough RAM installed.

Figure 15.6 and table 15.1 show you what happens when an application demands more of the system than it has available.

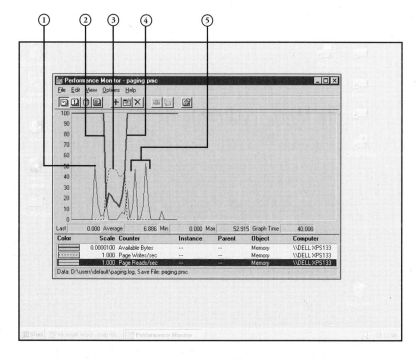

Figure 15.6

The big drop in Available Bytes (heavy line) is what you see when you exhaust the amount of RAM in your system.

TABLE 15.1
Chronology of Memory Events

Callout	Description
1	Some memory pages are read back in from virtual memory as the window that contains the program is brought to the foreground before launching it.
2	The program is launched and rapidly eats up all available memory.
3	As available memory falls below 4 MB, page writes increase dramatically as the system starts sending idle pages to the paging file.
4	The application terminates; available memory increases back to normal levels.
5	As available memory increases after the application finishes closing, the system starts to pull some of the memory pages back in from the virtual memory file.

This sequence illustrates, over a short period of time, how the system behaves as it becomes necessary to page memory out to disk. In a situation in which your system is thrashing, you would expect to see constant page reads and writes and pages that keep shuffling back and forth in order to satisfy the demands on various processes.

In the following section, you learn how to mediate thrashing problems, as well as how to address other memory performance problems in your system.

Solving Inadequate Memory Problems

Objective F.2

There are three ways to solve performance problems—such as thrashing—that relate to inadequate memory:

◆ Purchase and install more RAM in your computer.

◆ Reduce the number of programs you use simultaneously.

◆ Remove non-essential Windows NT services.

Add RAM

There are times when you simply must install more RAM. If you're still experiencing symptoms of inadequate memory after you've reduced the number of programs you run at once and removed all non-essential Windows NT services, you must add more RAM. First, you might look for ways to test if this will solve your problems. You can do this by borrowing memory from another computer or person, and then testing to see if it solves your problem.

> **Tip**   If you're experiencing thrashing and one of your applications is disk-intensive, you may be able to improve the situation somewhat by making sure that your paging file is located on a different physical disk than the one the disk-intensive application is using for its data or temporary files. This can also help you learn whether it is the application causing all of the disk activity or paging activity because you can monitor the activity of different disks and partitions with Performance Monitor.

Run Fewer Programs

When experimenting with reducing the number of programs you use for a particular performance problem area, you should restart your system and start the applications you absolutely need one-by-one. You do this instead of simply closing applications because some of the original running applications may have loaded or activated system services that remain in memory.

> **Tip**   If one of your required programs uses a different application subsystem than the others, see about upgrading it to a Windows NT-specific version. Even a single application that makes use of a different application subsystem (such as an OS/2 application) requires not only that the application be loaded into memory, but that all of the Windows NT code that supports that type of application be loaded, as well.

Remove Nonessential Windows NT Services

To reduce the memory requirements of Windows NT Workstation itself, consider the following actions:

◆ Remove any networking protocols that you're not using; each one consumes memory, even when not being used.

◆ Remove Dial-Up-Networking if you're not using it.

◆ Go through the Services icon in the Control Panel and disable services that aren't essential to the work you're trying to accomplish. Be careful with this because some services may be needed by your system even when you don't think they're being used. Generally, disable them one-by-one, or at least keep notes on which services you disable, so that you can reactivate them if a problem develops later.

◆ Reduce the resolution and number of colors displayed using the Display icon in the Control Panel.

◆ Turn off any screen savers.

◆ If you have Microsoft Office installed, remove all of the Microsoft Office tools from the Startup menu (Fast Start, Find Fast, and the Shortcut Bar) and restart your system.

◆ Remove unnecessary fonts from your system.

◆ Remove your sound card driver, if you have one, and restart the system.

Some of these measures are a bit draconian, but may make enough of a difference to let you accomplish a particular job in much less time (assuming you can reduce memory needs below those that cause excessive swapping).

End Note: You can use the Performance Monitor to see how much memory each of your running programs uses. To do this, use the Process object in Performance Monitor and select the Working Set counter, selecting each of the running processes available in the Instance window. Figure 15.7 shows four programs displayed this way in Performance Monitor.

As you can see from figure 15.7, Windows NT Imaging (wangimg in figure 15.7) is using up over 850 KB of available memory. Although the other displayed applications are using up more, they're all being used and cannot be closed in this case. Were the system shown in the figure experiencing inadequate memory, the first target for resolving the situation would be to close Windows NT Imaging (assuming that it is not being used). In other circumstances you might identify other programs that you're not using, but that are consuming memory. You can use Performance Monitor to measure their impact on your system and then decide if the impact is worth the convenience of leaving them open.

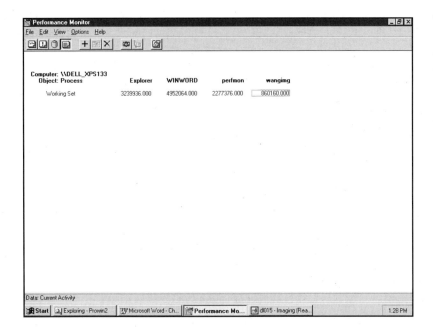

Figure 15.7

Performance Monitor can display the amount of working memory each process uses in Report View mode.

Test Your Knowledge

1. The best description for virtual memory is:
    A. Memory created by using compression algorithms against the data you have stored in RAM
    B. Disk-based storage that "masquerades" as system RAM
    C. Ghost RAM
    D. RAM borrowed from your video adapter board for running programs

2. The file that contains the virtual memory under Windows NT Workstation 4 is called:
    A. SWAPPER.DAT
    B. WIN386.SWP
    C. PAGEFILE.SYS
    D. VIRTUAL_MEMORY.DAT

3. In order to manage pages of virtual memory, the system uses a method called:

   A. First-In-First-Out (FIFO)

   B. Last-In-First-Out (LIFO)

   C. Just-In-Time Paging

   D. Demand Paging

4. On Intel-based computers, a page of memory is exactly:

   A. 2 KB large

   B. 4 KB large

   C. 8 KB large

   D. 4 bytes (32 bits)

5. You can locate part of the paging file on:

   A. Only one disk on the system

   B. Only SCSI-based disks

   C. Any and all fixed disks on the system

   D. Up to 3 disks on the system

6. If your system is thrashing (excessively paging), you should try:

   A. Closing programs that aren't being used

   B. Adding RAM

   C. Deactivating unessential system services

   D. Lowering the bus speed of the system

7. If you are using Windows NT on a dual-boot system and running the other operating system, you should *never*:

   A. Erase Windows NT's PAGING.SYS file.

   B. Activate paging by the other operating system.

   C. Add disk storage.

   D. None of the above restrictions exist.

8. You can examine paging file activity by:

    A. Running Performance Monitor and looking at the relevant statitics

    B. Using the Control Panel's Memory icon

    C. Viewing the paging file with a text editor

    D. You can't examine paging file activity under Windows NT Workstation 4.

9. "Thrashing" happens when:

    A. You use a very disk-intensive program.

    B. Your computer has an interrupt problem.

    C. You have excessive virtual memory usage.

    D. You use Intel MMX processors.

10. You can use the System Control Panel dialog box to control which aspects of the system's paging file?

    A. The minimum initial size, but only on your *WINNT_ROOT* partition.

    B. The minimum and maximum sizes for all partitions on which you have a paging file.

    C. Which partitions contain a paging file.

    D. Whether or not the system performs any paging at all.

Test Your Knowledge Answers

1. B
2. C
3. D
4. B
5. C
6. A,B,C
7. D
8. A
9. C
10. B,C

Chapter Snapshot

System services are special programs that provide system-wide functions. System devices are special programs that allow software, including the operating system, to communicate with hardware devices. Understanding what services and devices are and how they work is important to maintaining, optimizing, and troubleshooting your system. This chapter discusses the following topic areas:

Windows NT
Workstation 4

CHAPTER 16

Understanding System Services and Devices

S ystem services and system devices are special kinds of programs. These are "privileged" programs that operate at a very low level within the system. Because Windows NT is a secure operating system, normal programs are not allowed to access hardware directly, such as a hard disk, or other system objects, such as the Event Log. (The Event Log records noteworthy events, such as access violations or program failures.) System services and devices are the special programs that can access the hardware and system objects for other, normal programs.

Exploring System Services

System services are programs that Windows NT relies on to operate. These programs provide special functionality to other programs, such as reading and writing to the Event Log. The operating system itself relies on system services. Services include supporting network protocols, spooling print jobs, and logging events.

System services have several characteristics that make them different from "normal" programs. First, system services run automatically; they run in the background, waiting to be needed. Second, they don't require a user to log on. For example, the Event Log records whether or not the user successfully logged on. Therefore, the Event Log Service must be running before the User tries to log on. System services do need a user account because of the way the Windows NT security system works. Every running program, including services, must be associated with a user account. The user's User Profile is employed to determine security privileges. Windows NT provides a special user account—LocalSystem—for Services to use to establish security privileges before any real user has logged on. Although services may use other user accounts, most use the LocalSystem account.

| **Note** | See Chapter 5, "Understanding Profiles," for more information on User Profiles. |

Objective B.5

A number of default system services are automatically installed with Windows NT. These are listed in table 16.1. The actual services that are installed on your system will most likely be slightly different. You may have additional network services specific to your type of network, for example. You may choose to install additional services, such as the Internet FTP (File Transfer Protocol) Service.

TABLE 16.1
Default System Services

System Service	Description
Alerter	Notifies selected users and computers of administrative alerts that occur on the computer on which this service is running. Used by the Server (and other system services). Requires the Messenger service.
Clipbook Server	Supports the Clipbook Viewer application, enabling pages to be seen by remote Clipbooks.
Computer Browser	Maintains an up-to-date list of computers and provides the list to applications when requested. Provides the computer lists displayed in the Select Computer and Select Domain dialog boxes.

System Service	Description
Directory Replicator	Replicates directories, and the files in those directories, between computers.
Event Log	Records system, security, and application events in the event logs.
Messenger	Sends and receives messages sent by administrators or by the Alerter service.
Net Logon	For Windows NT Workstation, supports passthrough authentication of account logons. Used when the workstation participates in a domain. For Windows NT Server, performs authentication of account logons, and also keeps the domain's security database synchronized between the domain controller and the other Windows NT Servers of the domain.
Network DDE	The Network DDE (Dynamic Data Exchange) service provides a network transport, as well as security for DDE conversations.
Network DDE DSDM	The Network DDE DSDM service manages the shared DDE conversations and is used by the Network DDE service. DSDM stands for DDE Share Database Manager.
NT LM Security Support	Provides Windows NT security to RPC Provider applications that use transports other than named pipes.
Remote Procedure Call (RPC) Locator	Enables distributed applications to use the Microsoft RPC name service. The RPC Locator service manages the RPC name service database. The server side of a distributed application registers its availability with the RPC Locator service. The client side of a distributed application queries the RPC Locator service to find available compatible server applications.
Remote Procedure Call (RPC) Service	The RPC subsystem for Microsoft Windows NT. The RPC subsystem includes the endpoint mapper and other miscellaneous RPC services.
Schedule	Must be running if the AT command is to be used. The AT command can be used to schedule commands and programs to run on a computer at a specified time and date.

continues

TABLE 16.1, CONTINUED
Default System Services

System Service	Description
Server	Provides remote procedure call (RPC) support, and file, print, and named pipe sharing.
Spooler	Provides print spooler services.
UPS	Manages an uninterruptible power supply connected to the computer.
Workstation	Provides network connections and communications.

You may notice from table 16.1 that some services require other services. Windows NT handles these dependencies. Each service must register any dependencies it has with Windows NT. This enables Windows NT to load the services in an order so that each will have any service it needs already loaded. The Alerter system service requires the Messenger system service, for example. Therefore, Windows NT loads the Messenger service before it tries to load the Alerter service.

Services are installed and removed when you add or delete Windows NT components. When you add new networking protocols, additional network-related services may get installed. When you add UPS support, the UPS service will get installed.

Note See Chapter 20, "Installing Network Options," for more information.

In the rest of this section, you will learn how to manage system services. You will learn how to start, stop, and pause system services; how to control whether a service automatically starts; and how to specify startup parameters to control services.

Starting and Stopping Services

Objective B.5

There may be times when you need to start or stop a system service. Sometimes a service isn't automatically started by the system, and you need it. Perhaps a service became hung or stopped functioning properly, and you want to restart it. Starting a service means that you want to load it into memory and execute it. Stopping a service is exactly the opposite. When you stop a service, it stops executing, unloads from memory, and any resources it was using are released.

Perhaps you tried to print something, and for some reason your printer just stopped. You might need to stop the spooler service, turn your printer off and back on, and then restart the spooler service.

To start a service, follow these steps:

1. From the Start menu, choose Settings, Control Panel. The Control Panel window opens (see fig. 16.1).

2. Double-click on the Services icon. The Services dialog box appears (see fig. 16.2).

3. Select the service you want to start in the Service list box.

4. Choose Start. A message appears while the service is started.

5. Choose Close to finish configuring the service.

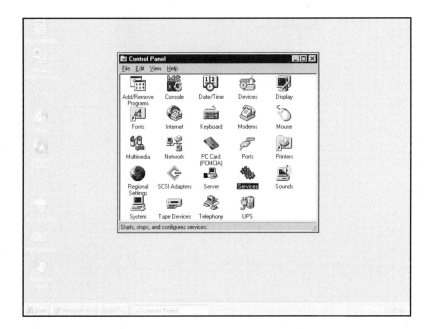

Figure 16.1

The Control Panel contains programs to configure both system services and devices.

To stop a service, follow these steps:

1. From the Start menu, choose Settings, Control Panel. The Control Panel window opens.

2. Double-click on the Services icon. The Services dialog box appears.

3. Select the service you want to stop in the Service list box.

4. Choose Stop. A confirmation dialog box appears (see fig. 16.3).

5. Choose Yes. A message appears that the operating system is stopping the service.

6. Choose Close when you are finished with the dialog box.

Figure 16.2

The Services dialog box lists all the system services, their current status, and startup settings.

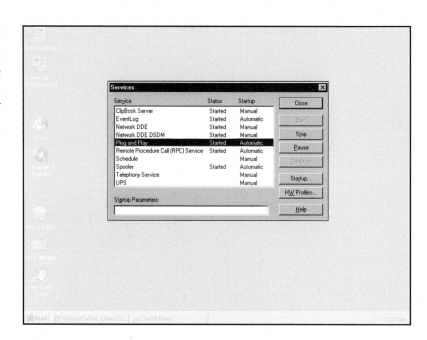

Figure 16.3

Before stopping a service, you will have to confirm that you really want to stop it.

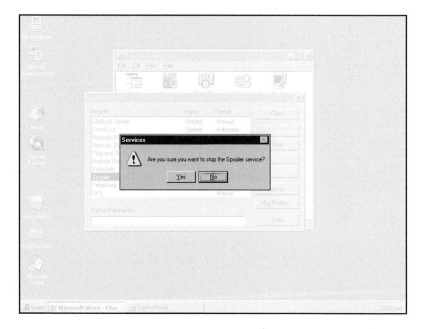

Pausing Services

If you want to stop a service, but other users are connected to your computer and using that service, you don't want to just stop the service. This could cause the users to lose data they are working with. You want to give them time to finish and disconnect from your computer. You don't want new users to start using that service while you are waiting for the first users to stop, though. The solution is to pause the service. Pausing a service means that no new users will be allowed to connect to it. After all the users have disconnected from the service, you can safely stop it.

To pause a service, follow these steps:

1. From the Start menu, choose Settings, Control Panel. The Control Panel window opens.

2. Double-click on the Services icon. The Services dialog box appears.

3. Select the service you want to pause in the Service list.

4. Choose Pause. A confirmation dialog box appears (see fig. 16.4).

5. Choose Yes to confirm that you want to pause the service.

6. Choose Close to finish with the dialog box.

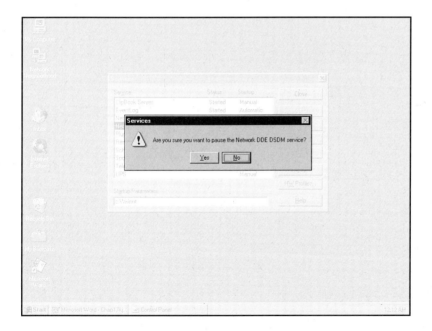

Figure 16.4

As with stopping a service, you must confirm that you really want to pause a service.

To restart a paused service, follow these steps:

1. From the Start menu, choose Settings, Control Panel. The Control Panel window opens.

2. Double-click on the Services icon. The Services dialog box appears.

3. Select the service you want to continue in the Service list.

4. Choose Continue.

5. Choose Close to close the Services dialog box.

Service Functions from Command Prompts

As with many Windows NT features, you can perform many of the service maintenance functions from a command prompt. If the Windows method doesn't work, you might want to try the command prompt versions. Although the command prompt program should not behave differently than the Windows program, sometimes the command prompt works when the Windows versions don't. You can use several NET commands to start, stop, pause, and continue system services. These commands are NET START *service_name*, NET STOP *service_name*, NET PAUSE *service_name*, and NET CONTINUE *service_name*.

You probably noticed that one of the problems with the command prompt versions is that you must know the name of the service with which you want to work. The command NET HELP SERVICES lists all the services. Also, typing in NET START lists all the currently running services.

If the name of the service is more than one word, you must put quotes around the service name in the command you issue.

Automatic Startup

Objective

B.5

You can configure your services to automatically or manually start. A service set to start automatically starts every time you start up your computer. A service that is configured to start manually must be explicitly started by you, another service, or an application.

To configure a service to automatically start every time you start your computer, follow these steps:

1. From the Start menu, choose Settings, Control Panel. The Control Panel window opens.

2. Double-click on the Services icon. The Services dialog box appears.

3. Select from the Service list the service you want to start automatically.

4. Choose StartUp. The Service dialog box appears (see fig. 16.5).

5. Choose Automatic as the Startup Type.

6. Choose OK to save the new startup type.

Choose Close to finish.

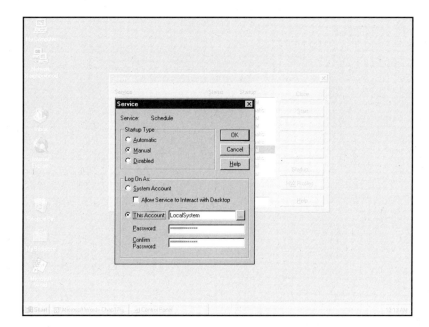

Figure 16.5

The Schedule service was scheduled to run manually.

Note   If you've accidentally disabled your system by changing some configuration for system services, reboot your system and revert to your Last Known Good setup. See Chapter 3, "Booting and Shutting Down Windows NT 4," for more information on solving booting problems and specifically for invoking the Last Known Good profile.

Manual Startup

To configure a service to start only when you want it to or when it is required by another service or application, follow these steps:

Objective B.5

1. From the Start menu, choose Settings, Control Panel. The Control Panel window opens.

2. Double-click on the Services icon. The Services dialog box appears.

3. Select the service you want to configure in the Service list.

4. Choose StartUp. The Service dialog box appears (refer to fig. 16.5).

5. Choose Manual as the Startup Type.

6. Choose OK to save the new startup type.

7. Choose Close to finish.

Disabling a Service

Objective B.5

You may install a service that you do not want a user to be able to start manually. You cannot simply remove this service from the computer—other services may need it. The answer is to disable the service. A disabled service cannot be manually started, but it can be started by the operating system (if it is required by another program).

To disable a service so that it cannot be started, follow these steps:

1. From the Start menu, choose Settings, Control Panel. The Control Panel window opens.

2. Double-click on the Services icon. The Services dialog box appears.

3. Select the service you want to configure in the Service list.

4. Choose StartUp. The Service dialog box appears (refer to fig. 16.5).

5. Choose Disabled as the Startup Type.

6. Choose OK to save the new startup type.

7. Choose Close to finish.

Using Different Logon Accounts

Objective B.5

Some services may be designed to use a certain user's account when they start instead of the default LocalSystem. This will be specified in the service's documentation. If you have installed such a service, you need to configure the service to use a different logon account.

To configure a service to use a different logon account, follow these steps:

1. From the Start menu, choose Settings, Control Panel. The Control Panel window opens.

2. Double-click on the Services icon. The Services dialog box appears.

3. Select the service you want to configure in the Service list.

4. Choose StartUp. The Service dialog box appears (refer to fig. 16.5).

5. Choose This Account and enter the new user account. You can choose the button to the right of the text field (the button is labeled with an ellipsis) to bring up the User Manager to select the account.

> **Tip**
>
> If you want to use an account other than the standard system account for a service, you must make sure that the account you want to use has been configured properly. The account must have the Log On as a Service user right assigned. This is an advanced user right. Otherwise, the service will fail to load.

6. Choose OK.

7. Choose Close to finish.

> **Note**
>
> See Chapter 5 for more information on user profiles.

Setting Startup Parameters

You may have a service installed on your system that requires some additional information when it starts. If you have such a device, it most likely came with documentation describing what information it needs at startup. A service might need to know the directory in which you installed the software, for example. Perhaps you can make the service turn on logging events by specifying the name of a log file (for example, C:\LogFile.txt). You need a way to get this information to the system service. Startup parameters are the means to do this.

Objective B.5

To start a service and specify startup parameters for it, follow these steps:

1. From the Start menu, choose Settings, Control Panel. The Control Panel window opens.

2. Double-click on the Services icon. The Services dialog box appears.

3. Select the service for which you want to set startup parameters in the Service list.

4. Type the parameters in the Startup Parameters text field (see fig. 16.6). For example, if the service needs to know the directory in which you installed some software, type that directory path (such as C:\\New Software) in the text field.

> **Note**
>
> The startup parameters specified for system services sometimes use escape codes. Escape codes start with a backslash (\); if the startup parameter you are using contains an actual backslash, you must type in two backslashes (\\). So if you want to specify the Windows root directory, you need to type c:\\winnt.

Figure 16.6

Specifying a drive path as a startup parameter requires that you use double slashes rather than single slashes.

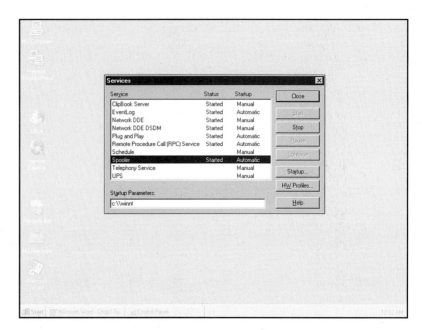

5. Choose Start. A message appears that the service is being started.

6. Choose Close to close the Services dialog box.

By specifying the startup parameters, you change the behavior of those services that are designed to be controlled in this manner. If you have installed a service, check the documentation that came with the software to see if it accepts any startup parameters.

Using Hardware Profiles

Objective

B.5

You can configure services so that they are available only under certain hardware profiles. (A hardware profile specifies a certain configuration of your hardware.) Perhaps you have a laptop and don't want certain services to be loaded when the laptop is undocked, but you want those services available when you are in your office with your docking station. After creating hardware profiles for both the docked and undocked states, you can then enable and disable services based on the active hardware profile. When you are in the office and connected to the network, you would want to start your networking related services, for example. When you are away from your office, you would not need to start these services.

To specify whether or not a service should be used with a specific hardware profile, follow these steps:

1. From the Start menu, choose Settings, Control Panel. The Control Panel window opens.

2. Double-click on the Services icon. The Services dialog box appears.

3. Select the service you want to configure in the Service list.

4. Choose HW Profiles. The Service dialog box appears (see fig. 16.7).

5. Select the hardware profile in the Profile list for which you want to either enable or disable the service.

6. Choose to either Enable or Disable the service. You can toggle between the two states.

7. Choose OK to close the Service dialog box.

8. Choose Close to finish.

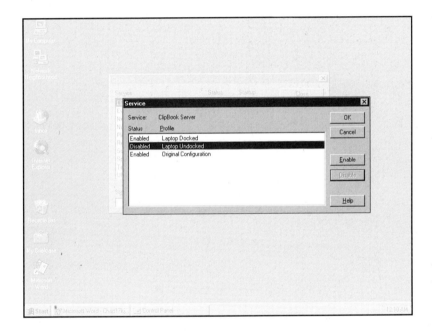

Figure 16.7

Here you see a service being configured to be enabled when the laptop is docked and disabled when it is undocked.

You will need to configure only a few system services based on hardware profiles; however, system devices are specifically designed to work with hardware devices. System devices are discussed in the following section.

Understanding System Devices

System devices are programs that allow other programs, including the operating system, to communicate with hardware such as mice, hard drives, and CD-ROMs. System devices are very similar to system services. The primary difference is that system services tend to provide communication between programs, and system devices tend to provide communication between software and hardware.

Another difference between system services and system devices is the naming convention. System services tend to have practical, understandable names, such as Computer Browser. System devices, because their names tend to be the same as their short file names, are rather cryptic. You find device names such as Aha154x, Null, and VgaStart.

Note

As with all rules, there must be exceptions. Here is one. UPS (Uninterruptible Power Supply) devices are managed by a system service, not a system device. So if you need to configure what you think is a device, but you can't find it listed as a system device, check for a system service that supports it.

In the rest of this section, you will learn how to manage system devices. You also will learn how to control devices. This includes starting and stopping the device, as well as configuring whether a device automatically starts.

Starting and Stopping Devices

Objective B.5

Starting and stopping devices is just like starting and stopping services, but you will find that you do it less often. First, because of the nature of devices, you won't find yourself in the position where you need to stop and restart a device. Second, the management of devices is handled automatically by Windows NT as actual devices are installed and removed. This is unlike services, which can be installed and removed by a user. You will most likely only need to stop a device when you are trying to resolve some problem with your system.

Caution

Be very careful if you start changing the automatic startup types for devices. By disabling devices or having them load in the wrong order (for example, changing a boot type to an automatic type), you can cause your system to be unable to start.

To start a device, follow these steps:

1. From the Start menu, choose Settings, Control Panel. The Control Panel window opens.

2. Double-click on the Devices icon. The Devices dialog box appears (see fig. 16.8).

3. Select the device you want to start in the Device list.

4. Choose Start. A message states that the device is starting. After the device has started, the message disappears.

5. Choose Close to finish configuring the device.

Tip

If a device is loaded, its status is listed as "Started" in the Devices list. If it isn't loaded, its status is blank.

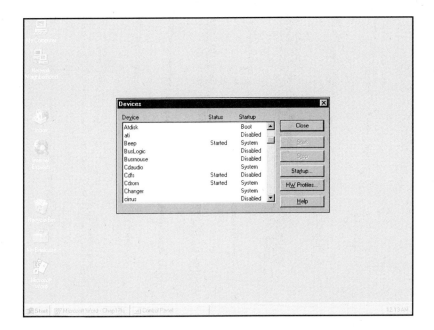

Figure 16.8

The Devices dialog box is almost identical to the Services dialog box; the difference is that devices cannot be paused.

To stop a device, follow these steps:

1. From the Start menu, choose Settings, Control Panel. The Control Panel window opens.

2. Double-click on the Devices icon. The Devices dialog box appears.

3. Select the device you want to stop in the Device list.

4. Choose Stop. A confirmation dialog box appears (see fig. 16.9).

5. Choose Yes. A message states that the device is being stopped. When the device has stopped, the message disappears.

6. Choose Close to close the dialog box.

Automatic Startup

You need to have some devices, such as your hard disk, start up automatically when you turn on your computer. Therefore, system devices need to be able to be configured to start automatically when you start your computer. Automatic startup devices come in three categories: Boot, System, and Automatic (see table 16.2). You need to determine how critical the device you are configuring is to proper system operation when you configure its startup options. For example, you need the system device that controls your hard disk to start immediately. Therefore, it is considered a critical device. However, your mouse device does not have to load immediately because it is not critical for your computer to function.

Objective

B.5

Figure 16.9

Before you can stop a device, you must confirm your action.

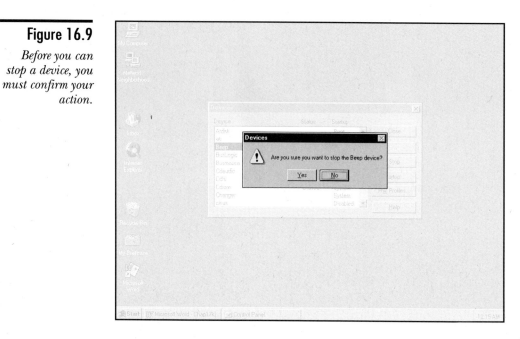

Table 16.2
Device Startup Types

Startup Type	Description
Boot	Boot devices are the most critical to system operation and are started first.
System	System devices are important to proper system operation and are started second.
Automatic	Automatic devices are usually not required for system operation and are started last.
Manual	Manual devices can be started by a user, a dependent system service, or another device.
Disabled	Disabled devices cannot be started by a user. They can be started by a system service or another device.

To configure a device to start automatically every time you start your computer, follow these steps:

1. From the Start menu, choose Settings, Control Panel. The Control Panel window opens.

2. Double-click on the Devices icon. The Devices dialog box appears.

3. Select the device you want to automatically start in the Device list.

4. Choose StartUp. The Device dialog box appears (see fig. 16.10).

5. Choose Boot, System, or Automatic as the automatic Startup Type. Refer to table 16.2 for more information about startup types.

6. Choose OK to save the new startup type.

7. Choose Close to finish.

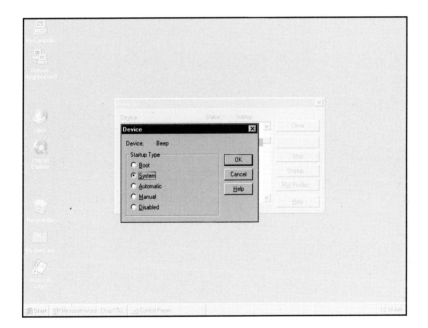

Figure 16.10

You use the Device dialog box to control how devices start.

Adding New Hardware

When you add new hardware, Windows NT does not necessarily remove the references to your old hardware. This is true for video boards, for example. Using the Event Viewer (see Chapter 29, "Using the Event Viewer"), examine the log and see which device failed to load.

continues

> Then go to the Device dialog box, find the device in the list, and change its startup type to Disabled.
>
> Anytime you are disabling devices or services, make sure you are disabling the correct service or device. If you make a mistake, your system could stop working properly and you may have to revert to the Last Known Good profile to correct the situation.

Manual Startup

Some devices do not need to be started automatically. With these types of devices, you can wait until you need the actual device before loading the corresponding system device.

To configure a device to start only when you want it to or when it is needed by another device or system service, follow these steps:

1. From the Start menu, choose Settings, Control Panel. The Control Panel window opens.

2. Double-click on the Devices icon. The Devices dialog box appears.

3. Select the device you want to configure in the Device list.

4. Choose StartUp. The Device dialog box appears.

5. Choose Manual as the Startup Type.

6. Choose OK to save the new startup type.

7. Choose Close to finish.

Using Hardware Profiles

You can configure devices so that they are available only under certain hardware profiles. Perhaps you have a laptop and don't want certain devices to be loaded when the laptop is undocked, but you do want those devices available when you are in your office with your docking station. After creating hardware profiles for both the docked and undocked states, you can then enable and disable devices based on the active hardware profile.

To specify whether or not a device should be used with a specific hardware profile, follow these steps:

1. From the Start menu, choose Settings, Control Panel. The Control Panel window opens.

2. Double-click on the Devices icon. The Devices dialog box appears.

3. Select the device you want to configure in the Device list.

4. Choose HW Profiles. The Device dialog box appears (see fig. 16.11).

5. Select the hardware profile in the Profile list for which you want to either enable or disable the device.

6. Choose to either Enable or Disable the device.

7. Choose OK to close the Device dialog box.

8. Choose Close to finish.

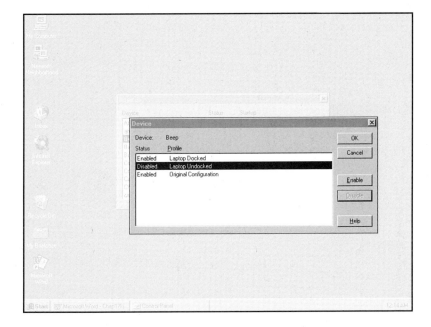

Figure 16.11

The Device dialog box looks and acts just like the Service dialog box.

End Note: If you are having problems, use the Event Viewer to find out which services or devices are causing problems. Then use the Devices and Services Control Panel programs to adjust the devices and services as needed. Windows NT maintains the Last Known Good configuration, so you can always restart and revert to the previous settings.

Also, Windows NT won't let you do things that would cause catastrophic problems. If a device is considered critical by Windows NT, the Stop button will be disabled, for example. You won't even get the opportunity to stop the device.

Test Your Knowledge

1. System services and system devices are:

   A. Programs that anticipate your every need and try to take care of you.

   B. Privileged programs that operate at a very low level within the system.

   C. Special application programs designed to monitor the activity of other application programs.

   D. There are no such things as system services and system devices in Windows NT.

2. Examples of valid system services include:

   A. Spooling print jobs

   B. Supporting network protocols

   C. Writing information to the event log

   D. Reformatting word processing documents

3. System services, by default, use which of the following user accounts for their security privileges?

   A. User

   B. System service

   C. LocalSystem

   D. Administrator

4. Which three of the following are system services?

   A. Server

   B. ScreenSaver

   C. UPS

   D. Schedule

5. How does Windows NT know the order in which to initialize services?

   A. You choose the exact order in which they start.

   B. Windows NT automatically starts them, making sure that any dependent services are started after the service on which they depend.

   C. They are started alphabetically.

   D. They are started numerically based on the internal service handle determined by the service programmers.

6. Which of the following statements about services are true?

   A. Services can be started and stopped on command.

   B. If you want to stop a service but want users to complete using the service first, you can pause the service. This causes new users to be denied access to the service, while letting existing users complete their service-dependent work.

   C. Services cannot be stopped and started at will.

   D. You can control service starts and stops with the NET command.

7. What is a system device?

   A. A special program that supports the use of some hardware device.

   B. A plan that the operating system executes.

   C. System devices are for the support of only pointing devices.

   D. There is no difference between a system device and a system service.

8. In what order do system devices start?

   A. Boot, System, Manual

   B. System, Boot, Automatic

   C. Boot, System, Automatic

   D. Automatic, Boot, System

9. You can view error messages generated by system device drivers with:

   A. Windows NT Diagnostics

   B. Dr. Watson

   C. Event Viewer

   D. The system log file

10. You can use the Control Panel's Services dialog box to:

    A. Start, Stop, and Pause system services.

    B. Change the order in which the services start.

    C. Change the logon account that a service uses.

    D. Remove services from the system entirely.

11. The Control Panel's Devices dialog box controls which aspects of the system?

    A. All the settings regarding any system device

    B. Whether a particular device's support software is active on the system

    C. Pausing devices

    D. The startup type of any installed devices

Test Your Knowledge Answers

1. B
2. A,B,C
3. C
4. A,C,D
5. B
6. A,B,D
7. A
8. C
9. C
10. A,C
11. D

Chapter Snapshot

No matter what applications you install and use in your Windows NT system, you eventually need to print something you have created. Before you can do that, you have to tell the operating system about the printer (or printers) you can use. This chapter covers everything you need to know to set up printing in Windows NT, focusing on the following topics:

Windows NT
Workstation 4

CHAPTER 17

Printing

Any Windows NT 4 workstation that has a printer connected to it can be used as a print server for other connected users. However, a print server that is workstation-based can only handle ten connections (computers running Windows NT Server can handle unlimited connections when they are configured as print servers).

The way you print and set up printers in Windows NT differs a bit from the way you did it in previous versions of Windows. The capability of an NT Workstation print server (providing printers for other computers on the network) to provide drivers for those computers at the time the printer is accessed is extremely efficient. Administrators who set up Windows 95 and Windows 3.x workstations to use printers connected to an NT 4 Workstation don't have to install drivers on those workstations.

Installing Printers

All printers expect specific instructions (codes) to tell them what to do. For instance, there are codes for fonts, margins, graphics, and ejecting the page. The codes (which vary from printer to printer) are in a software file called a printer driver. Every time you print, Windows NT intercepts the data when it leaves your software application, sends it to a file (the spool file), and then uses a Windows NT printer driver to send the document to the printer. The printer installation process is the installation of the correct printer driver on your Windows NT system (all of the other processes are controlled by software that is part of the Windows NT operating system).

Printers are installed by opening My Computer, then opening the Printers folder (you also can reach the Printers folder from the Start menu by choosing Settings, Printers). When you open the Printers folder, you see an icon named Add Printer—even if printers are already installed and displayed in the Printers folder.

Objective C.5

Double-click on the Add Printer icon to begin installing a printer with the aid of the Add Printer Wizard (see fig. 17.1).

After the first wizard page appears, the rest of the process depends on the location of the printer you want to install. If you're on a network, you can access printers that are connected to other computers on the network, either in addition to, or instead of, a printer attached to your computer.

Figure 17.1

Printer installation begins with the Add Printer Wizard, which walks you through the steps.

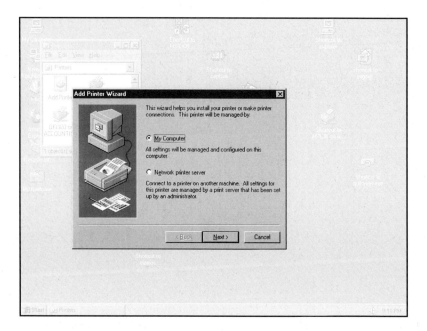

Installing a Local Printer

If the printer you want to install is attached to your computer, then it's a local printer. The settings and management of that printer all take place from your computer.

To install a local printer, follow these steps:

1. On the first wizard page, be sure that My Computer is enabled, and then press Next.

2. The Available ports list appears on the next page (see fig. 17.2). Select the port to which the printer is attached (usually LPT1:), and then choose Next.

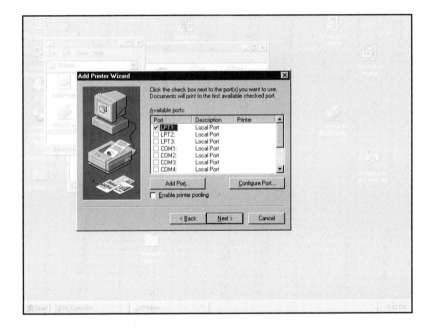

Figure 17.2

Select the port that connects the printer to your computer.

Note The port selection page has a check box labeled Enable Printer Pooling. A printing pool is two (or more) identical printers that are connected to your computer. If you enable this feature, you can select multiple ports, one for each printer. If a printer dies or for some other reason cannot complete the print job (a paper jam, the cable falling out, or some other calamity strikes), you can restart the print job and the second printer takes over and completes the printing process. To arrange for this convenient scenario to take place, you need to right-click on the original printer's icon and choose Properties. Then, on the Ports tab, change the port to the one occupied by the twin printer. This is a handy feature for mission-critical printing.

3. On the next wizard page, select the name of the Manufacturer of your printer from the left pane, and then choose the model from the right pane. Then choose Next.

4. The wizard inserts the Printer name, which you can change if you want (see fig. 17.3). You also must specify whether this printer is the default printer for all your Windows applications to use (unless it's the first printer you're installing, of course). Then choose Next.

Figure 17.3

In addition to needing a name for the printer, the wizard needs to know if this printer is the default Windows printer.

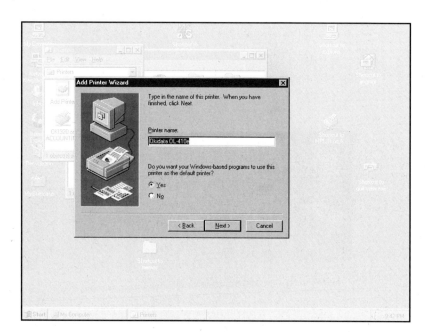

> **Note** Indicating that a printer is the default printer for Windows applications means that when a Print dialog box opens (after you choose File, Print), the printer is listed. You can change to another printer in the dialog box by pressing the arrow to the right of the current printer listing. The default printer automatically is used if you print by clicking on the Print icon on the toolbar—no dialog box appears to enable you to change to another printer.

5. The next wizard page asks whether other computers on the network will share this printer. For now, assume the printer isn't shared (sharing your printer is discussed later in this chapter). Choose Next.

6. The installation setup is complete and the next page offers an opportunity to print a test page. Choose Yes so you can make sure that the printer works. (The test page prints after the second stage of installation—the transfer of the printer driver files to your hard disk—is complete.) Click on Finish to complete this setup phase of printer installation.

7. If the setup program doesn't correctly identify the location of your Windows NT original media (it frequently asks for a disk in drive A, which is appropriate only if your NT software is on disks), enter the correct location of the files (usually D:\i386, where D represents whatever drive letter is assigned to your CD-ROM). Choose OK.

 Tip If your printer isn't listed and you have a Windows NT 4 driver available from the manufacturer, select Have Disk when you select the printer model. Then insert the disk into the floppy drive and tell the installation program to look there.

Completing these steps transfers the printer drivers to your hard drive. The icon for the printer is placed in your Printers folder. The icon represents the driver (it is the driver you configure, not the physical printer).

If you requested a test page, it is printed at this point. If it prints properly, answer Yes when you are questioned about it. If not, answer No and the printer troubleshooter will walk you through the steps to test each step of the installation process (make sure the printer is turned on, cabled correctly, and online).

Using the Printer Troubleshooter

If the test page didn't print right, a Windows NT Help window opens to begin troubleshooting the installation (see fig. 17.4).

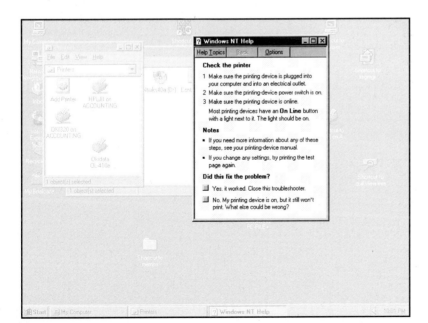

Figure 17.4

Windows NT Help troubleshoots printer installations that failed by asking questions and responding to your answers.

The troubleshooter asks questions. A Yes answer completes the troubleshooting process; a No answer brings up additional suggestions. If you tell the troubleshooter that the suggestion didn't work, it presents one or more alternative suggestions.

Suggestions usually are accompanied by a "click here" arrow, which brings up the appropriate dialog box to implement the suggestion.

If following every suggestion still results in failure, the troubleshooter eventually admits defeat and advises you to get some expert help.

 One of the problems that the troubleshooter doesn't address is an occasional conflict with some video drivers. To determine whether this is the problem, restart Windows NT in VGA mode and see if the problem has been resolved. If so, you need to change your video driver before you can install the printer driver.

Most of the time, however, the troubleshooter's suggestions do work.

Sharing Local Printers

If you're on a network and have a printer attached to your computer, you probably have to share your printer with other users. Providing a printer for every user is prohibitively expensive in large companies.

You can configure the printer for sharing during the installation process, as noted earlier in this chapter, or you can set up the sharing some time later after installing the printer. To configure sharing on an installed printer, right-click on its icon and choose Sharing.

 Most of the functions and features covered in the following sections require Administrator permissions to perform.

When you indicate that you want to configure a local printer for sharing, the Sharing tab in the printer's Properties dialog box appears (see fig. 17.5).

Follow these steps to create a shared printer:

1. Choose Shared to indicate that this printer will be shared with other users on the network. Then enter a Share Name for the printer.

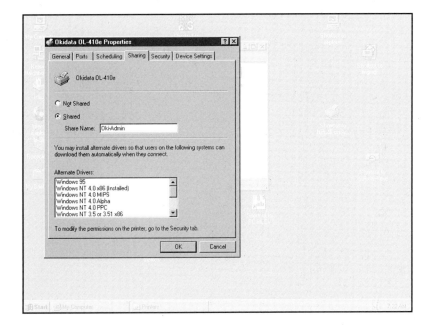

Figure 17.5

Establishing a network share for a printer requires a name. The name should identify the printer easily.

Tip   The name you give the printer share is presented to other users when they print. Use a name that makes it easy to identify this printer; reminding people where the printer is located usually is helpful (they have to walk to the printer to pick up their documents). In figure 17.5, the computer name (Admin, which matches the department name) is part of the printer share name.

2. Windows NT 4 furnishes the capability to provide the drivers for other users who access your shared printer. You should install printer drivers for all the Microsoft operating systems you know about on your network. Select every applicable entry.

Note   The capability to install drivers for other Microsoft operating systems as you configure a printer for sharing is unique with Windows NT 4. When other users install the printer on their own computers, they don't have to load drivers for the printer. Your computer simply copies the appropriate printer driver to the requesting computer.

One major advantage is that every user who wants to install a network printer doesn't have to have a copy of the CD (or disks) of the original files for their operating system. Finding original media is a constant problem in most companies.

3. Select the Security tab to begin giving permissions for users to access this shared printer. Click on Permissions to activate the Printer Permissions dialog box (see fig. 17.6).

Figure 17.6

The default permissions for a shared printer can be modified in the Printer Permissions dialog box.

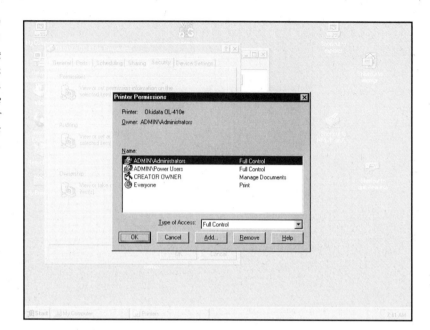

4. To change the Type of Access for any entity in the Name list, select it, and then select an access level. The choices are as follows:

◆ **Full Control.** Permits all administrative and management functions for this printer. This level of permission is required to make changes to the configuration of this printer.

◆ **Manage Documents.** Permits the user to open the printer window and manipulate the documents waiting to be printed.

◆ **Print.** Permits access to the printer by the user's software to print documents.

◆ **No Access.** Prohibits the user from using this printer.

5. Choose Add to put additional groups or individual users on the permissions list. The Add Users and Groups dialog box (see fig. 17.7) can display groups or individual names. Select any additional group or user and assign a Type of Access. Then choose OK.

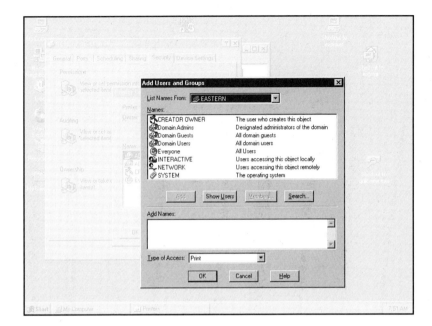

Figure 17.7

Choose a group or one or more individual users and assign permissions to use this printer.

Tip When you want to add groups or individuals to your permissions list, use the List Names From box to choose the list from which you want to work. If you're on a Microsoft Network domain, you see the groups from that domain. You also can display groups and users from another domain if it is available to you. Choose Show Users to see individual user names.

6. After you return to the Properties dialog box, choose OK to finish the configuration for sharing the printer. If you choose to load drivers for other operating systems, those files are transferred to your hard drive.

Audit a Shared Printer

You can view information about the use of the shared printer by choosing Auditing from the Security tab of the printer's Properties dialog box. Before you can track the use of a shared printer, however, you must enable auditing.

Enable System Auditing

You can establish the capability to audit events that occur on your computer. The audit record is logged in a security log file that you can examine. To enable auditing, follow these steps:

1. From the Start menu, choose Programs, Administrative Tools, User Manager to display the User Manager window.

2. Choose Policies, Audit from the menu bar to see the Audit Policy dialog box. Choose Audit These Events to make the events list available (see fig. 17.8).

Figure 17.8

Select the activities you want to audit as users access your computer's resources.

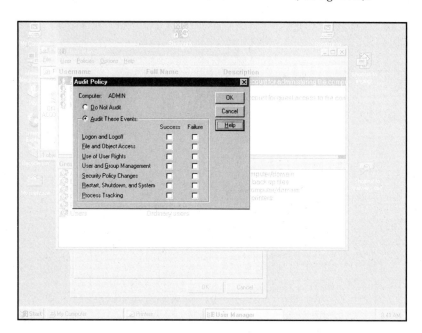

3. In this case, you're concerned only about the printer, so choose File and Object Access. Then choose whether you want to audit Success, Failure, or both.

> **Note** Choosing Success for an event tracks all successful accesses of the printer; choosing Failure tracks only the accesses that resulted in problems. Your choice depends on what you need to know.
>
> The security logs have a maximum size (which you can set in the Event Viewer), and you should choose auditing configuration options with that in mind. When the maximum size is reached, older events are deleted to make room for the newest event.

4. Choose OK and then close User Manager.

After you enable auditing for your computer, you can track all the activities you've configured for auditing.

Audit the Printer

To establish auziting for your shared printer, follow these steps:

1. On the Security tab of the printer's Properties dialog box, choose Auditing to display the Printer Auditing dialog box.

2. Choose Add to specify the groups and users you want to audit. When the Add Users and Groups dialog box appears, select the appropriate entities by selecting the name and choosing Add. The selected groups and users are displayed in the Add Names box (see fig 17.9). Choose OK after you finish adding names.

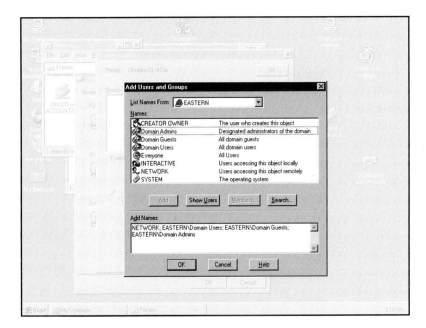

Figure 17.9

Add the users whose activities you want to track as they use your printer.

3. In the Printer Auditing dialog box, select the events you want to audit, indicating whether you want to track Success, Failure, or both (see fig. 17.10).

4. Choose OK. Then choose OK again to close the dialog box.

Hereafter, the security log will show the events you've configured. To see the log, choose Programs, Administrative Tools, Event Viewer from the Start menu. When the Event Viewer opens, choose Log, Security. Double-click on an event to see the audit details (see fig. 17.11).

Figure 17.10

Choose the events you want to audit.

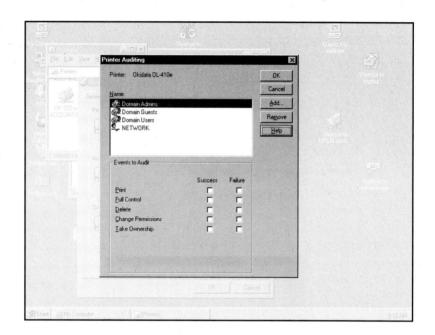

Figure 17.11

The Event Detail dialog box displays all the information about access to the printer.

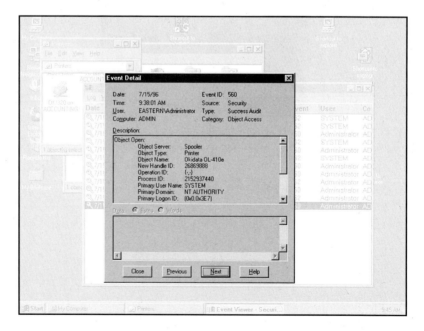

More information about using the Event Viewer is found in Chapter 29, "Using the Event Viewer."

Schedule a Shared Printer's Use

You can schedule a local printer that has been enabled for sharing. Use the Scheduling tab of the printer's Properties dialog box to configure a schedule for other users to have access. You can configure the following options:

Objective C.5

◆ Set the availability of the printer as Always or for a specific period of time during the day. Choose From and To times to create a specific period of availability.

◆ Set a default Priority level for documents. You should set the default priority to low in order to make moving a document to a high priority level easier if you need to do so in a hurry.

◆ Opt to Spool documents, meaning you can have the documents stored on the hard disk and then sent to the printer. After the sending application moves the document to the hard disk (which is much faster than sending it directly to the printer), the user can continue to work in the application. The spooler sends the document from the hard disk to the printer in the background.

◆ Specify that you want to Start Printing After Last Page is Spooled, which means that the spooler doesn't begin sending the file to the printer until it receives the entire file (the application sends an end-of-file marker to indicate the entire file has been sent). Or, select Start Printing Immediately, which means the spooler begins sending pages to the printer as they are received.

Tip   Waiting for the last page to spool before sending the document to the printer results in a slight delay before you can retrieve the finished document from the printer tray. It also guarantees that the whole document will print, however, and that nothing is wrong. You can choose between speed and safety; go with the one that best serves your needs.

◆ Use an option to Print Directly to the Printer; that is, bypass the spooler and move the file directly from the application software to the printer.

Caution   Printing directly to the printer usually isn't safe because there's no spooler to keep documents intact and to separate multiple documents from each other. Use this option only if you're having a problem using a spooler or if you need instant printing and are certain that no other jobs are going to the printer.

◆ Select Hold Mismatched Documents to force the spooler to match the printer codes in the document against the printer setup. If the printer codes for your document indicate legal length paper and the setup indicates that there isn't a legal paper tray, for instance, the spooler holds the job in the queue.

Other jobs that aren't mismatched can jump over the mismatched job and print normally. Eventually, you can change the tray in the printer, change the setup, and print the job (or reformat it in the software to eliminate the mismatched setup).

◆ Select Print Spooled Documents First to tell the spooler to print documents that have completed spooling before printing documents that are still spooling. If you don't select this option, a document with high priority prints first (even if the spooler has to wait a few minutes for the high priority document to finish spooling while a low priority document has already completed spooling).

◆ Select Keep Documents After They Have Printed if you want the spooler to retain the spooled file after the job has been sent to the printer. This makes printing the job again right from the queue possible, instead of having to re-send it from software. You don't normally have to do this, and it does use up disk space, so don't choose this option without good reason.

After you configure the options you want to use on the Scheduling tab, press OK to close the Properties dialog box.

Install a Network Printer

If you don't have a printer connected to your computer, you need to install a printer that is connected to another computer in order to print.

> **Tip** Even if you do have a printer connected to your computer, you sometimes end up needing to use a different printer. Many companies have preloaded forms in computers so if you want to print an invoice, a purchase order, checks, a label, or some other form, you have to access the appropriate printer, which may be connected to another computer. On the other hand, if you're in the accounting department and have job-specific printers attached to your computer so you can print checks and invoices, you occasionally may need to access a laser printer for correspondence or reports.

Install a Network Printer from Network Neighborhood

The quickest way to install a printer that is attached to a connected computer is to find it on the system and then install it. To do this, open Network Neighborhood and browse the network to find the computer that has the printer you need (see fig. 17.12).

Any computer that has set up a printer for shared access displays that share in Network Neighborhood. (In fact, it's displayed in Explorer when you expand the Network folder.) To install a printer from Network Neighborhood, follow these steps:

1. Right-click on the printer you want to use from your computer, and then choose Install from the shortcut menu. The Device Settings dialog box for this printer opens so you can see the settings for paper type and bins. Choose OK.

2. If the connected computer isn't running Windows NT 4 as an operating system, you receive word that there isn't a suitable driver available to use this printer from your computer. Click on OK to install the proper driver to your hard disk.

> **Tip**   If the connected computer is running NT 4, your computer (and applications) will use the driver on that connected computer to send documents to the printer.

3. The Add Printer Wizard appears to complete the installation. Select a Manufacturer from the left pane of the wizard page, and then select the Printer model from the right pane. Choose OK after you select the printer.

4. Follow the steps in the Add Printer Wizard to complete the installation of the printer drivers (as discussed earlier in this chapter for installing a local printer).

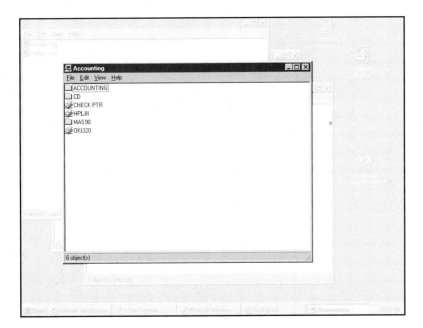

Figure 17.12

The computer named Accounting has three printers that have been configured for sharing.

You can close Network Neighborhood after the printer has been installed. Incidentally, if a number of Network Neighborhood folders are open as a result of browsing for the printer, you can hold down the Shift key while you click on the Close button of the last folder to close all the folders (which is faster than closing them one at a time).

Install a Network Printer with the Wizard

Objective C.5

You also can use the Add Printer Wizard to install a printer that's on another computer. To do so, follow these steps:

1. Open the Printers folder (from My Computer or from Settings on the Start menu) and double-click on Add Printer.

2. Select Network printer server on the first wizard page, and then choose Next.

3. The Connect to Printer dialog box opens (see fig. 17.13). Enter the printer name in the Printer field, using the UNC \\computername\printersharename. If you don't know the UNC, browse the network by double-clicking on the appropriate domain or workgroup shown in the dialog box. When you find the printer, choose it to insert its name in the Printer field. Choose OK.

Figure 17.13

Enter the printer name or browse through the network to find it.

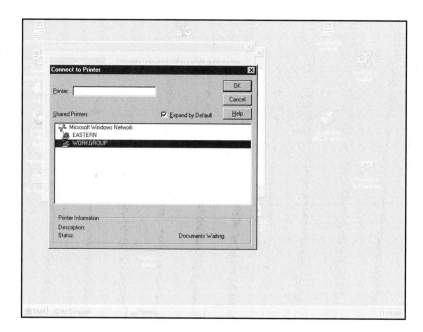

4. Tell the wizard whether you want this printer to be the default Windows printer for your computer (unless it's the only printer you're installing). Then choose Next.

5. Select whether you want to print a test page (you should—you learn the driver filename and version), and then choose Finish. The appropriate drivers are copied to your computer (unless the connected computer is running Windows NT 4, in which case the drivers are accessed from that computer whenever you print).

You can use the printer after it has been installed to your computer. If you open the Printers folder (from My Computer or via Settings on the Start menu), a list of all the printers you can use appears (see fig. 17.14).

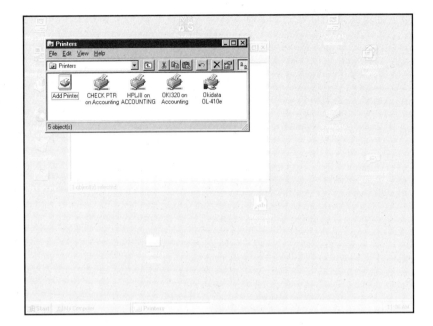

Figure 17.14

The Printers folder shows that three printers on the accounting computer and one local printer are available for printing.

Viewing Printer Activity

You can view and manipulate the current activity of a printer by opening (double-clicking on) the printer in the Printers folder. The printer window displays information about the status of any documents currently printing (see fig. 17.15). In previous versions of Windows, you would have used Print Manager to perform the tasks available in the printer window.

To manipulate the printer or the print jobs, use the menu bar options.

Printer Menu

From the Printer menu, you can perform the following commands on the printer:

◆ **Pause Printing.** Stops the printer. The Pause Printing command is checked, and you merely select the command again to uncheck it and resume printing.

◆ **Set as Default Printer.** Makes this printer the default printer for Windows applications. Print dialog boxes in application software display this printer's name (if other printers are installed, you can change the print job to use one of those), and clicking on the Print button on the toolbox sends the print job to this default printer automatically.

◆ **Set New Document Defaults.** Sets defaults such as paper size or printer tray, orientation, and number of copies.

◆ **Sharing Configuration.** Turns sharing off or on.

◆ **Purge Print Documents.** Empties the current print job queue.

◆ **Properties (the printer's Properties dialog box).** Accesses the Properties dialog box.

Figure 17.15

There is one document printing to this printer at the moment, and the printer window gives detailed information about it.

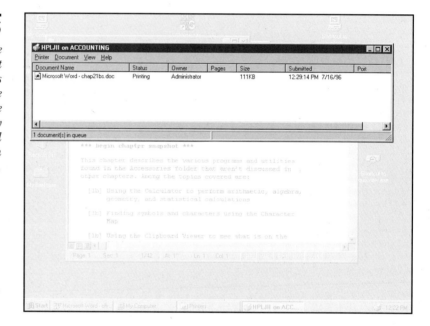

Document Menu

The commands available in the Document menu work on a print job, so you must select a print job before the commands are accessible. The available options follow:

◆ **Pause.** Stops the current document's printing and the next document prints.

◆ **Resume.** Starts the printing of a paused document. Printing is picked up where it left off.

◆ **Restart.** Starts a print job again after it has been stopped or paused (or had a problem). Restart means the document is printed from the beginning; the entire job is reprinted.

◆ **Cancel.** Removes the print job from the queue.

◆ **Properties.** Displays the properties information about the document. Use the Properties dialog box to change the priority of the print job. Drag the Priority slider lower or higher to change its print priority. If you make it high, it will move to the top of the queue. Making it low permits high priority documents to print first. You cannot change the priority of a document that has begun printing.

 Tip You can change the order of printing for documents of equal priority by dragging a document to a higher position (higher on the displayed list).

View Menu

Use the View menu to turn the printer window Status bar off and on, and to Refresh the display of print jobs so that any additional jobs sent to the printer after you open the printer window are visible.

Printing Documents

Luckily, all of the installation and configuration tasks you've been going through in this chapter are pretty much a one-time thing. After all the chores are complete, you can print documents.

Print from Windows Applications

All the Windows software you use is trained to look for your printer setup information and use it to print. You don't have to go through a software installation of printers, and you don't have to worry about whether the software knows how to format documents for your printer.

When you're ready to print a document from any Windows application, just choose File, Print. A Print dialog box opens (see fig. 17.16) so you can make choices about what you want to print and how you want to print it. The dialog box differs from software to software, but the one thing all Print dialog boxes have in common is the name of the printer that the print process is planning to use. This is always the current default printer.

If you want to use a different printer, click on the arrow to the right of the Name box to see a list of all the printers you've installed (both local and network). Then choose the printer you want to use for this print job.

Figure 17.16

For a Microsoft Word document, the printing options are quite extensive.

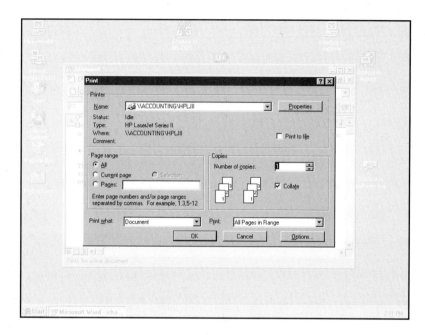

Print to a File

Notice the option on the Print dialog box to Print to File. This option is always available in Windows software. If you print to a file, you're prompted to name the print job.

There are a few good reasons for choosing Print to File, such as the following:

◆ You want to print the document later (perhaps the printer is down).

◆ You want to print the document from another location (perhaps you want to take it home). Take the print file with you and then send the file to the printer.

◆ You want to give the file to another user who will print it from his own workstation. You can transfer the file through the network, or put it on a floppy disk and use "sneaker net."

Note When you take a print file away from the office to print it at another location, the printer you use must be the same printer that was selected in the Print dialog box (or must emulate the original printer). The printer codes are included in the print file, and codes that tell one printer to print a graphical character may be a code to eject the page in another printer.

Although you have to have a similar printer to print this file at a different location, you don't need the software that created the file (because the codes are in the file).

You can use an MS-DOS command to copy the file to the printer. See the section on printing in DOS later in this chapter.

If you don't have a similar printer at another location and want to print this file directly to a printer without opening software, save it as a text file. Then you can send it to any printer from the command line (**copy filename prn**).

Drag and Drop Printing

You can drag a document to the printer object to print it. When you perform this action the software that prepared the document (or software able to load the document) opens, loads the document, issues a print command, and closes again. The advantage of drag and drop printing is that you don't have to perform all those keystrokes and mouse clicks; it's all on autopilot.

Before you can accomplish this, the document has to be associated with a software application. This means it either had to have been prepared in software installed in your computer, or you have to associate it with an application installed on your computer.

Note See Chapter 9, "Using Explorer," for more information on associating files.

You don't have to know in advance whether a file is associated with an application; the operating system will tell you if there is no association when you try to open it. The Open With dialog box displays and asks you to find a program to use to open the file (see fig. 17.17).

Tip Although you don't have to know what application, if any, is associated with a file you want to drag to the printer, you do need to know its content type. For example, you can't open a spreadsheet in a word processing application, and you can't open a document prepared in a word processor into a text editor (although you can do it the other way around, because all word processors accept text files).

To associate the file with an application, scroll through the list and select the appropriate software. Then choose OK. If the application you want to use isn't on the list but is installed on your computer, choose Other and enter the path and name of that application.

After the document is linked to an application, you can drag and drop it onto the printer. Just open Explorer or My Computer and find the document file you want to print. Then open the Printers folder and drag the file to the appropriate printer icon. You have to arrange the windows so both are visible.

Figure 17.17

Select an application in which to open this document.

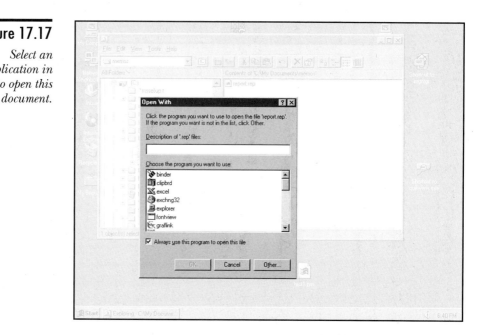

An even easier way would be to put a shortcut to the printer on the desktop. Just right-drag the printer icon from the Printers folder to the desktop. When you release the mouse, a menu opens; choose Create Shortcut(s) Here. Now you can drag files from an Explorer Window or My Computer to the desktop printer shortcut. You also can put the printer on the Send To submenu (right-click on any object to bring up the shortcut menu; then place your mouse pointer on Send To to see the choices).

Print from DOS

If your printer is connected to your computer, you won't notice a problem when you print from DOS software or from the command line.

However, if you use a printer that's located on a connected printer, printing from DOS software may not be a simple task.

If you're on a NetWare network system that captures and redirects ports to a network printer, your DOS software should print without problems. The same is true if the network uses a third-party software application to handle printing redirection.

During the printer installation, there is no way to configure the printer for DOS printing. (For those who have experience with Windows 95, which asks about DOS printing during printer installation, this is a major difference.)

To print from DOS software to a remote printer, you must manually issue the command to redirect printing. The basic command is:

```
net use lptx \\computername\printersharename
```

The x is the port you want to redirect (usually 1).

You can make this a permanent command by adding the parameter /persistent:yes to the command.

For example, on this author's machine, to enable DOS printing to the HPLJII (the name of the shared printer) on the computer named Accounting, the command is:

```
net use lpt1 \\accounting\HPLJII /persistent:yes
```

A number of other parameters are available for the net use command (see Appendix A, "Windows NT Command Reference," for more information).

After the redirection is in place, you can send files to the printer via the DOS command line. The command **copy filename prn**, for example, will send a file to the printer. This works for text files and for printer files that have been saved to disk (see the section on saving to a disk file earlier in this chapter).

The persistent parameter is really persistent; it survives shutdown and startup—it's always there. However, it is only always there for the user who entered the command. The state of LPT redirection is a user profile issue.

Understanding Banners

For shared printers, banners are a handy device. Banners are sheets of paper that identify the user who sent the print job to which they are attached. They are sent to the printer as the beginning of each print job and they are delivered to the printer tray in front of page one of each print job. Banners are also called separator pages.

If you're standing in front of a printer waiting for the job you sent from your computer to print, and a number of other people are waiting at the same place for the same thing, you'll appreciate banners. Without them, people tend to grab sheets of paper as they come out of the printer, read them, announce "This isn't mine," and then put them back in the printer tray. By that time, the next page has ejected (or several more pages have ejected) and the owner of that print job has to collate the pages.

The owner identified on the banner can take all the pages that come out of the printer until the next banner is seen. If the owner isn't standing at the printer, the pages can stay in the tray. Meanwhile, other owners hanging around the printer can ignore that print job and wait for the banner to announce the next job.

To enable banners for shared printers, follow these steps:

1. Right-click on the printer and choose Properties from the shortcut menu.

2. On the General tab, choose Separator Page to open the Separator Page dialog box (see fig. 17.18).

Figure 17.18

Choose a separator page that will print in front of every document to notify users who own each print job.

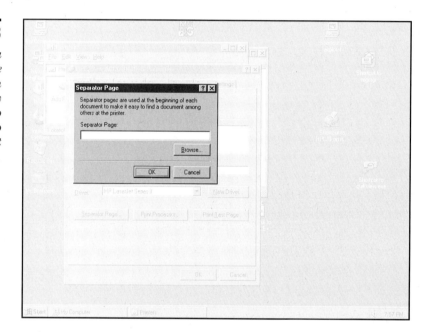

3. Enter the name of the separator file you want to use, or choose Browse to search for the file. You need one of the following files (which are found in the \system32 subfolder under your Windows NT software folder):

   ◆ **PCL.SEP.** Used for PCL printers.

   ◆ **SYSPRINT.SEP.** Used for PostScript printers.

4. Click OK after you select the separator file; then click OK to close the Properties dialog box.

Note   The \system32 subfolder actually contains three separator files: PCL.SEP, SYSPRINT.SEP, and PSCRIPT.SEP. PSCRIPT.SEP doesn't send a banner, even though it has a separator page file extension. It is a software program that switches the target printer to PostScript printing. This, of course, is only for those printers that are capable of PostScript printing and also use PCL commands. Sending the PSCRIPT.SEP files resets the printer to use PostScript. Sending PCL.SEP resets to PCL printing and prints a banner.

Note that if the printer is located on a Windows 95 computer, the banner configuration must be done at that computer using the local printer Properties page. It doesn't matter what your permissions are; a connected user cannot establish banners. If you attempt to configure a banner from a Windows NT 4 machine on a Windows 95-connected printer, you will not see an error message (you'll go through all the steps thinking you've successfully installed banners), but you also won't see banners.

Windows NT Print Processes

Although you have to install a specific driver for your printer, the operating system takes care of most of the processes involved in printing without any setup action from you. There are quite a few processes, and this overview should help you understand what the operating system is doing and what it is using to perform each process. The print processes include the following steps:

1. Printing begins when an application running on a computer sends a print job to a printer.

2. The printer driver is loaded into memory (so its information is available to all the operating system processes).

> **Note**   Some applications load the printer driver when the software is loaded in order to use the information in the driver for WYSIWYG.

3. The print job is converted into a metafile (output file) using the Windows NT Graphics Device Interface (GDI).

4. The output file is passed to the spooler (the local spooler regardless of the location of the printer). The spooler checks the file (actually it checks for the data type) and sends the job and information about the job's data type to the print processor.

5. The print processor translates the data into a format expected by the target printer (it gets the information it needs from the printer driver).

6. The job is passed to the spooler on the computer that has the printer (which may be the same as the sending computer) where it waits for the printer to be free. The jobs waiting in the spooler form the queue.

This overview is extremely brief, showing only the highlights and omitting plenty of details, but you should be able to understand how complicated printing is. This complication is what drives administrators crazy when trying to troubleshoot printing problems—there are so many places where things can get stuck or break down.

Administrative Troubleshooting

**Objective
G.2**
For an administrator, a print file provides the capability of doing some troubleshooting. Print files that are sent to the physical printer from the command line bypass the printer driver and the spooler, offering a fast way to eliminate the printer as the source of a printing problem. If there is output as a result of a command line printing process, you know you have to look elsewhere for the printing problem.

> **Tip** I've always had the theory that, when troubleshooting, you should try the easiest test first, then move on to more difficult procedures.

If the print file doesn't work, check the cable connection and then check the obvious stuff like online lights and paper-out messages.

If the print file works, try some of these troubleshooting techniques:

◆ Check the space on the hard drive for the computer that sent the print job. The temporary files created by the printer driver can be quite large and if the hard drive has insufficient space the job is corrupted.

◆ Check the Print dialog box in the application that sent the print job and make sure the selected printer is correct.

◆ Check the spool file—the spooler that receives the file is the local spooler even if the print job is being sent to a printer on another computer. The spool file is located in your Windows directory in the subdirectory \system32\spool\printers.

If the spool file is going to an NTFS partition and the user who sent the print job doesn't have Write permissions for the subdirectory, that's the problem.

Each print job in the spooler directory should have two files: the spool file that has the print job, which has a filename extension of .spl; and the shadow file, which has administrative information (user's name, priority of the print job, name of the target printer), and has a filename extension .shd. If a file is missing, or seems too small (couple of bytes) and may have been corrupted, try resending the job.

If the spool files are there but the job doesn't print, you can try stopping and starting the spooler: Open the Services applet in Control Panel; Select Spooler and choose Stop (you have to confirm the fact that you're stopping the Spooler). Then choose Start to restart the Spooler.

> **Note** I'm not sure why this last technique works, but it does.

◆ You can reinstall the printer drivers if you run out of other things to try. This one is the solution of choice if other Windows software applications (besides the one that first had the problem) fail to print or print incorrectly.

If disk space is a problem and there's an additional drive on the computer (either a partition or a physical drive), you can move the spooler directory. This change involves the Registry:

Objective G.6

1. Open the Registry with your favorite Registry editor.

2. Expand HKEY_LOCAL_MACHINE.

3. Move to \System\CurrentControlSet\Control\Print\Printers.

4. Change the data in the DefaultSpoolDirectory item by entering a new path.

5. Reboot to have the new path take effect.

If printing works but is extremely slow, you can also change the priority level for the spooler in the Registry. In HKEY_LOCAL_MACHINE, go to \System\CurrentControlSet\Control\Print. Double-click on the PriorityClass data item in the right pane and enter a higher priority.

> **End Note:** When you share the printer on your Windows NT 4 computer with others, your computer is a print server. It's possible to set up a print server that can provide all the printing services for up to ten simultaneously connected users. You might want to think about establishing a Windows NT 4 machine exclusively for printing services. This means you install a number of additional ports (an extra parallel port and several extra serial ports), and attach multiple printers to the computer (most laser printers have serial connectors available). The real advantage of using a Windows NT 4 machine in this manner is that it can provide drivers as well as printers for the attached users, regardless of the Windows operating system being used. When a connected computer accesses a printer, the correct driver is accessed at the same time. For an administrator, this is a time saver in terms of installation on the connected computers.

Test Your Knowledge

1. Select the correct statement(s) about a printer that you installed and configured as a shared printer:

   A. Users of computers running Windows 95 have to install Win95 drivers for your printer on their machines.

   B. All the users on the network can access your printer whenever they need it.

   C. Users who access your printer send their print job spool files to their own computer.

   D. Your computer holds the spool files for all the print jobs sent to your printer.

2. If you use a printer that is attached to another computer:

    A. You must install a local printer driver if the printer is on a Windows 95 machine.

    B. You cannot print from the command line.

    C. You cannot print from DOS software.

    D. You cannot place a shortcut to the printer on your desktop.

3. What does GDI stand for?

4. Choose the _____ tab from the Log menu to see the audit report for a printer in the Event Viewer.

5. Select the item(s) you can configure for a printer using the document defaults configuration options:

    A. Output Resolution

    B. Paper Orientation

    C. Available Hours

    D. Separator pages

6. Expand the _____ key to use the Registry for changes in the printing process.

7. The job of the print processor is to:

    A. Send the job to the correct spooler

    B. Create an output file using the GDI

    C. Send the data to the printer

    D. Keep the queue's priority list

Test Your Knowledge Answers

1. C

2. A

3. Graphics Device Interface

4. Security

5. A,B

6. HKEY_LOCAL_MACHINE

7. C

PART IV

Installing and Configuring Applications

Chapter Snapshot

Successfully installing programs is relatively simple with Windows NT 4, but you can increase your effectiveness by learning all the ins and outs of installation. This chapter focuses on the following:

Windows NT
Workstation **4**

CHAPTER 18

Running Windows Applications

Applications written for Windows, in all its different versions, are pretty straightforward to install. You do have options, depending on what's most convenient for you. Beginning users can use tools that walk them through the installation process easily; advanced users can take advantage of some time-savers that exist. This chapter first discusses the installation and running of programs for both levels, starting with the easiest methods and working up to methods that more experienced users will appreciate. The chapter also covers the act of uninstalling programs (which is not always as simple as installing them). Finally, this chapter discusses how to actually run Windows programs on the Windows NT Workstation 4 operating system.

Installing with Add/Remove Programs

Objective

B.5

The Control Panel contains an icon called Add/Remove Programs (see fig. 18.1) that has two purposes. First, the icon provides an easy way to install applications onto your system (and uninstall them). Second, it lets you add and remove Windows NT Workstation 4 components. You won't be learning about the second capability in this chapter; instead, you will learn how to install applications using Add/Remove Programs. For information on adding and removing Windows NT Workstation components, see Chapter 2, "Installing Windows NT Workstation 4."

Figure 18.1

Use the Add/Remove Programs icon to install and remove applications.

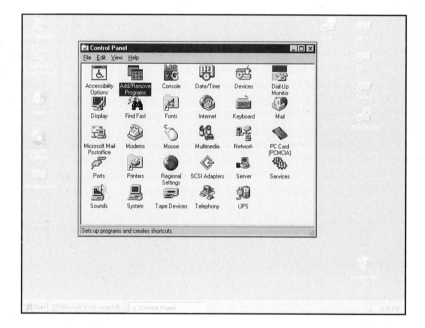

Double-clicking on the Add/Remove Programs icon activates the Add/Remove Programs Properties dialog box (see fig. 18.2), which is composed of two tabs. The first, Install/Uninstall, is used to add and remove applications from your system. The second, Windows NT Setup, lets you add and remove Windows NT Workstation components.

Click on the Install button to begin the process of installing a new application. Then start a wizard designed to help walk you through the installation. Figure 18.3 shows the first screen of the Install Program From Floppy Disk or CD-ROM Wizard.

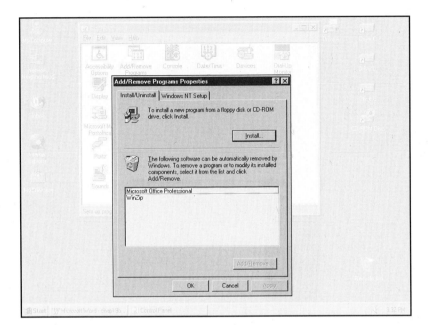

Figure 18.2

In the Add/ Remove Programs Properties dialog box, use the Install/Uninstall tab to control installed programs.

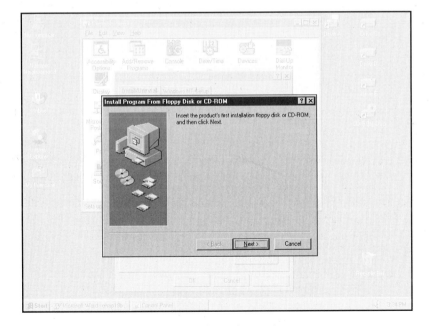

Figure 18.3

The Install Program From Floppy Disk or CD-ROM Wizard appears when you install a program using the Add/ Remove Programs icon.

At this point, you insert the installation disk or CD-ROM for your application into your system. After doing this, click on the Next button to continue. The wizard then searches any inserted disks or CD-ROMs for recognized installation programs (see fig. 18.4).

Figure 18.4

The wizard searches for installation programs automatically.

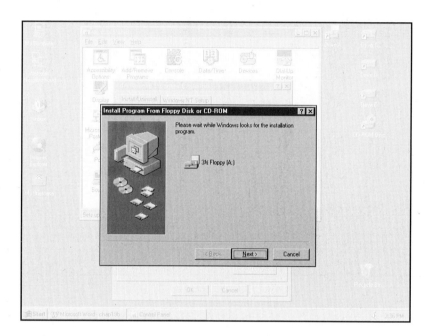

When the wizard finds what it regards as a valid installation program, the Run Installation Program dialog box shown in figure 18.5 appears. After confirming that it has found the correct installation program (refer to your program's documentation), click on the Finish button to automatically start that installation program.

If the installation wizard cannot find an installation program, you will see the message shown in figure 18.6 instead.

When the wizard fails to find a valid installation program, you should first confirm that you have properly inserted the installation disk or CD-ROM for your program into the appropriate drive. If not, insert the disk correctly, click on the Back button to back up one step, and then click on the Next button to have the wizard re-search for an installation program.

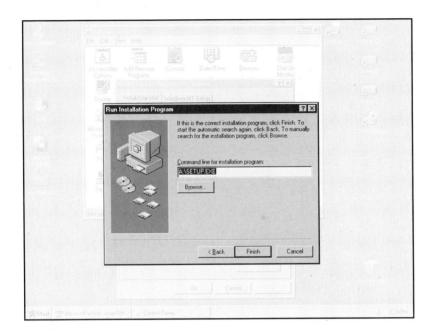

Figure 18.5

The wizard finds a valid installation program.

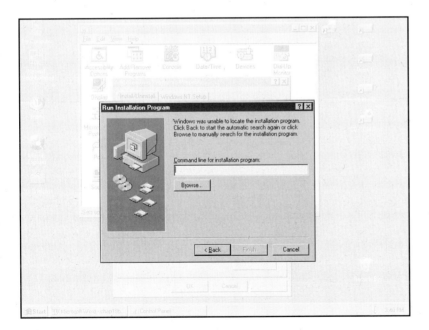

Figure 18.6

When an installation program is not found, the Run Installation Program dialog box appears, asking for input.

Sometimes an installation program will not be found simply because it uses an uncommon program name, such as ZINSTAPP.EXE. The wizard searches for common installation program names, such as SETUP (the most common) and INSTALL (the next most common). If it cannot find a program using one of the common names, you must specify the exact name of the correct installation program for your application. You discover the name either by checking the documentation that came with your program or by clicking on the Browse button to search for it yourself. Clicking on the Browse button brings up a Browse dialog box (see fig. 18.7) that lets you look through the files on your program's installation disk. When you find the program that installs the application, select it and click on the OK button.

Figure 18.7

Use the Browse dialog box to locate the installation program you need when it's not automatically found.

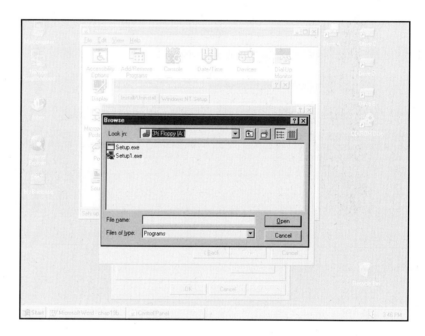

After the installation program is located—either by the automatic search or by using the Browse dialog box—proceed by clicking on the Finish button in the installation wizard's dialog box. This starts the installation program, from which point it walks you through its own installation process.

> **Tip** If an application uses the Install/Uninstall Applications Programming Interface (API), you will see it listed in the Add/Remove Programs dialog box after it is installed. Selecting it thereafter will activate its installation program, from which you can add or remove options or remove the application entirely. You will need to consult the application's documentation for instructions on doing so if it does not support the Install/Uninstall API.

Installing Programs Directly

There is a way to install programs that is faster than using the Add/Remove Programs icon discussed in the previous section. All you need to do is insert the installation disk or CD-ROM into your computer, and then open the drive using either the My Computer tool or Windows NT Explorer. Browse the installation disk, locate the installation program yourself, and double-click on it. Figure 18.8 shows both My Computer and Windows NT Explorer ready to run an installation program, using this method.

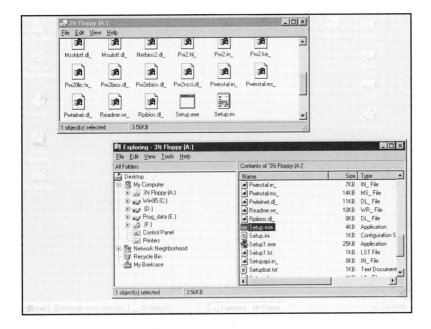

Figure 18.8

The Drive A window and Windows NT Explorer are both ready to launch SETUP.EXE.

You can also use the Start menu's Run command to start your program's installation program. Choose Run from the Start menu, which brings up the Run dialog box shown in figure 18.9. Type in the name of the installation program (from the installation instructions that came with the program) in the Open field and click on the OK button to start the program.

Note You should always refer to the instructions that came with your application for details about how it is best installed.

Figure 18.9

The Run dialog box is a "quick and dirty" way to launch an installation program.

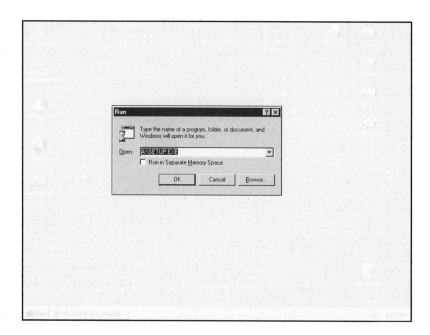

Adding Programs to the Start Menu

Objective E.1

Most Windows-based programs must be installed using their installation programs. During their installation, these programs often create key files in your Windows NT directory that they require in order to run. The installation programs also usually make necessary changes to your system's Registry or, in the case of Windows 3.1 programs, your WIN.INI file. Also, during their installation, they create their own menus or icons in your Start menu so that you can run them easily.

Sometimes there are programs that do not need to be installed in this way. These programs are self-contained (all necessary files only need to exist in one directory) in their own directories, and need to be started from their directory in order to run. This kind of program, which is admittedly becoming more and more rare, does not need to make changes to your system's setup files in order to run, nor does it need to copy support files into your \WINNT_ROOT directory. In these cases, after you've placed the program files in an appropriate directory, you'll want to add them to your Start menu so that you can more easily start them. This avoids having to browse their directory every time you want to use them or using some other method to start them.

You can modify the Start menu in many ways, but this chapter shows you the two methods that are most convenient. The first is for beginning users, while the second will be more useful to intermediate and advanced users of Windows NT Workstation 4.

Beginner Method for Adding Programs to the Start Menu

To have Windows NT walk you through the process of adding a program to your Start menu, follow these steps:

1. Open the Start menu.

2. Open the Settings submenu and choose Taskbar, as shown in figure 18.10.

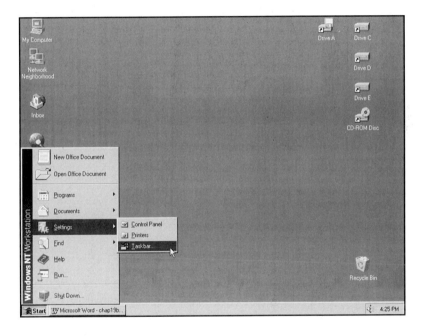

Figure 18.10

Use the Settings menu's Taskbar command to change the contents of Start menu.

3. The Taskbar command brings up the Taskbar Properties dialog box (see fig. 18.11). In this dialog box, select the Start Menu Programs tab.

4. To begin adding a program to your Start menu, click on the Add button. This calls up the Create Shortcut dialog box, shown in figure 18.12.

5. If you know the path and file names of the program you want to add, type it into the Command line field. You can also add any needed parameters to this line.

   If you do not know the file name of the program you want to add, click on the Browse button to access the Browse dialog box and locate the program on your computer. The Browse dialog box is a standard File Open dialog box that, after you select a program on your system, returns the full path name to the Command line field.

Figure 18.11

The Start Menu Programs tab lets you add and remove entries from your Start menu.

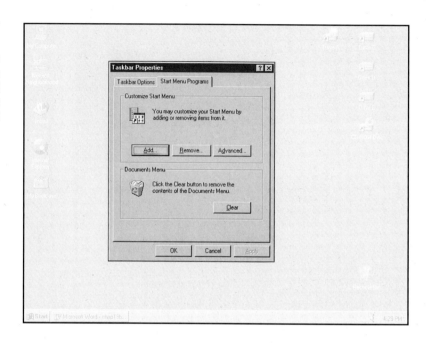

Figure 18.12

The Create Shortcut dialog box enables you to put an installed program onto your Start menu.

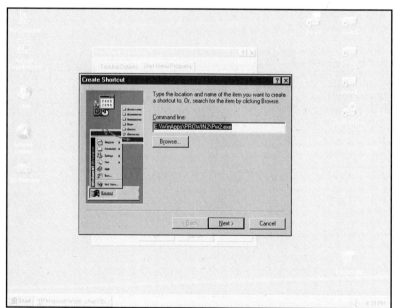

6. After locating the program and clicking on the Next button, you see the Select Program Folder dialog box, as shown in figure 18.13. Use the Select Program Folder dialog box to choose which folder your new shortcut will be placed into.

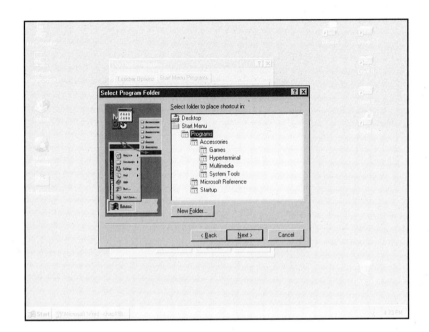

Figure 18.13

The Select Program Folder dialog box enables you to choose which Start menu folder contains the new program shortcut.

If you don't see a folder into which you want to place the shortcut, you can create a folder by clicking on the New Folder button. A folder is created with a generic name that you can edit, as shown in figure 18.14.

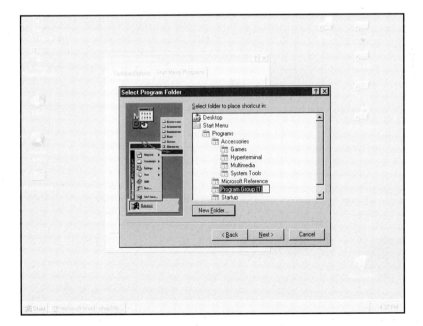

Figure 18.14

Creating a new folder automatically enables you to edit its name.

Tip

Before clicking on the New Folder button, first select the folder into which you want to create your new folder. By default, new folders are created at the top level of the Programs menu when you click on the New Folder button, and there is no provision to move them in the Select Program Folder dialog box.

7. After creating a folder, select it in the Select Program Folder dialog box by clicking on it and then clicking on the Next button. You are then shown the Select a Title for the Program dialog box (see fig. 18.15).

Figure 18.15

The Select a Title for the Program dialog box lets you name your new Start menu shortcut.

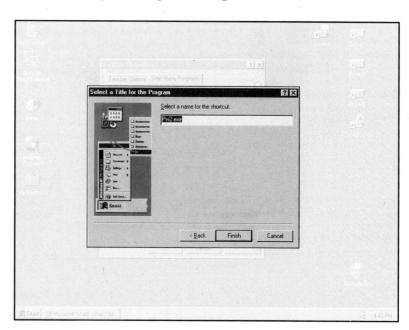

8. Type in the name that you want shown in the Start menu in the field offered. By default, the field contains the name of the executable file itself, but you will typically want a more descriptive name. After entering the name you want, click on the Finish button to complete the addition of the icon to the Start menu.

Advanced Method for Adding Programs to the Start Menu

Objective E.1

The beginner method for adding program icons to the Start menu takes quite a bit of time, although the user is led through the process in an easy fashion. More advanced users can use the Windows NT Explorer to add shortcuts to their Start menus more quickly.

Before using these more advanced methods, you should understand how Windows NT Workstation 4 stores its Start menus. First of all, each user has his or her own Start menu and desktop settings. User settings, including the Start menu, are stored in the \WINNT\Profiles folder. Figure 18.16 shows the Profiles folder selected in Windows Explorer.

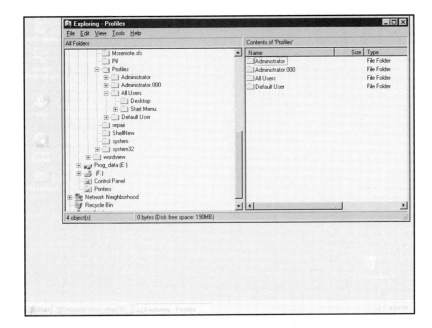

Figure 18.16

The Profiles folder contains each user's Start menu.

In the Profiles folder, there is a subfolder for each system user. In figure 18.16, you see folders for Administrator, Administrator.000, All Users, and Default User. The Administrator folders are specific user folders, while the shortcuts you see in All Users are shared automatically by all system users. Default User contains folders that are used when a new user is set up on the computer (they are copied to the folder created for the new user).

Within each of these user folders is a folder called Start Menu. This folder contains the shortcuts for that user's Start menu. If you have Administrative privileges on the system, you can directly modify all of these folders' contents. Changes that affect the Start menu folder immediately appear in the real Start menu when you open it.

There are three ways to start Windows NT Explorer and work directly with the various Start Menu folders:

◆ Start Windows NT Explorer from the Start menu, and then open the Start Menu folder for the profile you want to modify. You can open any of the user profiles for which you have access.

◆ Choose the Taskbar command in the Settings menu, move to the Start Menu Programs tab, and click on the Advanced button. This brings up Windows NT Explorer automatically and selects the Start Menu folder for your own account.

◆ Right-click on the Start menu. This action causes a pop-up menu to appear from which you can choose to edit the Start menu. From the pop-up menu, you can choose Explore (see fig. 18.17), which takes you to your own private Start Menu folder. You can also choose Open All Users or Explore All Users, which lets you modify the system-wide Start menu.

Figure 18.17

The Start menu's pop-up menu gives you quick access to some of its features.

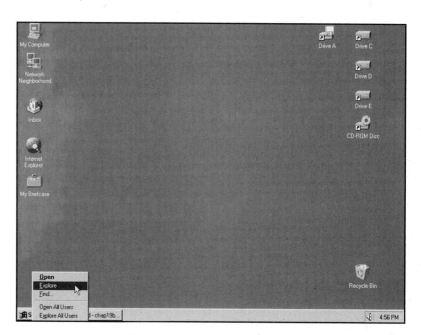

After you have accessed the appropriate Start menu, you can add, remove, and modify the shortcuts and folders within it to set up the Start menu in any way that you like. For instance, you can create a shortcut for an existing program and drag it into one of the Start menu subfolders. The shortcut instantly appears on your Start menu after you make changes.

Uninstalling Windows Applications

Because Windows-based programs typically add files to your Windows directories and make changes to your Registry and .INI files, you need to uninstall or remove them from your system. You typically cannot erase their directory and expect to fully remove them from your system.

There are two ways to remove Windows-based applications from your system, depending on whether they were designed for Windows 95 and Windows NT Workstation 4 or for previous versions of Windows. Older programs need to be removed by following the instructions that came with the specific program. Removing files often involves running the program's setup program and choosing a remove option. Other applications have specific programs designed to remove them from your system.

Applications designed for newer versions of Windows (those that support the Install/Uninstall API) can be removed more easily by using the Add/Remove Programs icon in the Control Panel. Consider the Add/Remove Programs Properties dialog box shown in figure 18.18. In the lower half of the dialog box, you can see Microsoft Office Professional and WinZip (a shareware utility) displayed. Programs that appear in this window can be removed by Windows itself.

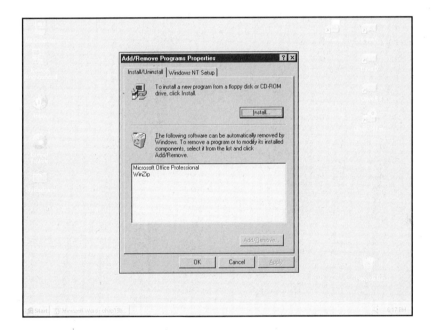

Figure 18.18

The Add/Remove Programs Properties dialog box enables you to remove programs from Windows.

To remove a program displayed in the Add/Remove Programs Properties dialog box, select the program and click on the Add/Remove button. Selecting WinZip and clicking on the Add/Remove button displays the WinZip dialog box shown in figure 18.19.

Programs designed for newer versions of Windows notify Windows about their removal procedures during their installation, and they automatically link their removal programs into Windows. Those specific removal programs are called automatically by the Add/Remove Programs Properties dialog box when you choose to remove the application from your system. Each program will use its own removal program.

Figure 18.19

The WinZip removal dialog box gives you a final chance to cancel the removal of the program.

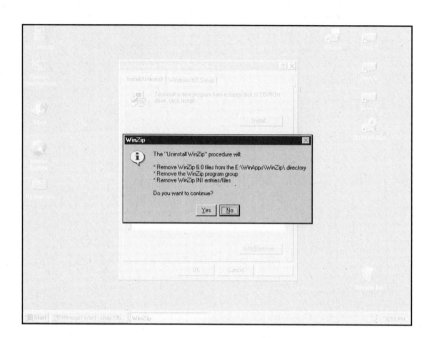

> **Note** | Many removal programs require you to reinsert the original program disks as part of the uninstall process.

Working with Windows 3.x and Windows 95 Programs on NT

You can run applications designed for Windows 3.x and Windows 95 on Windows NT Workstation 4. Windows 3.x applications are supported by a 16-bit Windows subsystem (Win16) that runs under Windows NT. Windows 95 applications typically make use of the 32-bit Windows subsystem (Win32) that supports both Windows NT and Windows 95 applications.

There are a number of restrictions to running Windows 3.x and Windows 95 applications under Windows NT Workstation 4, although most applications are not affected greatly:

◆ Applications cannot directly access the hard disk unless they are being run by someone with Administrative privileges, and nobody else is using the hard disk (for instance, across a network).

◆ Windows 95 uses a slightly different method to store long file names on FAT drives, and disk utilities designed for Windows 95 (such as Norton Disk Doctor) will cause problems on a Windows NT Workstation 4 system, possibly rendering your system unusable.

◆ Programs that use Interrupt 19 to reboot the computer don't actually do so; instead, they terminate the Virtual DOS Machine (VDM) in which they are running.

◆ Block-mode device drivers are not supported; however, these types of device drivers are exceedingly rare these days. Generally, they only existed for very early CD-ROM drives.

To maintain compatibility with Windows 3.x applications, Windows NT Workstation maintains WIN.INI and SYSTEM.INI files in the \WINNT directory. Applications written for Windows 3.x make use of these files. Windows NT Workstation reads these files when it boots and stores the information in its Registry, thereafter providing the information to the 16-bit Windows subsystem as required. Changes made to these files by Windows 3.x applications are maintained.

Start applications designed for Windows 3.x in the same way that you start Windows NT Workstation 4 or Windows 95 applications:

◆ Add their program icons to your Start menu.

◆ Double-click on their program icons in My Computer or in the Windows NT Explorer.

◆ Type the name of their program executable file at a Windows NT command prompt.

All of these methods start the program automatically, using the 16-bit Windows subsystem.

All Windows 3.x programs run within the 16-bit Windows subsystem, and exist in a single Virtual DOS Machine (VDM). Therefore, if one 16-bit Windows application crashes, all other 16-bit Windows programs running in that VDM will also be affected. When this happens, you can terminate the VDM by pressing Ctrl+Alt+Del to bring up the Windows NT Security dialog box, from which you can open the Task Manager. From within the Task Manager (see fig. 18.20), you can select the program.

Note You can see in Task Manager that all 16-bit Windows processes are running within a single VDM called NTVDM.EXE. Running in the VDM is WOWEXEC.EXE, one of the key components of Windows on Windows (the nickname for running 16-bit Windows programs on 32-bit versions of Windows).

Figure 18.20

You can end a process with Task Manager.

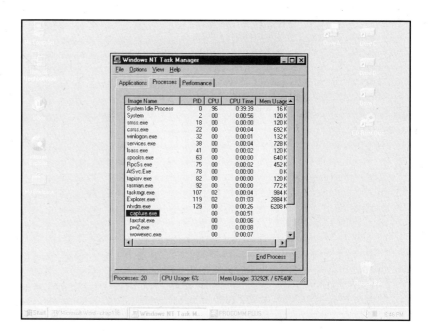

Using Separate VDMs for Win16 Programs

As mentioned previously, Win16 programs all run within a single Windows NT process—a VDM—called NTVDM.EXE. A poorly behaved Win16 program can adversely affect other Win16 programs running within that VDM. The adverse effects include slow performance or outright crashes of the other Win16 programs.

You can get around this hang-up by running selected Win16 programs in their own, private VDM. To do so, right-click on the shortcut for the program and access its Properties dialog box. Move to the Shortcut page, shown in figure 18.21.

On the Shortcut tab, select the box marked Run in Separate Memory Space. This action causes a new, private NTVDM to be started when you use that program shortcut in which the application runs. Even if other Win16 applications on the system are running, the application with the Run in Separate Memory Space box checked will not interfere with them.

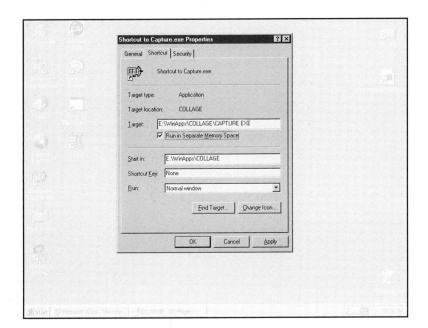

Figure 18.21

The Shortcut tab for a Win16 Application lets you choose to run the application in its own memory space.

Tip On multiprocessor systems, you can cause multiple Win16 applications to make use of the multiple processors by using the Run in Separate Memory Space checkbox for each program. Windows NT will only run NTVDM.EXE on a single processor at a time. If you have multiple NTVDMs running, each with its own program, Windows NT will evenly distribute their workload across the processors.

Changing Windows 3.x Program Priority

Windows applications that are 16-bit are written to use a cooperative multitasking scheme, in which all of the running 16-bit Windows programs cooperate in achieving multitasking. They are not designed to communicate with the operating system and adjust their relative priority levels as their needs change. This holds true under Windows NT Workstation 4; however, you can control the priority of the VDM that runs all of the 16-bit Windows applications and collectively raise or lower their priority with respect to other Windows NT processes.

Objective E.2

You do this with the Task Manager display shown in figure 18.20. You can right-click on the NTVDM.EXE process, which activates its pop-up menu. In the pop-up menu, you can choose the Set Priority command, and then the priority level at which you want it to run (see fig. 18.22).

Figure 18.22

Use a process's pop-up menu to change its priority in Task Manager.

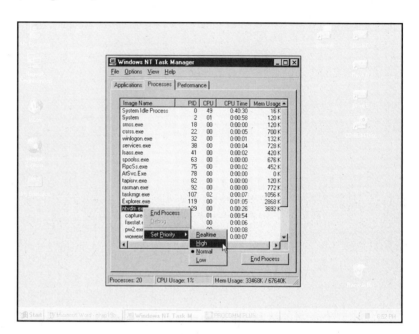

> **Note**   You should avoid setting the priority of the 16-bit Windows subsystem to the Realtime class, which is otherwise reserved for threads that absolutely must have control of the system on a regular and predictable basis. If you do, you risk starving the threads that really do need this level of priority in the system.

The priority levels range from 0 to 31. The base, or normal, priority is 7. Higher numbers represent more critical programs. Programs with priorities from 0 to 15 are known as *dynamic applications.* Programs with priorities from 16 to 31 are known as *real-time applications.* Real-time applications cannot be written out to the page file; they must reside in RAM at all times. Generally, only the operating system itself and its support programs operate in the real-time priority classes.

The settings available in the pop-up menu in the Task Manager are Low, Normal, High, and Real Time, and they correspond to priority levels 4, 7, 13, and 24, respectively.

You can also use a parameter with the START command to begin a program with a specific priority. The following settings are available with the START program:

- ◆ **/LOW.** Sets priority to 4.

- ◆ **/NORMAL.** Sets priority to 7.

- ◆ **/HIGH.** Sets priority to 13.

- ◆ **/REALTIME.** Sets priority to 24.

To open the calculator program at high priority, for example, you would type the following:

```
START /HIGH CALC.EXE
```

You should be careful about setting specific priorities (unless you are working to solve a particular problem). Setting a program's priority unnecessarily high can slow other programs in the system, possibly programs that you don't want to run more slowly.

Troubleshooting the Running of Windows Applications

Windows programs are generally well-behaved within Windows NT, and not much troubleshooting is required for them as a general class of programs. There are some common problems that occur, though. This section outlines a few of these common problems and suggests specified courses of action:

**Objective
G.4**

- ◆ Win16 (Windows 3.x) programs cannot run if they rely on virtual device drivers (VxDs). VxDs need to write directly to the computer's hardware, and therefore are not allowed under Windows NT. Games and utility programs are common program-types that sometimes violate this rule. Your only course of action for these types of programs is to seek a Windows NT-specific version, or to run them under Windows 95.

- ◆ Windows NT programs need to be compiled for the hardware platform on which they are to run. A program compiled for an Alpha-based Windows NT machine will not run on an Intel-based Windows NT machine. Make sure that you're trying to run a version of the Windows NT application that is compiled for the hardware platform you are using.

End Note: 16-bit Windows programs can make use of the drag-and-drop features of the Windows NT Workstation 4 desktop. If you want to open a particular graphics file with a graphics program written for a 16-bit version of Windows, you can still drag the file and drop it onto the program's icon.

Test Your Knowledge

1. What are generally valid ways of installing Windows programs onto Windows NT?

   A. Use the Add/Remove Programs icon in the Control Panel.

   B. Run the application's installation program directly.

   C. Copy all of the application's files to a directory and double-click on one of them to run the program.

   D. Use the Application Installer applet.

2. Two programs that the Install Programs from Floppy Disk or CD-ROM Wizard searches for include:

   A. INSTALL.EXE

   B. INST.COM

   C. SETUP.EXE

   D. NORMAL_INSTALL.EXE

3. Which of the following two methods will add a program shortcut to the Start menu?

   A. Run the Start Menu Maintenance tool.

   B. Open the Start menu, choose Settings, choose Taskbar, and use the Start Menu Programs tab.

   C. Right-click on the Start menu, choose Explore, and then drag the application shortcut into the appropriate Start Menu subfolder.

   D. You cannot directly control what goes on the Start menu.

4. Start Menu entries for a particular user are stored where?

   A. In \WINNT

   B. In \WINNT\Start Menu

   C. In \WINNT\Profiles*user_name*

   D. In \Desktop\Start Menu

5. Which of the following two ways are the best ways to remove Windows applications from a Windows NT system?

   A. Use the Add/Remove Programs icon in the Control Panel.

   B. Erase the application's directory structure with Explorer.

   C. Use the application's specific uninstall instructions.

   D. Remove the application's entry from the Registry.

6. Which of the following are valid restrictions for Win16 programs running under Windows NT Workstation 4?

    A. Programs that directly access the computer's hardware cannot run.

    B. Programs that use block mode device drivers cannot run.

    C. Programs that include Multimedia movies, like QuickTime, cannot run.

    D. Programs that use Interrupt 19 to reboot the computer do not reboot it; instead they merely terminate the VDM in which the Win16 program runs.

7. If you are running four Win16 programs on a computer with four processors, what are possible ways that you can improve the performance of those programs?

    A. Increase the programs' priority setting.

    B. Run the programs in separate memory spaces (VDMs).

    C. Install more RAM onto the system.

    D. Relocate the PAGEFILE.SYS to a different drive.

8. Which of the following lists the possible priority settings for Win16 programs from lowest to highest?

    A. Real, Low, High, Normal

    B. Real, Low, Normal, High

    C. Low, Normal, High, Real

    D. Low, Normal, Real, High

9. You can change a program's priority by:

    A. Using the proper START command parameter.

    B. Using the Windows NT Task Manager.

    C. Using the SET_PTY program.

    D. You cannot directly control the priority of a running program under Windows NT.

Test Your Knowledge Answers

1. A,B	6. A,B,D
2. A,C	7. A,B
3. B,C	8. C
4. C	9. A,B
5. A,C	

Chapter Snapshot

You'll find that Windows NT Workstation's support for DOS and OS/2 1.x applications is quite good. Applications for both generally run very well, sometimes exceeding the performance available when they run in their native environments. This chapter focuses on the following topics:

Windows NT
Workstation 4

CHAPTER 19

Running Non-Windows Applications

Early versions of OS/2 taught Microsoft and IBM a valuable lesson: you cannot come out with a new operating system and expect it to be successful if it cannot run most of the existing software available. Not only is it extremely expensive and difficult to move software applications from one operating system to another, in some cases there is no real need to do so. Even when companies might like to implement a new operating system for the features it offers, it makes no sense to upgrade if they cannot run their vital programs under the new operating system. After all, the operating system accomplishes no work; it merely enables the applications running under it to get the real work done.

Because of this essential truth, Windows NT Workstation runs virtually all legacy applications available. Whether you want to run applications designed for Windows 3.x, MS-DOS, OS/2 1.x, POSIX, or Windows NT, you can get your work done and access the software that's crucial to you. In this chapter, you learn about configuring and running MS-DOS, POSIX, and OS/2 1.x applications under Windows NT Workstation 4.

Starting Non-Windows Programs

Objective E.1

There are really three ways for you to start an application under Windows NT. First, you can simply double-click on the program itself (or its shortcut) in Windows NT Explorer, Network Neighborhood, or My Computer. Second, you can start a program from a command prompt, from the appropriate directory (or when the directory is in your PATH statement). Third, you can use the Windows NT START command, which is really a modification of the command prompt method, but gives you some additional controls when running the program that are specific to Windows NT (see the following section for more information on the START command).

When you start an application by double-clicking on it, or by typing its name at a command prompt, Windows NT inspects the application to determine what subsystem is needed to run the application. It then starts the necessary subsystem, if any, and proceeds to load and run the program.

Using the START Command

Objective E.1

Objective E.2

When you double-click on a program to start it, any settings associated with the program are used to open the program. Later in this chatper, for instance, you learn how to set application settings for DOS applications under Windows NT. However, there are times when you need to control how an application starts from the command line, and the default startup behavior may not be suitable to your needs. Or, perhaps, you are developing a batch file that starts a program and need that program to start in a particular way only when it is run from that batch file. You use the Windows NT START command to resolve these situations.

You can use the START command to control these properties for a started program:

- ◆ Its window state (minimized or maximized)
- ◆ Its startup directory
- ◆ The title displayed in the program window's title bar
- ◆ Whether or not the program is run in separate or shared memory space (16-bit Windows programs only)
- ◆ At what priority class the program will run

The syntax for the START command is as follows:

```
START ["window title"] [/Dpath] [/I] [/MIN] [/MAX] [/SEPARATE ¦ /SHARED]
[/LOW ¦ /NORMAL ¦ /HIGH ¦ /REALTIME] [/WAIT]
[/B] [command_or_program] [command_or_program_parameters]
```

Table 19.1 details the START command's parameters.

TABLE 19.1
START Command Parameters

Parameter	Description
"window_title"	Sets the program window's title
/D*path*	Sets the startup path for the program
/I	Specifies that the program will run in the original startup environment of the system, and not the current environment (which may have changes made to it)
/MIN	Starts the program window minimized
/MAX	Starts the program window maximized
/SEPARATE	Only for 16-bit Windows programs, this forces the program to run in a separate NTVDM memory space
/SHARED	Only for 16-bit Windows programs, this forces the program to run alongside any other running 16-bit Windows programs
/LOW	Starts the program with the IDLE priority class
/NORMAL	Starts the program with the NORMAL priority class
/HIGH	Starts the program with the HIGH priority class
/REALTIME	Starts the program with the REALTIME priority class (you must have Administrator-level privileges to do this)
/WAIT	Starts the program and waits for it to exit itself; no keyboard input is passed to the program
/B	Starts the program without creating a new window

Valid examples of the START command include:

```
START "My Program" /MAX /NORMAL myprog.exe

START "Separate Memory Space Program" /MAX /SEPARATE /HIGH win16prg.exe
```

Understanding Priority Levels and the START Command

Windows NT's application priority levels range from 0 to 31. The base, or normal, priority is 7. Higher numbers represent more critical programs. Programs with priorities from 0 to 15 are known as *dynamic applications*. Programs with priorities from 16 to 31 are known as *real-time applications*. Real-time applications cannot be written out to the page file; they must reside in RAM at all times. Generally, only the operating system itself and its support programs operate in the real-time priority classes.

You can use a parameter with the START command to begin a program with a specific priority. The following settings are available with the START program:

- ◆ **/LOW.** Sets priority to 4
- ◆ **/NORMAL.** Sets priority to 7
- ◆ **/HIGH.** Sets priority to 13
- ◆ **/REALTIME.** Sets priority to 24

So, for example, to open some DOS program at high priority, you would type:

START /HIGH DOSPROG.EXE

You should be careful about setting specific priorities unless you are working to solve a particular problem. Setting a program's priority to an unnecessarily high priority can slow other programs in the system, and possible programs that you don't want to run more slowly.

Understanding DOS Application Support

DOS applications running under Windows NT make use of a special Windows NT application called the NTVDM.EXE. "NT" stands for Windows NT, and "VDM" stands for *Virtual DOS Machine*. A Virtual DOS Machine is exactly that: a simulated Intel x86 system that, as far as the DOS application knows, is merely a standard PC on which DOS is installed and running.

DOS applications are typically written to make use of the PC hardware directly, without interference by the operating system. The NTVDM interfaces between the DOS program and Windows NT and simulates the PC hardware for the DOS application. The virtue of this approach is that it lets DOS applications, which are not cognizant of multitasking requirements, coexist with other running applications on the same computer. The NTVDM takes care of the details of apportioning system resources for the DOS application and ensures that it behaves itself within the system. Each DOS application uses its own, private NTVDM. Therefore, a failure of a DOS application will not affect other running DOS systems. Because of this fact, DOS applications are more reliable under Windows NT than under DOS itself.

Each NTVDM is made up of the following components:

◆ NTVDM.EXE, a protected-mode program written using the Win32 API. This program is the management program for the VDM.

◆ NTIO.SYS, which simulates DOS's IO.SYS.

◆ NTDOS.SYS, which simulates DOS's MSDOS.SYS.

◆ On RISC-based systems, there is also an Instruction Execution Unit (IEU) that simulates an Intel 80486 processor for those non-Intel computers.

| **Tip** | On Intel-based machines, DOS programs require no translation of their programming code to run; on RISC-systems, each instruction must be translated into instructions that the RISC processor understands. For this reason, DOS programs typically execute much more slowly on RISC-based systems, even those that are otherwise much faster than Intel-based systems. |

NTVDMs also include virtual device drivers that emulate the hardware devices on the system for the DOS application. These virtual device drivers are supplied to emulate COM ports, mice, keyboards, and printers.

Configuring DOS Applications

Objective E.1

DOS applications typically run without any special actions on your part. You can open a command prompt and run the program by typing its program name from within its directory; you can open My Computer and double-click on the icon for the program in its folder on your hard disk; or you can use Windows NT Explorer to do much the same thing. Usually the program simply starts and runs normally.

Sometimes, however, you might need to take advantage of some special settings available under Windows NT Workstation for DOS programs to get them to work well (or at all).

You access the settings for a DOS program through the program icon in the program's folder. Use My Computer to open the folder that contains the application and locate the program file (the program name you type to run the program, followed by an EXE or COM extension). Figure 19.1 shows an open folder from a hard disk that contains a DOS program called Onlan/PC that's used to dial in to a remote computer.

Figure 19.1

A DOS application's folder; the MS-DOS icon usually indicates the program file.

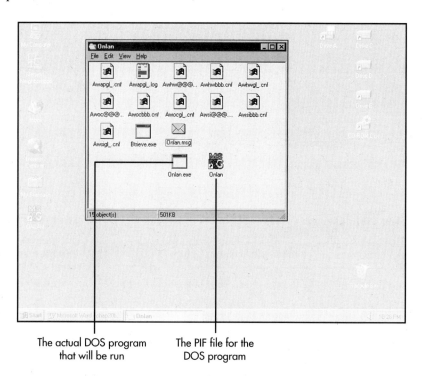

The actual DOS program that will be run

The PIF file for the DOS program

When you change the properties for a DOS program, the information you specify is automatically stored in a PIF file (Program Information File) that has the same name as the DOS program, but has the extension PIF. PIF files appear in folders as MS-DOS icons (see fig. 19.1), and they are created automatically whenever you change the properties for a DOS program from the default settings.

Note After a PIF has been created by Windows NT Workstation, changes made to the properties of the actual program icon or to the PIF icon automatically reflect in the other. Also, when you start a DOS program from a command prompt, its PIF settings aren't used.

To access a DOS program's settings, right-click on its icon and choose Properties from the pop-up menu. You will see the Properties dialog box for the program, as shown in figure 19.2.

| **Caution** | The Properties dialog box tabs you will learn about in the following section are very similar to the Windows 95 tabs. Unlike with Windows 95, some of these fields have no effect under Windows NT Workstation 4. For each tab field in the tables that follow, inactive fields or options will be mentioned. |

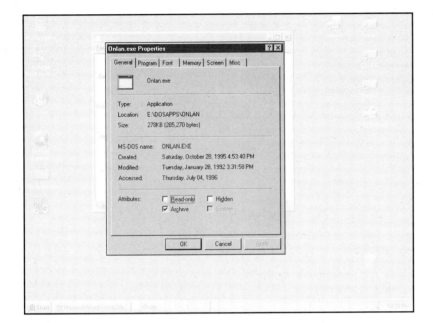

Figure 19.2

A DOS application's Properties dialog box contains its settings.

General Tab

The General tab of a DOS program's properties is primarily informational. You see the actual name of the program, its type, location, size, and date and time information about the file.

The General tab also contains four check boxes that you can use to control the file attributes of the program file. You can choose to set or clear the following attributes:

◆ **Read-only.** Specifies that the file cannot be erased, written to, or modified. (Actually, the file can be erased provided you have the appropriate security privileges. However, you are warned that it is a read-only file before the system removes it.)

◆ **Archive.** Indicates that the file has been modified since the last system backup and will be backed up during the next incremental backup.

◆ **Hidden.** Indicates that the file cannot be seen in a DIR listing at the DOS prompt (except by using certain commands, such as ATTRIB).

Objective

E.1

◆ **System.** Indicates that the program is a system file that is crucial to the proper functioning of the operating system. Certain commands will also not work when used with files flagged with the System attribute.

Program Tab

The Program tab (see fig. 19.3) of a DOS program's Properties dialog box contains many important settings that control how the program starts and runs.

Figure 19.3

The Program tab contains the basic settings for the DOS program.

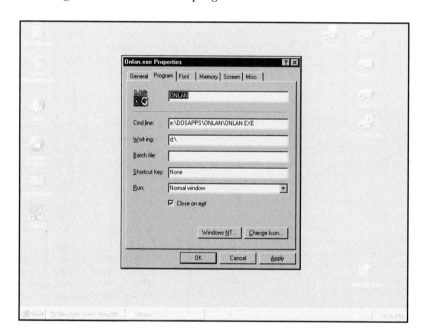

Table 19.2 details the fields on this page.

TABLE 19.2
Program Tab Fields

Field Name	Description
Top field	The top field, which doesn't have a field name, controls the name of the program that appears in the title bar when it's running in a window on your desktop.

Field Name	Description
Cmd line	The command line field specifies the exact path and file name that is used to run the program. If the program requires any parameters, add them to this line just as you would when typing the command and parameters at a DOS prompt.
Working	Use the Working field to control the working directory the program uses when it starts. When blank, the directory in which the program is stored is used. In most cases, this setting should be left unchanged, or the DOS program may not run properly.
Batch file	This field enables you to specify a batch file that is run whenever the program is started. This field is functional only when using the settings under Windows 95.
Shortcut key	Use this field to define a key combination that will instantly invoke the program from your Windows NT desktop. To use it, click in the field and then type the key combination you want to assign. You must include Ctrl or Alt (or both keys). For instance, if you hold down Ctrl and Alt and press the F10 key, the field will automatically show Ctrl+Alt+F10. Also, if the key combination you choose conflicts with a Windows shortcut key, the combination you define will not work. Conversely, a shortcut key defined for a program may override a shortcut key in an application.
Run	You can choose what type of window is used to run the program with this field. Your choices are Normal, Maximized, and Minimized. The program starts using whatever window choice you select.
Close on exit	If this box is checked, the VDM that is started to run the program automatically closes when the program terminates.

The Program tab also lets you choose a customized AUTOEXEC.BAT file to use with the program. To access this feature, click on the Windows NT button, which reveals the dialog box shown in figure 19.4.

In the Windows NT PIF Settings dialog box, you can define a custom AUTOEXEC.BAT and CONFIG.SYS file for the program by typing the file names you want to use in the fields provided. By default, AUTOEXEC.NT and CONFIG.NT are used, both of which are stored in the SYSTEM32 subdirectory of your main Windows NT Workstation directory. You can also select the Compatible Timer Hardware Emulation check box, which lets timer-sensitive DOS programs function normally.

Figure 19.4

The Windows NT PIF Settings dialog box enables you to choose a custom AUTOEXEC.BAT and CONFIG.SYS to use with the program.

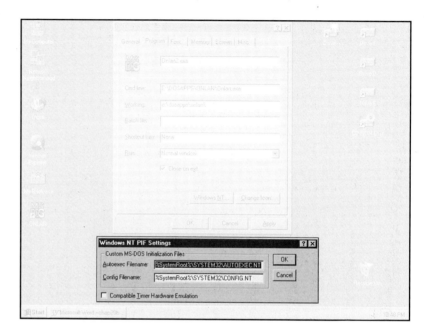

Finally, the Program tab enables you to choose a new icon for the DOS program. Click on the Change Icon button, which brings up the Change Icon dialog box (see fig. 19.5).

Figure 19.5

Spice up your desktop with new icons in the Change Icon dialog box.

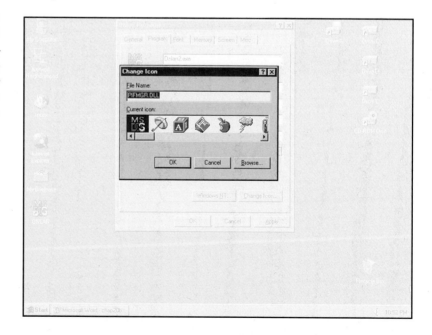

By default, you can choose from a selection of icons stored in the PIFMGR.DLL file. Simply select an icon and click on the OK button to use it. You can also use the Browse button to search for an appropriate icon file located on one of your disks. For instance, there are a number of icons in the file SHELL32.DLL that you can also use.

Font Tab

The Font tab of a DOS program's Properties dialog box lets you choose the font to use for the DOS program when you run it in a window on your desktop. You can choose a very small font that causes the DOS program to use a very small window on your desktop, or you can choose a larger font that makes it easier to read. Figure 19.6 shows the Font tab.

Objective
E.1

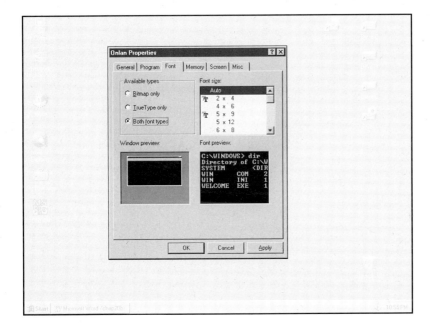

Figure 19.6

Use the Font tab to choose how the DOS program appears on your desktop.

In the Available types area, you can choose from Bitmap or TrueType fonts (or both font types). Generally, you would choose Both font types so you would have the most fonts available to choose from.

Tip On some systems, bitmap fonts may display more quickly than TrueType fonts.

Use the Font size window to choose the exact font size you want for the DOS program. Sizes are listed in terms of the number of pixels that are taken up horizontally and vertically. The font size bears a direct relationship to the size of the DOS window, which you can see in the Window preview box as you select different fonts. You can also preview how the font will appear on your desktop in the Font preview box. Depending on the type of program you're running, you may want to use a small font so that a minimum of screen space is taken up or choose a large font so that you can clearly see what you are working with.

Memory Tab

The Memory tab (see fig. 19.7) contains a number of settings that control how much memory the program "sees" when it runs. You want to control this because some programs require certain minimum values in order to work properly. Many DOS programs, however, being written for an operating system in which they could take control of the machine, will grab all the memory they can find and try to use it. A spreadsheet program, for example, might try to use a full 16 MB of EMS or XMS memory, even when it doesn't really need that much memory. You can use the Memory tab to provide exact limits on what a program can use.

Figure 19.7

The Memory tab enables you to control how much memory the DOS program can access.

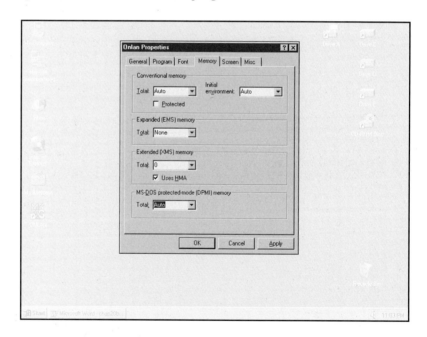

Table 19.3 describes the settings found on the Memory tab of a DOS program's Properties dialog box.

TABLE 19.3
Memory Tab Settings

Setting	Description
Conventional memory Total	This setting controls the amount of conventional memory (memory from 0 to 640 KB) that the program has available.
Initial environment	DOS programs make use of environment variables, and you can control the size of the environment with this setting.
Protected	Marking this check box specifies that the program will be run in a more protected mode than otherwise, where it has less access to the computer's hardware; however, this setting has no effect under Windows NT.
Expanded (EMS) memory	Controls the amount of LIM (Lotus-Intel-Microsoft) expanded memory available to your program. Up to 16 MB can be allocated.
Extended (XMS) memory	Controls the amount of XMS (eXtended Memory Specification) memory available to your program. Up to 16 MB can be allocated.
Uses HMA	If your program makes use of the High Memory Area available to XMS-aware programs, select this check box.
MS-DOS protected-mode	Controls the amount of DOS Protected-Mode Interface memory (DPMI) available to the program. Up to 16 MB can be allocated.

Screen Tab

The Screen tab affects various video-related settings for DOS programs. You see this tab in figure 19.8.

Table 19.4 describes the settings found on the Screen tab of a DOS program's Properties dialog box.

Objective

E.1

Figure 19.8

The Screen tab enables you to control how the window appears for the DOS program.

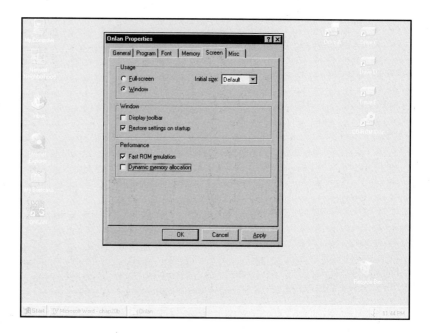

TABLE 19.4
Screen Tab Settings

Setting	Description
Full-screen	Enabling this option causes the program to start in full-screen mode.
Window	Enabling this option causes the program to start in win-dowed mode on your desktop (the settings on the Font page control how the window appears).
Initial Size	Some DOS programs can use a larger screen size than the traditional 80 characters wide by 25 characters tall. If you are using such a program, use this setting to control the size of the DOS window.
Display Toolbar	This setting has no impact under Windows NT.
Restore Settings on Startup	Selecting this check box causes all the program's window settings to be restored when you exit and restart the program.
Fast ROM Emulation	Activating this option causes most DOS programs to display more quickly than otherwise. Some DOS programs require

Setting	Description
	access to special features in the ROM on a video card and must have this setting turned off in order to function. If your DOS program isn't working right, try turning off this setting.
Dynamic Memory Allocation	Some DOS programs switch between graphics mode and text mode. Graphics mode requires more RAM in your system to display properly. If you select this check box, and you switch from a graphics mode to a text mode in your DOS program, the extra memory will be released back to the system until you switch back to graphics mode. There is some system overhead in managing this extra memory, so this option should only be selected if your system does not have ample RAM installed.

Misc Tab

Objective E.1

The final tab in a DOS program's Properties dialog box is the Misc tab (see fig. 19.9).

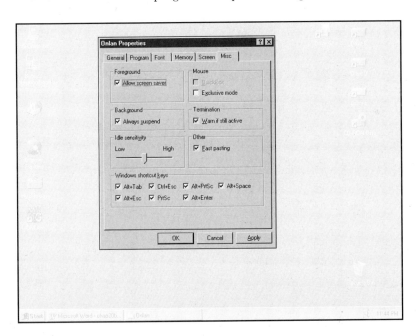

Figure 19.9

The Misc tab contains a number of miscellaneous settings for the DOS program.

Table 19.5 describes the settings found on the Misc tab of a DOS program's Properties dialog box.

TABLE 19.5
Misc Tab Settings

Setting	Description
Allow screen saver	When selected, your Windows NT Workstation screen saver will run, even when the DOS program is in the foreground. There is a very slight system performance overhead when this option is turned on.
Always suspend	Some DOS programs do no useful work when you are not actually using them. For such programs, you can speed up the rest of the system by making them inactive when they are minimized or otherwise put in the background by setting this option.
QuickEdit	This option enables you to drag across a DOS window to select text within it for use with the Clipboard. This option is functional only under Windows 95.
Exclusive mode	Under Windows 95, this option causes the mouse pointer to work only with the DOS program until the program is exited, even when the program runs in a window. This setting has no effect under Windows NT Workstation 4.
Warn if still active	When selected, you are warned if you try to terminate this program from Windows NT Workstation while it is still running.
Idle sensitivity	DOS programs typically poll the keyboard for input, and this polling consumes processor cycles. Setting Idle sensitivity to High causes Windows NT to assume that the program is merely polling for input sooner, at which point it reduces the amount of processor time allocated to the program to avoid wasting it. Low sensitivity causes Windows NT to be more lenient in assuming that the program is truly idle.
Fast pasting	You can copy text from the Windows NT Workstation Clipboard into DOS programs. There are two methods that accomplish this. When Fast pasting is selected, the quicker method is used. Some programs cannot accept input in this way, and in such cases you should turn off this option.
Windows shortcut keys	The key combinations that are checked are intercepted from being sent to the DOS program and are instead sent to Windows NT Workstation (they are Windows NT Workstation shortcut keys). In some cases, you want your program

Setting	Description
	to accept some of these key combinations. When this is true, you need to clear the check box for the key combination that your DOS program needs to accept.

Using the Clipboard with DOS Applications

Windows NT Workstation enables you to copy information from a DOS window and then paste it into a Windows application or another DOS application. You can also take text information stored on the Clipboard and paste it into the DOS application, just as if you had typed it yourself. You don't often use this capability, but when you need it, you really need it.

Each DOS window on your desktop has a control menu from which you can control certain characteristics of the running window. The control menu is accessed by clicking on the icon in the upper-left corner of the window (see fig. 19.10).

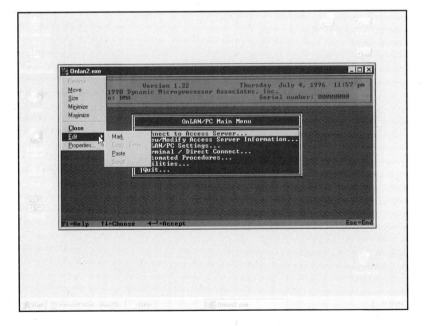

Figure 19.10

The DOS window control menu contains mark, copy, and paste commands that work with Windows NT Clipboard.

Of particular interest in the control menu is the Edit menu, which contains commands that let your DOS program interact with the Clipboard (even though DOS programs have no native capability to do so). The commands are as follows:

- ◆ **Mark.** Lets you select a portion of the text on the DOS window using your mouse.

- ◆ **Copy Enter.** Takes marked text and moves it to the Windows NT Workstation Clipboard.

- ◆ **Paste.** Takes Clipboard text and inserts it into your DOS application, just as if you were typing it directly into the DOS program.

- ◆ **Scroll.** When you resize a DOS program's window to a smaller size (scroll bars appear when you do this), the Scroll command lets you use your arrow keys to scroll the window to reveal the hidden portions of the screen. Press Esc to cancel scrolling.

To move text from what appears in the DOS window into the Clipboard, first mark the area of interest and then use the Copy command to move the text to the Clipboard. Move to the destination application and select its Paste command to insert the data. Remember that the receiving application must be able to use the raw text information (for instance, you may not be able to paste text from a DOS program into a graphics program).

Running OS/2 Applications

Objective E.1

Windows NT Workstation can run OS/2 1.x applications on Intel-based systems with little trouble. The properties for these programs work the same as those you've seen for DOS applications. Some limitations apply to the types of OS/2 1.x applications you can run:

- ◆ You can run only character-based applications, not graphical applications that make use of OS/2's Presentation Manager (the OS/2 graphical windowing capability).

Tip You can purchase a product from Microsoft called "Windows NT Add-on Subsystem for Presentation Manager," which allows some Presentation Manager-based OS/2 1.x applications to run. This product does not come with Windows NT Workstation and is designed as an aid to helping programmers port Presentation Manager OS/2 applications to Windows NT.

- ◆ You can run only OS/2 1.x applications on X86-based computers.

◆ OS/2 applications designed for OS/2 2.x or greater aren't supported.

◆ OS/2 programs that require that the OS/2 IOPL (Input-Output Privilege Level) setting be set to YES cannot run under Windows NT Workstation 4.

◆ Programs that require OS/2-based device drivers cannot be used with Windows NT Workstation 4.

◆ Some OS/2 API calls aren't supported.

◆ OS/2 programs will not run on RISC-based systems with one exception: FAPI programs (discussed in the following note) can run in MS-DOS mode within a NTVDM.

Note | Some programs are written using a technique that includes both OS/2 executable code and DOS executable code within the same program file. Such programs are called *Family API (FAPI) programs, bound applications,* or sometimes *Dual-Mode applications.* When you run such programs under Windows NT Workstation, they always run using the OS/2 subsystem and not the MS-DOS subsystem. You can force a FAPI application to run in DOS mode with the FORCEDOS command.

Even with those limitations, quite a number of OS/2 1.x applications run without trouble under Windows NT Workstation. Figure 19.11 shows a program called SlickEdit for OS/2 running in a window on the Windows NT Workstation desktop, for example.

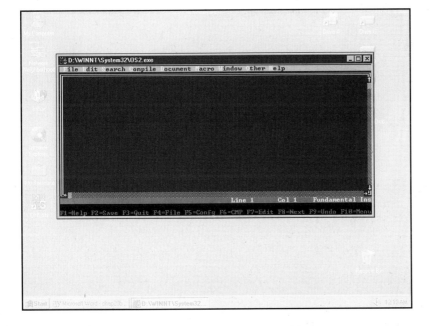

Figure 19.11

SlickEdit for OS/2 can run under Windows NT Workstation 4.

> **Note** If you look in the title bar of the OS/2 window in figure 19.11, you can see that the program is using the OS/2 subsystem in Windows NT, which is called D:\WINNT\System32\OS2.exe.

Understanding POSIX Applications

Objective E.1

POSIX is a standard Applications Programming Interface standard for Unix and psuedo-Unix systems. Programs using this API can run on any POSIX-compliant system. Under Windows NT, the POSIX subsystem is loaded whenever a POSIX application is run. The subsystem is made up of the following three files:

◆ **PSXSS.EXE.** A Win32 application that supports the entire POSIX subsystem.

◆ **POSIX.EXE.** A Win32 application that interacts between the POSIX subsystem and the Windows NT Executive Services.

◆ **PSXDLL.DLL.** A program that runs in the same memory space as the POSIX program and communicates between the POSIX program and the POSIX subsystem.

POSIX applications that need to access data files will only run with a disk partition formatted using NTFS. On an NTFS partition, POSIX applications use case-sensitive file names, unlike any other subsystem in Windows NT (or Windows NT itself), which are all case-insensitive. Also, NTFS supports the POSIX requirement for a feature called *hard links*, which is somewhat similar to shortcuts in Windows NT.

POSIX programs are compiled for specific types of computer systems. If you are using an Intel-based Windows NT system, you will need to make sure you're using an Intel version of the POSIX program.

Getting to an MS-DOS Command Prompt

You don't need to distinguish between a Windows NT command prompt and an MS-DOS command prompt; the Windows NT prompt automatically starts DOS programs (or other subsystem programs) and uses the same commands that you're familiar with from DOS. You access the command prompt by opening the Start menu, choosing Programs, and then choosing the Command Prompt command.

You use command prompts with DOS and OS/2 programs for a variety of purposes. For instance, you open a command prompt to install DOS or OS/2 programs, following whatever installation instructions come with the program. You can also use command prompts to execute DOS and OS/2 programs by typing the name of the program at the command line, with your current directory set to the location of the application.

Troubleshooting the Running of Non-Windows Applications

Provided a non-Windows application meets the compatibility requirements under Windows NT, there are few problems you will experience. There are some, however, to which you need to be able to respond.

**Objective
G.4**

DOS applications cannot take control of the computer hardware. Windows NT will prevent this from happening. Some DOS programs, however, may be dissatisfied with the hardware emulation that Windows NT provides. There is no real recourse to this problem; it's a fundamental incompatibility with the DOS program in question.

Similarly, some DOS programs require a specific version of DOS under which to run because they make use of some internal DOS memory structures; these change from DOS version to DOS version. There is no way to satisfy such requirements under Windows NT.

A checklist follows of possibilities you should pursue when you are having trouble with a non-Windows application:

◆ Are you certain that the application meets Windows NT's compatibility requirements? Does it require direct access to the computer hardware?

◆ Can the supplier of the program state whether it has been tested with Windows NT and whether it should work or not? Some software providers may have certain settings that you need to make in order to get their programs to run under Windows NT. Call the program's supplier if you're having trouble. They may tell you that their program is unsupported under Windows NT; however, they will also usually tell you if it *should* work or not (only that they won't take responsibility if it doesn't work properly).

◆ Have you made sure that the appropriate device drivers and other support programs for a DOS program are present in the CONFIG.NT and AUTOEXEC.NT files, and does the DOS program indicate the correct files in its Properties dialog box?

◆ If you are having trouble with a POSIX program, it may make use of unsupported API calls. If so, it cannot run under Windows NT.

◆ Are there any online discussion groups that concern the program you're trying to run? If so, has anyone else been successful in getting the program to run? Asking this question in support forums or USENET groups can often uncover successful tips to getting a program to run. You can also ask in discussion groups oriented to Windows NT.

◆ Have you made sure that a POSIX program is running on and using an NTFS-formatted partition?

◆ Have you tried methodically adjusting different settings in the program's Properties dialog box? Key settings to look at for DOS programs include everything on the Memory tab, the Fast ROM emulation and Dynamic Memory settings on the Screen tab, and the Compatible Timer Hardware Emulation on the Program tab.

◆ Sometimes, when a program appears to start but then never fully initializes, you simply have to wait for a while. Because of the virtualized hardware support in Windows NT, a given program may take much longer under Windows NT to completely initialize than it does under DOS. If possible, it's not a bad idea to start the program and let it continue to try to start for ten minutes.

◆ Make sure you examine the Windows NT Event Viewer if a non-Windows application fails to start. You may find error messages in the Event Viewer that indicate the cause of the problem and suggest a solution.

◆ Try searching the Microsoft Knowledge Base using the name of the program as your search word. Microsoft may have already learned about the program you're trying to use, and there may be an application note about running it, being unable to run it, needing a Service Pack of Windows NT first, or whatever.

◆ Do you have the latest Service Pack for Windows NT? Sometimes updates to Windows NT allow programs to run that otherwise wouldn't.

◆ You can try running an offending DOS program on another system, particularly one that is based on a different processor family than the one on which you've been trying. If you've been trying on an Intel-based system, try a RISC-based system, and vice versa.

End Note: You can create different sets of properties for a single DOS program. For instance, you may have a program that does different things when you use different command-line parameters. You can create multiple shortcuts to the program and then modify the properties for each shortcut. Unlike the relationship between a program and its PIF, shortcuts maintain their individual settings for the program they reference.

Test Your Knowledge

1. DOS programs run under Windows NT using what component?

    A. DOS Compatibility Box

    B. Virtual x86 Mode

    C. NT Virtual DOS Machine

    D. DOS on Windows (DOW)

2. Which of the following would cause a DOS program to *not* run under Windows NT?

    A. Requires a specific version of DOS

    B. Requires direct access to the computer hardware

    C. Uses a graphical mode under DOS

    D. Requires updates to a CONFIG.SYS or AUTOEXEC.BAT file

3. On RISC-based computers, DOS programs are supported with an additional mechanism not found on Intel-based systems:

    A. An add-on card that includes an Intel processor

    B. Virtual x86 Mode

    C. An Instruction Execution Unit that emulates an Intel 80486 processor

    D. DOS programs are not supported under Windows NT on RISC-based computers

4. Which of the following types of programs take advantage of the NTVDM subsystem, by default?

    A. MS-DOS applications

    B. OS/2 applications

    C. Family API (FAPI) applications

    D. Windows 95 applications

5. When you modify the Properties dialog box for a DOS application, the settings are stored in:

    A. The Windows NT Registry.

    B. A special NTVDM Registry.

    C. A .PIF file that shares the same main file name as the program file name and is stored in the same directory.

    D. You cannot change settings for DOS-based applications.

6. Which of the following statements are true about DOS applications under Windows NT?

   A. DOS applications require NTFS-formatted disk partitions.

   B. Each DOS application running uses its own private NTVDM.

   C. You cannot use the Windows NT clipboard with DOS applications.

   D. You can force a Family API (FAPI) program to use a NTVDM with the FORCEDOS command.

7. Which of the following statements are true about OS/2-based applications under Windows NT?

   A. OS/2 Presentation Manager programs are supported, so long as they are written for OS/2 1.x.

   B. Some OS/2 API calls are not supported under Windows NT.

   C. OS/2 programs require an NTFS-formatted disk partition on which to run.

   D. You can use OS/2-based device drivers to support an OS/2 program, but they must be loaded into the CONFIG.SYS file properly.

8. Which of the following statements are true about POSIX-based applications under Windows NT?

   A. POSIX applications must be compiled for the type of processor the computer is using.

   B. POSIX applications require an NTFS-formatted disk partition against which to perform file access.

   C. POSIX applications require case-sensitive file names.

   D. POSIX "hard links" are not supported under Windows NT.

9. Using the START command to start a program at the NORMAL priority corresponds to what priority level number?

   A. 4

   B. 7

   C. 13

   D. 26

Test Your Knowledge Answers

1. C
2. A,B
3. C
4. A
5. C
6. B,C
7. B
8. A,B,C
9. B

PART V

Networking with NT 4

Chapter Snapshot

With Windows NT Workstation 4, you can participate in peer-to-peer Windows Workgroups, in client/server network operating systems as part of a Windows NT Server-based domain, or with any other network operating system that enables Windows clients. To connect Windows NT to your network, you must familiarize yourself with the following topics in this chapter:

Windows NT
Workstation 4

CHAPTER 20

Installing Network Options

One of the great strengths of Windows networking is the large variety of network types in which this operating system can participate. Through software, Windows can be a client in Novell NetWare IPX networks, Internet/intranet TCP/IP networks, NetBUEI, and so on. You will learn about all these software protocols in this chapter. The good news is that most network add-in cards, called Network Interface Cards (NICs), support all these protocols.

To begin, you must install into your computer a network adapter that is compatible with the bus structure. For most client workstations these days, the common bus types are ISA or, more recently, PCI buses (although you might even have EISA workstations). In the sections that follow, you'll learn what you need to know to buy and install the correct network adapter card into your computer.

Installing a Network Adapter

In many instances, you order a Network Interface Card (NIC) for a computer to be used in a networking environment when you first purchase the computer—essentially, a NIC it is part of the package. The computer vendor matches your NIC with the type of bus that the computer has. The only question that arises is what type of network hardware you intend to use.

For example, several Ethernet configurations are available, including the following common types:

- ◆ **10BaseT.** This most common kind of Ethernet configuration uses coaxial cabling that looks like black rope connected with BNC connectors.

- ◆ **10Base5.** This Ethernet variety works with a maximum 500-meter cable length.

- ◆ **10Base2.** This Ethernet variety uses twisted-pair wiring that resembles your phone line.

- ◆ **100BaseT.** This configuration is a newer, fast networking Ethernet protocol.

Ethernet is a networking protocol in which packets are broadcast until the computer at the correct address answers the call. The first number in the name refers to the speed—this means that 10BaseT and 10Base2 both run at 10 Mbps. 100BaseT, used now in network backbones, runs at 100 Mbps. Ethernet has been codified as an IEEE standard and uses a standardized packet structure.

When you buy an Ethernet card, you must specify the type of Ethernet networking hardware protocol in which your NT Workstation 4 must participate. What you are really specifying is mostly the connection and cabling type. For 100BaseT, you specify not only a different connection and cable type but also a different packet structure.

In the case of similar speeds—10BaseT and 10Base2—you often can buy combo cards that contain two or more connection types. You should do so because there is little, if any, penalty for using them. In addition, you can buy adapters that convert the output of one Ethernet NIC to another. This isn't the case when one of the hardware protocols differs significantly from the other, such as a 100BaseT. In such a case, your decision to switch to another Ethernet protocol would require the purchase of a separate NIC.

Ethernet isn't the only network hardware protocol that is used in networking NT Workstation 4, but it is by far the most common one. Other networking standards you will find include the following:

- ◆ **Twisted-pair.** Many low-cost network boards used in peer-to-peer networking use twisted-pair wiring. This wiring is similar to, and in some cases identical to, phone wiring. Twisted-pair wiring can be either unshielded twisted-pair (UTP) or shielded twisted-pair (STP).

Some twisted-pair networking solutions can actually use the extra wires in your building's phone system for networking. This type of network is appropriate for low-speed connections and small workgroups.

◆ **Token Ring.** A Token Ring network is used in many companies that have made a hardware commitment to IBM products. The topology is that of a "logical" ring and a physical bus. You need a Token Ring board to participate in a Token Ring network.

◆ **Fiber-optic networks.** This form of cabling uses special light-transmitting glass. NIC cards for fiber-optic networks are expensive, so this type is rarely used in a workstation. Fiber-optic cabling is often used to connect servers in a WAN as a backbone connection.

◆ **Wireless LANs.** In this network, the NIC transmits network signals without cable. Signals are either infrared (and thus require line-of-sight or reflection from a hard surface) or RF (radio) transmissions.

An RF network can transmit about 500 feet through walls and floors. In either case, these methods are slow transmission media, appropriate for word-processing applications and data entry but not high-speed applications.

Each of these different types of networks requires a different type of network card, different cabling, and different connectors. Each offers different transmission speeds, lengths of cable before attenuation is required, and costs. As a measure of cost, I have worked with Ethernet combo cards costing as little as $30, and as much as $175, with both providing acceptable service. At the high end are wireless LANs requiring $300–$600 per node for the network interface. The cost of fiber-optic networks mainly results from the cabling. An average network card generally runs between $50 and $200.

The NICs you purchase will prove the axiom that you get what you pay for. Spend some money to get the following advantages:

◆ Better construction

◆ Improved installation software

◆ Faster direct memory access (DMA) through bus mastering

Note *Bus mastering* is a technique in which a direct memory access (DMA) chip on the NIC communicates directly with your computer's CPU.

◆ Release of updated network drivers for new operating system releases

◆ Companies that might survive into the next millennium

◆ Companies that have people who will answer the phones

For a network administrator, these are properties to be greatly treasured. Unless you are in a strict cost-cutting environment, using low-priced NICs is probably not the best way to achieve savings.

Most NIC cards are reliable, and they either work or don't work when you first try them in your computer. A preconfigured computer should have had its NIC cards already tested before an administrator's reputation is on the line in an important installation.

Installing the Card

Although some computers contain networking built into the motherboard, this is very uncommon. For the most part, you install a network card by placing that card into one of your computer's expansion slots. Depending on your computer's case, power supply, and bus configuration, most computers come with either three, five, or six expansion slots. Computers with special high-speed buses, such as VESA (used for video boards), have an extra expansion slot.

In most instances, you can install your NIC into any available slot.

Caution | Make very sure that you properly seat your NIC, because a loose network board can cause difficulties that are hard to track down. In the best case, a loosely seated NIC does not operate at all (if you are lucky); in the worst case, a daisy-chain configuration (coax Ethernet) interrupts one workstation, which brings down every workstation on that leg. It's like those Christmas tree lights that shut down if one bulb burns out.

Windows NT Workstation 4 is not yet Plug and Play (PnP) certified. Although Microsoft promises PnP in Windows NT Workstation 5, it is not there now, meaning your computer will not self-configure the network board to achieve hardware settings that do not conflict with other hardware in your computer. As with any board installation, you must pay particular attention to the IRQ number and the Base I/O address that the board uses. Common IRQ numbers are 3 and 10. There are many Base I/O addresses that can be used.

A NIC card can have its Interrupt Requests (IRQs) and Base I/O addresses set through hardware, software, or both. Less often, you will also have to concern yourself with direct memory access (DMA) channel settings. With a bus-mastered NIC you will not need to concern yourself with DMA. The on-board chip takes care of this detail.

If any of these terms are not familiar to you, you probably haven't suffered through a lost weekend of PC board installation—something many administrators suffer on a regular basis. However, this chapter is not the place to learn more about this topic, so you'll have to do a little homework on your own.

When hardware configuration is offered, as it is with older boards, switch the configuration of DIP switches, rocker switches, jumpers, or resistors to achieve a new setting. Your vendor's manual will show you the possibilities. When a NIC card can be software-configured, you run a program that comes on a disk that your vendor supplies to set the NIC card. Windows NT Workstation 4 Setup can change, test, and verify many software-configurable NIC cards.

You'll find that most newer NIC boards are software-configurable. As the world becomes more and more PnP (60 million Windows 95 clients and counting), software configuration is becoming the coin of the realm. I have purchased software/hardware configurable boards and had reasonable luck with them.

Software configuration is nice in that there is no fuss. If something doesn't work, you just run the configuration program again to try another setting. Depending on the vendor and the amount of care that was taken in writing the installation routine, the major difference in the "high price spread" NICs is that these NICs include software routines that can more readily discern and negotiate hardware conflicts. Because most NICs are based on standard chip sets these days, this (and the quality of construction of the board itself and, thus, its reliability) is the only difference. At the time of this writing, this is perhaps a major difference indeed. You want a NIC to install once, and you don't ever want to know about it again.

Before leaving this topic of IRQ and Base I/O settings, know this about it: setting configuration through software is convenient and doesn't require you to keep messing with the board and getting your hands dirty (or testing your eyesight with those teeny jumpers). However, when you set a board using hardware, at least you know where you are and what you have, and you only have to look at the board to determine the right settings.

Setting Up Windows NT 4 Networking

The last part of properly configuring NIC cards involves the installation of the driver software used to communicate between the Windows NT Workstation 4 operating system and the network card. As with all peripheral hardware devices, if Windows NT Setup recognizes your network card and can supply the appropriate driver, you're fine. The latest and greatest drivers most often ship on a new version of the operating system, and this is the one you definitely should use.

As your copy of the operating system ages, newer drivers generally are available from the vendor through a BBS, an Internet site, or a Windows library that Microsoft or others maintain.

If Windows either doesn't recognize your NIC or doesn't have the appropriate driver, you must use the Have Disk feature in Setup to locate the NIC driver that Windows will use. In this instance, a disk with your driver should have come with your computer, or with the NIC if you purchased it separately. Make sure that your driver is compatible with Windows NT 4—otherwise, you either might not be able to install it, or you might have difficulties. Different operating systems use different drivers for NIC cards.

NICs usually have their drivers installed during the installation of the operating system. Windows NT 4 Setup will do its best to recognize your NIC configuration, or you manually can select from a list of supported adapters and configure the proper settings for your PC or workstation.

An auto-detect feature in the networking portion of Setup detects your NIC automatically and also detects the IRQ and Base I/O addresses. If after installation your network card isn't operating properly, you can play with these settings, trying different ones until you find one that works.

> **Note** I have had the experience of selecting my network card manually and having my installation succeed where auto-detect failed. If you have difficulties with installation, you might try selecting your peripheral devices manually and configuring them after Windows NT Workstation 4 is up and running. This same technique once got me around a glitch with my video installation.
>
> In fact, in some troublesome installation procedures, I found it helpful to install the operating system with a blatant lie—I told the installation program I didn't have a network card. Then after a successful installation of the operating system (which would not have been successful if the network installation procedures had been permitted to run) I lied again and told NT 4, "Hey, I just installed a NIC; let's configure it."

You don't need to reinstall the operating system if you decide to swap NIC boards or update a driver. You can perform this feat using the Network dialog box. At most, Windows NT Workstation 4 will ask you to restart your machine to install your new settings.

Objective B.4

To configure a NIC, do the following:

1. Go to the Network dialog box by right-clicking on the Network Neighborhood icon on the Windows NT desktop and choosing Properties.

You also can click on the Start Button, choose Settings, then choose Control Panel, and double-click on the Network icon. In either case, you see the Network dialog box on your screen.

2. Click on the Adapters tab in the Network dialog box, as shown in figure 20.1.

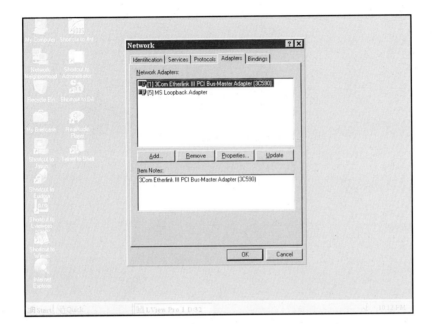

Figure 20.1

The Adapters tab of the Network dialog box is empty until you install an adapter.

A list of the network adapters that are currently installed on your system appears in the Network Adapter list. If no network adapters are installed, the list will be blank.

3. To add a network adapter to the list, click on the Add button.

   The Select Network Adapter dialog box shown in figure 20.2 appears.

4. Choose the NIC of the type installed in your computer from the list in the Select Network Adapter dialog box; then click the OK button.

5. Choose your NIC's IRQ, Base I/O address, and (if applicable) the Transceiver Type from the Network Card Setup dialog box. An example is shown in figure 20.3.

6. Click on the OK button, and the adapter with the settings you selected is installed on your list.

   You also can double-click on an installed adapter to view the current Network Card Setup dialog box and change its settings.

Figure 20.2

*The Select
Network Adapter
dialog box lists
supported NICs.*

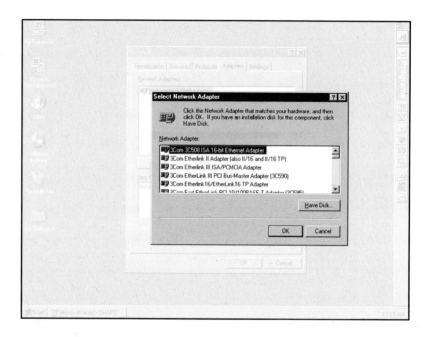

Figure 20.3

*This Network
Card Setup dialog
box reflects the
configuration for
a Novell NE2000
compatible
network card.*

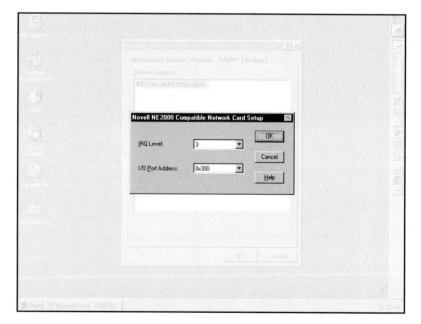

7. Click on the OK button to confirm your choices.

    Windows will post an alert box telling you to restart your computer to install the
    new settings. You can do this now or at a later time.

If your NIC is not listed, check with your NIC's manufacturer to see if it is compatible with any of the NICs in the Windows NT 4 Hardware Compatibility List (HCL) or if your NIC has a separate driver disk for Windows NT.

Many NICs can be installed using the Novell NE2000 Adapter because they are rated NE2000-compatible. For those who have been around networks a while (especially NetWare), these are all the NICs we used to call Anthem/Eagle.

If your NIC has a separate driver disk, or if you have obtained the driver files from the manufacturer and copied them to a directory on your hard disk, click on the Have Disk button. You will be presented with an Insert Disk dialog box that asks you to locate your driver. Normally you use a disk in drive A, or enter the path to a drive and directory containing the driver files and the OEMSETUP.INF file for your card. Click on the OK button to return to the Network dialog box and install your driver files.

Installation of an NT driver for your NIC card represents the last portion of the configuration of a NIC in Windows NT 4 Workstation. That isn't to say, however, that there aren't additional things that you should know about network installation.

Prior to your installation, you should check to see if your NIC is one of the following cards:

◆ **ISA.** This covers any ISA card (such as a 3C0M 3C509 Etherlink III or a Novell/ Eagle NE2000 compatible). For those cards, you must select the correct I/O port address, Interrupt Number, and Transceiver Type (if necessary).

◆ **PCI and EISA.** These NICs are typically self-configuring, and this extra step usually is not necessary. EISA cards should be installed with your PC's EISA configuration utility before you start Windows NT. The Interrupt Number for PCI interface cards is set using your PC's BIOS setup program and is associated with the slot in which the PCI card is installed. If your PC has more than one hardware bus (for example, a machine with both PCI and EISA) and you are installing an ISA card, you must specify which hardware bus you are using for the NIC, as well as the slot number in which the NIC is installed.

◆ **NE2000 clones.** These cards are set in software, although NT expects them to be set using jumpers. To install these cards correctly, you should run their installation program under DOS first to obtain the correct IRQ and Base I/O settings.

The annoying thing to watch out for is that because NT 4 expects these cards to use jumpers, it presents a limited number of choices in the configuration process (the old jumper-set cards offered just a few IRQ choices). Though the software-setup procedure lets you configure the NIC for INT 15, because that's not available in the old NE2000 NICs, it's not presented.

| Note | I've successfully installed an NE2000 clone set for INT 15 and I/O 0x280 by choosing a Novell NE2000 adapter rather than the "compatible" choice. Apparently NT 4 does know that the newer models can be software set with a larger range of settings but thinks the "compatible" model applies only to the old cards. |

To change the settings for a NIC, select that adapter in the Network Adapter list of the Network dialog box. Then click the Properties button to view the Network Card Setup dialog box. This action is the same as double-clicking on the name itself.

Objective B.4

To remove a NIC from the adapter list, click on the name to highlight it, and then click on the Remove button. Windows will ask you to confirm your action.

If the driver for your NIC is updated by your manufacturer at a later date, choose the adapter in the Network Adapter list and click on the Update button. You then will be prompted for a disk/directory path containing the driver files and the OEMSETUP.INF file for your card, just as you were when the driver wasn't one that Windows NT 4 Setup recognized.

Now that you have your networking hardware installed, you'll want to know more about networking protocols. Networking protocols are the things that make a Novell Network a "Novell Network" and an Internet an "Internet." and so on. They are software routines that use the hardware and driver software you have just installed.

Understanding Network Protocols

LANs, WANs, intranets, and networking in general require protocols to have information successfully transmitted and received. Protocols include the following:

- ◆ The way data is packaged for transmission
- ◆ The size of the data byte or word used in data transmission
- ◆ Any data-compression methods
- ◆ Error-correction methods
- ◆ Methods used to address transmissions and to signal that the transmission was received

Windows NT's networking foundation is based on NDIS(Network Driver Interface Specification). This is an abstractive data-link layer that enables multiple network protocols to talk to your NIC simultaneously. You can think of the NDIS as a special kind of multidriver interface that enables the Application layer (in the OSI/ISO 7-layer model) to talk to the hardware layer through your NIC card.

Before the wide implementation of NDIS in the computer industry, PC operating systems used monolithic device drivers to communicate with NIC cards and to transmit protocols on networks. These device drivers required that either the protocol driver or the NIC be swapped in order to implement a new networking protocol.

NDIS was created by 3COM and Microsoft to solve a design flaw of early monolithic device drivers in which PCs could only participate on one type of network at a time because the driver only enabled the use of one network transport protocol per NIC. So, using NDIS, you can have several network transport protocols operating simultaneously using the same NIC, without having to change or even know which protocol is in current use. Often two or more protocols are being used simultaneously.

For example, if you have the Peer Web Services installed on Windows NT Workstation 4, you might have TCP/IP data transmission occurring at the same time that a local computer is seeking data from a database using NetBEUI. Both services run in a multithreaded Windows NT operating system without conflict.

Novell also was able to solve the one-protocol-per-NIC problem by creating its own datalink standard, known as ODI (Open Datalink Interface). For compatibility reasons, NDIS 3.1 and 4.0 protocols can run on Windows NT with ODI data-link drivers and other ODI protocols.

The sections that follow describe the protocols supported by Windows NT 4 that are part of the NDIS 3.1 specification. Their intended applications are also described.

Installing Network Protocols

Transport protocols are what actually communicate with your LAN, WAN, and the Internet. Windows NT Workstation and Server are unique in that they support a wide range of network protocols, some or all of which can operate on the network at the same time. That's why a Windows NT Workstation (and Server) can be clients (and servers) on NT Server-based networks (using NetBEUI), on Novell NetWare networks (using IPX/SPX), on Internets/intranets (using TCP/IP), and so on. It is this support of different protocols that makes NT such a good networking neighbor—or, if you are Novell-centric, such a good Trojan horse.

The Setup program of Windows NT Workstation 4 prompts you for your networking protocol and offers you all three of the choices mentioned in the previous paragraph. If you know what protocols are in current use, select them. Setup will proceed. For TCP/IP, you must know the IP address and Subnet address, or network installation will fail (or appear to fail). You learn more about this later in the chapter. In the case of NetBEUI or IPX/SPX, no further information is required.

As in all things NT, you can install or modify a network protocol after the operating system is installed. It's easy and straightforward.

Objective D.1

To install a protocol, do the following:

1. Open the Network dialog box by double-clicking on that icon in the Control Panel.

2. Click on the Protocols tab in the Network dialog box.

   A list of your installed protocols appears on the Protocols tab (see fig. 20.4). If no network protocols are installed, the list will be blank.

Figure 20.4

The Protocols tab in the Network dialog box lists existing protocols.

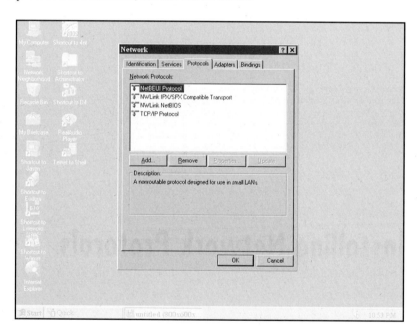

3. Click on the Add button to view the Select Network Protocol dialog box, as shown in figure 20.5.

4. Choose a network protocol from the list in the Select Network Protocol dialog box by clicking on its name and then clicking on the OK button.

   If any additional configuration steps are required, you will be presented with the appropriate dialog boxes.

Caution Several protocols, such as TCP/IP and AppleTalk, involve several additional steps for correct configuration. Please see the following sections on configuring network services and settings for more information on how to configure for your network.

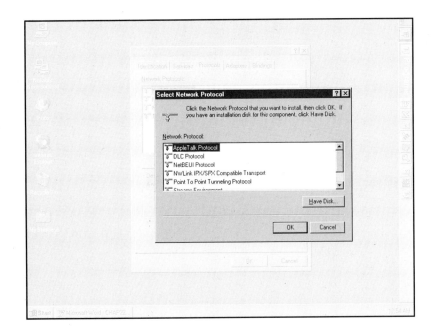

Figure 20.5

The Select Network Protocol dialog box shows the protocols available for installation.

5. After you have finished installing protocols, click on the OK button.

   Windows will inform you that your protocol was successfully installed and will prompt you to restart your computer for the changes to take effect.

One of the things you will notice immediately is you can install several other protocols manually (using the procedure above) that weren't available in the Setup program for Windows NT Workstation 4 itself. For example, the AppleTalk protocol, which is necessary for Apple Macintosh clients, requires manual installation after the fact.

NetBEUI or NBF

Microsoft's NBF implementation of the NetBEUI (NetBIOS Extended User Interface) protocol is automatically installed as a transport protocol whenever you install a LAN card in Windows NT. NetBEUI offers the advantage of being a very fast protocol that does not require a lot of resource overhead to run on your PC. NetBEUI is the default protocol used by Microsoft Windows for Workgroups, Windows 95 Peer Networking, Microsoft OS/2 LAN Manager, IBM OS/2 Peer Networking, and IBM OS/2 LAN Server. If you have any of these kinds of networks, Windows NT can share resources from all of these using NetBEUI.

Although NetBEUI is a good choice for smaller networks, such as a regional office or even a two-node peer-to-peer network installed in your home, it is not a good choice for large networks. This is because NetBEUI is non-routable (which is why it is not considered to be a true network transport protocol) and thus cannot communicate between multiple network segments. A primary limitation of the NetBEUI specification is that it uses an 8-bit Local Session Number, so NetBEUI networks are limited to 256 nodes on a single network segment.

Because NetBEUI uses the actual name of your computer as an address, you cannot have two computers with the same name on the same segment. Other networking protocols use machine addresses or a dynamic system of machine address assignment and are less sensitive to this kind of conflict.

NetBEUI should not be confused with NetBIOS, which is a programming interface. This mistake often is made because early versions of the NetBEUI transport protocol on OS/2 1.x and MS-DOS provided NetBIOS services using the NetBEUI device driver. Under Windows NT, NetBEUI can be unloaded from the system, and other protocols (such as IPX and TCP/IP) still can take advantage of programs that use the NetBIOS interface. For example, Windows NT's File and Print services and popular network applications such as Lotus Notes can operate correctly with NetBIOS unloaded from the protocol stack of the NDIS.

NWLink (IPX/SPX)

NWLink is Microsoft's implementation of a pair of protocols that include Novell's IPX (Internetwork Packet Exchange) and SPX (Sequenced Packet Exchange). *IPX* is a network-layer protocol that provides datagram services. *SPX* is a transport-layer protocol that provides network connection services. IPX enables you to map your drive resources to NetWare file systems. SPX commonly is used to connect to NetWare printer queues and to communicate with application servers such as Lotus Notes (which uses SPX) and Oracle database servers (which use the SPX-based SQLNet client). NWLink also has an interface to NetBIOS that enables you to communicate over Novell NetWare networks and multiple network segments, which are connected by routers.

NWLink does not enable you to connect to NetWare servers. You must use NWLink as well as Novell's Windows NT Requester, or NWLink and Microsoft's Client Services for NetWare (CSNW), which is described in the section "Client Services for NetWare," later in the chapter.

TCP/IP

Transmission Control Protocol/Internet Protocol (TCP/IP) is an industry-standard transport protocol that is used to provide communications between many types of computer systems. Originating on the Unix operating system, it was developed by the Department of Defense in the late 1960s to preserve the government's line of communication in the event of a nuclear conflict. This means that even if the standard established network routes were destroyed, TCP/IP could adapt to the changing network environment and deliver information completely.

Since the mid-1980s, TCP/IP has become the standard protocol for the Internet and is used for the integration of many varieties of disparate computer systems. Virtually every network operating system now supports TCP/IP, and because TCP/IP supports routing as a basic element of its design, it is used to communicate among many types of network applications (World Wide Web, UseNet newsgroups, Internet Relay Chat, FTP, Telnet, SQL database server access, and so on).

The two primary disadvantages of TCP/IP are the size of its protocol stack—it's more than twice the size of NetBEUI—and its slower speed compared to other network protocols. TCP/IP is also a fairly complicated protocol to configure, compared to the other protocols described in this chapter, but the section "Configuring Network Protocols and Installing Network Services" covers that in depth.

DLC

DLC, or *Data Link Control*, is a protocol usually associated with IBM Token Ring networks. Microsoft provides DLC in Windows NT so you can communicate with IBM mainframes and AS/400 minicomputers via 3270 and 5250. DLC also is used to communicate with devices that are attached directly to your network, such as HP laser printers, instead of attaching to a printer queue or through the parallel port driver.

AppleTalk

Microsoft provides the AppleTalk protocol so you can share resources with Macintosh computers on your LAN. AppleTalk is a very slow protocol (230 Kbps). Nevertheless, it's better than nothing. Many companies have enclaves of Macs doing such things as desktop publishing and image manipulation. If you want to send files back and forth between Macs and PCs, you need AppleTalk.

To communicate with Macs using AppleTalk under Windows NT, you also must run Windows NT Server on the network that is running Windows NT Services for Macintosh.

The later section "Configuring AppleTalk" briefly describes how to configure AppleTalk with your workstation. Configuring an NT network for use with Macs is outside the scope of this book, however. For more complete information, you should read the Services for Macintosh manual that comes with NT Server.

The only instance in which having AppleTalk installed is important from a Windows NT Workstation 4 point of view is if Windows NT Workstation 4 provides network services (such as file sharing or acting as a print server) that a Macintosh client requires. Even installing the Peer Web Services in Windows NT Workstation 4 doesn't require AppleTalk because Macintosh clients can use MacTCP to communicate using the TCP/IP protocol.

Streams Environment

Streams is a multiprotocol "wrapper" facility for NWLink and TCP/IP. Streams is popular in Unix-based environments for implementing the TCP/IP protocol. Streams surrounds both the NWLink and TCP/IP protocol drivers so that all calls to and from TCP/IP and NWLink first must go through the upper layer of the Streams driver and then through NDIS.

There are various reasons why your environment may choose to implement Streams for TCP/IP and NWLink, but primarily Streams enables protocols to be organized in a modular and stackable fashion (see fig. 20.6), which conforms to the ISO's (International Standards Organization) OSI (Open Systems Interconnect) Model of Data Communications.

Figure 20.6

The ISO's OSI Model of Data Communications.

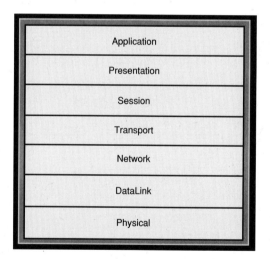

| Application |
| Presentation |
| Session |
| Transport |
| Network |
| DataLink |
| Physical |

The OSI model divides all the functionality of a computer network into seven layers: Physical, Data Link, Network, Transport, Session, Presentation, and Application.

Although it is outside the scope of this book to go into expansive detail about the OSI model and data communications in general, suffice it to say that the OSI model enables each layer to talk to the layer immediately above and below it. This section already mentioned how NDIS talks to the Data Link layer that communicates with your network card. The protocol stacks that reside on top of NDIS communicate with the Network layer. Streams just adds another layer of abstraction around TCP/IP and NWLink before those protocols can interact with the Network and the Data Link layers.

PPTP (Point-to-Point Tunneling Protocol)

PPTP enables a Windows NT 4 client using Remote Access Service (RAS) to access resources on a remote LAN by connecting to a Windows NT 4 RAS server through the Internet. This is possible by dialing into an ISP, or by connecting directly to the Internet via your LAN and a leased line to your local telecommunications provider (such as a T-1, ISDN, Frame Relay, or ATM connected to AT&T or MCI).

PPTP is new to Windows NT 4, and this network protocol supports multiprotocol virtual private networks (VPNs). This support enables remote users to access corporate networks securely across the Internet by dialing into an Internet service provider (ISP) or by connecting directly to the Internet.

Configuring Network Protocols and Installing Network Services

Now that you understand the basics of network transport protocols, you're ready to configure Windows NT with your network and install network services. This section covers connecting to various services, including Novell NetWare, Microsoft Networking, TCP/IP, SNMP, and AppleTalk. In addition, this section covers setting up Microsoft's peer version of Internet Information Server (IIS).

Objective B.5

For this section, you will use the Services tab in the Network dialog box to install network services (see fig. 20.7).

User Configurations for Mixed Network Environments

If you have a mixed NetWare and NT Server environment and you want to access resources from both of these servers simultaneously, you must make certain concessions. Windows NT Workstation 4, unlike Windows 95, requires identical UserIDs and passwords on each network operating system when both the Microsoft Networking and CSNW (Client Services for NetWare) are installed. At the very least, you will have to create a local user account on your NT Workstation for your NetWare logon name with an identical NT password as your NetWare password—otherwise, your workstation will not enable you to log on.

Many MIS environments require that you change your password after a certain period of time (usually 30 days) for your UserID in each network operating system. If your passwords expire at different times, this can become extremely inconvenient. You'll have to log on to NetWare on a non-Windows NT PC, change your password, and then log on to the NT Server and change your password to the same password you just changed it to on NetWare.

If you require that your NT Server domains and NetWare logons work simultaneously, make sure that your identical UserIDs have non-expiring passwords, or put a system in place for changing both passwords simultaneously.

Figure 20.7

Services are installed through the Services tab in the Network dialog box.

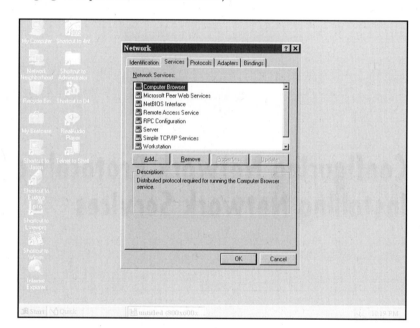

Client Services for NetWare

Novell NetWare represents roughly 70 percent of all installed network operating systems. Microsoft's support for NetWare has been traditionally somewhat less than optimal; if you required the use of NetWare NDS (NetWare Directory Services) on a NetWare 4.x LAN, you had to install Novell's ODI-based NetWare Requester for connectivity, which was ridden with bugs and known for its instability.

Fortunately, things have changed for the better in Windows NT Workstation 4. Microsoft includes Client Services for NetWare (CSNW), which enables you to connect not only to bindery-based 3.1x servers but also to NetWare 4.x NDS-based servers. You also must install the NWLink protocol to participate on a NetWare LAN. CSNW still does not support VLMs (Virtual Loaded Modules), which are a center-piece of how applications run in protected memory in NetWare.

To install Client Services for NetWare on your workstation, follow these steps:

Objective

D.3

1. Open the Network dialog box and click on the Services tab, as shown in figure 20.8.

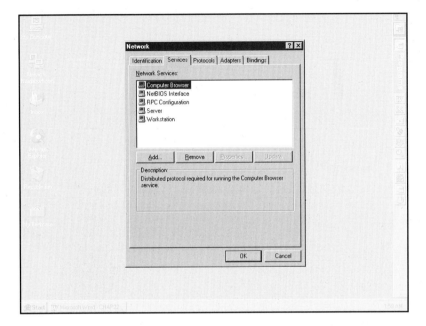

Figure 20.8

Start services configuration with the Services tab of the Network dialog box.

2. Click on the Add button.

   The system will bring up the Select Network Service dialog box, as shown in figure 20.9.

3. Highlight Client Service for NetWare, and then click on the OK button.

   You will be presented with a Windows NT Setup dialog box.

4. If the default path to the installation files is okay (such as your NT Workstation CD or a directory on your hard disk), click on Continue.

   Windows NT will copy files to your disk, and Windows will inform you that CSNW was installed. You will be asked to restart your computer to log on.

5. Restart your computer and log on to the NetWare server of your choice.

If you wish to configure CSNW, you can't just double-click on that service name in the Services tab of the Network dialog box. If you have an eagle eye, you might spot the CSNW icon that was installed in Control Panel during the previous installation. That icon is used to configure CSNW.

Figure 20.9

Choose the appropriate service from the Select Network Service dialog box.

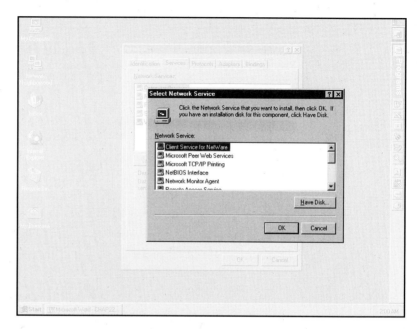

To configure CSNW, follow these steps:

1. Double-click on the CSNW icon.

   The CSNW dialog box appears, as shown in figure 20.10.

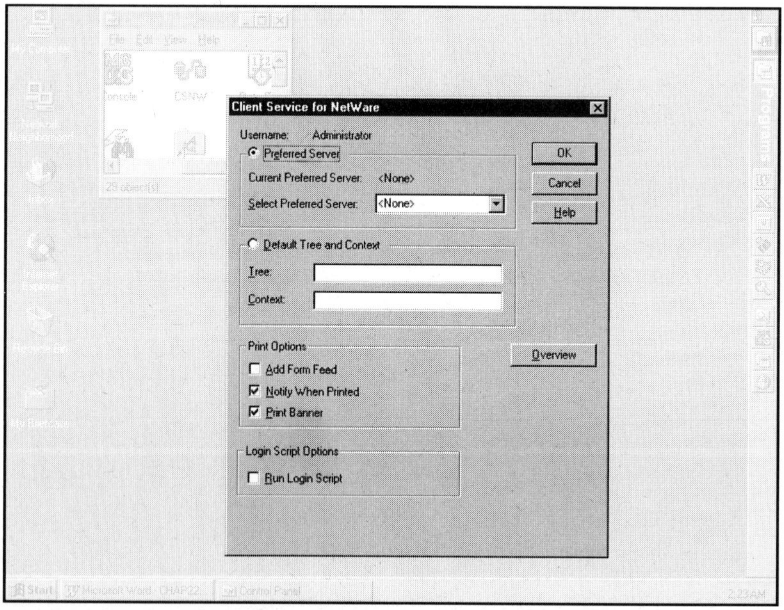

Figure 20.10

Configure CSNW with the Client Service for NetWare dialog box.

2. Enter your Preferred Server, Default Tree and Context, Print Options, and Login Script options.

   NetWare 4.x networks require you to provide the Default Tree and Context. Similarly, NetWare 3.x networks require you to enter a Preferred Server. Print Options applies to your NetWare network's local administration policy or your personal preferences.

3. Click on the OK button to enforce your selections.

   Shut down the computer and restart Windows NT to connect to your NetWare network using your new settings.

> **Tip** The Notify When Printed option can be very handy when you issue a large print job and the printer is not in your immediate vicinity or if your workgroup printer is very busy and you must wait in a long queue for your job to print.

Under the Login Script Options, deselect Run Login Script (this is enabled by default) if you want the NetWare Login Script for your user account to be processed during logon time. Some programs (such as Norton Administrator for Networks and Norton Antivirus) run during the logon process and can considerably lengthen your logon time. These programs also won't do anything useful or work properly under NT, so you might want to disable the logon script or obtain from your system administrator a different script with these programs disabled.

Configuring Microsoft Networking

To communicate with Windows NT Server, OS/2 LAN Server, Windows 95, and Windows for Workgroups, use Microsoft Networking. Because networking is part of Windows NT's core functionality, Microsoft Networking is installed by default if you add a NIC to your system. Setting up Microsoft Networking is also part of the Windows NT 4 installation because every computer on the network must belong to a Workgroup or a Windows NT Domain and have a unique name to participate on the network. Microsoft Networking can communicate with the NetBEUI, NWLink, and TCP/IP transport protocols.

When you first run Setup, you are prompted to select a Workgroup or a Domain when you set your networking settings. If your setup fails to install your network option correctly and your domain server cannot be found, one of several things could have gone wrong:

◆ Your network card might be configured improperly.

◆ Your TCP/IP protocol uses a different Subnet mask than the server.

◆ You don't have a domain, or your workstation isn't registered in the domain.

This is not an exhaustive list, but it does give you some idea of what can go wrong when you try to add NT Workstation 4 to a workgroup or, more often, to a domain.

To change the default settings for Microsoft Networking, do the following:

1. Open the Network dialog box and click on the Identification tab (this tab setting appears by default), as shown in figure 20.11.

Figure 20.11

The Identification tab of the Network dialog box shows the current computer information.

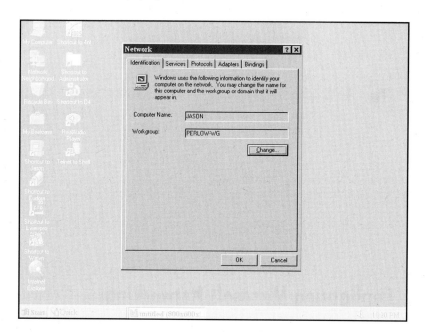

2. Click on the Change button.

   You will be presented with the Identification Changes dialog box, as shown in figure 20.12.

3. To participate in a Windows for Workgroups network or a Windows 95 peer-to-peer network, choose the Workgroup radio button and enter the name of your workgroup.

   Or, if your computer is to participate on a Windows NT or OS/2 LAN Server domain, select the Domain radio button and type in the name of your domain.

4. To add your computer to the Windows NT server domain, check the Create a Computer Account in the Domain check box and enter a user name with the right to add computers to the domain along with the password.

   In almost all instances, this is the Administrator account.

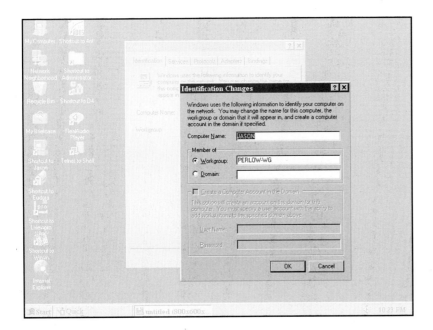

Figure 20.12

Make ID changes in the Identification Changes dialog box for Microsoft Networking.

5. Click on the OK button.

   You will be returned to the Network dialog box.

6. Click on the OK button in the Network dialog box.

   Windows will ask you to shut down your computer and restart Windows NT to connect to your Microsoft workgroup or Windows NT network.

If you have successfully installed your computer in the workgroup or domain, you will see that workgroup or domain appear in the logon dialog box when you restart your computer. After you see the Windows NT desktop, you also can determine if your installation was completed by the appearance of other workgroup or domain members in the Network Neighborhood, as well as the appearance of any network shares that exist in the Windows NT Explorer.

Configuring the NetBIOS Interface

The NetBIOS programming interface is installed automatically when you install a Network Adapter, TCP/IP, or NWLink. A set of Lana numbers is installed that lists the routes from the NetBIOS interface to the NIC drivers (see fig. 20.13). You can change the Lana number for the NetBIOS network routes by selecting the NetBIOS interface and clicking on the Properties button under the Network Services section. You normally would change these settings only if you were experiencing difficulties with NetBIOS transmissions.

Figure 20.13

The NetBIOS Configuration dialog box shows the current status.

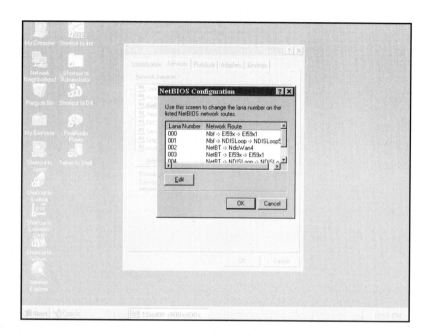

Caution │ Do not change the default Lana numbers for the NetBIOS network routes unless you are very familiar with the internal workings of Windows NT's networking subsystem. Changing the Lana number may produce unwanted or unpredictable results.

Configuring Microsoft TCP/IP

TCP/IP is becoming one of the fastest-growing network protocols in terms of popularity because it is a requirement if you want to communicate with the Internet or integrate with a myriad of other computer systems that use the TCP/IP protocol, such as Unix.

You need the following components before you begin TCP/IP installation:

◆ The IP address and hostname assigned to your personal computer (if your IP address is allocated using DHCP or WINS, you won't need to know what it is)

◆ The Subnet mask

◆ The IP address of the default router or gateway for your network segment

◆ The IP address of your Domain Name Server (DNS)

◆ The IP address of your WINS server (if your organization uses WINS)

◆ The name of your organization's domain (for example "MICROSOFT.COM" or "IBM.COM")

If any of the aforementioned terms are unfamiliar to you, you'll find a brief explanation in the following sections.

TCP/IP Basics

The inquisitive reader might be asking, "What do all those pieces of information mean?" If you represent the average Internet junkie, you are probably thinking, "Do I really need to read an introduction to TCP/IP if I'm just interested in getting my Web browser working and loading up the latest Dilbert?" For the readers who *do* want to know the significance of these things, some basic background is included here. If you're part of the second group of people who require immediate gratification and are suffering from "Net Withdrawal Syndrome," skip this section.

 Tip   If you want to learn about TCP/IP in more exhaustive detail, be sure to check out the following resource at the University of California, Davis:

gopher://gopher-chem.ucdavis.edu/11/Index/Internet_aw/Intro_the_Internet/intro.to.ip/

As previously mentioned in this chapter, TCP/IP was created by the DOD's Defense Advanced Research Project Agency (DARPA) in the late 1970s and early 1980s to deliver reliable computer data on ARPANET (the precursor to the modern Internet) in the event of a nuclear war. TCP/IP was designed to be robust, to adapt to battlefield-type conditions, and to recover automatically during a node or line failure. The upside of using TCP/IP is that it enables very large networks to be designed with little or no central management; the downside is that problems can go unnoticed for very long periods of time before they actually are diagnosed. As with any other data-communications protocol, TCP/IP is composed of layers. There are three primary layers: IP, TCP, and Sockets. A few others are used (such as UDP, ICMP, and ARP), but for the sake of brevity, these aren't covered here.

◆ **IP Layer.** IP's primary function is to move data from one node to the other, and to forward every packet of information based on a 4-byte destination address.

These destination addresses are governed by an organization known as the InterNIC, which assigns ranges of addresses to different organizations around the world. The organizations then take these ranges of addresses and partition them among their internal departments and groups. IP operates on gateway computers (or routers, as they are commonly called) that move data from department to department in an organization, to regional areas, and around the world.

◆ **TCP Layer.** TCP's primary function is to verify that the information carried by IP is correct. Whereas IP is an addressing scheme, TCP is the transmission-control protocol that determines how TCP/IP data is transmitted (packaged). Because data can be corrupted or lost between the client application and the server, TCP adds support for the detection of lost or corrupted data and re-initiates the data transfer until the data arrives at its destination in its original form.

◆ **Sockets Layer.** The Sockets layer defines how TCP/IP is implemented (it's a programming interface) on client computer systems. On many forms of Unix, TCP/IP is implemented using BSD Sockets, which is a standard that originated on Berkeley Unix or BSD. Windows NT 4 uses Winsock version 2.0, which is 32-bit and backward-compatible with applications that run on the 16-bit Winsock 1.x implementation used in Windows 3.1.

The following sections go into more detail on these three important building blocks for internetworking and intranetworking computers.

IP Addresses

On a LAN, the TCP/IP address is bound to the MAC address, which is composed of information unique to the NIC hardware vendor and a unique number. TCP/IP assigns a unique number to every IP address in the world. This IP number is a 4-byte value that is expressed by converting each byte into a decimal number (0–255) and separating the bytes with a period. For example, the Microsoft Web Server is 198.105.232.30.

To get a block of addresses, an organization sends an e-mail message to InterNIC requesting a network number assignment. IP networks are classified as Class C, Class B, or Class A, depending on their size and capacity. Class C networks are assigned to smaller organizations, of which the first three bytes identify the network and the last byte identifies the individual computer.

A Class C network has a capacity of 254 hosts in a universe of two million assignable C numbers. Larger organizations can obtain a Class B network, in which the first two bytes identify the network and the last two bytes identify each of up to 65,534 individual workstations out of a universe of 16,382 possible B assignments. The largest network available, Class A, enables 16 million (16,777,214) nodes on a network. Only 126 Class A addresses are available in the InterNIC scheme.

After it is assigned a network number, the organization connects to the Internet using a regional network provider (such as AT&T, MCI, NYNEX, Bell Atlantic, Pacific Bell, or BBN). The network provider then takes that network number and adds it to the routing configuration in its own machines and those of the other major network providers.

Although individual networks don't need to determine network numbers or provide explicit routing from one network to another, most Class B networks are managed internally as much smaller and simpler versions of the larger network organizations. Using a method known as subnetting, smaller organizations subdivide the two bytes available for internal assignment into a one-byte department number and a one-byte workstation ID. As the first three bytes designate the department, a subnet mask is defined as 255.255.255.0 (255 is the largest byte value and represents the number with all bits turned on). It is an MIS convention that station number 1 is reserved for the default gateway or router within a department's network segment.

DNS

Domain Name Server (DNS) is the computer on your network that translates these 4-byte IP addresses, such as "205.216.146.70," to the recognizable names such as "www.yahoo.com." Every organization must maintain its own DNS or, at the very least, have access to one at its network provider. Otherwise, you can't resolve a name into a pronounceable TCP/IP address. Because users are comfortable with referring to World Wide Web sites and FTP sites as names and not numbers, having a working DNS is extremely important when using any TCP/IP client-server application.

From the standpoint of your LAN running TCP/IP, a domain might have one or more servers providing TCP/IP services on it. Even an NT 4 workstation can provide TCP/IP services to other computers when the Peer Web Services are installed.

DNS resolves the different named servers in a TCP/IP network, just as it does on the Internet. If you log on to http://www.microsoft.com, the fact that a couple hundred or more servers provide services to World Wide Web clients is transparent to you, the browser. You enter an address such as http://www.microsoft.com/ntwork4/index.html, and wherever that document is located, your request for the document is serviced. Similarly, for NT Workstation 4 in a LAN, DNS provides this same transparent location service that frees the user from needing to know the actual name of your server in a Web application.

This is not the case for other services such as FTP or Gopher, two of the other services in IIS, and the Peer Web Services of NT Workstation 4. In these services, you are presented with hierarchical directories of server names in order to navigate to your documents.

Fully Qualified Domain Names

A Fully Qualified Domain Name Service (FQDNS) might be something like guido.funnyapps.com, where "guido" is the server or host in the domain "funnyapps.com." The suffix indicates that funnyapps is a commercial enterprise. Other common domain identifiers are edu for education, gov for government, mil for military, net for network service provider, and org for nonprofit organization.

The hostname (usually determined by your DNS administrator) is used by the DNS to resolve your IP address and to identify your station to other computers while using TCP/IP applications. Although it isn't an absolute requirement that you have a hostname, if you're going to run TCP/IP server applications on your workstation (such as Peer Web Services), you'll want to be able to give an easy-to-remember name to people who will connect to your computer rather than using just some numerical IP address.

With an FQDNS, you can compose a Uniform Resource Locator (URL) that can be used by any computer connected through the TCP/IP protocol to your network to locate and communicate with that computer.

The domain name is used by the DNS to resolve your IP network number and to identify your network to other computers while using TCP/IP applications.

DHCP and WINS

Dynamic Host Configuration Protocol (DHCP) is a Unix server protocol standard used for the random assignment of IP addresses to a workstation. Microsoft implements DHCP on NT Server and uses the database of computer names provided by Windows Internet Name Service (WINS) to resolve client names. When you connect a Windows NT or Windows 95 computer to your LAN and your NT server is running WINS, your computer is assigned an IP address automatically by WINS. The upside of using WINS or DHCP on your network is that after you assign a large block of addresses to give to your WINS or DHCP server, you don't have to keep track of those addresses or give them out on a gradual basis. The downside is that anyone who connects a new PC to your LAN can gain access to the Internet. In addition, tracing network problems through applications such as OpenView can be difficult because network administrators use the broadcasted MAC address to narrow down the problem (such as a collision, bad packets, or a bandwidth hog), which is usually associated with a static IP stored in a database.

Now that you have an idea of what happens behind the scenes on your TCP/IP network and you have your configuration information for your workstation in front of you (or committed to memory), you know enough to configure TCP/IP on Windows NT.

**Objective
D.4**

To configure TCP/IP on your workstation, follow these steps:

1. Install the TCP/IP protocol as instructed in the section "Installing Network Protocols" earlier in this chapter.

2. Click on the Protocols tab of the Network dialog box.

3. Highlight TCP/IP, and then click on the Properties button.

   You will be presented with the Microsoft TCP/IP Properties dialog box, as shown in figure 20.14.

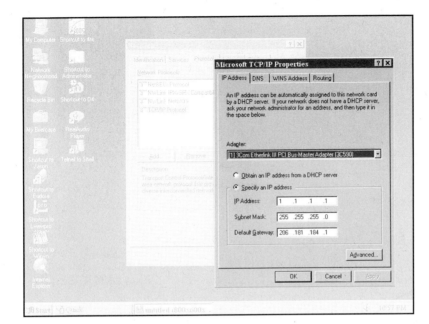

Figure 20.14

Specify your adapter in the IP Address tab of the Microsoft TCP/IP Properties dialog box.

4. Highlight the particular network adapter in the IP Address tab to which your IP address will apply.

5. If your computer's IP address is to be assigned by DHCP (Dynamic Host Configuration Protocol), select the Obtain an IP Address from a DHCP server radio button.

6. If your IP address is static, select the Specify an IP Address radio button. Enter the IP address, the Subnet Mask, and the Default Gateway in the spaces provided.

7. Click on the DNS tab in the Microsoft TCP/IP Properties dialog box, as shown in figure 20.15.

8. In the Domain Name System section, enter your computer's Host Name and the Domain name of your TCP/IP network in the spaces provided.

9. In the DNS Service Search Order section, click on the Add button.

10. Enter the IP Address for your Domain Name Server in the space provided in the TCP/IP DNS Server dialog box, and click on the Add button.

    If you have more than one DNS server, repeat step 8.

11. Click on the close button, then choose OK to back out through the dialog boxes.

    Windows informs you that you need to restart your computer to install your settings.

12. Shut down your computer and restart Windows NT to connect to your TCP/IP network.

Figure 20.15

The DNS tab of the Microsoft TCP/IP Properties dialog box is for host and domain information.

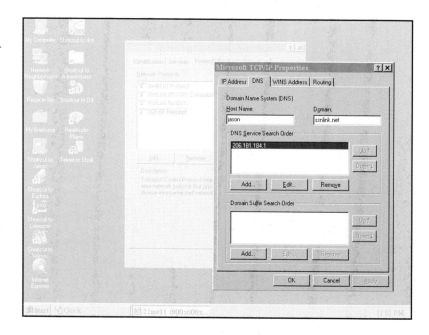

To install Windows Internet Name Service (WINS), follow these steps:

1. Click on the WINS Address tab in the Microsoft TCP/IP Properties dialog box, as shown in figure 20.16.

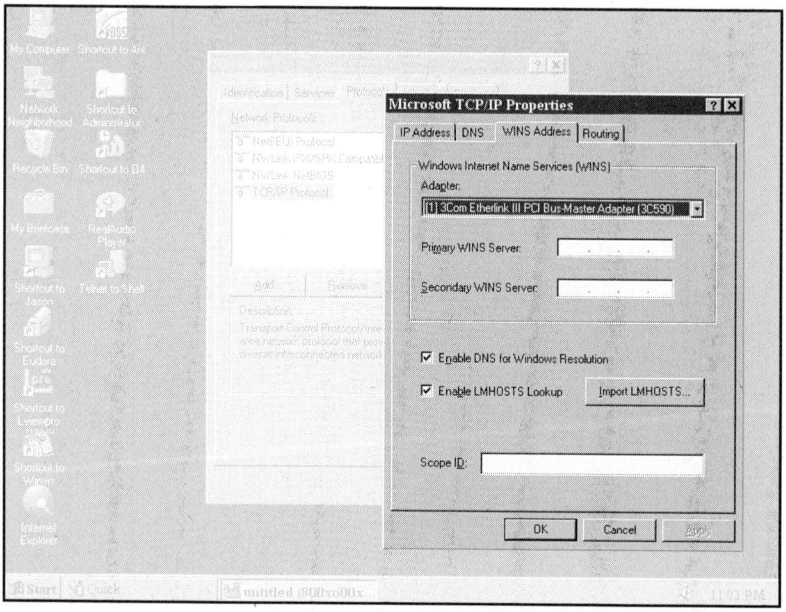

Figure 20.16

The WINS Address tab of the Microsoft TCP/IP Properties dialog box holds IP address information.

2. In the Windows Internet Name Services section, enter the IP Addresses for the Primary WINS Server and the Secondary WINS Server (if available).

   WINS resolves NetBIOS names on a TCP/IP network.

3. If you have a LMHOSTS file for looking up the names for hosts on your network, check off the Enable LMHOSTS Lookup box and click on the Import LMHOSTS button.

   You will be provided with a file dialog box to import the LMHOSTS file.

4. Choose the directory in which the LMHOSTS file is located (\%WINNTROOT%\SYSTEM32\DRIVERS\ETC\LMHOSTS), and click on the Open button.

5. To enable IP Forwarding on your system, or if your system uses RIP, select the Routing tab and check off Enable IP Forwarding (see fig. 20.17).

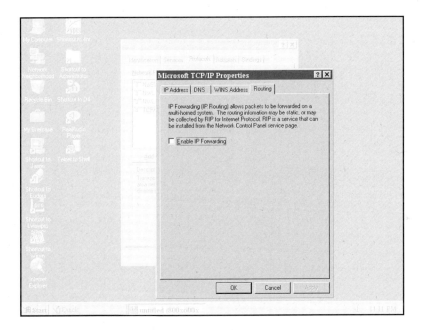

Figure 20.17

Enable routing on the Routing tab of the Microsoft TCP/IP Properties dialog box.

6. Click on the OK button in the Microsoft TCP/IP Properties dialog box.

   If you leave the WINS section blank in the Microsoft TCP/IP Properties dialog box, you will be presented with a warning dialog box. Click on Yes to proceed. You will be returned to the Network dialog box.

7. Click on the Close button.

   Windows informs you that you must restart your computer to install your settings.

8. Shut down your computer and restart Windows NT to connect to your TCP/IP network.

On an Internet, your specific addresses matter. You will be assigned a range of addresses you can use, and it is up to you to make sure that no two IP addresses on your network are the same. When you use DHCP and WINS, you set the network IP address, and your DNS server dynamically applies IP addresses on your network as required, mapping them to the names you created.

Configuring SNMP

Simple Network Management Protocol (SNMP) is actually a subset of the TCP/IP protocol used for remote data collection and statistics gathering for nodes on a network (primarily routers, hubs, and other network resources).

If you are familiar with the Windows NT Performance Monitor, the idea is similar. The performance counters used to monitor performance in the Performance Monitor administration tool are created by applications. You can control which counters are created and when, and by listening to any particular device, you can find performance bottlenecks and errors.

Similarly, SNMP defines unique MIB (Management Information Base) events. The data exported from these MIBs can be used to set triggers on SNMP-aware applications, such as Hewlett-Packard's OpenView, Computer Associates CA Unicenter, IBM's NetFinity, or even an intelligent network "sniffer" device.

To install the SNMP service on your system, do the following:

1. Open the Network dialog box and click on the Services tab.

2. Click on the Add button. Highlight the SNMP Service from the Select Network Service dialog box. Then click on the OK button.

   You will be presented with a source file dialog box.

3. If the source path to the Windows NT installation files is correct, click on the Continue button.

   Windows NT then will copy the files to your computer and present you with the Microsoft SNMP Properties dialog box.

4. Click on the Agent tab shown in figure 20.18.

5. Enter the Contact name and the physical Location of your computer in the appropriate fields.

   This data is used by the administrator at the SNMP monitoring application to diagnose problems that are reported by the SNMP service.

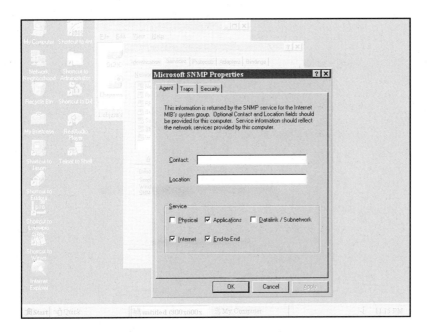

Figure 20.18

The Agent tab of the Microsoft SNMP Properties dialog box needs information about your computer.

6. Check the Applications and End-to-End check boxes if you wish to report data to those services.

7. Select the Traps tab (see fig. 20.19).

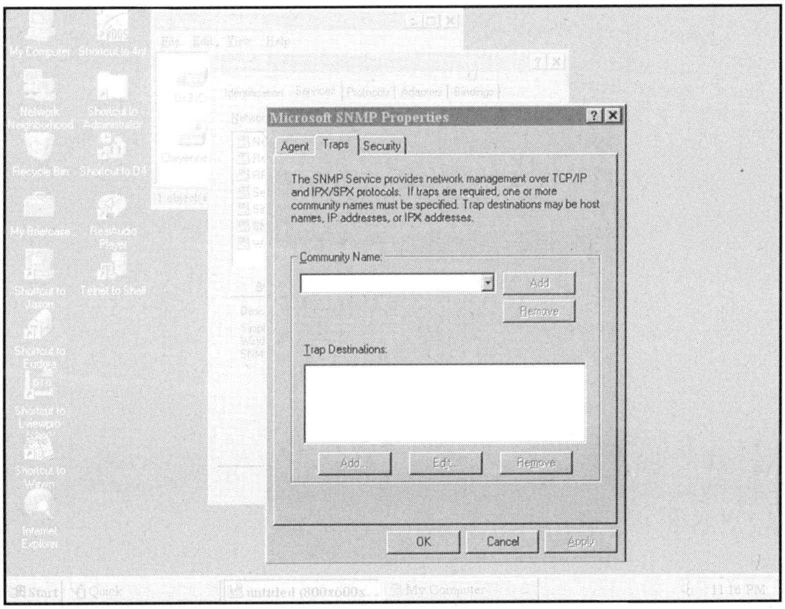

Figure 20.19

Use the Traps tab of the Microsoft SNMP Properties dialog box to specify recipients.

8. Enter the name(s) of the SNMP communities from which you wish to receive information during an error trap.

To limit access to the SNMP service to SNMP consoles in specific communities, follow these steps:

1. Click on the Security tab (see fig. 20.20) to enter the appropriate settings.

Figure 20.20

The Security tab of the Microsoft SNMP Properties dialog box needs community names.

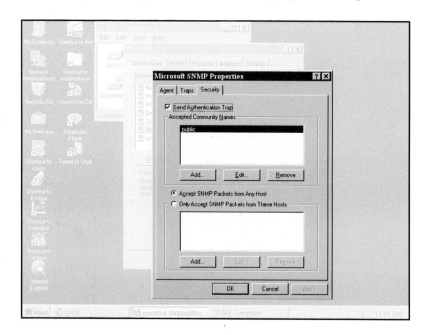

2. Click the Add button and enter the community names in the Accepted Community Names section.

3. Click on the Add button in the Accepted Communities Names section to add the community to the list.

   Repeat if necessary for multiple communities.

4. To further limit SNMP requests from this station, select the Only Accept SNMP Packets from These Hosts radio button.

5. Click the Add button and add the IP addresses of the host computers to which you want to limit access.

   Repeat if necessary for multiple hosts.

6. Click on the Apply button in the Microsoft SNMP Properties dialog box to effect your settings.

7. Click on the Close button in the Network dialog box.

   Windows NT will review your bindings and prompt you to shut down your workstation and restart Windows NT.

Configuring AppleTalk

The AppleTalk protocol can be very useful if you need to share data with Macintosh computers connected to your network.

To install and configure the AppleTalk protocol, do the following:

1. Open the Network dialog box and click on the Protocols tab.

2. Click on the Add button.

3. In the list of protocols, click on the AppleTalk Protocol, and then click on the OK button.

   Windows NT will prompt you for the source media.

4. Click on Continue to copy the files to your system.

   After installation, Windows NT will prompt you to shut down your computer and restart Windows NT.

After restarting Windows NT, return to the Network dialog box and click on the Protocols tab. Select AppleTalk Protocol from the list and click on the Properties button. You will see the Microsoft AppleTalk Protocol Properties dialog box shown in figure 20.21.

To complete your installation of Macintosh network services, follow these steps:

1. Select the NIC on which you want the AppleTalk protocol to be used.

2. Select the default AppleTalk zone from the drop-down list.

3. Click on the OK button; then click on the OK button in the Network dialog box.

You are now ready to share information with Macintosh computers on your network.

Installing and Configuring Microsoft Peer Web Services

New with Windows NT Workstation 4 is the Peer Web Services (PWS) version of Microsoft Internet Information Server (IIS). IIS enables you to run a World Wide Web server on your personal Windows NT workstation, so you can publish your very own home page within your organization or on the Internet.

Figure 20.21

Configure Microsoft AppleTalk in this dialog box.

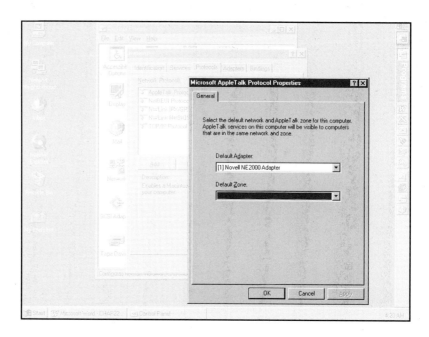

Caution | You must have Microsoft TCP/IP installed before you can continue with the Peer IIS installation. Refer to the earlier "Configuring Microsoft TCP/IP" section for instructions on how to install Microsoft TCP/IP.

In every possible instance, the PWS is identical to IIS. Early in the beta cycle, Microsoft sought to limit the number of simultaneous connections that a PWS could offer on the Internet to 10 simultaneous connections. This connection limit was removed due to protests in late beta of Windows NT Workstation 4. In any event, a 10-connection limit is a licensing issue only. A simple calculation suggests that NT Workstation 4, even when it abides by the 10 simultaneous connections limit, is capable of 500,000 hits a day. So, most users would not even notice the difference.

The files for Peer Web Services must be installed into the INETSRV folder. In addition, you are required to turn the services on after they're installed.

Objective D.6

To install and configure the Peer Web Services, do the following:

1. Open the Network dialog box and click on the Services tab.

2. Click on the Add button.

3. Choose Microsoft Peer Web Services from the Select Network Service dialog box.

4. Windows might post a Files Needed dialog box asking you to locate the files for PWS on disk. Enter the path and click on the OK button.

You will be presented with a Microsoft Peer Web Services Setup screen, as shown in figure 20.22.

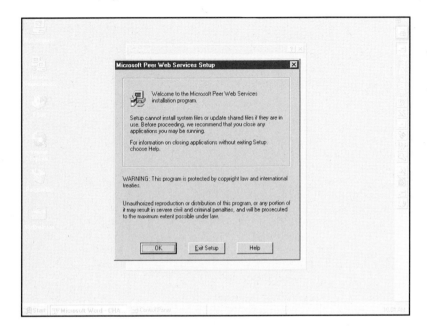

Figure 20.22

Microsoft Peer Web Services Setup screen starts the process.

5. Click on the OK button to proceed.

    You will be presented with the Microsoft Peer Web Services Setup dialog box, as shown in figure 20.23. By default, all the services will be checked off. You can choose which services you want by clicking on/off the check boxes in the Options section.

6. Click on the option(s) desired.

7. To change the directory, click on the Change Directory button.

    The Select Directory dialog box appears, as shown in figure 20.24. The Peer Web Services setup program will install IIS as the \INETSRV subdirectory of your Windows NT \SYSTEM32 directory by default if you don't change the location.

8. Click on the OK button to copy the files to your specified location.

    If you accept the default location and the folder doesn't exist, Windows will ask you to create it, as shown in figure 20.25.

Figure 20.23

Choose which services you want in the Microsoft Peer Web Services Setup dialog box.

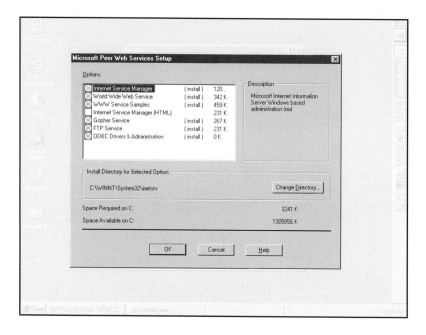

Figure 20.24

Enter the source directory in the Select Directory dialog box.

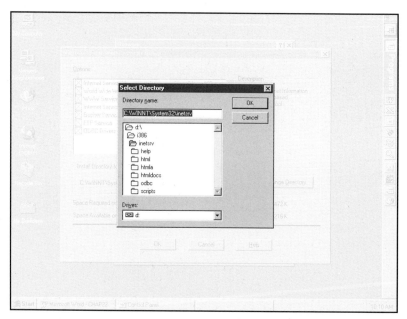

9. If Peer Web Services has not been installed before, you will get a confirmation dialog box to create the new directory. Click on the Yes button.

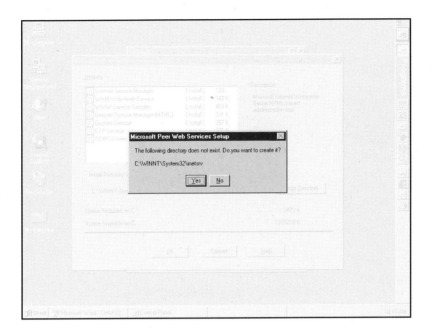

Figure 20.25

The Microsoft Peer Web Services Setup dialog box will ask you to create the folder.

The Publishing Directories dialog box shown in figure 20.26 then will appear. The Publishing Directories will contain your HTML directories, FTP directories, and Gopher directories. Peer Web Setup will create default paths for you.

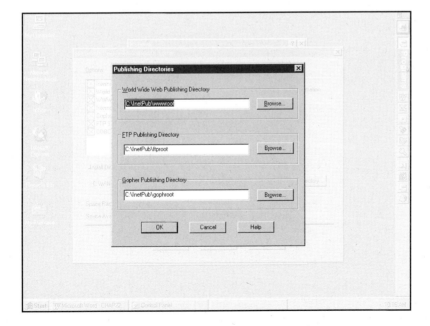

Figure 20.26

Configure the Publishing Directories dialog box with correct locations.

10. To change the names and locations of these directories, enter the correct path and names in the spaces provided. Then click on the OK button to continue.

11. You will be presented with a confirmation dialog box to create any new directories. Click on Yes.

Setup will copy files to your computer. Upon completion, you will get a confirmation dialog box that the setup completed successfully. If you don't have a domain name established for your workstation, you will see the alert box shown in figure 20.27.

Figure 20.27

The Internet domain name alert box appears if there's no domain name.

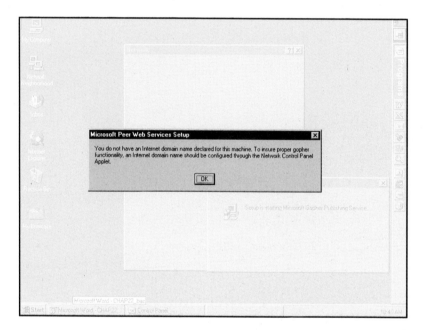

12. If you selected ODBC driver installation, you will see a list of drivers appear in the Install Drivers dialog box (see fig. 20.28). Select your desired driver(s), and then click the OK button.

13. Click on the OK button in the confirmation box (see fig. 20.29) to complete the installation.

To connect to your Peer Web, start Microsoft Internet Explorer and type in the TCP/IP hostname of your computer in the Address field. Press Enter and the default home page will load.

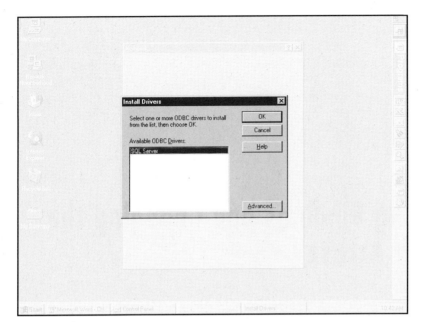

Figure 20.28

The Install Drivers dialog box.

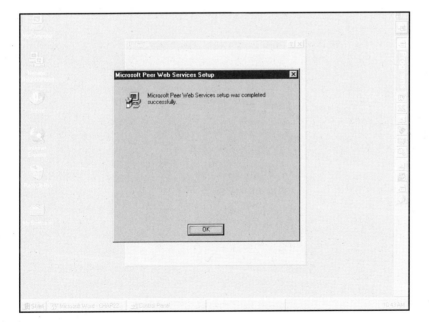

Figure 20.29

The PWS confirmation dialog box needs an OK to complete the process.

> **Tip**
>
> As an example, if your hostname is "mycomputer," type in **http://mycomputer** in the Address field, and press Enter. Others accessing your computer over the Internet and within your local network will have to add your domain name after your hostname. For example, if your domain name is "microsoft.com," they would have to enter **mycomputer.microsoft.com** in the Address or URL field (as used in Netscape) of their client browser.

Use the Internet Services Manager application installed in the Microsoft Peer Web Services folder to administrate your Web server.

Reviewing Bindings and Changing the Network Access Order

When you install a network protocol or a network service, Windows NT automatically configures your protocol bindings. Bindings are software components that let applications communicate using network protocols and through your network card driver to the NIC and beyond. Bindings exist for your services, your adapter cards (NICs), and your protocols. Bindings are stored in the Windows Registry.

You can adjust bindings and improve network performance by changing the order of preference in which protocols and NICs are accessed(in order to favor the protocols and NICs used most, or to configure the bindings so that the fastest protocols and NICs are accessed first). On the other hand, you could disable the bindings entirely if they are not used for a particular network service. This can be done in the Windows Registry as well, but the Bindings tab of the Network dialog box is cleaner and easier to work with.

For example, you should disable NWLink and NetBEUI for Remote Access Service if the primary protocol you are using to connect to your Internet Service Provider is TCP/IP and the WINS TCP/IP client should be on the top of the access hierarchy for RAS. This would be of particular importance for a laptop installation of Windows NT Workstation 4.

> **Caution**
>
> Do not disable or rearrange a NIC or protocol binding unless you are absolutely sure of what you are doing and are familiar with the nuances of Windows NT's networking subsystem. Disabling or rearranging NICs or protocol bindings may produce unpredictable and unwanted results.

To change your NIC or protocol bindings, do the following:

Objective

D.1

1. Open the Network dialog box and click on the Bindings tab, as shown in figure 20.30.

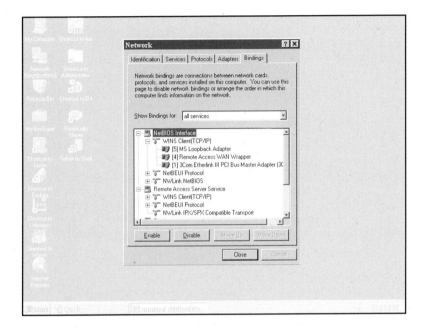

Figure 20.30

Configure the Bindings tab in the Network dialog box.

2. A hierarchical list of installed network services appears. To show additional bindings for a network service, click on the plus symbol (+) to the left of the PC-shaped symbol next to the service name. A second layer hierarchy is shown for the NIC bound to a particular protocol.

3. To disable a network protocol or NIC for a particular service, click on a protocol on the expanded list to highlight it, and then click on the Disable button.

4. To change the network access order for a protocol binding or a NIC, highlight the protocol name in the expanded list, and click on the Move Up or Move Down button to raise or lower the priority of that protocol or NIC for the listed network service.

In most instances, you don't alter the order of network bindings for desktop computers. However, it might be worth changing the binding order for a laptop computer on which Internet connections are used frequently. For more information on this topic, you might want to check in Microsoft's technical reference (*NT 4 Resource Kit*) or a book such as New Riders' *Windows NT Workstation 4 Professional Reference* for more details and registry information.

Sharing Directory Resources

Now that you have connected your Windows NT Workstation to your LAN and can access network resources on your server and other workstations, you might want to share files and folders with other people in your organization.

The improved Windows 95 style interface on Windows NT 4 makes it very easy for novice users to share resources on their computers. Sharing can be done directly on folders in the folder windows using the right-click context-sensitive menu's Sharing command. In addition, you can share resources using the Windows NT Explorer and, less conveniently perhaps (because you must know the path and syntax), using the Windows NT command line.

Sharing folders and the files contained in them is no different from creating other shared network resources, such as printer shares. If you have created other network shares before, you will be right at home creating and managing network shares for folders.

Sharing Files and Folders from the Windows Shell

Creating shares on a network in Windows NT Workstation 4 is easy. When you create a folder, you are automatically the owner of the folder and have full privileges to control sharing. If you are not the creator, in some instances you might need to have an administrator-level access to set up a network share. From Windows NT Workstation 4, you can create shares on your local disks or shares on the drives of remote computers.

Files are shared on the basis of their placement into folders. That is, you will not see a Sharing command when you select a file; you will see only that the container folder is available for sharing.

To share a folder(s), do the following:

Objective C.3

1. Double-click on My Computer.

    You will see the list of available hard disks that you can share on your computer. If they are currently shared, you will see that the icon for each drive depicts a hand holding the device. Figure 20.31 illustrates the icon for a shared disk. Figure 20.32 shows you the icon for a shared folder.

Figure 20.31

This icon depicts a shared disk device.

[D:]

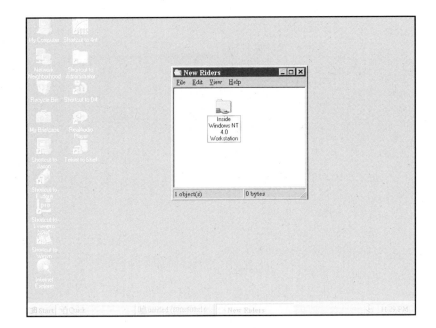

Figure 20.32

A shared folder has the sharing icon.

Note | The system creates a default share for the root directory on each logical device when you install Windows NT. C$ is the name of the C: drive root directory share, D$ is for the D: drive, and so on. These initial default shares are referred to as Administrative Shares and usually are not modified. Doing so can lead to an unusable system. For more information on Administrative Shares, read the following sections.

2. Double-click on the drive icon that contains the directory or file that you wish to share.

3. Navigate through the Explorer interface and highlight the directory of your choice.

   (Use the Ctrl key as you open folders to close the parent folder and keep your screen less crowded.)

4. Right-click on the directory you wish to share, and choose Sharing from the shortcut menu.

   You will be presented with the Sharing tab of the Properties dialog box (see fig. 20.33).

5. Click on the Shared As radio button.

   By default, Windows NT uses the name of the directory as the name of the new share.

Figure 20.33

*Configure the
Sharing tab of the
Properties dialog
box.*

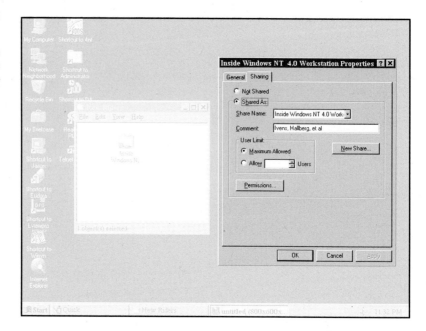

6. To change the name of the share, edit the text in the Share Name field
(optional).

7. To enter an additional comment that can be seen by users browsing for data on
your computer, enter a comment in the Comment field (optional), along with
the Share Name.

8. To limit the number of users you want to access the resource, click on the Allow
xx Users radio button and type the number of Users allowed in the field provided (the default is 10 users). (This is also optional.)

9. Click on the OK button.

Your resource is now shared. Any folders contained inside your network share
also will be shared (the folders inherit the sharing attributes) unless you specifically change this setting.

This discussion has centered on sharing as it exists on a FAT drive. Formatting a drive
as NTFS enables additional security options. For example, you will see a Tool tab in
the Sharing dialog box for NTFS file systems. Unless you need to give access to DOS
clients for NT Workstation 4 network services, you are strongly advised to use NTFS as
your file system.

To remove a share, follow steps 1 through 4 in the preceding list, and click on the
Not Shared radio button. Then click on the OK button to update the system.

To view the list of shared resources using the Explorer Shell, do the following:

1. Double-click on Network Neighborhood.

2. Double-click on the computer name from which you wish to display a resource list.

   The list of shared resources for that computer will be displayed, as shown in figure 20.34.

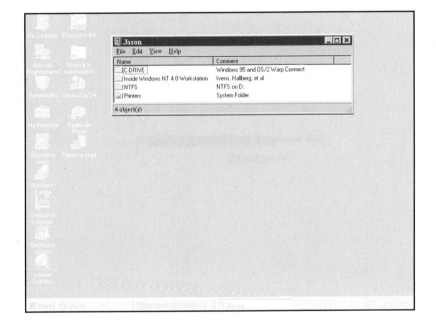

Figure 20.34

The shared folder list can be viewed through the Explorer Shell in Network Neighborhood.

Sharing Directories from the Windows NT Explorer

Another (easier) way to create a network share is by using Windows NT Explorer. To do so, follow these steps:

1. Navigate the directory structure of your hard drive using Windows NT Explorer, and find the directory you wish to share.

2. Right-click on the directory you wish to share, and choose Sharing from the pop-up menu.

   You will be presented with the Sharing dialog box that you saw previously. As an alternative, you can choose the Sharing command for a selected folder from the File menu.

3. Follow steps 4 and 5 from the previous directions given for sharing files and folders.

Sharing Directories with the Windows NT File Manager

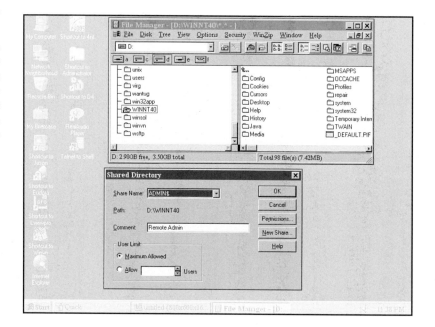

Objective C.3

The Windows NT 3.51 File Manager still is included in Windows NT Workstation 4 and is as useful as ever (see fig. 20.35). If you prefer File Manager over the Explorer Shell or the Windows NT Explorer, you can use it to create and delete shares just as you would with the Explorer.

Figure 20.35

You can accomplish many of the same sharing tasks under the File Manager as you can under the Explorer Shell.

To create shares with the Windows NT File Manager, follow these steps:

1. Highlight the directory you wish to share, and choose Share As from the Disk menu. You will be presented with a Shared Directory dialog box (refer to fig. 20.35).

2. Enter a comment for the shared directory in the Comment field (note, when using File Manager, you cannot change the default share name). You can limit the number of users you want to access the resource by clicking on the Allow xx Users radio button and typing the number of Users allowed in the field provided (the default is 10 users).

3. Click on the OK button in the Shared Directory dialog box. Your resource is now shared.

To unshare a resource, choose Stop Sharing from the Disk menu, choose the resource you wish to unshare in the Stop Sharing Directory dialog box, and click on OK.

Viewing, Creating, and Removing Shares from the Windows NT Command Prompt

The NET SHARE command can be extremely useful for quickly viewing, creating, and deleting shared resources after you learn the syntax.

To view the shares in use on your computer, type the following in the Windows NT command prompt:

NET SHARE

Alternatively, you can use NET VIEW \\COMPUTERNAME (where COMPUTERNAME is the computer whose resources you wish to view) to view the shares for any particular computer on your network. Figure 20.36 shows the command prompt setup for the NET SHARE command.

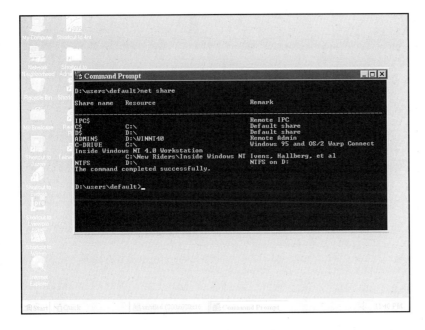

Figure 20.36

Use the NET SHARE command if you like to work from the command line.

To create or delete a share from the command line (see fig. 20.37), use the following syntax:

```
NET SHARE sharename
sharename=drive:path [/USERS:number ¦ /UNLIMITED]
[/REMARK:"text"]
sharename [/USERS:number ¦ /UNLIMITED]
[/REMARK:"text"]
{sharename ¦ devicename ¦ drive:path} /DELETE
```

Objective C.3

Figure 20.37

*Create shares
using NET
SHARE.*

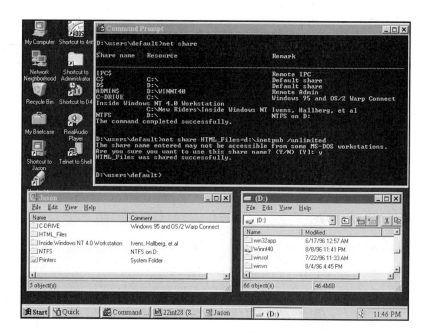

Figure 20.37

*Create shares
using NET
SHARE.*

Setting Access and Permissions for Sharing

After you have created shared directory resources on your computer, you probably
will want to limit those shares to users to whom you want to give trusted access.

Users can be granted access to a shared directory based on user name and group
membership.

**Objective
C.3**

To grant permissions to a network share, follow these steps:

1. Right-click on the directory in the Explorer Shell or in Windows NT Explorer.

2. Click on the Security tab.

3. Click on Permissions to view the Access Through Share Permissions dialog box
   (see fig. 20.38).

4. Select an access level (see following table).

5. Or, click on the Permissions button when creating a share. (See Chapter 26,
   "Understanding Shared Resources," for more information.)

The following table illustrates the permission characteristics of the four access levels
that can be assigned to a user for a particular share.

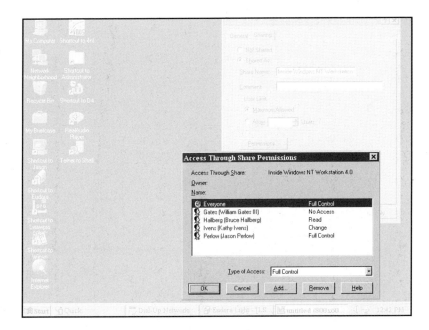

Figure 20.38

Use the Access Through Share Permissions dialog box to set permission levels.

Level	Permission Characteristics
No Access	None
Read	Read files, list subdirectories, view properties
Change	Write to file, create file/subdirectory, delete file/subdirectory, change attributes
Full Control	Write to file, create file/subdirectory, delete file/subdirectory, change permissions (NTFS only), take ownership (NTFS only)

Because you can add user names and groups to the Access Through Share Permissions dialog box, and because these different levels of access are available to you, you have a fine level of control over who can do what to a network share.

Understanding Administrative Shares

As mentioned in the previous section, Windows NT automatically creates an administrative default share on the root directory of all your disk devices, labeled as C$, D$, E$, and so on. These shares are created for the benefit of users who belong to the Administrators and Backup Operators groups so that they can administer the computer remotely using the administrative utilities programs. Only group members of Administrators and Backup Operators can use these shares, and only Administrators

Objective D.2

can change the properties of them. All the administrative shares are reserved by the operating system and cannot be used directly in the Windows NT interface or by the NET SHARE command.

Five other administrative shares are reserved by the operating system:

◆ ADMIN$ is assigned to the \WINNT directory or the directory to which Windows NT 4 system files were installed during Windows NT Setup.

◆ IPC$ is a resource sharing the named pipes that are essential for communication between programs. It is used during the remote administration of a computer and when viewing the computer's shared resources.

◆ PRINT$ is used by the operating system during the remote administration of printer devices.

◆ REPL$ is the default share provided for Windows NT Server computers that are configured as replication export servers. It is not used on Windows NT Workstation computers.

◆ NETLOGON$ is a resource used by the NET LOGON service of a Windows NT Server computer while processing domain logon requests. It is not used on Windows NT Workstation computers.

Usually, you do not make changes to administrative shares. As an administrator, you can view (and modify) the contents of these shares. For more information on working with administrative shares, consult *the Microsoft Windows NT Workstation 4 Resource Kit* or New Riders' *Inside Windows NT Workstation 4 Professional Reference.*

Viewing Resources and Sessions in Use

Occasions will arise, of course, when you will want to know which of your shared resources are being used and which users are using your computer at a particular time. To do that, you will want to use the Server dialog box. You also can use the Windows NT command prompt for this purpose.

Viewing Resources and Sessions in Use with the Server Dialog Box

To find out which resources are being used, follow these steps:

1. Go to the Control Panel and double-click on the Server icon. The Server dialog box appears (see fig. 20.39).

2. To display the list of Shares being used, click on the Shares button in the Server dialog box.

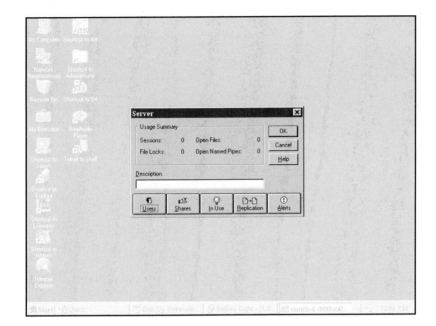

Figure 20.39

The Server dialog box displays current sharing activity.

You will be presented with the Shared Resources dialog box shown in figure 20.40.

3. Highlight a particular share to display the users who are connected to that share.

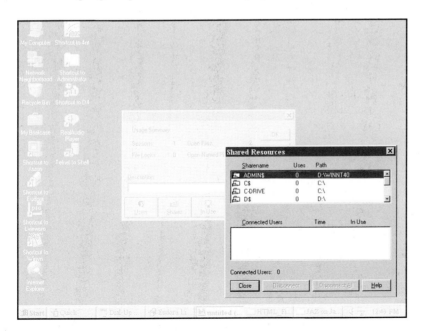

Figure 20.40

The Shared Resources dialog box displays current users.

4. To disconnect them, click on the Disconnect or Disconnect All buttons.

Caution | You are strongly advised to send a message to connected users before disconnecting them or closing a resource (see the following). Disconnecting a user can damage data open during a connected session.

5. To display the list of Open resources, click on the In Use button in the Server dialog box.

   The Open Resources dialog box is shown in figure 20.41.

Figure 20.41

Use the Open Resources dialog box to see what's going on.

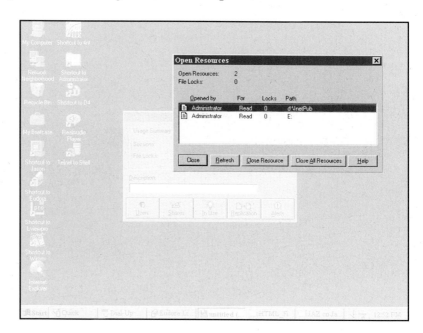

6. You can close a particular resource in use by clicking on the Close Resource or Close All Resources buttons.

7. To display the list of users who are logged on to your system, click on the Users button in the Server dialog box.

   The User Sessions dialog box is shown in figure 20.42.

8. You can disconnect those users from your computer by highlighting the users and clicking on the Disconnect button.

   If you wish to disconnect all users from your computer, click on the Disconnect All button.

Although you can disconnect users and remove network resources, notify your network users that this is about to take place so they can close their work in an orderly fashion.

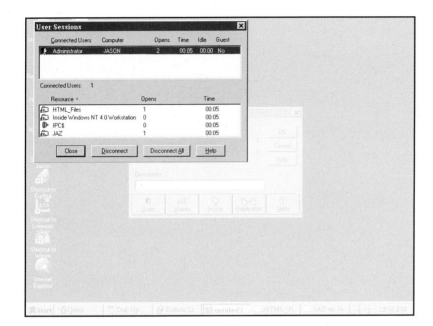

Figure 20.42

The User Sessions dialog box lets you see and disconnect users.

Viewing Resources and Sessions in Use with the NET Command

Alternatively, you can use net session and net file to display the sessions in use and the file locks, as well as to disconnect computers and users from your system from the Windows NT Command Prompt (see fig. 20.43).

The syntax of both commands follows:

```
net session [\\computername] [/DELETE]
```

\\computername lists the session information for the named computer.

/DELETE ends the session between the local computer and computername, and closes all open files on the computer for the session. If computername is omitted, all sessions are ended.

```
net file [id [/CLOSE]]
```

id is the identification number of the file.

/CLOSE closes an open file and removes file locks. Type this command from the server where the file is shared.

Figure 20.43

Use net session and net file if you work at the command line.

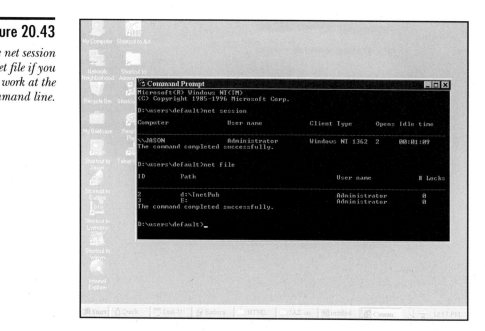

End Note: Windows NT Workstation 4's networking support can be overwhelming, to say the least. Now that you have mastered the basics of installing network adapters, installing your transport protocols, setting up your network services, and sharing your resources, you can try your hand at connecting to other computers (see Chapter 21, "Accessing Other Network Computers"), connecting to remote networks with Dial-Up Networking (see Chapter 22, "Using Dial-Up Networking and Remote Access Services"), and connecting to the Internet with Microsoft Internet Explorer and TCP/IP services.

Test Your Knowledge

1. NDIS permits adapters to use how many transport protocols?

    A. Up to 10 at any one time

    B. 1

    C. Unlimited

    D. 3

2. What setting(s) is/are always required for Network Interface Cards?

    A. DMA and IRQ

    B. IRQ and I/O

    C. DMA and I/O

    D. IRQ only

3. Ethernet is:

    A. A transport protocol

    B. A redirector protocol

    C. A hardware protocol

    D. A driver interface protocol

4. To install Peer Web Services, you must install:

    A. NetBEUI

    B. NetBIOS

    C. IPX/SPX

    D. TCP/IP

5. For an NT Workstation to act as a NetWare client, what must you install?

6. Which network protocol(s) cannot be installed and configured during the installation of the operating system?

    A. AppleTalk

    B. IPX/SPX

    C. TCP/IP

    D. DLC

7. Which resources can be shared and have permissions configured for the share?

    A. Printers

    B. Drives

    C. Program Files

    D. Subfolders

Test Your Knowledge Answers

1. C

2. B

3. C

4. D

5. IPX/SPX

6. A,D

7. A,B,D

Chapter Snapshot

The capability to connect computers together creates new application opportunities and can drastically improve productivity. When you're connected to a network, you can take advantage of other computers also on the network, including your main file servers. Even in a small office with no dedicated file server, Windows NT Workstation's built-in networking enables you to share resources among the workstations networked together. Accessing networked computers isn't much harder than accessing your own computer. This chapter focuses on the following:

Windows NT
Workstation 4

CHAPTER 21

Accessing Other Network Computers

A *network* is a collection of computers connected by some sort of cabling system. When the computers are connected with a network, they can communicate with each other over the network. They can also communicate with printers and other shared network hardware that otherwise would have to be directly connected to each computer.

Networks are used for two reasons: keeping computing costs as low as possible and improving productivity. Because networks enable you to easily share expensive resources such as printers, you can purchase far fewer of these resources and get more bang for your buck. Because networks help people share information quickly and easily, productivity is improved throughout the entire company.

If you're using Windows NT Workstation 4 on a network, you're probably going to have to access other computers through the network. You may be accessing a corporate file server or even someone else's computer down the hallway. You do this so that resources, such as files and programs, can be shared more easily. For instance, your department may have a shared network folder in which all the working project files are kept, so that everyone in the department can access them easily. In some companies, in fact, you'll store the vast majority of your files on a network computer—usually a file server—so that your files are backed up regularly and are protected by your network password.

Objective D.2

Windows NT Workstation 4 gives you easy access to other computers and printers across a network. Using Network Neighborhood, you can browse other computers' hard disks that you have permission to browse, and you can run programs, copy files, and save information with those other computers.

Browsing Network Computers

Just as you can browse your local computer using the My Computer icon on your desktop, you can browse networked computers using the Network Neighborhood icon. Opening Network Neighborhood shows you the computers available on your network, as shown in figure 21.1.

Figure 21.1

Opening Network Neighborhood shows you the computers on the network.

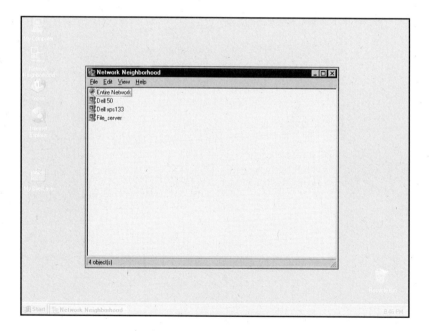

Double-clicking on one of the computers reveals the shared resources (the shares) available to you. (Chapter 26, "Understanding Shared Resources," explains permissions and security for shared resources). Figure 21.2, for example, shows that you can access a number of folders and a printer on the computer named Dell xps133.

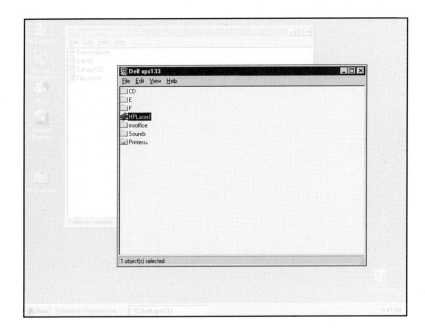

Figure 21.2

Opening a computer displays the resources available to you on that computer.

Opening up one of the shares reveals the files and folders to which you have access. Everything works as if it were a drive or folder on your local computer, except you're sending and receiving data across the network. Aside from the source of the information being different, Network Neighborhood works just like My Computer.

Mapping Drives

Current Windows programs—those that are Win32-based—enable you to access network shares through their File Open dialog boxes. Windows 3.x programs (Win16 programs) and DOS programs, however, do not. These older programs understand only drive letters and directories. Under such circumstances, you need to map a network share so that it appears to your Win16 and DOS programs as a drive letter. You could create a map from the msoffice share shown in figure 21.2, for example, and have it appear to your computer as your G: drive. After you create the map, you access the drive just like any other drive on your system; your programs don't know the difference between a mapped drive and a real, installed drive.

To map a share as a drive letter, right-click on the share in Network Neighborhood and choose the Map Network Drive command. You see the dialog box shown in figure 21.3.

Figure 21.3

Use the Map Network Drive dialog box to create drive maps.

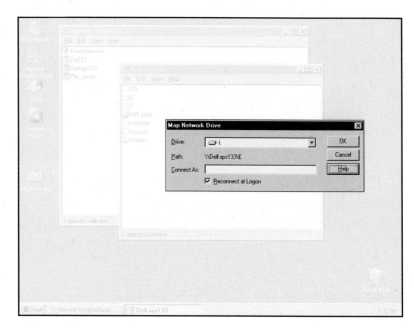

Use the Drive drop-down list to choose a drive letter for mapping the share (the list displays existing mapped drive letters). By default, the drive letter that appears in Drive is the first available drive letter on your system. You can choose a different drive letter or even an existing drive letter (which remaps the share). The Path field, which you do not edit, shows the computer name and share name to which you map. You also can use the Connect As field to map the drive using a different user name and password—by default, the user name and password that you used to log on to the computer are used when you leave the Connect As field blank.

After you supply the necessary information in the Map Network Drive dialog box and click on the OK button, the drive is mapped and the folder opens on your desktop. At this point, Win16 and DOS programs can access the share simply by using the drive letter that you chose.

A somewhat more advanced way to map network shares as drive letters is to right-click on the Network Neighborhood icon on your desktop and then choose Map Network Drive.

The advanced Map Network Drive dialog box (see fig. 21.4) works about the same as the one shown in figure 21.3. You can browse the network shares available more easily, however, by using the Shared Directories pane.

Note If you simply select a computer in the Shared Directories pane and click on the OK button, no drives are mapped. You need to select an actual share and see its name appear in the Path field before you click on OK.

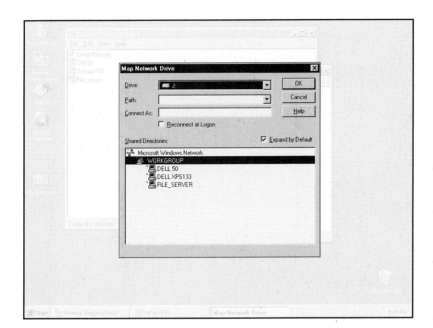

Figure 21.4

More technically savvy users can use the Map Network Drive dialog box from Network Neighborhood if they want.

Disconnecting Mapped Drives

Just as you can map drive letters, you also can disconnect, or remove, the mapping. You still have access to the shares through Network Neighborhood, but the drive letter no longer appears in My Computer and isn't available to Win16 and DOS programs.

You can disconnect maps by right-clicking on a drive in the My Computer icon and choosing the Disconnect command. Figure 21.5 shows this command, and you also can see the mapped drives in My Computer. (The Disconnect command only appears for mapped drives in My Computer.)

If any files are open on the mapped drive when you try to disconnect it, you see the message shown in figure 21.6. Even leaving a command prompt with the mapped drive as its active drive causes this warning to appear.

Caution   Forcibly disconnecting a drive being accessed by a program you're using can cause catastrophic loss of data from the application in question. You should carefully exit any programs that are being used on the mapped drive before you proceed with the disconnect.

Figure 21.5

Use a drive's pop-up menu to access the Disconnect command and remove a drive mapping.

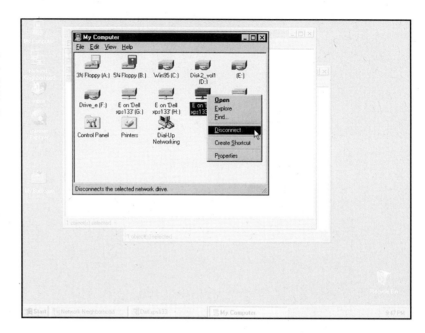

Figure 21.6

You see a warning when you try to disconnect a drive that has open files.

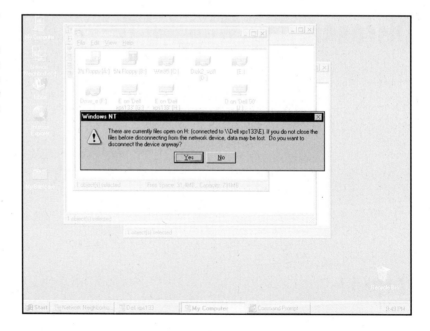

You also can use the Disconnect Network Drive command (to find it, right-click on the Network Neighborhood icon) to disconnect mapped drives. When you see the Disconnect Network Drive dialog box, select a map from the list and click on OK to disconnect the drive mapping.

Accessing a Network Printer

Just as you can access shared folders and files across a network, you can also access printers. Sharing printers, in fact, was one of the important reasons networks became popular. Early laser printers were expensive, and most companies had only a few of them. By networking them, many people could benefit from the use of the printer without the company having to purchase a printer for each individual employee. Because people generally use printers lightly (and can use the exercise from a walk to the printer!), sharing them over a network often makes sense.

These days, laser printers are much less expensive. However, there are still relatively expensive printers that provide great benefits for users, but are too expensive to install for everyone. High-end color printers, for example, can still cost more than $10,000 per printer.

To share a printer, the printer must be connected to the network. Most of the time, that means a printer is connected to a workstation or a file server on the network. You access the printer through that computer's icon in Network Neighborhood. (Some printers, however, contain Network Interface Cards and can be cabled as if they were workstations).

There are two ways to access printers across your network. You can use the Add Printer icon found in your Printers folder inside My Computer, or you can double-click on the printer after you open a computer's folder through Network Neighborhood. If the drivers for the printer are not yet installed on your workstation, an installation program begins automatically. If the printer is connected to an NT 4 workstation, the drivers will be supplied to your computer at the time you request printing services, and you don't have to install them.

Note For more information about configuring and using printers with Windows NT Workstation 4, see Chapter 17, "Printing."

Running Applications Across a Network

You can access files and folders on networked computers, and you also can execute programs located on those computers. You might want to do this when a program is installed on another machine, and you need occasional access, but you don't want to install it on your own machine.

To run that program, double-click on the program icon located in a share on the other computer. Because network drives work like local drives (for this purpose, at any rate), the program information is sent over the network automatically, loaded into your computer's memory, and the program executes.

When running programs across a network, you need to keep these considerations in mind:

◆ Many applications must be installed into Windows NT Workstation in order to work. Even though a program may be installed correctly on a networked computer, it may not work on your computer until it is installed locally. This application is program-dependent, so check the specs for the application you want to use across a network.

◆ Some programs, particularly Win16 and DOS programs, do not work if executed from a Network Neighborhood folder. Instead, you need to map the share that contains the program to a drive letter, then access the share using My Computer.

◆ Some programs may not work correctly if more than one person accesses the program files at the same time. The most common symptom of this problem is an error message indicating that files cannot be found or cannot be opened. You may also see file sharing violation error messages, either from Windows NT Workstation or from the application itself.

◆ Accessing a program across the network may be much slower than running the program from your own computer. This depends on the speed of your network, the speed of your network interface card, the speed of the remote computer, and how the program operates. Some programs run just fine, while others can be slower when running across the network. (Some rare programs can even run faster across the network.)

◆ The software license for a particular program may not allow it to be used on more than one machine, even if only one person is using it at a time. You need to read your software license for the program in question to see if this is the case—the legal language in software licenses varies considerably on this subject.

Even after taking all these considerations into account, running programs based on remote computers can be extremely useful, can conserve the total amount of disk space consumed on your network, and can make administering a program accessed by many workstations much easier.

End Note: Accessing shared CD-ROM drives across a network can be extremely useful. You can, for instance, place a CD-ROM on any computer, then sit at any other workstation and install the software on that CD-ROM to the workstation. Also, if users are working locally with a software application that keeps some resources on the CD-ROM in order to save local disk space (clip art, for example), set up a workstation that is designated as the keeper of the CD-ROM. If you install the software from that shared resource onto all the workstations, every time a file is needed the workstations will look to that share for the file.

Test Your Knowledge

1. Choose the correct statement(s) about accessing another computer on your network:

   A. You can see all the computers on the network in Network Neighborhood, regardless of whether they have shared drives or folders.

   B. Double-clicking on a computer icon in Network Neighborhood shows the folders on that computer, but you must have permissions for peripherals to see them.

   C. You cannot see folders on a connected computer unless you have permissions for them.

   D. You can only see folders that have been mapped with a drive letter.

2. Your computer has one floppy drive and one hard drive. Which letter(s) are available for mapping drives?

   A. B–Z

   B. C–Z

   C. D–Z

   D. F–Z

3. You do not have a printer connected to your computer. When you open Network Neighborhood, you find a printer on another computer. What must you do to use that printer? (Select all of the statements that are correct.)

   A. Double-click the printer icon to open the Properties dialog box and insert your name as a user.

   B. Right-click the printer icon and choose Install from the shortcut menu.

   C. Open the printers folder in your own computer and run the Install Printer Wizard for a network computer.

   D. Have the user at the printer's workstation use User Manger to add you to the Printing group for that computer.

4. Which object does NT 4 eliminate from becoming a shared resource?

   A. A floppy drive

   B. A subfolder without its parent folder

   C. A second hard drive

   D. All of the above

   E. None of the above

5. Software is installed on a server and shared by users for what reason? (Choose all that apply.)

   A. To save space on workstations.

   B. Only to run older (DOS and Windows 3.x) software.

   C. To speed up the program.

   D. It is the only way to keep the data files stored on the server.

Test Your Knowledge Answers

1. A,C

2. C

3. B,C

4. E

5. A

Chapter Snapshot

Dial-Up Networking (DUN) is a powerful tool for connecting your computer to remote systems and then interacting with them directly. This chapter discusses how to set up and use DUN, focusing on the following topics:

Windows NT
Workstation **4**

CHAPTER 22

Using Dial-Up Networking and Remote Access Services

Most companies have a need to let remote users connect to the company network at times. Perhaps someone works from home and needs to access e-mail and transfer files to and from his or her home system, or perhaps some employees travel frequently and need the same features, or perhaps you have very small remote offices that don't require a network but still need to exchange information with the main company facility. In any case, even small networks often need to help remote users connect over telephone lines.

Windows NT includes features that enable you to *provide* this service on the network end and to *use* the service from the client end. On the network, you can run Remote Access Service (RAS) on Windows NT. The RAS computer can be the main Windows NT-based file server for the network, or it can be a stand-alone RAS server that performs only that task. A RAS server running Windows NT Server (as opposed to NT Workstation) can support up to 256 remote connections. Keep in mind, however, that you would also need a modem bank of 256 modems, a very fast computer running RAS, and the necessary hardware in the computer to support that many serial connections. Most RAS computers are designed to support from two to four remote connections.

> **Note** | A computer running Windows NT Workstation is limited to one inbound RAS connection at a time.

When using Windows NT or Windows 95 as a client to a RAS computer, you use *Dial-Up Networking* (*DUN*). DUN enables you to connect to remote RAS servers and to remote Internet servers, such as those supplied by an Internet Service Provider (ISP). You can choose from a wide variety of configurations that give DUN broad usefulness.

One scenario using these DUN tools involves dialing in to your office's desktop computer, which runs the Remote Access Service software. Once connected to your office computer using DUN and RAS, you can access the corporate file server as if you were using the computer at work, although the connection is quite a bit slower, even over the fastest communications lines.

Understanding DUN Hardware Requirements

Before using either Dial-Up Networking or Remote Access Service, you must have the correct communications hardware installed on your system. This can be any of the following:

◆ A modem for access over dial-up telephone lines

◆ An X.25 card if you are using an X.25 network

◆ A network interface card for use over a cabled LAN (such as an Ethernet or a token ring network)

◆ An ISDN card for access over ISDN telephone lines

You can also use a mixture of the above hardware, then select which connection to use for different Dial-Up Networking connections.

If you are setting up both ends of a Dial-Up Networking connection, you can choose which method you want to use to connect to the remote site. Ordinarily, this connection will be over either modem, which is the least expensive way to connect, or ISDN lines, which offer better speed but are somewhat more expensive to set up. Modems communicate at 33,600 bits per second. ISDN connections can connect at either 64,000 bits per second or 128,000 bits per second, depending on whether you use both available channels—and this depends largely on the ISDN interface cards you install at each site.

What Is ISDN?

Integrated Services Digital Network (ISDN) is a digital telephone line from your local telephone company. It is available in most metropolitan areas, and usage costs are about the same as a normal telephone line (however, installation costs are often high). You need a special ISDN interface card in your computer to use an ISDN line, and the remote system needs one as well. These ISDN cards are *not* modems; they are digital networking cards that happen to use ISDN lines to connect. Because of this fact, ISDN cards cannot be used to connect to a remote modem; you still need a modem on your side for that. (Some ISDN interface cards include modems built into them for making analog telephone connections, but most do not.)

ISDN is carried over normal telephone wiring in your house (except for very old homes), but it is a digital connection rather than an analog connection. An ISDN Basic Rate Interface (BRI) line, the kind that you would install, supports three simultaneous channels: two that carry your data or voice (called *bearer channels*, or *B channels*) and one that carries control information and call setup information (called the *data channel*, or *D channel*). Accordingly, your local phone company might refer to a BRI ISDN line as a 2B+D line, which stands for two bearer channels plus one data channel. (Yes, the nomenclature is a bit confusing because you send data over the bearer channels rather than over the data channel.) Each bearer channel can carry up to 64 Kbps (thousand bits per second) of data, whereas the data channel carries only 16 Kbps of information. Sometimes you can use two bearer channels simultaneously; this raises your connection speed to 128 Kbps.

ISDN is not available everywhere; to get full benefit from it, you'll want to find out if your Internet Service Provider offers ISDN services in your area. You might be able to justify it for a DUN connection to your office; if you use it frequently enough and transfer enough data, the higher throughput makes it worth the extra expense.

You generally will not be using an X.25 connection because they are rather slow compared to ISDN connections. Some companies, however, have existing X.25 networks that you can tap into. To find out if this is the case, discuss an X.25 connection with your MIS department at work.

Understanding DUN Features

There are two different ways to establish DUN-to-RAS connections: *SLIP* and *PPP*. Both are used for Internet connections as well as for RAS connections. SLIP stands for Serial Line Internet Protocol; PPP stands for Point-to-Point Protocol.

SLIP supports the TCP/IP networking protocol only. You configure a SLIP connection using a predetermined Internet address for the client computer. This address also needs to be configured as a valid client address on the remote server (which can be RAS or another type of SLIP-compatible server). Also, you should be aware that passwords are sent using clear ASCII text over SLIP connections.

PPP is a newer connection type than SLIP. In fact, originally it was merely an improvement on SLIP. You can use a variety of networking protocols over PPP connections, including TCP/IP, NetBEUI, IPX, AppleTalk, and so forth. PPP is the preferred choice to connect most fully to remote servers. It is required for connection to remote NetWare servers, for instance, because of NetWare's reliance on IPX as a networking protocol.

A DUN connection to other Windows NT RAS servers is secure, and it is easy to administer. Because RAS uses the existing Windows NT security settings and participates in the security domain, you do not need to maintain a separate set of security permissions for people connecting over DUN/RAS. And because most DUN/RAS users also use the network locally, they generally have all their security permissions properly set and no additional security work is required. Moreover, DUN/RAS uses encrypted passwords rather than plain ASCII passwords, so security is maintained against anyone "listening in" on a DUN/RAS connection. Finally, you can configure DUN/RAS to use automatic callbacks, further improving security. (A remote intruder may discover a valid logon name and password, but he or she is extremely unlikely to also be located at a validated remote telephone number that the RAS server calls back when a connection is attempted.)

Installing and Configuring DUN Services

Objective D.5

After installing and configuring your hardware, you can install and configure the Dial-Up Networking software. By default, Dial-Up Networking is not installed when you install Windows NT Workstation. Instead, make sure you have your installation disks or CD-ROM available and follow these steps to install DUN:

1. If you installed Windows NT Workstation from CD-ROM, insert your CD-ROM before proceeding.

2. Open My Computer and double-click on the Dial-Up Networking icon. You will see the dialog box shown in figure 22.1. Click on Install to proceed.

3. Dial-Up Networking is then installed on your computer. If necessary, you will be prompted for the appropriate disks or to insert the Windows NT Workstation CD-ROM.

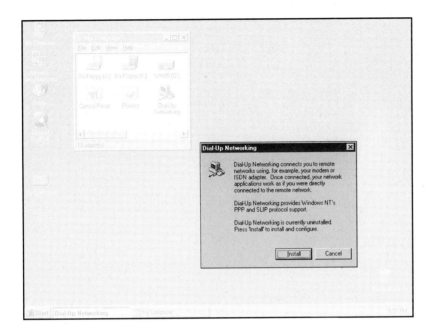

Figure 22.1

Begin installation with the Dial-Up Networking dialog box.

4. Assuming that you have not already installed a device capable of supporting Remote Access Service (if you have, you can skip to step 6), you automatically see the dialog box shown in figure 22.2. The message states that you need to install a modem that RAS can use in order to proceed. Click on Yes to proceed.

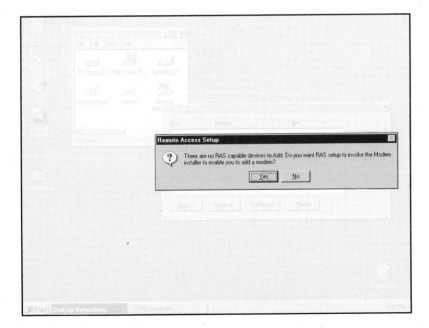

Figure 22.2

Use the Remote Access Setup dialog box to add devices capable of making RAS or DUN connections.

5. You are then walked through the process of installing a new modem. This is the same process you go through when installing a modem using the Modems icon in the Control Panel. Either let the Install New Modem dialog box detect your installed modem (if it can), or choose it from the list with which you are presented. When finished, you proceed automatically to the next step.

6. The Add RAS Device dialog box appears. In the drop-down list, you can select from all the RAS-capable devices installed on your system. Do so, and click on OK to proceed. If the device you want to use is not shown, use either the Install Modem or Install X.25 Pad button to add that device.

7. You see the Remote Access Setup dialog box, which should list the selected communications device and the port to which it is connected (see fig. 22.3). If the information is wrong, use the Add button to add a new device, or the Configure button to reconfigure the communications device. When the device is shown correctly, click on Continue to proceed.

Figure 22.3

The Remote Access Setup dialog box lists the selected communications device and the connected port.

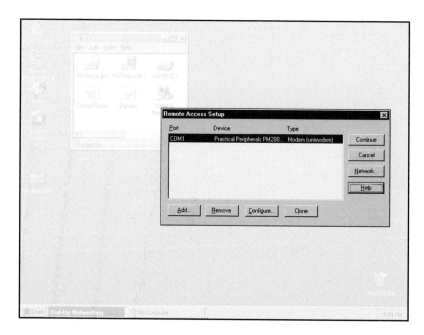

8. The Remote Access Service is now installed, and the setup has been analyzed and saved by Windows NT Workstation. You are now prompted to restart the computer, after which Dial-Up Networking is installed and ready to be used.

After installing DUN, you need to set up your phonebook entries, which define the parameters for the connection you make. This is discussed in the next section.

Using Phonebook

To begin using Dial-Up Networking, double-click on the Dial-Up Networking icon in My Computer. When you first start DUN, you see a dialog box telling you that your phonebook (the collection of DUN connections you use) is empty—you must first create a phonebook entry.

Creating Phonebook Entries

Click on OK in the dialog box to automatically create your first phonebook entry. You see the New Phonebook Entry Wizard shown in figure 22.4.

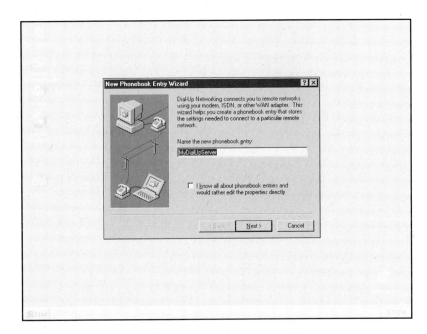

Figure 22.4

Begin defining a connection with the New Phonebook Entry Wizard.

For your new entry, enter a name in the Name the New Phonebook Entry field and then click on Next to continue.

> **Tip** After you know how to set up a Dial-Up Networking connection, you can click on the I Know All About Phonebook Entries and Would Rather Edit the Properties Directly field to proceed straight to the phonebook properties screen.

Next you see the Server dialog box in the wizard, shown in figure 22.5.

Figure 22.5

Define connection characteristics in the Server dialog box of the New Phonebook Entry Wizard.

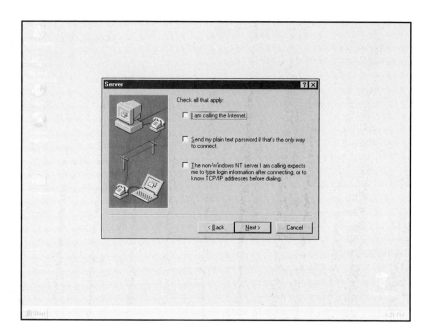

In this dialog box, you select the DUN parameters for making your connection. Choose from the following settings, selecting all that apply:

◆ I am Calling the Internet.

◆ Send My Plain-Text Password If That's the Only Way to Connect.

◆ The Non-Windows NT Server I am Calling Expects Me to Type Login Information After Connecting, or to Know TCP/IP Addresses Before Dialing.

Note For this example, it's assumed that you did not select any of the options, which is true when setting up a connection to a RAS server. You learn about setting other options in the section "TCP/IP for Internet Connections," later in this chapter.

You are now prompted for the phone number you will dial to make your connection, as shown in figure 22.6. Generally, you will enter the phone number in the field provided. If your computer is connected to a telephone system that makes use of Windows NT Workstation's Telephony drivers, however, select the Use Telephony Dialing Properties check box.

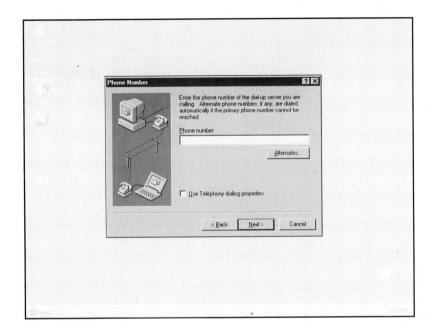

Figure 22.6

Type the number to which you are connecting into the Phone Number field.

If there are multiple connection numbers that you want to dial, click on Alternates to bring up the alternate Phone Numbers dialog box shown in figure 22.7. Enter each alternate phone number in the New Phone Number field and then click the Add button to add it to the list. You also can choose the order in which the phone numbers are dialed (if the first one is busy or can't connect for some reason) by selecting a number, then using the Up and Down buttons to reposition it in the list. If you select the Move Successful Number To the Top Of the List On Connection check box, the number that works becomes your first-dialed number on successive connections.

After returning to the original Phone Number dialog box and clicking on Next, you are shown the New Phonebook Entry Wizard Completion dialog box; click on Finish to complete the entry. You are taken to the Dial-Up Networking dialog box (shown in figure 22.8), which you will see from now on each time you start Dial-Up Networking.

Figure 22.7

Maintain multiple phone numbers in the alternate Phone Numbers dialog box.

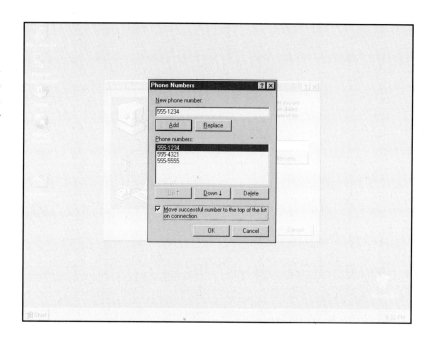

Figure 22.8

This is where your connection begins— the Dial-Up Networking dialog box.

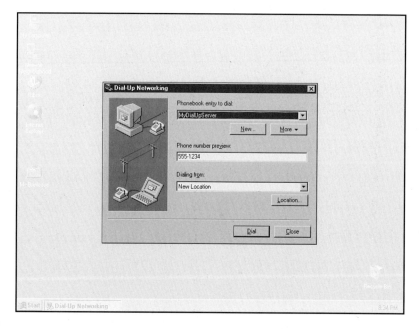

Advanced Phonebook Entries

After you have created your first phonebook entry and selected the Dial-Up Networking icon, you see the Dial-Up Networking dialog box shown in figure 22.8. From here,
you can define a new connection with the New button, or you can change the settings
for the selected connection with the More button.

**Objective
D.5**

The More button is a somewhat rare feature in that it's a button that opens a menu;
this type of interface element isn't used very often in Windows programs. Clicking on
it reveals the menu shown in figure 22.9.

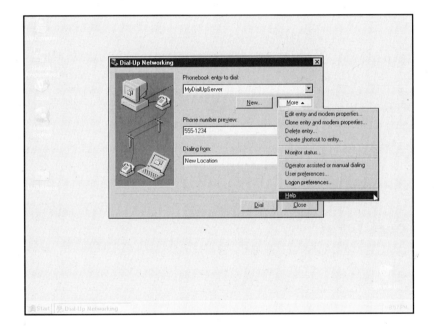

Figure 22.9

*The More button
menu is your
means of making
changes to your
DUN parameters.*

From the More button menu, you can perform these tasks:

◆ **Edit Entry and Modem Properties.** Enables you to change the connection
settings for the selected phonebook entry.

◆ **Clone Entry and Modem Properties.** Creates a copy of the current entry,
which you then can modify to suit your needs. This is often faster than creating
a new entry from scratch, particularly when you only need to change one thing,
such as the phone number dialed.

◆ **Delete Entry.** Deletes the entry from the phonebook.

◆ **Create Shortcut to Entry.** Saves a shortcut to the Dial-Up Networking entry. A dialog box appears that asks you to choose the folder in which to store the shortcut. By default, the dialog box enables you to save the entry onto your desktop. This can make opening a frequently used connection convenient.

◆ **Monitor Status.** Activates the Dial-Up Networking Monitor dialog box, which shows you statistics about your current connection.

◆ **Operator Assisted or Manual Dialing.** Enables you to dial the phone number for the connection by hand, assuming you have a telephone connected to your modem. This is often useful if you need to get operator assistance to place a call (as you might when calling overseas) or when the string of numbers that needs to be dialed is too complex to enter manually, such as when you have to wait for various tones when dialing from a hotel. Manual dialing also is useful when connecting from a location from which you will not be connecting in the future because you don't have to create a complete entry and save it for a temporary dialing situation.

◆ **User Preferences.** Activates the User Preferences dialog box in which you choose system-wide preferences for dialing and using Dial-Up Networking.

◆ **Logon Preferences.** Only available when you are logged onto the workstation as an administrator. Use this entry to set up Windows NT Workstation to log on to a remote system—from the Ctrl+Alt+Del logon screen—instead of to a local cabled LAN.

Editing Phonebook Entries

Objective D.5

When you select Edit Entry and Modem Properties from the More menu, you see the Edit Phonebook Entry dialog box (see fig. 22.10). In this dialog box, you choose all the necessary settings for the connection with which you are working.

Basic Tab

Objective D.5

The first tab, Basic, enables you to set the name and telephone number of the DUN connection. You also can choose which of the available connection devices are used when connecting with the Dial using field. If you want to configure the connection device, click on the Configure button to display the Modem Configuration dialog box shown in figure 22.11. In the Modem Configuration dialog box, set the speed and operating characteristics you want to use with your modem.

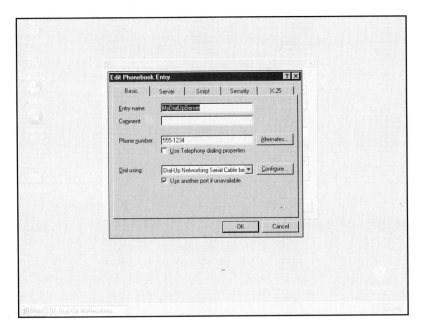

Figure 22.10

The Edit Phonebook Entry dialog box enables you to change parameters for the DUN connection entry.

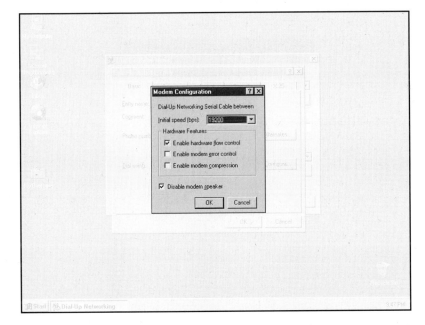

Figure 22.11

Tweak your modem settings for the best connection characteristics in the Modem Configuration dialog box.

| Tip | Sometimes enabling modem compression actually slows transmission, particularly when you are transmitting files that are already compressed, such as GIF or JPG image files. This is because additional overhead in the modem compresses the data, which is often unable to be further compressed. You should experiment with this setting turned on and off in the Modem Configuration dialog box to learn whether you derive any benefit from it. For some kinds of data, you can reap significant benefits from modem compression. For other types of data (compressed data), you might not see a benefit or you might even see some slowdown in transmission times. |

Server Tab

Objective D.5

The Server tab of the Edit Phonebook Entry dialog box enables you to choose the kind of server to which you are connecting, as well as the network protocols that will be available for the connection (see fig. 22.12). When using the TCP/IP protocol, as you would when connecting to the Internet, you also need to click on the TCP/IP Settings button in order to set the details of the Internet connection. You can select all protocols to be available for a connection; however, only the one that is used by the remote system will be used on your end. This process is automatic.

Figure 22.12

The Server tab enables you to define the type of remote system.

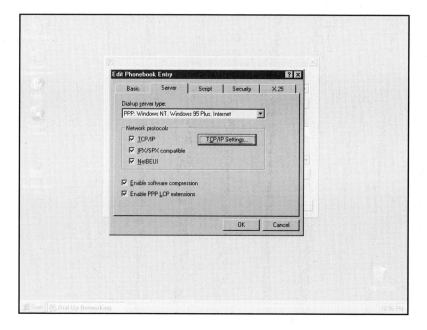

Script Tab

Use the Script tab to choose a connection script when connecting with the Dial-Up Network settings you are modifying (see fig. 22.13). Scripts are useful when the connection to the remote system requires uncommon logon procedures. You can write a script that automates this for you. You can also, if you choose to avoid writing a script, select the Pop Up a Terminal Window option, which enables you to manually complete the logon process on the remote system when establishing the DUN connection. You also can specify special actions to take before dialing the remote server by clicking on the Before Dialing button, which enables you to open a terminal window or run a script before the remote server is contacted (the need to do this is rare, however).

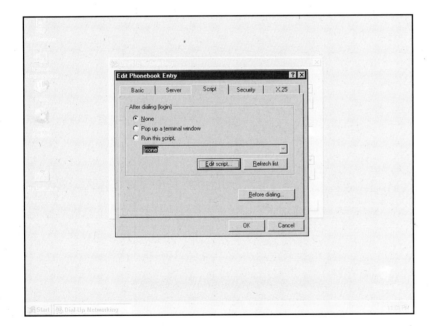

Figure 22.13

Use the Script tab to attach a script to a connection.

When you need to generate a script for your DUN connection, click on the Edit Script button on the Script tab. This causes Notepad to open automatically with a default script already loaded. You can modify the default script to meet your needs. The instructions for modifying the script are contained within the script itself as comment lines. Figure 22.14 shows you this default script in Notepad.

Figure 22.14

Notepad appears with the default script loaded and ready for editing.

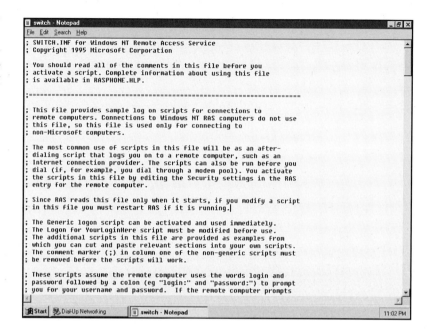

Security Tab

Objective D.5

The Security tab enables you to choose the level of security that the system will enforce for your connection (see fig. 22.15).

Figure 22.15

Use the Security tab to ensure that you don't send unsecured passwords across the network connection you make.

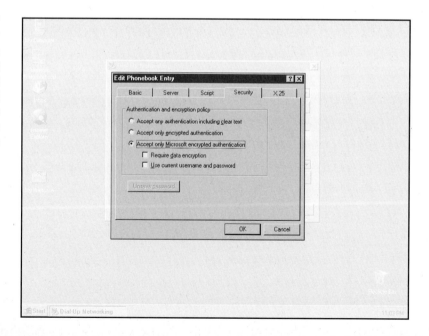

You have the following choices:

◆ **Accept Any Authentication Including Clear Text.** The lowest level of security, this setting allows any form of authentication required by the server to be used. For many Internet providers, you will have to use this setting.

◆ **Accept Only Encrypted Authentication.** Similar to the first choice, except that plain-text passwords will not be sent to the remote system; the server must use one of the accepted encryption techniques. This setting is secure because your password will not be sent in plain text, which could conceivably be intercepted.

◆ **Accept Only Microsoft Encrypted Authentication.** Requires that the remote system accept the MS-CHAP authentication method. You use this when connecting to a system running Remote Access Server.

X.25 Tab

On the X.25 tab (see fig. 22.16), set your X.25 parameters for DUN connections over an X.25 network card. You specify the following settings:

◆ **Network.** The X.25 network you will be using.

◆ **Address.** Holds the network address of the X.25 server to which you need to connect.

◆ **User Data.** Provided by your X.25 network administrator if it is required for your X.25 network.

◆ **Facilities.** Contains any additional settings you can use with your particular X.25 network. These are provided by your X.25 network administrator when you are given your account information.

Securing Your Phonebook

If you share a workstation with other users, you might not want them to access your DUN phonebook entries, in which you might have stored your passwords needed to connect to the remote systems that you use. If this is the case, you can specify to create a user-specific phonebook that is only available when you are logged on to the workstation using your user name and password. You choose this option by opening the User Preferences dialog box and then selecting the Phonebook tab (see fig. 22.17).

Objective
D.5

Objective
D.5

Figure 22.16

The X.25 tab enables you to set X.25 connection details.

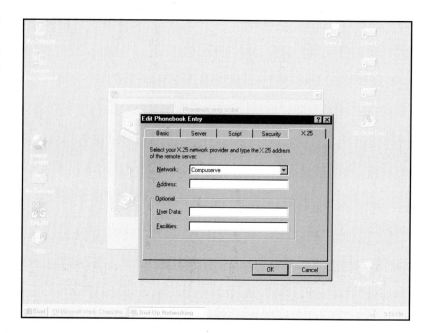

Figure 22.17

Choose which phonebook to use with the Phonebook tab.

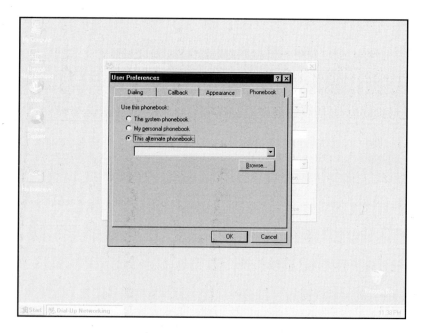

On the Phonebook tab, you can choose The System Phonebook, which is shared by all users of the machine, or My Personal Phonebook, which is automatically private to your logon account and is secured by your user name and password. If you want to access a different phonebook file, you can choose This Alternate Phonebook, which then enables you to enter a path and file name to be used (this can be in your home directory on the network server and will also be secure from other users).

Note | The security of selecting a personal phonebook works only when Windows NT Workstation 4 is installed on an NTFS-formatted drive. On FAT drives, other users will still be able to access your phonebook file.

Objective D.5

TCP/IP for Internet Connections

If you are using TCP/IP and selected that protocol on the Server tab of the Edit Phonebook Entry dialog box, you need to set your TCP/IP parameters. Click on the TCP/IP Settings button on the Server tab to access these through the PPP TCP/IP Settings dialog box, which you see in figure 22.18.

Objective D.4

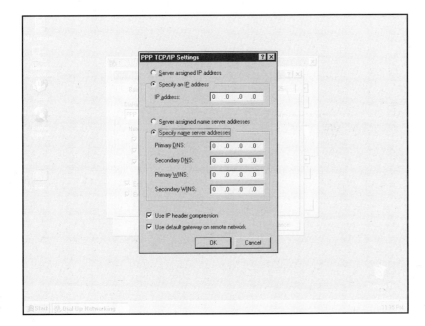

Figure 22.18

There are many TCP/IP details to be set in the PPP TCP/IP Settings dialog box.

Note | You must have the TCP/IP protocol installed to connect to the Internet with Dial-Up Networking.

Your Internet provider gives you the correct addresses to enter in this dialog box. Often, you will need to enter the primary and secondary DNS addresses, at a minimum. Some systems, however, automatically assign these to you every time you dial in.

Setting Dialing Preferences

You can control the dialing preferences used when trying to connect to a server with DUN. From the Dial-Up Networking More button menu (refer to fig. 22.9), choose User Preferences and then select the Dialing tab of the User Preferences dialog box that appears (see fig. 22.19).

Figure 22.19

Set your user choices in the Dialing tab of the User Preferences dialog box.

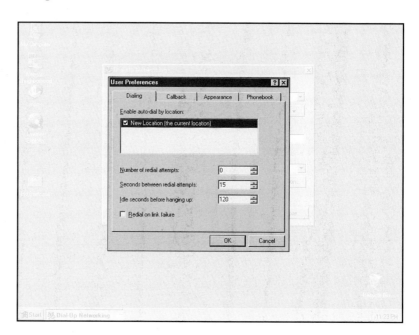

Use Enable Auto-Dial by Location to control from which locations numbers can be auto-dialed. Auto-dial is a feature that automatically establishes a DUN connection to a server when you open a shortcut to a resource stored on that server. For instance, you may have created a shortcut on your desktop to a file located on your office network server. When you use that shortcut, the system knows that a DUN connection is required to access that resource, and it will automatically make the connection for you to open the shortcut. Some locations cannot be auto-dialed, however, such as when you must perform manual tasks when connecting. The Enable Auto-Dial by Location window enables you to choose which locations can be automatically connected and which should not.

Also use the Dialing tab to choose how DUN attempts to reconnect when it can't connect to the server, such as when it encounters a busy signal. You can set the number of times it will automatically redial and how long it should wait between redial attempts. You also can set how long it should try to establish a particular connection before giving up and considering it a failed connection. Finally, if you check Redial On Link Failure, DUN will automatically try to reestablish your connection after it is lost (this sometimes happens due to a poor telephone connection).

> **Tip**   Sometimes it takes a long time to connect to a server because the telephone system takes a long time to connect the call (especially when connecting from overseas). If you are having trouble connecting for this reason, increase the Idle Seconds Before Hanging Up parameter.

Callback

You might want to enable the callback feature of DUN when connecting to a RAS server that has callback enabled. Callback is used to avoid incurring the telephone connection costs at your location, instead incurring them from the server's location. You enable this through the User Preferences dialog box on the Callback tab (see fig. 22.20).

Objective

D.5

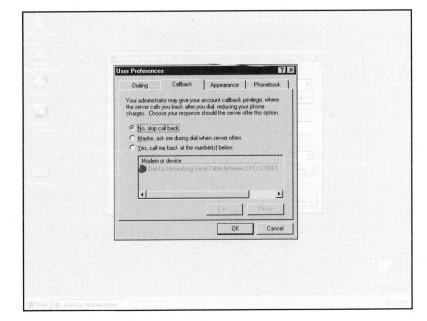

Figure 22.20

For some RAS servers, you must set the correct options on the Callback tab.

| Note | You can use callback only when the number you are calling from can be dialed directly from outside. For instance, you cannot use callback from a hotel in which the operator has to connect outside calls to your room. |

On the Callback tab, select whether you want to use the feature by choosing the No, Maybe, or Yes option buttons. If you choose Maybe, then you will be prompted for your callback phone number only if the RAS server has this feature enabled. If you choose Yes, you can choose one of the connection devices listed; then click on Edit to assign the telephone number at which the server will call you back to establish the DUN connection.

Monitoring DUN Connections

| Objective |
| F.1 |

You can view statistics about your DUN connection and can set your monitoring preferences with the Dial-Up Networking Monitor dialog box, shown in figure 22.21. You access the DUN Monitor by opening the Dial-Up Networking dialog box's More menu and choosing the Monitor Status command.

Figure 22.21

Keep an eye on your connection with the Dial-Up Networking Monitor.

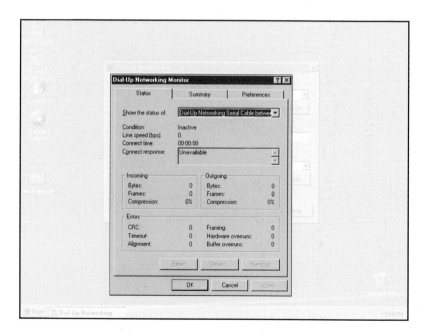

Use the Status tab to view statistics about your current connection. You can see how much data you have sent and received, the speed of your connection, and your connection time on this tab. You can also see error counts that might help you diagnose a poor telephone connection to the server.

The Preferences tab of the monitor enables you to choose how you view and monitor your connections outside of the Dial-Up Networking Monitor dialog box (see fig. 22.22). You can also choose which DUN events will cause a beep on your computer and how you view the modem status lights on your desktop.

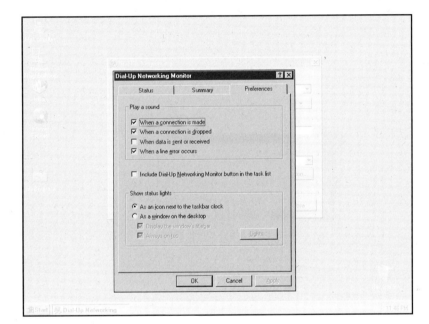

Figure 22.22

Choose your monitoring preferences with the Dial-Up Networking Monitor Preferences tab.

Installing and Configuring Remote Access Service

The flip side to DUN is *Remote Access Service (RAS)*. RAS is designed as a server that remote users can dial in to. You can run RAS on either Windows NT Server or Windows NT Workstation. It provides you with features that enable you to administer the remote users' connections.

> **Note**   Dial-Up Networking uses some of RAS's features, so if you've already installed
> DUN, parts of RAS are also installed. For this section, however, it is assumed that
> you are installing RAS onto a fresh system that has not had RAS or DUN previously
> installed onto it.

To install RAS, first ensure that you have your Windows NT Workstation disks or CD-ROM available. Open the Control Panel and double-click on the Network icon. Select the Services tab and click on the Add button. You see the Select Network Service dialog box shown in figure 22.23. Select Remote Access Service and click on OK to proceed. You will be prompted for your Windows NT Workstation disks or CD-ROM as the installation proceeds.

Figure 22.23

The Select Network Service dialog box enables you to choose which networking service you want to install.

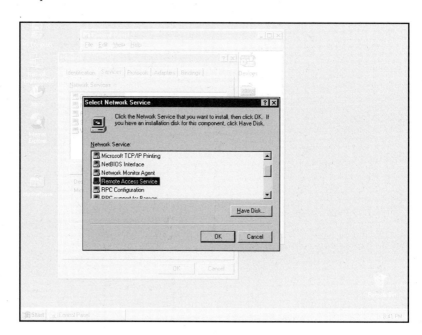

After the RAS files are copied onto your system, select the devices that you will use with RAS. You will see the Add RAS Device dialog box shown in figure 22.24. From the RAS Capable Devices drop-down list, choose the modem or communications connection hardware that you will use with RAS and click on OK. If the device you want to use is not yet installed into Windows NT Workstation, click on either the Install Modem button or Install X.25 Pad button to install those types of devices.

You now see the Remote Access Setup dialog box, which lists all your currently configured RAS devices (see fig. 22.25). You can add additional devices with this dialog box using the Add button, remove devices with Remove, and configure existing devices with Configure. You can also use the Clone button, which duplicates an existing port, to which you can then make minor changes rather than creating a new port.

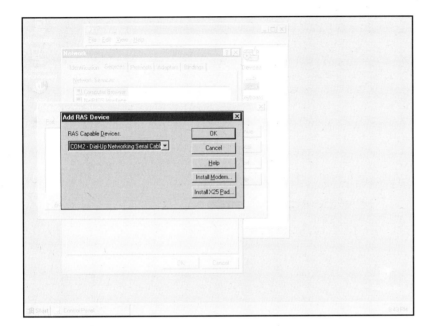

Figure 22.24

You can choose or add a device to use with the Add RAS Device dialog box.

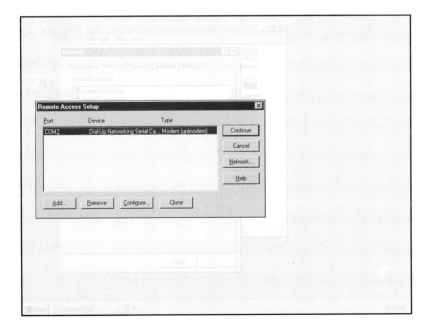

Figure 22.25

The Remote Access Setup dialog box enables you to configure the RAS devices.

> **Note** You can return to the Remote Access Setup dialog box in the future by choosing the Network icon in the Control Panel, selecting the Services tab, selecting Remote Access Service, and clicking on the Properties button.

The Configure button enables you to choose how the device is used. When you click on it, you see the Configure Port Usage dialog box, shown in figure 22.26. Choose whether you want this device to Dial Out Only, Receive Calls Only, or Dial Out and Receive Calls. Click on OK to return to the previous dialog box.

Figure 22.26

To maintain security (and manage your configuration), use the Configure Port Usage dialog box to set the port's capability to accept or place calls.

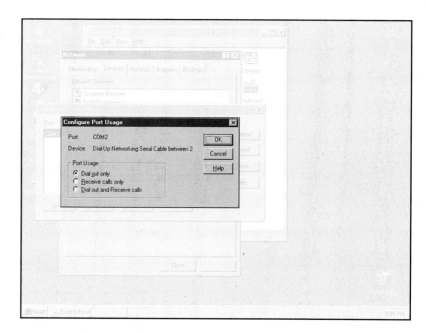

The Network button brings up the Network Configuration dialog box, in which you choose which protocols will be available for RAS connections (see fig. 22.27). Select the appropriate check boxes and click on OK.

Configuring RAS for Dial-Out

When you use the Configure button to also allow dial-out calls, the Network button displays different choices on the Network Configuration dialog box (see fig. 22.28).

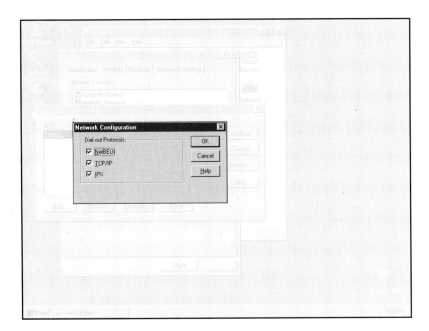

Figure 22.27

Choose the allowed network protocols in the Network Configuration dialog box.

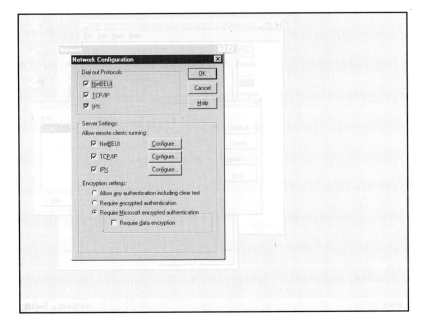

Figure 22.28

When dial-out is enabled, the Network Configuration dialog box contains some options that you don't otherwise see.

First, choose which protocols will be used for both Dial out and Dial in (the Server Settings box). After you've done that, configure each of your allowed dial-in protocols by choosing its respective Configure button.

Configuring NetBEUI

The RAS Server NetBEUI Configuration dialog box enables you to choose whether remote clients using the NetBEUI protocol can access the entire network to which the RAS server is connected or just the computer on which RAS is running (see fig. 22.29).

Figure 22.29

Set up your NetBEUI protocol information in the RAS Server NetBEUI Configuration dialog box.

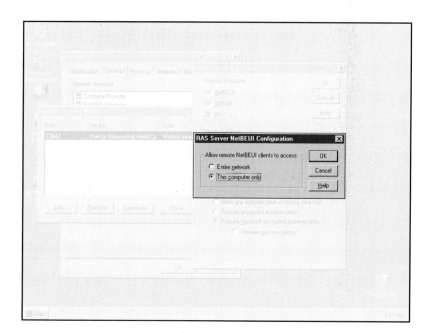

Configuring TCP/IP

The RAS Server TCP/IP Configuration dialog box contains a number of options (see fig. 22.30).

First, choose whether remote clients using TCP/IP can connect to the entire network through the RAS server or just the RAS server machine itself. Then, if you have the Dynamic Host Configuration Protocol (DHCP) service running on your network, you can choose to let it assign the TCP/IP addresses automatically when clients dial in.

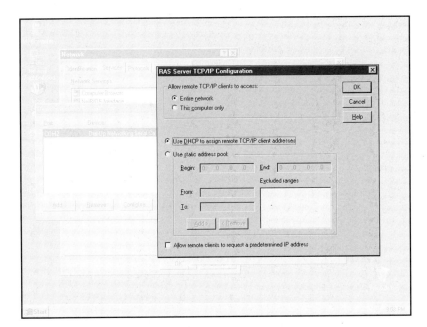

Figure 22.30

The RAS Server TCP/IP Configuration dialog box enables you to define TCP/IP settings.

If you choose not to use DHCP, you need to enter the appropriate TCP/IP address ranges. Select Use static address pool, then define a range of addresses that the RAS server can assign to remote clients dialing in. Enter the valid address range in the Begin and End fields. You then can exclude certain addresses from that range by using the From and To fields and clicking the Add button.

> **Note** You must define at least two addresses in the static pool: one for the server and one for the client.

If you select the check box Allow Remote Clients to Request a Predetermined IP Address, the remote system requests a particular address, which is specified in the Dial-Up Networking configuration.

Configuring IPX

The RAS Server IPX Configuration dialog box that is shown in figure 22.31 enables you to decide how IPX connections will be made. As with the other protocols, you first choose whether remote IPX clients can access the entire network or just the RAS server machine.

Figure 22.31

*The RAS
Server IPX
Configuration
dialog box
controls clients
dialing in with
the IPX protocol.*

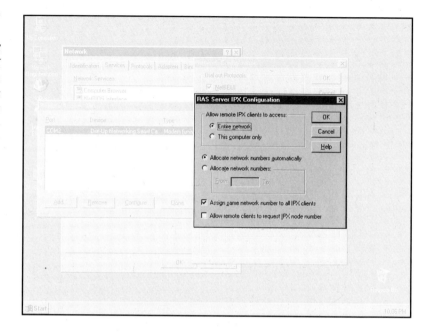

Generally, you will want to let the RAS server automatically assign IPX addresses to dial-in clients. You do this by selecting the Allocate Network Numbers Automatically option. You also can assign a static pool of numbers to be distributed. This is useful when you want to quickly identify RAS clients by their network number at the file server or through a protocol analyzer.

If your network is heavily routed, you might want to select the Assign Same Network Number to All IPX Clients check box. This reduces the number of Routing Information Packets on your network and can reduce network traffic. Finally, you can also let RAS clients request a specific IPX number, just as you can for TCP/IP clients. Select Allow Remote Clients to Request IPX Node Number, and the client then sets the desired IPX number in its DUN settings.

Configuring Encryption

Encryption is important for some sites with technically sophisticated users. It is possible to use software that can listen to traffic on the network for plain-text passwords. After the password is captured and the user name is known, the person who discovered it can then use it. Encrypted passwords reduce this threat significantly.

In the Network Configuration dialog box (refer to fig. 22.28), choose which encryption rules you will enforce for dial-in clients from the following choices:

◆ **Allow Any Authentication Including Clear Text.** The lowest level of security, this allows any form of authentication requested by the client to be used.

◆ **Require Encrypted Authentication.** Similar to the first choice, except that plain-text passwords will not be accepted; the client must use one of the accepted encryption techniques. This is secure because your password will not be sent in plain text, which could conceivably be intercepted.

◆ **Require Microsoft Encrypted Authentication.** Requires that the remote system use the MS-CHAP authentication method. DUN clients can and should use this setting.

Troubleshooting DUN and RAS

To get the most out of Dial-Up Networking when connecting to your company network, follow these tips and use these suggestions for resolving problems:

**Objective
G.5**

◆ Don't run software that is stored on the remote system. Instead, install the software you use on your local system and only access the data files that are stored on the network through DUN. Even this can sometimes be a problem because some applications use data files that are quite large. A good example is to run a word processor on your local system, only opening document files stored on the server. Better still, copy the files you need to your local system using your DUN connection, and then disconnect and use them locally. Reconnect later to copy the updated files back to the network.

◆ Use your e-mail program in its remote mail mode, in which it only transfers new messages to you over the DUN link. Some e-mail programs, particularly Microsoft Exchange Client, Microsoft Messaging, and Microsoft Outlook, use private e-mail files that can be quite large, too large to transmit quickly over a DUN connection.

◆ Never forget that sometimes it's much faster to simply bring the files you need when traveling or going home. Put them on a disk to carry between sites. Although RAS and DUN can be lifesavers at times, it's almost always easier to use disks to access files when you need to use them.

◆ DUN might work well with client-server applications, in which most of the work is done on a server and only screens and your input are transmitted over the connection. Client-server applications differ, however, and you should try this in a non-emergency situation first to find out if your application is usable over a DUN link.

◆ Problems with RAS or DUN in which a connection attempt fails usually generate an error in the Windows NT Event Viewer. Be sure to examine this source when a problem occurs for information that can lead to a solution.

◆ You can enable logging to diagnose PPP connection problems. Using the Registry Editor, modify the following key

> \HKEY_LOCAL_MACHINE\System\CurrentControlSet\Services\Rasman \PPP\Logging

and set its value to 1. After doing so, a file called PPP.LOG will be created on PPP logon attempts. This file is found in the *\winnt_root*\System32\RAS directory.

◆ If connection problems are happening in which the remote user cannot have his or her password authenticated, try changing the authentication rules. Allow all types of passwords and security, for instance, and then see if a connection is possible. If so, you can then increase the security back again gradually until you find the authentication level that is causing the problem. You can thereafter use the highest security level that works for the remote user authentication.

◆ Some information might be gleaned from the Dial-Up Networking Monitor that activates once a DUN machine initiates a connection. You can right-click on the DUN icon next to the time in the lower-right corner of the display and then choose Open Dial-Up Monitor to access the monitor.

End Note: When using Dial-Up Networking, you should keep in mind how it works and how you can best use it. You are forming a network connection to a remote system (the RAS server), through which you can use the network just as if you were sitting in the building using a cabled connection. However, telephone (even ISDN) lines run at a small fraction of the speed of a cabled LAN. Ethernet, for instance, runs up to 10 million bits per second of throughput (although the practical maximum is around 5 Mbps). The fastest modems available today run at 33,600 bits per second, which is less than half of one percent of the speed of Ethernet. ISDN connections aren't much better, at a maximum of 128,000 bits per second. So you can see you won't have a speedy connection to your network using Dial-Up Networking!

Test Your Knowledge

1. Remote Access Service is:

   A. A program that runs on a remote client computer and enables it to connect to a DUN server

   B. A way to provide Internet services to any client computer

   C. A server program that enables DUN computers to connect as clients and access the network to which the RAS server is connected

   D. A networking protocol for modems

2. Dial-Up Networking is:

   A. A server program that enables RAS computers to connect as clients and access the network to which the DUN server is connected

   B. A client program that enables DUN computers to connect as clients to RAS servers and other types of general Internet servers

   C. A method for managing a telephone connected to a computer

   D. A networking protocol for modems

3. Which of the following statements are true about RAS connections?

   A. Only TCP/IP can be used over RAS.

   B. You can use a wide variety of protocols over RAS, including TCP/IP, IPX, and NetBEUI.

   C. RAS connections only work over modems.

   D. RAS connections can support several remote access methods, including modems, ISDN connections, and X.25 connections.

4. A RAS server can support:

   A. 2 to 4 connections

   B. Up to 100 connections

   C. Up to 256 connections

   D. Up to 1,024 connections

5. Network security for a combination of a network and a RAS server is handled:

   A. Automatically, using the domain security privileges set in a Windows NT security domain.

   B. Using a special program called RAS Security Manager.

   C. Using the NET SECURITY command.

   D. You cannot control security for RAS servers.

6. The User Authentication Settings control:

   A. What files a user can access

   B. The method whereby a remote user is authenticated (logged on)

   C. How passwords and logon information are (or are not) encrypted before being sent over the RAS connection

   D. Which users have access to a RAS server

7. If you do not want other users accessing your DUN Phonebook, you can:

   A. Hide the file that contains the information.

   B. Do not give other users the key to your computer.

   C. Select the My personal phonebook option.

   D. Change your passwords frequently.

Test Your Knowledge Answers

1. C
2. B
3. B,D
4. C
5. A
6. B,C
7. C

PART VI

Communicating with NT 4

Chapter Snapshot

Windows NT Workstation 4 includes
two communications accessory applications, HyperTerminal and Phone
Dialer, that make it easy to communicate using your computer.
HyperTerminal is a program that
enables you to connect to remote
systems that run terminal server
software, such as a bulletin board
system (BBS). Phone Dialer enables
you to program your computer to dial
your phone using your modem. This
chapter discusses the following:

Windows NT
Workstation 4

CHAPTER 23

Using the Communications Accessories

The Internet is all the rage these days, and to use it you need access to the Internet network, the correct protocol stack (TCP/IP), a Web browser, and programs such as FTP, Telnet, and so on. You often need a much simpler connection to a remote system, however, using a terminal program instead of the Internet. Perhaps you're connecting to a local BBS system, or perhaps you're dialing in to the company mainframe. You can accomplish these tasks by using HyperTerminal, which comes free with Windows NT Workstation 4.

Windows NT Workstation 4 also includes a small telephone dialer application that enables you to dial your phone using your computer's modem. In this chapter, you will learn how to hook up and use Phone Dialer.

Using HyperTerminal

Start HyperTerminal by using its command in the Start menu's Accessories folder. Starting HyperTerminal opens the Connection Description dialog box shown in figure 23.1, in which you can define a new connection for HyperTerminal.

Figure 23.1

Start setting up a new communications session immediately when HyperTerminal starts.

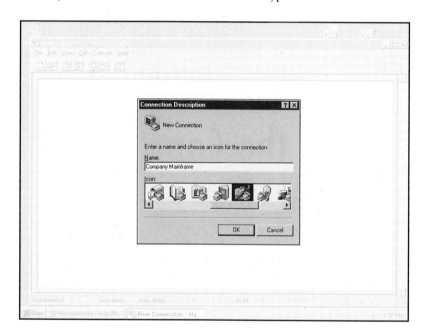

If you want to use existing settings for a connection that you've already set up and saved, click on the Cancel button to bypass this screen.

Defining a New Connection

To connect to a remote system, you must first set up a new connection in HyperTerminal. You can do this in the dialog box that appears right after you start HyperTerminal. Enter the name you want to use for the connection in the Name field (refer to fig. 23.1), and use the scrollable Icon window to select an icon that identifies this connection for you. Click on OK to continue.

You then see the Connect To dialog box shown in figure 23.2. In it, you choose the dialing parameters for the remote system.

Select the Country code for the connection, and enter the Area code and Phone number in the corresponding fields. If you have multiple modems or communications devices attached to your computer, use the Connect using field to select the one you want to use for this connection.

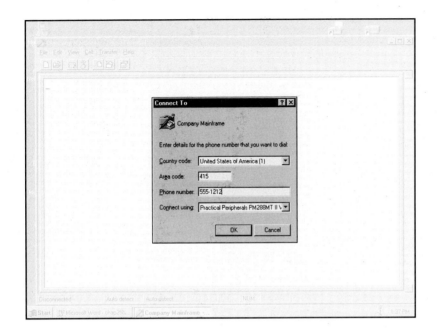

Figure 23.2

Enter the telephone number of the system to which you are connecting in the Connect To dialog box.

Tip

In the Connect using field, you see settings named Direct to Com1 through Direct to Com4 (among others). You can use these settings when direct-connecting over a null-modem cable.

You then see the Connect dialog box shown in figure 23.3. If your connection works using the default parameters (most do, but you have to try), you can connect immediately by clicking on the Dial button. You may have to define other settings that are specific to the remote system, however, before you can successfully connect.

Clicking on the Modify button brings up the Properties dialog box for the connection you're creating, as shown in figure 23.4. On the Properties dialog box's Connect To tab, you can choose a different icon for the connection and can change the telephone number and communications device to use (established in the initial Connect To dialog box). You also can select the Use Country Code and Area Code check box to dial those numbers each time you connect, and you can select the Redial On Busy check box if you want HyperTerminal to automatically keep trying to connect when it encounters a busy signal on the remote end.

Note

Busy signal detection is performed by your modem, which then sends a busy signal back to HyperTerminal. If your system isn't properly recognizing a busy signal, make sure you have installed the correct modem type into Windows NT Workstation and that your modem is operating properly.

Figure 23.3

The Connect dialog box enables you to initiate a connection to a remote system.

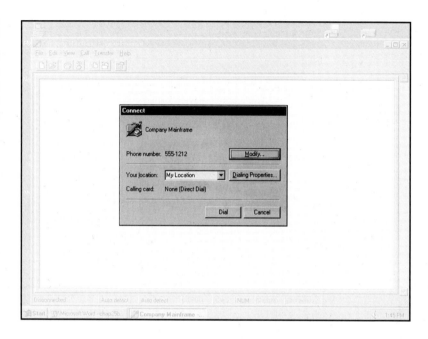

Figure 23.4

The Connect To tab of the connection Properties dialog box enables you to begin to define settings for your connection.

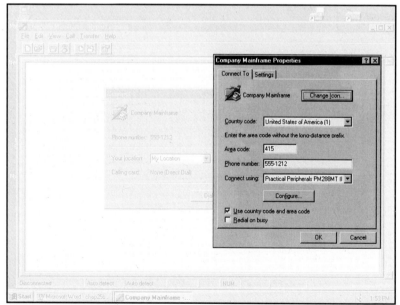

You can modify your modem settings by clicking on the Configure button in the connection Properties dialog box. This brings up the Windows NT Workstation dialog box that you otherwise see when you double-click the Modems icon in the Control Panel.

The Settings tab of the connection Properties dialog box also contains important settings (see fig. 23.5). Here, you define whether your computer will use normal terminal keys for the selected terminal type or the standard Windows keyboard mappings.

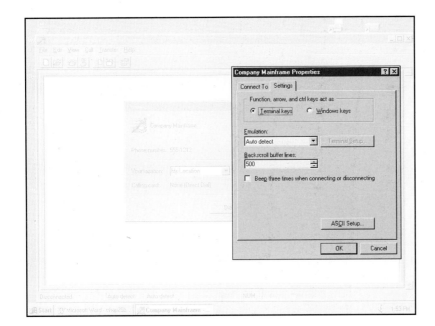

Figure 23.5

The Settings tab of the connection Properties dialog box enables you to choose what type of terminal HyperTerminal emulates.

Choose what type of terminal HyperTerminal will emulate in the Settings tab's Emulation drop-down list (for example, VT100, ANSI, and so on). Generally, you can set the option to Auto detect, but there will be cases when you want to manually select the type of terminal that HyperTerminal emulates. You must select the terminal type, for example, before you change any of the custom settings available for that terminal type with the Terminal Setup button.

The Backscroll buffer lines setting enables you to control how many lines of data HyperTerminal keeps before getting rid of them. You can reaccess these lines of data even when they're not visible by using the scroll bar in HyperTerminal.

For some remote systems, you have to change some of the ASCII character settings by clicking on the ASCII Setup button, which opens the ASCII Setup dialog box (see fig. 23.6).

Figure 23.6

The ASCII Setup dialog box enables you to fine-tune how characters are sent and received for a connection.

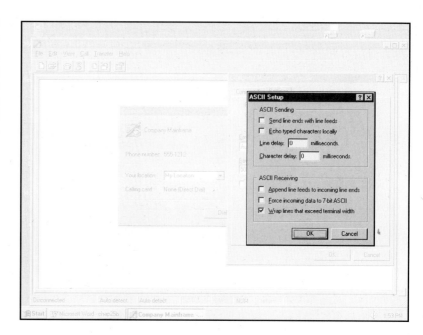

The options for the ASCII dialog box are shown in table 23.1.

TABLE 23.1
ASCII Setup Dialog Box Options

Setting	Description
Send Line Ends with Line Feeds	Causes a carriage return to be inserted at the end of a line when you press the line feed (Enter) key. Some systems do not want carriage returns sent, while others require them to work normally.
Echo Typed Characters Locally	Different remote systems can be set to send back an echo of what you type, or you can choose to echo the characters locally when the remote system doesn't do this. If you are seeing double characters when you type, such as LLOOGGIINN instead of LOGIN, turn this setting off. If you type and nothing appears on your screen, turn this setting on. You can adjust this setting when online by using the Properties command in the File menu of HyperTerminal.

Setting	Description
Line Delay	Some remote systems need time to process a line of data before they can accept additional characters. If this is the case and you lose characters at the beginning of lines, you can increase this setting to compensate.
Character Delay	More rare, some systems need a little time after processing each character before they're ready for the next character. If you sometimes lose characters when sending text to the remote system, try increasing this setting.
Append Line Feeds to Incoming Line Ends	If text displayed by the remote system continues to overwrite a single line on your screen, you need to turn this setting on.
Force Incoming Data to 7-Bit ASCII	Many terminal systems use 7-bit ASCII characters and do not properly deal with the 8-bit characters that are more common on PC-compatibles. If you are seeing gibberish on your screen from the remote system, try activating this setting.
Wrap Lines that Exceed Terminal Width	This setting, selected by default, automatically wraps lines of text that would otherwise extend off your screen to the right.

After you make your setting choices, close the ASCII Setup dialog box (click on OK) and the Properties dialog box (click on OK) to return to the Connect dialog box (refer to fig. 23.3). You can then choose how the call will be dialed by clicking on the Dialing Properties button. The Dialing Properties dialog box is shown in figure 23.7.

In the Dialing Properties dialog box, you can identify the location from which you're calling, which is useful when you use a notebook from multiple locations. You also can set other calling parameters, such as what you need to dial to access an outside line from your location, and what you dial to disable call waiting (usually *70). At the bottom of the dialog box, the number that will be dialed is shown, so you can double-check it.

Tip Some phone systems require you to dial a 9 before getting to an outside line. Often, these types of phone systems need a little pause while they are picking up the outside line. You often have better success using 9 followed by a comma rather than just a 9 for the outside line field. Adding a comma to a dialed number causes the modem to pause for two seconds when dialing.

Sometimes this trick also is needed when dialing long-distance dialing codes or when waiting for a credit card call tone to sound.

Figure 23.7

The Dialing Properties dialog box enables you to choose how HyperTerminal dials a remote system's phone number.

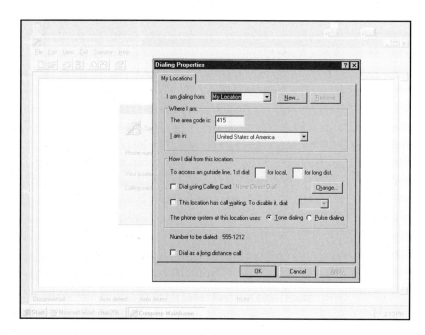

Connecting with HyperTerminal

After you check all the settings described in the previous sections, you can click on the Dial button in the Connect dialog box to connect to the remote system. You should hear your modem dialing and the squeal of the modem establishing a carrier signal, and then you should be connected. The remote system then displays whatever logon prompt it uses, or whatever opening screen it uses in the main HyperTerminal window. (The main HyperTerminal window is the white background you see when HyperTerminal starts.) You now use whatever instructions are appropriate for the remote system.

If, for whatever reason, you cannot make a connection, you can troubleshoot the problem a number of different ways. How you go about tackling a failed connection attempt depends on the symptoms of the problem. Table 23.2 lists common communication problems and what you can do to straighten them out.

TABLE 23.2
Communication Problems and Corrections

Symptom	Correction
Remote system rings without answering	Aside from checking to make sure you're dialing the right number, there's not much you can do about this except notify the remote system operator that their modem isn't working properly. The problem is on the remote end.

Symptom	Correction
Busy signal	This symptom indicates a problem on the remote system, in which someone else is using the modem. Some modems also can generate a busy signal by keeping the line open when system maintenance is being performed. In any case, contact the remote system administrator about the problem.
No dial tone before dialing	Sometimes you won't hear a dial tone before your modem dials, even though the modem speaker normally lets you hear them. This is usually caused by a faulty connection to the wall jack. You should test the jack and cable by plugging a normal everyday tele phone into the jack and finding out if it works. Also, some companies and hotels have digital phone systems installed, and you cannot directly use their wall jacks. In this case, there is usually a modem port on the telephone itself that you must use.
No dialing	If you hear no dial tone and no dialing noises (and no connection is established), then you probably have the modem installed on the wrong COM port on the computer.
No connection	When everything sounds great—you hear a dial tone, your modem dials, the remote system answers—and then the squealing keeps going on forever, your modems are unable to negotiate a successful communications rate to use. Often, they will time out after about a minute with a failed connection message. This can be due to a poor quality phone connection or to something set incorrectly in your modem. You should first turn your modem off and back on, and try again. (If you use an internal modem, shut down Windows NT, turn the computer completely off, and then restart the system.) If that doesn't work, try choosing a lower baud rate at which to connect. Also, confirm that you have the right modem type installed into Windows NT Workstation. Finally, contact the remote system administrator; the problem might be on their end.

continues

TABLE 23.2, CONTINUED
Communication Problems and Corrections

Symptom	Correction
Occasional "garbage" on the screen	This is usually caused by static on the telephone connection and can be solved by using the error-correcting features of your modem (assuming the zxremote system supports similar features). Enable this by accessing the modem properties' advanced settings tab. (Open the modem Properties dialog box in the Control Panel, select the modem, and click Properties. Then select the Connection tab and click on the Advanced button.) Select the Use Error Control check box.
Unexpectedly disconnects	This also is usually caused by a poor telephone connection. It also can be caused by a timer on the remote system that disconnects users after a certain amount of time has passed. Contact the remote system administrator for assistance with this problem.

Downloading and Uploading Files

Often, you need to transfer files from a remote system to your own, or from your system to a remote system. This is best done using a file transfer protocol, which transmits binary data without error.

To upload or download a file (after you're connected to the remote system with HyperTerminal), use the appropriate option on the remote system to begin an upload or download. When the remote system is ready, it should tell you to begin your transfer. At this point, access the Transfer menu in HyperTerminal and choose either Send File or Receive File. The Receive File dialog box (to download) is shown in figure 23.8.

In the dialog box, choose the directory to which you want to receive the file and the file transfer protocol that you will use. Your selection in the Use receiving protocol field must match what you selected on the remote system. A variety of different transfer protocols are available, and their efficiency varies based on line conditions and the speed of your connection. In general, you should choose the protocol in the order listed here (dropping down to the next choice when the remote system doesn't support your preferred choice):

◆ Zmodem with Crash Recovery

◆ Zmodem

◆ Ymodem-G (requires an error-correcting modem connection)

◆ Ymodem

◆ 1K Xmodem

◆ Xmodem

◆ Kermit

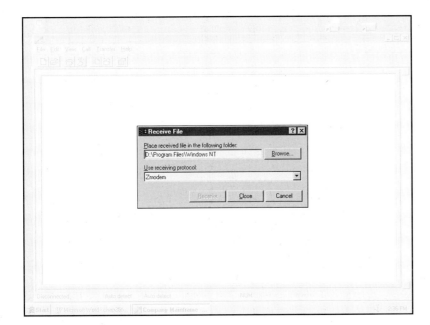

Figure 23.8

The Receive File dialog box enables you to choose the transfer protocol to use.

Tip | Zmodem with Crash Recovery resumes a file transfer when you have been inadvertently disconnected, without having to retransmit the entire file. This option, however, needs to be supported on the remote system before it can work.

Capturing Data

You can capture the text from an online session into a log file that you can read at your leisure—this is useful for minimizing online time. To start logging data to a file, pull down the Transfer menu and choose Capture Text, which opens the Capture Text dialog box (see fig. 23.9).

Use the File field to enter the name of the file to which you want to record the session. You also can use the Browse button to graphically locate a file and directory to use. Click on Start to begin logging. After you've started logging, the Capture Text command contains submenus that enable you to pause and stop the logging.

Figure 23.9

The Capture Text dialog box enables you to choose a file name into which captured text from a remote system is placed.

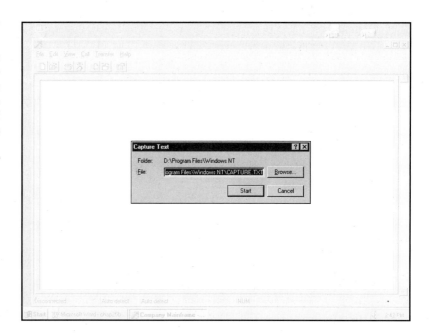

> **Tip**
>
> Sometimes you need to enter text into a remote system that can't be transferred using the Send File command. Instead of typing the text, you can use the Send Text File command in the Transfer menu to rapidly enter an ASCII text file into the remote system, just as if you had typed it yourself.

Starting and Stopping HyperTerminal

When you exit HyperTerminal, be sure to save your connection settings using File, Save. Later, when you restart HyperTerminal, you can use the Cancel button on the New Connection dialog box that automatically appears, and then use File, Open to reload your settings for a particular connection.

To reaccess the connection settings, first open the settings file and then choose File, Properties.

Using Phone Dialer

Windows NT Workstation includes a small accessory application that enables the computer to dial your telephone. Connect your modem to the telephone wall jack and your telephone to the Phone connection on the back of the modem. Then, use the Phone Dialer program to dial your phone. After you dial, you can pick up the phone and use it normally.

You start Phone Dialer from the Accessories menu. Figure 23.10 shows the Phone Dialer screen.

Enter the number you're calling into this field

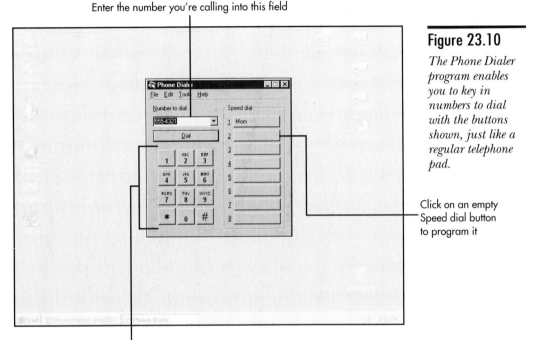

Figure 23.10

The Phone Dialer program enables you to key in numbers to dial with the buttons shown, just like a regular telephone pad.

Click on an empty Speed dial button to program it

Use these buttons to enter the phone number

To assign a name and number to a speed dial button, just click on a speed dial button to program the number. A dialog box appears into which you enter the name and number you want to assign to the speed dial button. After you program a speed dial number, clicking on it immediately dials the phone number. If you want to change speed dial numbers that are already programmed, use Edit, Speed Dial.

You can access a Dialing Properties dialog box—exactly the same as the one you use with HyperTerminal (refer to fig. 23.7)—by choosing Tools, Dialing Properties. This can automate dialing credit card numbers or dialing a 9 to access an outside line.

End Note: HyperTerminal is much like other communications programs, such as Procomm and QModem. Although it doesn't have all the bells and whistles that these other programs sport, it does provide the basics and makes most jobs sufficiently easy. Usually, when you use a terminal program to access remote BBS

continues

systems, you need to control how the connection is made, you need good support for different upload and download protocols, and you need control over what type of terminal the application emulates.

Commercial terminal programs like Qmodem (as well as HyperAccess, the commercial version of HyperTerminal) offer you scripting tools with which you can automate most routine tasks that you perform using a remote system. If you use a remote system and find yourself repeating a series of steps over and over again, you should strongly consider purchasing one of these commercial programs and automating your duties with their built-in scripting language.

Test Your Knowledge

1. You use HyperTerminal for:

    A. Browsing the World Wide Web

    B. Connecting to remote BBS systems

    C. Connecting to systems that expect a terminal over a modem

    D. Performing File Transfer Protocol (FTP) transfers between Internet sites and your computer

2. When trying to connect with HyperTerminal, when the remote modem rings without answering, you should:

    A. Restart your system.

    B. Turn your modem off and then back on again.

    C. After confirming that the phone number being used is correct, contact the remote system administrator; the problem is on their end.

    D. Dial the connection telephone number more slowly.

3. To transfer a binary file from a remote BBS system using HyperTerminal, you should:

    A. Use Copy and Paste to move the data from the HyperTeminal into a file on your computer.

    B. Use one of HyperTeminal's file transfer protocols, such as ZMODEM, to download the file.

    C. Use an ASCII transfer from the remote system to your own.

    D. HyperTerminal doesn't support file transfers, only terminal data.

4. You can use Phone Dialer to:

    A. Dial stored telephone numbers, after which you can use a telephone connected to the modem normally.

    B. Sequentially try different phone numbers in order to discover secret modem phone numbers.

    C. Automatically redial a phone number until someone answers.

    D. Connect to remote systems for HyperTerminal sessions.

Test Your Knowledge Answers

1. B,C
2. C
3. B
4. A

Chapter Snapshot

The Internet and, by extension, intranets are vital to Microsoft's computing strategy and are particularly important components of Windows NT.

Windows NT Server includes an Internet server package called Internet Information Server (IIS); Windows NT Workstation includes a similar, but more limited, offering called Peer Web Services (PWS). (PWS also comes with Windows 95.) Both have similar capabilities, but IIS is more suited to handling large numbers of Internet connections; PWS is more suited to handling intranet services in a departmental setting. This chapter covers the following topics:

Windows NT Workstation 4

CHAPTER 24

Understanding and Installing Peer Web Services

The Internet is quite an amazing creation—a network of millions of computers, spanning the entire world, opening up broad new vistas in our use of information. It's no wonder that the Internet has become key to Microsoft's strategy for much of their software offerings. These days, you either embrace the Internet or you get left behind.

The features inherent in the Internet are not limited to just the worldwide Internet. Private companies can build their own, much smaller, local internets. These private internets are called *intranets*. Intranets provide all the tools and capabilities of the Internet but can be used to provide more focused information-sharing tools to people within an organization.

In this chapter, you learn about Microsoft's strategy for the Internet and intranets. More importantly, and in greater detail, you learn about Peer Web Services, a package included with Windows NT Workstation that enables you to deploy an intranet for smaller numbers of users, such as those within a small- to medium-sized company or a department within a larger company.

Understanding the Internet and Intranets

Before discussing Peer Web Services, it is important to make sure you're grounded in the terms and concepts involved.

The *Internet* is a network of computers. This network spans the entire globe, comprises hundreds of thousands of links between computers, and includes thousands of computers that provide services to other computers through the network. The computers on the Internet are linked using a variety of network connections, ranging from simple modem-to-modem connections, to 56 Kbps dedicated connections, to ISDN BRI and PRI connections, and all the way up to high-speed DS-1 and DS-3 (also known as T-1 and T-3) connections. Usually, multiple routes exist between any two given computers on the Internet, so the network has built-in redundancy. If one link goes down somewhere in the world, often other links are available to take up the slack.

Over this network of computers, most of the computers communicate with one another using a networking protocol called *TCP/IP*. This protocol handles the packets of data, and in each packet, routing information is contained to ensure the packet ends up at its desired destination. These packets are similar to our road system, with millions of cars each taking a trip from a source to a destination.

The predominant service provided by servers on the Internet is *World Wide Web* service, also known as WWW or more simply as the Web. Using a technology called *HyperText Transport Protocol* (HTTP), pages of information can be linked together seamlessly. A page of information you view may have a link to another page. That other page may be located on the same server as the original, or on a server halfway around the world. Simply clicking on the link opens the linked page as quickly as your connection can send the data. Even over standard modems, most pages can be viewed very quickly.

The pages that make up the Web are designed using a sort of computer programming language called *HyperText Markup Language* (HTML). HTML is a graphics language that enables you to design pages of information that contain text, graphics, animation, sounds, and other types of information. HTML also encodes the links that connect any page with other pages to which the author wants to provide links.

A *web browser* is a program for viewing web pages and for displaying any embedded graphics, sounds, or movie files along with the text of the web pages. Windows 95, Windows NT Workstation, and Windows NT Server all come with Internet Explorer, Microsoft's web browser. Other web browsers can be used as well, such as Netscape's Navigator.

Other commonly used services on the Internet include *File Transfer Protocol* (FTP), used to transfer files between computers; *Telnet,* used to let remote computers connect to a server using a terminal connection; and *Gopher,* which provides a simple menu system to information on Internet servers.

Everything said here about the Internet is also true about intranets, the only difference being that intranets are smaller versions of the Internet, are typically found within a single company, and are carried over their own company network. Possible uses for a company or departmental intranet include the following:

◆ Publishing financial information for managers to view on their computers

◆ Providing access to databases of company information, such as human resources information, help desk information, legal information, and the like, in an easy-to-use format

◆ Allowing paperless systems to be built, such as ones that might accept and process purchase orders or expense reports

◆ Distributing files to people in the company or department

◆ Sharing information of all types

Microsoft is pursuing three key areas in order to take advantage of the Internet and intranets:

◆ Applications and operating systems are being extended so that they make easy use of the Internet and intranets. Office 97, for example, includes Internet features built into the applications that make up Office, and the next versions of Windows 95 and Windows NT will use an Internet-style user-interface as the primary way for users to interact with their systems.

◆ Microsoft is adopting and designing standards that extend the usefulness of the Internet. Examples of adopted standards include TCP/IP, HTML, HTTP, and Java. Examples of Microsoft-built standards include various flavors of ActiveX, such as ActiveSound, ActiveMovie, and others.

◆ Microsoft is working with other companies in the industry to further develop the Internet.

Microsoft is absolutely committed to the Internet and believes the Internet is absolutely essential to Microsoft's future success. It's important that you learn about and stay current with the Internet and with Microsoft's Internet products.

Learning the Features of PWS

Peer Web Services (PWS) comes with every copy of Windows NT Workstation 4. It is a service that runs on the workstation and that provides intranet services to other workstations across a network. Using PWS, you can provide HTTP, FTP, and Gopher services to other users.

After you have installed and enabled PWS, you can publish information using any of the services previously described, including web pages, files through FTP, and a menu system through Gopher. In most cases, web pages will be the primary focus of a PWS server.

The following list shows the key features available as part of PWS:

◆ PWS supports the Internet Server Application Programming Interface (ISAPI), which provides a method to publish and accept data from web pages.

◆ You can publish existing files located on a computer to other people running PWS.

◆ Support is included to control the security of web pages published using PWS. This support uses a combination of Windows NT security and special security keys administered through the Internet Service Manager application.

◆ Internet applications can be developed that use Common Gateway Interface (CGI) and PERL scripts.

◆ Virtually any web browser can access information published on a PWS computer, including browsers running on any version of Windows, Macintosh, and various Unix platforms.

◆ You can run PWS on any Windows NT Workstation 4 computer platform, such as Intel, DEC Alpha, or MIPS.

◆ PWS will integrate with the Microsoft BackOffice family of products.

Installing PWS

Objective D.6

Installing PWS is straightforward, but the following prerequisites must be met:

◆ You need your Windows NT Workstation 4 CD-ROM or access to the shared Windows NT Workstation 4 files over a network.

◆ The TCP/IP protocol must be installed and configured.

◆ You need an NTFS-formatted drive on which to store the PWS information to provide security.

To install PWS, perform the following tasks:

1. Open the Control Panel, and then open the Network icon and move to the Services tab.

2. Click on the Add button. This activates the Select Network Service dialog box, in which you select Microsoft Peer Web Server (see figure 24.1). Click on the OK button after you've selected Microsoft Peer Web Server in the list.

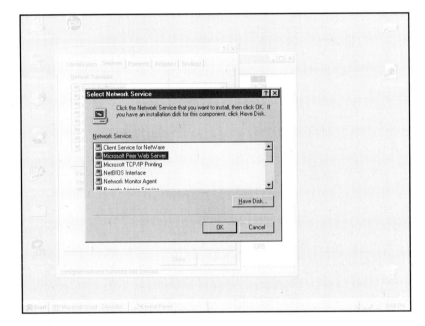

Figure 24.1

Add Microsoft Peer Web Server by using the Select Network Service dialog box.

3. You will be prompted for the source to use for the Windows NT Workstation 4 files. Select the CD-ROM drive or shared network folder that contains the operating system files and click on OK. You now see the welcome screen for the installation program, shown in figure 24.2. Click on OK to proceed.

4. You now see the Microsoft Peer Web Services Setup dialog box, shown in figure 24.3. In this dialog box, you choose which services and features to install and also choose where the files to be installed will be placed.

   The components you can choose to install are the following:

   ◆ **Internet Service Manager.** Enables you to administer the Peer Web Services.

   ◆ **World Wide Web Service.** Provides Web pages from PWS.

   ◆ **WWW Service Samples.** Installs sample HTML pages, including examples of the Internet Database Connector and ActiveX controls.

◆ **Internet Service Manager (HTML).** Extends the functionality of the Internet Service Manager so that you can administer the PWS through a Web browser.

◆ **Gopher Service.** Installs a Gopher publishing server.

◆ **FTP Service.** Enables computers to use the FTP program to transfer files between their workstations and the PWS server.

◆ **ODBC Drivers & Administration.** Open Database Connectivity drivers that enable you to link an application to Web pages through the ODBC mechanism.

Figure 24.2

The welcome screen for the Peer Web Services installation program offers a couple of tips you should read prior to beginning the installation.

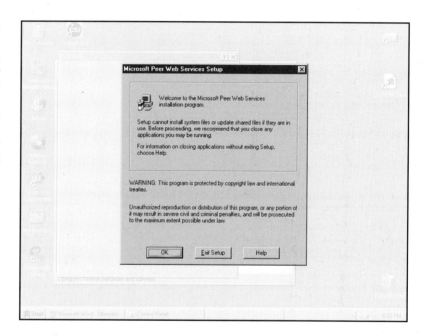

5. Choose the components you want to install and then use the Change Directory button, if necessary, to choose a destination for the PWS files. Click on OK to continue.

6. You next are prompted for the directories that will serve as the root directories for the different services you are installing, as shown in figure 24.4.

The directories you define in the Publishing Directories dialog box are those that contain the information you publish through the Peer Web Services program. The World Wide Web Publishing Directory, for example, is the one that will contain the Web pages you develop. If you want different directories than the defaults, type the new directories or use the available Browse buttons to locate the directories with a dialog box. Click on OK to continue after you have all the directories set as you choose.

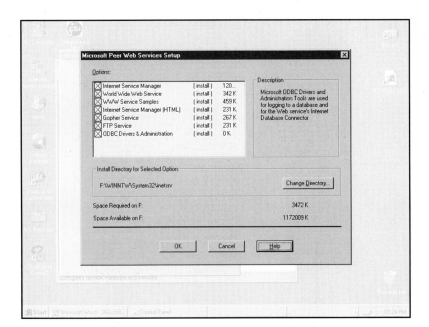

Figure 24.3

Use the Microsoft Peer Web Services Setup dialog box to choose features to install.

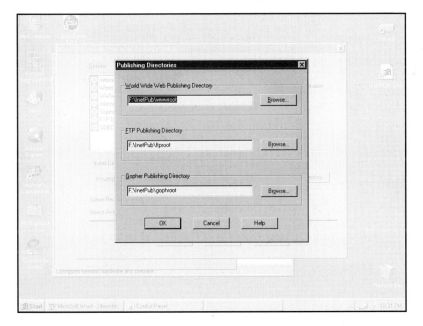

Figure 24.4

The Publishing Directories dialog box enables you to locate the root directories for the various services.

The components you chose are now installed, and the PWS service is started automatically when the installation completes. You should not have to restart the computer in order to start using Peer Web Services immediately.

Setting Up PWS

Objective

D.6

After installing PWS, you access and administer the service using the Microsoft Peer Web Services menu in the Start menu, as shown in figure 24.5.

Your first order of business should be to read the full documentation on the PWS product, which is accessed by choosing the Product Documentation command in the Microsoft Peer Web Services menu. This menu entry starts Internet Explorer (or whatever default Web browser you have installed) with the product documentation displayed. The product documentation is designed as web pages, as shown in figure 24.6. You should carefully read all of the product documentation found there.

Figure 24.5

Use the Microsoft Peer Web Services menu to access and administer PWS.

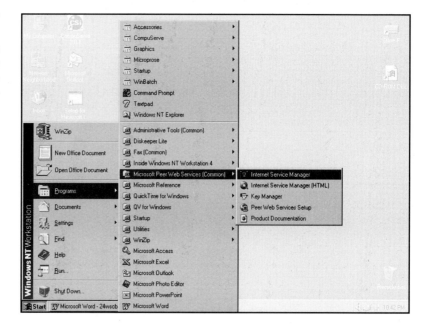

You complete the configuration of PWS through the Internet Service Manager, which can be run as a normal Windows NT program or through a web page. Both options are available in the Microsoft Peer Web Services menu and are shown respectively in figures 24.7 and 24.8.

For each of the running servers, you can select the server in the displayed screen and then edit its properties. Figure 24.9, for example, shows the properties for the web server under the Internet Service Manager.

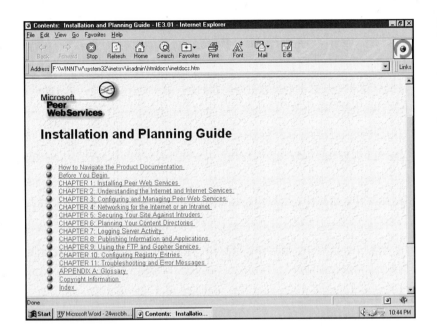

Figure 24.6

The Microsoft Peer Web Services documentation is made up of web pages you can access on the local computer.

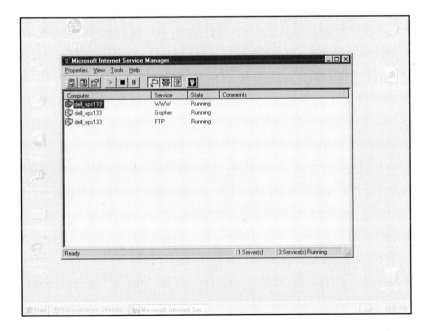

Figure 24.7

You can use the Windows NT–based Internet Service Manager to set up and administer PWS.

Figure 24.8

You can use a web page–based version of the Internet Service Manager to set up and administer PWS.

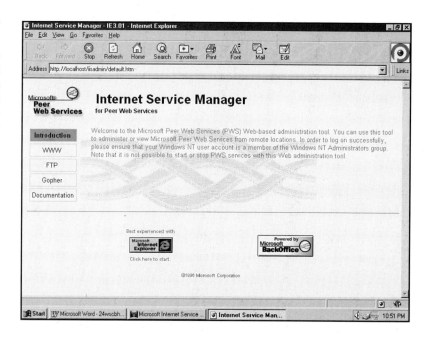

Figure 24.9

The Internet Service Manager contains property pages that enable you to configure the services.

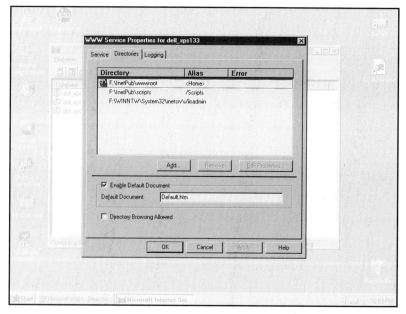

Removing PWS

Should you need to remove Peer Web Services, use the Peer Web Services Setup command in the Microsoft Peer Web Services submenu in the Start menu. The setup program appears, and here you can choose to remove all Peer Web Services components. You can also use the Setup program to Add or Remove components of PWS or to reinstall the product should some of the files become damaged.

Objective

D.6

End Note: Peer Web Services provides a fast and flexible way for you to embark on an exploration of how Internet servers work and are implemented. You can install Peer Web Services and start designing web pages quickly and easily, and you can let others access your web pages with a minimum of fuss under Windows NT Workstation.

Test Your Knowledge

1. Peer Web Services is designed to:

   A. Provide Internet server services for large numbers of users.

   B. Provide Internet and intranet services for smaller numbers of users.

   C. Provide WWW, FTP, and Gopher server services.

   D. Provide superior web browsing capabilities for accessing the Internet from a Windows NT Workstation computer.

2. Which of the following features does PWS support?

   A. CGI and PERL scripts

   B. ISAPI

   C. TCP/IP, HTML, HTTP, FTP, and Gopher

   D. Built-in capability for Internet commerce

3. Which of the following are prerequisites to installing PWS?

   A. The TCP/IP protocol must be loaded.

   B. A DS-1 digital link must be available to the Internet.

   C. An NTFS-formatted drive to contain the published files (if you want the files to be secure).

   D. A current web browser must be installed on the system.

4. You install PWS by:

   A. Using the Peer Web Services icon in the Control Panel

   B. Using the Services tab of the Networking icon to add the Peer Web Services service

   C. Simply starting the service in the Services icon in the Control Panel

   D. Through the Internet Service Manager application

5. You want to set up a web server that will provide confidential information to a select group of people, and you want to ensure that only those people can access the information. What do you do?

   A. You have to use Internet Information Server (IIS) through Windows NT Server in order to get web server security.

   B. You can enable strong security of web pages on PWS through a combination of Windows NT security and security keys in the Internet Service Manager.

   C. You must install the Peer Web Services Secure Sockets Layer before publishing secure web pages.

   D. You cannot have security for web pages.

Test Your Knowledge Answers

1. B,C
2. A,B,C
3. A,C
4. B
5. B

Chapter Snapshot

Microsoft's Internet Explorer 3 is now one of the most advanced Web browsing products available today. With the recent addition of optional e-mail, Usenet news reading, and chat capability, this browser has finally entered the halls of world-class browsers.

The latest version of Internet Explorer contains a wealth of new technology and features. As you read this chapter, expect to become adept at:

Windows NT
Workstation 4

CHAPTER 25

Using Internet Explorer 3

Internet Explorer 3 is Microsoft's third major release of its free Web browser software. In addition to furnishing a highly advanced Web browser, Microsoft has incorporated plenty of new technology into this version of Internet Explorer.

Microsoft has moved a long way in the Internet marketplace, making the Internet a major focus of its overall product strategies. The Internet Explorer interface is expected to become a major player in the development of future releases of Microsoft Windows. As part of the philosophy of developing the single document interface, Microsoft is aggressively developing Internet Explorer in a very competitive marketplace. Microsoft Internet Explorer 3 (MSIE 3) is gaining muscle power and integration into Office and BackOffice products, prompting many to expect Microsoft Internet Explorer to become the de facto standard web browser in the not-too-distant future.

In this brave new world of the Internet, new products mean new features and even newer technologies intended to help a product outdo its competition. In the case of Microsoft's Internet Explorer, the scope of this product's impact is much greater than just the marketplace it is intended to ultimately dominate. If Microsoft is to someday succeed in creating an environment in which users simply cannot do without a Microsoft product, the Office product line must be refitted with a single, common interface that offers the capability to view the most conceivable content, regardless of the file format, media, or geographic location. Expect future versions of Microsoft Internet Explorer to be tailored to achieve exactly that.

To support the ambitions of the marketing people in Redmond (the same people who canned such expressions as "robust" and "user centric"), Microsoft Internet Explorer 3 has been beefed up considerably, with many new features.

Internet Explorer 3 could very well take a considerable lead in functionality and ease-of-use in these distinct categories:

- ◆ **Exploring the new technology.** New methods are needed to overcome the pitfalls of that most arcane of rendering conventions: HyperText Markup Language (HTML). ActiveX and other new technologies accomplish much toward this end.

- ◆ **Securing your navigation.** Internauts agree: people don't trust charge card numbers or systems exposed to the Internet. Microsoft's slant at helping them feel secure when brandishing their plastic and exposing their client systems to attack from without does much to provide a more secure environment.

- ◆ **Finding what you want.** Sifting through the content of the Internet is a daunting task. Internet Explorer 3 helps you find the path-of-least-resistance to the content you want.

- ◆ **Customizing the look of Internet Explorer.** You don't have to stick with the generic look of Internet Explorer 3. This chapter details the different ways you can tailor the interface of Internet Explorer 3 to your needs.

- ◆ **Increasing your personal productivity.** Everyone needs to find ways to cut corners in a world where time is not readily available. Visit the later section titled "Increasing Your Personal Productivity" to find how to improve your productivity when using the Internet Explorer 3 browser.

- ◆ **Going beyond the basics.** You can expect much more out of Internet Explorer 3 than meets the eye. Reach beyond the obvious to become more of a master of your own domain.

Exploring the New Technology

The engineering focus on Microsoft Internet Explorer 3 is clearly directed at creating a more interactive environment for developers and users alike. The technology with the greatest impact on MSIE 3 is called ActiveX. *ActiveX*, in a nutshell, is an intranet/Internet-ready set of enhancements to OLE that enable greater interactivity between an ActiveX-compliant browser and other applications. Although ActiveX is the offspring of the engineers in Redmond, it is being adopted industry-wide and is by no means centric to MSIE 3. Expect to see ActiveX applets popping up on your browser's screen in the near future.

Some of the latest enhancements to HTML, such as style sheets and borderless frames, also are represented in MSIE 3. HTML authors finally can use elements like borderless frames to add nonscrolling banners and other static elements to their Web pages.

The following list includes some of the more promising technological enhancements in this release of Microsoft Internet Explorer:

◆ Background sounds are possible. Now you can drive your co-workers crazy with audio while viewing Web pages in an open workgroup environment.

◆ DirectX, which MSIE 3 takes advantage of, provides developers with shortcut access to hardware. Game developers now can help your PC render games at more exciting levels of performance.

◆ MSIE 3 utilizes Visual Basic, Java, JavaScript, VB Script, C/C++, Pascal, and ActiveX. No browser offers more interactivity with emerging programming conventions.

◆ Cross-platform availability is more complete and now includes Unix and the Mac. Microsoft has finally accepted the prolonged existence of Apple, among other competitors.

◆ MSIE 3's multimedia support is now the most advanced of all browsers. Internet Explorer 3 has the capability to offer the viewer more interesting moving pictures at the highest levels of performance possible today.

◆ Security has been beefed up for use in commerce, including full implementation of Security Certificates, which allow you to control which embedded program objects on Web pages can run on your machine.

◆ A content rating system has been integrated into MSIE 3, offering support for screening content at home and in the workplace. Now you can preclude your employees from viewing boss-bashing Web sites!

◆ MSIE 3 provides support for all HTML tags found in the HTML 3.2 standard, including style sheet proposals.

◆ With VRML 1 and 2 support, virtual reality becomes a reality of its own. If you have the time, VRML sites can now be viewed on older 486 systems.

◆ NetMeeting (a separate downloadable application not covered in this chapter) enables you to work with others in a whiteboard environment shared by anyone you choose.

Microsoft Internet Explorer 3 obviously is intended to be much more than just a Web browser. The following sections take a more detailed look at the top enhancements to date.

Using Enhanced Multimedia Support

Internet Explorer 3 provides support for all popular multimedia standards and many emerging standards. Bitmap support includes JPEG, GIF, and BMP. Two-dimensional animations are viewable when in the GIF file format. Audio support continues to center around MPEG, WAV, MIDI, AU, and the AIFF file formats.

In the realm of moving imagery, Microsoft Internet Explorer continues to support QuickTime and AVI file formats. A new technology named ActiveMovie leads Microsoft's effort to standardize MPEG-1 (Motion Pictures Experts Group) as the de facto format for high-quality moving imagery files.

Using Microsoft ActiveMovie

Microsoft ActiveMovie is Microsoft's model for streaming audio or video. When used by developers in conjunction with DirectX (see the following section), ActiveMovie can be extremely smooth in its rendering of well-timed video and audio playback, if your video card is advanced enough to support it. That advanced capability is being called DirectDraw, a technology integrated into the hardware products of business partners that promises to support enhanced, concurrent rendering of combinations of 3D and 2D elements. With its advanced support for streaming complex data, you can expect ActiveMovie to replace Video for Windows as Microsoft's standard video playback technology.

The foundation of ActiveMovie is in its ActiveMovie Streaming Format, or ASF. ASF provides the capability to combine multiple multimedia source files during download, enabling moving pictures to play during (and not just after) download. Synchronization is another paramount issue in streaming real-time multimedia, and it is greatly enhanced with Internet Explorer 3. ActiveMovie is easily moved across LANs and WANs via TCP/IP, UDP, RTP, IPX/SPX, and ATM protocols and transports.

Using Microsoft DirectX Technologies

Microsoft Internet Explorer 3 supports DirectX technologies. *DirectX* is a compendium of technologies based on providing developers with direct access to hardware previously shielded from their access by DOS and Windows. Promising full device independence, developers who produce action games and high-performance multimedia applications will be able to directly manipulate video and audio hardware to dramatically improve performance of their products.

Internet Explorer supports these DirectX APIs:

◆ **Direct3D.** Provides streaming services and direct video hardware access to improve 3D renderings.

◆ **DirectDraw.** Enables the developer to manipulate the video display card (including video memory) to enhance 2D renderings.

◆ **DirectInput.** Supports input devices—beginning with joysticks and extending to devices such as rudder pedals and virtual reality headgear—and can utilize six levels of axes.

◆ **DirectPlay.** Supports the movement of application data over TCP/IP networks or other medium.

◆ **DirectSound.** Provides high-quality sound playback and direct developer access to sound hardware.

Using Background Sounds

Internet Explorer 3 supports the use of background sounds that users can hear while viewing HTML pages. Background sounds can be tailored to play when a page is first opened, or they can be looped for continuous play. Expect to see WAV, MIDI, AU, and AIFF audio files used as background sounds.

Downloading with FTP and HTTP

Internet Explorer 3 offers more visible support for the user during FTP file transfers. In previous versions, a small amount of transfer detail appeared on the status bar. MSIE 3 now posts a dialog box that displays a progress bar (displaying estimated remaining download time), as well as an animation that keeps you apprised of the progress of the transfer. Moreover, downloads can proceed independently of the browser window, so that you can download files while viewing other web pages.

If the transfer hangs due to a constraint, the animation stalls and gives you a visual cue that it might be best to restart the download or choose another FTP server altogether to accomplish your download in minimal time.

Printing with Internet Explorer

Microsoft Internet Explorer has always supported the printing of HTML pages. Now, with version 3, you also have additional functionality in that you can print a table (or list) of links at the end of the printed document. Enable the Shortcuts option in the Print dialog box to create a list of the links in the current page.

You can print the contents of any HTML document to a file by enabling the Print to File option in the Print dialog box. The table of links is listed at the end of any HTML document that you print in this way.

Each shortcut appears in the left column of this two-column table. The URL appears in the right column. If you use hyperlinked buttons, the text substitution (for the button) appears in the Shortcut Text column. If you use a mailto: link, then <no text> appears in lieu of any other text in the Shortcut Text column.

If you use the Microsoft HTML driver by using the Print to File option described above to print out a Web site and to enable the printing of the table of links, the driver prints the contents of the current page (as well as the table of links) as an HTML file. Microsoft Internet Explorer 3 then opens the file, presenting the original HTML file with a table, minus any background images that were apparent in the original HTML document on the Web.

> **Note**   When using the HTML print driver, every graphic in the original HTML document is re-created in the directory where you assign the output file to be stored.

Finding What You Want

Browsing is all about getting around on the World Wide Web—bouncing between sites and browsing their contents. Finding what you want can be a bit of a daunting experience. Fortunately, Internet Explorer 3 is equipped to help you find content of interest to you—on your intranet, on the Internet, and on the disk drives of your NT Workstation 4.

Navigating to an Internet Site

Internet Explorer 3 has some useful features that help you find the Internet site of your choice. You don't have to type in **http://** anymore. Internet Explorer 3 often connects even if you leave out the **www.** in the URL for a site. Sites are parsed for protocol by Internet Explorer 3, making it possible to enter shorter Internet addresses. You could type **microsoft.com** into the text box, for example, and press Enter to successfully connect to this URL:

    http://www.microsoft.com

To browse any specific Web site, type the URL or domain name into the Address text box and then press Enter. That's it.

Searching the Internet

There are dozens of ways to search the Internet, and each search engine performs its search functions in different ways. Microsoft Internet Explorer 3 provides you with quick access to several Internet search engines.

To access the search engines offered by Internet Explorer 3, connect to the Internet and then click on the Search button on Internet Explorer's button bar. After a few seconds, Internet Explorer 3 opens the Search page of The Microsoft Network, or MSN (see fig. 25.1). MSN was originally intended to be a competitor to other online services but was re-purposed as an Internet-access and Web site resource. Today, you don't have to be a member of MSN to access much of the MSN content.

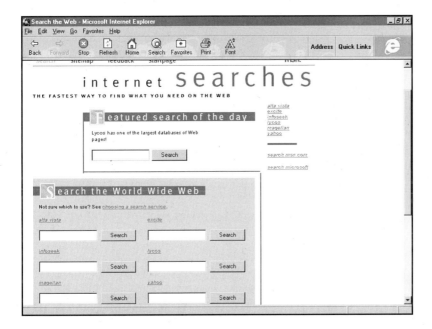

Figure 25.1

The Search page at MSN provides you with quick access to several search engines from a single page.

Using any search engine is fairly simple. Place the insertion point into the text box provided, enter your text, and then click on whatever button is provided to initiate your search.

Search engines display their results in various ways. Some search engines, for example, display only a succinct list of topics rather than a paragraph of text outlining the purpose of each Web site found during the search.

| Tip | You can buy third-party search utility programs (often referred to as intelligent agents) that specialize in searching all search engines at the same time. If you spend lots of time performing search tasks on the Internet, you would do well to look into these productivity-enhancing software products. Using your favorite search engine, try searching on "intelligent agents" or "software agents" to find out more about such software programs. |

You can even use a search engine to look for other search engines and then copy the found URLs to your Favorites folder. Some search engines have an extremely specific scope. Experimentation definitely is in order before you find the search engine that both serves you well and presents information in a way that is most helpful to you.

Working with Favorites and Bookmarks

Microsoft Internet Explorer 3 utilizes its own unique method of storing preferred, visited sites. You can save the location of any Web site for future visits by saving a copy of the page in the Favorites folder.

Netscape Navigator saves Bookmarks as lines of text in a single HTML file. Microsoft Explorer saves bookmarks as Favorites, shortcuts stored in the Favorites folder on your hard drive. You can create new, multiple folders to hold favorite sites, accessing them whenever you want to revisit that site.

These Favorites folders occupy actual space on your hard drive and can be viewed using Internet Explorer 3, Windows 95 Explorer, or any file management utility, such as Windows File Manager. The Favorites folder is a subfolder of the Windows folder.

Favorites can be copied to the Clipboard and then e-mailed to others. You can share a Favorites directory, folders, and shortcuts with others if they have access rights.

If you've been using another Web browser product and have created bookmarks using that product, Microsoft Internet Explorer 3 does its best to find and import those bookmarks for use with MSIE 3. Conversely, you can also find utilities on the Internet that can do the reverse to convert MSIE bookmarks to Netscape Navigator bookmarks.

This importing function happens during Internet Explorer's installation (see fig. 25.2). The original Netscape Navigator bookmark files remain intact, but aren't updated or subsequently synchronized between MSIE and Netscape Navigator.

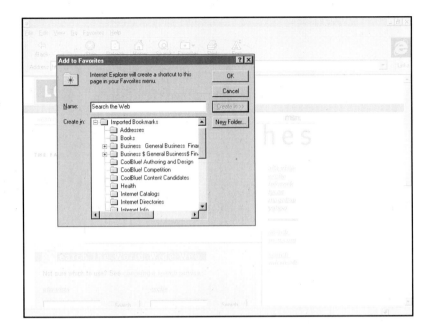

Figure 25.2

Internet Explorer imported this lengthy Netscape Navigator bookmarks file during its installation process.

Imported bookmarks are stored in the Favorites folder as well. If folders existed in the imported bookmarks file, these folders are represented as a subfolder in the Imported Bookmarks folder.

You can view and manage your collection of favorite sites by accessing them in your Favorites folder. Select Open Favorites Folder from Internet Explorer's Favorites menu to view both shortcuts and folders that can hold collections of shortcuts.

Managing your Favorites folder is just like using My Computer to work with any folder. Use any of the four views from Internet Explorer's View menu to see the contents of your Favorites folder in your preferred manner.

Tip You can copy or delete any shortcuts (or folders) using the same conventions that you would use in My Computer.

If you opt to view your Favorites folder in the Details view, for example, you can sort the displayed list by clicking on any of the buttons that serve as headers for the columns in that view. Double-click on any shortcut to go to the corresponding Web site or folder.

Viewing Your History

If you've recently been to a site that you would like to revisit, you often can find that site more quickly and easily by referring to your History, which is a list of the sites you've recently visited, sorted in order of visitation.

To review your History, click on the down arrow button at the far right of the browser's Address text box, or select Open History Folder from Internet Explorer's Go menu.

You can set the number of days that Internet Explorer 3 will keep track of your History. Select Options from the View menu to view your History options.

If you use Internet Explorer 3 to browse the hard drive contents of your own (or another) computer, you find that activity also included in your History.

Viewing Contents of Drives

Internet Explorer 3 can serve as a rudimentary replacement for Windows Explorer or My Computer. Although you can't manage multiple windows or work with files in the same manner, you can quickly view the contents of any drives and folders to which you have rights.

Here is how you use Microsoft Internet Explorer 3 to view drive contents:

1. Click on the contents of the Address text box to highlight those contents and then press Delete to clear the text box of all text.

2. Type C:\ (or some other drive letter) and press Enter. The drive you entered is outlined much in the same way it would be in My Computer.

3. From this point on, you are functionally working with My Computer.

When viewing drive contents using MSIE, you can further configure your view of your computer's contents by selecting any of these four menu items from the View menu:

◆ Large icons

◆ Small icons

◆ List

◆ Details

These four views enable you to present the same information in four distinctly different ways. Internet Explorer 3 keeps track of your preference, referring to your choice of view whenever you look at your workstation with Internet Explorer (see fig. 25.3).

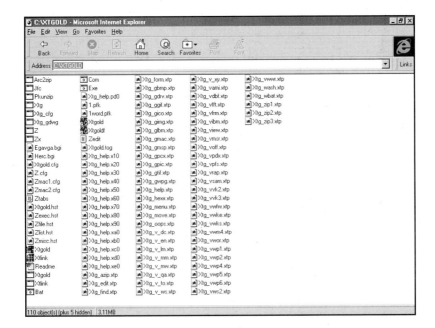

Figure 25.3

This folder contains a DOS application. Internet Explorer 3 can easily substitute as a rudimentary Windows File Manager.

You can further configure Internet Explorer 3 to arrange the icons in this view. Select Arrange Icons from the View menu and then choose the arrangement that best suits your preference. Note that these menu items do not appear when you are viewing HTML Web pages.

Navigating Safely

The word "security" is on the lips of every computer professional in touch with emerging technologies and the Internet. The development of protocols and mechanisms designed to protect access to information and the integrity of banking information has been well underway for quite some time now with only minimal results.

Microsoft has embarked on several missions to improve the integrity of commercial transactions on the Internet. While these efforts haven't yet popularized commercial transactions, they have resulted in general security improvements in Internet Explorer 3.

Security is about getting what you expect from a transaction or service. If you manage an HTTP server, you expect to be able to protect your resources from unwanted access and to prevent unauthorized users from damaging resources that your authorized users own.

The Internet Explorer line of browsers has grown to become one of the most competent, secure browsers on the market. The next section covers the security features built into Internet Explorer 3.

Code Signing

Microsoft Internet Explorer 3 uses *code signing,* a process in which you determine whether the code you're about to download is indeed the original code. Code signing is a matter of checking the size of the code and comparing it to what it's supposed to be.

Code (file) size is checked before you download the file and then again after you download the file. If the size of the code has changed during download, you are notified of this fact at the same time that you're prompted to name a location on your workstation to receive that code. You then can decide whether you want to accept the code despite the evidence of tampering.

> **Tip**   Some anti-virus products perform a function similar to code signing, as well as scanning the code for known viruses. If you are concerned about the integrity of the code you're downloading, you should go one step further than Internet Explorer 3's trusted code technology and look into products that check for viruses too.

Secure Channels

Internet Explorer 3 supports the latest security protocols, including SSL 2, SSL 3, and PCT 1. Internet Explorer uses a methodology that enables you to gain unique identification with certificates. MSIE 3 creates and uses certificates to identify you as the "real article" whenever an SSL server needs to verify your identity. These certificates are managed in what Microsoft and other security vendors refer to as *wallets.*

Both clients and servers are capable of requiring and presenting proof of authenticity in the form of certificates. You may be required to provide your own certificate (you will be prompted if it's necessary) to a server when you attempt to transact commerce or access valued data. As a workstation user, you also may require remote servers to authenticate themselves to you when you're poised to utilize secure information, such as bank and credit card account numbers or personal identification numbers.

> **Tip**   Although SSL and security have come a long way in the last year, industry pundits are advising that you select unique passwords or personal identification numbers for Internet use, rather than reusing your ATM (automatic bank teller machines) or other passwords on the Internet. In other words, don't use your ATM card's PIN for commerce accounts over the Internet.

You can determine how you want to be warned of a potential problem when viewing or sending information to a remote server. Figure 25.4 shows you the Safety Level dialog box you use to preset levels of security. (Use the View Options command, select the Security tab and click the Safety Level button.) Internet Explorer 3 can post a warning dialog box whenever you're about to send or receive data.

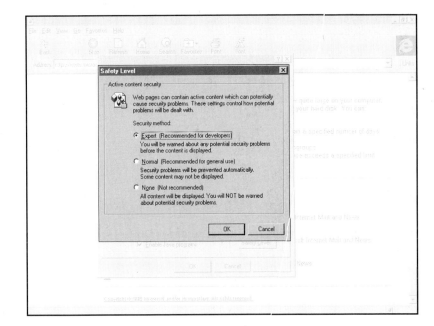

Figure 25.4

Three security levels give you the option to make judgments based on the context of the moment.

You access security settings choosing View, Options. After the Options dialog box appears, select the Security tab to review security options.

Safety Levels

The Security dialog box gives you control over when you are warned about potential hazards: either just before accessing programs through a Web page or just before sending information (like a credit card number) that might not be secure. Figure 25.5 shows the Security tab of the Options dialog box.

In a nutshell, you can be told you're about to be exposed to unsecure transmissions, then directed to choose one of the following:

◆ To let Internet Explorer protect you without your input

◆ To decide at the time of the warning

Figure 25.5

*Use the Security
tab of the Options
dialog box to
control MSIE's
security settings.*

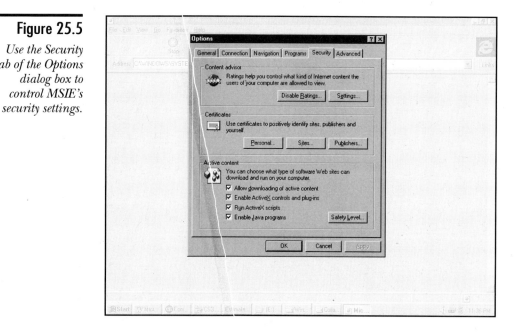

To disable these warnings altogether, use the Security tab and click on the Disable
Ratings button.

Ratings and Your Browser

Internet Explorer 3 is equipped to screen out Web sites that are not approved by a
password. This option is great for parents in the home and also can be set by network
system administrators to keep employees from viewing resources that have no place in
activities normally conducted in the enterprise.

The private sector has been developing rating systems for sites that parents might
want to keep their children from viewing. Sites are reviewed for content and then
assigned ratings according to the site's inclusion of these four content areas:

◆ Language

◆ Nudity

◆ Sex

◆ Violence

You can tailor the degree of allowable content in any of these four areas. You might
allow your teens to view obscene gestures, for example, but you may want to exclude
them from accessing sites where they would be able to view explicit sexual activity.

You determine and set the level of acceptance in these four content areas. After you set these levels, they can be turned off or changed only by using your password.

Remote administrator access of client ratings settings might not be available in the final release of Internet Explorer 3 for Windows NT Workstation 4. System or network administrators, however, can set ratings passwords on client machines when they install Internet Explorer 3 on that client machine.

To access your ratings options from the client, use this next set of steps:

1. With MSIE 3 running, choose View, Options and then select the Security tab. Click on the Enable Ratings button to enter a unique password.

2. Click on the Settings button to see and update your ratings options (see fig. 25.6).

3. Click on any of the four rating categories (Language, Nudity, Sex, and Violence) and then drag the slider that appears to adjust the content level that MSIE will allow. Click OK to close the dialog box.

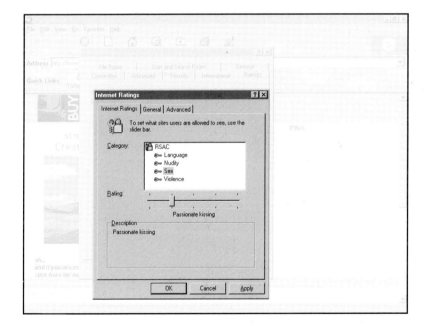

Figure 25.6

The ratings system is broken into four content areas.

You should be aware that the ratings systems are not yet widespread. This means that not many sites, other than adult sites, use ratings systems at all. After ratings systems are in play on a widespread basis (HTML authors must place an identifying tag on their home pages), you can choose different ratings systems tailored more closely to your needs.

The Proxy Server

Many Web servers today are protected from intrusion by unwanted or unauthorized entry. The most popular approach toward system security is to install firewall software on a proxy server, which runs on the network and maintains the security of the Web browsing on the network. Users then need to access the Web server via the proxy server.

If you need to access a Web server that uses a firewall maintained on a proxy server, you first need to tell Internet Explorer 3 that you require access to that proxy server and then enter settings that get you into that proxy server.

Here is a list of the settings you need:

◆ The HTTP address and port number

◆ The secure address and port number

◆ The FTP address and port number

◆ The Gopher address and port number

◆ The Socks address and port number

Proxy settings are located in the Options dialog box, which is available by selecting Options from Internet Explorer's View menu. Select the Connection tab to gain access to proxy settings as shown in figure 25.7.

Figure 25.7

Use the Connection tab of the Options dialog box to enable proxy settings.

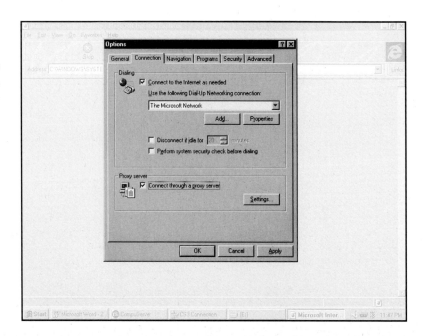

Note that you don't need Gopher settings if you don't use Gopher, and so on. You can exclude intranets by making the appropriate selection in the Exceptions group box. You can also exclude using a proxy server for selected sites by specifying the first characters in the names of those sites in the Exceptions group box.

Customizing the Look of Internet Explorer

Internet Explorer 3 has more interface tailoring options than any previous version. Most of these options are related to the button bars and how they can be configured.

This section explores the options for customizing button bars, color preferences, and the look of your Web pages.

Changing the Size of Fonts

With Internet Explorer 3, you can change the size of fonts shown in Web pages that you browse. This feature is especially useful when browsing a Web site authored in a different screen resolution, which makes text uncomfortable to read.

To change the size of the fonts used in a Web page you are viewing, click on the Font button on the toolbar until you find a font size that works for you. The font size toggles between five predetermined sizes: Largest, Large, Medium, Small, and Smallest.

 Some web pages use predetermined font sizes that are specified in the document's HTML code. You will not be able to use the Font button to change the size of such text on these pages.

You also can change global usage of fonts by choosing View, Fonts.

Setting Font and Page Color Preferences

You can set your own preferences for font colors and page colors. Your preferences override any color settings in the HTML code in the page you are viewing. The benefit is clear if you have a low-contrast environment and you want to use pre-defined color settings for page backgrounds and page fonts. The drawback here is that, if you change the color settings, you might not be able to see many of the unique design properties of some exciting web pages.

Choose View, Options, and then select the General tab (see fig. 25.8) to view and change text and page color options. Be sure you enable the option that uses "these colors instead of Windows desktop colors" to make the text and background color settings available.

Figure 25.8

The General tab lets you control different display options for Internet Explorer.

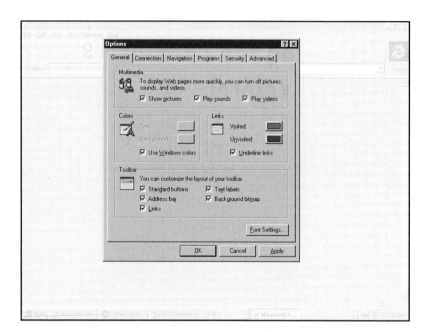

Customizing Your Toolbar and Status Bar

The button bars on the toolbar used by Microsoft Internet Explorer 3 can be configured in these ways:

◆ They can be made to appear or disappear.

◆ They can share a single bar of space, being scrolled in and out of view.

◆ They can be moved up or down on the interface, placing any toolbar on top, in the middle, or on the bottom.

◆ The Status bar can be made to appear or disappear.

Three button bars are on the toolbar. One holds navigation buttons, another hosts the text box in which you enter your URLs, and the third harbors established links to Web sites.

You can disable the display of the toolbar by deselecting it from View, Toolbars.

You can move any of the three bars up or down by dragging their borders in the direction you want to move them (see fig. 25.9).

The toolbar can be made to share a single horizontal space. Drag the bottom of the Links bar up until only one bar shows. Next, drag the anchors on the Address and Links buttons, sliding them horizontally to suit your viewing preference. You also can click on Links or Address to maximize them.

Drag in these places to
reposition the toolbars.

Figure 25.9

You can drag Internet Explorer's toolbars to suit your preferences.

Click on these bars to adjust the
horizontal position of the toolbar.

Increasing Your Personal Productivity

You can do several things to optimize your time with Internet Explorer 3 for Windows NT Workstation 4. You can create shortcuts that take you and readers of your documents to Web sites around the world. You can use keyboard shortcuts to get Internet Explorer 3 rolling faster. You can set up dialing preferences and configure how much space can be used when caching documents. This section discusses each of these time savers.

Creating Shortcuts

You can create shortcuts that get you to your destinations much faster if you use Internet Explorer 3's capability to store and organize destinations as shortcuts.

Internet Explorer 3 enables you to create shortcuts to Web site locations (URLs) to be referred to in the future. To save a shortcut (Web site URL) to your Favorites folder, select Favorites from the main menu and then select Add to Favorites to open the Add to Favorites dialog box.

Save your new Favorite as an entry on its own. You can save it in an existing folder or save it as a new folder. Be sure to select a meaningful name for the Favorite so you can quickly recognize it in the future.

Using Keyboard Shortcuts

You can use the keyboard to be productive with Internet Explorer 3. You might enjoy the power and speed of execution that goes along with the use of keyboard shortcuts. Of course, Windows NT Workstation 4 holds many shortcuts for you. Internet Explorer, however, has a few of its own (see table 25.1).

TABLE 25.1
Microsoft Internet Explorer 3 Keyboard Shortcuts

Shortcut Key	Action
Backspace	Go to the previous page
Shift+Backspace	Go to the next page
End	Go to the end of a document
Ctrl+N	Open a second browser window
Page Down	Page down
Page Up	Page up
Ctrl+P	Print the page or selected frame
F5	Reload the page

Shortcut Key	Action
Ctrl+S	Save the page as an HTML file
Down Arrow	Scroll down
Up Arrow	Scroll up
Shift+F10	Show a shortcut menu for a hyperlink
ESC	Stop a task
Ctrl+Tab	Toggle between frames
Shift+Ctrl+Tab	Toggle between frames in the opposite order from Ctrl+Tab
Ctrl+O	Open a dialog box from which you can open a file or
URLHome	Toggle to the top of the document

Customizing Your Start, Search, and Quick Link Pages

Internet Explorer 3 comes installed with preset, configurable default Start, Search, and Quick Link pages. The *Start page* is the page that always opens when you connect to the Internet or to your intranet with the browser. The *Search page* is the search page or engine you want to see when you are looking for something on the Internet or intranet. *Quick Links* are the buttons that take you places and are found on the Links part of the toolbar.

You can use any Web page as your preferred start page. Choose View, Options, Navigation to view the Start, Search, and Quick Link pages (see fig. 25.10). Select one of those three by clicking on the down arrow button next to the Page list box, then double-clicking on the one you want to view. Next, you can either type a new URL into the Address text box, click on Use Current to make the currently viewed Web page your new start page, or click on the Use Default button to make MSN your default Web page. Close the Options dialog box to save your selections.

If you want to replace the hyperlinks that are your current Quick Links, select any of the Quick Links on the list and then select a new URL to assign to any of them. Don't forget to name each Quick Link—you'll see this name, not the URL, on the toolbar.

Figure 25.10

Check out this list of default assignments that you can change to increase your productivity.

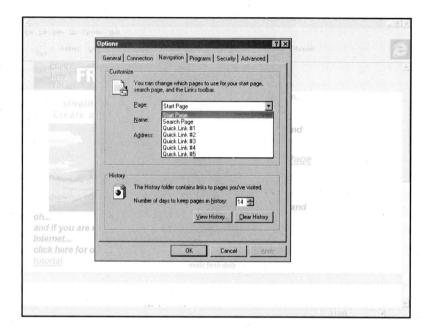

Enabling Pictures, Sound, and Video

By default, Microsoft Internet Explorer 3 is preconfigured to utilize pictures, sound, and video. You can change these settings if you find that many of the sounds are annoying your co-workers or are otherwise disruptive in the workplace. You also can toggle video on and off if you don't have the hardware or bandwidth to support this, or prefer not to wait to see such content. You can also disable sound and images in this way for the same reasons.

To toggle these three media on or off, open the Options dialog box found on the View menu, then select the General tab.

Going Beyond the Basics

Some of you might not be easily impressed with the general workings of Internet Explorer 3. You might want to go a bit farther with this new, world-class browser.

You can view source code for any page filled with HTML or CGI code. You can update your version of Microsoft Internet Explorer whenever it is revised by clicking on a button. Microsoft also is offering an Administration kit geared primarily for the networking support professional.

Internet Explorer users now have access to a dedicated resource at the Microsoft Web site. Avid learners can also quench their thirst for more knowledge by accessing the Tutorial area at the Microsoft Web site.

The following sections examine these five activities.

Viewing Source Code

Viewing source code doesn't get any easier with any other browser product. To see the actual hidden HTML code in any document being viewed, select Source from Internet Explorer's View menu. The current page is opened in Notepad, a text editor that shows the contents of files that are less than 64 KB in size.

After you open Notepad, you can review the code and save it to disk. Remember, you can't save it to a remote server if that's where it came from, but you can save it to a local or network drive. If you're authorized to have read/write access to the Web where the document originated, you might be able to edit the document and then save it back to the Web. If you aren't clear about your right to directly write to the Web server, consult with your in-house Webmaster or network professionals.

Updating Your Version of Internet Explorer

Internet Explorer 3 offers a new feature on its toolbar, a Quick Link button called Product Update. This button automatically links you to the Microsoft Internet Explorer 3 home page, where you can download the latest and greatest versions of Internet Explorer, along with several add-on products such as Mail and News, NetMeeting, and so on.

 Tip Although you can use HTTP (the browser) to download updates, downloading files from the Microsoft FTP site is often a time-saver:

ftp.microsoft.com

FTP can be at least two times faster than using Internet Explorer 3 or any FTP utility program. To use Internet Explorer 3 as an FTP utility, enter the address of the FTP site in the Address box and then press Enter. After you can see the file structure of the FTP site, select MSDOWNLOADS and then go to the MSIE 3 folder to download the NT or Windows 95 version of the product.

You'll also find the other Microsoft utility programs, enhancements, and add-ons at the same FTP site. Don't be afraid to download software from the Microsoft FTP site to the hard drive on your NT Workstation 4 machine. You can save time, and the worst that can happen is an unexpected disconnection, requiring you to restart the download process.

Using the Internet Explorer Administration Kit

The Administration Kit available for use with Microsoft Internet Explorer 3 helps you customize Internet Explorer for use on all NT Workstations on the network. You also can add your company's logo (animated, even!) to the Internet Explorer toolbar.

If that's not enough, you can fully configure every option before you install Internet Explorer on NT Workstation 4. You can, in essence, give every NT Workstation 4 user in your company a fully customized, company-specific installation of Internet Explorer 3.

The Internet Explorer Administration Kit is a great support tool for ISPs or Webmasters who are motivated to create and employ a true plug-and-play solution for their users. A wizard steps you through customizing and creating a self-installing product ready for distribution. The CD-ROM version includes virtually every freeware Internet- and intranet-specific offering in play by Microsoft.

The catch: Your company must sign a distribution agreement with Microsoft. Although there isn't any fee, you should take certain restrictions and requirements seriously. The current URL that leads you to this agreement is

http://198.105.232.4/ie/ieak/iedist.htm

The Internet Explorer Home Page

Microsoft has built a home page dedicated to users of Internet Explorer 3. You can head straight for this page by clicking on the Product Update button on Internet Explorer's Links bar. For those of you who insist on doing it the hard way, the URL is

http://www.microsoft.com/ie

Although everyone knows that Web pages can change often, figure 25.11 offers a glimpse of the Internet Explorer home page.

You learn everything you ever wanted to learn about Microsoft's plans for you and its premier Web browser, Internet Explorer 3, at this site.

Using the Internet Tutorial

So you want more help using Microsoft Internet Explorer 3 with the World Wide Web? Microsoft has built a Web page dedicated to helping you learn more about using MSIE 3 on the Web. If you haven't already changed the Quick Link that leads to this tutorial, click on the link that reads Web Tutorial. It takes you to a page at the Microsoft Web site and offers a good beginner tutorial for your use if you're new to the World Wide Web.

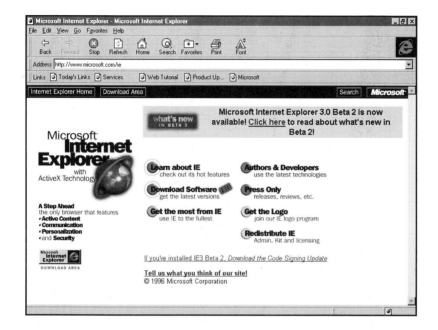

Figure 25.11

The Internet Explorer home page displays a globe that animates once every second.

If you have already changed the link that leads you to Microsoft's Internet tutorial, use this URL instead:

http://home.microsoft.com/tutorial/default.html

End Note: Although you can ignore the obvious advantages of using Microsoft Internet Explorer 3, you would be wise to consider that many software developers and Web authors are embracing the standards and achievements of Microsoft's Internet directions and standards.

In the quest for robust performance and feature sets that rival the competition, browsers are getting larger with every product release. This product has become significantly larger in the amount of space it occupies on your hard drive. Expect the product to demand 50 MB of hard disk space but to actually use about 15 MB of space.

Browsers are being expanded to incorporate the most popular and common add-on technologies—many of which are part of Microsoft's global quest to dominate all areas of the software industry. Expect future versions to provide increasingly high levels of compatibility and interactivity, leveraging proprietary Microsoft enhancements in other products in the lineup.

Test Your Knowledge

1. Which of the following technologies are supported by MSIE 3?

    A. ActiveMovie

    B. Direct3D

    C. DirectAccess

    D. DirectPlay

2. If you want to set up a company-specific version of Internet Explorer for use on your company network, you can:

    A. Edit the CONFIG.WEB file with the appropriate changes.

    B. Purchase the corporate license version of Internet Explorer.

    C. Acquire the free Internet Explorer Administration Kit from Microsoft.

    D. You cannot modify Internet Explorer.

3. Which graphics file formats does Internet Explorer support?

    A. JPEG

    B. GIF

    C. Encapsulated Postscript

    D. BMP

4. You can extend the functionality of Internet Explorer to access pages using VRML, ActiveMovie, and other emerging technologies by:

    A. Buying the Microsoft Plus! for Internet Explorer package.

    B. Support for all emerging technologies already exists in Internet Explorer 3.

    C. You can download or purchase the appropriate add-in module from its provider.

    D. You cannot take advantage of any technologies not supported by Microsoft.

Test Your Knowledge Answers

1. A,B,D

2. C

3. A,B,D

4. C

PART VII

Administering NT Workstation 4

Chapter Snapshot

Windows NT Workstation lets you seamlessly share your computer's resources with others over a network. In order to effectively manage the shared resources of your workstation, you need to understand the tools that are available to you as well as how the security of the system is designed. Once you're familiar with Windows NT Workstation 4's abilities to share its resources, it becomes easy to do so and to also ensure that confidential work on your computer is safe from prying eyes. This chapter focuses on the following topics:

Windows NT
Workstation 4

CHAPTER 26

Understanding Shared Resources

If you use Windows NT Workstation 4 within a company, chances are that you may want to share some resource of your workstation with other users over the network. Perhaps you might want to share a printer, files stored on your computer, or other resources. As part of this, however, you must also handle the security of your workstation so that information or resources that you don't want to share aren't made available to others without your permission. Because Windows NT Workstation 4 is designed to be both a network client and a network server whereby others on your network can access your computer, it needs to be administered if you want to control who can access your stored work and the devices connected to your computer. Windows NT Workstation 4 includes many tools that enable you to control access flexibly, so that you can exert control over who can do what on your computer.

In this chapter, you learn how to share resources (files, folders, and printers) on your computer with others on the network. As part of sharing these resources, you also learn how to administer them and control their security. Along the way, you also learn how to create and maintain the list of users who can access your computer and how to set security policies for your system.

Sharing Resources

You control which devices on your computer are shared with other users and which ones are kept private. You can control whether drives (including disk drives and CD-ROMs), individual folders, and printers are shared. When you are setting up the share (a shared device is often called a share), you can control who can access the device and what permissions they have.

Sharing Drives

When you open My Computer, you can tell which of the drives on your computer are shared by the wrist and hand icon next to the drive icon. In figure 26.1, for example, you can see that drives C, D, and E are shared.

The drive icons with the hands displayed are shared.

Figure 26.1

Shared drives in My Computer display with hand icons superimposed.

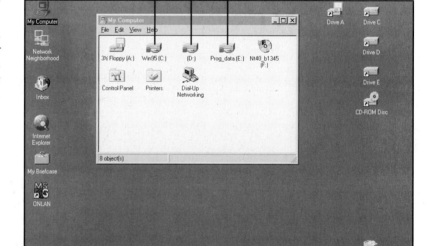

> **Note** | Sharing of drives works the same whether the drive is a floppy disk drive, hard disk drive, or CD-ROM drive.

To share a drive, right-click on the drive and choose Sharing from the pop-up menu. You then see the dialog box shown in figure 26.2.

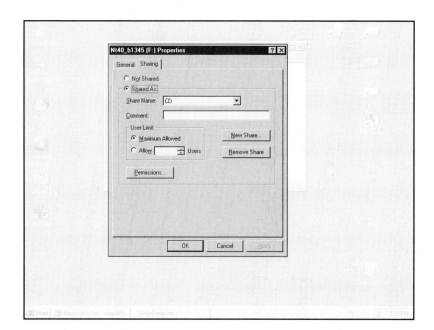

Figure 26.2

The drive's Properties dialog box enables you to control how drives are shared.

To enable the share, select the Shared As radio button and then assign a name that other computers will see in the Share Name field. You also can control how many users can simultaneously access the share with the User Limit choices. To control access rights to the share, click on the Permissions button, which displays the Access Through Share Permissions dialog box shown in figure 26.3.

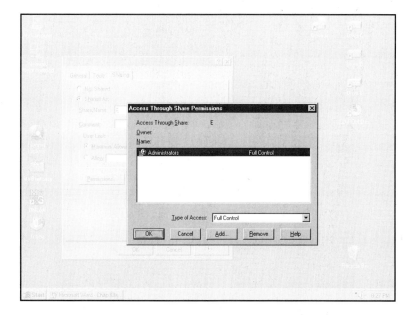

Figure 26.3

View and set access privileges with the Access Through Share Permissions dialog box.

> **Note** You can have multiple shares for a single resource. Using the Share Name field's drop-down list, you can see each of the shares that have been defined.

By default, the group Everyone is assigned Full Control rights to the share. You can change the access level for Everyone by selecting a different level with the Type of Access drop-down list. You can choose from No Access, Read, Change, and Full Control.

> **Caution** Full Control means users who have that type of access can, for NTFS-formatted drives, change the permissions for the share and take ownership of the share.

You should carefully consider the type of access you grant and how you grant it. *No Access* means just that; the selected user or group has no access to the drive. *Read access* means the user can view files and run programs stored on the share. *Change access* means the user can additionally modify or delete any files; *Full Control* means the user can administer the share if it's for an NTFS-formatted drive.

Also remember that users are given the fullest access that applies to them—access rights are said to be *cumulative*. If you grant Full Control access to Everyone and then add a specific user with Read access, the user will still have Full Control access to the share because he is a member of the Everyone group. To control things more tightly, you would use a more limited group instead of Everyone or explicitly grant access to the users that you want to access the resource and grant No Access levels to groups.

> **Note** On NTFS-formatted drives, the No Access level overrides other granted rights, even cumulative rights.

To add a user or group to the share's access permissions, click on the Add button. This displays the Add Users and Groups dialog box shown in figure 26.4.

To assign rights to a group, follow these steps:

1. Select the group in the window.

2. Click the Add button.

3. Choose the type of access you will grant.

You can select multiple groups and assign them access all at the same time, as long as you are granting them all the same level of access. If you want to add more than one group and want the groups to have different access types, you must re-access the Add Users and Groups dialog box for each type of access granted.

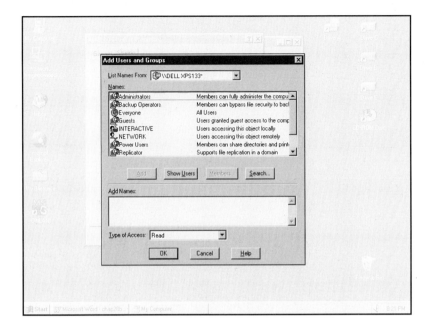

Figure 26.4

The Add Users and Groups dialog box enables you to add access permissions.

The Add Users and Groups dialog box can display individual users if you click on the Show Users button; by default, only groups are shown. Also, when you select a group, you can click on the Members button to see a dialog box that displays the members of the group.

Sharing Folders

Individual folders are shared just like drives. Right-click on a folder and choose Sharing from the pop-up menu. The dialog boxes function exactly the same way as they do when sharing a drive (refer to the preceding section for complete instructions).

Objective C.3

Understanding Inherited Rights—FAT versus NTFS

When you share a folder on FAT-formatted drives, you are not only giving access to that particular folder, you are also giving access to all the folders within it, down as many levels as there are folders. You cannot arbitrarily restrict access to lower-level folders. If you've given Full Control access to Everyone for \FOLDER1, for example, you cannot set \FOLDER1\FOLDER2 to a more limited access. Also, new directories created under \FOLDER1 automatically inherit the rights of \FOLDER1.

NTFS-formatted drives behave this way by default, but you can set different permissions for lower-level folders.

Setting Drive, Directory, and File Permissions on NTFS Drives

Objective C.4

When you format your disk drives using the NTFS file system, you gain important additional security features that aren't available on FAT-formatted drives. To access these features, use the Security tab of a folder's Properties dialog box, which isn't visible for FAT drives. The Security tab is shown in figure 26.5.

Figure 26.5

The Security tab of a folder's Properties dialog box enables you to exert more control over an NTFS-formatted drive's security.

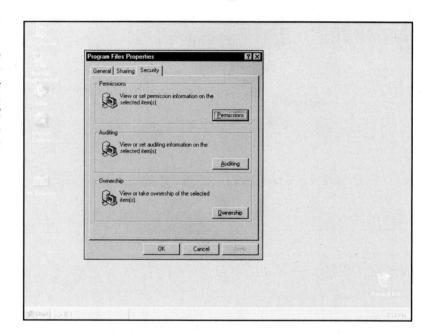

Note | Changing permissions for drives, directories, or files works exactly the same way, and the dialog boxes you use are identical except for their title bars.

Objective C.3

Clicking on the Permissions button shows you the Directory Permissions dialog box displayed in figure 26.6.

Tip | You can select multiple directories or files before accessing the Properties dialog box. Your permission changes will be applied to all the preselected objects.

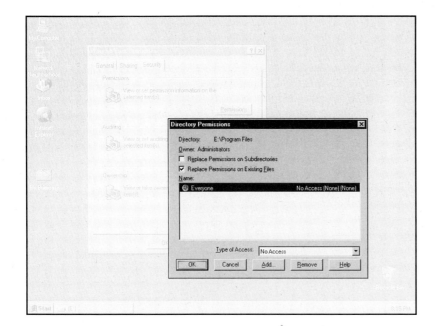

Figure 26.6

The Directory Permissions dialog box enables you to set permissions on NTFS drives.

The Directory Permissions dialog box, at first glance, appears similar to the Add Users and Groups dialog box, but there are important differences:

◆ The owner of the share is tracked and displayed.

◆ You can choose two new options for replacing permissions on subdirectories and files.

◆ Additional access types are available.

When you set permissions on directories using the Directory Permissions dialog box, the change you make only applies to the directory you selected. Although lower-level directories will inherit your setting, they will only do so if they have no conflicting security settings. Suppose you have a drive called D:, for example, and it contains two directories: \TOP_DIR and \TOP_DIR\SUBDIR. You start a share for drive D: with Change-level access for Everyone. You then modify \TOP_DIR\SUBDIR so that Everyone has only Read access to that directory. Later, you set the permission of \TOP_DIR for Everyone to Full Control access. The change you make, by default, does not change the permissions you earlier assigned to \TOP_DIR\SUBDIR. You can, however, select the Replace Permissions on Subdirectories check box on the Directory Permissions dialog box. This causes your new change to be applied to any subdirectories that exist. The Replace Permissions on Subdirectories check box then overwrites any existing permissions contained in subdirectories with the new setting.

A similar situation exists with regard to files. By default, the Replace Permissions on Existing Files check box is selected (while the Replace Permissions on Subdirectories is not selected by default) so that any changes you make to the directory's permissions are automatically asserted to any files in the directory. If you clear this check box, however, your changes will not apply to any existing file permissions.

The Directory Permissions dialog box for NTFS-formatted drives also contains additional types of access (in addition to No Access, Read, Change, and Full Control) that you can choose:

- ◆ **List.** Lets users view directory names, file names, subdirectories, but they cannot open or access files.

- ◆ **Add.** Lets users create files and subdirectories, but they cannot access existing files (even the ones they just created). This is useful if you want to set up a folder into which people can put things, but you do not want them viewing the folder's contents. The folder becomes like a black box into which they can put files but can take nothing out.

- ◆ **Read.** Lets users view directory and file names, view file contents and run programs, and create new files or subdirectories.

You also can choose Special Directory Access and Special File Access in the Type of Access field, both of which display dialog boxes. The dialog boxes are identical; the Special Access dialog box is shown in figure 26.7.

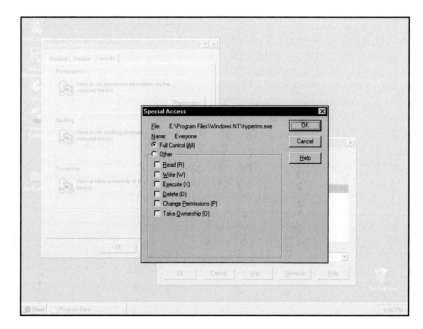

Figure 26.7

Set custom permissions with the Special Access dialog box.

If you need to set permissions that are not possible with the types of access you've learned about so far, you can use the Special Access dialog box to build your own custom permissions. The permissions that you can choose are:

◆ **Read (R).** Directory and file names can be seen.

◆ **Write (W).** New files and directories can be created.

◆ **Execute (X).** The user can change to subdirectories and can execute programs.

◆ **Delete (D).** Files and directories can be deleted.

◆ **Change Permissions (P).** Permissions can be changed for the directory or file.

◆ **Take Ownership (O).** The user can take ownership of the directory or file.

Changing Ownership

Creating a file or directory on an NTFS-formatted disk records that you are the owner of the resource. You can grant others permissions to the resource, including the ability for them to take ownership away from you. (Only members of the Administrative group can otherwise take ownership away from an owner.)

**Objective
C.4**

Ownership is an important tool for preserving the security of your files and directories. Although members of the Administrative group on the system can take ownership from you, they cannot grant it to others (including back to you). If you've placed a No Access permission on a resource, and an administrator takes ownership of the resource and then grants different permissions, you can see that the ownership of the resource has changed. Because administrators cannot change the ownership back to you, they cannot hide this change from you. For very important resources, you might want to check the ownership regularly to ensure that your permissions are intact.

You can view the ownership of a resource, and take ownership if you have the necessary permissions, with the Ownership button on the Security tab of the resource's Properties dialog box. This brings up the Owner dialog box (see fig. 26.8).

To take ownership as your own, click on the Take Ownership button.

Sharing Printers

If you want to share a printer over the network, you must create a share for the printer. This is done by accessing the printer's pop-up menu and choosing the Sharing command. You see the Sharing tab of the printer's Properties dialog box, as shown in figure 26.9.

Figure 26.8

Use the Owner dialog box to take ownership of a resource.

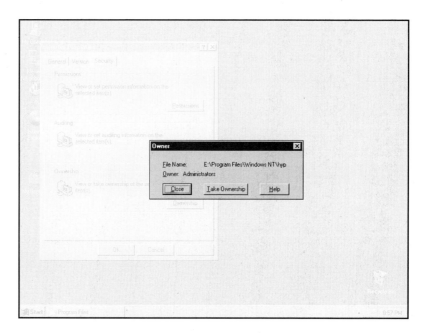

Figure 26.9

The Sharing tab of a printer's Properties dialog box lets you control whether printers are shared across the network.

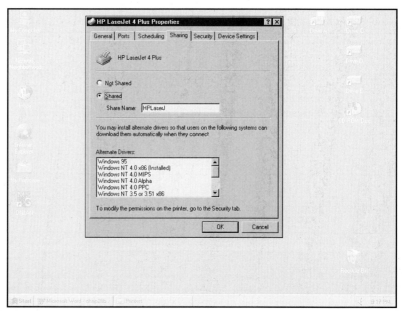

To enable sharing of the printer, select the Shared radio button and assign a network name for the printer to the Share Name field.

With printers you can set detailed permissions, whether your system uses FAT- or NTFS-formatted drives. You access these permissions through the Security tab of the printer's Properties dialog box. Then use the Permissions button to access the Printer Permissions dialog box shown in figure 26.10.

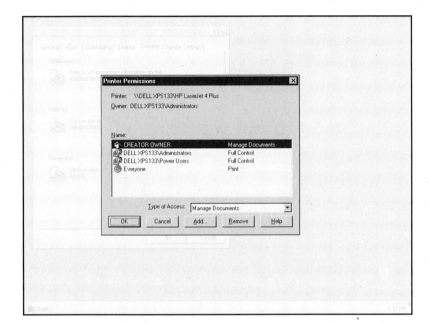

Figure 26.10

The Printer Permissions dialog box displays current permissions.

By default, as you can see in figure 26.10, the creator or owner of a print job can manage his documents, while the Everyone group can only view jobs in the queue. Administrators can, of course, fully control the printer queue.

You can grant four types of access : No Access, Print (allows the user to use the printer), Manage Documents (allows the user to access the printer and manage any documents waiting to be printed), and Full Control (full access to the printer, including the capability to take ownership and to set access permissions for others).

Understanding User Manager

Complete management of your system's security includes managing user accounts on the system. The user accounts are what enable a person to log on to your system across a network. You need to be able to create, modify, and delete user accounts. In this section, you learn how to do this.

Objective

C.1

You administer User Manager, which is found in the Administrative Tools menu. User Manager enables you to add, modify, and delete users from your system, and it also enables you to set security policies and audit capabilities. Figure 26.11 shows you the main User Manager screen.

Figure 26.11

User Manager enables you to maintain user accounts for the system.

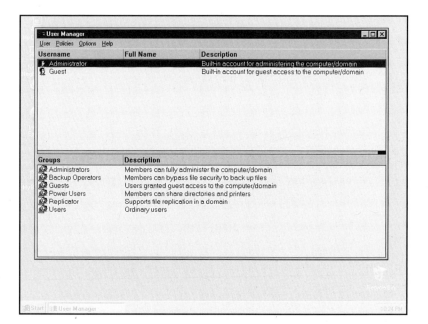

On a freshly installed system, two users are defined: Administrator and Guest. (The Guest account is disabled by default.) The groups you see in figure 26.11 also are defined. You can assign new users to these pre-existing groups.

Adding and Maintaining User Accounts

Objective C.1

You add new users with the New User command in the User menu. The New User dialog box is shown in figure 26.12.

Table 26.1 shows you the fields and options in the New User dialog box.

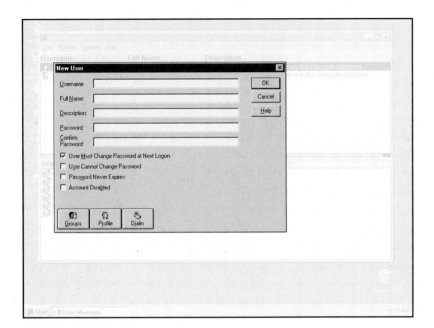

Figure 26.12

A number of fields need to be completed when using the New User dialog box.

TABLE 26.1
New User Dialog Box Fields

Field	Description
Username	The name by which the user is known on the system. User names should not have spaces and can be up to 20 characters long.
Full Name	The user's full name; this field is not used except to more fully define for you who the user account belongs to (this can be helpful if the actual user name isn't based on the person's name).
Description	Any description you want to note about the user.
Password	Type the opening password for the user in this field. The password displays as asterisks. The maximum length of a password is 14 characters.
Confirm Password	Retype the opening password for the user in this field, which should exactly match the Password field entry.

continues

TABLE 26.1, CONTINUED
New User Dialog Box Fields

Field	Description
User Must Change Password at Next Logon	This check box forces the user to choose his own password, which only he knows, after he first logs on to the system.
User Cannot Change Password	If an account is being used by multiple users, you might want to select this check box to ensure that one of the users doesn't change the password to the account without informing the other users.
Password Never Expires	The policies you set determine how often passwords expire and need to be changed. If this check box is selected, the user account being added or modified does not need to change its password.
Account Disabled	When selected, this check box disables all access for this user but does not delete the account.
Groups	Activates a dialog box in which you choose to which groups the user belongs. By default, everyone belongs to the Everyone group.
Profile	Lets you define information about the user's profile, such as his home directory and login script.
Dialin	Enables you to grant dial-in access for the user.

To modify an existing account, select the user name and then access the Properties command in the User menu. You also can rename existing users by selecting the user and then selecting Rename from the User menu.

To delete a user, select the user and then choose Delete from the User menu.

> **Caution** In Windows NT, user permissions are said to be "unique across space and time." If you delete a user, then re-create the user using exactly the same name and password, any previous permissions assigned will *not* exist. Every time you create a user you must assign the appropriate permissions to the account. Therefore, if you need to inactivate a user for a specific period of time—but there is a chance they will require the account's use again in the future—you should instead use the Account Disabled property in the User Manager to turn the account off temporarily without disturbing the permissions for the account.

Setting User Policies

You set user security policies in the Account Policy dialog box, which you open by choosing the Account command in the Policies menu of User Manager. The Account Policy dialog box is shown in figure 26.13.

Objective

C.1

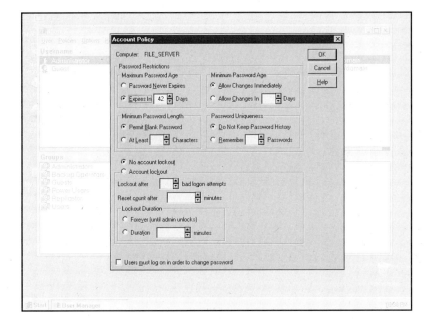

Figure 26.13

System-wide policies are set in the Account Policy dialog box.

Table 26.2 details the options available in the Account Policy dialog box.

TABLE 26.2
Account Policy Dialog Box Fields

Setting	Description
Password Never Expires	No user passwords ever expire on the system.
Expires In *xx* Days	Sets the number of days (up to 999) in which passwords expire and need to be changed by the users. Each user's expiration date is tracked separately.
Allow Changes Immediately	Lets users change their passwords immediately.

continues

TABLE 26.2, CONTINUED
Account Policy Dialog Box Fields

Setting	Description
Allow Changes In *xx* Days	Requires that users keep their selected passwords for the number of days selected, which can range from 1 to 999.
Permit Blank Password	Lets a user choose a password that has no characters.
At Least *xx* Characters	Requires that user passwords be at least the length specified (although they cannot exceed 14 characters).
Do Not Keep Password History	The system does not store previously used passwords for each user.
Remember *xx* Passwords	When selected, the system stores the number of passwords selected (up to 24) for each user and does not permit the user to reuse the passwords while they are still in the list.
No Account Lockout	If someone tries to access an account illegally, the system allows the repeated attempts.
Account Lockout	When selected, the system locks an account if someone meets the criteria listed in the Account Lockout box.
Lockout After *xx* Bad Logon Attempts	Inactivates the account after a wrong password is entered the selected number of times in a row.
Reset Count After *xx* Minutes	The system keeps track of how many incorrect passwords are entered in a row. After *x* minutes have passed, the system starts counting incorrect passwords over again.
Forever (Until Admin Unlocks)	Inactivates the account until an administrator reactivates it.
Duration *xx* Minutes	After an account is locked due to a series of wrong passwords being entered, the account is automatically reactivated after *x* minutes have passed.
Users Must Log On in Order to Change Password	This check box specifies that the user must logon using a valid password (and not an expired one) before changing his password. If his password expires, he cannot choose a new password without the administrator's help.

Auditing Users

In order to keep your workstation secure, not only do you have to control access, but you also need to audit access. Auditing means that you track and review successful and unsuccessful attempts to access some resource. Setting up auditing and keeping an eye on it are important for top-notch security management.

Objective
C.1

Windows NT Workstation 4 includes advanced auditing capabilities that enable you to view how very confidential resources are being accessed. Auditing must first be enabled in the User Manager, after which you specify auditing for each resource (drive, directory, file, and printer) that you want to audit.

Note   Auditing for drives, directories, and files is only available on NTFS-formatted drives.

Audited events are viewable in the Event Viewer's Security view. The system only keeps a certain number of audited events, which you control in the Event Viewer. The maximum log file size is a little over 4 MB.

Enabling Auditing

You enable auditing with the User Manager. Access the Audit command in the Policies menu to view the Audit Policy dialog box shown in figure 26.15.

Objective
C.1

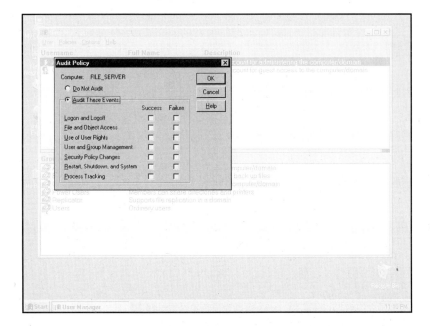

Figure 26.15

The Audit Policy dialog box enables you to choose which events you will audit. By default, no events are selected.

You can choose to audit successful and failed access attempts for the events shown in table 26.4.

TABLE 26.4
System-Wide Audit Events

Event	Description
Logon and Logoff	Logons and logoffs are audited.
File and Object Access	This option must be selected to enable specific drive, directory, file, and printer auditing.
Use of User Rights	All uses of the user rights listed in table 26.3 are audited.
User and Group Management	Changes to users or groups are audited.
Security Policy Changes	Any changes to the policies of the system are audited.
Restart, Shutdown, and System	Restarts and shutdowns are audited, as are any activities that affect system security or the security log.
Process Tracking	Detailed process activities are logged (this option is not typically useful except for programmers).

Auditing File and Object Access

Objective C.1

After you have activated the File and Object Access audit setting in the User Manager (see preceding section), you can set audit flags on drives, directories, files, and printers. Drives, directories, and files must be located on NTFS-formatted drives in order for auditing to be available.

For each of the auditable objects, you control auditing in the same way. You access the object's Properties dialog box, select the Security tab, and then click on the Auditing button. Figure 26.16 shows the Auditing dialog box for directories.

The events that can be audited include all the access permissions available for the object. If you view the auditing page for a printer, for example, you see that you can audit Manage Documents. Drives, directories, and files all use the same access permissions and, therefore, have the same events that can be audited. For each event that you want to audit, select either the Success or Failure check box or both. Auditing Success events shows accesses to the resource; auditing Failure events shows failed attempts to use the resource.

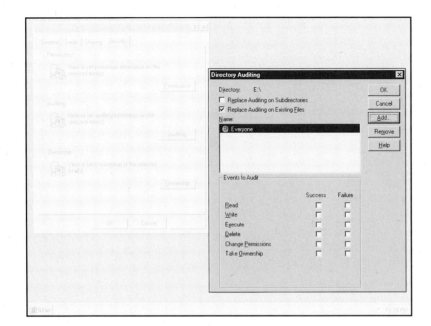

Figure 26.16

The Directory Auditing dialog box enables you to control which events for the selected resource are audited.

Audited events are placed into the Windows NT Event Viewer. In Event Viewer, you use the Security command in the Log menu (assuming you have the appropriate privileges to do so). Figure 26.17 shows the Security Log with some audited events.

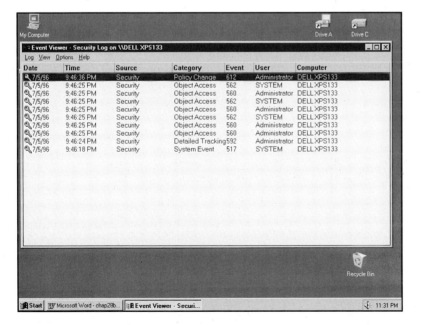

Figure 26.17

Viewing the Security Log in Event Viewer lets you see whatever security events for which you have enabled auditing.

For each of the audited events shown in Event Viewer, you can view more detailed information by double-clicking on the event. Figure 26.18 shows the information you see when you examine the details of an object-access audit entry.

Figure 26.18

The Event Detail dialog box lets you see all the details about any particular event.

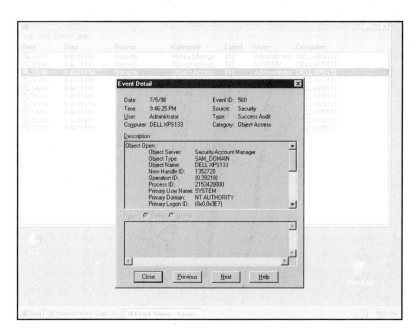

Note For more information about using the Event Viewer, see Chapter 29, "Using the Event Viewer."

Locking the Workstation

Many times, you might want to leave your computer unattended for an extended period of time but do not want anyone to be able to see what's on your screen or to access your system. You could log off the workstation, but this is often time-consuming because you must save all your open work and restart all your applications when you return. A simpler and easier approach is to use the Lock Workstation feature.

To use Lock Workstation, press Ctrl+Alt+Del while using Windows NT. The Windows NT Security dialog box appears. Click on the button marked Lock Workstation. Your computer will immediately be locked and will require your password or the workstation administrator's password in order to unlock it.

End Note: Security is a double-edged sword. When deciding on your system security policies and practices, you should balance the need for security against the hassle you and the users will face in working with the security measures on a day-to-day basis. You can set up a Windows NT Workstation 4 system that is more secure than Fort Knox, but it won't be very easy to use or to administer on an ongoing basis.

You also want to be careful that you don't overdo some of your security policies. You can insist that users use 14-character passwords, for example, but because those are passwords they can't remember, they are certain to write them down somewhere at their desks, which ends up being much less secure than if they were able to use a shorter password that they could remember.

Similarly, if you cause passwords to expire too frequently, users will start using the same password over and over but will just append a number to the end of the password to make it unique. You balance short expiration times against letting them keep their passwords for too long, which increases the risk that someone will learn their passwords and use them.

Think carefully about the security policies you want to use, and consider that the tightest security policies can sometimes reduce system security more than they help. You always have to consider the "human factor" when designing and implementing security policies.

Test Your Knowledge

1. You can share which of the following resources under Windows NT?

    A. Drives and Folders

    B. Printers

    C. Modems

    D. Sound cards

2. If you want a user to have a particular set of permissions to a folder, but then want them to have more limited permissions for a subfolder, which of the following is true?

    A. The folders in question must be on an NTFS-formatted drive.

    B. You must specifically set the more limited permission on the subfolder; otherwise, it will inherit the permissions from the parent folder.

    C. You cannot give more limited permissions to subfolders. Instead, you need to structure your folders in such a way that this requirement doesn't exist.

    D. You can grant the more limited permissions to a subfolder on both FAT- and NTFS-formatted drives.

3. In terms of security, which of the following benefits exist on NTFS-formatted drives that do not exist on FAT-formatted drives?

   A. Auditing file access.

   B. File-specific permissions.

   C. Tracking of object ownership.

   D. You can set Full Control, Read, Change, and No Access permissions.

4. On an NTFS-formatted drive, if you want to limit a user's access to a folder and all its subfolders, and there are hundreds of subfolders, you should:

   A. Change the permission on the top folder only; the change you make will be inherited to lower-level folders.

   B. Change the permission on the folder and all the subfolders, one by one.

   C. Change the permission on the top folder, but use the Replace Permissions on Subdirectories and Replace Permissions on Existing Files check boxes when making the change.

   D. Select all the relevant folders in Windows NT Explorer first, then use the Properties dialog box to make the permission change. Your change will be applied to all the folders you selected by Ctrl+clicking in Windows NT Explorer.

5. If you want to create a folder into which other users can place files for you but cannot see the files in the folder or affect them in any other way, you would need to grant them which of the following permissions?

   A. List

   B. Add

   C. Add and Read

   D. Change

6. If you want to grant access to a folder on an NTFS-formatted drive in which a user can delete selected files using Windows NT Explorer but cannot modify any of the file's contents and cannot create new files, you would do which of the following:

   A. Grant Change access.

   B. Use the Special Directory Access dialog box to grant them List and Delete privileges.

   C. Grant them the Administrator Delete privilege.

   D. This is impossible; you cannot grant the combination of rights described.

7. Which of the following statements are true about ownership tracking for files or folders under Windows NT?

    A. Ownership tracking is purely used as an aid to producing reports showing the amount of space being used on the system by each user account.

    B. Someone with Administrator group privileges can set the ownership of a resource to belong to any user on the system.

    C. Ownership tracking is a powerful security tool that even users with Administrator group privileges cannot circumvent.

    D. A user with Take Ownership privileges to a resource can take ownership of the resource, but an administrator is required to change the ownership back to the original user account.

8. If you need to grant a user access to the system in order to perform backups, but you don't want them to have access to all the files on the system, you can:

    A. Use the Backup Files and Directories user right; they can perform backups using Windows NT Backup but cannot access the files using other tools simply as a result of having this user right.

    B. Make a decision: You can choose to let them back up the entire system with the Backup Files and Directories user right, but you cannot limit their access to any file on the system; or you can grant them access to the limited set of files, but those are the only files they will be able to back up.

    C. Use the Backup All but Limited Files user right.

    D. Only the owner of a file can perform backups on that file.

9. To audit activities by users on the system, you can:

    A. Simply view the Event Viewer's Security log; all user activities are automatically audited.

    B. Activate auditing in User Manager, then set the events you want to audit on each resource.

    C. Auditing is only available on Windows NT Server.

    D. You must first enable the AuditEvent service in the Services icon, after which you can perform the actions described in answer B.

Test Your Knowledge Answers

1. A,B	6. B
2. A,B	7. C
3. A,B,C	8. B
4. C	9. B
5. B	

Chapter Snapshot

There's no such thing as a problem-free computer system. Things happen—mysterious hardware problems that render drives or peripherals useless, user errors that do damage, the hard-drive gremlins that destroy sectors. You can't stop these horrors, but you can prepare your system to fight back. This chapter discusses how to protect your computer and covers the following topics:

Windows NT
Workstation 4

CHAPTER 27

Protecting Your Workstation

The problem of protecting a computer is an ongoing issue for all users. There is no passive way to do this; you have to develop an understanding of the dangers that lurk, and you must take the necessary steps to protect your computer and its data. This chapter examines some of the problems that can affect your workstation, such as drives going bad, electrical problems destroying computer equipment, and other disasters. Some of the solutions you can apply are also discussed.

Protecting the Hardware

The hardware in your computer is susceptible to all sorts of damage and is extremely vulnerable if you don't take precautions to protect it. Many hardware problems can be prevented, but few can be fixed; take care to ensure that your computer operates in a safe environment.

Electrical Problems

The two entities that can cause the most damage are Mother Nature (especially if you live in an area that experiences lightning storms) and your local power company. Take a paranoid view of them, and protect your computer from their attacks.

Lightning storms can cause surges, and the power company occasionally is the source of brownouts (lowered voltage). You can purchase equipment to shield your computer from the effects of some of these electrical problems. It's important to understand what is happening and how you can protect your hardware.

Power Surges

Power surges are sudden rises in voltage and are extremely dangerous to all the hardware in your computer. Chips get fried, wires burn or melt, and power supplies blow up, destroying everything attached to them.

The way to protect against the damages caused by surges in voltage is to use a surge protector, which most computer users do use. Surge protectors vary widely in their effectiveness; sometimes, even the best of them provides no protection at all.

A surge protector that isn't built to fight back with the right level of defense when a substantial rise in voltage occurs is not much more than an expensive multi-outlet extension cord. Before you buy a surge protector, do some research by reading reviews, articles, and even the labels on the surge protector.

A good surge protector does whatever it takes to protect your computer, including performing a self-meltdown or some other form of suicide. When a surge protector destroys itself to save your equipment, you just replace it.

However, no surge protector will protect you from a direct hit by lightning. If lightning strikes the line, the size of the surge can be devastating, and you'll lose the surge protector, your computer, and probably everything connected to your computer (peripherals, other computers, and so on).

If a lightning storm is expected, unplug the computer from the wall outlet—there is no other protection available from lightning.

Many office buildings have lightning arresters or lightning rods, so it's probably not necessary to run all over the building unplugging every computer. But if you work in a small office environment or at home, don't take any chances.

Brownouts

A brownout is a lowering of the voltage level that comes from the electrical line, and low voltage can destroy electronic equipment. Even before the voltage drops enough to see lights flicker, your hard drive can suffer damage from low voltage. The computer's power supply can have its life shortened by continuous low voltage, as can the power supply on your printer or other peripherals.

Brownouts occur much more frequently than surges. You should investigate two sources of these brownouts: the local power company and your own use of power.

The power company generally tries to put out enough power to maintain the optimum of 120V. But sometimes conditions make it difficult to maintain that voltage. As a result, most power companies consider anything within six percent of the optimum to be totally acceptable. As far as your computer is concerned, you don't really have to worry about voltage as long as it measures between 105 and 125V. Any deviation above or below those levels, however, can be dangerous.

The power company battles two obstacles in its path as it tries to provide 120V:

◆ At certain times of the day, especially around 9 a.m., it is almost impossible to maintain the optimum voltage because copiers, laser printers, and other power-consuming devices are being switched on in offices throughout the area.

◆ During the summer, when air conditioners run constantly, the voltage falls all throughout the grid on which the power company relies. There is usually nowhere to go for additional power because every power supplier in the grid experiences the same problem.

Sometimes, low voltage is the result of user error. Laser printers and copy machines should be plugged in to dedicated outlets, a maxim that is true of any equipment that uses a lot of amps and requires a lot of voltage. You should never put your computer into the same circuit as a laser printer.

As you purchase and use equipment, you must adopt a certain level of common sense. You don't need to be an expert in electricity to achieve this; you just have to read the technical specifications for the equipment you buy and use the expert advice available in the media. Otherwise, you might end up with a self-inflicted dangerous environment for your computer.

To boost low voltage before it harms your computer, you can use a line conditioner. A line conditioner works by measuring the voltage of the power coming out of the wall and then adjusts the voltage it's too low or too high. A line conditioner can't defend against extremely high voltage, though; you need a good surge protector for that.

Line conditioners are sold by wattage. A 600W unit (sufficient for most workstations) generally costs less than $100.

Telephone Lines

Many computers and networks destroyed by lightning receive that fatal surge through the telephone line that's connected to a modem.

When this happens, the surge goes from the telephone line to the modem, through the serial port, to the motherboard, where it finds (and fries) the network interface card (NIC). The NIC sends the surge through the network cable, spreading the zap to every NIC on the system. Some cards pass the surge on to their own motherboards, destroying the workstation.

Although most electric companies protect their lines at the transformer with lightning arresters or some other type of protection, almost no telephone companies in the United States use any form of line protection. Telephone lines conduct electricity, so if a line is charged with high voltage, it burns everything in its path. If you use surge protectors, be sure to purchase the type that includes protection for telephone lines. Even with surge protectors, you should pull the telephone line out of the wall jack when you're preparing your defense against electrical storms.

You also can protect your telephone system (and thereby include modems and computers) by using a gas plasma protection device on the lines as they enter the building (before each line is sent to a wall jack). A good telephone-line protection system is easy to install and provides some protection against lightning hits.

Conditioning Electrical Lines

If low voltage problems occur all over the office, it's probably easier and cheaper to solve the problem at the breaker box instead of buying line conditioners for every computer. Symptoms to look for include the following:

◆ Power supply problems on computers, laser printers, and other peripherals

◆ An increasing number of bad sectors on hard drives

◆ Constant signs of activity (usually clicking noises) from any line conditioners in use

You should check the voltage at various outlets over an extended period of time with a diagnostic machine that prints the results. You can rent testing machines or have an electrician bring the testing equipment.

If you find that voltage throughout the office is too low too frequently, put line conditioning on the breaker box. Any electrician can handle this task.

Intelligent line conditioners can be installed on the box to maintain a minimum voltage. "Intelligent" means that the line-conditioning device reads the voltage and corrects it only if necessary. Some line conditioners are set to raise existing voltage automatically, but these dumb line conditioners aren't safe.

The Dangers of Re-Tapping

Many office buildings have transformers that feed the building or multiple transformers that feed established in the building. These transformers can be configured to raise voltage, which is called re-tapping. Re-tapping can be very dangerous, and it is definitely not advisable. Some electricians, after measuring the voltage coming out of your wall outlets and finding low voltage, recommend re-tapping as a solution. However, there are side effects that make this a potential nightmare instead of a solution.

The problems arise because re-tapping provides a permanent solution to a temporary problem, and applying the solution when the problem no longer exists is dangerous.

If an electrician measures the voltage every day for a week while the office is running and everyone is working, and finds 106V coming out of every wall outlet, it makes sense to push the voltage up about 12 points. That brings you to 118V, still under the 120V optimum, but close enough for your hard drive to stay happy.

However, on the weekend, the building's elevators aren't running as often, the copy machines and laser printers are turned off, all the coffee pots in the building are off, and the computers are not being used. Now it's entirely possible that the voltage coming out of the box is the expected 120V or something very close to it. Of course, the permanent boost to the box means the voltage coming out of the wall outlets is 132V. This can toast the motherboards, hard drives, and most other devices in the office computers.

Installing a UPS

An Uninterruptible Power Supply (UPS) should be attached to any network servers or any computers used for mission-critical applications. Corrupted data due to a power failure is more than an annoyance; it frequently leads to revenue loss.

Two types of UPS units exist:

◆ **Always On.** This UPS itself supplies the power to the computer and charges itself with the power coming from the wall outlet. The computer never sees the power that comes from the wall, but runs completely from the UPS unit. This provides steady and safe power. These UPS units are quite expensive, require fresh batteries every couple of years, and are large, bulky, and heavy. Such units frequently are used for large servers that have many users attached, especially where user access is constant, as in branch offices or retail outlets connecting to the system constantly and around the clock.

◆ **On When Needed.** In this UPS unit, the battery is active when the power fails. Actually, the batteries kick in when voltage drops to the point at which the UPS believes the power might be going off, so you never really experience a total computer shutdown.

If you install an On When Needed UPS, Windows NT provides software that adds to the features available with the basic UPS device. The operating system has software available that communicates with the UPS and initiates an orderly shutdown of files and services when the UPS senses a loss of electrical power.

Three steps are involved in the installation of a UPS that is controlled by Windows NT UPS software:

◆ Physically install the unit and its cable.

◆ Run the Windows NT installation and configuration software.

◆ Start UPS services in Windows NT 4.

Attach the UPS Device

The physical installation is simply a matter of plugging the UPS unit into the wall and then moving the plugs for the computer and monitor into the UPS. Follow the manufacturer's instructions for connecting the cable between the UPS and one of the computer's serial ports.

> **Tip** Although the following section covers the installation and configuration of Windows NT software that controls your UPS device, software programs available for specific UPS devices might work as well as or better than the application provided by Windows NT.

Configure Windows NT UPS Settings

To install and configure the UPS in Windows NT Workstation, follow these steps:

1. Choose Settings, Control Panel from the Start menu (or open the Control Panel folder in My Computer).

2. Double-click the UPS icon to bring up the UPS dialog box (see fig. 27.1). Select the Uninterruptible Power Supply is Installed On check box.

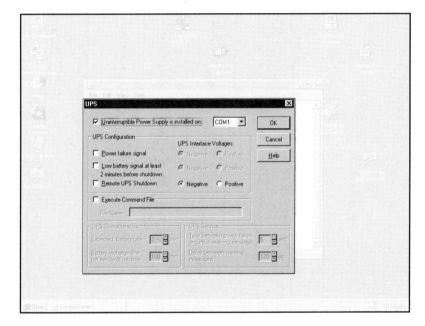

Figure 27.1

Use the UPS installation dialog box to configure the features you want to install.

3. Specify the features that are available with your UPS in the UPS Configuration section of the dialog box. The following options could be available:

   ◆ Select the Power Failure Signal check box if your UPS unit can send a message when the power fails. To your serial port, this message is the same as a clear-to-send (CTS) signal.

   ◆ Select the Low Battery Signal at Least 2 Minutes Before Shutdown check box if your UPS unit can issue a warning when the battery power is low. To your serial port, this is similar to a data-carrier-detect (DCD) cable signal.

   ◆ Select the Remote UPS Shutdown if you want the UPS application to run shutdown through a remote computer. Although this usually is configured in this manner for servers, you could select this option if your workstation is accessible by another computer. To your serial port, this is similar to a data-terminal-ready (DTR) cable signal.

4. For each item you selected, you must specify UPS Interface Voltage, either Negative or Positive, so that the serial port communication works properly. The documentation that came with your UPS system provides this information.

5. Select Execute Command File if you want the system to execute a command file before the system shuts down. This is useful to ensure that specific events occur before shutdown. For example, you might want to log off a network or close another type of connection. The following circumstances must exist for the command file:

   ◆ It can be installed from a third-party source that provides files for this purpose, or it can be written by a user.

   ◆ It must have a filename extension of BAT, EXE, or COM.

   ◆ It must reside in the \SYSTEM32 directory under the system root directory. For most computers, this means the path is \WINNT\SYSTEM32.

   ◆ It must complete the execution of its program in less than 30 seconds to make sure it completes running before shutdown is complete.

6. Specify the name of the command file in the File Name box.

7. In the Expected Battery Life box, specify the number of minutes that the system can run on battery power. Check the specifications for your device (the available range is 2–720 minutes).

8. In the Battery Recharge Time Per Minute of Run Time box, specify the number of minutes it takes to recharge the battery. This means the number of recharge minutes needed to create each minute of battery running time (the available range is 1–250 minutes).

9. In the Time Between Power Failure and Initial Warning Messages box, enter the number of seconds that should elapse between the loss of power and the first message notifying anyone using the computer (the available range is 0–120 seconds).

| **Tip** | You don't have to worry about setting the time between power failure number to a short interval. For one thing, the UPS device probably will begin beeping (most of them do). Secondly, it is not always necessary to be notified and then take some action, because many power failures last only a few seconds. |

10. In the Delay Between Warning Messages box, enter the number of seconds that should elapse before the second warning message is sent (the available range is 5–300 seconds).

11. Choose OK when you have finished configuring the dialog box. The system then establishes the communication between the serial port and the UPS device.

If there are times when you don't want to use the Windows NT management features with your UPS, you can open the UPS dialog box and deselect the Uninterruptible Power Supply Is Installed On check box.

Note   Remember that the deselection of the Windows NT UPS software does not stop the battery from working; it merely prevents the software from performing its configured steps to shut down in an orderly fashion. Sometimes, there's no need to go through all those steps because the power returns quickly. The software, however, having received the signal, moves inexorably toward the goal of shutting down. Without it, the battery would just stop providing power (and beeping at you), and you would proceed with your work.

If you experience short blackouts or think there might be a serious chance of a blackout (perhaps it's a very hot summer day and your local power company is having a problem keeping up), you might want to keep working with the power the battery provides rather than be forced to go through a shutdown.

Configure Service Startup

The installation and configuration of the UPS device is followed by the startup of UPS services. To accomplish this last step, follow this process:

Objective B.5

1. Open the Control Panel.

2. Double-click the Services icon to see the Services dialog box (see fig. 27.2). Select UPS from the Service list.

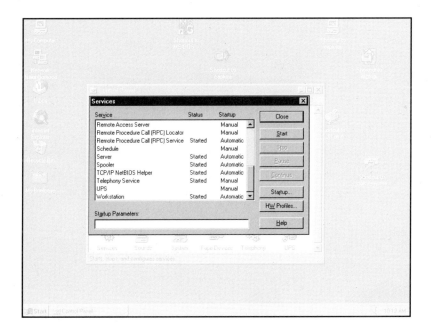

Figure 27.2

You must tell the system how you want to launch the UPS services you've installed.

3. Click on Startup, and choose one of the following methods for starting the service:

   ◆ Select Automatic to start the service automatically every time your system starts.

   ◆ Select Manual to start the service manually after the system is up and running. This means that when you want to start the service, you move to the Services dialog box. Then highlight UPS services and choose Start.

   ◆ Select Disabled if you don't want the service to start.

4. Close the Services dialog box when you are finished configuring the start mode.

Backing Up

Backing up is the most important task you do. All hard drives die eventually—there's even a life-expectancy statistic for hard drives, called an *MTBF* (mean time before failure). Manufacturers know the statistics for their own drives; if you're curious and the documentation doesn't provide the information, you can call and obtain the MTBF rating. The number doesn't mean some pre-ordained failure date, but it's important to understand that you cannot expect your hard drive to last as long as you might need it.

However, backing up isn't just a hedge against the day your drive dies; it's also protection for recovering from mistakes. More backup tapes are used to restore files that were accidentally removed than for recovering from major disk disasters.

Planning a Backup Strategy

Objective A.2

Backing up shouldn't be done haphazardly. You should have a backup plan. Several approaches exist for backing up, and you must make a number of decisions as you design your backup plan.

The first decision to make is the one regarding the media you will use for backing up. The following choices exist:

   ◆ Copy files to a connected computer (usually a server) that is backed up to tape.

   ◆ Back up to floppy disks.

   ◆ Back up to tape.

You also must make decisions about the type of backups you will be performing. You can choose from these possibilities:

◆ Partial backups

◆ Full backups

Planning Server-Based Backup

In some network environments, the application software and data are both on the server. When users access the software on the server, the configuration options point to the network drive as the container for the application data. Because most networks are backed up regularly, your individual work is safe and secure, and you don't have to initiate backups.

However, if you access software on a network drive but save your application data to a local drive, you should worry about getting the data backed up.

Furthermore, if you are linked to a network only for printer sharing or e-mail and your application software, along with the data, exists on your local drive, you need to make sure your data is backed up.

Setting Up Directories

The easy way to back up your data is to create a system for copying it to the server. Usually, it is best to perform this task before the end of the day, making sure you finish before the server backup process begins. You can use any of several approaches, and your choice depends on the way you store data on your local drive. For example, you can establish protocols that permit your copying operations to take place in one of the following configurations:

◆ Create a personal data directory on your local drive, and save all data from all application software in that local data directory. Also create (or have an administrator create) a data directory in your name on the server. Then you can just copy the local data directory to your personal data directory on the server.

◆ Create separate data directories for each application on your local drive, and then copy all those data directories to one personal data directory that is established for you on the server.

Caution   If you copy files from multiple local directories into one target directory, be very careful about file-naming conventions. Files that have the same name but are stored locally in separate directories will end up as one file (the second file you copy will overwrite the first). An easy way to avoid problems is to use file-name extensions. For instance, all the files in the data directory for your word-processing documents might have the extension DOC, while your database files carry an extension of DTA. This way, if you're creating different types of data files for customer ACME, you won't replace a letter named ACME1 with a database report named ACME1.

◆ Create data directories for each application on your local drive, and create the same directory structure on the server. Then you can copy each local directory to its counterpart on the server.

After you have a plan and have established the necessary directory or directories on the server, copying the files is an easy process. You can use Explorer or My Computer to copy and paste the files, or you can use a batch file that you create for this purpose.

Dragging and Dropping the Files

The easiest way to copy the files is to use Explorer, Network Neighborhood, My Computer, or a combination of any of these.

The first time you copy a folder from your local drive to the network drive, a subfolder with the same name as your source folder is created in the target folder. Subsequently, be sure to drag the local folder to the original target folder; the files will be copied automatically to the appropriate subfolder. If you drag the source folder to the newly created subfolder, yet another subfolder will be created.

Some guidelines make it easier to do this with dispatch and efficiency:

◆ When you drag folders or files between drives, you do not have to hold down the Ctrl key to make sure the files are copied instead of moved.

◆ If you use Explorer, you'll want to make sure there is a way to see both the source and target files in the same Explorer window.

◆ If you cannot see both source and target folders in Explorer, you can open another instance of Explorer, open Network Neighborhood in addition to Explorer, or open My Computer in addition to Explorer.

◆ If you want to use My Computer for the target (network) drive, you must map the drive in order to display it in the folder.

◆ If you want to use Explorer or Network Neighborhood for the target drive, you do not need to map the drive to display it and access it.

Using a Batch File

If you don't want to spend time dragging and dropping, you can write a batch file that copies the contents of one or more local directories to one more server directories. The server must be a mapped drive, because the batch file requires a drive letter in order to work.

A batch file is a text file that contains a series of MS-DOS commands. One command exists on each line, and the file is executed in the order in which the commands are listed.

You can create a batch file in any text editor and save it with the file extension BAT. Then move to a command prompt and type the file name to launch the batch file.

For instance, you can write a batch file that copies files to a network server from individual data folders that are connected to software. The following batch file assumes that a folder has been established on the server for this individual user and that the folder contains subfolders for each set of data files. Also, if you are using an NT server, you must be sure to map the drive in order to reference the drive letter.

```
COPY C:\WPAPP\MYDATA\*.* F:\MYFILES\WPDATA
COPY C:\DBAPP\MYDATA\*.* F:\MYFILES\DBDATA
COPY C:\SSAPP\MYDATA\*.* F:\MYFILES\SSDATA
EXIT
```

The EXIT command in the last line closes the command prompt session, so you don't have to click the Close button on the command session window.

 Tip If you do take advantage of the speed of a batch file, make a shortcut for it so you don't have to open a command session manually and enter the batch file's name at the prompt.

Backing Up to Floppy Disks

Although you can perform a backup of the important files to floppy disks, this process takes more willpower than most people have. Sitting in front of a computer and putting one floppy disk after another into the disk drive can be an incredibly boring exercise.

In fact, this process takes so long and is so boring that it's difficult to talk yourself into performing the task. As a result, many times you won't. In fact, you'll skip the backup for days, weeks, or even months at a time. The computer demons somehow know this and take this opportunity to destroy your hard drive.

Floppy disk backups, however, are better than no backups at all. If you do use them, you have several approaches at your disposal:

◆ Use Explorer and drag your data directories to the disk.

◆ Use a file-compression software application that writes to floppy disks and spans them, requesting additional disks as needed.

◆ Use the MS-DOS BACKUP command from a command prompt. Just follow any prompts to insert disks after you enter the command BACKUP x: where "x:" is the drive you want to back up (usually C). You can learn about some additional parameters for more advanced features in backup by typing **BACKUP/?**.

The best disk-based backup approach is to stop using this method when you find you're skipping it, and buy a tape drive or a supported removable drive.

Using Windows NT Backup

Windows NT Backup software is included with the operating system. This software works with your tape drive and supports both FAT and NTFS file systems. (Not all tape software supports these file systems.)

Using a tape backup system provides some distinct advantages over copying files to the server or backing up to floppy disks:

◆ Backups are unattended because you don't have to do anything except start the backup with a click of the mouse.

◆ You can copy every file in your system when you are making a backup.

◆ You can restore files easily if a major disaster occurs with your hard drive.

◆ You can store backup media off-site so that if disaster strikes the building, your data is safe.

Determine a Tape Backup Philosophy

With the convenience of tape backup comes the ability to back up every file on your computer, not just data files. This provides a full range of choices about what you want to back up and how. (The question of how often is not up for debate—backing up is a daily task.) The following list details your choices:

◆ Back up your entire drive every day. This is called a full backup.

◆ Back up your entire drive once. Then back up only your data every day. This is called a data-only backup. (When you add software or otherwise change the file system, you must back up the entire drive again.)

◆ Back up your entire hard drive once a month (or once a week), and then back up only the files that have changed since the last backup. This is called an incremental backup.

The more files you back up, the longer the backup takes. The great advantage of tape backup is that it doesn't matter because you don't have to baby-sit the procedure—you can leave.

> **Tip**   All the convenience of tape backup is lost if you purchase a tape system that can't handle all your files. Make sure the system handles tapes that hold as many bytes as your hard drive can. If you have to wait for the first tape to fill up and then change tapes, you've made your backup procedure almost as inconvenient as using floppy disks. In fact, the best approach is to buy a tape system twice as large as your drive because you might one day install a larger drive or add a second one.

The way to decide which type of backup to perform is to ask yourself why you're backing up. What is the use of the backup tape? The answer should be, "So when disaster strikes, I can get back to work quickly."

This means that the reason for backing up is to restore things as quickly as possible so that you don't have to reinvent all the work you've done. If you follow that logic to its natural conclusion, you realize that you create a backup philosophy to make restoring convenient, not to make backing up convenient. If you do anything except a full backup, restoring your system is going to be time consuming.

If you choose to perform data-only backups, you will have to reinstall every piece of software on your system, go through the configuration process for each of them, and then restore your data.

If you choose incremental backups, you will have a pile of tapes that are incremental backups of files that have changed. You have to restore each tape in the same order in which you backed up to ensure you have restored the right version of each data file. This could take a very long time.

If you choose a total backup, then after a disk death you only have to install the operating system, open the backup software on your new drive, and then click on Restore. Go have a cup of coffee and, when you return, everything is the way it was before the disaster. The poor users who chose backup schemes that made backing up each night a quick process will be putting tapes in and taking them out long after you're back to work, generating revenue with your computer.

Install and Configure the Tape Device

Before you can use the Windows NT tape backup software, you must install your tape device and copy the drivers to your system.

The physical installation of the tape device is accomplished by following the instructions that come with the unit. You'll have to open your computer, install the device into a bay, secure it with screws, and connect the cable to a controller.

Then you must install the drivers for your unit. This assumes that you've purchased and installed a tape device that is compatible with Windows NT (check the hardware compatibility list that came with your operating system software). You also will need your original Windows NT CD-ROM. Then follow these steps:

1. Open the Control Panel, and then double-click the Tape Devices icon to see the Tape Devices dialog box. The Devices tab displays a message indicating that no tape devices are found.

2. Select the Drivers tab, and then choose Add.

3. In the Select Tape Driver dialog box, move through the list to find your tape device.

4. If your unit isn't listed, you must have a disk from the manufacturer that contains the driver files. Choose Have Disk.

5. Enter the drive and path for the disk or CD-ROM you're using for this driver, and then choose Continue. The files are copied to your hard drive.

6. When the files are copied, Windows NT will load and start the drivers.

Run Windows NT Tape Backup Software

After the installation and configuration is complete, you can back up your system.

 Caution Because Windows NT is a multitasking operating system, you might be tempted to continue to work while performing a backup. Files that are in use won't be backed up, though, so it's not a very good idea to work during a backup.

Insert a tape in the drive and follow these steps:

1. Choose Programs from the Start menu, and then choose Administrative Tools, Backup. The NT Backup Program launches (see fig. 27.3).

2. If you want to view information about the Tape, double-click its minimized icon. If the tape has a backup on it, information about that backup is displayed, including the drive that was backed up, the date, and other information.

You can begin your backup according to the type of backup protocol you decide on.

Full Backup

To perform a full backup, follow these steps:

1. Select the drive(s) you want to back up and click the Check button on the toolbar (or choose Select, Check).

2. Click the Backup button on the toolbar, or choose Operations, Backup.

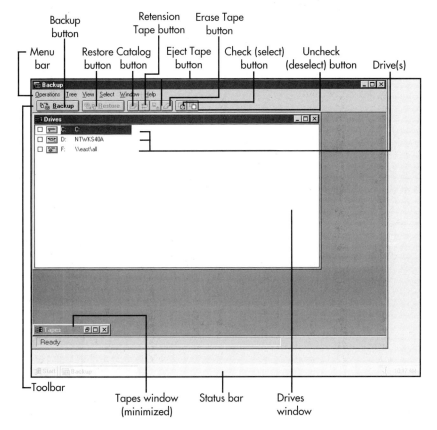

Backup
button

Retension
Tape button

Erase Tape
button

Menu
bar

Restore Catalog
button   button

Eject Tape
button

Check (select)
button

Uncheck
(deselect) button

Drive(s)

Toolbar

Tapes window
(minimized)

Status bar

Drives
window

Figure 27.3

*The Windows NT
Backup software
window opens
with the Drives
window
displaying all the
drives found.*

Partial Backup

To back up specific files or directories, follow these steps:

1. Double-click the drive that contains the files you want to back up. The contents of the drive are displayed (see fig. 27.4).

2. Use the options in the Tree menu to expand and collapse the view of the drive.

3. Select the folders or files you want to include in the backup, and then click Check on the toolbar. If you want to deselect a file, highlight it and click Uncheck.

4. Click Backup to begin. If the tape fills up before all the files are backed up, you are prompted to insert another tape.

Before beginning the backup, you can configure the software for a variety of backup options.

Figure 27.4

Display the folders and files on a drive. Then pick and choose the ones you want to back up.

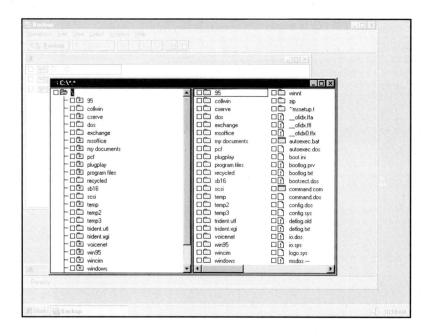

Set Backup Options

After you've selected the drives or files to back up, you can configure options for the manner in which you want to back up. When you choose Operations, Backup, the Backup Information dialog box offers a range of options.

Backup Operation Types

Windows NT Backup offers five specific backup types, or protocols, from which to choose:

◆ **Normal.** This protocol backs up all the selected files and marks the files on the disk to indicate that they have been backed up.

◆ **Copy.** This protocol backs up all the selected files but does not mark the disk with any attributes to indicate that they've been backed up.

◆ **Incremental.** This backup type looks at the selected files and backs up only those that have changed since the last backup. Files are marked with an attribute to indicate that they were backed up.

◆ **Differential.** This protocol backs up only files that have changed since the last backup but does not mark the files as having been backed up.

◆ **Daily.** This type backs up only those files that have been modified or added today. No attributes are marked on the disk to indicate that the files were backed up.

Tip | The best use of the daily backup type is to back up the files you worked on today so that you can take them home to continue your work.

Tape Options

You can configure the way in which tapes are used by setting the tape options:

◆ You can append this backup to the tape, putting it after the last backup already on the tape.

◆ You can replace (overwrite) any backup already on the tape.

◆ You can enter a name for the tape (many people use the day of the week and use that tape whenever that day is current).

◆ You can decide whether or not you want to verify the backup, which means the software makes sure it can read the file that was just backed up. This differs from the verify or compare function found on many third-party backup applications, which matches the file on the tape to the original file on the drive.

◆ You can choose to copy the Windows NT Registry files to the tape (if they are on the drive being backed up).

Caution | Never back up onto the tape that has the last good backup. The safest method is to have a unique tape for each day of the week.

Failing that, use a two-tape system in which one tape is marked Odd and the other Even. Use the Odd tape on odd dates and the Even tape on even dates.

A tape for each day also provides the greatest chance for restoring specific files that might have been erased. If the erasure isn't noticed for a day or two, a rotating odd/even system will not provide a tape with the file on it. The ability to go back several days or a week means that the chances of finding the file you need are much greater.

Logging Options

You can have Windows NT write a log file to the disk following the backup. You can choose from three logging options:

◆ Don't Log.

◆ Summary Log Only, in which the major processes are logged, including the time the backup began and a list of any files that couldn't be backed up.

◆ Full Detail Log, in which the operations are logged along with the names of every backed-up file and directory.

If you choose to log the backup operation, enter the name of the file to use for logging in the Log File box.

Restoring a Tape Backup

Depending on your need, you can restore all or part of the tape backup. If a major hardware disaster occurs, you will need everything on the tape. But if you need the original contents of a file you accidentally deleted or overwrote, you can restore an individual file.

To begin a restore, put the tape you want to restore into the tape drive. Then follow these steps:

1. Launch the Windows NT Backup software and double-click the Tapes icon to open the Tapes window.

2. Double-click the appropriate backup set to display a catalog of the tape's contents.

3. To restore all the contents of the tape, select the tape's check box. To restore individual files, select the check box for each file you need.

4. Click the Restore button.

> **Tip** You can configure the system to verify the files that are restored to the disk against the files on the tape. Any differences are written to a log file.

Maintain Tapes

Tapes require a certain amount of care, and maintenance features are built into the Windows NT Backup software. In addition to the functions available through the computer, you should take steps to make sure that your tapes are safe and secure—in terms of your work, your life is on those tapes.

Off-Site Storage

The most important step you can take to keep your backup tapes safe is to get them out of the building. This is your only guarantee that you'll be back in business in the event of a major calamity in the building in which your computer resides. If you have specific tapes for each day of the week and an office full of people to choose from, assign a Monday person, a Tuesday person, and so on. If your tape backup is performed unattended (either by scheduling it in the middle of the night through the software or by beginning the backup just before you leave for the day), you can establish a schedule that sends the Monday tape off-site on Tuesday, and so on.

If it is difficult to make a schedule like this work (the hardest part is having people remember to bring the tapes back), then at least make sure the Friday tape is taken out of the building.

If you can't set up an official office schedule, or if there aren't a lot of people working in your office, take it upon yourself to take one tape a week home. Or, find a friend who works somewhere else and make a trade—"I'll give you mine if you give me yours."

Physical Tape Maintenance

Most tape-drive manufacturers will sell or recommend a cleaning kit. The tape drive, especially the heads that read/write to tape, occasionally needs cleaning. Some of these kits are nothing more than special tapes that you insert into the drive and then use software features to move that tape across the heads. Other cleaning kits involve swabs and liquids for cleaning the unit. Follow the manufacturer's instructions.

> **Note** Dust is a big problem with tape devices. A regular squirt of canned air into the tape drive can prevent many problems caused by dust. Dust scratches tapes, which can make it impossible to restore any files that sit on that section of the tape. Dust also can prevent the drive from seeing the end of the tape (which is a transparent spot on the tape). This sometimes means that the tape rolls off the end of the spool, making the tape cartridge useless.

Software Tape Maintenance

The Windows NT Backup software contains features for tape-maintenance chores. All the tape-maintenance commands are found in the Operations menu:

◆ Choose Erase Tape to erase the tape. You can choose Quick Erase, which deletes the header (you must know how to hack to get information from a tape with no header), or Secure Erase, which deletes the entire tape. The latter can take quite a bit of time.

◆ Choose Retension Tape to have the tape fast-forwarded to the end and then rewound. This eliminates any loose tension in the tape and ensures smooth movement.

◆ Choose Format Tape to format an unformatted tape. This command is necessary only for mini-cartridge tapes.

Run NT Backup with a Batch File

You can use a batch file to run NT Backup, setting the parameters you need at the command line. The syntax for the batch file is

> ntbackup operation path /parameters

where operation is the operation you want to perform—backup is the normal choice (the only other available operation from the command line is eject)—and path is the path(s) of the directories you want to back up. Only directories are backed up; you cannot specify files and you cannot use wildcards.

Parameters include the following:

/a	Appends the backup set to the tape (otherwise, any existing backup sets are overwritten)
/v	Verifies the backup
/b	Backs up the Registry (only the local Registry can be backed up; if additional drives are being backed up, those registries will not be included)
/hc:on	Turns on hardware compression
/hc:off	Turns off hardware compression
/t[option]	Specifies the type of backup: normal, incremental, copy, differential, daily
/l	"Filename" calls for a backup log with the indicated file name
/e	Indicates a backup log with exceptions only in the report
/tape:n	Where n is a number from 0 through 9 that indicates the tape drive to which files are backed up (when multiple tape drives are installed, these numbers are assigned)

Note If /a is not used and tapes are to be overwritten, the first drive backup overwrites any existing backup sets on the tape; multiple drive backups will be appended to the first drive set backup.

Backing Up to Large Removable Storage

You have several choices for large, reasonably priced removable storage devices, all of which make excellent targets for backup. Because the removable storage drive can be shared, installing one can give multiple workstations backup media. You can purchase additional disks and give each workstation its own backup disks.

Windows NT Backup does not support these devices, but you can use them with third-party backup software. You also can copy files, which makes restoring easier (especially if it's only one file you have to restore).

I use a 1 GB jaz drive and wrote a batch file to copy the contents of my hard drive. The safest and best way to perform such a backup is to use Xcopy and take advantage of the switches available. For example, my batch file reads as follows:

```
xcopy c:\*.* d:\ /c
xcopy c:\artfiles\*.* d:\artfiles /s/e/h/i/r/c
xcopy c:\collwin\*.* d:\collwin /s/e/h/i/r/c
xcopy c:\exchange\*.* d:\exchange /s/e/h/i/r/c
xcopy c:\lightshp\*.* d:\lightshp /s/e/h/i/r/c
xcopy c:\mas90\*.* d:\mas90 /s/e/h/i/r/c
xcopy c:\mydocu~1\*.* d:\mydocu~1 /s/e/h/i/r/c
xcopy c:\netsca~1\*.* d:\netsca~1 /s/e/h/i/r/c
xcopy c:\office97\*.* d:\office97 /s/e/h/i/r/c
xcopy c:\pcf\*.* d:\pcf /s/e/h/i/r/c
xcopy c:\progra~1\*.* d:\progra~1 /s/e/h/i/r/c
xcopy c:\sb16\*.* d:\sb16 /s/e/h/i/r/c
xcopy c:\scsi\*.* d:\scsi /s/e/h/i/r/c
xcopy c:\fedex\*.* d:\fedex /s/e/h/i/r/c
xcopy c:\voicenet\*.* d:\voicenet /s/e/h/i/r/c
xcopy c:\winnt\*.* d:\winnt /s/e/h/i/r/c
xcopy c:\winzip62\*.* d:\winzip62 /s/e/h/i/r/c
xcopy c:\xy\*.* d:\xy /s/e/h/i/r/c
exit
```

These switches take care of all the copying commands and also any potential problems:

◆ **/s** copies all subdirectories except empty ones

◆ **/e** copies empty subdirectories

◆ **/h** copies hidden and system files

◆ **/i**, if destination does not exist and more than one file is being copied, assumes the destination is a directory (and creates it if it doesn't exist on the target)

◆ **/r** overwrites read-only files

◆ **/c** continues copying when an error occurs

A shortcut to the backup file on the desktop makes full backups a very easy task.

Backing Up the Registry

If you are backing up to tape using NT Backup, you can configure the backup to include the Registry. Most third-party backup software offers the same configuration option.

You also can back up the Registry manually. This is not a backup in the traditional sense—it's not any type of file copy. The Registry is backed up by exporting it to a text file. It is restored by importing that file to the Registry.

You should use this method of backing up the Registry whenever you are going to make changes to the Registry. Messing around with the Registry can be dangerous, so this gives you a fall-back position to recover from any damage you do.

Registry backup is accomplished from the Registry, which you can launch by choosing Run from the Start menu and entering **regedit** in the Open box.

To export the Registry, follow these steps:

1. Choose Registry, Export Registry File from the menu bar.

2. The Export Registry File dialog box is displayed (see fig. 27.5). This is really a File Save dialog box.

3. Choose a folder and enter a file name in the File name box.

> **Tip** It's a good idea to create a folder specifically for Registry export files. It's also a good idea to copy the files in the folder to disk as extra insurance.

4. In the Export range section of the dialog box, choose All to export the entire Registry, or choose Selected Branch to export only a branch of the Registry.

> **Tip** If you want to export only a branch of the Registry, select that branch before you choose the Export command from the Registry menu. The selected branch will be filled in automatically in the Selected Branch box when the Export Registry File dialog box appears.

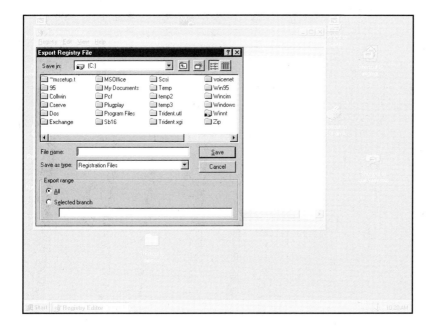

5. Choose Save to save the file.

If you need to restore the Registry, you have to import the Registry file you created when you exported the Registry. Choose Registry, Import Registry file. Select the file from the Import Registry File dialog box and double-click on it.

Setting Permissions for Backup

Many of the backup scenarios discussed in this chapter require you to give the appropriate permissions to the users who perform the chores.

To copy files from a local computer to the server in order to include those files in the server's backup, users must have permission to write to a target directory on the server. Create a directory for the backup and then use the Permissions button on the Sharing tab of the directory's Properties dialog box. Give specific users or all users Full Control.

Objective C.3

To perform a backup of the Workstation, users must have Backup rights (or better). Backup rights supersede any other file or directory rights during the backup process. In User Manager, make the user a member of the Backup Operators group (unless his or her existing rights are already at a higher level).

Objective C.1

If you use User Manager for Domains on the server to give Backup rights, the right extends to PDC and BDC servers in the domain. In User Manager for Domains (on the server), make the user a member of the group Backup Operators to effect this.

End Note: The most important thing to remember about keeping your workstation safe is that the onus is on you. You can't shrug your shoulders at the vagaries of the fates when there's an electrical problem or even a disastrous fire that burns down your office. You have no excuse for not being able to recover from disasters, because it only takes planning and the will to execute the plan.

Test Your Knowledge

1. Choose the correct statement(s) about Uninterruptible Power Supplies and Windows NT software support.

   A. A UPS must be connected to the computer via a serial cable to use Windows NT UPS software.

   B. A UPS must be connected to the computer via a parallel cable to use Windows NT UPS software.

   C. Windows NT UPS software works independently from cable; you do not have to install any cable between the UPS and the computer.

   D. Windows NT UPS software works only with "on demand" battery systems and not with "always on."

2. Installation and configuration of the Windows NT support software for a UPS is performed in which of the following?

   A. In the Devices applet of the Control Panel

   B. In the UPS applet of the Control Panel

   C. In both the UPS and System applets of the Control Panel

   D. In both the System and Ports applets of the Control Panel

3. Windows NT support for UPS devices results in which scenario when the power fails?

   A. A dialog box that enables you to choose whether you want to shut down the system

   B. An immediate shutdown of all open applications

   C. A dialog box that asks if you want Windows NT to shut down all open applications

   D. A dialog box announcing a system shutdown

4. On Monday you did a normal backup to tape. From Tuesday through Friday you want to back up only those files that are new or have changed each day. Which backup type accomplishes this?

5. On Monday you did a normal backup to tape. From Tuesday through Friday you want to back up only those files that are new or have changed since Monday. Which backup type accomplishes this?

6. Which solution for backup will work with Windows NT Backup software?

    A. Use a drive letter to map shared folders on other computers and back up to your hard drive.

    B. Use the UNC name of a shared folder on other computers and back up to your hard drive.

    C. Use either the UNC or a mapped drive letter for shared folders on other computers and back up to the server.

    D. None of the above.

7. What scenario will result if you start Windows NT Backup software from a batch file?

    A. You will not be able to compress files.

    B. You will not be able to verify files.

    C. You will not be able to append the backup.

    D. None of the above

Test Your Knowledge Answers

1. A,D
2. B
3. D
4. Incremental
5. Differential
6. D
7. D

Chapter Snapshot

To correct bottlenecks and speed up the operation of your software, you need to identify the bottleneck and then take appropriate action. As you hunt down and improve bottlenecks, you invariably learn things about your system that you didn't know before. Finding a pesky bottleneck and fixing it is a satisfying experience, much like solving a difficult puzzle. This chapter focuses on the following topics (all aimed at optimizing performance):

Windows NT
Workstation 4

CHAPTER 28

Optimizing Performance

Computers and operating systems are very complex. This complexity often gives rise to unexpected behavior when one part of the system isn't working well with another part. Perhaps a device isn't interacting well with another device or a program is hogging the system, preventing other applications from getting much work done. The computer almost becomes like a community of parts, and sometimes parts don't get along well together.

Other times, your bottlenecks might not be due to anything wrong in the system at all. Bottlenecks can be encountered simply based on the normal operation of the system.

How do you know you have a bottleneck, though? Think of it this way: If you want to improve the performance of an application, there's *always* a bottleneck that can be impacted. Sometimes the solution isn't worth the cost, but there's always a solution. It can be something simple such as using NTFS disks instead of FAT disks (or vice-versa), or it can be an expensive solution such as adding a lot more RAM or adding processors to your system. Your job is to identify what component in the system is keeping your program from running faster, and then decide how to address the issue.

In this chapter, you learn how to find bottlenecks and what actions you can take to correct them. To do this, you learn how to use a powerful performance testing tool that's included with Windows NT Workstation 4—Performance Monitor. You also learn about other ways in Windows NT Workstation to monitor and affect the performance of your system, such as Windows NT Diagnostics, the Task Manager, and changing the foreground application priority system-wide.

Enabling Disk Performance Counters

Objective F.1

Before embarking on a hunt for performance demons, you should first enable a key set of performance counters in Windows NT that measure disk performance. By default, these counters are inactivated because they carry a very slight overhead when they are running. You can enable and disable them at will, however, depending on your needs.

> **Note** A *performance counter* is a variable in the system that keeps track of certain performance characteristics on your system. Some performance counters know how busy your processor is or how often a read request is made from a particular disk. Many performance counters built into Windows NT are designed expressly for measuring and tuning your system's performance. Also, as you install software, some applications add new performance counters to the system that help you measure the application's performance.

To enable the disk performance counters, follow these steps:

1. Open a Windows NT command prompt.

2. Type the command **DISKPERF -Y** and press Enter.

You see a confirmation message that the disk performance counters are now set to start the next time you boot your system. Restart your system to activate them.

> **Note** On a 486-based workstation, the disk performance counters carry about a three to five percent performance overhead (in other words, they slow your overall system performance by about that much). On a Pentium-class machine, you will see no perceptible impact by enabling them.

You can deactivate the disk performance counters with the command **DISKPERF -N**.

Using Performance Monitor

Windows NT Workstation 4 includes an extremely powerful tool in your bottleneck-hunting toolbox—Performance Monitor. This program enables you to take a very close look at how the resources in your computer are being used, both by the system itself and by individual programs. With it, you can learn that a program (or your system) is processor-bound, memory-bound, or disk-bound in fairly short order. Performance Monitor is shown in figure 28.1.

Objective F.1

Note | Performance Monitor is exclusive to Windows NT. Windows 95 includes a somewhat similar tool called System Monitor, which is far simpler.

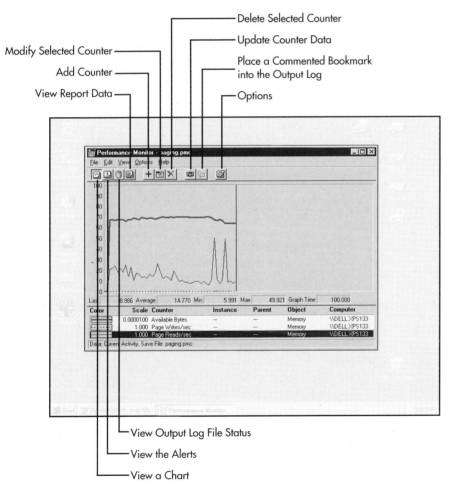

Figure 28.1

Windows NT Workstation's Performance Monitor helps you find hidden bottlenecks.

> **Note** Bottlenecks are often expressed as a program being "bound" by some element in the system. If a program is "processor-bound," for example, it is the processor that is inhibiting the program from running faster. Any component of your system can impact the performance of a program.

The main window displays the currently selected display option, which can be a graph of current activity, alerts that you set on certain performance counters, a log file status, or report data. A number of entries displayed at the bottom of the window show the actual data for the selected counter when in graph mode. The bottom portion of the window lists the currently displayed counters, displays their graph color, and enables you to select each one individually by clicking on it.

Adding and Modifying Performance Counters

Objective F.1

You add selected performance counters by clicking on the Add Counter button in the toolbar. This brings up the Add to Chart dialog box shown in figure 28.2, in which you select the counter you want to add to the display.

Figure 28.2

The Add to Chart dialog box lists all available performance counters.

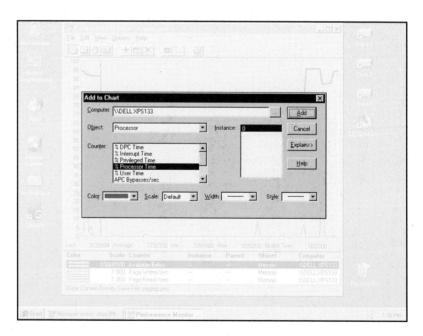

To add a specific counter, first select the category of counter you want from the Object drop-down list. Then select an actual counter in the Counter list and click Add to start watching the counter. Table 28.1 lists all the counter categories.

TABLE 28.1
Counter Object Categories

Object	Description
Browser	Network browser (Network Neighborhood) counters.
Cache	Statistics from the Cache Manager, which controls caching from both local disks and network interfaces.
Logical Disk	Counters for each of the partitions on your hard disk(s). You can monitor each partition individually by using this object.
Memory	Memory Manager activities, including page faults and memory-swapping activities.
NetBEUI	Statistics about the performance of the NetBEUI protocol stack (only appears if the protocol is installed).
NetBEUI Resource	More detailed NetBEUI counters that are selectable for different network resources (only appears if the protocol is installed).
NWLink IPX	IPX statistics, when IPX is installed.
NWLink NetBIOS	NetBIOS over IPX statistics, when NetBIOS is installed.
NWLink SPX	SPX over IPX statistics, when IPX is installed.
Objects	Counts the number of active objects in the system, broken into Events, Mutexes, Processes, Sections, Semaphores, and Threads.
Paging File	Percent usage of the paging file, and maximum percent usage.
Physical Disk	Performance counters that monitor physical disk drives installed in the system.
Process	A performance counter category that enables you to select individual running processes in the system. There are a number of counters for each process, and only running processes are capable of being selected.
Processor	Detailed statistics about processor usage. On multiprocessor machines, you can select these for each individual processor.

continues

TABLE 28.1, CONTINUED
Counter Object Categories

Object	Description
Redirector	Performance characteristics concerning the network redirector.
Server	Monitors performance of server activities (when someone else is connected to your machine over the network) on Windows NT Workstation 4.
Server Work Queues	Monitors the backlog of server-type requests waiting for service from your computer.
System	System-wide performance statistics. These are often aggregates of other counters that are available for specific devices, such as individual processors.
Telephony	Counters for telephony applications running.
Thread	Statistics about each running thread in the system.

Each of the performance counter objects contains many individual counters. You can get an explanation for each one using the Explain button. First select the particular counter you are interested in from the Counter list and then click the Explain button. The Explain window stays open, enabling you to select other counters to read about.

When you add a counter, you can choose how it is displayed in the graph window. Use the Color, Scale, Width, and Style fields to tune how the counter displays. When you are monitoring many counters, changing these makes the display easier to follow.

You can edit existing chart lines by double-clicking on the performance counter entry in the bottom portion of the window. Doing this brings up the Edit Chart Line dialog box shown in figure 28.3.

The Edit Chart Line dialog box enables you to change the display characteristics for the selected counter. To display a different counter, you must add it (deleting one of the existing counters if you want).

To delete a counter, select it in the bottom portion of the Performance Monitor window and click on the Delete Selected Counter button (refer to fig. 28.1), or choose the Delete From Chart command in the Edit menu. You also can press the Del key when the counter is selected.

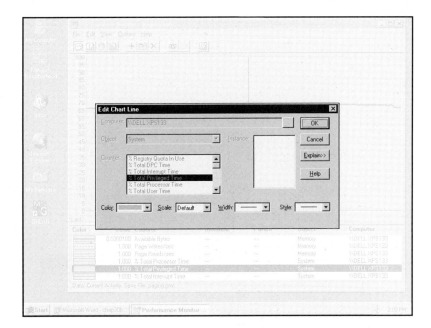

Figure 28.3

Edit existing chart lines in the Edit Chart Line dialog box.

Saving Performance Monitor Settings

Often, you will want to save a particular set of selected counters so you do not have to go through the trouble of reselecting them when you next use Performance Monitor. To do this, choose the Save Chart Settings As command in the File menu. Your current settings are saved into a file with a PMC extension, which you can open during subsequent Performance Monitor sessions.

Objective

F.1

Using Alternate Performance Monitor Views

Performance Monitor enables you to use one of several different views for the data it collects. Different views are used for different purposes. You've already seen the Chart view in the preceding sections. Three other views also can be useful:

Objective

F.1

◆ **Alert view.** Used to watch for system alerts, Alert view is a handy tool for system administrators who want to keep an eye on some of the system's counters to watch for trouble.

◆ **Log view.** This view tracks performance data over time and stores the detailed information in a file. You can "play back" the data in the file in order to look at a particular event in a number of different ways. It's almost like making a movie of something you did with the system, then replaying it to find out exactly what went on during that time period.

◆ **Report view.** With Report view you can create a report containing performance monitor data. The data does not show trends over time; it shows averages
or totals depending on the counters being displayed.

In the following three sections, you learn more about these different views and how to
use them.

Alert View

Performance Monitor can be set to monitor your system's counters, only alerting you
when certain conditions you set are met. An alert log also is maintained that contains
the most recent 1,000 alerts, along with the date and time at which they occurred.

To access the Alert view in Performance Monitor, choose Alert from the View menu
or press Ctrl+A. You see the screen shown in figure 28.4.

Figure 28.4

*The Alert view
gives you a heads-
up for system
events.*

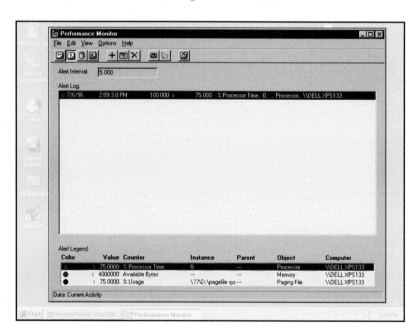

Alerts are shown in the main window, with the newest alerts appearing at the bottom
of the screen. Add new alerts you want to monitor by clicking on the Add Counter
button, which displays the Add to Alert dialog box shown in figure 28.5.

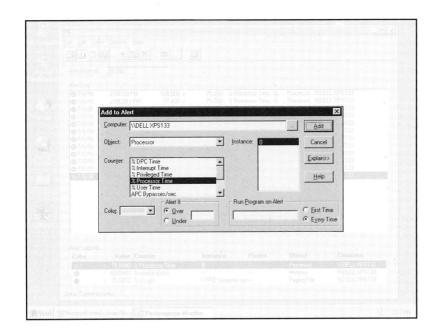

Figure 28.5

The Add to Alert dialog box contains a couple of settings not found in the Add to Chart dialog box.

Select the Counter you want, then select the Color of the counter. Then specify whether an alert should be logged if the value of the counter is over or under a value that you specify. You also can choose to run a program after a specific alert occurs using the Run Program on Alert field. You can run the program you enter here the first time the alert occurs or every time the alert occurs.

> **Tip**
>
> Running a program based on an alert is a powerful feature for administering a system. You can monitor the percentage of free space on each of your disks, for example, and then use a file-grooming program (a program that automatically erases files that haven't been accessed in a long time) whenever any of them becomes dangerously full. You also can use programs designed to beep the administrator of the system or that send a message across the network to another user.

> **Note**
>
> When you delete a counter from the list, all alerts logged for that counter are removed from the alert log.

You can set some useful options for the Alert window. Access its options using the Alert command in the Options menu, which displays the Alert Options dialog box shown in figure 28.6.

Figure 28.6

The Alert Options dialog box enables you to control how the alerts you program are acted upon.

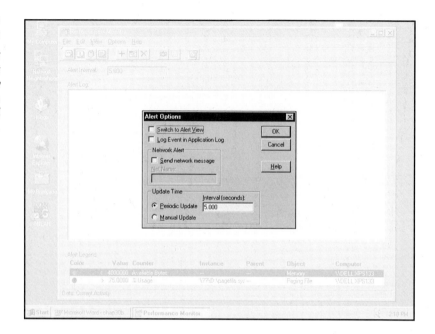

Table 28.2 shows you the options available.

TABLE 28.2
Alert Options

Option	Description
Switch to Alert View	Specifies that when an alert occurs, Performance Monitor automatically switches from whatever view you are looking at to the Alert view.
Log Event in Application Log	Adds the alert to the application log, which can be viewed using the Windows NT Event Viewer.
Send Network Message	If selected, a network message is sent to a user when an alert occurs.
Net Name	Specifies the user name to which network messages will be sent.
Periodic Update	Controls how often alert conditions are checked.

Option	Description
Manual Update	If selected, this means you must manually tell Performance Monitor to check for alert conditions with the Update Now command in the Options menu (Ctrl+U).

Log View

The Log view (available in the View menu) is different from the alert logger. When you use the Log view, you log all Performance Monitor activity to a log file that can be replayed later to analyze your system, perhaps during a particular event. All selected counter details are logged to the file. The Log view can be very useful to look at an event or series of events that happen very quickly or are difficult to reproduce. Consider, for example, that you are trying to make a particular event perform better. Usually, when you invoke the event, the graph is too complex to easily see and think about what's happening. In cases like this, you can enable the Log View, then cause the event, and then use the log to play back—in greater detail—what happened during the event.

Objective F.1

When you select the Log view, you see the display shown in figure 28.7.

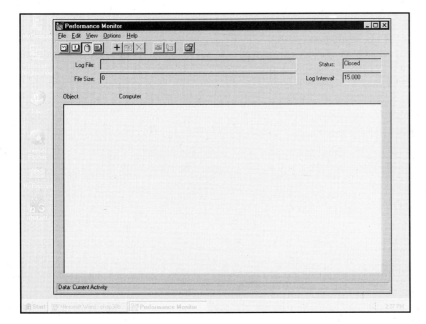

Figure 28.7

The Log view displays the counter objects that are being logged.

Clicking on the Add Counter button brings up a different dialog box than those you've seen for the other views (see fig. 28.8). This is because the log records entire counter objects, not just individual counters. You select which counters you want to view when you replay the log later.

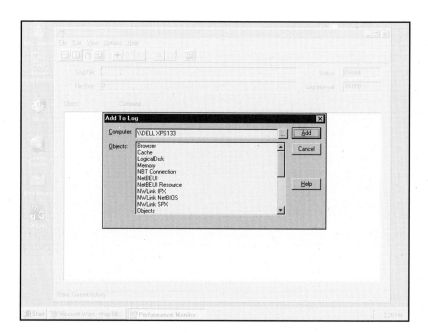

After selecting the objects you want to log, you then need to activate the logging. Choose the Log command in the Options menu to display the Log Options dialog box shown in figure 28.9.

Use the File Name field to choose a file name in which to store the log information, then use the Interval setting to select how often you want the log counters stored in the log file. After doing this and clicking on the Save button, reaccess the Log Options dialog box and click on Start Log. You can stop the log at any time by using the Stop Log button in the Log Options dialog box.

Tip You can click on the Start Log button to save your file name choice and to start logging in one step.

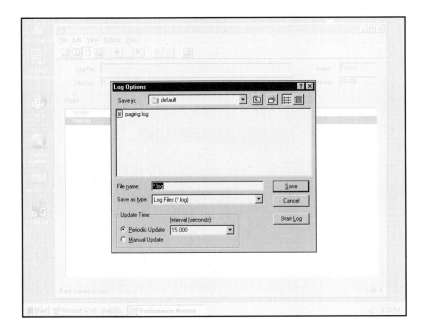

Figure 28.9

The Log Options dialog box controls how the log file is stored.

Viewing Log Counters

You view the log entries by switching to the view in which you want to work, then using the Data From command in the Options menu. This displays the Data From dialog box (see fig. 28.10), in which you choose the log file that contains the data you want to view.

After choosing to use the log file as your data source, you then add counters to the active display, just like you do when viewing real-time data. Only the counters for the objects you logged are available. The display is static and does not update with new data.

You can narrow the time period that you view using the Time Window command in the Edit menu. Accessing this command displays the Input Log File Timeframe dialog box shown in figure 28.11.

When dragging the timeframe boxes, a vertical line moves across your screen enabling you to see the activity to which you will be restricting your view.

Objective

F.1

Figure 28.10

Choose which log file's data you want to view in the Data From dialog box.

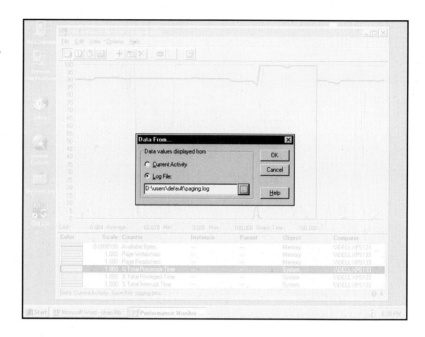

Drag these two boxes to change the time period that you view.

Figure 28.11

Narrow your search using the Input Log File Timeframe dialog box.

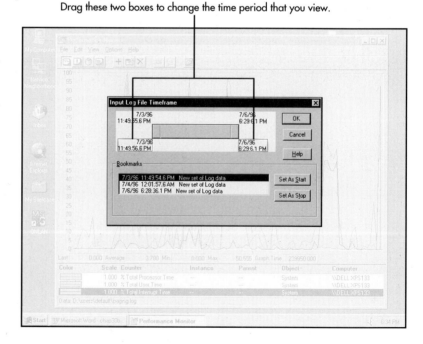

Report View

You also can view Performance Monitor data in a report format. This is useful for viewing fairly static data about the computer, such as the utilization statistics for disk drives. Report view only shows you current data from the last update interval and doesn't display any historical or moving averages. Report view is shown in figure 28.12.

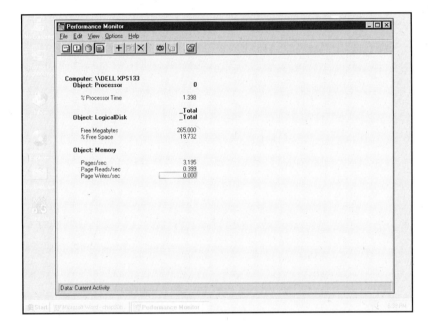

Figure 28.12

Report view shows you performance data in a report format.

> **Note** If you are using Report view with a logged source of data, be sure to set your Time view before switching to Report view. This way, Report view shows you the values for the area of interest, instead of the latest values in the log file.

Looking for Bottlenecks

Bottlenecks can be very hard to corral and tame; finding them often can be more art than technology. Experience and knowledge about Windows NT Workstation 4 helps tremendously, as does a thorough understanding of Performance Monitor.

Some of the counters in Performance Monitor are more useful than others in finding bottlenecks. (This is because some of the counters are more useful to programmers

Objective F.1

Objective F.1

Objective F.2

tuning their code than to users or administrators who want to tune their system.)
Table 28.3 discusses some of the key performance counters you can use to add more
zip to your system.

TABLE 28.3
Key Performance Counters

Object	Counter	Notes
Cache	Copy Read Hits %	Shows the overall efficiency of your cache in terms of satisfying application requests. It reflects the percentage of time that data requests are satisfied by data in the cache instead of by forcing a disk to be read. If you are using an application that works with a relatively small set of data, and this number is not as high as you expect, check Memory:Cache Bytes to check the size of your cache. If it is not as large as you would like, add memory or reduce the memory footprint of your system (stop other running programs or remove services). Also, look at Cache:Copy Reads/sec to see how active the cache really is (you can have a great hit rate with little activity going on).
Cache	Copy Reads/sec	Displays how much data is being retrieved from the cache to satisfy application requests. This measurement goes hand-in-hand with Copy Read Hits % to assess the efficiency of the cache.
Cache	Data Map Hits %	Shows you the hit rate for requests of file system meta data, such as directory information, folder information, and so on. Also look at Cache:Data Maps/sec. Applications that work with large numbers of files will make heavy use of Data Maps.
Cache	Data Maps/sec	Shows how much data is being moved to satisfy meta data requests. A high number here indicates lots of directory operations, such as you might see when manipulating a large number of very small files.

Object	Counter	Notes
Cache	Data Flushes/sec	Number of cache flushes to disk, which occur when dirty cache pages are flushed to disk. This is often an indication of file write activity.
Logical Disk	% Disk Read Time	Percentage of system time that the system is busy retrieving data from a partition. Use the Instance window to select which drive letter you want to watch.
Logical Disk	% Disk Time	Percentage of system time that the system is busy reading or writing a logical disk. This is the sum of Logical Disk:% Disk Read Time and Logical Disk:% Disk Write Time.
Logical Disk	% Disk Write Time	Percentage of system time that the system is busy writing data to a logical disk.
Logical Disk	% Free Space	Although not very helpful for detecting bottlenecks, this is a very useful counter to use with the Alert window in Performance Monitor to keep an eye on how much free space you have remaining on each logical disk drive.
Logical Disk	Avg. Disk Queue Length	Shows the average queue for requests to a logical disk. A high number here indicates that processes are having to wait on the disk excessively.
Logical Disk	Avg. Disk sec/Read	Shows the average time needed to satisfy read requests from the drive. When measuring with the same benchmark or application using different drives, this can show you which disk is more efficient for read operations.
Logical Disk	Avg. Disk sec/Write	The average time needed to satisfy write requests to a drive. Use this along with Logical Disk:Avg. Disk sec/Read to gauge the relative speed of your disks.

continues

TABLE 28.3, CONTINUED
Key Performance Counters

Object	Counter	Notes
Logical Disk	Current Disk Queue Length	The current size of the queue of requests waiting for the drive. A high number here indicates contention for the disk, or requests that outstrip the capability of the disk to respond.
Logical Disk	Disk Bytes/sec	The number of bytes read or written from the disk per second. Use Logical Disk:Disk Read Bytes/sec and Logical Disk:Disk Write Bytes/sec to find out if the data is composed of more reads than writes.
Logical Disk	Free Megabytes	Another useful Alert counter, this measures the free space of the disk in MB.
Memory	% Committed Bytes in Use	The utilization of the pagefile.sys file; a high percentage (75% or greater) may indicate that you should increase the size of your swap file.
Memory	Available Bytes	The amount of free working memory in the system. When this number drops below 4 MB, the memory manager immediately starts aggressively reducing the working set size of running processes (the system pushes unused pages to the page file more aggressively than normal). As a result, you typically won't see this number fall below 4 MB for very long.
Memory	Cache Bytes	The number of bytes in use by the system cache, which caches both disk and LAN accesses.
Memory	Cache Bytes Peak	Used in conjunction with Memory:Cache Bytes, this counter helps you see if the system is increasing or decreasing the size of the system cache. Massive decreases in the size of the system cache may mean that memory pressure from running processes is excessive; add more RAM or reduce the number of running processes to improve this situation.

Object	Counter	Notes
Memory	Page Reads/sec	The number of times the system had to retrieve memory from the pagefile.sys virtual memory file. Multiple pages can be retrieved for each Page Read operation, so this is not necessarily a good indicator of the amount of data being moved from virtual memory to physical memory.
Memory	Page Writes/sec	The number of writes from memory to the pagefile.sys file.
Memory	Pages Input/sec	The number of pages (a "page" is 4 KB on most systems) read from virtual memory per second. This counter tells you how much data is being moved from virtual memory to physical memory.
Memory	Pages Output/sec	The number of pages written to virtual memory per second.
Memory	Pages/sec	The number of pages read or written from virtual memory per second. This counter is a sum of Memory:Pages Input/sec and Memory:Pages Output/sec. Consider using this counter to measure overall virtual memory activity, then using Pages Input/sec and Pages Output/sec to see what kind of virtual memory activity is occurring.
NetBEUI	Bytes Total/sec	The number of bytes being read or written to the LAN using the NetBEUI protocol.
NWLink IPX	Bytes Total/sec	The number of bytes being read or written to the LAN using the IPX protocol.
NWLink NetBIOS	Bytes Total/sec	The number of bytes being read or written to the LAN using the NetBIOS protocol.
NWLink SPX	Bytes Total/sec	The number of bytes being read or written to the LAN using the SPX protocol.
Paging File	% Usage	The utilization of the pagefile.sys file. A high usage percentage may indicate that you should expand the initial size of your paging file.

continues

TABLE 28.3, CONTINUED
Key Performance Counters

Object	Counter	Notes
Paging File	% Usage Peak	The peak utilization of the pagefile.sys file. Use this in conjunction with Paging File:% Usage to watch the overall activity of the paging file.
Physical Disk	% Disk Read Time	The amount of system time spent reading data from the physical disk. A high number indicates a disk bottleneck.
Physical Disk	% Disk Time	The amount of system time spent reading from or writing to a physical disk. A high number indicates a disk bottleneck. This counter is the sum of % Disk Read Time and % Disk Write Time.
Physical Disk	% Disk Write Time	The amount of system time spent writing to a physical disk. A high number indicates a bottleneck.
Physical Disk	Avg. Disk Queue Length	Shows the average queue for requests to a physical disk. A high number here indicates that processes are having to wait on the disk excessively.
Physical Disk	Avg. Disk sec/Read	Shows the average time needed to satisfy read requests from the drive. When measuring with the same benchmark or application using different drives, this can show you which disk is more efficient for read operations.
Physical Disk	Avg. Disk sec/Write	The average time needed to satisfy write requests to a drive. Use this along with Physical Disk:Avg. Disk sec/Read to gauge the relative speed of your disks.
Physical Disk	Current Disk Queue Length	The current size of the queue of requests waiting for the drive. A high number here indicates contention for the disk or indicates requests that outstrip the capability of the disk to respond.

Object	Counter	Notes
Physical Disk	Disk Bytes/sec	The number of bytes read or written from the disk per second. Use Physical Disk:Disk Read Bytes/sec and Physical Disk:Disk Write Bytes/sec to find out if the data is composed of more reads than writes.
Process	% Processor Time	The amount of system time spent running the selected process. Use this measure for each available process to learn the distribution of processor time between processes.
Process	Page File Bytes	The number of bytes the selected process is using in the pagefile.sys file.
Process	Private Bytes	The number of bytes the selected process has allocated for its own use. This counter can show you the relative memory usage of each process.
Process	Working Set	The amount of physical memory (RAM) actually being used by the process on a regular basis. This number can decrease markedly when Memory:Available Bytes falls below 4 MB and the memory manager aggressively trims working set pages from running processes. Until Available Bytes falls below 4 MB, the system is lazy about keeping the working set as low as possible.
Processor	% Processor Time	Use this counter to measure the relative activity of different processors installed in the system. On uni-processor systems, use the System object's counters instead.
System	% Total Processor Time	The amount of time the processors are actually doing work in the system. High numbers here can indicate a processor bottleneck.
System	% Total User Time	The amount of time the processor spends running user code. When this number is markedly higher than System:% Total Privileged Time, the system is spending most of its time running application code.

continues

TABLE 28.3, CONTINUED
Key Performance Counters

Object	Counter	Notes
System	% Total Privileged Time	The amount of time the processor spends running privileged code, which is usually the code of the operating system itself. When this number is higher than System:% Total User Time, your system is spending more of its time running the operating system than the applications. Consider using the Process object to find out which processes are using the most privileged time, and consider possibly terminating services that are not in use but are consuming privileged time.
System	File Read Bytes/sec	The total number of bytes being read from the entire file system.
System	File Write Bytes/sec	The total number of bytes being written to the entire file system.
System	Processor Queue Length	The number of threads waiting for the processor to become available. Higher numbers indicate more contention for the processor (and more waiting threads). You can consider adding processors when this number stays too high (consistently more than two to four queued threads).

Dealing with Bottlenecks

Objective F.3

You can do a variety of things after you have identified bottlenecks. Generally, bottlenecks will occur in the processor, the disk subsystem, the system cache, or system memory.

To deal with processor bottlenecks, consider the following options:

Objective F.2

◆ Upgrade your processor or add more processors to your system. Adding processors will benefit you only if there are multiple threads vying for processor time simultaneously. If one particular thread is bound by the processor, all you can do is use a faster processor; a single thread cannot be distributed across more than one processor.

◆ If your system can accept more secondary cache memory—memory usually on the motherboard that caches the processor's memory requests—consider increasing it if you are either processor- or memory-bound.

◆ If the network and the processor are both busy, try upgrading an 8-bit network adapter to a 16- or 32-bit adapter, which will consume fewer processor cycles when communicating with the network. You also can look into bus-mastering network boards, which can make additional positive impacts on the capability of your processor to do more work.

◆ If your disk controller does not use Direct Memory Access (DMA) to transfer data from the disk to the system, consider upgrading it to one that uses DMA. DMA transfers are more economical for the processor.

◆ If your system is busy running a system service when you're trying to get the best possible speed out of an application, look into which system service is consuming the processor and look for ways to relieve it. If your system is spending a lot of time paging, for example, adding more memory will reduce the amount of time spent paging (and using the disk, too). (On a recent performance benchmark using Windows NT on an Intel-based system, extremely high database transactional benchmarks were achieved on a system that had 512 MB (!) of RAM installed.)

◆ If a process other than the one you want to speed up is using an appreciable amount of the system's CPU time, you can use the Task Manager to adjust the Base Priority settings of the process you're interested in (to raise it) and the one that appears to be using too much of the system (to lower it). See the section "Using the Task Manager for Performance Monitoring" later in this chapter to learn how to do this. Realize that changing base priority settings demands great caution—you can make the system unstable or unusable by changing these.

◆ Using the System icon in the Control panel, you can control the amount of priority boost given to whatever application is in the foreground. See the section "Changing Foreground Responsiveness" near the end of this chapter for more information on this subject.

Disk bottlenecks are also troublesome and, depending on the application, can be far more common than processor bottlenecks. Consider the following when you encounter a disk bottleneck:

◆ Before upgrading your disk subsystem, first make sure that you don't actually have a memory bottleneck. Excessive paging activity caused by insufficient memory can often appear to be a disk bottleneck. Make sure your paging counters are somewhat low relative to the total disk activity before deciding that you have a bona fide disk bottleneck.

◆ FAT-formatted disks tend to be faster for sequential file access, while NTFS-formatted disks tend to be faster for random accesses. Try running your application on a drive that uses a different formatting scheme. This can some-times yield enormous benefits, depending on the pattern of disk activity generated by the application.

◆ Consider creating a stripe set out of multiple physical disks. When you do this, your data is scattered across multiple disks; therefore, more read and write heads are available to access your data. For an application that is bound by the seek time of your disk heads, this change can really speed things up. For example, a two-disk stripe set can seek data, on average, twice as fast as a single disk. A four-disk stripe set can seek data, again on average, four times faster than a single disk.

◆ If you are already using a Windows NT stripe set, consider purchasing a RAID disk controller. A *RAID controller* can handle striping in its hardware, freeing up the processor for work other than managing the striping process. These controllers often perform faster than software-based striping, such as that included with Windows NT.

◆ Look into upgrading your disk controller to one that uses one of the local bus slots in your computer. PCI- and VLB-based disk controllers are faster than those that use ISA or EISA slots. Also, find a disk controller that performs 32-bit data transfers instead of 8- or 16-bit transfers. If you're stuck with an ISA bus-based disk controller, check to see whether your computer has a switch that increases the bus speed. Although this can sometimes cause hardware incompat-ibilities, it's worth trying to see if you can increase disk transfer speed.

◆ If you are using multiple disks in your system, you can add an additional disk controller to further segregate the load between the disks. Sometimes, because the disk controller is the bottleneck, two disk controllers that each control half of your disks can improve performance.

◆ ISA busses can reference only 16 MB of memory. Therefore, disk controllers installed in an ISA bus when the system has more than 16 MB of memory can suffer. Because the system cannot directly address a disk controller above 16 MB, it has to perform an extra memory transfer before sending data to the disk. This generally is only true with SCSI controllers because IDE controllers these days use Programmed Input/Output (PIO), which eliminates this problem even in ISA bus computers.

◆ A number of caching disk controllers on the market can further improve performance, particularly if the application is dealing with a relatively small amount of data. If you pursue this approach, install a generous amount of memory on the caching disk controller to maximize its benefit.

◆ Under Windows NT Workstation, SCSI disks often can perform faster than IDE disks. (This generally isn't true under DOS, Windows 3.x, or Windows 95, but it is true for Windows NT.) When purchasing a SCSI disk subsystem, be sure to get one that uses SCSI-2 and preferably uses both Fast and Wide SCSI, both of which increase the speed at which data can transfer from the disks to the computer. Also purchase disks with the fastest seek time you can find. When purchasing a new disk subsystem, consider buying many smaller disks instead of one gigantic disk and then creating a stripe set out of the multiple disks.

Windows NT Workstation is a big operating system. Today's applications also are large and consume lots of memory. There isn't much you can do to address memory bottlenecks except to reduce the number of processes you're running—including removing unused network protocols—or purchase and install more memory. See Chapter 15, "Configuring Memory Usage," for more information about monitoring memory in your system.

Performance Monitor is an important tool to use when delving into your system to see what it's doing. Another important tool is Windows NT Diagnostics, which displays important information about your system and can help you when troubleshooting. The next section discusses this tool.

Using Windows NT Diagnostics

Windows NT Workstation 4 includes another important tool, in addition to the Performance Monitor, that provides you with current statistics about your system quickly and also provides information useful in troubleshooting. Windows NT Diagnostics is a program that displays key data about the configuration of your computer. You start Windows NT Diagnostics using the Administrative Tools menu in the Start menu. Figure 28.13 shows the Version tab of Windows NT Diagnostics.

Objective

F.1

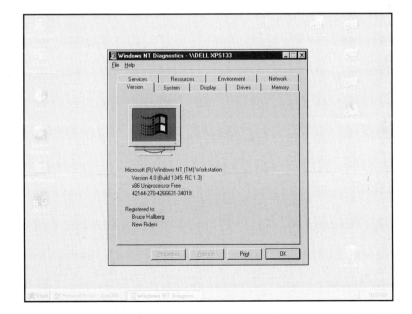

Figure 28.13

Windows NT Diagnostics' Version tab shows basic information about the system.

In the following sections, you learn about other tabs of Windows NT Diagnostics that show you detailed information about different aspects of your system.

System Tab

The System tab shows you basic information about the system, including the BIOS-version information and the version of the Hardware Abstraction Layer (HAL) that you are using (see fig. 28.14). You also see all installed processors listed, along with their stepping level. (*Stepping levels* are just like version numbers but are used for processor revisions.)

Figure 28.14

The System tab shows basic information about the system.

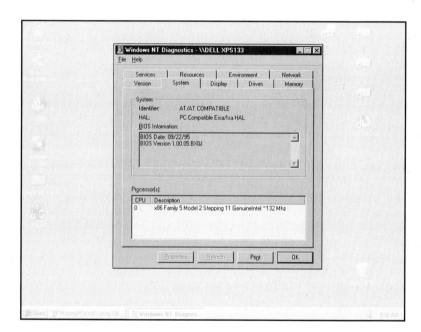

Display Tab

The Display tab shows you which video driver you are using as well as the current screen settings (resolution, color bit depth, and vertical refresh rate of the monitor). Figure 28.15 shows the Display tab.

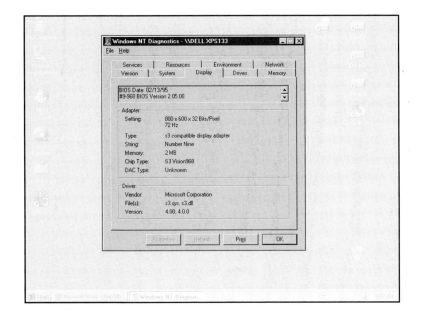

Figure 28.15

The Display tab shows information about your video setup.

Drives Tab

The Drives tab lists all attached physical disk drives. You can double-click on a particular drive to see statistics about that particular disk drive. Figure 28.16 shows both the Drives tab and the statistics for one of the physical disks attached to the system.

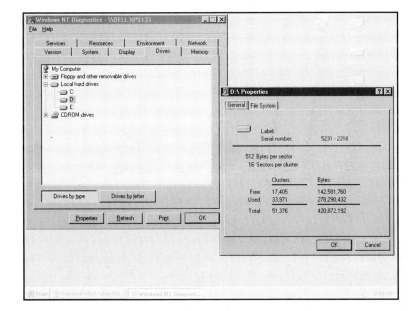

Figure 28.16

The Drives tab and the Properties dialog box enable you to see details about your disks.

Memory Tab

One of the most useful tabs in Windows NT Diagnostics is the Memory tab, shown in figure 28.17. Here you can get quick statistics about how the memory in your system is being used. In particular, the Available and File Cache measurements in Physical Memory are useful, as are the various Pagefile Space measurements.

Figure 28.17

The Memory tab shows detailed information about memory usage on your system.

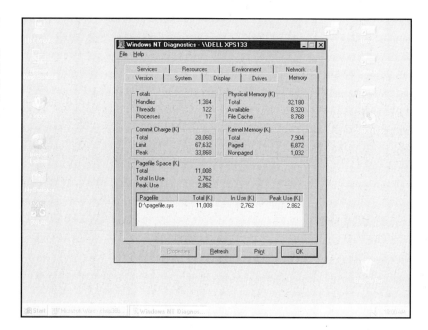

Services Tab

The Services tab, shown in figure 28.18, shows you two things: running services and running devices. Click on either the Services button or the Devices button to switch views on this tab. You also can view statistics about the services and devices by double-clicking on them or by selecting them and using the Properties button.

> **Note** It can sometimes take a few seconds to display the details about one of the services or devices when you open their properties.

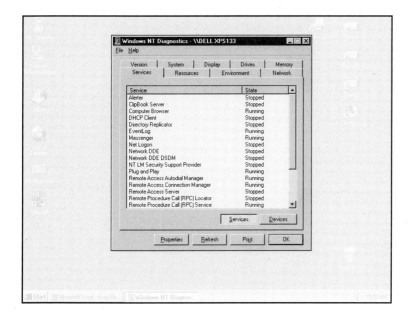

Figure 28.18

View running services and devices on the Services tab.

Resources Tab

Use the Resources tab to learn how key resources in your system are allocated. You can view assigned IRQs, I/O Ports, Direct Memory Access (DMA) channels, memory address ranges, and hardware devices. For each resource, you can view its details by selecting it and then clicking Properties. You see the Resources tab in figure 28.19.

Objective F.1

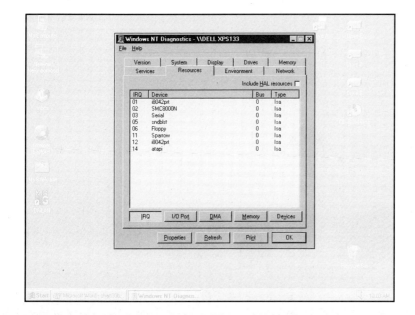

Figure 28.19

When troubleshooting hardware conflicts, the Resources tab is very helpful.

Tip If you select an installed device using the Devices button and then select its Properties, you can see all system resources used by the device.

Environment Tab

Objective F.1

To view currently set environment variables, select the Environment tab (see fig. 28.20). You can view system-wide variables with the System button and user-specific settings with the Local User button. (You can change the environment settings with the System icon in the Control Panel.)

Figure 28.20

The Environment tab shows environment variable settings currently in use.

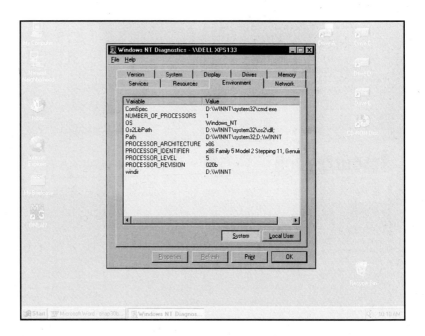

Network Tab

Objective F.1

Of particular interest on the Network tab is the Statistics button, which gives you overall network statistics for the local machine. You can view how many users are attached to the machine, how many bytes have been sent and received, and how many network errors have occurred. The General button shows basic statistics such as which domain you are connected to, your user name on the system, the computer name, and so on. The Transports button shows currently running network transports and their network addresses. The Settings button displays various networking settings on your machine. Figure 28.21 shows the Network tab set to Statistics view.

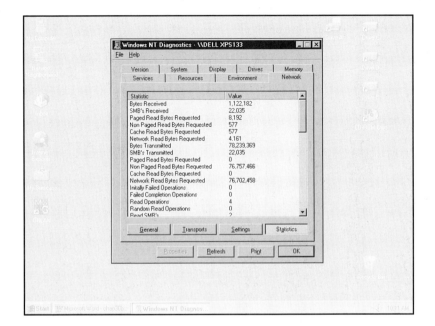

Figure 28.21

The Network tab enables you to examine network statistics.

Using the Task Manager for Performance Monitoring

Though not as comprehensive as Performance Monitor, you also can use the Windows NT Workstation Task Manager to get a quick glimpse of system performance and the impact of different processes. Often, you use Task Manager as a more general-purpose monitor of system performance, then use Performance Manager to take a closer look when you detect a problem.

Objective
F.1

The easiest way to activate the Task Manager is to right-click on a blank area of the Task Bar and then choose Task Manager from the shortcut menu. This action displays the Task Manager, which has several tabs available. The Performance tab is shown in figure 28.22.

Figure 28.22

The Performance tab of the Task Manager gives you a quick performance overview.

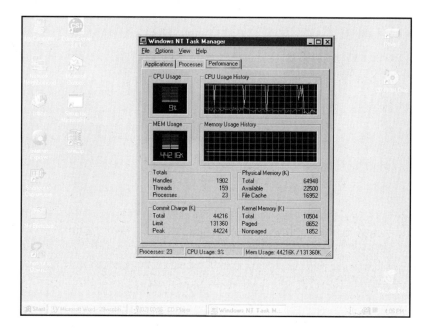

Understanding the Performance Tab's Display

Objective F.1

The CPU Usage display shows the utilization of the processor on an instantaneous basis. This information also is reflected in the status display at the bottom of the window. Impacts to the system show up immediately. To the right is the CPU Usage History display, which graphs changes over time. You can also monitor the amount of time the processor spends in Kernel Mode (operating system processor impact) by choosing Show Kernel Times from the View menu. In figure 28.22, the somewhat static graph line in the bottom of the CPU Usage History chart shows the Kernel Time usage of the processor.

> **Tip**
>
> To see more detail of the CPU Usage and CPU Usage History, double-click on either graph. Task Manager changes its display so that the CPU graphs take up the entire window, as shown in figure 28.23.

The next graphical display on the Performance tab of the Task Manager concerns memory usage. To the left, MEM Usage shows the amount of total memory (physical plus virtual) that the entire system—the operating system and all processes—is consuming. To the right, the Memory Usage History graph shows changes to memory usage over time.

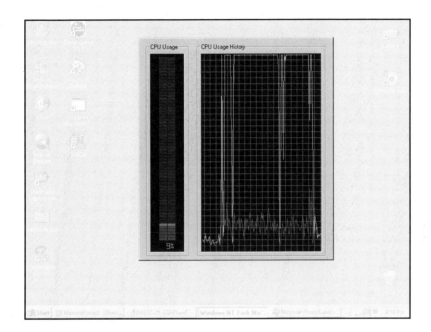

Figure 28.23

The CPU graphs appear in a full window.

Table 28.4 discusses the text information found on the Performance tab of the Task Manager.

TABLE 28.4
Performance Tab Information

Name	Description
Totals	
Handles	The total number of handles in use. Handles are used to access files, areas of memory, and semaphores.
Threads	The total number of running threads in the system.
Processes	The total number of running processes in the system. Note that there will always be fewer processes than threads because every process is made up of one or more threads.

continues

TABLE 28.4, CONTINUED
Performance Tab Information

Name	Description
Physical Memory (K)	
Total	The total amount of RAM installed into the system.
Available	The amount of unused RAM in the system.
File Cache	The amount of RAM being used to cache file reads and writes.
Commit Charge (K)	
Total	The amount of committed (used) memory.
Limit	The total possible amount of committed memory. This is the sum of the physical memory plus the paging file size.
Peak	The total amount of committed memory used since Windows NT was last booted.
Kernel Memory (K)	
Total	The amount of memory committed by the kernel; the "core" of the operating system.
Paged	The amount of kernel memory located in the paging file.
Nonpaged	The amount of kernel memory located in RAM.

You can make a couple changes to the display of the Performance tab in Task Manager. These changes are found in the View menu when the Performance tab is visible:

◆ **Update Speed.** You can choose to have Task Manager update the performance information at different speeds: Low, Normal, and High. You can also choose Paused to stop the display of data temporarily. Keep in mind that higher update speeds cause more processor overhead to collect and display the performance data. When you choose Paused, you can use the Refresh Now command on the View menu to get a quick update of the system's state.

◆ **CPU History.** This command on the View menu enables you to determine how multiple processors are displayed. You can have each processor on its own graph, or you can display them together on one graph.

◆ **Show Kernel Times.** Selecting this command (it is an on/off toggle) causes the amount of processor time spent dealing with the operating system kernel to be displayed on the CPU graphs in red.

When Task Manager is open, even if it is minimized, a small display appears on the Task Bar next to the current system time. A small green bar shows the current processor utilization and enables you to keep an eye on it without consuming much screen space. Furthermore, you can see a summary of the CPU usage and memory usage on the Task Manager's status bar.

Understanding the Processes Tab's Display

The other key performance-based information display in Task Manager is on the Processes tab. On this tab, you can see all the processes running on the system, along with valuable statistics about each one. Though you can view the same information with the Performance Monitor, it is often faster and easier to see important information with Task Manager. A sample Processes tab is shown in figure 28.24.

Objective F.1

Figure 28.24

Use the Processes tab to see information about running processes.

Image Name	PID	CPU	CPU Time	Mem Usage	Page Faults	VM Size	Paged Pool	NP Pool	Base Pri	Handles	Threads
System Idle Process	0	94	0:20:37	16 K	1	0 K	0 K	0 K	Unknown	0	1
WINWORD.EXE	116	00	0:02:26	572 K	2518	2732 K	43 K	6 K	Normal	98	4
System	2	00	0:00:42	200 K	1516	36 K	0 K	0 K	Normal	263	27
TASKMGR.EXE	58	06	0:00:15	1816 K	467	340 K	13 K	2 K	High	29	3
EXPLORER.EXE	42	00	0:00:15	4212 K	1773	1420 K	15 K	3 K	Normal	55	3
cdplayer.exe	178	00	0:00:13	148 K	561	512 K	12 K	2 K	Normal	49	1
NTVDM.EXE	185	00	0:00:00	1748 K	7940	2468 K	29 K	4 K	Normal	65	3
capture.exe		00	0:00:11						Normal		1
wowexec.exe		00	0:00:00						Normal		1
PHOTOED.EXE	189	00	0:00:06	1196 K	2869	1868 K	16 K	3 K	Normal	40	2
services.exe	40	00	0:00:04	3008 K	1041	1312 K	17 K	180 K	Normal	256	25
csrss.exe	24	00	0:00:01	2052 K	795	1412 K	33 K	4 K	High	260	9
WINLOGON.EXE	34	00	0:00:01	200 K	1046	1116 K	19 K	11 K	High	51	1
SPOOLSS.EXE	85	00	0:00:00	2268 K	637	3024 K	14 K	691 K	Normal	93	8
smss.exe	20	00	0:00:00	200 K	1974	164 K	0 K	1 K	High	30	6
RASMAN.EXE	136	00	0:00:00	1420 K	817	1012 K	16 K	6 K	Normal	105	10
RPCSS.EXE	98	00	0:00:00	520 K	908	724 K	15 K	1043 K	Normal	104	6
faxsvc.exe	155	00	0:00:00	404 K	774	3732 K	17 K	15 K	Normal	67	11
lsass.exe	43	00	0:00:00	620 K	683	740 K	11 K	11 K	Normal	87	11
OSA.EXE	104	00	0:00:00	1404 K	426	356 K	20 K	2 K	Normal	31	1
TAPISRV.EXE	82	00	0:00:00	200 K	515	716 K	13 K	12 K	Normal	88	11
faxstat.exe	114	00	0:00:00	1028 K	833	2652 K	12 K	14 K	Normal	41	6
popmenu.exe	126	00	0:00:00	812 K	430	504 K	12 K	2 K	Normal	21	1
TCPSVCS.EXE	111	00	0:00:00	1380 K	393	496 K	13 K	498 K	Normal	43	2
systray.exe	102	00	0:00:00	216 K	334	304 K	11 K	2 K	Normal	24	2
nddeagnt.exe	72	00	0:00:00	828 K	281	308 K	9 K	1 K	Normal	16	1

End Process

Processes: 24   CPU Usage: 6%   Mem Usage: 46480K / 131360K

You change the columns that are displayed for each process by accessing the Select Columns command in the View menu. Doing so displays the Select Columns dialog box shown in figure 28.25. In this dialog box, you can enable or disable different information displays for the processes.

Figure 28.25

The Select Columns dialog box selects the information displayed about each process.

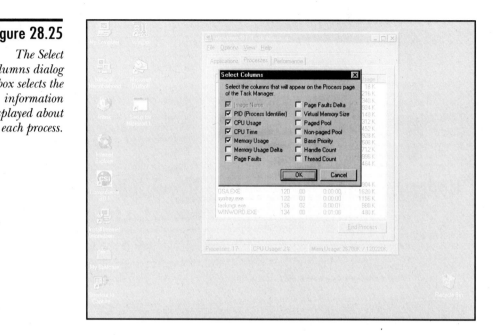

Table 28.5 details the settings shown in the Select Columns dialog box and discusses what the column display shows when they are activated.

TABLE 28.5
Column Displays for Processes in Task Manager

Display Name	Description
Image Name	You cannot turn this option off. It displays the name of each process.
PID	The Process Identifier (PID) shows the process number assigned by Windows NT.
CPU Usage	Displays the percentage of time, during the update interval, that the process uses the processor.
CPU Time	Displays the total amount of processor time used by the process since the process was started. The display is in Hours, Minutes, and Seconds.
Memory Usage	Displays the amount of memory used by the process.

Display Name	Description
Memory Usage Delta	Displays the change in memory usage since the last time the Task Manager Processes display was updated. Using this setting, you can see changes in memory usage.
Page Faults	Displays the number of times the process requested memory that had to be retrieved from the system paging file.
Page Faults Delta	Shows any changes in the number of page faults recorded since the previous information update.
Virtual Memory Size	Displays how much of the paging file is being used by the process.
Paged Pool	Exhibits the amount of the paged pool used by the process.
Non–paged Pool	Shows the amount of the non–paged memory pool used by the process.
Base Priority	Lists the base priority of the process.
Handle Count	Shows how many handles are being managed by the process. A *handle* is an object being referred to by the process, such as a region of memory, a file, a network stream, and so forth.
Thread Count	Lists the number of threads associated with a process.

Just as you can do with the Performance tab, you can adjust the update frequency of the Processes tab. Use the View menu, choose Update Speed, and then choose from Low, Normal, High, and Paused. When paused or whenever you want an immediate update, use Refresh Now from the View menu.

Changing a Process's Base Priority

The Task Manager enables you to adjust the base priority of a process. Within that base priority you set, the threads of the process are adjusted accordingly. You can use the capability to change a process's base priority to compensate for performance problems.

Objective F.3

First, you should review the information about thread priorities in Chapter 1, "Understanding Windows NT Workstation 4." There you will learn about Windows NT's priority-based scheduling scheme that apportions the processor's time among the running processes and threads in the system. Also, take great caution when you adjust base priorities. You can make the operating system unusable or unstable by making inappropriate changes. In certain cases, you can even prevent your capability to shut Windows NT down properly. You could be forced to reset Windows using the reset button on the computer or by powering the system down and then back up.

To change the base priority of a process, use the Processes tab of Task Manager. Right-click on a particular process and then choose Set Priority. You can then choose from the available choices: Low, Normal, High, and Realtime. Avoid setting any application programs to the Realtime priority, as you will then preempt some crucial system processes from running properly.

To apply this information, consider this scenario: You are trying to maximize the performance of an application, and you learn that the important application can't go faster because some other, perhaps inconsequential, process in the system is taking up too much of the system's CPU time. In cases like this, you can try lowering the priority of the process detracting from your main application's performance, or you can boost the priority of the application you are most interested in. After doing so, use Task Manager and Performance Monitor to inspect the results of your changes.

Assuming you use a change in base priority to effect a beneficial change, another problem arises: You will need to adjust the selected processes' base priority every time you start those applications or every time you start the system. Otherwise, they will use their programmed default base priorities. You can ease this task by starting the affected processes using the Windows NT START command, which accepts command-line parameters that enable you to control the base priority of the processes that you start.

> **Tip**   If you decide to use the Start command to begin an application at a certain priority, don't forget that you can establish a batch file with the appropriate command, and then use a shortcut to that batch file on your desktop or in your Start menu.

Changing Foreground Responsiveness

Objective F.3

Windows NT Workstation is designed as a network-able operating system. In some cases, Windows NT Workstation is used as a person's primary desktop operating system, on which they run various programs and use the system. In other cases, it provides some sort of service to other computers across a network. Because Windows NT Workstation is designed to serve both of these roles—which require different priority settings for the system—you can adjust the amount of priority boost foreground applications receive.

When using the system as a primary desktop system, you want the foreground application—the one you are working with—to take a certain amount of precedence over other processes in the system, including those that service requests from remote computers across a network. When using the system to provide a network service, you generally want the network service being provided (such as a Web server) to take priority over any programs being run on the machine itself. In these sorts of cases, generally only administrative programs will be run on the server, and you typically do not want them to have priority over the system performing its primary mission.

To adjust the overall relative priority of foreground applications, open the System icon in the Control Panel and then move to the Performance tab. You can see this tab in figure 28.26.

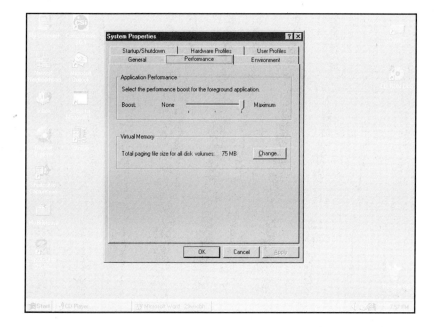

Figure 28.26

You can access the Performance tab with the System icon in the Control Panel.

When you are using the system as a primary desktop system, you generally want the Boost slider to be as far toward Maximum as possible. When using a system as a network service provider, you want the slider to be set to None. At other times, when a machine serves dual roles, you might want some setting in between; try different settings and experiment until you find one that is most satisfactory.

End Note: If you are a computer support person helping people realize better performance, keep these tips in mind:

◆ Sometimes you need to suggest that the users' behavior changes in order for them to realize better performance. Sometimes people take advantage of multitasking—they could get a lot more work done if they did work sequentially because they then make more appropriate demands of their computer hardware. Often, running ten tasks simultaneously is a lot slower than running two or three tasks at a time, with each group being run after the previous set finishes.

◆ It is crucial that you set realistic expectations for users who are complaining about poor performance. Explain to them the trade-offs to making changes, including the relative costs and benefits. Most people are reasonable about their expectations when they understand the cost and effort involved in making improvements.

◆ Conversely, many users just accept crummy performance because they don't know what to expect or what is possible. Often, there are very minor things you can do to make radical improvements. Keep an eye on what people do with their computers. Sometimes you can find little productivity nuggets that have a huge payoff for the company but cost little or nothing to implement.

The art of helping others with their computers requires more than technical knowledge on your part. It also requires excellent communication skills coupled with good business sense. Many great technical people sometimes do more harm than good because they don't pay attention to the larger picture of what they do and the impacts their changes have.

Test Your Knowledge

1. The most powerful tool you can use to uncover performance bottlenecks is:

    A. Task Manager

    B. Performance Monitor

    C. Ziff-Davis Benchmarking Tools

    D. A stopwatch

2. If you want to improve the performance of an application, your best initial course of action is to:

    A. Examine the system, using the tools discussed in this chapter to look for bottlenecks.

    B. Reprogram the application so that it uses more efficient algorithms.

C. Buy a faster computer.

D. Take a class in developing patience.

3. Consider a system on which the most important application is found to be processor-bound. The system is a Pentium-class computer using an ISA-based SCSI disk controller that has 24 MB of memory installed. The system uses an 8-bit network adapter. Which of the following are likely ways to improve the performance of the application?

A. Upgrade the CPU to a faster model.

B. Switch to a PCI- or VLB-based SCSI disk controller.

C. Lower the base priority of other processes that are using the CPU, or increase the priority of the process you want to speed up.

D. Install more RAM.

4. Consider a system on which the primary application is found to be disk-bound. The system is a dual-Pentium Pro system with 24 MB of RAM installed and uses a SCSI-2 hard disk formatted with NTFS. The application makes large sequential writes to disk as it builds and uses large temporary files. Which of the following are likely ways to improve the performance of the application?

A. Try running the application on a disk formatted using the FAT file system.

B. Diagnose the swap file. If it is being used heavily, add more RAM to the system.

C. Add two more processors to the system.

D. Use an EIDE-based hard disk.

5. Consider a system on which the primary application is found to be memory-bound. The system is a Pentium system (200 MHz) with 64 MB of RAM installed and uses a SCSI-2 hard disk formatted with NTFS. The application appears to be limited by its ability to move 1 MB "chunks" of memory around and manipulate that memory. Which of the following are likely ways to improve the performance of the application?

A. Decrease the number of running processes.

B. Remove any unused networking protocols.

C. Add more memory, whether or not the paging file is being used at all.

D. Add a RAID disk controller.

6. You can use Task Manager to:

A. Get a quick glimpse of the performance of the system.

B. Watch how many page faults a given process generates.

C. See how fast your hard disks are performing.

D. Raise or lower the base priority of a process.

7. On a system that is providing network services to other computers across a
   network as its primary mission, you should:

   A. Make sure the base priority of the EXPLORER process is raised to the
      Realtime priority class.

   B. Adjust the foreground boost to None using the System icon in the
      Control Panel.

   C. Adjust the Network Boost setting to Maximum using the Network icon in
      the Control Panel.

   D. There is nothing special you should do in this circumstance.

8. Working Set refers to:

   A. The total amount of memory controlled by a process

   B. The amount of a process's memory present in physical RAM

   C. The amount of the paging file in use

   D. The running services

9. You watch the Processor Queue Length in Performance Monitor to see:

   A. The number of events the processor is working on at any given instant in
      time

   B. The number of threads with work to do that are waiting for the processor

   C. The amount of system overhead on multiprocessor systems to manage the
      two processors

   D. The number of memory requests waiting to be filled

10. If you want to run something on the system that will cause an alert if a given
    event happens, such as the disk becoming too full, you:

    A. Use Task Watcher to set up the alert criteria.

    B. Use Performance Monitor's Alert View.

    C. Set up a system counter and an outcome using the AT command.

    D. Use the ALERTER utility in the Windows NT Resource Kit.

Test Your Knowledge Answers

1. B
2. A
3. A,B,C
4. A,B
5. A,B
6. A,B,D
7. B
8. B
9. B
10. B

Chapter Snapshot

This chapter describes events and event logging in Windows NT 4 Workstation. *Events* are actions and occurrences that can be monitored by your system in the Event Viewer. There are system events, security events, and application events. With a picture of the events that occur on your computer, you can optimize your system or correct many malfunctions that occur. This chapter focuses on the following topics:

Windows NT
Workstation 4

CHAPTER 29

Using the Event Viewer

The *Event Viewer* is an application that monitors your system's performance and records activity that is different from what is expected. The Event Viewer classifies this activity as system, security, and application events, and records these events in event logs. Obvious errors are recorded in your Event Viewer, but you can also configure the Event Viewer to show events of any type—errors or not—to suit your purpose.

When a critical event occurs, the event is displayed on your screen. For non-critical events, the information is recorded into a log file. You can audit log files, as you will subsequently see in this chapter.

To open the Event Viewer, open the Start menu, click on Programs, then Administrative tools. You will see the Event Viewer shown in the list of Administrative Tools programs, as shown in figure 29.1.

Figure 29.1

You can open the Event Viewer from the Start menu.

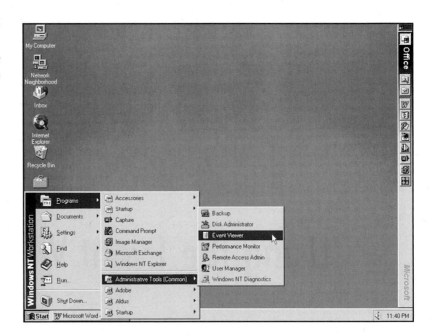

The Event Viewer is shown in figure 29.2. Notice that running services can record many events in the Event Viewer. Windows NT Workstation 4 starts recording events as soon as the operating system starts loading, so that some categories of events apply to startup operations.

Figure 29.2

The Event Viewer is shown here with the System Log open.

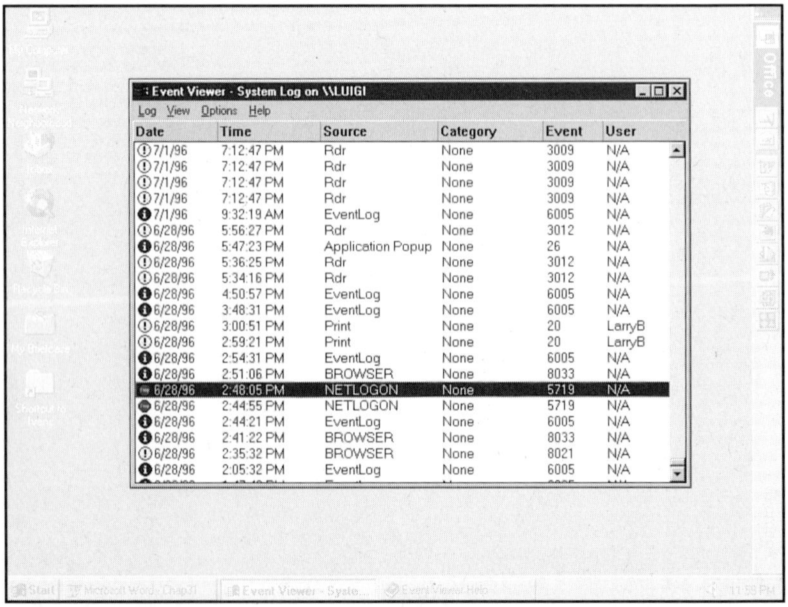

You will notice five different icon types in the extreme left column of the Event Viewer window. Their descriptions follow:

◆ **Warning icon.** This yellow circle with an exclamation mark in it indicates that an event occurred that required tracking, but it wasn't important enough to require a posted warning. Eliminating these errors can be used to optimize your system and prevent more serious problems in the future.

◆ **Information icon.** The blue circle with an "i" in it informs you of a successful service operation, an application, a properly functioning access of a device by a device driver, and so on. In a healthy system, the bulk of your entries in the logs should be of this type.

◆ **Error icon.** This red octagonal sign (like a stop sign) indicates that an event occurred in which data was lost or a function failed. These events can be caused by a program that crashed, a system service malfunction, a failure of a device driver, and so on. In some cases, they are not reproducible. When they are, it's worth tracking them down to attempt to correct the situation.

◆ **Success Audit icon.** The key icon indicates that an audited security-access event was successfully applied. These events typically are security modifications or usage of a security resource in NT. You would see these events, for example, when you make changes in the User Manager, set privileges or access to resources in NT Explorer, make security changes in the Clipboard Viewer to ClipBooks, change the Registry with the Registry Editor, or make changes to any other application that is audited.

◆ **Failure Audit icon.** The lock icon indicates that an audited security-access event failed.

The following data is displayed about specific events in the Event Viewer:

◆ **Date and Time.** These two columns record the time the event occurred and was logged in the Event Viewer.

◆ **Source.** The part of the operating system, service, driver, or application that records the event.

◆ **Category.** The event's classification, as recorded by the source of the event in the log.

◆ **Event.** The Event ID is a tag that describes the event. Using this ID number, a service representative for the application or for Microsoft can give you specific help to resolve the problem. You'll find a listing of these error ID codes in technical manuals.

◆ **User.** The User column specifies text that matches text in the User field name.

Event logging is one of the things that makes NT Workstation 4 a robust operating system. Using the Event Viewer, you can diagnose problems in your system and correct them. The Event Viewer's services come with a price, however. They can slow down your system, particularly when you enable security auditing.

In the sections that follow, you'll learn how to view the event logs and glean information from them.

Viewing Event Logs

When you open the Event Viewer, you see one of the event logs in the Event Viewer window. An *event log* is a history of events in a particular category. You can save these logs to text files or database files to load them into another application and work with them there, or you can print them out to analyze your system's history. Through careful analysis, you can eliminate problems in your system, optimize system performance, and locate hardware and software errors.

You can view any of the following three log types:

◆ System events

◆ Security events

◆ Application events

Each of these three classes of events is described in more detail in the sections that follow.

Once opened, the Event Viewer does not display additional events that occur for that particular log. Use the Refresh command on the View menu, or press F5, to update your log and view recent events. Archived logs cannot be updated, thus no refresh is possible.

To select a log for viewing, select either the System, Security, or Application command in the Log menu. You then see the events recorded for that particular log.

To sort or filter the events in a log or to find a particular event, see the following sections.

Sorting Events

The Event Viewer enables you to sort your events by date and time so as to get an accurate picture of the sequence of different events. By knowing which events occur in sequence, you can more successfully identify the cause and effect of different events. The date and time of an event are taken from your computer's system clock.

To set a chronological sort, select the Oldest First or Newest First command on the View menu.

Oldest First puts the first events recorded at the top of the Event Viewer and the newest events at the bottom of the Event Viewer window. Newest First puts the first events recorded at the bottom of the Event Viewer and the newest events at the top of the Event Viewer window. Newest First is the default view.

Viewing Events by Type

You can view events by type by filtering the event log.

To filter events by type, follow these steps:

1. Choose the Filter Events command on the View menu.

2. Enter the parameters desired in the Filter dialog box shown in figure 29.3.

3. Click on OK.

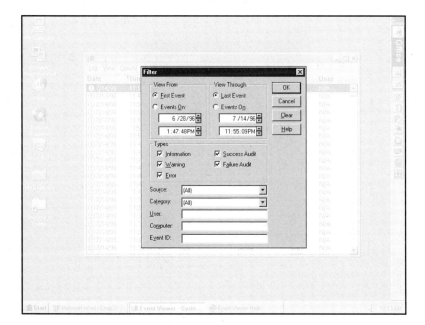

Figure 29.3

The Filter dialog box enables you to look at events of a particular type.

The Filter dialog box offers you many different ways to filter your view. Among your selection criteria are these:

◆ **View From section.** You can choose to view events starting with the First Event, or starting on any date or time you set in the Events On field.

◆ **View Through section.** You can choose to view events ending with the last one recorded by clicking the Last Event radio button. Or, you can enter the last event date and time in the Events On field.

The combination of View From and View Through sections in the Event Viewer enables you to set a range of dates and times to filter your view of the Event Logs.

> **Note** When you open the Event Viewer, you see all the events you specify up to the time you open the application. Windows NT Workstation 4 is still recording events, but they do not appear in the Event Viewer window. To see your most recent events after the Event Viewer was opened, use the Refresh command on the View window, or press F5.

◆ **Information check box.** The Information check box enables you to filter your view to see events of the Information type. These events take an icon with a blue circle and a small "i" in them.

◆ **Warning check box.** The Warning check box enables you to filter your view to see events of the Warning type. These events take an icon with a yellow circle and an "!" in them.

◆ **Error check box.** The Error check box enables you to filter your view to see events of the Error type. These events take an icon with a red octagon, just like a stop sign.

◆ **Success Audit check box.** The Success Audit check box enables you to filter your view to see events in which audited security events are altered. These events take a key icon.

◆ **Failure Audit check box.** The Failure Audit check box enables you to filter your view to see events in which audited security events could not be successfully altered. These events take a lock icon.

◆ **Source combo box.** The Source combo box filters your events by an application, system component, or device driver that you specify.

◆ **Category combo box.** The Category combo box filters your events by category. When viewing the security log, for example, you can filter your view to Logon and Logoff, Policy Change, Privilege Use, System Event, Object Access, Detailed Tracking, and Account Management.

◆ **User text box.** You can filter your view to a particular user name by entering that name in the User text box. If you are viewing the event log of a remote computer, then that user must be in the domain of that computer. Not all events are associated with a particular user; system events, for example, are often unclassified in this regard. Events without an associated user take the N/A entry in the User column of the event log.

◆ **Computer text box.** You can filter your view to a particular computer by entering the name for that computer in the Computer text box.

◆ **Event ID text box.** You can filter your view to a particular event ID type by entering the number for that event in the Event ID text box. Specific Event ID numbers are associated with a very specific event type.

You can, of course, mix and match the different events you want to view. When you set two or more different criteria, the Event Viewer performs a find based on a Boolean AND. All the criteria you enter must be satisfied in order for the event to appear in the Event Viewer. That means every condition narrows the search and makes it even more specific.

When you use the Filter dialog box to set the desired criteria, all the events that match those criteria appear in the Event Viewer for your current log.

Finding a Specific Event

You can search for a specific event using the Find command. Using the Find command isn't much different from setting up a filter, as you can tell by comparing the Filter dialog box and the Find dialog box in figures 29.3 and 29.4, respectively.

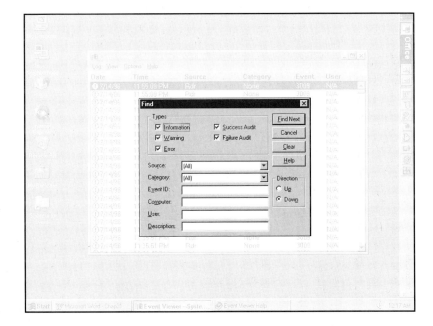

Figure 29.4

The Find dialog box enables you to locate an event using criteria you enter.

To find a specific event, follow these steps:

1. Choose the Find command on the View menu, or press F3.

2. Enter the characteristics of the event(s) you need to search for in the Find dialog box (refer to fig. 29.4).

3. Click on the direction of your search—the Up or Down radio button (Down is the default).

4. Click on Find Next; the first matching selection appears highlighted in the Event Viewer and the Find dialog box disappears.

5. To continue with your search, press F3 to open the Find dialog box again.

6. Click on Find Next again to view the next matching event. (Your criteria are remembered from session to session.)

7. Continue your search until complete, or click Cancel to dismiss the Find dialog box.

Viewing Event Details

You can get more specific information about a particular event by viewing the details of the event. Details include a variety of information about where and when the event was recorded, the error type, and a more complete description of the actual event itself. This information is important to you whenever you need to fully analyze a specific event.

To view details for an event in the Event Viewer, do one of the following:

◆ Double-click on an event to view its description in the Event Detail dialog box.

◆ Click once to highlight the event and select the Detail command on the View menu.

◆ With the event highlighted, press the Enter key.

In any instance, the Event Detail dialog box appears, as shown in figure 29.5.

Viewing a Remote Computer's Event Log

If you are connected to a network with NT Workstation 4, you can view Event Logs on other computers, provided you have the permission to access that computer. Use the Select Computer command on the Log menu to access the computer from the Select Computer dialog box (see fig. 29.6). If you are connected by modem, click the Low Speed Connection check box before closing the Select Computer dialog box.

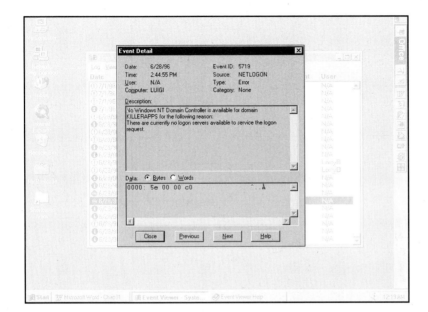

Figure 29.5

The Event Detail dialog box gives you descriptions and other information about events.

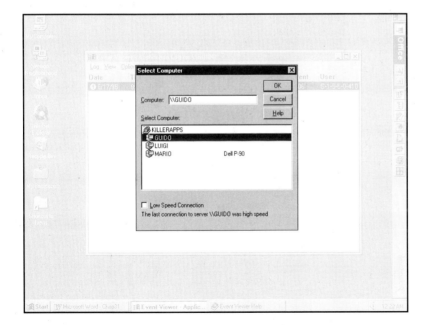

Figure 29.6

The Select Computer dialog box enables you to open event logs on other connected computers for which you have access rights.

Stopping and Starting Event Logging

If you want to turn event logging off, you can do so in the Services Control Panel. You might, for example, want to turn event logging off to improve performance. In most instances, though, you would leave these services running.

The *Event Log* is an automatic service that launches at startup. In order to turn this service off, you must do so in the Startup dialog box, and you must have sufficient privileges to access that dialog box.

Follow these steps to turn the Event Log on and off:

1. Choose the Control Panel command from the Settings submenu of the Start menu.

2. Double-click on the Services icon, as shown in figure 29.7.

Figure 29.7

The Services icon is found in the Control Panel folder.

Services icon ———

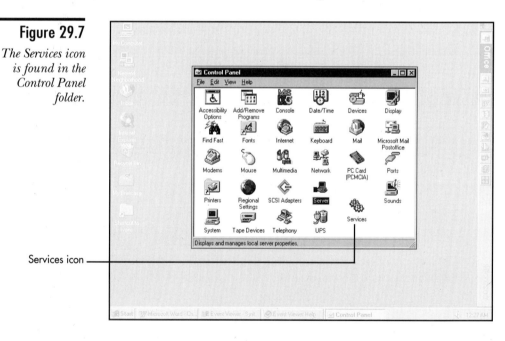

3. In the Services dialog box (see fig. 29.8), highlight the EventLog choice in the Service list.

4. Click on Startup to view the Service startup dialog box (see fig. 29.9).

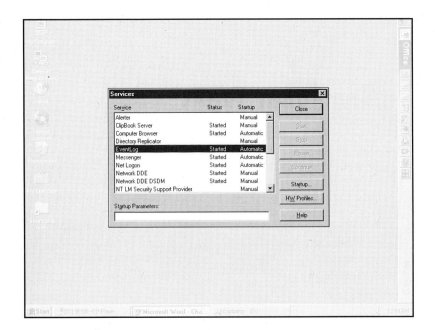

Figure 29.8

The Services dialog box enables you to turn event logging on and off.

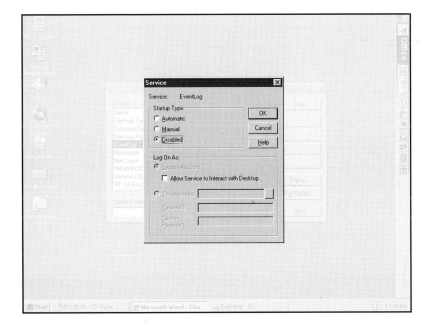

Figure 29.9

The Service startup dialog box enables you to have event logging start up when your computer boots.

5. Click on Disabled to disable the EventLog, or click on Automatic to enable it.

6. Click on OK.

7. Click on Close in the Services dialog box to effect your setting.

Understanding Event Types

The three different event logs are capable of recording a very large number of events. In a standard system, literally hundreds of events are recorded in a typical week for an NT workstation. For an NT server, that number can be in the thousands. The number of events you see in the three event logs (System, Security, and Applications) is determined by:

◆ **Configuration Errors.** How well your workstation (or a server) is configured can greatly affect the number of events you see, particularly in the System log. Configuration errors generate a lot of events, particularly warning events.

◆ **Application and Services.** The application and services you have installed can affect the events you see in the event logs. Many applications can be specifically configured to provide events whenever an action occurs. The Internet Information Server, for example, can register logon events so that an administrator can check out who has accessed the application.

◆ **Auditing Policies.** If you set a password that expires and have chosen to audit passwords, you will see log entries for changes of this type. Auditing these types of events are much less an issue for NT Workstation 4 than they are for NT Server. Events of this type register as Success Audit or Failed Audit events.

◆ **Programming Conflicts.** If an application conflicts with the operating system in some way, or if an application fails, then you will see events for these failures. Generally, you see warning events for application failure.

> **Note** In some instances, errors will not only be logged in the event logs, but may also generate a Dr. Watson error (*Dr. Watson* is a program that starts automatically to help you identify the source of the problem when certain types of events occur). You can use Dr. Watson errors to debug your system, as the technical description of this class of errors can be useful to a service technician. Dr. Watson is a highly technical application that is really of interest only to qualified Microsoft service technicians and not to the average or even the power user.

In the sections that follow, you will briefly learn about the different events that are tracked in the event logs. Knowing where an event type is tracked will help you locate that event more easily.

System Events

Windows NT Workstation 4 keeps track of a set of events relating to system components, device drivers, or other procedures such as network logons that occur during startup in the System log. These events obviously are determined by your hardware configuration and the device drivers installed to service those devices. In many instances, device driver errors can be eliminated by installing a new device driver. The System log is helpful in resolving these types of issues.

Security Events

The Security log is used to record events relating to the NT security scheme. In that regard, it is probably the easiest log to document. It records logon attempts, file and directory access that requires auditing, changes in security policy, and so on. The auditing policy for a domain is set in the User Manager for Domains in NT Server. In NT Workstation 4, the auditing policy is set in the User Manager application in the Administrative Tools folder. This application was discussed in Chapter 26, "Understanding Shared Resources."

Following are some of the events tracked in the Security log:

◆ **Logon and Logoff.** Whenever a user logs on to NT Workstation 4, a security event is recorded.

◆ **File and Object Access.** When a user accesses a folder or file that is set for auditing in the NT Explorer, or if a user sends a print job to a printer that is set for auditing in the Print Manager, then a security event is recorded.

◆ **User and Group Management.** If a user (machine) account or group is created, modified, or deleted; if a user account is renamed, disabled, or enabled; or if a password is modified; then a security event is recorded.

◆ **Security Policy Changes.** When you make a change to the User Rights or to the Audit policies in the User Manager application, a security event is recorded.

◆ **Restart, Shutdown, and System.** Whenever the system is restarted or shut down, or an event occurs that affects NT Workstation 4's security system or log, then a security event is recorded.

◆ **Process Tracking.** Events such as program activation, some types of handle duplication, indirect object accesses, and process exits initiate the recording of a security event.

Figure 29.10 shows you the Audit Policy dialog box from the User Manager application where these events are specified. Open this dialog box by selecting the Audit command from the Policy menu in that application.

Figure 29.10

The Audit Policy dialog box enables you to specify what events are tracked.

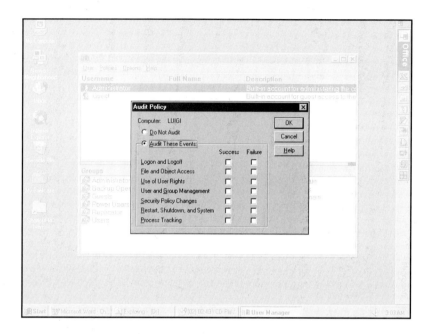

Application Events

The Applications log records events that applications track in your system. If you have SQL Server or the Internet Information Server running on your workstation, for example, both these applications record application-related events in the application log. (SQL Server actually keeps its own event log as well.) These events can be access of application files, file errors, logons and logoffs, and so on.

Because the range of applications you can install in NT Workstation 4 is large, the types of application errors you can view is almost limitless. Understanding these errors, however, can affect how well your applications run. You should make certain to check this log from time to time, particularly when an application error occurs.

Dr. Watson, I Presume

Windows NT Workstation 4 ships with the Microsoft Dr. Watson utility. You can't find it on the Start menu, but the executable file DRWTSN32.EXE is located in the \WINNT\System32 folder. Dr. Watson for Windows NT is a program error debugger. It detects and diagnoses program errors, and it records the error type in a log. When there is a program error, Dr. Watson may load automatically when you start NT Workstation 4.

Dr. Watson records fatal application and system errors and provides a technical description of the problem. It's rare to have a Dr. Watson error, but if it reoccurs, it generally requires a service call. If you are having problems of this type, when you call Microsoft, they might have you start up your computer and reproduce the error. Dr. Watson can then help them diagnose your system.

Setting Log Options

Administrators can set some options for the Event Viewer. They can set the size of the log, when the log is updated, when events are discarded, and so on. As your event log fills, you will need to begin discarding events so that the files stay a manageable size. The Event Log Settings dialog box enables you to control this behavior.

To change log settings, follow these steps:

1. Choose the Log Settings command from the Log menu.

2. In the Event Log Settings dialog box (see fig. 29.11), select the log in the Change Settings For drop-down list.

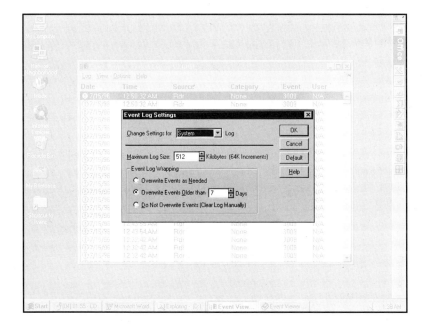

Figure 29.11

The Event Log Settings dialog box enables you to control different log properties.

3. Specify the log size (in KB) in the Maximum Log Size field.

4. In the Event Log Wrapping section, select your choice for events to be kept or discarded from the log.

   Or, click the Default button to restore the original system settings.

There are many instances in which you will want to save an Event Log to record system behavior, analyze problems, or optimize performance. Because the size of an event log is limited, you can save an event log to an archive file. Archiving event logs can be very valuable and can provide a snapshot of your system over a period of time.

Follow these steps to archive an event log:

1. Choose the Save As command on the Log menu.
2. In the Save As dialog box, select a file type, either Event Log Files (*.EVT), Text Files (*.TXT), or Comma Delim. Text (*.CDT).
3. Enter a file name in the File Name text box for the archived log file.

NT Workstation 4 saves your entire log file in the archive, without considering any filters or finds that you might have done previously. Text files or comma-delimited text files will stay sorted if you sorted the log, but the binary data for each event does not stay sorted. All categories of events (security, system, and applications) are stored in the archive.

To view an archived log (EVT) file in the Event Viewer, follow these steps:

1. Choose the Open command from the Log menu.
2. Select the EVT file in the standard file Open dialog box with the EVT file type selected in the Files of type drop-down list.
3. Click on OK.
4. The Open File Type dialog box appears, as shown in figure 29.12.

Figure 29.12

You can open an archived event log with the Open File Type dialog box.

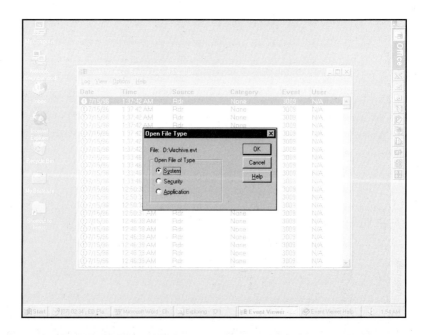

5. Click on either System, Security, or Application to view that log.

6. Click on OK.

The Event Viewer displays the archive in its window. An archive looks similar to a log, the only difference being the title of the window. The Event Viewer cannot display text files, nor can it refresh or clear the viewed archive in the window. You can switch back to the live logs by selecting them from the Log menu. To delete an archive saved to disk, do so in the Windows NT Explorer.

You can view your event log in TXT format inside a word processor, WordPad, or even Notepad (provided you don't exceed Notepad's small file-size limitation). If you saved your archive in the comma-delimited format, you should be able to import that file into most spreadsheets or databases for further analysis.

End Note: Windows NT Workstation 4 records many events in an event log. You can view these events in the Event Viewer and separate out three different main event types: system, security, and application events. Events are categorized and can be identified. Knowing an event happened can help you optimize your system or correct an error. You also can connect to a remote computer and view its log, if you have the access rights to do so.

You can save your event log to an archive file. That archive file can give you a picture of your system over a period of time and an understanding of its health. The concept of event logging is a powerful one that separates a robust operating system, such as Windows NT Workstation and Server, from a less robust one, such as Windows 95.

Test Your Knowledge

1. The Event Viewer:

    A. Records and displays everything that happens in Windows NT

    B. Records and displays certain events that occur in Windows NT

    C. Can be used to archive error logs

    D. Is a calendaring application for setting and viewing your backup rotation scheme

2. Which of the following are valid icon types displayed in the Event Viewer?

    A. Information

    B. Success Audit

    C. Stop

    D. Error

3. Which of the following are event logs you can see with the Event Viewer?

    A. System

    B. Hardware

    C. Application

    D. Security

4. In a large event log, you can more easily see the information that interests you by:

    A. Using the Selective Delete command to remove events that don't interest you

    B. Using the Filter Events command to show only events that interest you

    C. Using the Filter Archive command to archive off events that don't interest you

    D. Using the Select Events command to select the events that interest you

5. To view event logs on other computers on the network, you can:

    A. Use the Select Computer command in the Event Viewer to connect to the remote computer through a network.

    B. Copy the event logs from the remote computer to your local computer's *winnt_root*\\LOG directory, after which you can use Event Viewer to browse the log files.

    C. Start Event Viewer with the /N /R parameters.

    D. Windows NT's security scheme prevents the viewing of a remote computer's event log.

6. On a stable computer in which you never really need to view events, you can improve the system's performance slightly by:

    A. Stopping the EventLog service

    B. Preventing events from being logged by avoiding use of the Event Viewer

    C. Erasing the log files regularly

    D. Setting up a special user account to use that has event logging turned off

7. Which of the following types of events generate an event in the Event Viewer?

    A. Hardware configuration errors or hardware failures

    B. Security access violations

    C. Application conflicts with Windows NT

    D. Adding and deleting users

Test Your Knowledge Answers

1. B,C
2. A,B,D
3. A,C,D
4. B
5. A
6. A
7. A,B,C,D

Chapter Snapshot

Managing hard disks can be complicated. Windows NT Workstation 4 comes with a graphic tool, the Disk Administrator, to help you configure and maintain your disks. In addition to the Disk Administrator, certain features such as file compression can be administered from the Windows NT Explorer.

This chapter focuses on the following topics:

Windows NT
Workstation 4

CHAPTER 30

Managing Disks

MS-DOS provided for only a single file system—the FAT file system. Windows NT is designed to support multiple file systems. The two disk-based file systems available are FAT from MS-DOS and New Technology File System (NTFS) from Windows NT. (The CD-ROM file system called CDFS also exists, although this is used only with CD-ROMs.) Unlike the very rigid FAT system, NTFS has several different ways of managing your disks. These options enable you to optimize how your disks are used.

You usually will use Disk Administrator to manage your disks. This tool is used to prepare your disks for use and to segment your disks into volumes. When you compress specific folders and files, such as a folder full of documents, however, you will use the features built into the Windows NT Explorer.

The Disk Administrator enables you to view your disks either by volume (see fig. 30.1) or by disk configuration. Most examples in this book use the Disk Configuration mode, but many of the tasks also can be accomplished in the Volume view mode.

Figure 30.1

The Disk Administrator can use the Volume view mode to view hard disks.

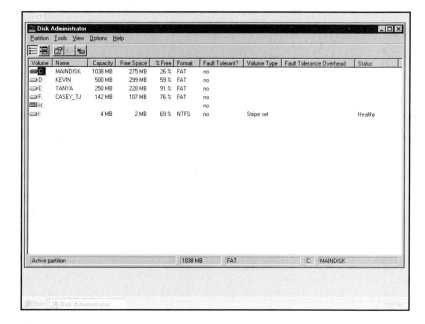

In this chapter, you learn how to use the different features of the Disk Administrator. You also learn how to customize the Disk Administrator to your tastes. By using the Disk Administrator, you can effectively configure and manage your disks, which affords two major benefits. First, you can optimize the performance of your hard disks. Second, you can effectively organize your disks for your particular needs. For example, if you only use Windows NT Workstation 4 on your computer, you will want to consider using NTFS. However, if you also use Windows 95 or DOS, you might want to use two drives, one for each operating system.

Converting to NTFS

Objective A.3

Windows NT supports a file system called New Technology File System (NTFS), which offers several benefits over the FAT file system used by DOS. With Windows NT, you can better utilize your hard disk, as well as obtain better performance and, perhaps most importantly, better security. If you don't have a reason to stick with the DOS file system, you should seriously consider converting your partition(s) to NTFS.

When you install Windows NT 4, you are given the option of converting DOS partitions to NTFS. If you don't take advantage of the option at that time, don't worry—you can convert FAT partitions to NTFS partitions later. If you want to save files that are on the partition, you can convert the entire partition in a process that retains the existing files. However, if you want to start from scratch with a clean disk, you can reformat the partition altogether.

To convert a FAT partition to an NTFS partition, follow these steps:

1. From the Start menu, choose Run. The Run dialog box appears.

2. Type **convert [drive:]**. To convert the D: drive, for example, you would type convert d:.

3. Choose OK to start the conversion.

> **Tip**
>
> You might encounter two problems when trying to convert a volume. First, you cannot convert the current drive. You must change the logged drive before attempting to convert it. Second, if the files have unusual file names, they might fail to convert. If this happens, try running the conversion with the /nametable:filename option. For example, if you want to convert the D: drive and it has unusual file names, type **convert d: /nametable:convert.log**.

To reformat a FAT partition to an NTFS partition, follow these steps:

1. From the Start menu, choose Programs, Administrative Tools [Common], Disk Administrator. The Disk Administrator program starts. If this is the first time you have run Disk Administrator, it takes a little extra time to start while it saves its configuration information.

2. In either Disk Administrator view (Volume or Disk Configuration), select the drive you want to change (see fig. 30.2).

3. Choose Tools, Format. The Format dialog box appears, as shown in figure 30.3.

4. Select the format you want in the File System drop-down list.

5. Type in the new label for the partition.

6. Select Quick Format if you do not want to check for bad sectors. Using Quick Format is not recommended for hard disks.

> **Tip**
>
> You cannot use Quick Format on either mirror sets or stripe sets with parity.

7. Choose OK. The partition is now converted.

After you convert a partition to NTFS, you have a new tool at your disposal— file compression. This feature is so useful that it alone makes the process of installing NTFS worthwhile. You must understand exactly how file compression works, however, so that you can use it effectively.

Figure 30.2

You usually use the Disk Administrator in Disk Config-uration view mode, as shown here.

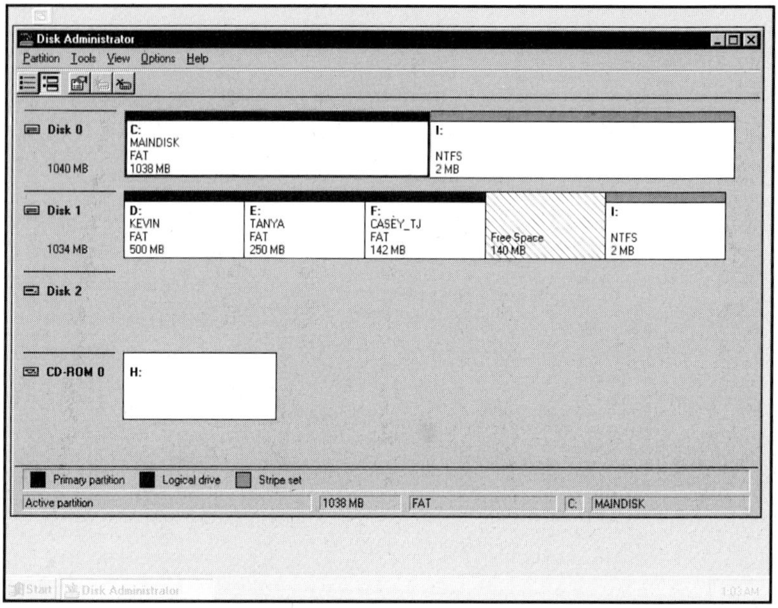

Figure 30.3

You can format disk partitions with the Format dialog box.

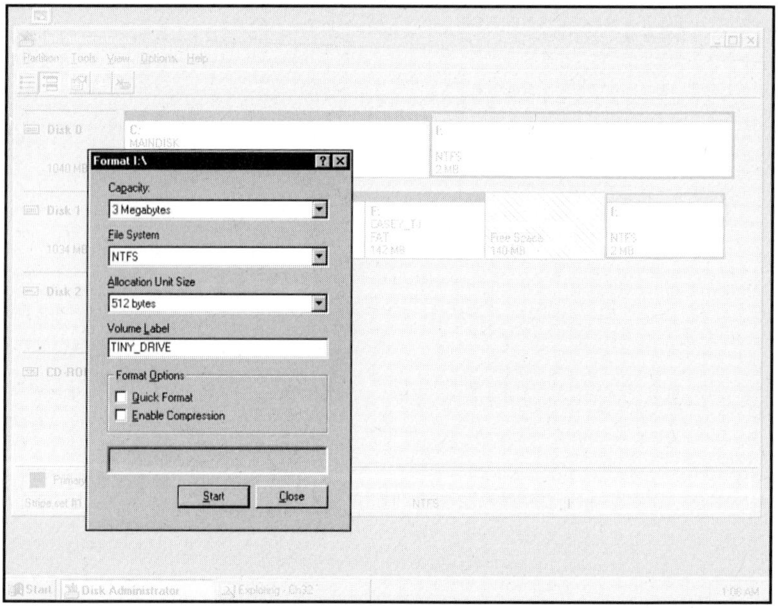

Understanding Compression

Although the size of hard disks continues to get larger, you still might find that you don't have enough hard disk space. That 1 GB hard disk that you thought you would never fill up could be stuffed with application programs, graphics files, and various data files. You might now be eyeing a 2 GB drive. Before you buy another hard disk, however, Windows NT 4 provides a solution to this problem if you are using the NTFS file system.

On an NTFS volume, Windows NT provides transparent file compression. Before a file is written to the disk, Windows NT compresses the file. Then, as the system reads the file back off the disk, Windows NT reverses the compression—it expands the file. Expanding files is very similar to using zipped files, but with one great advantage. Zipped files require you to unzip them before you work with them, but this is not so with the built-in Windows NT file compression. The file compression is transparent to you, the user, as are the application programs. In the following sections, you learn how to compress certain folders or only certain files, what to do when file compression doesn't help that much, and finally, how to work with Explorer and file compression.

Compressing Drives and Volumes

If you want to use file compression on an NTFS volume, you can compress the entire drive, specific folders, or specific files. If you have a fast computer and you want to produce maximum file space, you can compress the entire drive. However, you might choose to compress only certain folders or files. If you installed all of Microsoft Word, for example, you might choose to compress the sample files and the clip art, while leaving the application files uncompressed. This provides a balance between performance and space savings. In general, the file compression is very fast and you probably will not notice perceptible delays.

 Tip   You might think that to save space, you will first compress a file to a zipped file and then save it by using Windows NT file compression. Unfortunately, this doesn't work very well. After a file has been compressed, it will not compress much more, if at all. Trying to compress an already compressed file sometimes takes up more room.

To compress a drive, follow these steps:

1. Select the drive you want to compress in either Explorer or My Computer.

2. Choose File, Properties. The Properties dialog box appears, as shown in figure 30.4.

Figure 30.4

*You can enable
compression for a
drive by using the
Disk Admin-
istrator.*

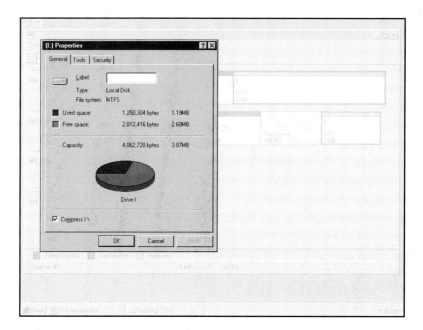

Tip In Windows NT Explorer, you can quickly get to the Properties page of any file system object—drive, folder, or file—by clicking on the object with the right mouse button. This brings up a shortcut menu with the Properties option at the bottom.

3. Choose Compress.

4. Choose OK. A message box appears.

5. If you want to compress all the files and folders on the drive, select Also Compress Subfolders.

6. Choose OK.

Compressing Folders

If you have decided not to compress the entire drive, you still can compress specific folders. When you compress a folder, you have the capability of compressing only the files in the folder or compressing the folder and all its subfolders. For example, if you installed a program in a folder called PROG1 and it contained two folders called DATA and SAMPLES, you have two choices. You can compress only the files in PROG1, or you can compress all the files in PROG1, DATA, and SAMPLES.

To compress a folder, follow these steps:

1. Choose the folder you want to compress.

2. Choose File, Properties. The Compressed Properties dialog box appears (see fig. 30.5).

3. Select Compress in the Attributes section of the dialog box.

4. Choose OK. A message box appears.

5. If you want to compress all the files and folders on the drive, select Also Compress Subfolder.

6. Choose OK.

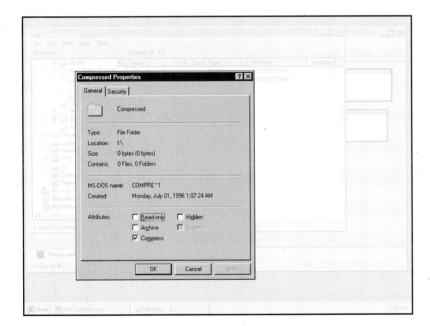

Figure 30.5

You can use the Windows Explorer to turn on compression for an empty folder.

Compressing Files

If you find that compressing all the files on your system causes your system to slow down but you still need to save room on your hard disk, you can compress only specific files. For example, you can compress only the really large data files. Ideally, these would be files that you do not need to access frequently.

To compress a file, follow these steps:

1. Select the file you want to compress in either Explorer or My Computer.

2. Choose File, Properties. The Compressed Text File Properties dialog box appears (see fig. 30.6).

3. Select Compressed.

4. Choose OK.

Figure 30.6

You can use the Windows Explorer to compress a text file.

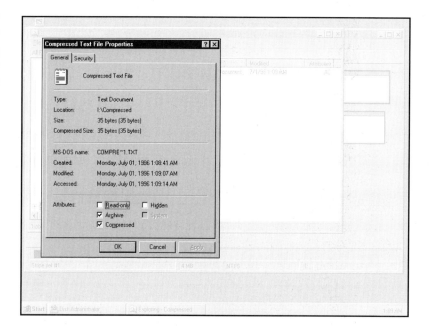

Displaying Compressed Files and Folders in Alternate Colors

You can choose to have Windows Explorer display compressed files or folders in a color different from the color in which normal files or folders are usually displayed. By adjusting the color, you can quickly make sure that you compress the correct files. To display compressed files and folders in an alternate color, follow these steps:

1. In either My Computer or Explorer, choose View, Options. The Options dialog box appears.

2. Select the View tab.

3. Choose Display Compressed Files and Folders with Alternate Color.

4. Choose OK to turn on this feature.

Using the Compact Command

In addition to using Windows NT Explorer to access file compression, you can compress files, folders, drives, and volumes using the Compact command line program. Although the Windows NT Explorer provides a very visual interface for selecting and compressing specific files and folders, it still can be very time-consuming. If you know that you want to compress all files of a particular type, the Compact command enables you to compress all files of that type on a drive in a single command. For example, to compress all the bitmap files on the C: drive, you would type **compact /c /s:\ *.bmp**.

To run the Compact program, follow these steps:

1. From the Start menu, choose Run. The Run dialog box appears.

2. Type in the Compact command and any parameters. See figure 30.7 for all the parameters.

3. Choose OK to run the Compact command.

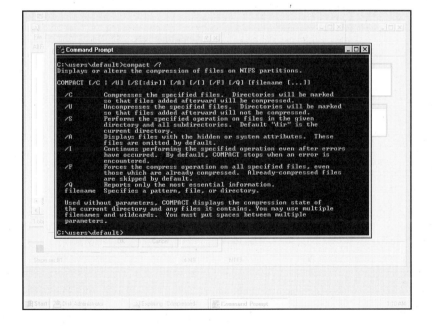

Figure 30.7

The Compact command line program offers many options.

| Tip | If the Compact program did not finish properly because of a system crash or some other unexpected event, rerun the Compact command and use the /f option. This forces Compact to try to recompact every file and finishes the compression on any partially compressed file. |

Understanding Disk Administrator

The Disk Administrator is the Windows NT 4 visual tool for managing your hard disks. With the Disk Administrator, you can perform all the management tasks you need to configure and maintain your hard disks, including the following:

◆ Create and delete partitions

◆ Format partitions

◆ Assign drive letters

◆ Change volume labels

◆ Create volume sets and stripe sets

Because the Disk Administrator tool can cause unrecoverable data loss if misused, you must log on as the administrator or as a user who has administrator privileges.

Creating and Deleting Partitions

Partitions are sections of your hard disk that are treated as separate drives. Each partition can be formatted to use different file systems. With Windows NT, you have two options: the FAT file system and NTFS. If you use only Windows NT on your computer, NTFS is your best choice because it provides advanced features as well as enhanced security options. If you use more than one operating system on your computer, then you must use the FAT file system on the boot device. If you use NTFS for any partition, files stored on that partition will be available to you only when you run Windows NT.

Each physical hard disk can have a primary partition and an extended partition. The primary partition of your first hard disk is the boot drive. The extended partition can further be divided into different logical drives.

Using Partitions

You might be wondering why you must deal with partitions instead of treating a physical hard disk as a single drive. Two reasons exist: First, partitions enable you to have two distinct file systems. This is especially useful if, for example, you run Unix and DOS off a single hard disk. Second, partitions enable you to get around DOS limitations. DOS supports only hard disks of a certain size. This means that if you have a really large hard disk, you either can't use all of it or you must use it very inefficiently. Partitions enable you to break the physical hard disk into smaller pieces so that you can efficiently use the entire hard disk.

To create a primary partition, follow these steps:

1. In the Disk Administrator, choose View, Disk Configuration.

2. Choose the free space in which you want to create the partition. A thick black border appears around the free space (see fig. 30.8)

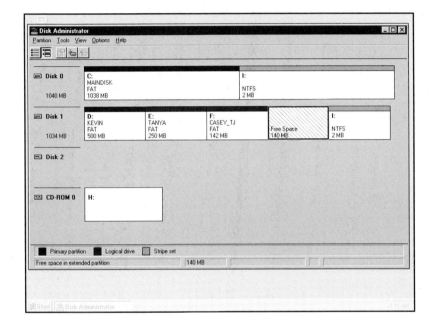

Figure 30.8

Select free space in the Disk Administrator to use when creating a partition.

3. Choose Partition, Create. The Create Logical Drive dialog box appears (see fig. 30.9).

4. Enter the size, in megabytes, of the partition you want to create in the Create logical drive of size field.

5. Choose OK to create the partition.

6. Choose Partition, Commit Changes Now. A confirmation message box appears.

7. Choose Yes to commit the new partition information to disk. The partition is now ready to be formatted.

8. Another message box appears telling you that you were successful. Choose OK.

Caution If you add or remove partitions such that your home partition for Windows NT changes drive letters, take care to update the BOOT.INI file on your C: drive (with a text editor) to reflect any changes.

Figure 30.9

Use the Disk Administrator to create a logical drive of the maximum allowed size.

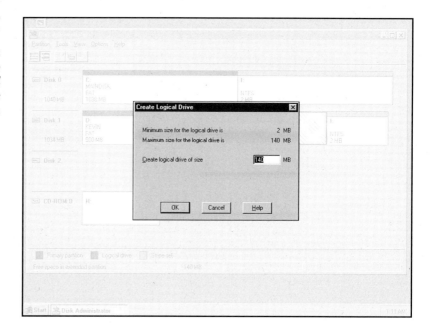

To create an extended partition, follow these steps:

1. In the Disk Administrator, choose View, Disk Configuration.

2. Choose the free space in which you want to create the partition. A thick black border appears around the free space.

3. Choose Partition, Create. The Create Extended Partition dialog box appears (see fig. 30.10).

4. Enter the size, in megabytes, of the partition you want to create in the Create partition of size field.

5. Choose OK to create the partition.

6. Choose Partition, Commit Changes Now. A confirmation message box appears (see fig. 30.11).

7. Choose Yes to commit the new partition information to disk. The partition is now ready to format.

8. A message box appears telling you that you were successful. Choose OK (see fig. 30.12).

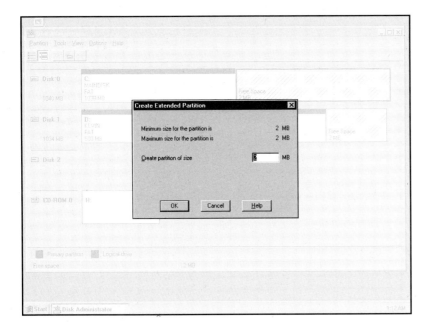

Figure 30.10

Create a partition with the Create Extended Partition dialog box.

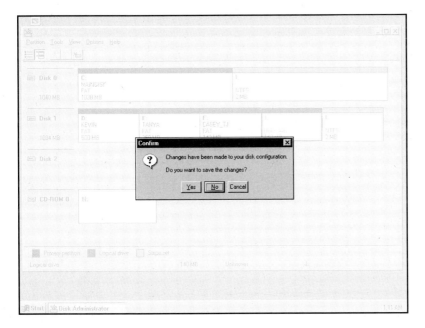

Figure 30.11

You must confirm any changes made to the disk when using Disk Administrator.

Figure 30.12

After a successful change to your disk information, you should update your Emergency Repair Disk.

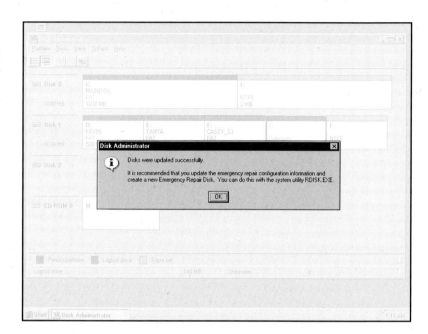

Note After you change any partition information, you should run RDISK to update your emergency disks. If you don't, the disks will not be able to correctly get your system up and running again.

To delete a partition, follow these steps:

1. In the Disk Administrator, choose View, Disk Configuration.

2. Choose the partition you want to delete. A thick black border appears around the partition.

Note A partition can be either a primary partition or an extended partition. The partition does not have to be formatted before it can be deleted; therefore, the partition can be indicated as free space in the Disk Administrator.

3. Choose Partition, Delete.

4. If the partition has been formatted, a confirmation dialog box is displayed. Choose Yes.

Formatting a Partition

After you have created a partition, you must decide what file system to use on the partition. If you need to access files on that partition from more than one operating system, such as Windows 95 and Windows NT, then you should format the partition with the FAT file system. However, if you access only files on that partition from Windows NT, you should use the NTFS file system.

To format a partition, follow these steps:

1. In the Disk Administrator, choose View, Disk Configuration.

2. Choose the partition you want to format. A thick black border appears around the partition.

3. Choose Tools, Format. The Format dialog box appears (refer to fig. 30.3).

4. Choose either FAT or NTFS as the File System by using the drop-down list.

5. Choose the Allocation Unit Size using the drop-down list. Usually, you should use the Default Allocation Size.

6. In the Volume Label field, type in the name you want to use for this volume.

7. If you want to skip checking for bad sectors, choose Quick Format.

8. If this is an NTFS volume and you want to enable compression for this drive, choose Enable Compression.

9. Choose Start. A warning message box appears.

10. Choose OK. A progress message box is displayed as the drive is formatted.

11. After the drive is formatted, a Formatting complete message box is displayed. Choose OK.

12. Choose Close to close the dialog box.

Changing Volume Labels

Each drive that you create can be given a volume label. This volume label can help you identify a volume and its use, especially if you share the volume on a network. For a FAT volume, you can use up to 11 characters. A drive label for an NTFS volume can contain up to 256 characters.

To change the volume label of a drive, follow these steps:

1. In the Disk Administrator, choose View, Disk Configuration.

2. Choose the drive you want to name or rename. A thick black border appears around the partition.

3. Choose Tools, Properties. The Properties dialog box appears (refer to fig. 30.4).

4. Choose the General tab.

5. Type in the new name in the Label field.

6. Choose OK.

Changing Drive Letter Assignments

You can assign any unused drive letter to any partition. You can do this to maintain consistent drive mappings between different computers. If you want all applications stored on the I: drive, for example, you can create a partition and assign it the letter I:, regardless of how many partitions each computer has.

To change the drive letter of a volume, follow these steps:

1. In the Disk Administrator, choose View, Disk Configuration.

2. Choose the partition to which you want to assign or reassign a drive letter.

> **Caution** You should be very careful if you reassign the drive letter for a drive that contains application programs. Some programs might save path information for ancillary files, and if you change the drive, the path information will be incorrect. An incorrect path can cause the program to stop working. This also can cause problems with installation programs when you try to either re-install or install new components.

3. Choose Tools, Assign Drive Letter. The Assign Drive Letter Dialog box appears (see fig. 30.13).

4. Choose Assign Drive Letter and choose the drive letter you want by using the drop-down list.

5. Choose OK.

Up to this point, this chapter discussed creating a single partition out of a single contiguous free space, which is all that you can do with the DOS file system. With NTFS, however, you can combine several different free spaces together to make a single, logical partition. Combining free spaces can have several benefits, which are discussed in the next sections.

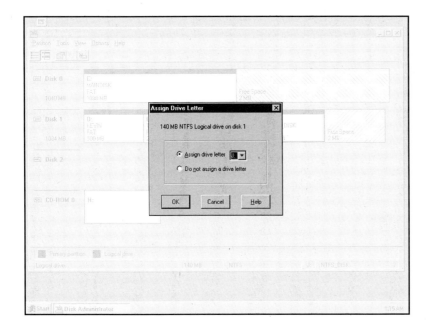

Figure 30.13

Assign the drive letter J: to the new partition in the Disk Administrator.

Understanding Volume Sets

Volume sets are very similar to normal volumes. The difference is that a normal volume is created from a contiguous free space area, whereas a volume set can be created from two or more free space areas.

You might choose to use volume sets for two reasons. First, volume sets enable you to collect several small, free space areas that are not very useful by themselves into a single, larger, more useful volume. The second reason is that if you have several drives, you can create volume sets that span the drives. This evens out the disk access between the different drives and can improve disk performance.

In the rest of this section, you learn how to effectively use volume sets, how to create and delete volume sets, and how to extend the size of a volume set by incorporating additional free space.

Creating and Deleting

Creating a volume set is very similar to creating a standard volume. To create a volume set, follow these steps:

1. In the Disk Administrator, choose View, Disk Configuration.

2. Select the free spaces you want to use for the volume set by holding down the Ctrl key and clicking on each free space with the mouse. Each selected free space should have a thick dark border (see fig. 30.14).

Figure 30.14

Select tiny free spaces at the end of each disk.

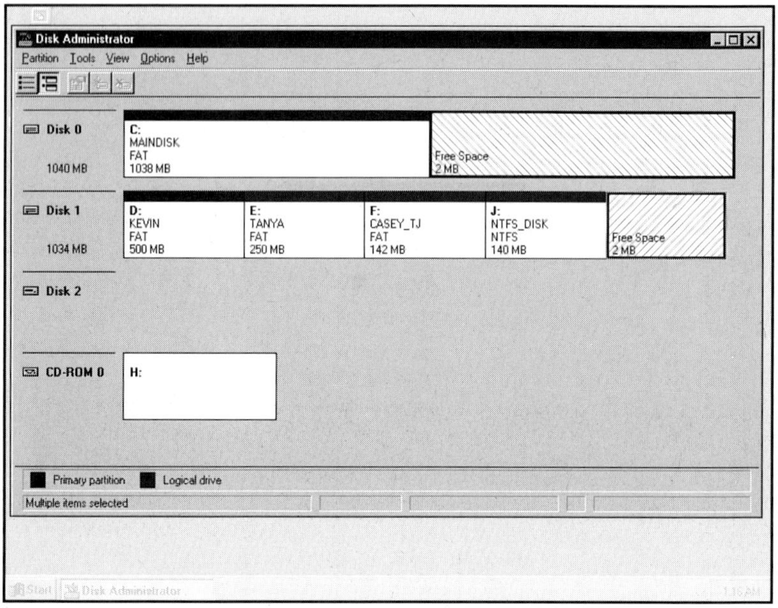

3. Choose Partition, Create Volume Set. The Create Volume Set dialog box appears (see fig. 30.15).

Figure 30.15

Create a 4 MB volume set out of two 2 MB free spaces left over from DOS partitions.

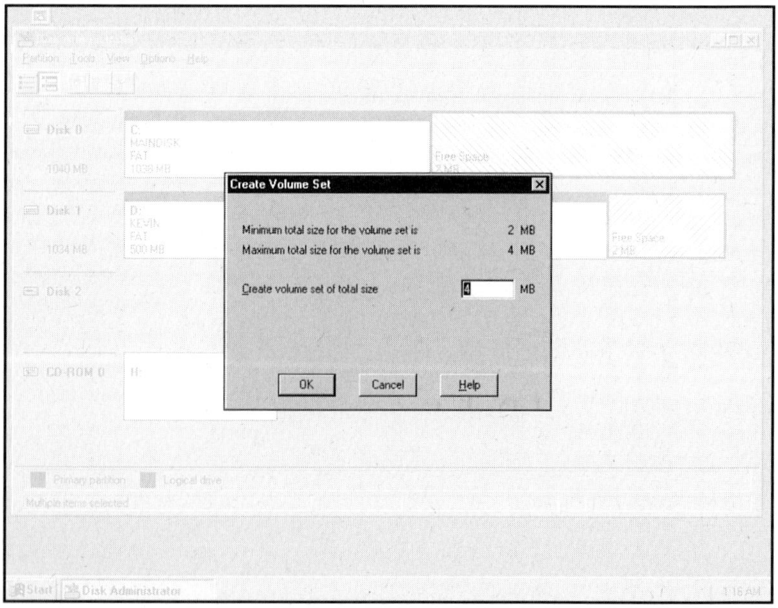

4. In the Create volume set of total size field, type the size, in megabytes, that you want the volume set to be.

5. Choose OK.

6. Choose Partition, Commit Changes Now. A confirmation message box is displayed.

7. Choose Yes. Another message box appears.

8. Choose OK. The volume set is now ready to be formatted.

To delete a volume set, follow these steps:

1. In the Disk Administrator, choose View, Disk Configuration.

2. Select the volume set you want to delete by clicking on any one of the pieces of the volume set.

3. Choose Partition, Delete. A confirmation message box appears.

4. Choose Yes to delete the volume set.

Extending NTFS Partitions

After you have created an NTFS volume or volume set, you can increase the size of the volume set by incorporating additional free space into the volume or volume set.

To extend a volume or volume set, follow these steps:

1. In the Disk Administrator, choose View, Disk Configuration.

2. Select the volume or volume set you want to extend by clicking on any one of the pieces of the volume or volume set.

3. Hold down the Ctrl key and click on the free space you want to add to the volume. Both the volume pieces and the free space should have dark borders (see fig. 30.16).

4. Choose Partition, Extend Volume Set. The Extend Volume Set dialog box appears (see fig. 30.17)

5. Type in the new amount of free space, in megabytes, that you want for the volume set.

6. Choose OK to extend the volume set.

Tip   You can extend a volume or volume set only if it has been formatted as an NTFS volume. You cannot extend a FAT volume.

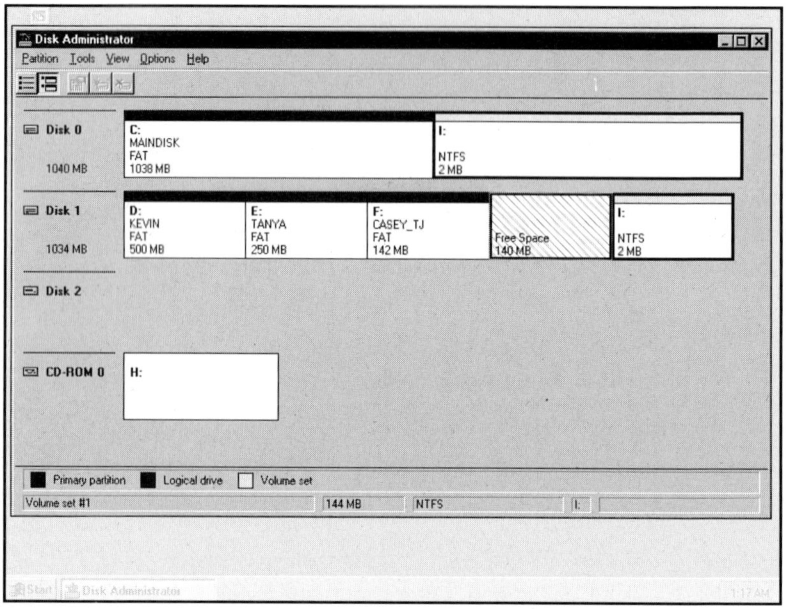

Figure 30.16

Extend the 4 MB volume set by adding another free space.

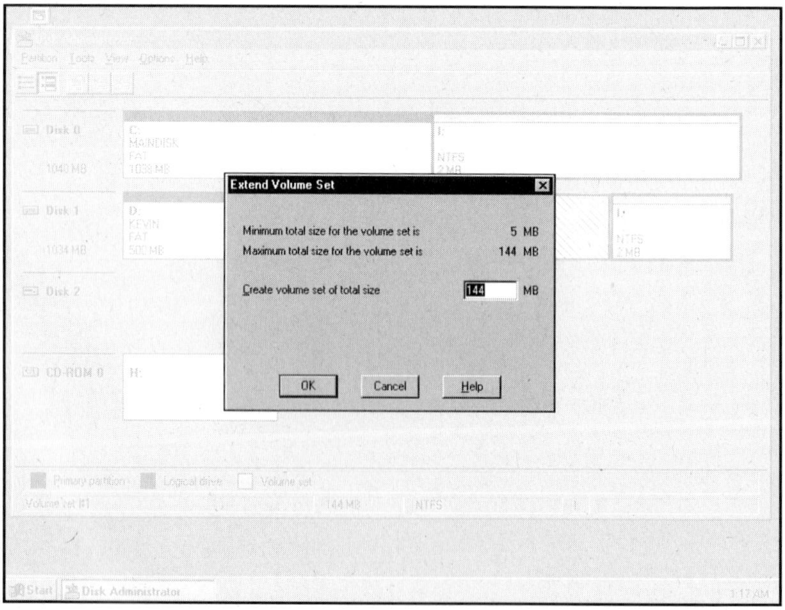

Figure 30.17

You can create the partition between 5 MB and 145 MB.

Understanding Stripe Sets

Stripe sets are similar to volume sets in that stripe sets are created from discreet pieces of free space. Unlike volume sets that can be created from pieces on the same disk and can vary in size, however, the free space pieces that make up a stripe set must be on a different drive and must be approximately the same size.

The reason for these constraints can be traced to the process by which Windows NT reads and writes data to volume sets and stripe sets. With volume sets, Windows NT starts writing data at the beginning of the first free area. It continues writing to the first free area until that area becomes full. Then Windows NT begins writing to the next free area. This means that when normal file reading and writing occurs, the reading and writing occurs across all the physical drives. This helps to optimize hard-disk performance.

With stripe sets, Windows NT writes a stripe of data to the first free area and then a stripe to the next free area. After writing a stripe to the last free area, it goes back and writes a second stripe to the first free area. This process balances reads and writes across all the disks of the stripe set.

Creating a stripe set is very similar to creating a volume set. To create a stripe set, follow these steps:

1. In the Disk Administrator, choose View, Disk Configuration.

2. Select the free spaces you want to use for the stripe set by holding down the Ctrl key and clicking on each free space with the mouse. Each selected free space should have a thick dark border.

3. Choose Partition, Create Stripe Set. The Create Stripe Set dialog box appears (see fig. 30.18).

4. In the Create Stripe Set of Total Size edit field, type in the size, in megabytes, that you want the stripe set to be.

5. Choose OK.

6. Choose Partition, Commit Changes Now. A confirmation message box is displayed.

7. Choose Yes. Another message box appears.

8. Choose OK. The stripe set is now ready to be formatted.

Figure 30.18

You can use the free space left over from DOS partitions to create a small stripe set.

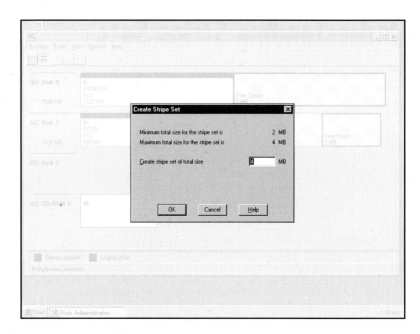

Customizing Disk Administrator

The Disk Administrator enables you to customize its display. You can modify the colors and patterns used, the way in which Disk Administrator displays the disks and partitions, and the buttons on the toolbar.

Changing Colors and Patterns

You can change the color and patterns that are used in the graphical display of the Disk Administrator. You might do this, for example, if you have certain color preferences or if your monitor does not display certain colors well.

To change colors and patterns used in the Disk Administrator program, follow these steps:

1. In the Disk Administrator, choose Options, Colors and Patterns. The Colors and Patterns dialog box appears (see fig. 30.19).

2. Select the type of object that you want to change in color or pattern. Such objects can include partitions, logical drives, and stripe sets, among others.

3. Choose the color you want to use in the Colors box.

4. Choose the pattern you want to use in the Patterns box.

5. Repeat steps 2–4 for each object you want to change.

6. Choose OK to change the color and patterns.

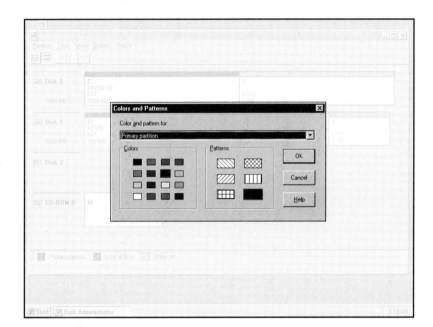

Figure 30.19

You can use a solid blue color for the primary partition display.

Changing Display Formats

Tip | You might want to display the disks equally if you have partitions that vary in size. If you don't, small disks can be so small that they won't be noticeable.

To change the display format for the disks, follow these steps:

1. In the Disk Administrator, choose Options, Disk Display. The Disk Display Options dialog box appears (see fig. 30.20).

2. If you want to display each disk so that the display area is the same size, select Size All Disks Equally.

3. If you want to display each disk so that the display area is proportional to the size of the disk, select Size Disks Based on Actual Size.

4. Choose OK to set the display option.

Figure 30.20

Showing each disk based on its actual size can help you visualize actual usage.

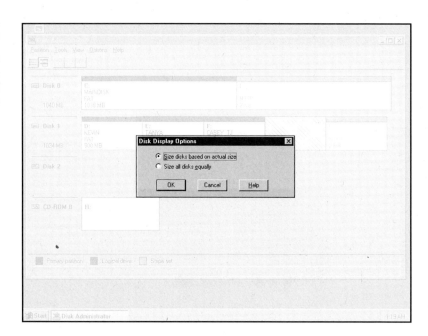

Tip If you want to have a visual indication of how large the different partitions are in relation to each other, you can choose to display the information based on the partition size.

To change the display format for each region of a disk, follow these steps:

1. In the Disk Administrator, choose Options, Region Display. The Region Display Options dialog box appears (see fig. 30.21).

2. If you want to set all the disks to use the same setting, select All Disks in the Which Disk box.

3. If you want to set each disk to use different settings, select For Disk in the Which Disk box, and select the disk for which you want to set the option. You can repeat the following steps for each individual disk.

4. If you want to display each partition so that its display area is the same, select Size All Regions Equally.

5. If you want to display each partition so that the display area for each partition is proportional to its size, select Size Regions Based on Actual Size.

6. If you want to allow the Disk Administrator program to decide between the two options for you, select Let Disk Administrator Decide How to Size Regions.

7. Choose OK to set the display options.

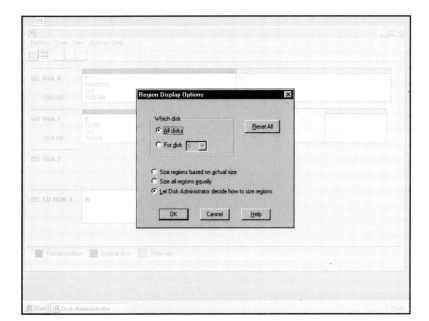

Figure 30.21

You can let the Disk Administrator decide how to display each disk region.

Customizing the Toolbar

To customize the toolbar in the Disk Administrator, follow these steps:

1. In the Disk Administrator, choose Options, Customize Toolbar. The Customize Toolbar dialog appears (see fig. 30.22).

2. Choose each command you want to add to the toolbar in the Available Buttons list and choose Add.

3. Choose each command you want to remove from the toolbar in the Toolbar Buttons list and choose Remove.

4. You can rearrange the buttons on the toolbar by selecting a button in the Toolbar Buttons list and choosing either Move Up or Move Down.

5. Choose Close to customize the toolbar.

Figure 30.22

You can add buttons to create and delete partitions to the toolbar.

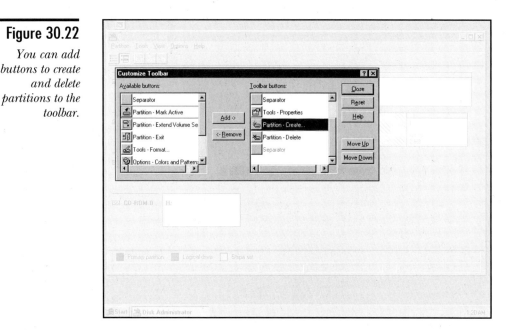

End Note: You will not need to regularly manage your disks because you won't run Disk Administrator on a daily basis. Instead, you should spend more time deciding how to configure your hard disks.

If you know that you will need to share files between different operating systems, you do not have much choice. You must configure at least one partition as a FAT partition.

If you will run only Windows NT 4, then you can format all your partitions as NTFS partitions. This gives you lots of extra features, including greater control over how your disks are utilized. To make sure that every bit of free space is used, you can collect all the free space into a single logical volume. If you have several disks, you can optimize performance by using stripe sets.

Test Your Knowledge

1. To make more free space available on NTFS-formatted partitions, you can do which two of the following?

    A. Erase excess files.

    B. Use the built-in file-compression feature.

    C. Use a disk-defragmentation program.

    D. Convert the partition to FAT and use the file compression only available on FAT drives.

2. To compress a file under Windows NT Workstation, you should do which two of the following?

    A. Use the FILECOMP command.

    B. Use the file's Properties dialog box.

    C. Use the COMPACT command.

    D. Use the File Compression Utility.

3. To use the Disk Administrator program, you must do which of the following?

    A. Start the system in maintenance mode.

    B. Enable the Disk Administrator service.

    C. Be logged in with Administrator privileges.

    D. Boot Windows NT from an NTFS-formatted partition.

4. You can use Disk Administrator to accomplish which three of the following?

    A. Create, modify, and delete partitions.

    B. Extend NTFS-formatted partitions.

    C. Create volume sets.

    D. Compress files.

5. To convert a FAT partition to NTFS, you can do which two of the following?

    A. Use Disk Administrator to reformat the partition using NTFS.

    B. Use the CONVERT command.

    C. Convert only from NTFS to FAT.

    D. Use the Services icon in the Control Panel.

Test Your Knowledge Answers

1. A,B
2. B,C
3. C
4. A,B,C
5. A,B

Chapter Snapshot

Windows NT stores all the information about your computer in a database called the Registry. The Registry contains information about your installed software; the rights, privileges, and preferences of all users; and the configuration settings of your hardware. This database is crucial to keeping your system up and running properly. Equally important is understanding what the Registry is and how it works, not only so you have the knowledge to maintain your system, but also so you can safely modify the Registry should the need to make certain changes arise. This chapter focuses on the following topics:

Windows NT
Workstation 4

CHAPTER 31

Using the Registry

The Registry is the central storage place for all the configuration information in your computer. Windows NT stores information about users and their security access privileges, hardware configuration, and system services. Applications can store information such as user preferences and history lists.

Normally, Control Panel programs, applications, or other system services make the necessary modifications to the information in the Registry, but occasionally you might need to modify the Registry yourself. You might need to clean up after removing a program, to change some undocumented setting, or to restore settings after a system crash.

This chapter focuses on the Registry and its construction. It also covers how to use two tools Microsoft provides for directly manipulating the Registry.

Understanding the Registry

The Registry functions like the configuration files in Windows 3.x (WIN.INI, SYSTEM.INI, CONFIG.SYS, and AUTOEXEC.BAT). When Windows NT starts, it loads information from the Registry about the device drivers it needs to load, hardware installed in your system and how to configure it, user security information, and much more. The Registry, however, also serves other functions.

The Registry also serves as the central repository for applications that support Object Linking and Embedding (OLE). All OLE-enabled applications store information about themselves—information that other OLE applications need to know—in the Registry. This kind of information enables you, for example, to embed a Microsoft Excel spreadsheet into a Microsoft PowerPoint presentation.

Well-behaved Windows applications store data (such as the last window position or default font) in the Registry. Before Windows NT, applications stored the same kind of information in INI files, which resulted in INI files being stored all over the place on your hard disk. Now, each application can create a section within the Registry to neatly and efficiently store its information.

> **Note** You probably still run one or more 16-bit Windows applications. These programs don't use the Registry and still read and write to their own private INI files. They also expect WIN.INI, SYSTEM.INI, and other standard INI files to be available. Windows NT goes to great lengths to make these old programs coexist with newer programs using the Registry, but the bottom line is that you still have INI files on your system.

The rest of this section discusses the Registry's origins, explains the Registry's organizational structure, and finally, tells you how to make the Registry and INI files coexist on your computer.

The History of the Registry

The Registry can trace its beginning to the Registration Database in Windows 3.1. The Registration Database was what enabled Windows to make Object Linking and Embedding (OLE) possible between applications. It acted as the central place to which all the information about the programs and interfaces used to support OLE (such as displaying, editing, and printing object data) could be stored.

Microsoft decided to extend the functionality of the Registration Database when it began to design Windows NT. Microsoft decided to create a single database in which to store all the configuration information about the computer—its hardware, software, networking, security, and user profiles. This information (and the database that contains it) has come to be known collectively as the Registry.

> **Note** Windows 95 also has a Registry. Although both Registries contain the same type of information, the files that form them are different. Despite other differences—some good and some bad—the Registry will eventually completely replace INI files.

Structure of the Registry

The Registry is a hierarchical database; in other words, it is organized in a tree structure. The Registry tree is divided into subtrees as listed in table 31.1. Each branch or subtree is called a key.

TABLE 31.1
Registry Keys

Key Name	Description
HKEY_CLASSES_ROOT	Contains information about programs; used for working with files (opening, printing, and so on) and OLE.
HKEY_CURRENT_USER	Contains information about the active user (currently logged on), including preferences, the User Profile, and network settings.
HKEY_USERS	Contains information about all the users on this machine.
HKEY_LOCAL_MACHINE	Contains information about the local computer, including hardware settings, startup options, and system parameters.
HKEY_CURRENT_CONFIG	Contains information about the hardware profile used by the computer at boot time.

> **Note** If you use REGEDIT as your registry editor, you'll see an additional key: HKEY_DYN_DATA. This key holds all the information that must be stored in RAM and it should never be altered.

Each key provides a primary function and is further divided into additional keys. These subkeys also can be further divided, and those keys divided again, and so on. Each key has a unique name within its subkey and can have one or more values associated with it. Each value has three parts: a name, a data type, and an actual data value. Each key has a default value without a name. Any other values must have a name. In my system, for example, the key HKEY_CLASSES_ROOT\DOC has a default value of type REG_SZ and an actual value of "Word.Document.8."

Table 31.2 lists the five possible data types for Registry values.

TABLE 31.2
Registry Data Types

Data Type	Description
REG_BINARY	Contains raw binary data.
REG_DWORD	Contains a four-byte value.
REG_EXPAND_SZ	Contains a string (text) that contains a replaceable parameter; for example, in the string paint.exe %1, the %1 will be replaced with a valid file name.
REG_MULTI_SZ	Contains several strings, separated with a NULL character.
REG_SZ	Contains a text string. This is often used for description values, program names, and so on.

HKEY_CLASSES_ROOT

HKEY_CLASSES_ROOT contains the information that the Registration Database contained under Windows 3.1. This information defines all the file associations and Object Linking and Embedding data. The data is divided into two types of keys: file name extensions and class definitions. The file name extensions map file types to class definitions. The file type key .XLS, for example, has the value "Excel.Sheet.8" in my system. The data necessary for performing basic shell and OLE functions is stored under the class definitions. This type of data, for example, enables you to double-click on an Excel spreadsheet in Explorer to have the system launch Excel and automatically load the selected spreadsheet.

This key's only real purpose is to provide compatibility with Windows 3.1 applications that read and write to the old Registration Database. The entire HKEY_CLASSES_ROOT key actually is stored as a subkey in HKEY_LOCAL_MACHINE\ SOFTWARE\CLASSES.

HKEY_CURRENT_USER

HKEY_CURRENT_USER contains all the information required for Windows NT to set up the computer for the user logging on, including information such as environment settings, application preferences, and user rights. The seven default keys (your system may have more keys) under HKEY_CURRENT_USER are these:

◆ Console

◆ Control Panel

◆ Environment

◆ Keyboard Layout

◆ Printers

◆ Program Groups

◆ Software

> **Tip** If you browse the Registry, you might notice that the same types of data appear in different parts of the Registry. You might also notice that some keys of HKEY_LOCAL_MACHINE and HKEY_CURRENT_USER are identical but have different values. In such cases, the values in HKEY_CURRENT_USER override the values in HKEY_LOCAL_MACHINE. HKEY_LOCAL_MACHINE contains the default values that every new user gets. As each user changes his preferences, however, these new values are saved in HKEY_CURRENT_USER.

HKEY_USERS

HKEY_USERS contains the data for each user (user profiles). When a user logs on to the computer, his profile data is copied from HKEY_USERS\Security ID String to HKEY_CURRENT_USER. The key HKEY_USERS\.DEFAULT contains the default data for any new users added to the computer.

HKEY_LOCAL_MACHINE

HKEY_LOCAL_MACHINE contains all the data required to specify the hardware and operating system configuration of the local machine. It does not contain data about software or information about the users defined for this computer. It is divided into several subkeys—HARDWARE, SAM, SECURITY, SOFTWARE, and SYSTEM.

The HARDWARE key is a dynamic subkey that is constructed each time the computer is booted. It contains information broken down into three more keys: DESCRIP-TION, DEVICEMAP, and RESOURCEMAP. Together, these keys contain data that Windows NT requires to boot up your computer to the logon screen. These keys describe the hardware in your computer, where configuration information about each device can be found within the Registry, and the resources that each device requires (for example, interrupts and I/O addresses).

The SAM key contains data about users and group accounts. This data is referred to as the Security Account Manager database—hence, the key name SAM. The majority of the data in this key can be changed using the User Manager program. This key also is mapped to the key HKEY_LOCAL_MACHINE\SECURITY\SAM.

The SECURITY key contains security-related information, such as the password policy, local group membership, and user rights. To change most of the information in this key, you must use the User Manager program, not the Registry.

The SOFTWARE key contains information about the software installed on the computer. The information is not user specific; rather, it is general configuration information. User-specific information is stored under HKEY_USERS\SOFTWARE. The SOFTWARE key is subdivided into Classes, Program Groups, Secure, and Description keys. Classes is the same key as HKEY_CLASSES_ROOT (see the section "HKEY_CLASSES_ROOT" earlier in this chapter). The Program Groups key contains information about programs shared by all users of the local computer. (Information about programs used by specific users are stored under HKEY_CURRENT_USER.) The Secure key provides a secure location in which applications can store information that should only be changed by a system administrator. Finally, the Description key contains the names and version numbers of the software installed on the computer.

The SYSTEM key contains information needed during the startup of the computer. Similar to the HARDWARE key, the SYSTEM key contains information about the computer. (The HARDWARE key contains data computed at startup.) Because this data is critical to getting your computer up and running, multiple copies of the settings are maintained in control sets. These copies appear as ControlSet00x keys, where "x" is replaced with a number (for example, HKEY_LOCAL_MACHINE\ SYSTEM\ControlSet001). These copies are kept so that if you (or someone else, such as a system administrator) make a change to the Registry that prevents you from starting your computer, you can revert back to an earlier, good configuration. For further details, see the section "What to Do When a System Won't Start" later in this chapter.

Making INI Files and the Registry Work Together

Among other functions, the Registry fulfills a function similar to the Windows 3.x INI files. That is, programs use it to save information between sessions and to store startup information and user preferences. If you look in the Windows NT folder of your system, you will notice that you still have INI files, including the standard WIN.INI and SYSTEM.INI files.

You might be wondering why Windows NT has INI files. INI files are used for backward compatibility. Even if you run Windows NT, you probably still need to use at least one 16-bit Windows 3.x program—a program that doesn't know anything about the Registry, a program that tries to read and write data to and from WIN.INI and SYSTEM.INI.

You have a problem when one program writes data to an INI file and another program tries to read the same data from the Registry. To keep the old and new programs working together, Windows NT can synchronize data contained in an INI file to particular keys in the Registry. This mapping is defined by the data contained under HKEY_LOCAL_ MACHINE\SOFTWARE\MICROSOFT\WINDOWS NT\ CURRENTVERSION\INI FILEMAPPING. This key has subkeys that define particular INI files and particular entries within those INI files. To understand how to read the values for these keys, you need to know five symbols. These symbols are listed in table 31.3.

TABLE 31.3
INI Mapping Symbols

Symbol	Description
!	Write any data to both the Registry and the INI file.
#	When a user logs on, set the Registry value to the value contained in the INI file.
@	Don't read data from the INI file if the data isn't in the Registry.
USR	The INI file data for the entry should be mapped to HKEY_CURRENT_USER plus the text value for the key.
SYS	The INI file data for the entry should be mapped to HKEY_LOCAL_MACHINE\Software plus the text value for the key.

The value for HKEY_LOCAL_MACHINE\SOFTWARE\MICROSOFT\WINDOWS NT\ CURRENTVERSION\INIFILEMAPPING\WIN.INI\WINDOWS\BORDERWIDTH, for example, is "#USR:Control Panel\Desktop." The # means that the value for the BorderWidth should be reset from the WIN.INI file each time a new user logs on. The USR means that the value for the border width itself should be stored at HKEY_CURRENT_USER\ CONTROL PANEL\DESKTOP\BORDERWIDTH.

Modifying the Registry

Microsoft doesn't recommend directly changing data in the Registry. Changing Registry data can result in data loss, program failure, or startup failure. Despite the inherent dangers, you might sometimes want or need to edit the Registry. Windows NT comes with two Registry editor tools to help you edit the Registry. And to make matters confusing, both are called Registry Editors. You cannot find these programs on the Start menu. Microsoft does not want novice users carelessly editing the Registry, most likely because of the technical support nightmare that would result. These tools are available, however, for the informed user.

Note | Windows NT 3.51 had a Registry Editor called the Registration Info Editor, which was used to add file association information (that is, information about how to open and print each particular type of file—for example, *.DOC, *.XLS, *.TXT). The Registration Info Editor has been removed from Windows NT 4 and replaced with a Registry Editor similar to the Registry Editor in Windows 95.

The Registry Editor, REGEDIT.EXE, is located in the Windows NT root folder (for example, C:\WINDOWS). It looks like the Registry Editor found in Windows 95 (see fig. 31.1). It provides an Explorer NT-like view of the Registry, using a single window split into two panes for viewing the Registry data. This editor is best suited for advanced users who want to make adjustments to their own Registry settings, such as user preferences. It is not a good idea to let the average user near this program, and many administrators remove it from client workstations.

Figure 31.1

You can view Registry data using the Registry Editor.

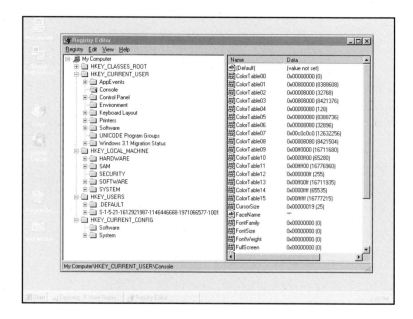

The other Registry Editor, REGEDT32.EXE, is located in the Windows NT \system folder. This Registry Editor uses multiple child windows to view Registry data, with each major key showing in its own window. REGEDT32 provides some additional functionality to that found in REGEDIT.EXE; for example, it allows loading individual hives, setting user security permissions, and auditing settings. Consequently, it's better suited for administrators to use.

Caution	When you use the Registry Editor, you might make a mistake that could stop one of your programs from running correctly or even from running at all—if you are lucky. If you aren't so lucky, that mistake could disable your computer or prevent you from connecting to the network or accessing devices attached to your computer. You will read this again and again in this chapter: Be careful when you modify the Registry! If you aren't sure about the changes you're making, create a backup of the Registry before you alter it.

Using Regedit

Regedit looks like the same Registry Editor that comes with Windows 95, and it is the Registry Editor best suited for individual use. Because the Registry is actually stored on the disk differently for Windows NT than for Windows 95, however—and because Windows NT has more security features than Windows 95—the internals of the programs differ.

Regedit provides plenty of functionality, and you can use it to modify the Registry. It enables you to import and export pieces of the Registry, as well as print out specific portions. Finally, you can use Regedit to work with the Registry of any other networked computer.

Note	The Windows NT Registry is stored on the hard disk as different files (discussed in the section "Understanding Hives" later in this chapter). The Windows 95 Registry is stored as two files, SYSTEM.DAT and USER.DAT (with backups of each— SYSTEM.DA0 and USER.DA0).

Working with Registration Files

Many applications come with a registration file (*.REG) that contains all the Registry keys required for that application to function properly. The following is a portion of a registration file that comes with Microsoft's Word for Windows. This particular portion contains all the information Word needs to make its wizards function properly:

```
HKEY_CLASSES_ROOT\Word.Wizard = Microsoft Word Wizard
HKEY_CLASSES_ROOT\Word.Wizard\DefaultIcon = winword.exe,4
HKEY_CLASSES_ROOT\Word.Wizard\CLSID = {00020900-0000-0000-C000-000000000046}
HKEY_CLASSES_ROOT\Word.Wizard\shell = New
HKEY_CLASSES_ROOT\Word.Wizard\shell\New\ddeexec = [FileNew("%1")]
HKEY_CLASSES_ROOT\Word.Wizard\shell\New\ddeexec\Application = WinWord
HKEY_CLASSES_ROOT\Word.Wizard\shell\New\ddeexec\Topic = System
HKEY_CLASSES_ROOT\Word.Wizard\shell\New\command = winword.exe /n
```

Using the Registry Editor, you can merge these settings into the Registry. You also can export a portion of the Registry to a registration file. You might do this to make a backup of some Registry settings or to copy some settings from one Registry to another. It comes in handy for saving the settings before you make any changes. Then you can restore the original settings if necessary.

Importing a Registration File

To import a registration file, follow these steps:

1. Choose Registry, Import Registry File to open the Import Registry File dialog box (see fig. 31.2).

Figure 31.2

Microsoft Word's registration file is imported using Regedit.

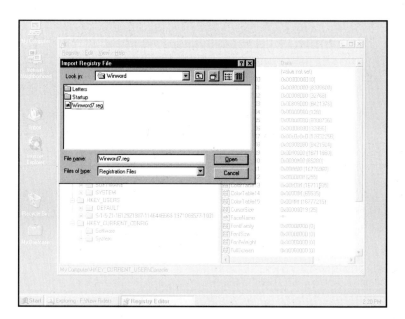

2. Browse to find the folder that contains the Registry file you want to import.

3. Choose Open or press Enter.

4. A message box appears, telling you whether the file was successfully imported. Click on OK.

Exporting a Registration File

To export a portion of the Registry, follow these steps:

1. In Regedit, browse to find the key that you want to export and select it. If you want to export the entire HKEY_CLASSES_ROOT key, for example, select that key in the left-hand pane. If you only want to export the "txtfile" key (found within the HKEY_CLASSES_ROOT), expand the HKEY_CLASSES_ROOT key and select only the "txtfile" key.

2. Choose Registry, Export Registry File to open the Export Registry File dialog box (see fig. 31.3).

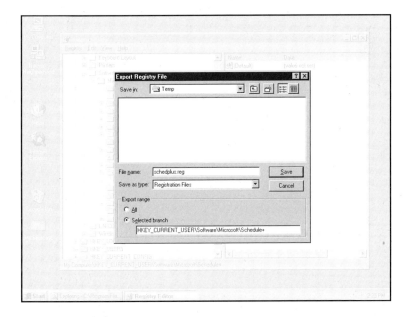

Figure 31.3

You can export even a single key (such as Microsoft's Schedule+) to a temp folder using Regedit.

3. Browse to find the folder where you would like to store the Registry file.

4. Type the name you want to use for the Registry file in the File name field.

5. You can choose to export the entire Registry by choosing All in the Export range box.

6. Choose Save or press Enter.

Connecting to a Remote User's Registry

You can use the Registry Editor to connect to a remote user's Registry, enabling you to view his Registry to try to diagnose problems, check settings, and make any necessary adjustments. Before you can connect to another user's Registry, you must have proper access permissions.

To connect to a remote user's Registry, follow these steps:

1. Choose Registry, Connect Network Registry to open the Connect Network Registry dialog box.

2. If you don't know the computer name to which you want to connect, choose Browse. Choosing Browse opens the Browse for Computer dialog box, in which you can select the computer to which you want to connect; then click on OK.

3. If you know the computer name to which you want to connect, type the name in the Computer Name field.

4. Click on OK.

 Tip   When you use REGEDIT.EXE to connect to a remote user's Registry, you can connect only to the Registry for the active user (the user currently logged on). If you use REGEDT32.EXE, however, you can load the Registry settings for a user who isn't logged on because you can load specific hives.

Disconnecting from a Remote User's Registry

After you finish looking at or working with another user's Registry, you can disconnect from it. To disconnect, simply follow these steps:

1. Choose Registry, Disconnect Network Registry.

2. Click on OK.

Printing the Registry

If you want to print out the entire Registry, follow these steps:

1. Choose Registry, Print to open the Print dialog box (see fig 31.4).

2. In the Printer box, use the Name drop-down list to select the printer you want to use.

3. Choose the All radio button in the Print range box.

4. Click on OK.

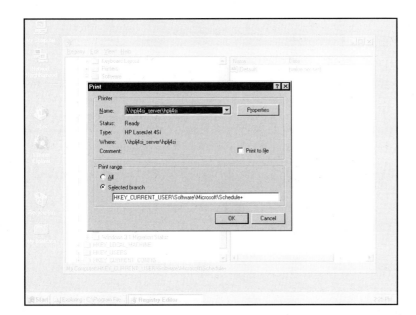

Figure 31.4

You can print any branch of the Registry with Regedit.

If you want to print a specific portion of the Registry, follow these steps:

1. Select the key in the Registry Editor that you want to print. If you want to print the "txtfile" key under HKEY_CLASSES_ROOT, for example, you would expand the HKEY_CLASSES_ROOT key and select the "txtfile" key.

2. Choose Registry, Print to open the Print dialog box.

3. Use the Name drop-down list in the Print box to select the printer from which you want to print.

4. Choose the Selected Branch radio button in the Print range box. The edit field contains the name of the key you selected. Check the name. If it is wrong, type the correct name.

5. Click on OK.

Editing the Registry

Sometimes you need to edit the Registry directly. Some programs, for example, do not provide a method for making the changes that need to be made. Perhaps a program uses a value in the Registry to control how often a backup copy is made.

Unfortunately, it doesn't provide any way for you to change that value from within the program. The only way to change this value then is to use one of the Registry editors and make the change yourself.

When you edit the Registry, you can add, change, or delete keys and values. The following sections cover each of these tasks.

 Tip In Windows NT 4, much of the Registry Editor's functionality is accessible directly from context menus. The steps listed in the following sections use the standard Registry Editor menus to perform the tasks. Instead, try directly selecting the key or value and then clicking with the right mouse button, which brings up a context menu that might contain the command you want.

Adding a New Key

To add a new key, follow these steps:

1. In the left pane, select the Registry key under which you want to add your new key. If you want to add a new file extension, for example, you would select HKEY_CLASSES_ROOT. On the other hand, if you want to add a DefaultIcon key for a particular file type, you would select that file type (HKEY_CLASSES_ROOT\wrifile) in the left pane.

2. Choose Edit, New. A cascading submenu appears (see fig. 31.5).

Figure 31.5

The submenu contains the commands for adding a key or data item using Regedit.

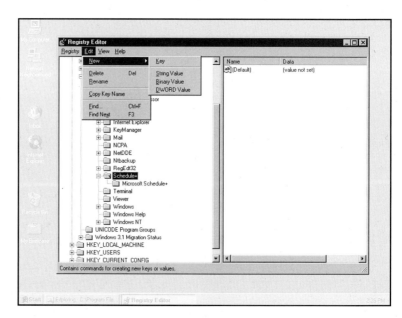

3. Choose Key.

4. The new key appears in the left pane. The name will be New Key # and will already be selected and ready for renaming. Type the key name you want.

5. Press Enter.

Deleting a Key

You might want to delete a Registry key for several reasons. One example is when you uninstall a program, it should clean the Registry by deleting all its keys. Sometimes, however, this doesn't happen. If you discover that this has not happened, the only way to remove the keys is to delete them yourself.

To delete a key, follow these steps:

1. In the left pane, select the Registry key that you want to delete.

2. Choose Edit, Delete.

3. A message box appears asking you to confirm that you really want to delete the key. Click on OK.

Renaming a Key

If you aren't positive about how your changes will affect the Registry, you might want to consider renaming keys before you delete them. If the change has an unwanted effect, you can easily restore the key.

To rename a key, follow these steps:

1. In the left pane, select the Registry key that you want to rename.

2. Press F2 to put the key in edit mode, then enter the new key name.

3. Press Enter.

Adding a New Value

Adding a value is similar to adding a new key. The reasons to add a value are typically similar.

To add a new value, follow these steps:

1. In the left pane, select the Registry key under which you want to add the new value.

2. Choose Edit, New. A cascading submenu appears.

3. Choose the type of value you want to add—String Value, Binary Value, or DWORD Value.

4. The new value appears in the right pane with the name New Value #. The value name is selected and ready for renaming. Type the new name you want and press Enter.

 Tip The REGEDIT.EXE Registry Editor allows you to add only three types of values: string, binary, and DWORD. If you want to add one of the additional string types—expandable strings or multi-strings—you need to use REGEDT32.EXE.

Deleting a Value

To delete a value, follow these steps:

1. Select the Registry key in the left pane that contains the value you want to delete.

2. Select the value you want to delete from the right pane.

3. Choose Edit, Delete.

4. A confirmation message box appears, asking whether you really want to delete the value. Click on Yes.

Renaming a Value

To rename a value, follow these steps:

1. In the left pane, select the Registry key that contains the value you want to rename.

2. In the right pane, select the value you want to rename.

3. Choose Edit, Rename.

4. The value name is selected. Type the new value name.

5. Press Enter.

Changing a Value's Data

To change a value's data, follow these steps:

1. In the left pane, select the Registry key that contains the value you want to change.

2. In the right pane, select the value you want to change.

3. Choose Edit, Modify. An edit dialog box appears.

4. Type the new value.

5. Press Enter.

Using Regedt32

REGEDT32.EXE is the most powerful Registry Editor available with Windows NT. Be careful! If you make a mistake using the Registry Editor when working with file-type information, an application might not work properly. It might not even run. OLE functionality, such as In Place editing, might stop working. If you make a mistake using the Registry Editor when you work with other Registry information, you can cripple Windows itself or even prevent another user from using the computer. If you can, you should use the various administrative tools and Control Panel programs to modify the Registry. On the other hand, some applications might not provide tools to modify all their keys, or you might need to create or modify the keys for an application by hand. When you need to directly modify the Registry, the REGEDT32.EXE Registry Editor allows you full and complete access to all the Registry keys.

Although you can perform many of the same operations using either Registry Editor, you should be aware of the differences. Because Regedt32 gives you a little more control, the following sections discuss hives (portions of the Registry) before discussing how to handle the typical operations, such as adding and deleting Registry keys.

To run the Registry Editor, follow these steps:

1. From Program Manager, choose File, Run, to open the Run dialog box.

2. Type **regedt32** in the Command Line field.

3. Click on OK. The Registry Editor starts.

Understanding the Display

Unlike the simpler display of the Registry Editor, REGEDT32.EXE has a multiple document interface (MDI). It displays several windows (normally five), each of which displays the contents of one of the five major keys (see fig. 31.6). In much the same way that File Manager displays the contents of a drive (folders and files), the Registry Editor displays the contents of a root key (subkeys and values). You can expand and collapse keys by double-clicking on the folder icons. Icons with a "+" in the folder icon indicate that the key has subkeys. You also can expand and collapse the tree using the keyboard in the following ways:

Figure 31.6

You can view Registry data by using REGEDT32.EXE.

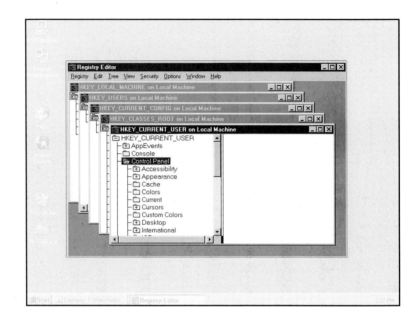

◆ Expand the selected level by choosing Tree, Expand One Level or by pressing the + (plus sign) key.

◆ Collapse the selected branch by choosing Tree, Collapse Branch or by pressing the – (minus) key.

◆ Expand the entire branch (all the keys underneath the selected key) by choosing Tree, Expand Branch or by pressing the * (asterisk) key.

◆ Expand the entire tree by choosing Tree, Expand All or by pressing Ctrl+*.

Understanding Hives

The Registry actually is stored on your hard disk as distinct files. Each file, along with a backup copy (with a LOG extension) is called a hive. Table 31.4 lists the standard hives. Because the system hive is so critical, it also has an additional backup copy (with the ALT extension). By default, these files are stored in the SYSTEM32\ CONFIG folder off the root Windows folder (that is, C:\WINNT\SYSTEM32\CONFIG).

> **Note** | LOG files are used to make sure Registry hives aren't corrupted when they get updated. To prevent corruption, Windows NT writes all changes to the LOG file, then it marks the Registry to indicate that it's about to update the Registry. It then performs the update by processing the changes stored in the LOG file. Finally, it

unmarks the Registry, indicating that it has finished processing the LOG file. If your computer crashes during the update, Windows NT can use the list of changes in the LOG file to recover the hive when Windows NT restarts.

TABLE 31.4
Standard Hives

Hive	File Names
HKEY_LOCAL_MACHINE\SAM	SAM(.LOG)
HKEY_LOCAL_MACHINE\SECURITY	SECURITY(.LOG)
HKEY_LOCAL_MACHINE\SOFTWARE	SOFTWARE(.LOG)
HKEY_LOCAL_MACHINE\SYSTEM	SYSTEM(.LOG) and SYSTEM.ALT
HKEY_USERS\DEFAULT	DEFAULT(.LOG)

When you use REGEDT32.EXE, you can actually load and work with hives of another user and with hives from another computer. You might need to load such a hive if you make changes to another user's hive because of changes in software or because the other user is having problems running Windows NT.

To load another hive, follow these steps:

1. Choose File, Load Hive.

2. Browse to the drive and subdirectory in which the hive you want to load is located.

3. Select the file and click on OK.

After you work with the hive, you need to unload it so that it can be loaded by the other user or machine. To unload the hive, choose File, Unload Hive.

Editing the Registry with the Registry Editor

The Registry Editor provides a much richer set of controls when you need to edit the Registry. Not only does it enable you to add keys and values, it also enables you to work with all types of values: binary, string, expandable string, DWORD, and multi-string. See table 31.5 for descriptions of each data type.

TABLE 31.5
Registry Data Types

Data Type	Description
Binary (REG_BINARY)	Simple binary data. It is often used to store configuration information for hardware components.
String (REG_SZ)	Text data. It is often used for file names, component descriptions, and so on.
Expandable string (REG_EXPAND_SZ)	Text that contains a variable that will be replaced. For example, many system components add Registry entries that contain %SystemRoot%. When this value is requested by an application, %SystemRoot% is replaced by the actual path of the Windows system files.
DWORD (REG_DWORD)	A number four bytes long.
Multi-string (REG_MULTI_SZ)	Multiple text strings. Each string is separated by a NULL byte (a byte of all zeros). It is often used for device driver information.

Adding a Key

To add a key, follow these steps:

1. Select the primary key under which you want to add your new key by clicking in the child window's title bar or by choosing Window, primary key name (for example, HKEY_CLASSES_ROOT).

2. Navigate down the subkey tree until you reach the subkey under which you want to add your new key (for example, \AVIFILE\SHELL). Navigate by double-clicking on the key names in the left pane.

3. Choose Edit, Add Key to open the Add Key dialog box.

4. Enter the key name in the Key Name field (for example, PRINT). Although there is a field for entering the class of the Registry key, you can ignore this field. This might be used in the future, but not now.

5. Click on OK.

Adding a Value

To add a value, follow these steps:

1. Select the primary key under which you want to add your new value key by clicking in the child window's title bar or by choosing Window, primary key name (for example, HKEY_CLASSES_ROOT).

2. Navigate down the subkey tree until you reach the subkey under which you want to add your new value (for example, \AVIFILE\SHELL\PRINT\COMMAND). Navigate by double-clicking on the key names in the left pane.

3. Choose Edit, Add Value to open the Add Value dialog box (see fig. 31.7).

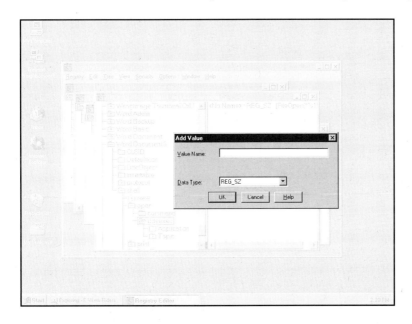

Figure 31.7

Add a string value to the DDEXEC Registry key.

4. Enter the name of the new value in the Value Name field (for example, PRINT). Each key can contain one value that doesn't have a name, represented in the display by <No Name>. The <No Name> value for the key HKEY_CLASSES_ROOT\ TXTFILE\SHELL\OPEN\COMMAND, for example, is notepad.exe %1. This is often used when the key only has one data value.

5. Select the class of the key in the Data Type drop-down list.

6. Click on OK.

7. An editor dialog box (one exists for each data type) appears. Type the actual data value.

8. Click on OK.

Deleting a Key or Value

To delete a key or value, follow these steps:

1. Select the primary key that contains the key or value you want to delete by clicking in the child window's title bar or by choosing Window, primary key name (for example, HKEY_CLASSES_ROOT).

2. Navigate down the subkey tree until you reach the subkey or value you want to delete (for example, \AVIFILE\SHELL\PRINT). Navigate by double-clicking on the key names in the left pane.

3. Select the key or value you want to delete.

4. Choose Edit, Delete or press the Delete key.

5. A prompt appears asking you to confirm that you want to delete the key or value. Click on Yes.

Editing a Value

To edit a value, follow these steps:

1. Select the primary key that contains the value you want to edit by clicking in the child window's title bar or by choosing Window, primary key name (for example, HKEY_CLASSES_ROOT).

2. Navigate down the subkey tree until you reach the subkey that contains the value you want to edit (for example, \AVIFILE\SHELL\PRINT\COMMAND). Navigate by double-clicking on the key names in the left pane.

3. Choose Edit, data type, in which data type is one of four values: Binary, String, DWORD, or Multi-String. Although you can edit any value by choosing any data type, choosing the same data type command as the value's data type is the most useful.

4. The data type editor dialog box appears (for example, DWORD Editor). Type the new data for the value.

5. Click on OK.

Changing the View

The default view of REGEDT32.EXE usually works well. If you work with a low-resolution monitor such as on a laptop (640×480), however, you might find that you want to view only the key pane or the value pane. To change between these different views, do one of the following:

◆ Choose View, Tree and Data to view both the keys and data values.

◆ Choose View, Tree Only to view only the keys (the left pane).

◆ Choose View, Data Only to view only the values (the right pane).

When you work with REGEDT32.EXE in the Tree and Data mode, you can increase the width of either the Tree or Data pane. Doing so naturally decreases the width of the other pane. To adjust the widths of the panes, follow these steps:

1. Choose View, Split or click on the separator between the Tree and Data window panes.

2. Move your mouse right to increase the width of the Tree pane, or left to increase the width of the Data pane.

3. After you adjust the widths to your liking, single-click the left mouse button.

Finally, you can control when REGEDT32.EXE refreshes the contents of display. In other words, the data that appears in the Registry Editor is a view of the Registry's data at the time you started the Registry Editor. Some of the data has probably changed since you started, especially if you are working with a Registry on another computer. To update the view so that it displays the most current data, you need to force the Registry Editor to refresh its display by doing one of the following:

◆ Turn on the automatic refresh by choosing Options, Auto Refresh. If the command already has a check mark beside it, Auto Refresh is already turned on.

◆ To refresh the entire Registry, choose View, Refresh All or press Shift+F6.

◆ To refresh just the contents of the active child window, choose View, Refresh Active or press F6.

> **Caution** Auto Refresh only works if you're editing your own local Registry. If you work with the Registry of a remote computer and turn on Auto Refresh, it doesn't update to reflect changes in the remote Registry. To make matters worse, Refresh All and Refresh Active are also disabled. To avoid problems when you work with a remote computer's Registry, turn off Auto Refresh and periodically refresh the data yourself.

Using the Security Features of the Registry Editor

Avoid using the Registry Editor carelessly—you don't want to disable your computer or your programs. On the other hand, it's also important to protect the Registry from changes from other users. You can help protect the Registry on your computer from other users in three primary ways:

◆ Use the security features available within the Registry Editor to allow users to have access only to certain keys.

◆ Set up auditing of Registry changes.

◆ Protect the actual files themselves using the file security features of Windows NT.

You have two other easy precautions you can take to protect your Registry. First, remove or restrict access to REGEDIT.EXE and especially, REGEDT32.EXE. Second, if you choose to restrict access, make sure access is granted to administrators only. No other user should need access to your Registry.

Restricting Users from Registry Keys

In much the same way that you can use Explorer to restrict access to folders and files on a user/group basis (assuming the folders and files are on an NTFS volume), you can restrict access to Registry keys on a user/group basis using the Registry Editor. The Registry does not have to be located on an NTFS volume for the user-based restriction to work. To set user permission for Registry keys, follow these steps:

1. Select the primary key that contains the key to which you want to restrict access by clicking in the child window's title bar or by choosing Window, primary key name (for example, HKEY_CLASSES_ROOT).

2. Navigate down the subkey tree until you reach the subkey to which you want to restrict access (for example, \AVIFILE\SHELL\PRINT). Navigate by double-clicking on the key names in the left (Tree) pane.

3. Select the key to which you want to restrict access.

4. Choose Security, Permissions to open the Registry Key Permissions dialog box (see fig. 31.8).

Figure 31.8

Set access permissions on the HKEY_LOCAL_MACHINE Registry key.

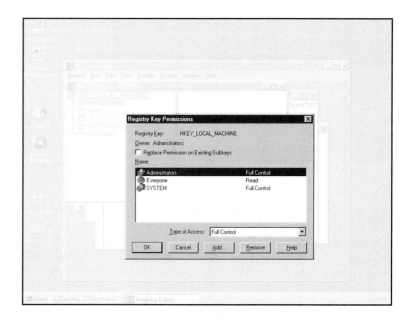

5. Select the user or group for which you want to set the access privileges. If you don't see the user or group, click on Add to add that user or group to the list.

6. Set the type of access by choosing one of the options in the Type of Access drop-down list.

7. If the key you are restricting has subkeys and you want your new settings to override the subkey setting, enable the Replace Permission on Existing Subkeys check box.

8. Click on OK.

 Tip If you set restrictions on any Registry keys, make sure that administrators and the system still have full access to all keys. That way, if something does go wrong, an administrator can go back in and reset the changes.

As a general rule, auditing changes to those keys you've restricted and testing your system are good ideas. Log on as different users and administrators to make sure that the restrictions you've set haven't caused any problems in the normal running of your computer and programs. After you are sure everything is functioning normally, you can turn off auditing.

Note Although the system automatically assigns permissions to all the hives (except for user profile hives), the Registry Editor allows permissions to be set on any key. You normally don't need to override this behavior.

Auditing Registry Editor Changes

If you want to monitor changes in your Registry and the people who are making those changes, you can turn on auditing features of the Registry Editor. You must follow three steps to use auditing:

1. Use the User Manager administrative tool to turn on auditing.

2. Use the Registry Editor to set up the auditing parameters for Registry changes.

3. Use the Event Manager to view the audit logs.

To set the auditing parameters using the Registry Editor, follow these steps:

1. Select the primary key that contains the key you want to audit by clicking in the child window's title bar or by choosing Window, primary key name (for example, HKEY_CLASSES_ROOT).

2. Navigate down the subkey tree until you reach the subkey you want to audit (for example, \AVIFILE\SHELL\PRINT). Navigate by double-clicking on the key names in the left (Tree) pane.

3. Select the key you want to audit.

4. Choose Security, Auditing to open the Registry Key Auditing dialog box (see fig. 31.9).

Figure 31.9

Set auditing parameters on the HKEY_LOCAL_ MACHINE Registry key.

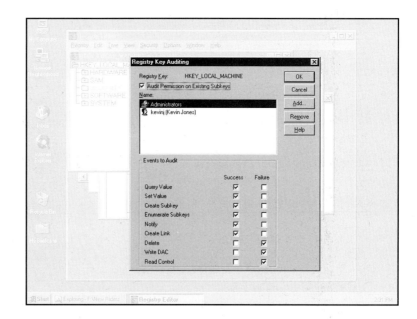

5. Select the user or group that you want to audit. If you don't see the user or group, click on Add to add that user or group to the list.

6. Set the type of auditing by choosing one or more of the options in the Events to Audit box. (See table 31.6 for more details.) You can choose to audit Success, Failure, or both. You can choose, for example, to audit every time a key is successfully set, every time a failure occurs when trying to set a key, or both events.

7. If the key you audit has subkeys and you want to audit those keys as well, enable the Audit Permission on Existing Subkeys check box.

8. Click on OK.

TABLE 31.6
Auditing Options

Audit Event Type	Description
Query Value	Audit any event that tries to open a key for the purpose of reading its value.
Set Value	Audit any event that tries to open a key for the purpose of setting its value.
Create Subkey	Audit any event that tries to open a key for the purpose of adding a new subkey.
Enumerate Subkeys	Audit any event that tries to open a key for the purpose of reading its subkeys.
Notify	Audit any event that tries to open a key for the purpose of monitoring when the key will be changed.
Create Link	Audit any event that tries to open a key for the purpose of creating a symbolic link.
Delete	Audit any event that tries to open a key for the purpose of deleting the key.
Write DAC	Audit any event that tries to open a key for the purpose of finding out who has access to the key.
Read Control	Audit any event that tries to open a key for the purpose of determining the owner of the key.

Making Common User Changes

So far, this chapter has covered the Registry and how to use the tools provided to modify it. But it hasn't discussed *when* you should modify the Registry or how to protect yourself from careless editing mistakes. Usually, you use tools other than the Registry Editor(s) to make changes. You might not even realize that you're changing the Registry. Control Panel applications and the User Manager program, for example, all make changes to the Registry. Sometimes, though, you need to roll up your sleeves and work directly on the Registry.

Objective
G.6

Making Safe Changes

You should take the following two precautionary measures when you modify the Registry:

◆ Export the key of the Registry you're going to change to a registration file. Then if your change causes unwanted problems, you can merge that exported file back in, overwriting your changes.

◆ Change the name of the original key. If the key name or data name was SIZE, for example, you would change the name to X_SIZE. Then you would add a new key or data item using the original name. If you need to revert back to the original settings, you can delete the new key and rename the original key its original name.

Increasing the Size of the Registry

The size of the Registry is limited, so that it can't grow too large and prevent your system from working. By default, the size of the Registry is set to be 25 percent of the size of the paged pool. The paged pool by default is 32 MB. That makes the default maximum size of the Registry 8 MB. This means that, by default, the Registry cannot grow beyond 8 MB.

Why would the Registry grow? The primary reason for Registry growth is the addition of new users. At 8 MB, the Registry can support about 5,000 users. Unless you maintain a very large network, you probably would never exceed 5,000 users.

To improve performance, you can restrict the Registry from growing very large at all. If you are the only user on your computer, you might want to restrict the size of the Registry to only a few megabytes.

To approximate the current size of your Registry, look in the SYSTEM32\CONFIG subdirectory of the directory to which you installed Windows NT (for example, C:\WINNT4\SYSTME32\CONFIG). Total the size of the following files:

◆ SAM and SAM.LOG

◆ SECURITY and SECURITY.LOG

◆ SOFTWARE and SOFTWARE.LOG

◆ SYSTEM and SYSTEM.LOG

◆ USER#### and USER####.LOG (for the current user; for example KEVIN000 and KEVIN000.LOG)

◆ ADMIN### and ADMIN###.LOG (if present)

◆ DEFAULT and DEFAULT.LOG

Although this figure isn't exact, it serves as a quick approximation of the amount of memory the Registry takes. To set the maximum size of the Registry, follow these steps:

1. Run the Registry Editor, REGEDT32.EXE.

2. Select the HKEY_LOCAL_MACHINE\SYSTEM\
   CURRENTCONTROLSET\CONTROL key.

3. Add (or if it's already there, modify) the value RegistrySizeLimit. This value should be a REG_DWORD type.

4. Set the value to the maximum size (in megabytes) to which you want the Registry to be able to grow.

5. Choose File, Exit to exit the Registry Editor.

What to Do When a System Won't Start

When a system fails to boot, you can do a number of things. If you've been proactive—creating an emergency repair disk and making regular backups of critical system files—you have a great leg up. If you haven't, you probably have a lot of work in front of you.

If your system has just failed to start properly, you can force Windows NT to start using the Last Known Good configuration. To do this, follow these steps:

1. Reboot your computer.

2. At the startup prompt, select Windows NT. Press Enter.

3. Immediately press the spacebar.

4. From the Configuration Recovery menu, select Use Last Known Good Configuration. Press Enter.

This tries to start your computer using a previously known good configuration.

> **Note**   Two criteria must be met during system boot for a configuration to be considered good. First, all startup drivers must successfully load. Second, a user must have successfully logged on to the computer. After these two events have been met, Windows NT copies the current configuration information to the Last Known Good Configuration key in the Registry.

If your computer still fails to load, you might have corrupted one or more of the Registry hives (actual files). To solve this problem, see the next section.

Restoring Damaged System Files

If you think parts of the Registry are actually damaged—that it isn't a configuration problem—then you need to restore the damaged files. Before you can restore damaged files, you must have backup copies of your Registry. If you do, you'll also be interested in the section "Changing the Registry on a Remote System" later in this chapter.

 Note Windows NT keeps a second backup copy of the system hive, called SYSTEM.ALT. During startup, if Windows NT can't load the system hive, it automatically tries to load this second backup copy.

The following procedure backs up your Registry files:

1. Boot your computer into another instance of Windows NT, or if Windows NT is installed on a FAT volume, you can boot into MS-DOS.

2. Copy the files in the Windows SYSTEM32\CONFIG subdirectory to another directory. These are your backup copies.

To restore these files, reverse the process by following these steps:

1. Boot your computer into another instance of Windows NT, or if Windows NT is installed on a FAT volume, you can boot into MS-DOS.

2. Copy the backup files to the Windows SYSTEM32\CONFIG subdirectory.

3. Restart your computer, booting into Windows NT.

Remember that you will lose any changes you made to the Registry between the time that you backed up and restored the files. If you installed a new program, for example, any Registry keys created by the new program are lost. You must reinstall the program or merge the program's registration file into the Registry. If you don't have a registration file, you might try exporting information from another user's Registry, although this is rarely successful unless all the client machines in your system are configured the same way and have the same software installed.

Changing the Registry on a Remote System

If booting into the Last Known Good configuration doesn't get your system running properly (and you don't have backup Registry files), or if restoring the backups doesn't fix your problems, you might still be able to fix your problem by using the Registry Editor from another Windows NT system.

If your system doesn't start into Windows NT because you had to replace some failed hardware (maybe a hard disk controller card), for example, but you can boot into

MS-DOS and connect to the network, you can make configuration changes using the Registry Editor on another system.

To load the Registry of a remote computer, after you've connected to the network via MS-DOS commands, follow these steps:

1. Run the Registry Editor.

2. Choose File, Select Computer.

3. Select the computer in the Select Computer list.

4. You now can edit HKEY-USERS and HKEY_LOCAL_MACHINE if you aren't a member of the Administrators group. If you are a member, you can edit all keys. This is subject to any access controls that might be in place for the remote Registry.

Using the Registry Editor to Find Configuration Problems

One of the most useful ways of using the Registry Editor isn't to perform any editing. You can quickly view configuration data using the Registry Editor. Then you can use another program—a Control Panel program or the User Manager program—to actually make the changes.

Couple the capability to view configuration data with the capability to view the Registry on a remote computer, and one user (usually an administrator) can help another user diagnose problems.

If a user has problems running software and environment variable problems are suspected, for example, an administrator can try to solve the problem by following these steps:

1. Run the Registry Editor.

2. View the Registry on the remote computer. See the section "Changing the Registry on a Remote System" earlier in this chapter.

3. View the values of the HKEY_LOCAL_MACHINE\SYSTEM\ CURRENTCONTROLSET\CONTROL\SESSION MANAGER\ENVIRONMENT.

4. If an incorrect value is found, the administrator can immediately fix the problem—remotely.

Tip Although the Registry Editor is useful for viewing data, sometimes the data in the Registry is in a rather unhelpful format, especially when viewing the data for the HKEY_LOCAL_MACHINE\HARDWARE key. This data tends to consist mainly of binary data, and looking at a bunch of bytes just isn't particularly edifying. To see this data in a friendlier form, run the Windows NT Diagnostics program, which organizes and displays the data in a readable format.

Customizing Your Windows NT Logon

You can customize the Windows NT logon in two ways. First, you can have your computer automatically log on when it boots up. You might want to do this if your machine is running a service—such as Peer Web Services—and you want the machine to restart automatically if the power should go out and come back on. To do this, follow these steps:

1. Run the Registry Editor.

2. Select the HKEY_LOCAL_MACHINE\SOFTWARE\MICROSOFT WINDOWS NT\CURRENTVERSION\WINLOGON key.

3. Add a value called AutoAdminLogon (should have a data type of REG_SZ and a data value of 1).

4. Add a value called DefaultPassword. This should have a data type of REG_SZ, and the data value should be set to the password of the user listed in the DefaultUserName value.

Second, you can have Windows NT display a custom logon prompt. Because users have to choose OK to get rid of this prompt, you're reasonably certain they'll read it. You might use this for a licensing agreement or disclaimer. To add the custom logon prompt, follow these steps:

1. Run the Registry Editor.

2. Select the HKEY_LOCAL_MACHINE\SOFTWARE\MICROSOFT\WINDOWS NT\CURRENTVERSION\WINLOGON key.

3. Add a value called LegalNoticeCaption. This should have a data type of REG_SZ, and the data value should be the text that appears as the caption for the logon prompt.

4. Add a value called LegalNoticeText. This should have a data type of REG_SZ, and the data value should be set to the text of the message for the logon prompt.

End Note: Modifying the Registry is not something you should do carelessly. If you are careful and take adequate precautions, however, you can control the behavior of your computer, Windows NT, and your installed programs. You have access to setting values that enable you to adjust programs to your liking. Using the Registry Editors to view the data in the Registry can offer insights into how programs work and the kinds of control you have.

Test Your Knowledge

1. You are a programmer and your software uses templates that have a file extension .TLX. Into which part of the Registry do you import this fact during installaton?

2. You have opened the Control Panel and tweaked your keyboard settings to change the repeat rate. Which part of the Registry gets the information?

3. For the previous question, give the complete path to the key that holds the information.

4. In which part of the Registry would you find data about your modem?

5. What is the Registry information that is stored as a file on your hard drive called?

6. In what subdirectory will you find the Registry information that is stored as a file on your hard drive?

7. Which Registry Editor enables you to work directly with the Registry information that is stored as a file on your hard drive?

Test Your Knowledge Answers

1. HKEY_CLASSES_ROOT

2. HKEY_CURRENT_USER

3. HKEY_CURRENT_USER\Control Panel\Keyboard

4. HKEY_LOCAL_MACHINE

5. Hive

6. \WindowsRoot\System32\Config

7. Regedt32

PART VIII

Understanding Server Features

Chapter Snapshot

Windows NT Workstation 4 can serve as the host of many network services. You will find these services to be valuable for file sharing, fault tolerance, and remote computing applications, among other uses. This chapter covers the following topics:

Windows NT
Workstation 4

CHAPTER 32

Using the Workstation's Server Properties

Windows NT Workstation 4 can host network services typically run on a server. You could run the Peer Web Services on NT Workstation 4, for example, and other users on your network could connect to your Peer Web Services server to view its contents on an intranet. In this instance, Windows NT Workstation 4 plays the role of a server.

You have no control over domain properties; machine, user, or group accounts; or other aspects of network security. You do have local control, however, over your workstation's host capabilities and server properties. This chapter explains how to get information about your workstation's server configuration and how to control who's connected, how and when directories are replicated, and other technical properties.

Managing Workstation Server Functions

Objective

A.2

In Windows NT Server, you can view and manage any computer in the server's domain using the Server Manager. When you launch the dialog box on an NT server, a list of computers appears. You can double-click on any computer in that list or choose Computer, Properties to view the computer's properties. The Server Manager has a counterpart dialog box in Windows NT Workstation 4 called the Server dialog box.

Windows NT Workstation 4 lacks the capability to adjust other network computers' properties. It also lacks the capability to view and alter domain properties or domain security features. You can, however, adjust the properties for your own computer. Server displays the exact same dialog box that you would see for a computer's properties in the NT Server's Server Manager.

Figure 32.1 shows the Server icon. Launching this icon brings up the dialog box shown in figure 32.2.

Figure 32.1

The Server icon is found in the Control Panel.

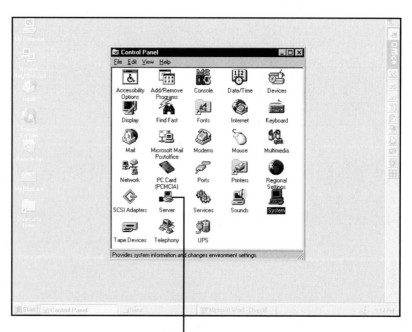

The Server icon

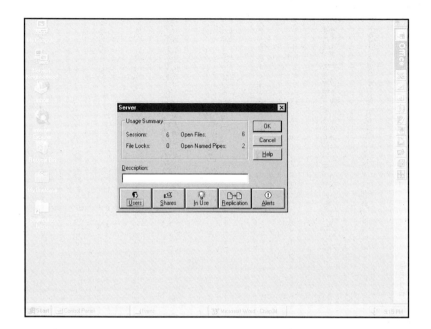

Figure 32.2

The Server dialog box enables you to control a number of resource and session properties.

From the Server dialog box, you can do any of the following:

◆ See who is currently using your computer (user sessions)

◆ Check what resources (shares) are in use

◆ Determine how long a resource has been in use

◆ Determine how long a session has been idle

◆ Get information on the disposition of resources—open file locks, resources, and so on

◆ Send alert messages to users and receive alerts from the system

◆ Replicate selected directories

Tip	The Description text box in the Server dialog box enables you to display a description about NT Workstation 4 that appears in the Comment field for the computer in the Network Neighborhood. It's an optional field, but it can help other users and network administrators to locate (physical location) your computer and to determine its proper usage as a service provider.

Many people put the manufacturer and model of their computer in the Description field. You also can indicate in the Description field who should be contacted in case of difficulties.

The preceding list is useful indeed. You can, for example, check the usage of your workstation by other users to determine what activities are currently in progress. By knowing your workstation's normal server activity, you can spot unusual activity. You can also see what resources are in use and if any particular resource (such as a directory share) is being overused. Knowing that a resource is heavily used enables you to create additional resources and share the load.

> **Note**
>
> You can have only ten network simultaneous connections to NT Workstation 4, thus limiting its use as a serious network server. Performance issues aside, certain serious security considerations suggest that you should run any shared services on NT Server.

The following sections survey the functionality of the Server dialog box, which is central to NT Workstation 4's server capabilities. You can learn all you need to know about NT Workstation 4's server capabilities by taking a close look at the Server dialog box.

Sessions

Objective F.1

The Usage Summary area of the Server dialog box (refer to fig. 32.2) displays a summary of the usage of your workstation as measured by the number of sessions. A *session* is a single connection by a user for a period of time. Generally (but not always), a single user establishes a single connection to your workstation. Thus you can roughly correlate sessions with the number of users connected to NT Workstation 4.

The four statistics displayed in the Usage Summary area are these:

◆ **Sessions.** Indicates the number of connections to your workstation.

◆ **Open Files.** Indicates how many shared resources are in use.

◆ **File Locks.** Tells you the total number of file locks that exist in open resources. A locked file cannot be used or modified in any way by another user while the lock is in place.

◆ **Open Named Pipes.** A *pipe* is a directed process. Generally, a pipe also requires that a portion of memory be set aside so that information can be passed from one process to another.

The buttons beneath the Description text box enable you to obtain additional information about your workstation's server usage and to control that aspect of its use.

Users

The Users button opens the User Sessions dialog box (see fig. 32.3). The User Sessions dialog box shows you who is connected to your workstation and the resources that are currently being used in the top and bottom list boxes, respectively. You also can use this dialog box to disconnect one or all connected users.

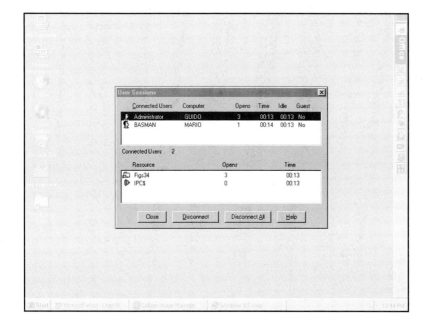

Figure 32.3

The User Sessions dialog box shows who is connected to services on an NT workstation.

The Connected Users list box contains the following information:

◆ **Connected Users icon column.** In the extreme left (unnamed) column of the Connected Users list box, you see an icon for a connected user (person in profile).

◆ **Connected Users column.** A *connected user* is a user account who is logged on to the network and is currently using a resource on your computer. In some cases, you might see a user's computer name in place of the user name in the Connected Users column.

Tip
While the User Sessions dialog box is open, new connections do not automatically appear; that is, the dialog box doesn't refresh automatically. To refresh the User Sessions dialog box, click on any user name in the Connected Users section.

◆ **Computer column.** Shows the name of the computer for the connected user.

◆ **Opens column.** Displays the number of resources that are currently opened by that user.

◆ **Time column.** Displays the time that has elapsed since the session was established. If two or more resources have been accessed, then the time relates to the time elapsed since the first resource was accessed.

◆ **Idle column.** Displays the time that has elapsed since a (any) resource was last used by this user.

◆ **Guest column.** Tells you whether this user logged on to your system as a guest. You see "Yes" or "No" in this column.

Below the Connected Users list box is the total number of connected users.

The Resource list box is the lower of the two list boxes in the User Sessions dialog box. It displays the resources currently being used by the user highlighted in the Connected Users list box. Only one user can be current and selected (highlighted). The information you see in the Resource list box applies to the resources used by the selected user. You do, however, see all the connected users in the Connected Users list box at all times.

The Resource list box contains the following items:

◆ **Resource icon column.** The four icons available for the Resource list box are shown in figure 32.4. These include a shared directory, a named pipe, a shared printer, and an unrecognized resource icon.

Figure 32.4

The four resource icons show you the types of resources in use. (These will appear in the Resource icon column of the Resource list box.)

Shared directory

Named pipe

Shared printer

Resource of an unrecognized type

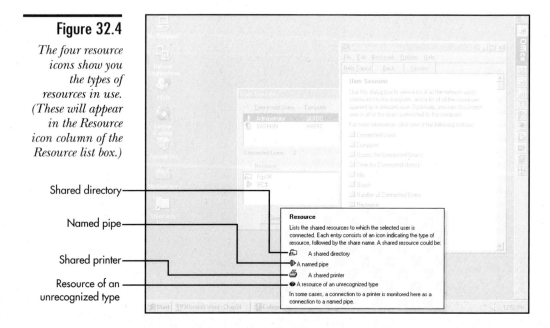

◆ **Resource column.** Shows the name of the resource. Some resources are unnamed. When that's the case, a generic name appropriate to the resource type appears.

◆ **Opens column.** Displays the number of opens for that resource by the selected user.

◆ **Time column.** Refers to the time that has elapsed since the user connected to the resource. Time is in hours and minutes, so 3:21 indicates a time of 3 hours and 21 minutes.

Note Sometimes a connection to a printer shows up as a connection to a named pipe.

The Disconnect and Disconnect All buttons are used to end a user's access to the resource. If the user currently is working in the file, any changes are lost. Sometimes disconnecting a user can result in file corruption. NT Workstation 4 warns you of this fact with the alert box shown in figure 32.5. It doesn't, however, warn your connected users. Before disconnecting users, therefore, you should warn them about the disconnection. Send them a message using Microsoft Exchange or whatever method of communication you have at your disposal.

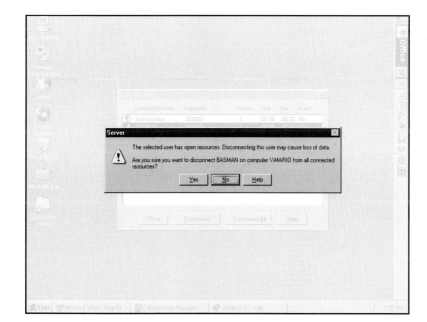

Figure 32.5

The Disconnect alert box informs you that a user's service is about to be shut off.

When you are logged on as an administrator to a remote computer, your administrator account is listed as a user connected to an $IPC resource. It cannot be disconnected.

Tip Use the Alerts function in the Server dialog box to inform users before you disconnect them. See the section "Generating Alerts" later in this chapter.

Sharing

The Shares button in the Server dialog box opens the Shared Resources dialog box (see fig. 32.6). Here you can view shared resources and the users who are sharing them (if any), as well as disconnect users from shared resources.

Figure 32.6

The Shared Resources dialog box enables you to view shared resources and the users who are sharing them.

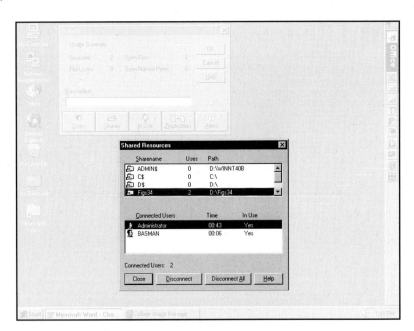

The Sharename list box shows the following information:

◆ **Sharename icon column.** The four icons available for the Sharename list box were shown in figure 32.4. These include a shared directory, named pipe, a shared printer, and an unrecognized resource icon. Remember that a printer can sometimes show up as a connection to a named pipe.

◆ **Sharename column.** Shows the name of the resource. Some resources are unnamed. When that's the case, a generic name appropriate to the resource type appears.

◆ **Uses column.** Displays the number of connections to this resource.

◆ **Path column.** Displays the location of the resource in your file system.

Only one resource is the current resource for the Shared Resources dialog box. You can click on the name of another resource to make it current. What you see in the Connected Users list box refers to the current resource.

The Connected Users list box gives you the following information:

◆ **Connected Users column.** Lists user accounts currently logged on to the network and using a resource on your computer. You might sometimes see a user's computer name in place of the user name.

◆ **Time column.** Refers to the time (in hours and minutes) that has expired since the user connected to the current resource.

◆ **In Use column.** Tells you whether the user has a file open in the current resource.

Below the Connected Users list box is the total number of connected users.

As you may recall, you can set up sharing for directories using the Sharing command in the File menu of the Windows NT Explorer. You also can select the Sharing command from the context-sensitive menu for a directory by right-clicking on the directory in the Folders or Contents panel of the Windows NT Explorer.

You work with shared printers by opening the Printers folder and creating or modifying the printers it contains. To open the Printers folder, choose Settings, Printers from the Start menu. With a printer selected, set up or modify sharing by choosing File, Sharing or by choosing the Sharing command from that printer's context-sensitive menu.

| **Note** | For information about establishing and modifying network shares, see Chapter 20, "Installing Network Options." Chapter 17, "Printing," describes printer sharing in detail. |

You use the Disconnect and Disconnect All buttons in the Shared Resources dialog box to end users' access to the current resource. The discussion in the previous section about users potentially losing information or files getting corrupted during the disconnect applies here as well. You should always warn users before disconnecting them. As before, post a message on Exchange, use smoke signals, or send out couriers on SneakerNet to let them know.

Shared resources are directories, printers, communication devices, and many other services provided by a network. Shares can be accessed by users (through their user account), guests, or administrators.

The NT operating system creates some special shares that the system uses and administers. These shares are often followed by a dollar sign. Among the special shares you might see in the Shared Properties dialog box are these:

◆ **driveletter$.** The root directory of an NT Workstation 4 storage device; typically, the C$ directory. For additional drives (logical ones as well as physical ones), you might see D$ and so on. Only Administrators, Server Operators, or Backup Operators logged on to your workstation can see these volumes.

◆ **ADMIN$.** The ADMIN$ resource appears when a user logs on remotely. It is located in the same directory as Windows NT.

◆ **IPC$.** An IPC$ resource is a named pipe. *Pipes* are communication pathways between processes. You view this resource when viewing the workstation's shared resources, or when an administrator or owner of the workstation is remotely connected to the workstation.

◆ **PRINT$.** A PRINT$ resource contains the files necessary to administer a local or networked printer.

◆ **REPL$.** The REPL$ resource is used for export replication. NT creates this resource whenever the workstation is set up to perform directory replication. See the section "Managing Replication" later in this chapter for more information.

◆ **NETLOGON.** A NETLOGON resource is used to process domain logon requests for the Net Logon service.

Some or all of the preceding special shares may appear in the Shared Resources dialog box, depending on your workstation's configuration and who currently is logged on to your workstation.

Do not delete or modify these special shares or essential server services or your workstation can fail. Playing with special shares is hard to do on NT Workstation 4 because it lacks the Properties button that would enable you to change a resource from within the Shared Resources dialog box. NT Server's Server Manager, however, has this feature in its Shared Resources dialog box. NT Server also enables you to create a new share within its version of the Shared Resources dialog box.

Also, the $ that follows the resource name hides the resource from view in NT Explorer. So although it is possible to get in and modify special resources on an NT Workstation 4, you have to do so by logging on remotely as an administrator.

Uses

Clicking on the In Use button in the Server dialog box opens the Open Resources dialog box (see fig. 32.7). This dialog box tells you what shared resources currently are in use and enables you to close them. You can see the actual number of shared resources that are open and the number of current file locks in place at the top of the dialog box.

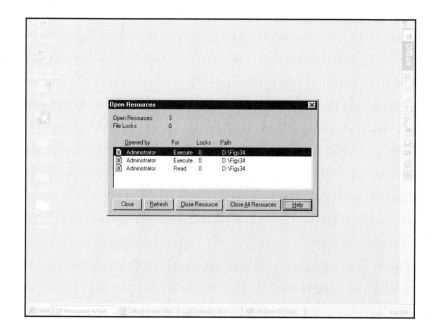

Figure 32.7

The Open Resources dialog box shows you what resources are currently in use.

The Opened by list box gives you the following information:

◆ **Opened By icon column.** The four icons available for the Opened By list box are shown in figure 32.8. These include an opened file, a named pipe, a print job in a print spooler, and a resource of an unrecognized type. Remember that a print job can sometimes show up as a named pipe. For a remote administering computer, the connection also appears as a named pipe.

◆ **For column.** Tells you the current condition of the opened resource.

◆ **Locks column.** Indicates the number of locks placed on the resource.

◆ **Path column.** Indicates the location of the resource in your file system.

While the Open Resources dialog box is open, resources that logged-on users open and close aren't reflected in the Opened by list box. Use the Refresh button to make the Open Resources dialog box current.

You also can use the Close Resource and Close All Resources buttons to close one or all resources, respectively. As before, whenever you close connected users, you run the risk of losing their data or corrupting their files. Therefore, you should alert these users before you disconnect them.

Figure 32.8

The Opened Resources icons indicate the type of resource. (These will appear in the Opened by list box of the Open Resources dialog box.)

Opened file —
Named pipe —
Print job in a print spooler —
Resource of an unrecognized type —

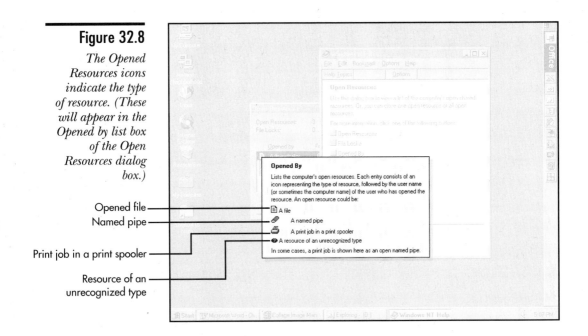

Exploring Replication

NT Workstation 4 has a directory replication feature that can duplicate directories. In NT Server, the replication service can operate in two modes: exporting directories from NT Server 4 to other servers or workstations, or importing directories from other servers or workstations to NT Server 4. NT Workstation 4 doesn't support export replication; that is, it can't be the source of the duplicated directory. NT Workstation 4 can, however, import replicated directories from other computers. The following sections tell you how.

The source of the directories that contain the original copy is called the *export server*. The target of the replication where the directory(s) is copied is called the *import computer*. NT Workstation 4 can be an import computer but not an export server.

Replication Uses

Objective F.3

Replication has any number of uses, but four stand out in particular. You can replicate a directory as a fault tolerance method. The duplicate directory (hopefully on a different computer) provides a backup copy of the original. This feature is the equivalent of a mirrored drive; any changes to the directory ripple through to the replicated copy on the import computer. Of course, NT Workstation 4 must be connected before the changes can propagate back to your workstation from the export server.

Replication also is useful for providing load distribution. If you have services that depend on access to a particular directory or set of directories, having multiple copies of this file in different locations spreads out the load as network users access this file. This can help improve network performance and enable more network users to access the directory's contents.

Replication also ensures data consistency when consistency is necessary. You could, for example, replicate system configuration files to ensure that the working environment of all users on a network is the same. Or you could replicate a database held locally on NT Workstation 4 to make sure that everyone on a network has access to the same data set at the same time.

Finally, you can take a replicated directory on the road with you. When you get the chance, you can call in for Remote Access Services (RAS) and perform a Dial-Up Networking connection. Then you can update your data. Directory replication is one of the major features that made Lotus Notes such a popular groupware application.

Managing Replication

The Server dialog box is used to configure replication using machine accounts. A domain can serve as the export server or import computer. If a domain is named as the import computer, all computers in the domain will have access to the replicated directory in the target. Because NT Workstation 4 is the primary focus here, you won't be using the domain feature as an import computer (just NT Workstation 4) or as an export server (NT Workstation 4 cannot play that role.) But you should be aware of the capabilities in NT Server that are lacking in the Workstation version of the operating system.

When you export or import using a domain on a WAN, you often experience problems at the bridge between networks. In this case, you're better off specifying individual computers by name. If you export replicated directories across a bridge to NT Workstation 4, for example, you should name the import computer(s). When you import replicated directories across a bridge, name the export server in place of the domain name.

The Replicator Account

Before you can configure NT Workstation 4 as an import computer, you need to create a user account in the Backup Operators group under any name other than "Replicator," which is a reserved group name.

To create a replicator account, follow these steps:

1. On the Start menu, choose the User Manager command from the Administrative Tools folder in Programs.

2. Choose User, New User.

3. Fill in the Username (account name), Full Name (person's real name), and Description fields of the New User dialog box, as shown in figure 32.9.

Objective C.1

Figure 32.9

The New User dialog box is where you can create the replicator account.

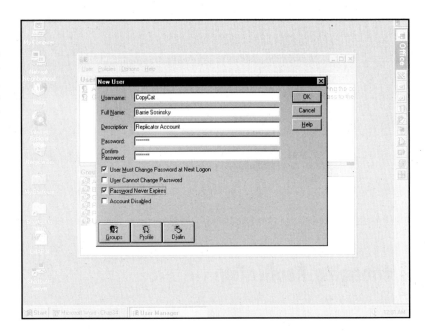

4. Enter the password twice in the Password and Confirm Password text boxes.

5. Enable the Password Never Expires check box and disable the User Must Change Password at Next Logon check box.

6. Click on the Groups button to open the Group Memberships dialog box (see fig. 32.10.)

7. Click on the Replicator group in the Not Member Of list box to highlight it.

8. Click on the Add button to move that group into the Member Of list box.

9. Click on OK twice to return to the User Manager dialog box.

10. Click on Close to close the User Manager dialog box.

Figure 32.11 shows the User Manager dialog box with the new replicator account, "CopyCat," added to it. You want to have the Directory Replicator service log on to your replicator account automatically. To set that up, you must specify the action in the Services dialog box.

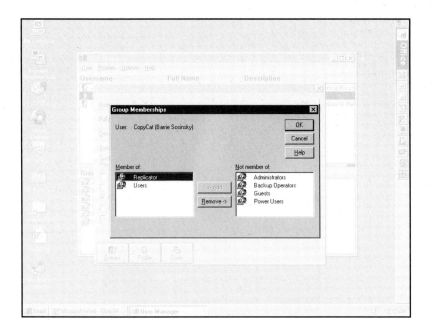

Figure 32.10

The Group Memberships dialog box enables you to create the replicator group into which you can place specific accounts.

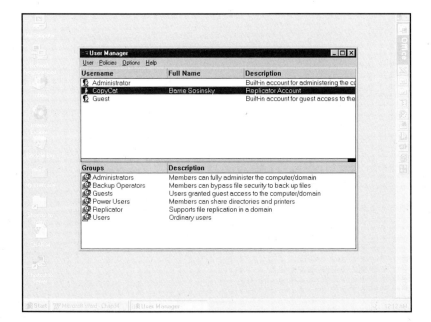

Figure 32.11

The User Manager dialog box shows the new replicator account.

Objective

B.5

To specify the directory replication account, follow these steps:

1. Open the Services dialog box in the Control Panel (see fig. 32.12) and select Directory Replicator in the Service list box.

2. Click on the Startup button to open the Service dialog box (see fig. 32.13).

Figure 32.12

Select the Directory Replicator service in order to configure its behavior.

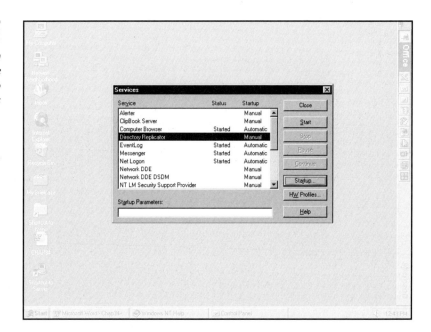

3. Click on the Automatic radio button in the Startup Type area.

4. Specify the replicator account in the This Account text box.

5. Enter the password in the Password and Confirm Password text boxes.

6. Click on OK to close the Service dialog box. If NT Workstation 4 can add the account as the default replication account, it posts the alert box shown in figure 32.14. This works for a specific account but not for a system account.

7. Click on Close to close the Services dialog box.

The replicator account should have a password that never expires, and it should be available at all times so that replication can take place unattended. Create this special account in the User Manager, which you can find in the Administrative Tools folder.

After you specify the account to use to log on when performing directory replication, you can specify which directories to import. NT Workstation 4 uses the replicator account you just specified to automatically log on to the network and to import the directories you specify.

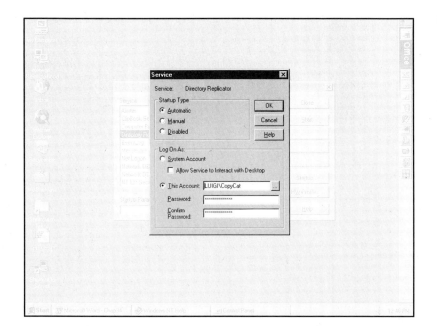

Figure 32.13

The Service dialog box is where you can specify the startup characteristics of a service.

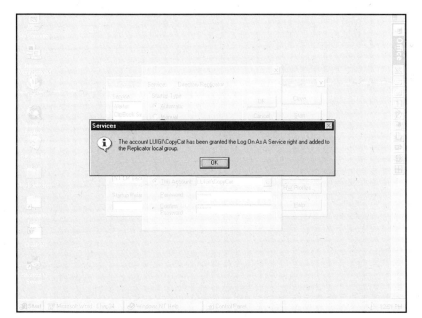

Figure 32.14

This alert box indicates that the rights were granted to add the account as a default replication account.

Exporting from NT Server

Only NT Server can be an export server. Importing computers can be Windows NT Server, NT Workstation, or OS/2 LAN Manager. Windows 95, Windows for Workgroups, Windows 3.1, MS-DOS, and Macintosh client computers cannot be import computers in a directory replication scheme.

When you export directories from one operating system to another, if the NTFS file system is used on the export server, you must use that same file system on the import computer.

To configure the directory replication services on NT Server, follow these steps:

1. Open the Server dialog box and click on the Replication button to open the Directory Replication dialog box (see fig. 32.15).

Figure 32.15

NT Server's Directory Replication dialog box enables you to configure a directory replication scheme.

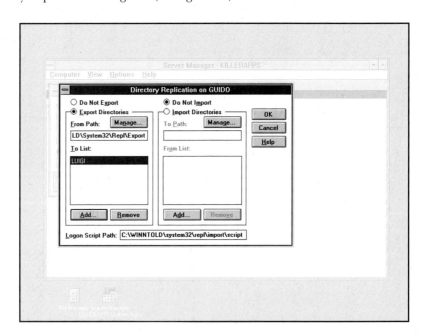

2. Select the Export Directories radio button and enter the name of the path you want to export (or leave the default path if that's the directory you want to use).

3. Click on Add under the To List box to view the Select Domain dialog box (see fig. 32.16).

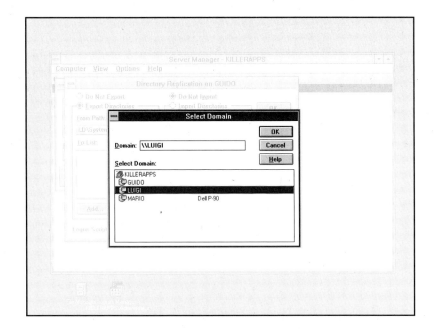

Figure 32.16

NT Server's Select Domain dialog box enables you to determine the domain of the computer that will serve as the import computer.

4. Double-click on the domain your workstation is in, click on your workstation's name, and then click on OK.

5. Click on OK to set up your replication.

6. Choose File, Exit (or press Alt+F4) to close the Server Manager.

Before you can replicate a directory from NT Server to NT Workstation, the directory on the Server must grant Full Control to the Replicator local group. Otherwise, files that are copied contain improper permissions. An error event is posted with an "access denied" label. You won't be able to work with that directory in NT Workstation 4.

The Manage button in NT Server's Directory Replication dialog box enables you to specify which subdirectories you want to export in the Manage Exported Directories dialog box (see fig. 32.17). Use this dialog box to manage locks, monitor stabilization status, and set subtree replication status for exported directories.

You also might notice a Logon Script Path text box at the bottom of the Directory Replication dialog box. A *logon script* is a batch file(s) that can be run when a particular user account logs on. These scripts are assigned as part of a user's profile, and the system looks for that logon script. In NT Server 3.51, you will find the replication export logon script in C:\WINNT35\SYSTEM32\REPL\EXPORT\SCRIPTS. An import logon script exists in the same path but in the \IMPORT\SCRIPTS subdirectory.

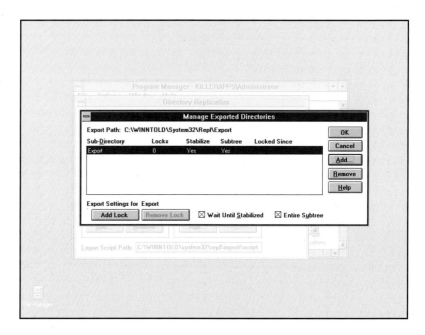

Figure 32.17

*NT Server's
Manage Exported
Directories dialog
box is where you
specify which
subdirectories in
the export server to
export.*

The three options in the Manage Exported Directories dialog box for NT Server are
these:

◆ **Add Lock button.** A lock prevents a subdirectory from being exported.
Multiple locks can be applied, but only a single lock is needed to prevent
export. There is also a Remove Lock button for this option.

◆ **Wait Until Stabilized check box.** The Wait Until Stabilized check box
checks for the last file modification time and waits two minutes from that time
before it replicates the change in the replicated directory on your workstation.
The default is to not wait.

◆ **Entire Subtree check box.** This exports all the contents of a directory.
If you don't check this option, only the top directory is replicated; all other
subdirectories are ignored during replication.

When you set up NT Server for export to an NT Workstation 4, you are counting on
NT Server to be configured properly for the replication. The replicator machine
account must exist, and the replicator service must be enabled on NT Server.

Importing to NT Workstation 4

With NT Workstation 4, you can configure your computer as an import computer.
An *import computer* is the recipient of replicated directories from an export server. An
import computer can import directories from one or more export servers and can
import from domain names and specific machine accounts.

Setting up NT Workstation 4 to import replicated directories is similar to the procedure in the preceding sections.

To specify import options, follow these steps:

1. Create the replicator account, add it to the Replication local group, and configure the account to automatically start up as you saw in previous sections.

2. Open the Server dialog box and click on the Replication button.

3. In the Directory Replication dialog box (see fig. 32.18), click on the Import Directories radio button.

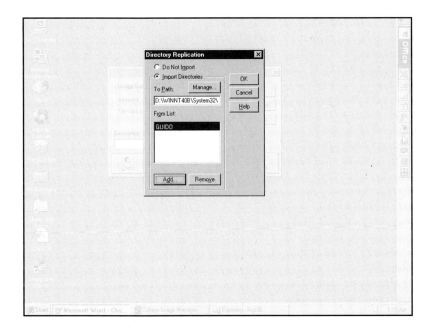

Figure 32.18

NT Workstation 4's Directory Replication dialog box enables you to set import options.

4. Click on Add to open the Select Domain dialog box.

5. Double-click on the Domain name, then click on OK to add the domain to the From List in the Directory Replication dialog box; or, double-click on a server or workstation name that you want to add to the list.

6. In the To Path text box, enter the folder you want to import.

7. Click on the Manage button to view the Manage Imported Directories dialog box (see fig. 32.19).

Figure 32.19

NT Workstation 4's Manage Imported Directories dialog box enables you to determine which directories to import.

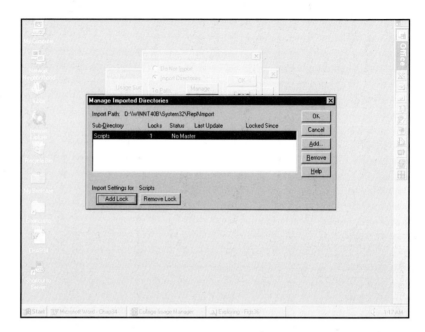

8. Add any subdirectories desired to the list and use the Add Lock button to apply locks.

9. Click on the OK buttons three times to back out to the Server dialog box and close it.

You will notice several differences between the Directory Replication and Manage Imported Directories dialog boxes for NT Workstation 4 and those shown previously for NT Server version 3.51. First, because you can only import directories in NT Workstation 4, the export section is absent from NT Workstation 4's Directory Replication dialog box. Additionally, you cannot specify the stabilization or subtree options that you saw previously for NT Server. You can, however, apply a lock on subdirectories involved in replication so that they aren't replicated on NT Workstation 4.

You have seen how to use the Server dialog box to view and modify services provided by NT Workstation 4 to a network. When you modify services—and particularly when you remove those services or a user(s) from those services—it's a good idea to provide them with an alert message. Doing so enables users to close their work without potentially losing valuable data. The next section tells you how to create alerts in NT Workstation.

Generating Alerts

NT Workstation 4 posts alerts whenever critical system events occur. When your hard drive is full, for example, you get an error when you try and write a file to disk. Most of the events you see are related to system events, security, hardware errors, or resource usage; but the range of events that generate alerts is wide.

Using the Server dialog box, you can send alerts of your own fashion to users whenever you choose. You have seen numerous examples throughout this chapter of why doing this can be useful. When you disconnect a user or close a resource, an alert can help users connected to your workstation to close their work safely. Messages are not stored and will time out if the destination computer is not on or properly configured.

Before you can send alerts, the Alerter service must be turned on in NT Workstation 4. Both sending and receiving computers must have the Messenger services on. Only NT, Windows 95, Windows for Workgroups, and OS/2 clients install the Messenger service on a network as part of their standard installation. Therefore, you can't use this service to send alerts to any Windows 3.1, MS-DOS, or Macintosh clients on a network.

Microsoft offers the Workgroup Connection client software for MS-DOS workstations that provide network connection. The Workgroup Connection, however, doesn't include the Messenger Service. If you install the Microsoft Network Client 3.0 for DOS, you can install the "Network Client and Load Pop-Up" option (which provides the Messenger service for MS-DOS clients) during the installation.

Now that you've seen why sending alerts is important, the following two sections look at how to build a list of users who will receive the alerts and how to send alerts.

Notification List

From the Server dialog box in Control Panel, click on the Alerts button to open the Alerts dialog box (see fig. 32.20). The Alerts dialog box enables you to build a notification list for the administrative alerts you want to send.

Objective B.5

To add recipient(s) to the notification list, follow these steps:

1. Open the Server dialog box and click on Alerts to open the Alerts dialog box.

2. In the New Computer or Username text box, enter the username or computer name for the user or machine account of a connected user.

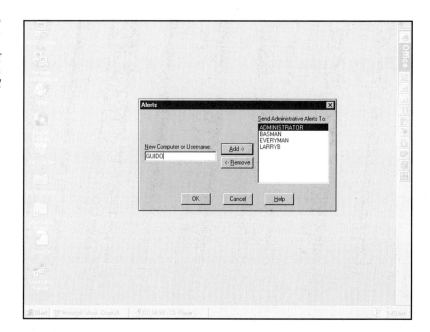

3. Click on Add to move that name into the Send Administrative Alerts To list box.

4. Or, to remove a name from the notification list, click on the name to highlight it, and then click on Remove.

5. Click on OK.

Sending Alerts

If you are familiar with NT Server, you know that you can send custom alerts to the users on your notification list whenever you want. In NT Server, that feature is supported using the Send Message command on the Computer menu. NT Workstation 4 doesn't support this feature. That is, you cannot send administrative alerts with a custom message at a time of your choosing. However, automatic system messages due to some failure, resource, or security problem will be posted.

You might wonder why Microsoft chose not to support this feature in NT Workstation 4. In a word (excuse me, two words), Microsoft Exchange. With built-in messaging support, you now can send any message you want to users on the network when you have Exchange installed. And that's what you should do before you disconnect a user or turn off a resource.

End Note: NT Workstation 4 is a robust network citizen. Although it doesn't have all the capabilities of NT Server, Workstation can perform many network server functions. Other users can connect to your computer and to shared resources. You can view connected users and open resources in the Server dialog box. You also can disconnect users and close resources if you want.

Additionally, NT Workstation 4 can serve as an import computer in a directory replication scheme. If you have a directory that you want mirrored from another source, you can set up replication so that any changes in the source directory are reflected automatically in the target directory on your workstation. Replication can be very useful for providing fault tolerance, ensuring data uniformity, and distributing network loading.

Test Your Knowledge

1. When a Windows NT 4 Workstation is acting as a server, the maximum number of connections is _____.

2. Choose the correct statement(s) about the Server dialog box in Control Panel:

   A. You can view the number of sessions and open file.

   B. You can view the name of the computer for a connected user.

   C. You can move a connected user to a specific folder.

   D. You can set a time limit for a connection.

3. To see which users are accessing a printer on your computer, use:

   A. The Shares button on the Server dialog box

   B. The In Use button on the Server dialog box

   C. The Printer's dialog box

   D. The Users button on the Server dialog box

4. To replicate from NT Server to NT Workstation (select all correct statements):

   A. Set up replication on the Workstation; it is established by default on the Server.

   B. Make the user who performs replication a member of the Backup group.

   C. Both computers must be using the same file system.

   D. You can only replicate entire drives or first-level folders.

5. For replication, which computers cannot import?

    A. Those running Windows NT Server

    B. Those running Windows for Workgroups

    C. Those running Windows 95

    D. Those running OS/2 Lan Manager

6. To set up a replicator account for a user:

    A. Open User Manager.

    B. Open the Server icon in Control Panel.

    C. Open the Replication icon in Control Panel.

    D. Turn on Replication in the Services icon in Control Panel and enter the user name in the dialog box that appears.

7. Choose the correct statement(s) about alerts in NT 4 Workstation:

    A. A user with Administrative permissions can send an alert at any time to all computers on the network by entering text in the Alert Text dialog box.

    B. An alert can be sent to any user on the domain.

    C. An alert can be sent to a computer without specifying a user name.

    D. To be able to send alerts, set up the sending computer for messaging services.

Test Your Knowledge Answers

1. 10

2. A

3. B,D

4. C

5. B,C

6. A

7. B,C

Chapter Snapshot

This chapter serves as a brief tour of the features of Windows NT Server 4. If you are connected to a Windows NT server, this chapter will give you an explanation of some of the features in Windows NT Server and help you understand its relationship to the tasks you perform at your workstation. The following list details the major topics covered in this chapter:

Windows NT
Workstation 4

CHAPTER 33

Understanding NT Server Functions

The Server version of Windows NT 4 is essentially the same as the Workstation with additional features that enable it to perform as a versatile network operating system (NOS).

Microsoft's approach offers significant advantages. With Windows NT, you can buy workstation and server products that are managed nearly identically and run the same programs and software drivers. You buy only the capabilities you need for a given computer.

> **Note** One of the advantages of Windows NT Server 4 is its capacity for managing multiple hard drives efficiently, providing plenty of disk space for software and user data. This efficiency provides a productive network environment. Windows NT Workstation can support disk striping, but only simple stripe sets and volume sets. NT Server supports striping with parity (RAID5) and mirroring.

Understanding NT Server and NTFS

Objective A.3

Servers running Windows NT 4 should use NTFS as the file system. The FAT file system is not well suited to network servers. It cannot compensate for disk flaws dynamically and cannot secure individual files against intruders who have access to the server.

NTFS compensates for disk flaws by using a hot-fix feature that automatically redirects data in a bad disk sector to a substitute sector.

NTFS also builds security into the file system. A user cannot gain access to an NTFS file volume by rebooting the computer from a bootable floppy disk. To access the files, the user must have a suitable user account and password.

Understanding Server Security

Windows NT can be configured to maintain a very high level of security. By using the proper procedures, it is possible to configure a network using Windows NT computers for Class C2 security, defined by the U.S. Department of Defense as providing "discretionary (need-to-know) protection and, through the inclusion of audit capabilities, for accountability of subjects and the actions they initiate."

Windows NT Workstation security is based on securing shared network directories. The same set of access restrictions is assigned to entire directory structures.

Security on Windows NT Server is much more detailed. Administrators of Windows NT Server determine who will access the network and what resources they are permitted to access, right down to the file level.

Windows NT Server includes several security classes that solve LAN administrator headaches. Consider the problem of the nightly tape backup. To be any good, the backup should include every file on the server. Ordinarily, access to all files requires full administrator privileges, something you probably don't want to give to the night operators who might perform the backups. Windows NT Server provides a special set of user privileges that enables tape-backup operators to archive files without having the run of the network.

Windows NT design incorporates some clever security features. You will notice, for example, that you log on to a Windows NT computer by pressing Ctrl+Alt+Del. This is a protection against programs that attempt to intercept passwords by substituting themselves for the normal logon program. The Ctrl+Alt+Del sequence always directly invokes the logon routine in the Windows NT program, an area of Windows NT that cannot be modified by users or intruders.

Another aspect of Windows NT security is that computers as well as users must be permitted access to the network. Even though a user has a valid user account, he can't log on from any Windows NT computer. The computer itself must have been added to the network. A network can be made very secure if it consists only of Windows NT computers.

Administering Server Tasks

More than 90 percent of Windows NT administration tasks are performed with graphics utilities. As a result, the user interface is consistent, and there are few commands to remember. The GUI interface is not the only feature that makes an administrator's life easier, however. Windows NT Server provides all the necessary tools to run a network easily and efficiently.

Centralized User Profiles

Windows NT computers can utilize profiles that describe a user's working environment in great detail. Centralized profiles fall into the following two categories:

◆ **Roaming profiles.** Locally stored user profiles can be modified by individual users. The same modifiable profile can be stored on the network. The advantage of a centralized user profile is that users can access their profiles from any Windows NT computer on the network, effectively making their working environment portable. For this reason, Microsoft refers to these centralized user profiles as roaming profiles.

◆ **Mandatory profiles.** Mandatory profiles cannot be modified by users. They enable an administrator to define a fixed environment for use by individuals or by large groups. A mandatory profile is a great means of ensuring that all users in a particular area have a common working environment. Support is greatly simplified.

For more information on user profiles, see Chapter 5, "Understanding Profiles."

Domain-Based Administration

Without some form of enterprise-based server administration, multiserver LANs are nightmares for an administrator. In some LAN environments, when you create a user account on one server, you must create an identical account on every other server on the LAN. Two accounts are more than double the work because you must cross-check everything, and problems inevitably arise.

Windows NT Server supports an administration approach that organizes multiple servers into commonly managed groups called domains. Users are not just given logon privileges for an individual computer. Instead, their account gives them permission to log on to the domain and gain access to all computers in the domain based on their security permissions. Domain-based administration significantly reduces the effort required to manage user accounts.

Domains also operate well in conjunction with workgroups. Therefore, Windows NT Workstation and Windows for Workgroups users can continue to use peer-to-peer resource sharing even as they access central resources on Windows NT servers.

Directory Replication

To distribute files to several servers, Windows NT Server uses directory replication. *Directory replication* enables you to designate an export directory on one server and import directories on other computers. The directory-replication service takes responsibility for ensuring that any changes made to files in the export directory are copied to all import directories without any further intervention from the administrator. Directory replication is a great way to distribute newsletters, phone lists, and commonly used files.

Task Scheduling

Frequently, you'll have a need to schedule tasks at particular times. The most common example of a timed task is kicking off the nightly tape backup job, which usually happens in the wee hours of the morning when users have gone home. Windows NT has a built-in task scheduler that can execute batch and EXE files at any designated time on a daily, weekly, or monthly basis.

Remote Administration

All network management functions can be performed remotely, enabling administrators to manage all your network servers from a central location.

Auditing

The more critical a LAN becomes, the more the administrators will want to keep track of who is using and abusing it. Windows NT Server has a powerful, easy-to-use auditing feature that can track many file-access and printing activities. This data can be exported in formats used by spreadsheet and database programs, enabling administrators to track events and statistics on your network.

Remoteboot Service

Windows NT Server is capable of starting Windows and DOS computers across the network. The Remoteboot Service is a program that runs on Windows NT Server as part of the Network Administration services.

Network Client Services

A number of programs in Windows NT Server are used to provide direct services to clients (workstations). These programs are part of the Windows NT Server feature called Network Client Administrator. For example, installation of the NT Workstation 4 operating system can be performed from the server (the jargon for this is a push installation). In fact, the server can install Windows for Workgroups, network clients for DOS workstations, and the client software for client/server applications such as Microsoft Exchange Server.

Understanding Network Protocols

To communicate with each other, computers must employ protocols (methods of communicating) that they agree upon. Windows NT includes support for the three most common protocol suites on LANs: NetBEUI, Novell's IPX/SPX, and TCP/IP.

> **Note** The Network Basic Input Output System (NetBIOS) has long been the standard API for Microsoft network products. Windows applications access the network through the NetBIOS interface. With Windows NT 4, Microsoft has ensured that NetBIOS applications can network with all three transport protocols that are included. NetBIOS applications can participate in a wide area network (WAN) using the NetBIOS over the TCP/IP feature of Windows NT Server 4, for example.
>
> The Network Driver Interface Specification (NDIS) is a key component in Windows protocol support. NDIS enables a computer to run multiple protocol stacks over the same network adapter card. NDIS effectively enables a computer to speak three network protocol languages at the same time.

NetBEUI

NetBIOS Extended User Interface (*NetBEUI*) was designed for running NetBIOS applications on local area networks. NetBEUI is a simple, efficient protocol that provides high performance on small networks. Prior to Windows NT version 3.5, NetBEUI was the standard protocol for Microsoft networking products. NetBEUI is a great fit for Windows networking because it is essentially a plug-and-play protocol that requires no configuration other than a simple installation procedure. Therefore, NetBEUI is well-suited to networks such as Windows for Workgroups that will be administered by end users.

NetBEUI has a significant limitation in that it cannot be routed and therefore cannot be used as the transport protocol on larger, multisegment networks.

NWLink

NWLink is an NDIS-compliant transport that is network-compatible with Novell's IPX/SPX protocols. The IPX/SPX protocols offer high performance and good functionality on WANs while requiring little setup. NWLink conforms to TDI and can support applications written to the NetBEUI and Windows Sockets APIs.

Another benefit of NWLink is that it simplifies the interface between Windows NT and NetWare networks. Windows NT includes NetWare client software and a NetWare gateway, both of which enable Windows network users to access resources on NetWare LANs.

TCP/IP

TCP/IP is named after the two primary protocols in the suite: Transmission Control Protocol (TCP) and Internet Protocol (IP). TCP/IP is a robust, versatile protocol suite that is the most widely used protocol suite in terms of the number of devices networked and the variety of supported computers. TCP/IP is particularly well suited to WANs when reliable delivery is essential.

The downside of TCP/IP is that considerable and expert work is required to install and maintain the networks. A plug-and-play TCP/IP network does not exist.

That said, Microsoft has made great strides in simplifying TCP/IP installation and support. Administrators are burdened with relatively little manual editing of configuration files, which is a significant consumer of labor on TCP/IP networks. The Domain Host Configuration Protocol (DHCP) can be used to assign addresses dynamically to network computers. The Windows Internet Naming Service (WINS) also adds a relatively low-effort naming service (NetBIOS name resolution) to Windows NT networks using TCP/IP.

TCP/IP is installed on a network in several situations:

◆ The network must interface with a TCP/IP network, such as the Internet.

◆ TCP/IP is the corporate standard.

◆ TCP/IP is required to connect devices on the network.

◆ The network includes two or more network segments, possibly in a WAN, and requires a protocol that can be routed among the segments.

NetWare Interoperability

NetWare is still a major player in the LAN world because it is highly desirable for other LAN products to enable users to access resources on NetWare LANs.

Windows NT Server provides the following two means of connecting users to NetWare servers:

◆ Client software that can access NetWare servers. Prior to Windows NT 4, only bindery-mode servers, such as NetWare 3.12, were supported. Starting with Windows NT 4, support has been added for NetWare Directory Services as well.

◆ A NetWare gateway that enables users to access NetWare services as if the services resided on the Windows network.

Companies sometimes have NT Servers and NetWare Servers on the same network. If everything is configured properly, it should be transparent to users as they move to different servers when choosing software applications.

Providing Internet Services

Windows NT Server has become a popular platform for providing services on TCP/IP Internets. That popularity is likely to increase because Windows NT Server 4 includes the Internet Information Server (IIS). This bundled software makes adding these three services to your TCP/IP network extremely easy:

◆ World Wide Web

◆ FTP server

◆ Gopher server

End Note: For server administrators, the *Windows NT Resource Kit*, the official reference on Windows NT, is an important resource. This kit consists of four fat volumes, and although there is some overlap with the product manuals, the Resource Kit contains material that is unavailable anywhere else. The Resource Kit also contains a CD-ROM and several floppy disks of programs and data.

continues

Microsoft's TechNet is another important resource. A subscription to TechNet costs only $295 a year, a profound bargain in the computer-support industry. Each month you receive two CDs containing product and troubleshooting databases, program patches, and information about Microsoft programs.

Test Your Knowledge

1. What are the available file systems for Windows NT 4 Server?

2. To log on to Windows NT Server you must do which of the following?
    A. Have a registered logon name, and your computer must be registered separately
    B. Have a registered logon name that includes the name of the computer
    C. Log on from a registered computer, and register your user name after you have logged on to the server
    D. All of the above

3. To see the same desktop and configuration of a workstation no matter which computer you're using, you must have what kind of profile on the server?

4. A Mandatory Profile is which of the following?
    A. The default profile that is installed when you install Windows NT Workstation
    B. The profile that loads when you reboot after you make changes to your profile
    C. The backup profile that is used when you use "Last Good Configuration" during bootup
    D. A profile that cannot be changed by the user

5. In a multiserver domain, administrators can administer the domain from which of the following?
    A. Any server on the domain
    B. Only from the Primary Domain Controller
    C. Only a Primary Domain Controller or a Backup Domain Controller
    D. Only from his/her workstation

6. What is the network protocol needed to access the Internet?

7. What is the network protocol needed to communicate with a Novell NetWare server?

Test Your Knowledge Answers

1. FAT and HPFS
2. A
3. Roaming
4. D
5. A
6. TCP/ICP
7. IPX/SPX

PART IX

Appendices

Windows NT Command Reference

Although you can execute most Windows NT functions by using graphic utilities, there are several reasons to use commands at the command prompt. Sometimes entering a command at the command prompt is faster than starting a graphic utility and stepping through menus.

Of greater significance is that you can put most commands into batch files, which are useful for building login scripts, executing commands at scheduled times, or performing functions when events are triggered. The UPS command, for example, can be configured to execute a batch file before shutting down Windows NT. Although the commands are described in online help displays, they are summarized here for your convenience.

The following conventions are used to indicate command syntax:

◆ **Bold** letters are used for words that must be typed as shown.

◆ *lowercase italic* letters are used for items that vary, such as file names.

◆ The [and] characters surround optional items that can be supplied with the command.

◆ The { and } characters surround lists of items. You may select one of the items in the list.

◆ The | character separates items in a list. Only one of the items can be included with the command.

For example, in the following syntax, you must type NET COMMAND and either OPTION1 or OPTION2. Supplying a name is optional.

```
NET COMMAND [name] {OPTION1 | OPTION2}
```

◆ The [...] characters mean you can repeat the previous item, separating items with spaces.

◆ The [,...] characters mean you can repeat the previous item, separating items with commas or semicolons, not spaces.

◆ When service names consist of two or more words, enclose the service name in quotation marks. For example, NET PAUSE "FTP SERVER" pauses the FTP server service.

Special Command Symbols

Windows NT's command prompt includes some special symbols that you can use to issue multiple commands on a single line. Some of the symbols enable you to create command lines that act conditionally based on the results of a previous command. Table A.1 shows these command symbols.

TABLE A.1
Windows NT Command Symbols

Symbol	Meaning
>	Redirects the output from one command into another, or to a file or device
>>	Appends the output from one command into another, or to a file or device
<	Redirects data from a file into a command
&	Separates multiple commands on a single line
()	Groups commands together
; and ,	Separates parameters from one another
^	Allows you to use a special command symbol literally
&&	Causes the following command to execute only if the preceding command is successful
‖	Causes the following command to execute only if the preceding command is *not* successful

Grouping Multiple Commands

To group multiple commands, simply separate them with a single ampersand. For instance, **DIR & TYPE \AUTOEXEC.BAT** will cause both commands to execute, one after the other.

You also can use the double ampersand (&&) and double pipe (‖) symbols to process multiple commands on a single line conditionally. For instance, consider the actions of the following commands:

◆ **TYPE C:\NOFILE && DIR **

Since the file C:\NOFILE does not exist, the DIR command is not executed.

◆ **TYPE C:\NOFILE ‖ DIR **

In this case, even though C:\NOFILE does not exist, the DIR command executes because the double pipe symbol processes the next command upon failure of the first command.

You can get more sophisticated with the conditional processing symbols and the parentheses grouping operators. For instance, consider this command:

TYPE C:\NOFILE &&(ECHO SUCCESS) ||(ECHO FAILURE)

If the file C:\NOFILE does not exist, the word FAILURE will be echoed to the screen. If C:\NOFILE does exist, the word SUCCESS will be echoed. You can further extend this idea by adding additional commands within each of the parentheses groups, remembering to separate each command with the appropriate symbol. Using these tools, you can build quite complex and "intelligent" commands.

Redirecting Output

Most commands display results on your screen. You can capture these results into a file using special *redirection symbols*. The most basic redirection symbol is the greater-than sign (>), which takes the output of a command and redirects it to a file or device. For example, this command directs the output of a DIR command into a file called LISTING.TXT:

DIR >LISTING.TXT

The greater-than symbol used to redirect data in this way will create the file named if it does not already exist. Also, you can redirect output to a device. For instance, this command redirects the same data to the printer:

DIR >PRN:

 DIR >PRN: may not immediately result in a printout from your printer, as no form feed character was added to the output, and most page-oriented printers require this to complete printing a page. You would have to press the Form Feed button on your printer to cause the data to complete printing.

You can use the double greater-than symbol to append output into an existing file. Text already in the file is maintained. For instance, this command will add the new directory information to the existing LISTING.TXT file, while maintaining the results of the first directory listing:

DIR C:\WINNT >>LISTING.TXT

There is also a case where you can redirect information *from* a file into a command. For instance, you can create a text file that contains responses needed by a command, and then direct that file's contents into the command, which causes the text in the file to be sent to the command just as if you had typed the input yourself. Follow these steps to create such a file and test it:

1. At the command prompt, type **COPY CON TEST** and press Enter. Your cursor moves to a new, blank line.

2. Type **12:05** and press Enter. Your cursor moves to the next line.

3. Save the file by pressing the F6 key and pressing Enter. `^Z` appears on the screen as you press F6, and then when you press Enter, you see the message `1 File(s) Copied`.

4. Test the redirection by typing **TIME <TEST** and pressing Enter. The time command's output appears displaying the correct time, and then the new time, 12:05, being set. You return to the command prompt automatically, and the time has been changed to 12:05.

Windows NT Command

The following commands are organized alphabetically. For each command, you see a description of what the command does, the syntax of the command (some commands have more than one syntax), a description of the command options, and any notes that pertain to the command.

ACLCONV

Migrates OS/2 HPFS386 permissions to NTFS volumes.

Syntax

```
ACLCONV /DATA:datafile /LOG:logfile [/NEWDRIVE:drive] [/DOMAIN:domain]
[/CODEPAGE:n]

ACLCONV /LIST /LOG:logfile /CODEPAGE:n
```

Options

/DATA:datafile   Specifies the LAN Manager backacc data file.

/LOG:logfile   Specifies the logging file.

/NEWDRIVE:drive   Specifies the drive to which permissions are restored. You only need to use this parameter when permissions are backed up from a different drive letter.

/DOMAIN:domain   Restricts the search for account names to the specified domain.

/CODEPAGE:n   Specifies the Code Page to be used with the backacc data file.

/LIST   Lists the contents of the specified log file.

APPEND

APPEND lets programs open files stored in other directories as if they were in the current directory.

Syntax

APPEND [;] [[drive:]path[;...]] [/X:{on | off}][/PATH:{on | off}] [/e]

Options

;   Cancels the appended directories.

[drive:]path   Specifies the drive and directory that you want to append to the current directory. Using semicolons to separate directories; you can reference multiple directories.

/X:{on | off}   Controls whether the MS-DOS subsystem searches appended directories for executable programs called by the program you initially run. /X:on means that appended directories are searched for executable files. If you use the /X:off switch, on the other hand, appended directories are not searched for executables. To use /X:on, you must use it the first time you use the APPEND command after starting your system.

/PATH:{on | off}   Stipulates whether a program searches appended directories for a data file when the path is already included with the name of the file for which the program is looking. By default this is set to /PATH:on.

/E   Using /E creates an environment variable named APPEND, which contains the list of appended directories. You must use this switch the first time you use APPEND after starting your system. This command is useful to view appended directories with the SET command.

ARP

ARP (short for Address Resolution Protocol) displays and modifies the IP-to-Ethernet or Token Ring address translation tables. This command is available only when the TCP/IP protocol is installed.

Syntax

```
arp -A [internet_addr] [-N [interface_addr]]

arp -D internet_addr [interface_addr]

arp -S internet_addr ethernet_addr [interface_addr]
```

Options

-A   Queries TCP/IP and displays the current ARP entries. If you specify *internet_addr*, only the IP and physical addresses for the specified address display.

-G   Same as -A.

internet_addr   Lets you enter an IP address using decimal notation.

-N   Displays the ARP entries for the network interface specified by *interface_addr*.

interface_addr   If present, specifies the IP address of the interface whose translation table should be modified. By default, the first applicable interface is used.

-D   Deletes an entry specified by *internet_addr*.

-S   Adds an entry to the ARP cache that associates the IP address *internet_addr* with the physical address *ethernet_addr*. Physical addresses are specified with six hexadecimal bytes separated by hyphens. The IP address is specified using standard dotted decimal notation.

ethernet_addr   Specifies a physical Ethernet address.

ASSOC

Displays or modifies associations for file extensions.

Syntax

```
ASSOC [.extension[=[filetype]]]
```

Options

.extension   Specifies the file extension to associate with a specified file type.

Filetype   Specifies the file type to associate with the file extension.

Notes

Typing ASSOC with no options displays the current extension assignments. To view the associations for a given extension, type **ASSOC .EXT**.

You can delete associations by typing **ASSOC .EXT=**.

AT

One of the more useful commands in Windows NT, AT lets you schedule commands or programs to run at a given time.

Syntax

```
AT [\\computername] [[ID] [/DELETE [/YES]]
AT [\\computername] time [/INTERACTIVE] [/EVERY:date[,...] | /NEXT:date[,...]]
"command"
```

Options

\\computername   Lets you specify a remote computer. By default, commands are scheduled for the local computer.

ID   Each scheduled command has an identification number assigned to it. You can specify this ID number when deleting scheduled commands.

/DELETE   When specified with the ID parameter, the scheduled command is deleted. If you use /DELETE without ID specified, all scheduled commands are deleted.

/YES   Forces a yes answer to all queries from the system when deleting scheduled events.

Time   Specifies when the command is to run, in 24-hour notation using hours:minutes. For example, 13:45 specifies 1:45 p.m.

/INTERACTIVE   When you specify /INTERACTIVE, the scheduled command can interact with the user of the computer.

/EVERY:date[,...]   Causes the command to run on every specified day of the week or month. You specify the date as one or more days of the week, using the abbreviations M, T, W, Th, F, S, and Su. Specify particular days of the month using the numbers 1 through 31. You can enter multiple dates by separating each date entry with a comma. By default, if you do not specify the date, the current day of the month is used.

/NEXT:date[,...]   Causes the command to run on the next occurrence of the day specified. Specify date as one or more days of the week using the abbreviations M, T, W, Th, F, S, and Su. Specify days of the month using the numbers 1 through 31.

"command"   In place of *command*, you specify the program or batch file that you want to run at the scheduled time.

When the command requires a path as an argument, use the absolute path, that is, the entire pathname beginning with the drive letter. If command is on a remote computer, specify the server and sharename, rather than a remote drive letter. You may use quotation marks around the command, whether you are using AT at the command line or in a batch file. If the command includes switches that are used by both the command and AT, you must enclose the command in quotation marks.

Notes

The Schedule service must be running in order for AT to function. By default, Schedule must be started manually using the Services icon in the Control Panel.

Type AT with no options to list all scheduled commands.

When you need to pass a path to the scheduled command as a parameter, make sure you use the absolute path and not a relative path reference, and include the drive letter.

Surround *command* with quotation marks when you need to pass a parameter to the *command* that conflicts with one of the AT parameters.

If the command you specify is not an executable file, you must precede the command with CMD /C. For example, you would use `CMD /C TYPE file.ext > C:\CAPTURE.TXT` because TYPE is a command that is part of the command processor and is not a free-standing executable file.

ATTRIB

ATTRIB lets you view or change file attributes (flags). With it, you can affect a file's or directory's read-only, archive, system, or hidden attributes.

Syntax

`ATTRIB [+R|-R] [+A|-A] [+S|-S] [+H|-H][[drive:][path] filename] [/S]`

Options

[[drive:][path] filename]   Specifies the file or directory with which you want to work.

+R   Sets the read-only attribute.

-R   Clears the read-only attribute.

+A   Sets the archive attribute.

-A   Clears the archive attribute.

+S   Sets the system attribute.

-S   Clears the system attribute.

+H   Sets the hidden attribute.

-H   Clears the hidden attribute.

/S   Use this parameter to process files in the current directory and all subdirectories that match the given file specification.

Notes

ATTRIB with no parameters displays all of the files in the current directory and their attributes. ATTRIB can be used to quickly view the present hidden files.

BACKUP

Backs up files. You can use either the hard drive or disks as your destination, or go from one disk to another.

Syntax

```
BACKUP source dest-drive: [/S] [/M] [/A][/F[:size]] [/D:date [/T:time]]
[/L[:[drive:][path]logfile]]
```

Options

source   *Source* is the specification of the files you want to back up. Use whatever combination of drive letter, directory, and file specification that's appropriate to select the desired files.

dest-drive: This parameter controls the drive onto which you will back up the files.

/S   Specifies that all subdirectories will be included in the backup.

/M   Selects files that have their archive attribute set (in other words, have been modified since the last backup). Also turns off the archive attribute of the backed-up files.

/A   Appends the selected backup files to an existing backup set.

/F[:size]   Forces the destination disk to be formatted at the size you specify with *:size*. *:Size* is specified as kilobytes per disk. Acceptable values for *:size* are 160, 180, 320, 360, 720, 1200, 1440, and 2880.

/D:date   Selects only files modified on or after the specified date to be backed up.

/T:time   Selects only files modified on or after the specified time to be backed up.

/L[:[drive:][path]logfile]   Creates a log file of the backup.

Notes

The backup files are stored as BACKUP.*nnn* and CONTROL.*nnn* (one each per disk used). Nnn is replaced with a number starting with 001. The stored files are marked read-only, so you will have to use ATTRIB to remove the read-only attribute if you wish to erase them from the destination disk (or, alternately, you must format the disk).

CACLS

Displays or changes the access control lists (ACLs) of files.

Syntax

```
CACLS filename [/T] [/E] [/C] [/G user:perm] [/R user [...]]
 [/P user:perm [...]] [/D user [...]]
```

Options

filename   Specifies the desired files.

/T   Modifies the ACLs of specified files in the current directory and all subdirectories.

/E   Edits the ACL instead of replacing it.

/C   Causes CACLS to continue changing ACLs instead of stopping on errors.

/G user:perm   Grants access rights to the specified user. The *perm parameter* can be:

◆ R   Read

◆ C   Change (write)

◆ F   Full control

/R user   Revokes a user's access rights.

/P user:perm   Replaces a user's access rights. The *perm* parameter can be set to:

◆ N   None

◆ R   Read

◆ C   Change (write)

◆ F   Full control

/D user   Denies access.

CHDIR (CD)

Changes the current working directory.

Syntax

```
CD [/D] [drive:][path] [..]

CHDIR [/D] [drive:][path] [..]
```

Options

/D   Lets you change the current drive. For instance, if you are in the D:\ directory, you can type CD /D E:\TEST to move to the specified drive and directory. Without the /D parameter the CD command will not change drives.

[drive:][path]   Specifies the drive and directory to which you want to change.

[..]   This parameter specifies that you want to move to the parent directory of your current working directory.

CHKDSK

Checks the integrity of a disk and displays a status report. CHKDSK can also repair errors on a disk.

Syntax

```
CHKDSK [drive:][[path] filename] [/F] [/V] [/R]
```

Options

none   Typing CHKDSK with no parameters causes the current drive to be checked.

drive: Specifies the drive that you want to check.

[path] filename   Specifies files that you want to check for fragmentation.

/F   Repairs (fixes) errors that are found. In order to use this option, CHKDSK must be able to lock the disk. If it cannot, it offers to perform the repair the next time you start the system.

/V   Displays a verbose listing of all files checked.

/R   Locates bad sectors and recovers readable information. The disk must be locked.

Notes

If CHKDSK cannot lock the drive because it is locked by another process, it offers to perform the check the next time you start the computer.

You must be a member of the Administrators group to use CHKDSK on one of the system's hard disks.

CLS

Clears the screen.

Syntax

```
CLS
```

CMD

Invokes the Windows NT Workstation command processor.

Syntax

```
CMD [/X | /Y] [/A | /U] [/Q] [/T:fg] [ [/C | /K] string]
```

Options

/C   Executes the command you specify and then stops.

/K   Executes the command you specify and then continues.

/Q   Turns console echoing off.

/A   Outputs ANSI characters.

/U   Outputs Unicode characters.

/T:fg   Lets you set the foreground and background colors for the command processor you invoke. See the COLOR command for more details.

/X   Turns on extensions to CMD.EXE. These extensions give you more control over the command processor.

/Y   Turns off extensions to CMD.EXE.

string   Specifies the command you want carried out.

Notes

The CMD.EXE command interpreter is a special program that accepts and executes commands that you type at the command prompt.

You can use the EXIT command to exit the current command processor and return to the previous one.

COLOR

Lets you set the foreground and background colors for the command prompt.

Syntax

COLOR bf

Options

bf   Two hexadecimal digits that contain the foreground and background color selection; *b* specifies the background color and *f* specifies the foreground color. Use the following values for the color selections:

0   Black

1   Blue

2   Green

3   Aqua

4   Red

5   Purple

6   Yellow

7   White

8   Gray

9   Light blue

A   Light green

B   Light aqua

C   Light red

D   Light purple

E   Light yellow

F   Bright white

Notes

If you specify no arguments, the default colors are restored.

COMP

Compares the contents of two files or sets of files byte-by-byte.

Syntax

COMP [first_set] [second_set] [/D] [/A] [/L] [/N=number] [/C]

Options

first_set   Controls the file specification for the first set of files to be compared.

second_set   Controls the file specification for the second set of files to be compared.

/D   Uses decimal format to display any differences. By default, differences are displayed using hexadecimal.

/A   Displays differences as ASCII characters.

/L   Shows the line number in which a difference is detected, instead of the file offset.

/N=number   Restricts the comparison to the first *number* of lines.

/C   Looks for differences in a case-insensitive manner.

Notes

COMP can compare files on the same drive or on different drives, in the same directory or in different directories. As COMP compares the files, it displays their locations and filenames.

COMPACT

Shows the compression level of files and directories. You can also change the compression level using COMPACT.

Syntax

```
COMPACT [/C] [/U] [/S] [/I] [/F] [/L] filename
```

Options

none   If you specify no parameters, you are shown the compression state of the current directory and files.

/C   Compresses a directory or file.

/U   Uncompresses a directory or file.

/S   Applies the chosen action (/C or /U) to all subdirectories.

/I   Ignores errors.

/F   If a file is left in a partially compressed or uncompressed state, you must use the /F option to force the file to be compressed or uncompressed.

filename   Contains the file specification for the COMPACT command.

Notes

COMPACT only works on NTFS-formatted disks.

CONVERT

Lets you dynamically convert a drive from FAT to NTFS while maintaining the data on the drive.

Syntax

```
CONVERT [drive:] /FS:NTFS [/V] [/NAMETABLE:filename]
```

Options

drive   Selects the drive to be converted.

/FS:NTFS   Tells CONVERT to use NTFS as the destination file system type.

/V   Selects verbose mode in which all messages are displayed during conversion.

/NAMETABLE:filename   If you have trouble converting some files that have unusual file names, you can create a name translation table in the root directory of the drive to be converted, and can specify that file name with the */NAMETABLE* option.

Notes

Converts FAT volumes to NTFS. You cannot convert the current drive. If CONVERT cannot lock the drive, it will offer to convert it the next time the computer reboots.

COPY

Copies files.

This command can also be used to combine files. When more than one file is copied, Windows NT displays each file name as the file is copied.

Syntax

```
COPY [/A|/B] source [/A|/B] [+ source [/A|/B] [+...]] [destination [/A|/B]]
[/V] [/N] [/Z]
```

Options

source   Contains the file specification of the source files.

destination   Contains the file specification (or simply the drive or drive and directory) of the destination files.

/A   Copies files in ASCII mode, in which copying stops when an End-Of-File marker
(Ctrl+Z) is found. If you use /A at the beginning of the command (before *source*),
ASCII mode is used for all files until a /B switch is encountered in the command.

/B   Copies files in binary mode, which copies the entire contents of a file. Binary
mode is the default for the COPY command.

/V   Verifies that the copies are accurate.

/N   Forces COPY to create short file names for the destination.

Notes

You can combine files with the copy command by using the + character. For instance,
typing **COPY** *file1+file2 file3* creates a file called *file3* that is the contents of *file1* plus
file2. When you combine files in this way, COPY uses ASCII mode by default, which
terminates copying of each file at any EOF markers. To combine files regardless of
EOF markers, use the /B parameter, like this: **COPY** */B file1+file2 file3*.

DATE

Displays or sets the system date.

Syntax

```
DATE [mm-dd-yy]
```

Options

[mm-dd-yy]   Lets you set the current date using numbers in place of the options, where *mm* is the month, *dd* is the day number, and *yy* is the year. You can specify *yy* with four numbers to specify the century.

DEL (ERASE)

Erases files.

Syntax

DEL [drive:][path] filename [;...] [/P] [/F] [/S] [/Q] [/A[:attributes]]

ERASE [drive:][path] filename [;...] [/P] [/F] [/S] [/Q] [/A[:attributes]]

Options

[drive:][path] filename   Contains the file specification of the files to be erased.

/P   Prompts for confirmation before erasing the specified file.

/F   Causes (forces) read-only files to be erased.

/S   Causes subdirectories to be included for the given file specification.

/Q   Runs the DEL command in quiet mode, which does not ask for confirmations.

/A:attributes   Lets you control which files are erased based on their attributes. Attributes allowed are R (read-only), H (hidden), S (system), and A (archive). You can also use a hyphen to exclude files with a specified attribute. For instance, DEL *.* /A:-A will not erase files with the archive flag set.

Notes

DEL and ERASE work exactly the same. Both are commands that are internal to the command processor CMD.EXE.

DIR

Displays the contents of a directory.

Syntax

```
DIR [drive:][path][filename] [;...] [/P] [/W] [/D] [/A[[:]attributes]][/
O[[:]sortorder]] [/T[[:]timefield]] [/S] [/B] [/L] [/N] [/X]
```

Options

none   If you do not use any parameters with the DIR command, the current directory's contents are displayed.

[drive:][path]   Specifies the drive and directory for display.

[filename]   Lets you restrict the display of files to those specified by *[filename]*.

/P   Pauses the display after each screen fills and waits for a key to be pressed.

/W   Displays files using a wide format, which lists only file names, not associated information.

/D   Uses the wide format, but sorts files by column.

/A[[:] attributes]   Restricts the display to only those files specified by *attributes*. Use /A to cause files with the system or hidden attributes set to be displayed. Attributes allowed are D (directories), R (read-only), H (hidden), S (system), and A (archive). Precede the attribute with a hyphen to cause files that do *not* have the attribute set to be displayed.

/O[[:] sortorder]   Lets you sort the display of files. By default, sorting is not performed. Allowed *sortorder* values are: N (by name), E (by extension), D (by date), S (by size), and G (lists directories first, followed by files). You can precede any of these values with a hyphen to reverse the sort order.

/T[[:] timefield]   Specifies which time is shown in the display. Allowed values are C (creation date), A (last access date), and W (last write date).

/S   Applies the DIR command to all subdirectories.

/B   Displays only file names.

/L   Outputs the display using lowercase letters.

/N   Forces the long version of each file name to appear at the right side of each file's display.

/X   Changes the order of the output display so that short names are shown to the immediate left of the long file names.

Notes

You can use **DIR filespec /S** to search a volume for a given file.

DISKCOMP

Compares the contents of two disks, byte-by-byte.

Syntax

```
DISKCOMP drive1 drive2
```

Notes

DISKCOMP is used to compare two disks to ensure that they are an exact match. The comparison does not compare files to one to another, but instead compares the contents of each disk byte-by-byte.

If drive1 and drive2 are the same, the system prompts you to swap the disks during the comparison.

DISKCOPY

Copies one disk to another, making an exact duplicate of the source disk onto the destination disk.

Syntax

```
DISKCOPY drive1: drive2: [/V]
```

Options

drive*x*: Specifies the drive letter of the source and destination disks.

/V   Causes the copy to be verified after it is written.

Notes

Using the /V parameter slows the copy process, but ensures a reliable copy.

DISKPERF

Enables and disables the system disk performance counters.

Syntax

```
DISKPERF [-Y|-N] [\\computername]
```

Options

none   With no parameters specified, DISKPERF reports whether the disk performance counters are enabled or disabled.

-Y   Turns on the system disk performance counters at the next system boot.

-N   Turns off the system disk performance counters at the next system boot.

\\computername   Lets you control the disk performance counters on a remote computer over a network.

Notes

By default, the system disk performance counters are not enabled. Enabling them may cause a slight performance decrease on the system, which can be noticeable on 80486-based systems. On Pentium-based systems, the overhead is negligible.

DOSKEY

DOSKEY recalls Windows NT Workstation commands and lets you edit them. You also use DOSKEY to create command macros.

Syntax

```
DOSKEY [/REINSTALL] [/LISTSIZE=size] [/MACROS:[ALL | exename] [/HISTORY]
[/INSERT|/OVERSTRIKE] [/EXENAME=exename] [/MACROFILE=filename][MACRONAME=[text]]
```

Options

/REINSTALL   Clears the command history.

/LISTSIZE=size   This parameter lets you control the maximum number of commands held by DOSKEY.

/MACROS   Using this parameter displays a list of all defined DOSKEY macros.

ALL   Causes a list to be displayed of all executable-based macros.

exename   If you define an executable file with this parameter, any DOSKEY macros attached to that executable are displayed.

/HISTORY   Using the /HISTORY parameter displays all commands stored in the DOSKEY buffer.

/INSERT | /OVERSTRIKE   These two parameters, which are mutually exclusive, control whether command-line editing defaults to overstrike mode or insert mode.

/EXENAME=exename   Controls the executable file for which the DOSKEY macro runs.

/MACROFILE=filename   This parameter lets you define a file that contains predefined DOSKEY macros, which are installed automatically.

MACRONAME=[text]   This parameter defines a new macro. *MACRONAME* is the name of the macro that, when typed at the command prompt, executes the commands given in *[text]*. Leaving the *[text]* portion blank erases the macro.

DOSONLY

Ensures that only MS-DOS programs are called from a command prompt using COMMAND.COM.

Syntax

DOSONLY

Notes

If you use a COMMAND.COM prompt (COMMAND.COM is the MS-DOS command interpreter, as opposed to Windows NT's CMD.EXE command interpreter), you can use the DOSONLY command to ensure that only MS-DOS programs are run at the prompt. This command is provided so that MS-DOS TSR (Terminate-and-Stay-Ready) programs are not interfered with.

FIND

Finds a specified string within one or more text files.

Syntax

FIND [/V] [/C] [/N] [/I] "search_string" [[drive:][path]filename[...]]

Options

"search_string"   This parameter contains the characters for which you are searching. You need to enclose the search string in quotation marks.

[drive:][path] filename   Specifies the file names to be searched.

/V   This parameter displays all of the lines in the searched text files that do *not* contain the search string.

/C   Using this parameter causes FIND to display a count of matching lines, rather than the contents of any matching lines.

/N   Specifying /N causes the line number to be displayed before the found text.

/I   Causes the search to be case-insensitive.

Notes

FIND can be used as a filter program, into which you can redirect output from other programs through it. For instance, you can type this command to find all files on a drive that contain the letters WIN: **DIR *.* | FIND "WIN"**

FINDSTR

FINDSTR lets you search files for matching text using either literal or regular expressions.

Syntax

```
FINDSTR [/B] [/E] [/L] [/C:string] [/R] [/S] [/I] [/X] [/V] [/N] [/M] [/O]
[/G:file] [/F:file] strings files
```

Options

/B   Causes a match if the target is at the beginning of a line.

/E   Causes a match if the target is at the end of a line.

/L   Causes a literal search of the search strings.

/C:string   Causes *string* to be used as the literal search string.

/R   Causes FINDSTR to search using regular expressions. See the following notes for regular expression characters allowed.

/S   Causes FINDSTR to search files in the current directory and any subdirectories.

/I   Causes the search to be case-insensitive.

/X   Displays lines that match the search exactly.

/V   Displays lines that do *not* match the search strings.

/N   Displays the line number before the matching text.

/M   Displays only the file names of files that contain matching strings.

/O   Displays the file offset before the matching text.

/G:file   Uses *file* to read in the search strings.

/F:file   Uses a list of files in *file* to define what files are searched.

Strings   The search strings.

Files   The files to be searched.

Notes

You can use spaces to separate multiple search strings.

FINDSTR can use regular expressions to search for matches in an ASCII file. Regular expressions let you use wildcards and other pattern-matching notation as part of the search text.

Allowed notations for a regular expression include:

.   Matches any single character

*   Matches any number of occurrences of the previous character.

^   Matches at the beginning of a line

$ Matches at the end of a line

[class]   A set of allowed characters can be surrounded by square brackets to match those allowed characters.

[^class]   Preceding the allowed characters with a carat (^) causes those characters to be excluded from a match in that position.

[x-y]   You can define a range of matching characters with a hyphen.

\x   At times, you may need to match one of the regular expression metacharacters, such as a carat or an asterisk. To do this, precede the character for which you are searching with the \x metacharacter, which stands for escape.

FORCEDOS

Forces a program to run in the MS-DOS subsystem.

Syntax

```
FORCEDOS [/D directory] filename [parameters]
```

Options

/D   Causes the current directory to be used to run the program.

Filename   Controls which program is started.

[parameters]   Contains any parameters that need to be passed to the program you run.

Notes

There are some programs that are written both for OS/2 and MS-DOS. Such programs are called dual-mode applications, or sometimes FAPI applications (Family API). By default, Windows NT runs such programs using the OS/2 subsystem. The use of FORCEDOS causes such programs to be run in the MS-DOS subsystem instead.

FORMAT

Formats a disk.

Syntax

```
FORMAT drive: [/FS:file-system] [/V[:label]] [/A:unitsize] [/Q] [/F:size]
[/T:tracks /N:sectors] [/1] [/4] [/8]
```

Options

drive: Controls which drive is formatted. By default, the drive is formatted based on the drive type.

/FS:file-system   Controls the file system that is used. You can choose from FAT and NTFS file systems.

/V:[label]   If specified, sets the volume label for the formatted disk.

/A:unitsize   Controls the allocation unit size on NTFS-formatted disks. Unitsize can be 512, 1024, 2048, and 4096.

/Q   Performs a quick format in which the root directory and the file table is erased. The entire disk is not formatted. Use this command to quickly erase a previously formatted disk.

/F:size   Controls the size of the disk that is formatted. Size represents kilobytes and can be 160, 180, 320, 360, 720, 1200, 1440, 2880, and 20.8 (for optical disks).

/T:tracks   Controls the number of tracks formatted on the disk.

/N:sectors   Controls the number of sectors formatted per track.

/1   Causes a single-sided disk to be formatted.

/4   Quickly formats a 5.25-inch, 360K, DSDD disk in a 1.2 MB drive.

/8   Formats a 5.25-inch disk with 8 sectors per track for use on systems running MS-DOS versions up to 2.0.

Notes

You must be a member of the Administrators group on the machine on which you want to format a hard disk.

FTYPE

Displays and controls file types used for associations.

Syntax

```
FTYPE [filetype[=[command]]]
```

Options

filetype   Controls the type of file for which you want to display its associations.

command   Controls the command to be used when a file of *filetype* is launched.

Notes

Type FTYPE with no parameters to display all defined and associated file types.

HELP

Displays help on a particular command.

Syntax

```
HELP [command]
```

Options

[command]   Specifies the name of the command for which you want help.

Notes

The HELP command is synonymous with typing /? after a particular command. For instance, DIR /? displays the same output as HELP DIR.

INSTALL

Loads Windows NT memory-resident programs.

Syntax

```
INSTALL=[drive:][path] filename [command-parameters]
```

Options

[drive:][path] filename   Specifies the name of the program that you want to load.

command-parameters   Enter parameters for the memory-resident program in place of *command-parameters*.

LABEL

Sets the volume label for a disk.

Syntax

```
LABEL [drive:] label
```

Options

[drive:]   The drive for which you want to change the label.

label   The label you want to assign to the drive.

MKDIR (MD)

Creates a directory.

Syntax

```
MKDIR [drive:]path
MD [drive:]path
```

Options

[drive:]   The drive on which you want to create a directory.

path   The complete pathname that you want to create.

MOVE

Moves files from one directory to another.

Syntax

```
MOVE [source] [target]
```

Options

source   Controls the path and name of the files to be moved.

target   Controls the destination path to which the files will be moved.

NET ACCOUNTS

NET ACCOUNTS is used to maintain the user account database. It can modify password and logon requirements for all user accounts. When entered without options, NET ACCOUNTS displays current settings for the password, logon limitations, and domain information for the logged-on account.

Syntax

```
NET ACCOUNTS    [/FORCELOGOFF:{minutes | NO}]
                [/MINPWLEN:length]
                [/MAXPWAGE:{days | UNLIMITED}]
                [/MINPWAGE:days]
                [/UNIQUEPW:number]
                [/DOMAIN]
NET ACCOUNTS [/SYNC] [/DOMAIN]
```

Options

/FORCELOGOFF:{minutes | NO}   *Minutes* specifies the number of minutes a user has before being automatically logged off when an account expires or logon hours expire. NO is the default value and specifies that forced logoff will not occur.

/MINPWLEN:length   *Length* specifies the minimum number of characters required for a password. The range is 0–14 characters. The default is 6 characters.

/MAXPWAGE:{days | UNLIMITED}   *Days* specifies the maximum number of days a password is valid. The UNLIMITED option specifies that no limit is imposed. /MAXPWAGE cannot be less than /MINPWAGE. The range is 1–49710 and the default is 90 days.

/MINPWAGE:days   *Days* specifies the minimum number of days that must pass before a user can change his password. A value of 0 specifies no minimum time. The range is 0–49,710; the default is 0 days. /MINPWAGE cannot be greater than /MAXPWAGE.

/UNIQUEPW:number   Specifies that the user's passwords must be unique for the number of changes specified by *number*. The maximum value is 8.

/SYNC   Synchronizes the account database.

/DOMAIN   Include this option to perform the specified action on the entire domain controller instead of the current computer. This option is effective only when executed on Windows NT computers that are members of a domain.

Examples

NET ACCOUNTS can be used to make global changes to all user accounts. To change the minimum wait before changing passwords for all user accounts to five days, enter the following command:

```
NET ACCOUNTS /MINPWAGE:5
```

Notes

NET ACCOUNTS options to take effect, the following conditions must be true:

◆ User accounts must have been set up by the User Manager or the NET USER command.

◆ The Net Logon service must be running on all domain controllers.

NET COMPUTER

Use this command to add or delete computers from the domain database.

Syntax

```
NET COMPUTER \\computername {/ADD | /DEL}
```

Options

\\computername   The name of the computer to be added or deleted.

/ADD   Adds the computer to the domain.

/DEL   Deletes the computer from the domain.

Example

To add a computer named GEORGE to the domain, enter this command:

```
NET COMPUTER \\GEORGE /ADD
```

Notes

This command is available only with Windows NT Server.

NET CONFIG SERVER

Use this command to display or change settings for the Server service. This command affects only the server on which it is executed.

You must be logged on as a member of the Administrators group to configure the server.

Syntax

```
NET CONFIG SERVER    [/AUTODISCONCONNECT:time]
                     [/SRVCOMMENT:"text"]
                     [/HIDDEN:{YES|NO}]
```

Options

/AUTODISCONNECT:time   *Time* specifies the number of minutes an account can be inactive before it is disconnected. Specify -1 to never disconnect. Range is 1–65,535 minutes. Default is 15.

/SRVCOMMENT:"text"   The message in "*text*" specifies a message that is displayed along with the server in many Windows NT screens. The message can consist of up to 48 characters and must be enclosed in quotation marks.

/HIDDEN:{YES | NO}   Determines whether a computer name is advertised in listings of servers. YES hides the server. NO includes the server name in lists.

Example

To display the current configuration for the Server service, type NET CONFIG SERVER without parameters.

NET CONFIG WORKSTATION

This command displays and changes settings for the Workstation service.

Syntax

```
NET CONFIG WORKSTATION    [/CHARCOUNT:bytes]
                          [/CHARTIME:msec]
                          [/CHARWAIT:sec]
```

Options

/CHARCOUNT:bytes   Specifies the *bytes* of data that are collected before data is sent to a communication device. If /CHARTIME is set, Windows NT relies on the value that is satisfied first. Range is 0–65,535 bytes. Default is 16 bytes.

/CHARTIME:msec   *msec* specifies the number of milliseconds that Windows NT collects data before sending it to a communication device. If /CHARCOUNT is set, Windows NT relies on the value that is satisfied first. Range is 0–65,535,000 milliseconds. Default is 250 milliseconds.

/CHARWAIT:sec   Specifies the number of seconds Windows NT waits for a communication device to become available. Range is 0–65,535 seconds. Default is 3,600 seconds.

Notes

To display the current configuration for the Workstation service, type NET CONFIG WORKSTATION without parameters.

NET CONTINUE

NET CONTINUE reactivates a Windows NT service that has been suspended by NET PAUSE.

Syntax

```
NET CONTINUE service
```

Options

service   Is any of the following paused services:

- ◆ FILE SERVER FOR MACINTOSH
- ◆ FTP SERVER
- ◆ LPDSVC
- ◆ NET LOGON
- ◆ NETWORK DDE
- ◆ NETWORK DDE DSDM
- ◆ NT LM SECURITY SUPPORT PROVIDER
- ◆ REMOTEBOOT
- ◆ REMOTE ACCESS SERVER
- ◆ SCHEDULE
- ◆ SERVER
- ◆ SIMPLE TCP/IP SERVICES
- ◆ WORKSTATION

NET FILE

Use this command to list ID numbers of files, to close a shared file, and to remove file locks. When used without options, NET FILE lists the open files on a server along with their IDs, path names, user names, and number of locks.

Syntax

```
NET FILE [id [/CLOSE]]
```

Options

id   The identification number of the file.

/CLOSE   Include this option to close an open file and remove file locks. This command must be typed from the server where the file is shared.

Notes

This command works only on computers running the Server service.

NET GROUP

This command adds, displays, or modifies global groups on servers. Enter the NET GROUP command without parameters to display the group names on the server.

Syntax

```
NET GROUP [groupname [/COMMENT:"text"]] [/DOMAIN]
NET GROUP groupname {/ADD [/COMMENT:"text"] | /DELETE} [/DOMAIN]
NET GROUP groupname username [...] {/ADD | /DELETE} [/DOMAIN]
```

Options

groupname   This parameter specifies the name of the group to add, expand, or delete. This parameter is also included when user names are to be added to or deleted from a group. Supply the group name alone to see a list of users in a group.

/COMMENT:"text"   This switch adds a comment of up to 48 characters, as specified by *text*. Enclose the text in quotation marks.

/DOMAIN   Include this switch to perform the operation on the primary domain controller of the current domain. Without the /DOMAIN switch the operation affects only the local computer.

username[...]   Specifies one or more user names to be added to or removed from a group. Multiple user name entries must be separated with a space.

/ADD   Adds a group to a domain or adds a user name to a group.

/DELETE   Removes a group from a domain or removes a user name from a group.

Examples

To view membership of the local group Server Operators, enter this command:

```
NET GROUP "SERVER OPERATORS"
```

To add a group named Blivet Engineers, you would use the following command:

```
NET GROUP "Blivet Engineers" /ADD
```

NET HELP

Use this command to display a help listing of the options available for any NET command.

Syntax

```
NET HELP command
```

or

```
NET command /HELP
```

Options

Help information is available for the following commands:

NET ACCOUNTS	NET HELP	NET SHARE
NET COMPUTER	NET HELPMSG	NET START
NET CONFIG	NET LOCALGROUP	NET STATISTICS
NET CONFIG SERVER	NET NAME	NET STOP
NET CONFIG WORKSTATION	NET PAUSE	NET TIME
NET CONTINUE	NET PRINT	NET USE
NET FILE	NET SEND	NET USER
NET GROUP	NET SESSION	NET VIEW

Notes

NET HELP command | MORE displays Help one screen at a time.

NET HELP SERVICES lists the network services you can start.

NET HELP SYNTAX explains how to read NET HELP syntax lines.

I ET HELPMSG

The NET HELPMSG command displays explanations of Windows NT network messages, including errors, warnings, and alerts. Type NET HELPMSG along with the 4-digit number of the Windows NT error. Although network error messages include the word NET (for example, NET1234), you do not need to include NET in the message# parameter.

Syntax

```
NET HELPMSG message#
```

Options

message#   The 4-digit number of the Windows NT message with which you need help.

I ET LOCALGROUP

Use this command to modify local groups on computers. Enter the NET LOCALGROUP command without parameters to list the local groups on the computer.

Syntax

```
NET LOCALGROUP [groupname [/COMMENT:"text"]] [/DOMAIN]
NET LOCALGROUP groupname {/ADD [/COMMENT:"text"] | /DELETE} [/DOMAIN]
NET LOCALGROUP groupname name [...] {/ADD | /DELETE} [/DOMAIN]
```

Options

groupname   *groupname* specifies the name of the local group to add, expand, or delete. Supply a group name without parameters to list users or global groups in the local group. If the group name includes spaces, enclose the name in quotation marks.

/COMMENT:"text"   This switch adds a comment of up to 48 characters, as specified by *text*. Enclose the text in quotation marks.

/DOMAIN   Include this switch to perform the operation on the primary domain controller of the current domain. Otherwise, the operation is performed on the local computer. By default, Windows NT Server computers perform operations on the domain. This option is effective only when executed on a computer that is a member of a domain.

name [...]   Specifies one or more user names or group names to be added to or removed from the local group. Multiple entries must be separated with a space. Include the domain name if the user is from another domain (Example: WIDGETS\CHARLES).

/ADD   Adds the specified group name or user name to a local group. User and group names to be added must have been created previously.

/DELETE   Removes a group name or user name from a local group.

Examples

To display the membership of the local group "Domain Admins," enter the following command:

```
NET LOCALGROUP "DOMAIN ADMINS"
```

To add the user Harold to the local group Widgets, enter the command:

```
NET LOCALGROUP WIDGETS HAROLD
```

NET NAME

The NET NAME command adds or deletes a messaging name at a computer. A messaging name is a name to which messages are sent. Use the NET NAME command without options to display names accepting messages at this computer.

A computer's list of names comes from three places:

◆ Message names, which are added with NET NAME.

◆ A computer name, which cannot be deleted. The computer name is added as a name when the Workstation service is started.

◆ A user name, which cannot be deleted. Unless the name is already in use on another computer, the user name is added as a name when you log on.

Syntax

```
NET NAME [name [/ADD | /DELETE]]
```

Options

name   The name of the user account that is to be added to names that will receive messages. The name can have as many as 15 characters.

/ADD   Adds a name to a computer. /ADD is optional. Typing NET NAME *name* is the same as typing NET NAME *name* /ADD.

/DELETE   Removes a name from a computer.

NET PAUSE

Use the NET PAUSE command to suspend a Windows NT service or resource. Pausing a service puts it on hold. Use the NET CONTINUE command to resume the service.

Syntax

```
NET PAUSE service
```

Options

service   The service to be paused. Please see the NET CONTINUE command for a list of services that can be paused.

Notes

If the Server service is paused, only users who are members of the Administrators or Server Operators groups will be permitted to log on to the network.

NET PRINT

Use this command to list print jobs and shared queues. For each queue, the command lists jobs, showing the size and status of each job, and the queue status.

Syntax

```
NET PRINT \\computername\sharename
          [\\computername] job# [/HOLD | /RELEASE | /DELETE]
```

Options

\\computername   Specifies the name of the computer sharing the printer queue(s).

sharename   Specifies the share name of the printer queue.

job#   Specifies the identification number assigned to a print job. Each job executed on a computer is assigned a unique number.

/HOLD   Assigns a "hold" status to a job so that it will not print. The job remains in the queue until it is released or deleted.

/RELEASE   Removes the "hold" status on a job so that it can be printed.

/DELETE   Removes a job from a queue.

Examples

To display active print jobs on a computer named Blivets, enter the following command:

```
NET PRINT \\BLIVETS
```

To hold job number 234 on the computer Blivets, for example, the command is

```
NET PRINT \\BLIVETS 234 /HOLD
```

NET SEND

This command sends messages to other users, computers, or messaging names on the network.

Syntax

```
NET SEND {name | * | /DOMAIN[:domainname] | /USERS} message
```

Options

name   Specifies the user name, computer name, or messaging name to which the message is sent. If the name contains blank characters, enclose the name in quotation marks.

*   An *, when substituted for *name*, sends the message to all the names in your group.

/DOMAIN[:domainname]   Specifies that the message should be sent to all users in the domain. If *domainname* is specified, the message is sent to all the names in the specified domain or workgroup.

/USERS   Sends the message to all users connected to the server.

message   The text to be sent as a message.

Examples

To send a message to everyone in a domain, type a command similar to the following:

```
NET SEND /DOMAIN:WIDGETS A message for everyone in Widgets
```

You can also specify a user (in this case, Mabel):

```
NET SEND MABEL A message for Mabel
```

Notes

The Messenger service must be running on the receiving computer to receive messages.

You can send a message only to a name that is active on the network.

NET SESSION

The NET SESSION command lists or disconnects sessions between the computer and other computers on the network. When used without options, NET SESSION displays information about all sessions running on the computer that currently has the focus.

Syntax

```
NET SESSION [\\computername] [/DELETE]
```

Options

\\computername   Lists the session information for the named computer.

/DELETE   Ends the session between the local computer and *computername*. All open files on the computer are closed. If *computername* is omitted, all sessions are ended.

Notes

This command works only when executed on servers.

NET SHARE

The NET SHARE command is used to share a server's resources with network users. Use the command without options to list information about all resources being shared on the computer. For each shared resource, Windows NT reports the device name(s) or path name(s) for the share along with any descriptive comment that has been associated with the share.

Syntax

```
NET SHARE    sharename
NET SHARE    sharename=drive:path
             [/USERS:number | /UNLIMITED]
             [/REMARK:"text"]
NET SHARE    sharename [/USERS:number | /UNLIMITED] [/REMARK:"text"]
NET SHARE    {sharename | devicename | drive:path} /DELETE
```

Options

sharename   Specifies the network name of the shared resource. Typing NET SHARE with a share name only displays information about that share.

devicename   Specifies one or more printers (LPT1 through LPT9) shared by *sharename*. Use this option when a printer share is being established.

drive:path   Specifies the absolute path of a directory to be shared. Use this option when a directory share is being established.

/USERS:number   Specifies the maximum number of users that will be permitted to simultaneously access the shared resource.

/UNLIMITED   Specifies that no limit will be placed on the number of users that will be permitted to simultaneously access the shared resource.

/REMARK:"text"   Associates a descriptive comment about the resource with the share definition. Enclose the text in quotation marks.

/DELETE   Stops sharing the resource.

Examples

To share the directory C:\APPLICATIONS with the share name APPS, enter the command:

```
NET SHARE APPS=C:\APPLICATIONS
```

You can limit the number of users who can access a share by using the /USERS options. The following example limits the number of users to 10:

```
NET SHARE APPS=C:\APPLICATIONS /USERS:10
```

To stop sharing the printer on LPT3, enter the following command:

```
NET SHARE LPT3: /DELETE
```

Notes

Printers must be shared with Print Manager. **NET SHARE** may be used to stop sharing printers.

NET START

Use the NET START command to start services that have not been started or have been stopped by the NET STOP command. Enter the command NET START without options to list running services.

Syntax

```
NET START [service]
```

Options

service   One of the following services to be stopped:

- ◆ ALERTER
- ◆ CLIENT SERVICE FOR NETWARE
- ◆ CLIPBOOK SERVER
- ◆ COMPUTER BROWSER
- ◆ DHCP CLIENT
- ◆ DIRECTORY REPLICATOR
- ◆ EVENTLOG
- ◆ FTP SERVER
- ◆ LPDSVC
- ◆ MESSENGER
- ◆ NET LOGON
- ◆ NETWORK DDE
- ◆ NETWORK DDE DSDM
- ◆ NETWORK MONITORING AGENT
- ◆ NT LM SECURITY SUPPORT PROVIDER
- ◆ OLE
- ◆ REMOTE ACCESS CONNECTION MANAGER
- ◆ REMOTE ACCESS ISNSAP SERVICE
- ◆ REMOTE ACCESS SERVER
- ◆ REMOTE PROCEDURE CALL (RPC) LOCATOR
- ◆ REMOTE PROCEDURE CALL (RPC) SERVICE
- ◆ SCHEDULE
- ◆ SERVER

- ◆ SIMPLE TCP/IP SERVICES

- ◆ SNMP

- ◆ SPOOLER

- ◆ TCP/IP NETBIOS HELPER

- ◆ UPS

- ◆ WORKSTATION

These services are available only on Windows NT Server:

- ◆ FILE SERVER FOR MACINTOSH

- ◆ GATEWAY SERVICE FOR NETWARE

- ◆ MICROSOFT DHCP SERVER

- ◆ PRINT SERVER FOR MACINTOSH

- ◆ REMOTEBOOT

- ◆ WINDOWS INTERNET NAME SERVICE

Notes

To get more help about a specific service, see the online Command Reference (NTCMDS.HLP).

When typed at the command prompt, service names of two words or more must be enclosed in quotation marks. For example, NET START "COMPUTER BROWSER" starts the computer browser service.

NET START can also start network services not provided with Windows NT.

NET STATISTICS

NET STATISTICS displays the statistics log for the local Workstation or Server service. Used without parameters, NET STATISTICS displays the services for which statistics are available.

Syntax

```
NET STATISTICS [WORKSTATION | SERVER]
```

Options

SERVER   Displays the Server service statistics.

WORKSTATION   Displays the Workstation service statistics.

NET STOP

NET STOP stops Windows NT services.

Syntax

```
NET STOP service
```

Options

service   Is a Windows NT service that can be stopped. See the NET START command for a list of eligible services.

Notes

NET STOP can also stop network services not provided with Windows NT.

Stopping a service cancels any network connections the service is using. Because some services are dependent on others, stopping one service can stop others.

You must have administrative rights to stop the Server service.

The EVENTLOG service cannot be stopped.

NET TIME

Use the NET TIME command to synchronize the computer's clock with that of another computer or domain. NET TIME can also be used to display the time for a computer or domain. When used without options or a Windows NT Server domain, it displays the current date and time at the computer designated as the time server for the domain.

Syntax

```
NET TIME [\\computername | /DOMAIN[:domainname]] [/SET]
```

Options

\\computername   Specifies the name of the computer with which you want to check or synchronize.

/DOMAIN[:domainname]   Specifies the domain with which to synchronize time.

/SET   Synchronizes the computer's time with the time on the specified computer or domain.

NET USE

This command connects a computer to a shared resource or disconnects a computer from a shared resource. NET USE without options lists the computer's connections.

Syntax

```
NET USE [devicename | *]
        [\\computername\sharename[\volume] [password | *]]
        [/USER:[domainname\]username]
        [[/DELETE] | [/PERSISTENT:{YES | NO}]]
NET USE [devicename | *] [password | *]] [/HOME]
NET USE [/PERSISTENT:{YES | NO}]
```

Options

devicename   Specifies a name to assign to the connected resource or specifies the device to be disconnected. Device names can consist of the following:

- ◆ disk drives (D through Z)

- ◆ printers (LPT1 through LPT3)

Type an asterisk (*) instead of a specific device name to assign the next available device name.

\\computername   Specifies the name of the computer controlling the shared resource. If the computer name contains blank characters, enclose the double backslash (\\) and the computer name in quotation marks. The computer name may be from 1 to 15 characters long.

\sharename   Specifies the network name of the shared resource.

\volume   Specifies the name of a volume on a NetWare server. You must have Client Services for NetWare (Windows NT Workstations) or Gateway Service for NetWare (Windows NT Server) installed and running to connect to NetWare servers.

password   Is the password needed to access the shared resource.

*   Produces a prompt for the password. The password is not displayed when you type it at the password prompt.

/USER   Specifies a different user name with which the connection is made.

domainname   Specifies another domain. If *domainname* is omitted, the current logged on domain is used.

username   Specifies the user name with which to log on.

/HOME   Connects a user to his home directory.

/DELETE   Cancels a network connection and removes the connection from the list of persistent connections.

/PERSISTENT{YES | NO}   YES saves connections as they are made, and restores them at next logon. NO does not save the connection being made or subsequent connections; existing connections will be restored at next logon. The default is the setting used last.

Examples

To connect drive M to a directory with the share name APPS on the server BLIVETS, which has the password LETMEIN, you would type the following:

```
NET USE M: \\BLIVETS\APPS LETMEIN
```

If you do not want the password displayed on the screen, include an * in the password position as follows, so that you will be prompted to enter one:

```
NET USE M: \\BLIVETS\APPS *
```

You can access a share that is secured to another user account if you have a valid password. To access the share using Mabel's account, enter this command:

```
NET USE M: \\BLIVETS\APPS * /USER:MABEL
```

NET USER

NET USER creates and modifies user accounts on computers. When used without switches, it lists the user accounts for the computer. The user account information is stored in the user accounts database.

Syntax

```
NET USER [username [password | *] [options]] [/DOMAIN]
NET USER username {password | *} /ADD [options] [/DOMAIN]
NET USER username [/DELETE] [/DOMAIN]
```

Options

username   Specifies the name of the user account to add, delete, modify, or view. The name of the user account can consist of up to 20 characters.

password   Assigns or changes a password for the user account. A password must meet the minimum length requirement set with the /MINPWLEN option of the NET ACCOUNTS command. The password can consist of up to 14 characters.

*   Displays a prompt for the password, which is not displayed when typed.

/DOMAIN   Specifies the action that should be performed on the primary domain controller of the current domain.

This parameter is effective only with Windows NT Workstation computers that are members of a Windows NT Server domain. By default, Windows NT Server computers perform operations on the primary domain controller.

/ADD   Adds a user account to the user accounts database.

/DELETE   Removes a user account from the user accounts database.

options   The available options are shown in table A.2.

TABLE A.2
Available Options

Option	Description
/ACTIVE:{YES | NO}	Activates or deactivates the account. When the account is deactivated, the user cannot access the server. The default is YES.
/COMMENT:"text"	Adds a comment consisting of up to 48 characters, as specified by *text*. Enclose the text in quotation marks.
/COUNTRYCODE:nnn	*nnn* is the numeric operating system country code that specifies the language files to be used for a user's help and error messages. A value of 0 signifies the default country code.
/EXPIRES:{date | NEVER}	Specifies a date when the account will expire in the form *mm,dd,yy* or *dd,mm,yy* as determined by the country code. NEVER sets no time limit on the account. The months can be a number, spelled out, or abbreviated with three letters. The year can be two or four numbers. Use commas or slashes(/) to separate parts of the date. No spaces may appear.
/FULLNAME:"name"	Specifies a user's full name (rather than a user name). Enclose the name in quotation marks.
/HOMEDIR:pathname	Specifies the path for the user's home directory. The path must have been previously created.
/HOMEDIRREQ:{YES | NO}	Specifies whether a home directory is required. If a home directory is required, use the /HOMEDIR option to specify the directory.
/PASSWORDCHG:{YES | NO}	Specifies whether users can change their own password. The default is YES.
/PASSWORDREQ:{YES | NO}	Specifies whether a user account must have a password. The default is YES.
/PROFILEPATH[:path]	Specifies a *path* for the user's logon profile.

Option	Description
/SCRIPTPATH:pathname	*pathname* is the location of the user's logon script.
/TIMES:{times | ALL}.	*times* specifies the hours a user account may be logged on. *times* is expressed as day[-day] [,day[-day]],time[-time][,time [-time]], limited to one-hour increments. Days can be spelled out or abbreviated. Hours can be specified using 12- or 24-hour notation. With 12-hour notation, include am, pm, a.m., or p.m. ALL means a user can always log on. A blank value means a user can never log on. Separate day and time entries with a comma, and separate multiple day and time entries with a semicolon.
/USERCOMMENT:"text"	Specifies a comment for the account.
/WORKSTATIONS: {computername[,...] | *}	Lists as many as eight computers from {computername[,...] | *} from which a user can log on to the network. If */WORKSTATIONS* has no list or if the list is *, the user can log on from any computer.

Examples

To display information about a user named Charles, type the following:

```
NET USER Charles
```

To create an account for a user named Harold, while prompting for a password to be assigned, enter the following command:

```
NET USER Harold * /ADD
```

Notes

This command works only on servers.

If you have large numbers of users to add, consider creating a batch file with the appropriate NET USER command. Following is a simple example of a file:

```
NET USER %1 NEWUSER /ADD /HOMEDIR:C:\USERS\%1 /PASSWORDREQ:YES
```

Of course, you would include other options as required. This file makes use of a batch file parameter %1 to pass a command argument to the batch file commands. %1 will pass a user name you specify to the NET USER command where it is used to name the user account and the user's home directory.

If the file is named ADDUSER.BAT, you could add the user Mabel by typing this:

```
ADDUSER Mabel
```

NET VIEW

The NET VIEW command lists resources being shared on a computer. NET VIEW without options displays a list of computers in the current domain or network.

Syntax

```
NET VIEW [\\computername | /DOMAIN[:domainname]]
NET VIEW /NETWORK:NW [\\computername]
```

Options

\\computername   Specifies a computer whose shared resources you want to view.

/DOMAIN:domainname   Specifies the domain with computers whose shared resources you want to view. If *domainname* is omitted, NET VIEW displays all domains in the local area network.

/NETWORK:NW   Displays all available servers on a NetWare network. If a computer name is specified, the resources available on that NetWare computer are displayed.

Examples

To list the resources shared by the computer Widgets1, enter the following command:

```
NET VIEW \\WIDGETS1
```

If Widgets1 is in another domain, include the domain name with the /DOMAIN option:

```
NET VIEW \\WIDGETS1 /DOMAIN:WIDGETS
```

To list all available domains, omit the *computername* parameter:

```
NET VIEW /DOMAIN
```

NTBOOKS

Invokes the online manuals for Windows NT.

Syntax

```
NTBOOKS [/S] [/W] [/N:path]
```

Options

/S   Use /S from a Windows NT Workstation machine to access documentation stored on a Windows NT Server.

/W   Use /W from a Windows NT Server to access documentation for a Windows NT Workstation.

/N   This parameter lets you specify the path to where the online books are stored. By default, the last used location is automatically used.

NTCMDPROMPT

From a COMMAND.COM prompt, NTCMDPROMPT invokes the Windows NT command prompt.

Syntax

```
NTCMDPROMPT
```

PENTNT

Tests for the Pentium floating point bug.

Syntax

```
PENTNT [-C] [-F] [-O] [-?|-H]
```

Options

-C   Turns on conditional emulation wherein floating point emulation will be turned on if the program detects the Pentium floating point bug.

-F   Forces floating point emulation to begin and disables hardware floating point calls.

-O   Disables forced emulation and turns the hardware floating point access back on.

PRINT

Prints a text file in the background.

Syntax

```
PRINT [/D:device] [drive:][path] filename[...]
```

Options

none   Displays the contents of the PRINT queue.

/D:device   Specifies the name of the print device, such as LPT1, COM2, and so on.

[drive:][path] filename   Specifies the file to be printed.

RENAME (REN)

Renames files.

Syntax

```
RENAME [drive:][path] filename1 filename2
REN [drive:][path] filename1 filename2
```

Options

[drive:] [path] filename1   Specifies the source file names.

filename2   Specifies the destination file names.

Notes

Files cannot be renamed across drives.

REPLACE

Replaces files in a specified directory with files in a different directory that have the same name.

Syntax

```
REPLACE [drive1:][path1] filename [drive2:][path2] [/A] [/P] [/R] [/W]
REPLACE [drive1:][path1] filename [drive2:][path2] [/P] [/R] [/S] [/W] [/U]
```

Options

[drive1:] [path1] filename   The source files.

[drive2:] [path2]   The destination files.

/A   Adds new files to the destination directory.

/P   Prompts for confirmation before replacing files.

/R   Forces replacement of read-only files.

/S   Includes all subdirectories.

/W   Causes REPLACE to wait for a disk to be inserted before searching for source files.

/U   Updates files in destination directory, where only files with dates older than the source files are replaced.

RESTORE

Restores files backed up with the BACKUP command.

Syntax

```
RESTORE drive1: drive2:[path[filename]] [/S] [/P] [/B:date] [/A:date] [/E:time]
[/L:time] [/M] [/N] [/D]
```

Options

drive1:   The source drive.

drive2:   The destination drive.

path   The destination directory. This must be the same directory as the one from which the files were backed up.

filename   The files you want to restore from the backup set.

/S   Include subdirectories.

/P   Prompts for confirmation when restoring over files that are read-only or that are newer than those stored in the backup set.

/B:date   Restores files modified since *date.*

/A:date   Restores files modified after *date.*

/E:time   Restores files modified at or earlier than *time.*

/L:time   Restores files modified at or later than *time.*

/M   Restores files modified since the last backup.

/N   Restores only files that do not exist in the destination directory.

/D   Displays files that would be restored, but does not actually restore any files. Use this command to test which files will be restored given other parameters that you've specified.

RMDIR (RD)

Removes directories.

Syntax

```
RMDIR [drive:]path [/S]
RD [drive:]path [/S]
```

Options

[drive:]path   The name of the directory that you want to remove.

/S   Removes an entire subdirectory tree, including files.

SORT

Sorts ASCII files.

Syntax

```
SORT [/R] [/+N] [<] [drive1:][path1] filename1 [> [drive2:][path2] filename2]
[command |] SORT [/R] [/+N] [> [drive2:][path2] filename2]
```

Options

[drive1:][path1] filename1   The file that you want to sort.

[drive2:][path2] filename2   The destination for the sorted output.

command   The command that is generating data that will be sorted by redirecting its output into SORT.

/R   Reverses the sorting order (performs a descending sort)

/+N   Sorts the file based on column n.

START

Executes a given command in a new window.

Syntax

```
START ["title"] [/dpath] [/I] [/MIN] [/MAX] [/SEPARATE] [/LOW] [/NORMAL]
[/HIGH] [/REALTIME] [/WAIT] [/B] [filename] [parameters]
```

Options

none   Opens a new command window.

"title"   The new window's title (displayed in the title bar).

/dpath   The directory to which the new window defaults.

/I   Automatically passes environment variables from CMD.EXE to the new window.

/MIN   Starts the new window minimized.

/MAX   Starts the new window maximized.

/SEPARATE   Runs Win16 applications in a separate address space.

/LOW   Runs the application at idle priority.

/NORMAL   Runs the application at normal priority.

/HIGH   Runs the application at high priority.

/REALTIME   Runs the application at realtime priority.

/WAIT   Begins the application; waits for it to terminate.

/B   Runs the application in the background, without a new window.

filename   The program to run in the new window.

SUBST

Creates a virtual drive letter from a specified path.

Syntax

```
SUBST [drive1: [drive2:]path]
SUBST drive1: /D
```

Options

none   Displays all virtual drives.

drive1:   The virtual drive that will be created.

drive2:   The actual drive that contains the path.

path   The path to use for the virtual drive.

/D   Deletes a virtual drive.

TIME

Displays or sets the computer's time.

Syntax

```
TIME [hours:[minutes[:seconds[.hundredths]]][A|P]]
```

Options

none   Displays the currently set time and lets you set a new time interactively.

hours   The hour you want to set, in military time format (0–23).

minutes   The minutes you want to set, from 0 to 59.

seconds   The seconds you want to set, from 0 to 59.

hundredths   The hundredths of a second that you want to set, from 0 to 99.

A|P   If you set the time using a 12-hour format, you must specify A or P for a.m. or p.m.

TITLE

Sets the title bar for the current command prompt window.

Syntax

```
TITLE title_name
```

Options

title_name   The title you want to appear in the window's title bar.

TREE

Graphically displays the directory tree of a drive.

Syntax

```
TREE [drive:][path] [/F] [/A]
```

Options

drive: The drive for which you want to see a directory tree.

path   The directory for which you want to see a directory tree.

/F   Causes the files for each directory to be displayed.

/A   Uses ASCII characters to represent the tree instead of the extended characters used by default.

TYPE

Outputs a file to the standard output device.

Syntax

```
TYPE [drive:][path] filename [...]
```

Options

[drive:][path] filename   The file you want to display.

Notes

If you are using TYPE with a file containing spaces, surround the file name with quotation marks.

You can pipe the output of TYPE through the MORE command, like this:

```
TYPE LONGFILE.TXT | MORE.
```

VER

Displays the version number of the command prompt you're using.

Syntax

VER

XCOPY

Copies files and offers more control than the COPY command.

Syntax

XCOPY source [destination] [/W] [/P] [/C] [/V] [/Q] [/F] [/L] [/D[:date]] [/U]
[/I] [/S [/E]] [/T] [/K] [/R] [/H] [/A |/M] [/N] [/EXCLUDE:filename] [/Z]

Options

source   The source files to be copied.

destination   The destination for the files to be copied.

/W   Waits for user input before copying files.

/P   Prompts for confirmation when creating destination files.

/C   Continues copying after errors are encountered.

/V   Verifies the integrity of each copied file.

/Q   Runs XCOPY in quiet mode.

/F   Displays file names during the copy.

/L   Lists files that would be copied, but does not copy any files.

/D[:date]   Copies files modified on or after *date*.

/U   Only copies files that already exist in the destination directory.

/I   Assumes that the destination specified is a directory and not a file.

/S   Copies subdirectories, except empty ones.

/E   Copies all subdirectories, including empty ones. Use this with the /S switch.

/T   Copies only the subdirectory tree and not any files.

/K   Retains the read-only attribute for destination files. By default, the read-only flag, if present in source files, is not set for destination files.

/R   Forces read-only files to be overwritten if they exist.

/H   Includes files that have the hidden or system flags set.

/A   Copies files that have the archive flag set.

/M   Copies files that have the archive flag set, and removes the archive flag from the source file.

/N   Copies files using the NTFS short file names.

/EXCLUDE:filename   Excludes files specified in *filename.*

Overview of the Certification Process

To become a Microsoft Certified Professional, candidates must pass rigorous certification exams that provide a valid and reliable measure of their technical proficiency and expertise. These closed-book exams have on-the-job relevance because they are developed with the input of professionals in the computer industry and reflect how Microsoft products are actually used in the workplace. The exams are conducted by an independent organization—Sylvan Prometric—at more than 700 Sylvan Authorized Testing Centers around the world.

Currently Microsoft offers four types of certification, based on specific areas of expertise:

◆ **Microsoft Certified Product Specialist (MCPS).** Qualified to provide installation, configuration, and support for users of at least one Microsoft desktop operating system, such as Windows NT Workstation 4.0. In addition, candidates may take additional elective exams to add areas of specialization. MCPS is the first level of expertise.

◆ **Microsoft Certified Systems Engineer (MCSE).** Qualified to effectively plan, implement, maintain, and support information systems with Microsoft Windows NT and other Microsoft advanced systems and workgroup products, such as Microsoft Office and Microsoft BackOffice. The Windows NT Workstation exam can be used as one of the four core operating systems exams. MCSE is the second level of expertise.

◆ **Microsoft Certified Solution Developer (MCSD).** Qualified to design and develop custom business solutions using Microsoft development tools, technologies, and platforms, including Microsoft Office and Microsoft BackOffice. MCSD also is a second level of expertise, but in the area of software development.

◆ **Microsoft Certified Trainer (MCT).** Instructionally and technically qualified by Microsoft to deliver Microsoft Education Courses at Microsoft authorized sites. An MCT must be employed by a Microsoft Solution Provider Authorized Technical Education Center or a Microsoft Authorized Academic Training site.

You can find complete descriptions of all Microsoft Certifications in the Microsoft Education and Certification Roadmap on the CD-ROM that comes with this book. The following sections describe the requirements for each type of certification.

Note For up-to-date information about each type of certification, visit the Microsoft Training and Certification World Wide Web site at http://www.microsoft.com/ train_cert. You must have an Internet account and a WWW browser to access this information. You also can call the following sources:

◆ Microsoft Certified Professional Program: 800-636-7544

◆ Sylvan Prometric Testing Centers: 800-755-EXAM

◆ Microsoft Online Institute (MOLI): 800-449-9333

How to Become a Microsoft Certified Product Specialist (MCPS)

Becoming an MCPS requires you pass one operating system exam. Passing the "Implementing and Supporting Microsoft Windows NT Workstation 4.0" exam (#70-73), which this book covers, satisfies the MCPS requirement.

Windows NT Workstation is not the only operating system you can be tested on to get your MCSP certification. The following list shows the names and exam numbers of all the operating systems from which you can choose to get your MCPS certification:

- ◆ Implementing and Supporting Microsoft Windows 95 #70-63

- ◆ Implementing and Supporting Microsoft Windows NT Workstation 4.0 #70-73

- ◆ Implementing and Supporting Microsoft Windows NT Workstation 3.51 #70-42

- ◆ Implementing and Supporting Microsoft Windows NT Server 4.0 #70-67

- ◆ Implementing and Supporting Microsoft Windows NT Server 3.51 #70-43

- ◆ Microsoft Windows for Workgroups 3.11–Desktop #70-48

- ◆ Microsoft Windows 3.1 #70-30

- ◆ Microsoft Windows Operating Systems and Services Architecture I #70-150

- ◆ Microsoft Windows Operating Systems and Services Architecture II #70-151

How to Become a Microsoft Certified Systems Engineer (MCSE)

MCSE candidates need to pass four operating system exams and two elective exams. The MCSE certification path is divided into two tracks: the Windows NT 3.51 track and the Windows NT 4.0 track. The "Implementing and Supporting Microsoft Windows NT Workstation 4.0" exam covered in this book can be applied to the Windows NT 4.0 track of the MCSE certification path.

Table B.1 shows the core requirements (four operating system exams) and the elective courses (two exams) for the Windows NT 3.51 track.

TABLE B.1
Windows NT 3.51 MCSE Track

Take These Two Required Exams (Core Requirements)	Plus, Pick One of the Following Operating System Exams (Core Requirement)	Plus, Pick One of the Following Networking Exams (Core Requirement)	Plus, Pick Two of the Following Elective Exams (Elective Requirements)
Implementing and Supporting Microsoft Windows NT Server 3.51 #70-43	Implementing and Supporting Microsoft Windows 95 #70-63	Networking Microsoft Windows for Workgroups 3.11 #70-46	Microsoft SNA Server #70-12
AND Implementing and Supporting Microsoft Windows NT Workstation 3.51 #70-42	*OR* Microsoft Windows for Workgroups 3.11–Desktop #70-48	*OR* Networking with Microsoft Windows 3.1 #70-47	*OR* Implementing and Supporting Microsoft Systems Management Server 1.0 #70-14
	OR Microsoft Windows 3.1 #70-30	*OR* Networking Essentials #70-58	*OR* Microsoft SQL Server 4.2 Database Implementation #70-21
			OR Microsoft SQL Server 4.2 Database Administration for Microsoft Windows NT #70-22
			OR System Administration for Microsoft SQL Server 6 #70-26

Take These Two Required Exams (Core Requirements)	Plus, Pick One of the Following Operating System Exams (Core Requirement)	Plus, Pick One of the Following Networking Exams (Core Requirement)	Plus, Pick Two of the Following Elective Exams (Elective Requirements)
			OR Implementing a Database Design on Microsoft SQL Server 6 #70-27
			OR Microsoft Mail for PC Networks 3.2-Enterprise #70-37
			OR Internetworking Microsoft TCP/IP on Microsoft Windows NT (3.5–3.51) #70-53
			OR Internetworking Microsoft TCP/IP on Microsoft Windows NT 4.0 #70-59
			OR Implementing and Supporting Microsoft Exchange Server 4.0 #70-75
			OR Implementing and Supporting Microsoft Internet Information Server #70-77
			OR Implementing and Supporting Microsoft Proxy Server 1.0 #70-78

Table B.2 shows the core requirements (four operating system exams) and elective courses (two exams) for the Windows NT 4.0 track. Tables A.1 and A.2 have many of the same exams listed, but there are distinct differences between the two. Make sure you read each track's requirements carefully.

TABLE B.2
Windows NT 4.0 MCSE Track

Take These Two Required Exams (Core Requirements)	Plus, Pick One of the Following Operating System Exams (Core Requirement)	Plus, Pick One of the Following Networking Exams (Core Requirement)	Plus, Pick Two of the Following Elective Exams (Elective Requirements)
Implementing and Supporting Microsoft Windows NT Server 4.0 #70-67	Implementing and Supporting Microsoft Windows 95 #70-63	Networking Microsoft Windows for Workgroups 3.11 #70-46	Microsoft SNA Server #70-12
AND Implement- and Support- Microsoft Windows NT Server in the Enterprise #70-68	*OR* Microsoft Windows for Workgroups 3.11-Desktop #70-48	*OR* Networking with Microsoft Windows 3.1 #70-47	*OR* Implementing and Supporting Microsoft Systems Management Server 1.0 #70-14
	OR Microsoft Windows 3.1 #70-30	*OR* Networking Essentials #70-58	*OR* Microsoft SQL Server 4.2 Database Implementation #70-21
	OR Implementing and Supporting Microsoft Windows NT Workstation 4.0 #70-73		*OR* Microsoft SQL Server 4.2 Database Administration Microsoft Windows NT #70-22
			OR System Administration for Microsoft SQL Server 6 #70-26

Take These Two Required Exams (Core Requirements)	Plus, Pick One of the Following Operating System Exams (Core Requirement)	Plus, Pick One of the Following Networking Exams (Core Requirement)	Plus, Pick Two of the Following Elective Exams (Elective Requirements)
			OR Implementing a Database Design on Microsoft SQL Server 6 #70-27
			OR Microsoft Mail for PC Networks 3.2–Enterprise #70-37
			OR Internetworking Microsoft TCP/IP on Microsoft Windows NT (3.5–3.51) #70-53
			OR Internetworking Microsoft TCP/IP on Microsoft Windows NT 4.0 #70-59
			OR Implementing and Supporting Microsoft Exchange Server 4.0 #70-75
			OR Implementing and Supporting Microsoft Internet Information Server #70-77
			OR Implementing and Supporting Microsoft Proxy Server 1.0 #70-78

How to Become a Microsoft Certified Solution Developer (MCSD)

MCSD candidates need to pass two core technology exams and two elective exams. Unfortunately, the "Implementing and Supporting Microsoft Windows NT Workstation 4.0" (#70-73) exam does NOT apply toward any of these requirements. Table B.3 shows the required technology exams, plus the elective exams that apply toward obtaining the MCSD.

> **Caution** | The "Implementing and Supporting Microsoft Windows NT Workstation 4.0" (#70-73) exam does NOT apply toward any of the MCSD requirements.

TABLE B.3
MCSD Exams and Requirements

Take These Two Core Technology Exams	Plus, Choose from Two of the Following Elective Exams
Microsoft Windows Operating Systems and Services Architecture I #70-150	Microsoft SQL Server 4.2 Database Implementation #70-21
AND Microsoft Windows Operating Systems and Services Architecture II #70-151	*OR* Developing Applications with C++ Using the Microsoft Foundation Class Library #70-24
	OR Implementing a DatabaseDesign on Microsoft SQL Server 6 #70-27
	OR Microsoft Visual Basic 3.0 for Windows– Application Development #70-50
	OR Microsoft Access 2.0 for Windows– Application Development #70-51
	OR Developing Applications with Microsoft Excel 5.0 Using Visual Basic for Applications #70-52
	OR Programming in Microsoft Visual FoxPro 3.0 for Windows #70-54
	OR Programming with Microsoft Visual Basic 4.0 #70-65

Take These Two Core Technology Exams	Plus, Choose from Two of the Following Elective Exams
	OR Microsoft Access for Windows 95 and the Microsoft Access Development Toolkit #70-69
	OR Implementing OLE in Microsoft Foundation Class Applications #70-25

Becoming a Microsoft Certified Trainer (MCT)

To understand the requirements and process for becoming a Microsoft Certified Trainer (MCT), you need to obtain the Microsoft Certified Trainer Guide document (MCTGUIDE.DOC) from the following WWW site:

> http://www.microsoft.com/train_cert/download.htm

On this page, click on the hyperlink MCT GUIDE (mctguide.doc) (117 KB). If your WWW browser can display DOC files (Word for Windows native file format), the MCT Guide displays in the browser window. Otherwise, you need to download it and open it in Word for Windows or Windows 95 WordPad. The MCT Guide explains the four-step process to becoming an MCT. The general steps for the MCT certification are as follows:

1. Complete and mail a Microsoft Certified Trainer application to Microsoft. You must include proof of your skills for presenting instructional material. The options for doing so are described in the MCT Guide.

2. Obtain and study the Microsoft Trainer Kit for the Microsoft Official Curricula (MOC) course(s) for which you want to be certified. You can order Microsoft Trainer Kits by calling 800-688-0496 in North America. Other regions should review the MCT Guide for information on how to order a Microsoft Trainer Kit.

3. Pass the Microsoft certification exam for the product for which you want to be certified to teach.

4. Attend the MOC course for which you want to be certified. This is done so you can understand how the course is structured, how labs are completed, and how the course flows.

> **Caution** You should use the preceding steps as a general overview of the MCT certification process. The actual steps you need to take are described in detail in the MCTGUIDE.DOC file on the WWW site mentioned earlier. Do not misconstrue the preceding steps as the actual process you need to take.

If you are interested in becoming an MCT, you can receive more information by calling 800-688-0496.

All About TestPrep

The electronic TestPrep utility included on the CD-ROM accompanying this book enables you to test your Windows NT Workstation knowledge in a manner similar to that employed by the actual Microsoft exam. When you first start the TestPrep exam, select the number of questions you want to be asked and the objective categories in which you want to be tested. You can choose from one to 51 questions, and from one to seven categories, of which the real exam consists.

Although it is possible to maximize the TestPrep application, the default is for it to run in smaller mode so you can refer to your desktop while answering questions. TestPrep uses a unique randomization sequence to ensure that each time you run the program you are presented with a different sequence of questions—this enhances your learning and prevents you from merely learning the expected answers over time without reading the question each and every time.

Question Presentation

TestPrep emulates the actual Microsoft "Implementing and Supporting Microsoft Windows NT Workstation 4.0" exam (#70-73), in that radio (circle) buttons are used to signify only one correct choice, while check boxes (squares) are used to signify multiple correct answers. Whenever more than one answer is correct, the number you should select is given in the wording of the question.

You can exit the program at any time by choosing the Exit key, or you can continue to the next question by choosing the Next key.

Scoring

The TestPrep Score Report uses actual numbers from the "Implementing and Supporting Microsoft Windows NT Workstation" exam. For exam #70-73, a score of 705 or higher is considered passing; the same parameters apply to TestPrep. Each objective category is broken into categories with a percentage correct given for each of the seven categories.

Choose Show Me What I Missed to go back through the questions you answered incorrectly and see what the correct answers are. Choose Exit to return to the beginning of the testing routine and start over.

Non-Random Mode

You can run TestPrep in Non-Random mode, which enables you to see the same set of questions each time, or on each machine. To run TestPrep in this manner, you need to create a shortcut to the executable file, and place the CLASS parameter on the command line calling the application, after the application's name. For example:

```
C:\TESTENG\70_73.EXE CLASS
```

Now, when you run TestPrep, the same sequence of questions will appear each and every time. To change the sequence but stay in Non-Random mode (for example, if you're in a classroom setting, where it is important that everyone see the same questions), choose Help, Class Mode on the main screen. This lets you enter a number from 1 to 8 to select a predefined sequence of questions.

Instructor Mode

To run TestPrep in Instructor mode (seeing the same set of questions each time, or on each machine), create a shortcut to the executable file, and place the INSTR parameter following CLASS on the command line calling the application, after the application's name. For example:

```
C:\TESTENG\70_73.EXE CLASS INSTR
```

Now, when you run TestPrep, the same sequence of questions will appear each and every time. Additionally, the correct answer will be marked already, and the objective category from which the question is coming will be given in the question. To change the sequence of questions that appear, choose Help, Class Mode on the main screen. This prompts you to enter a number from 1 to 8 to select a predefined sequence of questions; increment that by 100 and the sequence will be presented in Instructor mode.

Flash Cards

As a further learning aid, you can use the FLASH! Electronic Flash Cards program to convert some of the questions in the database into a fill-in-the-blank format. Run the FLASH! program and select the categories on which you want to be tested. The engine then goes through the database in sequential order and tests your knowledge without multiple choice possibilities.

I N D E X

Getting Started with the CD-ROM

This page provides instructions for installing software from the CD-ROM.

Windows 95/NT 4 Installation

Insert the disc into your CD-ROM drive. If autoplay is enabled on your machine, the CD-ROM setup program starts automatically the first time you insert the disc.

If setup does not run automatically, perform these steps:

1. From the Start menu, choose Programs, Windows Explorer.

2. Select your CD-ROM drive under My Computer.

3. Double-click SETUP.EXE in the contents list.

4. Follow the on-screen instructions that appear.

5. Setup adds an icon named CD-ROM Contents to a program group for this book. To explore the CD-ROM, double-click on the CD-ROM Contents icon.

How to Contact New Riders Publishing

If you have a question or comment about this product, there are several ways to contact New Riders Publishing. You can write us at the following address:

New Riders Publishing
Attn: Publishing Manager
201 W. 103rd Street
Indianapolis, IN 46290

If you prefer, you can fax New Riders Publishing at 1-317-817-7448.

To send Internet electronic mail to New Riders, address it to support@mcp.com.

You can also contact us through the Macmillan Computer Publishing CompuServe forum at GO NEWRIDERS. Our World Wide Web address is http://www.mcp.com/newriders.

MCSE Training Guide: Windows 95

ISBN: 1-56205-746-4, $59.99 USA/$84.95 CAN, CD

by Michael Wolf and Rob Tidrow

Written by MCSEs and one of the most well-known trainers in the industry, this resource contains all the insider tips, notes, tricks, strategies, and helpful advice users need to achieve Microsoft certification.

Accomplished-Expert

MCSE Training Guide: Networking Essentials

ISBN: 1-56205-749-9, $49.99 USA/$70.95 CAN, CD

by Joe Casad and Dan Newland, MCSE, MCT

Based on the highly successful *MCSE Training Guide* series, this updated edition has all the information users need to pass the Networking Essentials exam. Organized in a concise, easy-to-read manner, this is the most effective and least expensive study tool for achieving Microsoft Certification.

Accomplished-Expert

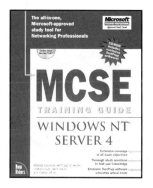

MCSE Training Guide: Windows NT Server 4

ISBN: 1-56205-768-5, $49.99 USA/$70.95 CAN, CD

by Joe Casad, Wayne Dalton, and Steven Tate, et al.

Organized in a concise, easy-to-follow format, this resource saves users countless hours and thousands of dollars in MCSE courses. This edition is filled with insider tips and notes from MCSE and Microsoft Certified Trainers.

Accomplished-Expert

Inside Windows NT Server 4, Certified Administrator's Resource Edition

ISBN: 1-56205-789-8, $59.99 USA/$84.95 CAN, CD

by Drew Heywood, et al.

This bestseller is the best book available for readers preparing for the MCSE core exams. This resource offers Microsoft training material enhanced with hands-on, performance based exercises covering BackOffice, NT clustering, and other NT Server strategies.

Accomplished-Expert

REGISTRATION CARD

Inside Windows NT Workstation 4 Certification Administrator's Resource Edition

Name _____ Title _____

Company _____ Type of business _____

Address _____

City/State/ZIP _____

Have you used these types of books before? ☐ yes ☐ no

If yes, which ones? _____
_____

How many computer books do you purchase each year? ☐ 1–5 ☐ 6 or more

How did you learn about this book? _____

Where did you purchase this book? _____

Which applications do you currently use? _____
_____

Which computer magazines do you subscribe to? _____
_____

What trade shows do you attend? _____
_____

Comments: _____
_____
_____

Would you like to be placed on our preferred mailing list? ☐ yes ☐ no

☐ **I would like to see my name in print!** You may use my name and quote me in future New Riders products and promotions. My daytime phone number is: _____

New Riders Publishing   201 West 103rd Street ◆ Indianapolis, Indiana 46290 USA

Fax to 317-817-7448

Fold Here

- -

NO POSTAGE
NECESSARY
IF MAILED
IN THE
UNITED STATES

BUSINESS REPLY MAIL
FIRST-CLASS MAIL PERMIT NO. 9918 INDIANAPOLIS IN

POSTAGE WILL BE PAID BY THE ADDRESSEE

NEW RIDERS PUBLISHING
201 W 103RD ST
INDIANAPOLIS IN 46290-9058

MACMILLAN COMPUTER PUBLISHING USA

A VIACOM COMPANY

Technical

Support:

If you cannot get the CD/Disk to install properly, or you need assistance with a particular situation in the book, please feel free to check out the Knowledge Base on our Web site at **http://www.superlibrary.com/general/support**. We have answers to our most Frequently Asked Questions listed there. If you do not find your specific question answered, please contact Macmillan Technical Support at **(317) 581-3833**. We can also be reached by email at **support@mcp.com**.